INDEX

TO

GENEALOGICAL PERIODICALS

Together With
"MY OWN INDEX"

By
DONALD LINES JACOBUS, M.A.

Three Volumes in One

Baltimore
GENEALOGICAL PUBLISHING CO., INC.
1981

INDEX TO GENEALOGICAL PERIODICALS

INTRODUCTION

This INDEX is in two sections, the first listing surnames, and the second, places and subjects.

It covers *periodicals,* not family genealogies nor (with a few exceptions) occasional publications issued by historical societies in book or pamphlet form. Many historical periodicals have been consulted, but indexed only so far as strictly genealogical matter is concerned. Strictly historical matter, memoirs of persons not long dead, and other reading matter not germane to the subject of genealogy, have not been indexed.

It has been our aim, in indexing, to make our listing as accessible as possible to genealogical students. Hence we have thrown overboard all rules for indexing and bibliography. An article with the title "To the Public" was found to pertain to loyalists of Topsham in 1775, and was indexed accordingly. Another entitled "A Lost Battalion of the Revolutionary War" was not indexed under "Lost," since no person seeking the Revolutionary service of an ancestor would ever think of looking under "Lost" for a muster roll. An article headed "Gleanings from Historical Records Concerning Maine, in Mass. Archives," we indexed under "Maine; garrisons and forts." The common sense of a practical genealogist, we believe, is capable of producing a more serviceable index than could be achieved by a scholastic worship of cut-and-dried rules. If we have erred in this, we cheerfully shoulder the responsibility for our blunders.

The foundation of this INDEX is the card index which the author made for his own use of the complete sets of the New York Genealogical and Biographical Record through 1931 (sixty-two volumes) and of the New England Historical and Genealogical Register for the volumes 51 to 85 inclusive, which covers the set of the latter through 1931 except for the first fifty volumes which are covered by the Register's own index. These are the two oldest publications of this type in the country, and they contain a tremendous mass of material.

In order to make this INDEX more useful, many other periodicals have been indexed. Some of the older periodicals which are no longer published have been indexed only with respect to the records of *places,* since it was found that Munsell's Index of 1900-1908 adequately covered the surnames of families of which some genealogy was published. Two or three publications have their own subject index covering the earlier volumes, hence we indexed only the later volumes. The reference list published herein contains the full titles of all periodicals, included in this INDEX, explains the extent to which they have been indexed, and refers to other indexes for supplemental information and guidance. Those who use this INDEX will find it well to read through this list and to note the supplementary sources there mentioned.

It was our hope and intention to index every genealogical publication in the country or such portions as were not adequately covered in other indexes. It has been necessary to depart slightly from that ambition. In the first place, it was learned that Dr. Stewart's Index to Printed Virginia Genealogies (1930) covers Virginia periodicals so far as surnames are concerned, while the Virginia Historical Guide which Dr. E. G. Swem is preparing will contain 900,000 entries and thoroughly cover the Virginia periodicals. Since it was felt that our space could better be devoted to periodicals and sections of the country which need indexing much more than does Virginia and its periodicals, and since we did not wish our work to conflict with that of Dr. Stewart and Dr. Swem, we reluctantly halted our own indexing of Virginia periodicals.

In the second place, we were unable to obtain access to full sets of a few periodicals. Several times, our desire to include periodicals was so great that we wrote to the individuals or societies which issued them, asking whether a set could be loaned to us for a few weeks for this purpose, and offering to pay the carrying charges both ways. When this request was ignored or refused, as it was in two instances, we abandoned the attempt to include these periodicals. We hope, therefore, that we shall be acquitted of any charge that favoritism has been shown or valuable periodicals wilfully omitted.

Not all of the periodicals indexed are of equal value or accuracy, and the fact that we have included them does not of itself warrant the assumption that we regard them as authorities of the first class. However, it can and should be stated with emphasis that even the best periodicals contain errors, and that even the poorest periodicals contain some valuable information. We have not scrupled to omit entirely such useless items as the descent of Julius Caesar from the goddess Venus; and also a few articles which we knew to be teeming with misstatements, when more reliable articles on the same families had been found in other periodicals. But in general, our attitude has been that the function of the indexer is to indicate what may be found in print and where, rather than to appropriate the prerogatives of a critic.

D. L. J.

HOW TO USE THIS INDEX

Look in Part I for the surname in which you are interested. If this does not produce results, look in Part II for the *place* where your ancestor lived, trying the *town,* the *county,* and the *State.* Sometimes the desired information can be located in Part II under *Passenger Lists, Revolutionary War and Soldiers, French and Indian Wars, Loyalists, England, Germany,* etc. Look in the key below, or inside the cover, for the name of the periodical. The reference is to *volume* and *page* on which the information *begins,* and it is assumed that the user will consult the next following pages. When three figures are given in the reference, as "(4-3-16)," the first is to volume, the second to part or issue, the third to page.

This is an index to *genealogical* periodicals; hence, although many *historical* periodicals are included, the INDEX covers only such material in them as is genealogically helpful.

Consult the heading *Genealogy* in Part II for much information of a miscellaneous nature.

As a further aid, below will be found a valuable list of other *general reference sources.* These are considered by the writer to be the most useful sources of a *general* nature, though there are many additional publications which are more limited or more local in scope. To this list, the genealogist should add a good atlas and a postal gazeteer.

Following this list will be found a complete key to the periodicals covered in the present INDEX, with an explanation (when necessary) of the extent to which they are included. In *small* type are entered the names of a few additional periodicals, which for one reason or another are *not* included in the present INDEX, the purpose being to call them to the attention of the inquiring student. After this key has been consulted, the inquirer will find it more convenient, for quick reference, to use the condensed key provided inside the front and back covers of the book.

GENERAL REFERENCE SOURCES

[1] Annual Report of the American Historical Association for the Year 1905. Vol. II. pp. 1374.

(Contains bibliography of all publications of all American historical societies through 1905, with *full tables of contents; indexed.*)

[2] Index to American Genealogies. Fifth Edition. Albany, N. Y., Joel Munsell's Sons, 1900. Supplement, 1908.

[3] American and English Genealogies in the Library of Congress. Second Edition. Government Printing Office, 1919.

[4] A Guide to Massachusetts Local History. Compiled by Charles A. Flagg. Pub. The Salem Press Company, Salem, Mass., 1907.

[5-a] Index to Printed Virginia Genealogies. Robert Armistead Stewart, 1930.

[5-b] Virginia Historical Guide, by E. G. Swem. 2 vols.; 900,000 entries. To be published at $100. Address the editor, 119 Chandler Court, Williamsburg, Va.

[6] Annual Report of the American Historical Association for the Year 1906. Vol. II.

(Contains description and location of public archives of Arkansas, Connecticut, Delaware, Florida, Georgia, Ohio, Tennessee, with bibliography of public archives of the thirteen original States to 1789. A trifle out of date as to *present location* of some records, but extremely useful.)

[7] Index (4 vols.) to the New England Historical and Genealogical Register, vols. 1-50.

[8] Catalogue of the Genealogical and Historical Library of the Colonial Dames of the State of New York. New York, 1912. pp. 518.

(A valuable bibliography, and very useful to the genealogist as a supplement to other indexes; it lists surnames of families genealogically treated in the books then in the Library of the Society.)

[9-a] A Century of Population Growth from the First Census of the United States to the Twelfth, 1790-1900. Government Printing Office, 1909.

(Contains maps, changes in county lines, distribution of surnames, and much other useful data.)

[9-b] Heads of Families at the First Census of the United States taken in the year 1790. Government Printing Office.

(Separate volumes for each State.)

[10-a] The Original Lists of Persons . . . . . who went from Great Britain to the American Plantations 1600-1700, edited by John Camden Hotten. New York, 1874.

[10-b] The Planters of the Commonwealth [Settlement in Massachusetts 1620-1640], by Charles Edward Banks. Boston, 1930.

(A useful supplement to [10-a], which however it does not supplant; especially valuable for English origins.)

[11] A Genealogical Dictionary of the First Settlers of New England, by James Savage, 4 vols. Boston, 1860-1862.

(A mammoth work still useful for a quick survey of the early distribution of surnames and individuals in New England; but its information should always be verified and supplemented by consultation of works containing results of more recent investigations.)

KEY TO PERIODICALS

A1   The New England Historical and Genealogical Register. vols. 51-85. 1897-1931.
     (See [7] and [2] for vols. 1-50.)

A2   The New York Genealogical and Biographical Record. vols. 1-62. 1870-1931.

B1   The Genealogical Magazine of New Jersey. vols. 1-6. 1925-1931.

B2   The Nebraska and Midwest Genealogical Record. vols. 1-9. 1923-1931.

B3   The Connecticut Quarterly (4 vols.). The Connecticut Magazine (8 vols.). 1895-1908.
     Numbered consecutively, vols. 1-12.

B4   New Haven Genealogical Magazine. [Conn.] vols. 1-8. 1923-1931.

B5   The Vineland Historical Magazine. [N. J.] vols. 1-15. 1916-1930.

B6   Somerset County Historical Quarterly. [N. J.] vols. 1-8. 1912-1919.

C1   The Salem Press Historical and Genealogical Record. vols. 1-2. 1890-1891.

C2   Putnam's Monthly Historical Magazine. vols. 1-7. 1892-1899.

C3   The Genealogical Quarterly Magazine. vols. 1-5. 1900-1905.

C4   The Genealogical Magazine. vols. 1-4. 1905-1907, 1915-1917.

D   The Mayflower Descendant. vols. 1-28. 1899-1930.

Dx   Pilgrim Notes and Queries. vols. 1-5. 1913-1917.

E   The "Old Northwest" Genealogical Quarterly. vols. 1-15. 1898-1909.

F1   Bangor Historical Magazine. vols. 1-9. 1885-1895.
     (Records of *places* are included in the present INDEX; for surnames, see [2].)

F2   Maine Historical Recorder. vols. 1-9. 1884-1898.
     (Records of *places* are included in the present INDEX; for surnames, see [2].)

F3   New Hampshire Genealogical Record. vols. 1-7. 1903-1910.

F4   Narragansett Historical Register. vols. 1-8. 1882-1890.
     (Records of *places* are included in the present INDEX; for surnames, see [2].)

F5   Dedham Historical Register. vols. 1-14. 1890-1903.
     (Not included in the present INDEX; see [2] for surnames, and [1] for tables of contents.)

G1   Records of the American Catholic Historical Society of Philadelphia. vols. 1-43. 1887-1931.

G2   The Journal of the American-Irish Historical Society. vols. 1-29. 1898-1931.

H   North Carolina Historical and Genealogical Register. vols. 1-3. 1900-1903.

J   South Carolina Historical and Genealogical Magazine. vols. 1-30. 1900-1929.

K   The Genealogical Advertiser. vols. 1-4. 1898-1901.

HOW TO USE THIS INDEX

M   The National Genealogical Society Quarterly. vols. 1-19. 1912-1931.

N1   The Transalleghany Historical Magazine. [West Virginia] vols. 1-2. 1901-1902.

N2   The West Virginia Historical Magazine. vols. 1-5. 1901-1905.

N3   Register of Kentucky State Historical Society. 21 vols. to 1923.
(A complete set was not available for indexing.)

N4   The American Historical Magazine. Pub. Nashville, Tenn. vols. 1-9. 1896-1904.
(Not included in the present INDEX; amply covered in [2].)

N5   Tennessee Historical Magazine. vols. 1-9. 1915-1926.
(Not included in the present INDEX; contains very little genealogical data.)

P   Publications of the Genealogical Society of Pennsylvania. vols. 1-11. 1895-1931.
(Indexed through vol. 11, No. 2, March 1931.)

Pw   Proceedings and Collections of the Wyoming Historical and Geological Society. vols. 1-20. 1858-1926.

Q1   The Pennsylvania Magazine. vols. 1-54. 1877-1930.
(The present INDEX omits *surnames* in the *earlier* volumes which were included in [2].)

Q2   Pennsylvania-German Society Proceedings. vols. 1-39. 1891-1928. Has a subject and name index, vols. 1-6, 1898.

Q3   Historical Register: Notes and Queries, Historical and Genealogical, relating to Interior Pennsylvania. Egle. Pub. Harrisburg, Pa. vols. 1-2. 1883-1884.
(Records of *places* are included in the present INDEX; for surnames, see [2].)

Q4   Western Pennsylvania Historical Magazine. vols. 1-12. 1918-1929.
(Not included in the present INDEX.)

Q5   Lancaster County Historical Society Papers. vols. 1-34. 1896-1930.
(Not included in the present INDEX.)

R1   Publications of the Southern History Association. Pub. Washington, D. C. vols. 1-11. 1897-1907.

R2   Gulf States Historical Magazine. Pub. Montgomery, Ala. vols. 1-2. 1902-1904.

S1   Americana, Illustrated. Pub. by The American Historical Society, Inc.
(A complete set not available; vols. 12-18, 1918-1924, are included in the present INDEX.)

S2   The Granite Monthly. Pub. Concord, N. H. vols. 1-30. 1877-1901.
(Later volumes not included in the INDEX, as they contain little genealogical data.)

S3   The Bulletin of the California State Society Sons of the Revolution. vols. 1-6. 1928-1932.
(The present INDEX covers genealogical data except queries and answers.)

T1   Reports and Papers, Fairfield County Historical Society. Pub. Bridgeport, Conn. Irregular, 1882-1899.

T2   New Haven Historical Society Papers. vols. 1-9. 1865-1918.

T3   Connecticut Historical Society Collections. vols. 1-22. 1860-1928.

T4   Bulletin of the Newport Historical Society. 81 issues, 1912-1931.

T5   Rhode Island Historical Tracts. First Series, 20 issues; Second Series, 5 issues; 1877-1895. Has its own index of First Series (No. 20). (Not included in the present INDEX.)

T6   Publications of the Rhode Island Historical Society. vols. 1-8. 1893-1900.

T7   Collections of the New York Historical Society. vols. 1-64. 1868-1931.

U   The Utah Genealogical and Historical Magazine. vols. 1-22. 1910-1931.

V1   Tyler's Quarterly Historical and Genealogical Magazine. vols. 1-12. 1919-1931.

V2   The Researcher. A Magazine of History and Genealogical Exchange. Richmond, Va. vols. 1-2. 1926-1928.

V3   The Virginia Magazine of History and Biography. vols. 1-38. 1894-1930. (Not included in the present INDEX; see [5].)

V4   Virginia County Records. Pub. Hasbrouck Heights, N. J. vols. 1-10. 1905-1912. (Not included in the present INDEX; see [5].)

W1   William and Mary Quarterly. vols. 1-27. 1892-1919. Has its own index, vols. 1-17. (Not included in the present INDEX; see [5].)

W2   William and Mary Quarterly. New Series. vols. 1-10. 1921-1930. (Not included in the present INDEX; see [5].)

X1   Maryland Historical Magazine. vols. 1-26. 1906-1931.

X2   Maryland Genealogical Bulletin. Pub. Robert F. Hayes, Jr., Baltimore, Md. vols. 1-2. 1930-1931.

Y1   Collections of Essex Institute. vols. 1-67. 1859-1931. Has its own subject index, vols. 1-40, and vols. 41-50.

     (For tables of contents of first 41 vols., see [1], p. 307; for *surnames* in first 49 vols., see [2]; the present INDEX covers vols. 51-67.)

Y2   The Essex Antiquarian. vols. 1-13. 1897-1909.

     (For *surnames* in vols. 1-11, see [2]; the present INDEX covers records of *places*, vols. 1-13, and of *surnames*, vols. 12-13.)

Z   The American Monthly (42 vols.). Daughters of the American Revolution Magazine (22 vols.). Numbered consecutively, vols. 1-64. 1892-1930.

     (Through the kindness of Mrs. Mary Knight Crane, Erie, Pennsylvania, we have been permitted to use her fine index covering vols. 1-56; and have included in the present INDEX all general items of a genealogical nature, such as records of places and muster rolls, vols. 1-64; *surnames* are *not* included in the present INDEX.*)

---

* The bulk of family statistics in this magazine are found in the Query and Answer Department. Apply to Mrs. Crane for references to surnames, and offer a small fee for the use of her index.

NAME INDEX Aarse—Alexander

Aarse, Artse; see Aert Willemszen.
Abbott, Daniel; Cambridge, Providence; F4 (6-81).
Abbott, George; Andover; English ancestry; A2 (61-224); A1 (85-79); S2 (9-278).
Abbott, George; Rowley; C2 (4-41; 5-26; 7-33).
Abbot, James; English origin; A1 (66-187).
Abbot, John; Philadelphia; English clue; A1 (59-419).
Abbott, Robert; Watertown, Branford; B4 (1-8; 4-943).
Abbot; Amwell, N. J.; M (17-8).
Abbott; Canton, Worthington; E (9-45).
Abercrombie; Md.; English clue; A1 (59-419).
Abercrombie; Bible records, Philadelphia; P (8-284).
Abernathy, William; Wallingford; B4 (1-9; 2-508; 7-1788).
Abington; Md.; X1 (25-251).
Achey; Bible record, Heidelberg, Pa.; Q1 (24-393).
Ackerman, David; Dutch ancestry; B1 (1-8).
Ackley, Thomas; Md.; English clue; A1 (59-419).
Ackley [Hackley]; Wallingford; B4 (3-692).
Acrill; Va.; V1 (7-212).
Adams, George; Va.; English clue; A1 (59-419).
Adams, George; E (1-101).
Adams, Henry; Braintree; A1 (66-187; 79-217; 85-382); A2 (12-9; 42-338); Dx (2-49); M (17-10); S (16-380); (Chelmsford branch); C2 (4-85); English ancestry; A1 (59-320).
Adams, Jeremy; Hartford; A1 (59-315; 67-89).
Adams, John; Boston; (N. H. branch); F3 (6-1).
Adams, John; Cambridge; C2 (4-91).
Adams, Nathaniel; Boston; A2 (58-188); M (1-67).
Adams, Robert; Newbury; E (1-21).
Adams, Roger; Roxbury, Brookline; A1 (53-214).
Adams, Samuel; Hunterdon County, N. J.; B6 (5-238; 6-155).
Adams, William; Ipswich; A1 (58-91; 60-314).
Adams, William; Milford; B4 (1-11, 255).

Adams; Settlers; M (9-38).
Adams; York County, Pa.; M (17-57).
Adams; Sudbury, Canterbury, Pomfret; C2 (7-247).
Adams; Family records, Mass.; Y2 (1-16).
Adams; Family record, Ipswich; Y2 (4-37).
Adams; Md.; X1 (22-304).
Adams; Bristol, Vt.; B5 (4-10).
Adams; Richmond, Va.; V1 (1-69).
Adams; Honington, co. Warwick, Eng.; C3 (5-195).
Addison, John (Col.); Md.; X1 (14-387).
Adee, William; New Haven; B4 (1-12; 4-943).
Adrianse; see A2 (8-62).
Aertszen; see Aert Willemszen.
Aglionby; Nunnery, Eng.; N2 (2-3-44).
Agnew, James; Lancaster, Pa.; Z (62-346).
Aires, Simon (Dr.); Watertown, Boston; English ancestry; A1 (69-248).
Akers; Amwell, N. J.; M (17-9).
Albertson; Bible records; A2 (46-289).
Albridgton; York County, Va.; V1 (9-209).
Alburtis; see Burtis.
Alcock; Boston; A1 (59-324).
Alcott, Thomas; Boston; B4 (1-12, 255); A2 (50-285).
Alden, John; Plymouth, Duxbury; A1 (51-427; 52-54, 162, 362, 435; 54-180); A2 (49-311); D (3-10, 120; 6-71, 110, 174, 193, 239; 9-129, 145, 193; 10-76; 12-72; 14-140; 20-12, 49, 76; 21-126; 22-189; 23-111, 129; 24-74, 165; 25-145); M (4-37; 11-2). Family record; Dx (3-77). Family record, Randolph; D (16-46).
Alden, John; English clue; A1(55-332).
Alden, John; note; A1 (51-69).
Alder; Prince George's County, Md.; M (17-11).
Alder; W. Va.; E (15-136).
Aldrich, George; Dorchester, Mendon; E (12-55).
Aldrich; Bible records; A1 (51-219).
Aldus, Nathan; Dedham; English ancestry; A1 (64-240).
Alexander, James; New York; A2 (12-13, 60, 111, 155, 174).
Alexander, James; S. C.; M (17-57).
Alexander; Baltimore; X1 (1-316).
Alexander; Conn., N. Y.; M (17-24).
Alexander; New York (Wills); A2 (18-173; 19-27).

Alexander; Spartanburg, S. C.; M (17-11, 45).
Alexander; (Wills); Z (42-187).
Alford; Boston; A1 (62-199).
Allen, Bozoune; English data; A1 (53-23).
Allen, Charles; Portsmouth, Greenland, N. H.; A1 (56-26).
Allen, George; Sandwich; S1 (12-449).
Allen, Hope; Boston; A1 (66-282).
Allen, Joseph; Braintree, Boston; A1 (54-349).
Allen, Lewis; Watertown; A1 (54-396).
Allen, Matthew; Windsor; English data; A1 (51-212).
Allen, Samuel; Cambridge, Windsor; C1 (2-102).
Allen; Founders of American families; C2 (1-286; 2-119).
Allen; Bible records, Brimfield; A1 (84-461).
Allen; New Haven [see also Alling]; M (17-24).
Allen; Pembroke; M (17-12).
Allen; Shrewsbury, N. J.; A1 (53-127).
Allen; N. J.; M (17-25).
Allen; Family record, N. J.; P (2-216).
Allen; Sturbridge; M (17-12).
Allen; Welliston, Vt.; M (17-11).
Allen; Cumberland County; V1 (8-253).
Allen; Fauquier County; V1 (9-277).
Allen; Bible record, Va., Mich.; V1 (9-259; 10-158).
Allen; Bible records, N. C., Tenn.; V1 (10-156).
Allen; Bible records, Brookfield, Craftsbury; D (3-135).
Allen; Bible records, Morristown; A2 (46-412).
Allen; Family record, Tisbury; A1 (83-507).
Allen; Family record; A1 (78-271).
Allen; Ira (Colchester, Vt.); C3 (1-255).
Allen [Allyn]; co. Devon, Eng.; B3 (8-810).
Allerton, Isaac; Plymouth, New York, New Haven; A2 (43-294); B2 (1-11); D (2-155; 4-109; 7-129, 173; 25-97); M (4-38); S1 (15-91).
Allerton; Bible records, Pa.; P (10-178).
Alley; New Haven; B4 (1-14).
Alling, Roger and John; New Haven; B4 (1-15, 255; 3-762; 4-943; 8-2044).
Allison; Wallingford, Newark; B4 (1-39).
Allyn; Hartford; A1 (65-382).
Allyn; Inscriptions, New London; M (16-25).
Almy, William; Portsmouth; English ancestry; A1 (71-310; 78-391).
Alrichs, Jacob and Peter; Delaware, New York; A2 (24-125; 44-226; 55-241).

Alsop, Joseph; New Haven; B4 (1-39).
Alsop; Conn. branches; English data; arms; C2 (6-33).
Alsop; Spotsylvania County, Va.; M (17-12).
Alston, John; St. John's, Berkeley; J (6-114).
Alston; Inscriptions, S. C.; J (10-181; 12-38).
Alvord; Bible record, Wilmington; A1 (61-306).
Ambler, Richard; Yorktown, Va.; N2 (2-4-52).
Ambler; Danbury, Conn.; M (17-13, 25).
Ambrose, Joshua and Nehemiah; English origin; A1 (61-386).
Ambrose; Salisbury; B4 (1-39).
Ames, Robert; Boxford; S1 (17-303; 18-338).
Ames, William and John; Braintree; U (20-108).
Ames; Bible record, N. H.; B5 (14-103).
Ammonet, Jacob; Henrico County, Va.; R1 (3-35).
Anderson, Rebecca (Wilson); Irish clue; Q1 (40-190).
Anderson; Va.; E (11-233); Hanover County, Va.; V1 (1-111); Va., Ky.; V1 (11-65).
Anderson; York County, Pa.; Q1 (31-243, 507).
Anderson; Bible records, Ky.; M (16-17).
Anderson; Family record, Westmoreland County, Pa.; M (19-55).
Anderson; arms; M (6-37).
Andrew; Bible records, Milford, Woodbury; A1 (84-236).
Andrews, Henry; Taunton; A1 (51-453; 52-16).
Andrews, John; Essex, Mass.; A2 (46-188).
Andrews, John (Lieut.); Ipswich (Norwich branch); A1 (70-102, 197).
Andrews, William; New Haven; B4 (1-40, 255; 2-508; 3-762; 5-1242; 8-2044).
Andrews; Berlin, Conn.; M (17-26).
Andrews; Montague, Mass.; Ohio; E (6-179).
Andrews; Bible records, Taunton; A1 (60-312).
Andrews; Bible record, Ky.; M (6-27).
Andrus; Norwich, Montgomery; M (7-60).
Angevine; Bible records; A2 (54-267).
Annable, Anthony; Plymouth, Scituate, Barnstable; English data; A1 (65-380).
Annesley; Philadelphia; Q1 (21-125).
Anno; New Haven; B4 (1-58).
Anthony; Philadelphia; Q1 (30-109).

Appleby, Francis; English clue; A1 (61-199).
Appleton, Samuel; Ipswich, Rowley; English ancestry; arms; C2 (6-137); A1 (56-184).
Appleton; Bible records; C4 (3-48).
Arbuthnot; Boston; D (24-7).
Archer; English data; A1 (64-347).
Ardis; Bible records, S. C.; M (9-40).
Armington, Joseph; Boston; S1 (14-168).
Armistead; York County, Va.; Clarke County, Ala.; V1 (6-124, 249; 7-139; 10-43).
Armitage; Boston; A1 (57-415).
Armitt; Philadelphia; P (9-45, 193).
Armstrong, Martin; Jamaica; English clue; A1 (59-109).
Armstrong, Nathan; Frelinghuysen, Warren County, Johnsonburg, N. J.; A2 (43-200).
Armstrong, Robert; Londonderry; S2 (8-191).
Armstrong; Kittanning; E (11-159).
Armstrong; Washington County, Md.; E (15-150).
Armstrong; Pa.; Q1 (29-483).
Armstrong; Juniata, Pa.; M (17-27); N. C.; M (17-27).
Armstrong; Bible records; P (5-112).
Arnold, William and Thomas; Providence; English ancestry; A1 (69-64); a line of descent; S1 (12-235).
Arnold, William; Boston; S. C.; J (22-60).
Arnold; Gloucester, R. I.; F4 (8-340).
Arnold; Marshfield; D (25-35).
Arnold; New London; A1 (66-284).
Arnold; (Benedict); R1 (9-42; 10-363).
Ash; S. C.; J (22-53); Bible records; J (26-175).
Ash; Family records; B2 (2-144).
Ashbridge; Bible record; P (5-173).
Ashburn, Joseph; Milford; B4 (1-59).
Ashfield; Monmouth County, N. J.; A2 (29-92).
Ashley, Robert; Springfield; S2 (14-301).
Ashley; Windham; M (17-28).
Ashton, James (Rev.); Monmouth County, N. J.; A2 (30-203).
Ashton; Marblehead; C2 (5-95).
Askew; Chester County, Pa.; P (11-199).
Aspinwall, Peter; Dorchester, Brookline; A2 (26-26).
Aspinwall; Norfolk, Conn.; M (17-28).
Aspinwall; B4 (1-59).
Astor, John-Jacob; New York; A2 (22-115; 23-15; 44-1).
Aten, Adrian Hendrickse; Flatbush; M (15-9).
Atherton, Humphrey (Maj.-Gen.); Boston; C2 (7-98); M (1-60).

Atherton, James; Milton, Sherburne; C2 (7-181).
Atherton; Bible records, Lancaster, Sharon, Wyoming; P (7-264).
Atkins, John; Va.; English data; A2 (42-173).
Atkins, Thomas; Me.; A1 (65-293).
Atkins; Bible records; A1 (60-154).
Atkinson, Luke; New Haven; B4 (1-59).
Atkinson; Bucks County, Pa.; Q1 (30-57, 220, 332, 478; 31-157, 429).
Atwater, David; New Haven; B4 (1-59, 255; 2-508).
Audley, John; Boston; T6 (2-208).
Augur, Nicholas and Robert; New Haven; B4 (1-87).
Austen, Jonas; Cambridge, Hingham, Taunton; English ancestry; A1 (67-161).
Austin, John and Leonard; New Haven; B4 (1-90, 255; 5-1242).
Austin, Richard; Suffield branch; A1 (85-451).
Austin; Inscriptions; B2 (5-61).
Austin; Conn., Texas; B3 (9-513, 803; 10-187).
Austin; Preston, Conn.; M (17-28).
Austin; Bible records; M (14-44).
Avery, Edward; Baltimore County, Md.; A2 (36-150).
Avery, William; Dedham, Boston; A2 (51-84); English data; A1 (63-362).
Avery; Dedham; M (17-57).
Avery; Groton; B3 (9-395); M (17-29).
Avery; Truro; D (22-163).
Avery; Wallingford; B4 (1-98).
Avery; Conn.; A1 (62-93).
Axson; S. C.; M (3-2-2).
Axtell, Daniel; S. C.; J (6-174).
Axtell, Thomas; Sudbury; A1 (53-227, 359); U (20-109).
Axtell; Bible records; A2 (53-136).
Ayer; Bible record, Haverhill; A1 (65-294).
Ayers, John; Salisbury; English data; A2 (40-233, 236).
Ayers; Bible record, Portsmouth, N. H.; A1 (67-88).
Ayers; Springfield, Mass.; M (17-29).
Ayrault, Pierre (Dr.); F4 (3-199).
Ayres, John (Capt.); Ipswich; A2 (46-82).
Ayres; Newbury, Basking Ridge; B6 (7-29).
Babbage, Agnes (Triggs); English ancestry; A1 (68-59).
Babbage, Christopher; Salem; English ancestry; A1 (68-56).
Babcock, James; Portsmouth, Westerly; U (5-20).
Babcock; New Haven; B4 (1-763).
Bachenberg, Peter; Dodgville, Ia.; B2 (1-54).

Bachiler, Stephen (Rev.); Hampton; A1 (74-319); S2 (29-215).
Bachman; Bible records; P (5-269).
Backer; Boston; A1 (62-93).
Backus; B3 (1-408).
Bacon, Michael; Dedham; A1 (56-364; 57-223, 329); A2 (48-312, 413).
Bacon; co. Suffolk, Eng.; A1 (57-310).
Bacon; English data; A2 (40-133).
Badcock; see Babcock.
Badger; Cheshire; B4 (1-98).
Bagley; Sedgeley, co. Stafford, Eng.; Q1 (37-87).
Bagnall, Walter; Me.; F2 (1-61).
Bailey, Francis; English clue; A1 (61-69).
Bailey, John; Newbury; S2 (12-216).
Bailey, John; Hartford, Haddam; A1 (61-60, 201); M (1-8; 5-10).
Bailey; Rowley; Y2 (1-69).
Bailey; Bible records, Scituate; A1 (55-276).
Bainbridge; Lancaster County, Pa.; M (19-98).
Baird, Alexander; Bushwick; B6 (7-132).
Baker, Alexander; Boston; C4 (3-128).
Baker, Henry; Bucks County; R1 (5-388, 477).
Baker, James; Prattham, N. Y.; B5 (15-209).
Baker, John; Ipswich; U (20-26).
Baker, Thomas; East Hampton; S1 (17-112).
Baker, William; Concord; B5 (12-148).
Baker; Easthampton, N. Y.; M (17-30).
Baker; Marshfield; D (24-27).
Baker; Northampton; M (17-30); S2 (2-17).
Baker; Bible record, Ga., Ala., Texas; M (17-48).
Baker; Bible records; P (5-116).
Baker; see Becker.
Baldwin, John; Milford; S1 (14-74).
Baldwin, Joseph; Milford, Conn., Hadley, Mass.; A2 (42-333).
Baldwin; Milford, Woodbridge, Derby; B2 (7-49); B4 (1-99, 255; 5-1242).
Ball, Allen and William; New Haven; English data; A1 (54-96; 61-118); descendants; B4 (1-107; 2-508).
Ball, William (Col.); Lancaster County, Va.; R2 (2-404).
Ball; Hampshire County, Va.; M (17-30).
Ball; Lancaster County, Va.; A1 (59-418).
Ball; Va.; Q1 (36-217).
Ball; Bible records, Philadelphia; P (7-29).
Ballantine, William; Boston; A1 (63-381).
Ballantyne, Richard; Scotland; Utah; U (2-170).

Ballard, William; English clue; A1 (61-69).
Ballou, Maturin; Cumberland, R. I.; S2 (4-13).
Bancker, Gerrit; Albany; A2 (2-68).
Bancker, Laurens Matthysen; New York, Sleepy Hollow; A2 (40-87).
Bancroft, John; Lynn; English ancestry; A1 (56-84, 196); a line of descent; E (10-67; 11-47).
Bancroft; New England settlers; Y2 (2-94).
Bancroft, Thomas; Reading; M (4-28).
Banister, Thomas; Boston; A1 (69-345; 73-156; 77-238).
Banks; Penobscot; F1 (7-25).
Banks; English data; A1 (51-262).
Banta; N. Y.; M (17-31).
Barbarie, John; New York; A2 (5-6).
Barber, Patrick; Montgomery, N. Y.; A2 (62-3, 120, 249).
Barber; Exeter, R. I.; M (17-31); Harwinton, Conn.; M (17-31).
Barber; New Haven; B4 (1-114).
Barker, Edward; Branford; B4 (1-114).
Barker, James; Newport; English ancestry; A2 (41-59, 176).
Barker, Robert; Marshfield, Duxbury; A1 (53-426).
Barker, Robert; Cape Ann; M (17-32).
Barker; Pembroke; D (24-7).
Barker; R. I., N. C.; H (1-515).
Barlow; Family records, Sandwich, Amenia; A1 (68-105).
Barlow; English data; A1 (54-218).
Barnard, Bartholomew; Hartford; A1 (64-81).
Barnes, Thomas; New Haven, Middletown; B4 (1-115, 256; 2-508; 3-763; 8-2044).
Barnes; Easthampton, L. I., Branford, Conn.; A2 (37-140, 213, 261; 38-34; 41-275).
Barnes; Trenton; B5 (13-78).
Barnes; Bible records, Trenton; B5 (8-115).
Barnes; Hereford, Pa.; M (17-32).
Barnett; New Haven; B4 (1-130).
Barney; Taunton; M (17-32); New Haven; B4 (1-131).
Barnwell, John; S. C.; J (2-47, 154).
Barrell, George; Boston; English data; A1 (61-69; 65-74).
Barrell; Scituate; D (19-145).
Barrell; Family record, Canaan, Hartford, N. Y.; A1 (75-77).
Barrett; Bible record; A1 (53-400).
Barrows; Family record; Dx (4-11).
Barry; (Commodore John); G1 (7-155; 8-86, 257).
Barstow; Family record, Duxbury; D (28-47).
Barstow; Hanover, Mass.; D (8-234).
Bartell, William; Boston; C4 (4-28).

Bartholomew, William; Roxbury (Branford branch); B4 (1-132).

Bartlett, George; Guilford; A1 (56-155).

Bartlett, Richard; Newbury; S2 (6-281).

Bartlett, Robert; Plymouth; D (3-105; 6-44; 12-14; 18-177, 242; 19-72; 20-117, 125; 21-131, 167; 25-16); Dx (5-17).

Bartlett, William; Guilford; A1 (56-160).

Bartlett; N. H.; F3 (2-95).

Bartole, John; Marblehead; English origin; A1 (61-385; 63-160).

Barton, Edward; Salem, Marblehead, Portsmouth, N. H., Kennebunkport; A1 (84-400; 85-455).

Barton, Roger; New York, Brookhaven; A2 (59-239, 361; 60-32).

Barton; Family records, Warwick; A1 (65-380).

Bartow, John (Rev.); Westchester; A2 (3-30).

Bartow; N. Y.; N. J.; Pa.; Q1 (22-125).

Bass, John; Braintree; D (4-202; 18-105); Dx (2-49).

Bassett, John; New Haven; B4 (1-145).

Bassett, William; Duxbury; D (10-25).

Bassett, William; Plymouth; S1 (13-275).

Bassett, William; New Haven; B4 (1-134, 256; 2-509; 3-763).

Bassett, William; Va.; V1 (2-140).

Bassett; Derby; M (17-32).

Bassnett; Bible records, S. C.; J (26-173).

Batcheller, Joseph; Salem, Wenham; A2 (46-321).

Batchelor; New Haven; B4 (1-146).

Bate, James and Clement; Dorchester and Hingham; A1 (51-268); English data; A1 (66-54).

Bateman; Cumberland County, N. J.; B5 (13-55).

Bateman; Bible records, N. J.; M (7-29).

Bates, Henry; Wallingford; B4 (1-147, 256; 2-509).

Bates; White Plains; A2 (49-386).

Bathurst, Lancelot (Capt.); New Kent Co.; V1 (11-172).

Batt, Nicholas; Newbury; English ancestry; A1 (51-181, 348; 52-44, 321).

Battell; Family record, Del.; Q1 (30-247).

Batten; Bible record, N. J.; Q1 (30-379).

Batten; Family records, Pa.; P (10-83).

Batterson; Fairfield, Conn.; M (17-33).

Battescomb, Richard; Hingham; English origin; A1 (63-161).

Baughman; Bible record, Pa.; M (17-72; 18-18).

Baxter, Thomas; Westchester; A2 (31-3, 74, 178, 204; 38-84).

Baxter, Thomas; Yarmouth; D (12-218; 13-247).

Baxter; Dorchester; M (17-34).

Baxter; Family record, Philadelphia; P (7-89).

Bayard, Peter and brothers; New York; A2 (9-188; 16-49); English inscriptions; A2 (21-26).

Bayard, Samuel; New York; A2 (10-36; 23-1).

Bayer; Bible records, Antigua; P (10-172).

Bayley; S. C.; J (12-106).

Beach, John; Note; A2 (6-157).

Beach, Richard, Thomas and John; New Haven; B4 (1-147; 2-509; 3-763).

Beach, Thomas; New Haven, Milford; A1 (80-107; 83-127).

Beach; Stratford; B2 (9-24).

Beach; Litchfield; M (17-37).

Beadles; Salem, Wallingford; B4 (1-161).

Beakley, Isaiah; Bethel, N. Y.; A2 (52-169).

Beal, John; English clue; A1 (57-224).

Beale, Henry; English clue; A1 (65-298).

Beale, Thomas; Cambridge; English ancestry; A1 (66-344).

Beale, Thomas (Col.); York County, Va.; C4 (3-111).

Beall; Georgetown; Q1 (21-507).

Beall; Bible record, Md.; M (18-20).

Beals; Bible record; B5 (6-204).

Beamon, George; Derby; B4 (1-162).

Bean; Exeter; Y2 (10-77).

Bean; Family record, Maine; A1 (62-201).

Bean; Bucks County, Pa.; M (17-37).

Beardsley; Fairfield, Conn.; B2 (4-291).

Beasman; Bible records; X2 (1-17).

Beaton; Pa.; English clue; A1 (55-337).

Beatty; E (8-141); Q1 (44-193).

Beatty; Orange County, N. Y.; B5 (15-259).

Bechtel, John; Bethlehem; Q1 (19-137).

Beck, Henry; Portsmouth, N. H.; A2 (38-98).

Beck; Bible records; A1 (60-299).

Becker; Bible records, Philadelphia; P (11-189).

Beckwith; Lyme; M (17-37).

Bedant; Bible record, Cumberland County, N. J.; Q1 (37-253).

Bedford, Gunning; Jamestown, Va.; A2 (31-1).

Bedlow; Bible record; A2 (31-51).

Bee; N. J.; P (5-168).

Beecher, Isaac; New Haven; B4 (1-162, 256; 2-509; 3-763; 4-943, 948; 8-2044).

Beecher; Bible records; Woodbridge-Sharon; A2 (51-27).

Beeckman, Marten; Albany; A2 (16-133; 28-156).

Beekman, Wilhelmus; New York; A2 (19-41); Probate, N. J.; A2 (33-42).

Beekman, William; New York; Bible records; A2 (28-52; 30-83).

Beeckman; Bible record, Albany; A1 (51-337).

Beeks; Va.; V2 (2-109).

Beeman; Amenia, Shoreham; M (17-60).

Beeman; Morris County, N. J.; M (17-38).

Beers, Richard, Anthony and James; Watertown, Roxbury, Fairfield; A2 (13-85).

Beers, Richard (Capt.); Watertown; U (20-148).

Beers; Stratford; M (17-26).

Beers; Conn.; B4 (1-182).

Belcher; New England families; A1 (60-125, 243, 358).

Belcher; Bible records, Halifax, N. S.; A1 (58-335).

Belden, Richard; Wethersfield; S1 (I3-393).

Belden, William; Wethersfield, Conn.; A2 (37-87).

Belden; West Haven; B4 (1-183).

Belfield, John; Va.; with English clue; V1 (11-167; 12-141).

Belknap, Abraham; Lynn; English ancestry; A1 (68-83, 190; 85-265); a line of descent; B5 (12-149).

Bell, Francis (Lt.); Stamford; A2 (28-153, 201; 29-59, 245).

Bell, John (Rev.); Lancaster County; C4 (3-18).

Bell, John; Londonderry; S2 (4-460).

Bell; Lancaster County, Pa.; M (17-38).

Bellamy, Matthew; Stamford, New Haven; B4 (1-183); A1 (61-338).

Bellingham, Richard; Boston; A2 (41-284).

Bellis; Amwell, N. J.; M (17-58).

Bellows, John; (Lunenburg, Mass., Springfield, Vt.); C3 (2-73; 3-99).

Belt, Humphrey; Anne Arundel County, Md.; X1 (8-195).

Bender; Bible records, Beach Island, S. C.; M (9-40).

Benham, John; New Haven; B4 (1-186, 256; 2-509; 4-956; 5-1242).

Benham; Bible record; A2 (54-66).

Benjamin, John; A1 (85-446).

Bennett, George; Lancaster; A1 (56-241; 58-199).

Bennett, Richard (Gov.); Va.; Md.; X1 (1-73).

Bennett; Middleborough; D (21-171).

Bennett; Bible record; Q1 (33-377).

Bennion; Utah; U (8-97, 145; 9-22).

Benson; Bergen, N. J.; M (17-59).

Bent, John; Sudbury; U (21-12) .

Bentley; English clue; A1 (61-66).

Benton, Andrew; Milford, Hartford; A1 (60-300, 340).

Benton, Edward; Guilford; A1 (54-175).

Beorgheart; Bible record; A1 (51-345).

Bergen, Hans Hansen; New York; A2 (12-152).

Bergh, John; Rhinebeck; A2 (19-122).

Bernard, Gabriel (Col.); Charleston; J (17-129).

Berrien, Cornelis Jansen; Flatbush, Newtown; A2 (14-144).

Berringer; Barbadoes; J (25-173).

Berry, John (Dep.-Gov.); Barbadoes, Bergen, N. J.; A2 (15-49).

Berry, Richard; Barnstable; English clue; A1 (61-278).

Berry, Samuel (Dr.); Charles County, Md.; X1 (23-14).

Berry; Boston, Meriden; B4 (1-197).

Berry; Philadelphia, Zanesville; E (10-91).

Berry; Bible record, King George's County, Va.; M (8-47).

Berry; Bible record; B5 (13-53).

Bertholf, Guillian (Rev.); Bergen County, N. J.; A2 (55-359).

Betts, Richard (Capt.); Ipswich, Newtown, L. I.; A2 (48-81).

Betts, Thomas; Guilford, Milford, Norwalk; A2 (46-303).

Besbeech, Thomas; Scituate, Sudbury; English ancestry; A1 (67-33).

Besson; Bible records, Md.; X1 (14-77).

Bethune, George; Boston; A1 (60-238, 401).

Betscomb; see Battescomb.

Beyer; Pa.; M (10-81).

Bibbe; Bible record; Q1 (31-251).

Biddle, John; Cecil County, Md.; P (11-1).

Biddle, William; N. J.; Q1 (14-364; 16-299).

Bieber; Berks County, Pa.; M (12-20).

Bierer, John M.; Greensburg, Pa.; B2 (5-39, 64, 69).

Bigelow, John; Watertown; English data; A1 (63-363).

Bigelow; Southampton, Middletown; A1 (60-95); A2 (37-72).

Bigelow; Vt.; Utah; U (3-121).

Bigge; English data; A1 (66-54).

Biggs; Va.; M (17-58).

Biggs; Bible records, Md.; M (10-110).

Biles, William and Charles; N. J.; Pa.; Q1 (15-503; 26-58; 45-393).

Billings, William; Dorchester, New London; A1 (81-156).

Billopp; Manorial family, N. Y.; A2 (40-207).

Bills; New Haven; B4 (1-199).

Bingham, John; Evesham, Philadelphia; P (9-207).

Bingham, Thomas; Norwich; Lempster, N. H., branch; S2 (5-353).

Bingham; Philadelphia; S1 (17-128).

Bingham; Norwich; B2 (4-292).

Bingham; King William County; V1 (10-47).

Bingham; Family records; A2 (48-77).

Bininger, Abraham; Pa.; N. Y.; M (15-45; 17-59); A2 (33-135).

Binkele; York County, Pa.; Q1 (31-243).

Bird; Dorchester, New Haven; B4 (1-200).

Bird; Bible records; P (10-174).

Birkhead; Md.; English data; X1 (4-194).

Bishop, Henry; Newport, New Haven, Boston; C2 (6-6).

Bishop, James and Henry; New Haven; B4 (1-201; 2-510; 3-764; 8-2045); C2 (5-120).

Bishop, John (Rev.); Taunton, Stamford; A2 (28-89, 129).

Bishop, John; Guilford, Conn.; C2 (3-241, 288, 311; 4-15, 53, 114, 169, 199).

Bishop, John (Dr.); Bradford, Medford, Mass.; A2 (34-77).

Bishop, John; Newbury; Y1 (63-252).

Bishop, Thomas; Ipswich; M (16-63); Conn. branch; C2 (4-239, 271).

Bishop; Salem; C2 (7-162).

Bishop; Drayton, co. Sussex; C2 (6-251).

Bishop; Bible record (Levi); M (14-58).

Bissell; Family records, R. I.; A1 (65-345).

Bittleston, William and Thomas; Cambridge; English clue; A1 (61-69).

Bixby; Redding; M (17-60).

Black; Berkshire County, Mass.; Cheshire, Ohio; E (12-109).

Blackburn; Fairfax County, Va.; V1 (2-263).

Blackfan; Family record, Bucks County; Q1 (27-111).

Blackford; Somerset County, N. J.; B6 (5-1).

Blackleech, Elizabeth (Bacon); English origin; A1 (63-159).

Bladen, William; Annapolis, with English ancestry; X1 (5-297; 8-302).

Blagge; New York; B4 (1-212).

Blair, George; Edenton, N. C.; H (2-458).

Blair; Amelia County, Va.; M (17-60).

Blair; Bible records, Pa.; P (9-311).

Blaisdell; Chelmsford, Newbury; ("Johnny"); Y2 (8-150).

Blaisdell; Bible records; A1 (84-461).

Blake; S. C.; J (1-153, 265).

Blake; Inscriptions, Wappoo Creek, S. C.; J (20-149).

Blake; Bible records; B5 (4-38, 78).

Blake; English data; A1 (70-366).

Blakeslee, Samuel; New Haven; A1 (56-277); B4 (1-213; 2-510; 6-1528).

Blakistone, George, etc.; St. Mary's County, Md., with English ancestry; X1 (2-54, 172).

Blanchard; Family records; A1 (72-150).

Blanchard; Family records, Andover; A1 (60-373).

Blanchard, Thomas; English data; A1 (68-107).

Bland; Va.; V1 (1-40).

Bland, John, Edward, Theodorick; Va.; X2 (1-11).

Blatchley, Thomas; Branford; A1 (58-357; 59-105).

Blauvelt [Gerret Hendricksen]; New York; A2 (28-158).

Blauvelt; Rockland County, N. Y.; M (17-61).

Blauvelt; Bible records; B1 (6-29, 92).

Bleakley [Bleakney]; Buchanan Valley, Pa.; B2 (1-6).

Blinman, Richard (Rev.); Marshfield; English data; A1 (53-234; 54-39).

Bliss; Rehoboth; A1 (62-202).

Blodgett, Thomas; Cambridge; B2 (2-120).

Blood, Edmond (Capt.); Albany; A1 (53-322).

Bloodgood, Frans (Capt.); Flushing; P (6-229).

Blott, Robert; Boston; U (22-117).

Blue; E (7-48).

Bly, John; Va.; A2 (40-180).

Boden, Ambrose; Scarborough, Me.; C3 (4-158).

Bogardus, Everardus (Rev.); New York; A2 (56-206; 57-81, 295, 373; 58-190; 59-255).

Bogart; Family records, N. Y.; A2 (55-119).

Bogart; see Outen Bogart.

Bogert, John; New York; A2 (9-191).

Boisseau, Joseph Ehyrr; St. Christopher's; V1 (10-118, 280).

Bolles, Joseph; Wells, Me.; arms; A1 (52-185).

Bonaparte; N. Y.; S1 (18-151).

Bond, Jacob (Capt.); Christ Church Parish, S. C.; J (25-1).

Bond; Md.; X1 (3-184); English clue; X1 (4-196).

Bond; Bible record, Arundel; A1 (51-71).

Bond; Bible records, Woburn; A1 (52-464).

Bond; Bible records; A1 (66-185); P (5-122, 124); Q1 (36-254).
Bond; co. Cornwall, Eng.; E (1-61).
Bonnell; N. J.; S1 (18-466).
Bonner, Thomas, James and William; Md.; Beaufort County, N. C.; H (2-115, 171, 405).
Bonticou, Pierre; New York; B4 (1-232).
Booge, John; Haddam; A2 (3-62).
Booker; Va.; V1 (4-437; 12-266).
Boone, George; Family record, Berks County; Q1 (21-112).
Boone, Nicholas; Boston; A1 (71-92).
Boone; Berks County, Pa.; G2 (27-73); Q3 (2-190).
Booth, John; Shelter Island, N. Y.; A2 (32-235).
Booth, Richard; Stratford; S1 (14-81).
Booth; Enfield; A1 (65-382).
Booth; Southold, Hamden, Woodbridge; B4 (1-234).
Booth; English clue; A2 (42-176).
Borden, Joane (Fowle); English ancestry; A1 (75-226).
Borden, John; Saybrook; A1 (84-227, 286).
Borden, Richard; Portsmouth, R. I.; A1 (75-233); T6 (2-244); English ancestry; A1 (84-70, 225).
Bordman, William (Maj.); Cambridge; English ancestry; A1 (77-305).
Bordman; Family records, Cambridge; A1 (76-312).
Boreman, Thomas; Ipswich; English clue; A1 (62-303).
Borton; Bible records; P (7-132).
Boss, Edward; S. Kingston, R. I.; S1 (18-177).
Bosworth, Edward; Hingham; S1 (12-251).
Bosworth; Plymouth; D (27-79).
Botts; Bible records, Va.; A2 (46-163).
Bouldin; Charlotte County, Va.; V1 (4-438).
Boult, John; Martha's Vineyard, Boston; C4 (1-303).
Bourne, Richard; Sandwich; A1 (62-139); D (19-36).
Bourne; English data; A1 (51-110 ff.).
Bourn; Bible records, Scituate; A1 (55-276).
Boush, Maximilian; Princess Anne County; V2 (1-118, 194).
Bowcock; Williamsburg; V1 (3-299).
Bowden, Benjamin; New Haven; B4 (1-236).
Bowditch, John; Braintree; A1 (79-175, 268).
Bowditch, William; Salem; English ancestry; A1 (72-223; 78-144; 82-303; 83-128).
Bowdoin [Baudouin], Pierre; Boston; A2 (45-109).

Bowen, Griffith; Boston; A2 (42-203).
Bowen, Richard; Rehoboth; D (17-247; 18-204).
Bowen; Pa.; N. C.; M (17-62).
Bower; Bible records, Philadelphia; P (9-162).
Bowers, George; Scituate, Plymouth; A1 (64-186; 79-286; 80-278); B4 (1-236).
Bowker; New England settlers; M (4-41).
Bowles; St. Mary's County, Md.; X1 (2-181).
Bowling; Fairfax County, Va.; V1 (1-168).
Bowman, Nathaniel; A1 (64-185).
Bowne, Thomas; Flushing, L. I.; A2 (42-206).
Bowne, William; Gravesend, L. I., Monmouth Co., N. J.; A2 (4-24); S1 (16-86).
Bowton, John; Norwalk; A1 (51-330).
Boyd, John; Franklin County, Pa.; B6 (7-280).
Boyd; Bible records, Pa.; B2 (5-73).
Boyer; Pa.; M (10-81).
Boyes, Matthew; Rowley; English origin; A1 (61-385).
Boykin, Jarvis; Charlestown, New Haven; B4 (1-237).
Boylan, Aaron; Basking Ridge, N. J.; B6 (6-98; 8-234).
Boyle, John; Washington; G2 (18-224).
Boyse, Luke; Charles City, Va.; A2 (42-173).
Bozeman; Bible records, N. C.; H (3-472).
Brackenridge; Inscriptions, D. C.; M (15-20).
Brackett; Boston; G1 (7-395).
Bracy, Thomas; New Haven, York; A1 (61-92).
Bradford, Robert; Boston; English data; A2 (41-72).
Bradford, William (Gov.); Plymouth; D (2-228; 3-144; 4-143; 5-217; 7-65; 9-65, 115; 16-114; 17-65, 254; 20-133; 21-189; 22-63; 23-14, 155, 181; 24-154; 25-25; 27-41, 129; 28-105); Dx (1-10); M (4-39); P (8-102).
Bradford, William (Gov.); English ancestry; A1 (83-439; 84-5).
Bradford, William (Gov.); Letter book; D (5-5, 75, 164, 198); 6-16, 104, 141, 207; 7-5, 79); Bible record, Canterbury; D (15-65); Bible records; Dx (3-104).
Bradford, William; New York; S1 (15-190).
Bradford; Bible records; A2 (56-60).
Bradley, William, etc.; New Haven; B4 (2-261, 510; 3-764; 4-949; 7-1788; 8-2045); Guilford branches; A1 (57-134).

Bradley, William; Philadelphia; A2 (4-183).
Bradley; Haverhill; S2 (4-395).
Bradstreet, Humphrey; English data; A1 (65-69).
Bradstreet, Simon (Gov.); Andover, Salem; Y2 (2-159); Y1 (64-301); C1 (2-83).
Bragg, Benjamin; Family record; A2 (48-88).
Brailsford; S. C.; J (26-237).
Braine, Thomas; Flushing, N. Y.; A2 (34-225).
Branch, Christopher; Kingsland, Va.; A2 (40-180); V2 (1-33).
Brand, Benjamin; English clue; A1 (65-298).
Brasier, Henry; New Haven, New York, Gravesend; A2 (27-37; 47-308).
Bratt, Albert Andriesz; Albany; A2 (35-45).
Brattan; Family record, Pa.; P (11-73).
Brattle; Bible record; B5 (12-234).
Bray; Southington, North Haven; B4 (2-307).
Brayton; Coventry; M (17-62).
Brazelton; Bible records, Md.; B2 (5-74, 85).
Breck, John; Sherborn; A1 (56-380).
Breck; Sherborn, Dorchester; A1 (51-71).
Breckenridge; Bible records, Va.; Z (45, 346).
Breestede; see Van Breestede.
Brengle, Jacob; Frederick County, Md.; X1 (7-91, 219).
Brenneman; Bible record, Conestoga, Pa.; M (18-82).
Brent, Giles; Va.; E (3-64).
Brent; Va.; X1 (1-189).
Brenton; Bible records, Newport; A1 (67-161).
Brevoort, Hendrick Janszen; New York; A2 (7-58).
Brewen; Md.; X1 (5-293).
Brewster, Francis and Nathaniel; New Haven, Brookhaven; A2 (46-4).
Brewster, William (Elder); Plymouth; A2 (42-211, 336; 44-214; 48-204); B2 (1-25, 194); A1 (53-109, 283, 439); D (2-203; 3-15; 5-193; 8-164; 20-112; 22-1, 97, 145; 23-75, 97; 24-97, 123; 28-145); Dx (4-56); K (2-29; 4-95); M (4-40).
Brewster, William (Elder); Family records (Jonathan); D (1-1, 71, 168, 193; 2-21, 112; 5-24).
Brewster; Early notes; D (1-224).
Brewton, Miles (Col.); S. C.; J (2-128, 241; 3-174).
Brick; Bible record; B5 (15-255).
Brickell; Fayette County, Pa.; E (15-143).
Bridgers; Bible record, N. C.; M (16-9).

Bridges, Edmund; Ipswich; Y2 (12-26).
Brigden; New Haven; B4 (2-307).
Briggs; Military records, Mass.; A1 (52-14).
Brigham, Thomas (Lt.); Cambridge; U (22-19).
Bright, William; R. I.; English clue; A1 (59-109).
Brimblecome, John; Marblehead; Y2 (12-34).
Bringhurst; Philadelphia; Q1 (16-468).
Brinker; Northampton County, Pa.; Q1 (39-119).
Brinley, Francis; Boston; A1 (61-394).
Brinley; R. I.; T4 (No. 32).
Brinson, Daniel; Somerset County, N. J.; B6 (3-289).
Brintnall, William; Rutland, New Haven; B4 (2-308; 4-943).
Brinton, William; Pa.; English data; Q1 (37-86).
Brisbane, William (Dr.); Charleston, S. C., with Scots ancestry; J (14-115, 175).
Briscoe, Philip (Col.); Md.; X1 (22-40).
Briscoe; Milford; B4 (2-309).
Bristol, Henry and Richard; New Haven and Guilford; A1 (57-263; 59-167); A2 (45-68, 170, 226, 319; 46-63, 164); B4 (2-309); B5 (13-90, 92; 14-114); (Ohio branch); E (6-179).
Bristol; Pa.; Q1 (17-118).
Bristowe; English data; X1 (22-211).
Brittain; Family record, Pa.; P (11-73).
Broaddus; Bible records, Mo.; B2 (9-49).
Brockett, John; New Haven; B4 (2-323, 511); S1 (13-374).
Brockholst, Anthony (Capt.); New York; A2 (9-115, 188).
Brocklebank, Mrs. Jane; Rowley; Y2 (12-54); U (20-33).
Brokaw [Bourgeon Broucard]; L. I.; B6 (7-293); see Broucard.
Bromfield; Boston; English data; A1 (52-262 ff.; 53-9).
Bromham; New Haven; B4 (2-335).
Bronson, John; Hartford, Farmington; B4 (2-335).
Bronson; Bible records; A2 (56-108).
Brooke, Mary (Wolseley); Md.; English ancestry; X1 (9-113).
Brooke, Robert; Calvert County, Md., with English ancestry; X1 (1-66, 184, 284, 376; 26-323); English origin; A1 (61-385); X1 (19-401).
Brooking, John; Boston; A1 (63-381).
Brooks, Beriah; Lynn; Y2 (12-61).
Brooks, Henry; Concord, Woburn; A1 (58-48, 125, 216); E (7-89; 8-95).
Brooks, John and Henry; New Haven; B4 (2-336, 511; 3-764).

Brooks, Robert; D (1-238).
Brooks, William; Springfield; A1 (72-142).
Brooks; Bible records, N. J.; M (7-26).
Brooks; Bible records; P (10-75).
Broom, Charles; Pa.; English origin; Q1 (22-250).
Broome; New Haven; B4 (2-344).
Broucard, Bourgon; Bushwick, L. I., Dutch Kills; A2(43-98); see Brokaw.
Broughton, John; Marblehead; Y2 (12-65).
Broughton; East Haven; B4 (2-345).
Broughton; S. C.; J (15-171, 183).
Broun; Lancaster County, Va.; R2 (2-402).
Brouwer, Adam; Brooklyn; A2 (8-132; 9-126; 61-254).
Browne, Chad; Providence; A1 (80-73, 170); English data; A1 (65-84).
Brown, Charles; Rowley; Y2 (13-26).
Brown, Cornelius; Boxford; Y2 (12-172).
Brown, Edmund; Dorchester; A2 (46-409).
Browne, Edmund; Plymouth, Sudbury; English clues; A1 (56-184).
Brown, Edward; Ipswich; Y2 (12-125).
Brown, Francis; New Haven; B4 (2-346; 3-764; 4-943; 7-1788).
Brown, George; Pipe Creek, Md.; B2 (1-13).
Brown, Henry; Salisbury; Y2 (12-97).
Brown, James; Newbury; Y2 (13-164).
Brown, James; Middletown, Guilford; A1 (62-334; 65-5, 84, 133).
Brown [Bruyn], Jan; New York, Fordham; A2 (28-1).
Brown, John; Gloucester; Y2 (13-118).
Brown, John; Ipswich; Y2 (12-156).
Brown, John (Elder); Salem; Y2 (13-147).
Brown, John; Rehoboth; D (7-163; 17-193; 18-14, 94; 20-178; 21-128).
Brown, John; Pemaquid, New Harbor; A2 (51-29, 165).
Brown, Nicholas; Haverhill; Y2 (13-24).
Browne, Peter; Plymouth; D (5-29; 23-75, 76); Dx (4-87); M (4-41).
Brown, Peter; Windsor; A2 (26-1).
Brown, Peter; Rye branch; A2 (49-300).
Brown, Richard; Newbury; Y2 (13-168).
Browne, Richard (Lt.); Southold; A2 (31-65, 166).
Brown, Thomas; Lynn; Y2 (13-102).
Brown, Thomas; Newbury; Y2 (13-120).
Brown, William; Marblehead; Y2 (13-55).
Brown, William; Marblehead; Y2 (13-119).

Browne, William; Salem; A1 (63-361); Y2 (13-159).
Browne, William; Saybrook and L. I.; English data; A1 (61-116; 62-199; 63-99, 100).
Brown, William; Chester County, Pa.; X1 (10-262).
Brown; Leicester, Mass.; E (9-28).
Brown; Reading; Y2 (13-40).
Brown; Bible record, Canterbury, Conn.; C4 (4-26).
Brown; Bible record, Richmond, R. I.; B5 (3-36).
Brown; St. Anne's Parish, Md.; X2 (1-32).
Brown; Newburgh, N. Y.; S1 (15-283).
Brown; Pittsburgh; M (17-38).
Brown; Bible record, Framingham; M (11-41).
Brown; Bible records, Md.; M (10-94).
Brown; Bible records, Va.; M (14-44).
Brownell, Thomas; Little Compton; B2 (4-239).
Browning, Nathaniel; Portsmouth; S1 (14-153).
Bruce; Va., Kans.; B2 (3-191).
Brundage, John; White Plains; A2 (49-293).
Bruner; Bible record, Philadelphia; Q1 (21-415).
Brunson; N. J.; P (7-198).
Brush; Dutchess County, N. Y.; Ohio; E (10-235).
Brush; Huntington, L. I.; A2 (33-107).
Bruyn, Jacobus; Kingston; A2 (20-26).
Bryan, William; Isle of Wight County, Va.; N. C.; H (1-577; 2-557).
Bryan; Bible records, King George County, Va.; M (19-104). .
Bryant, Abraham; Reading; S1 (13-64).
Bryant; Family record; A1 (54-101).
Buck, Emanuel; Wethersfield; E (12-118).
Buckingham, Thomas; Milford; (Norwalk branch); A2 (18-73); E (13-1).
Buckley, William; Ipswich, Salem; A1 (60-208).
Buckman; Medford; M (11-53).
Buckminster; Framingham; E (14-74).
Budd; Bible records; A2 (54-266); P (5-265).
Budge, William; Utah; with Scots ancestry; U (3-8).
Buell; B3 (11-501); B4 (2-357).
Buffum, Robert; Salem; S1 (12-263).
Bulkley, Grace (Chetwood); English data; A1 (52-351; 76-307).
Bulkley, Jane (Allen); English data; A1 (52-252).
Bulkeley, Peter (Rev.); Concord, Mass.; A1 (58-201; 63-199; 70-185); K (1-120); A2 (60-234); C4 (1-123); wife's ancestry; A1 (76-307).
Bull, Dixie; Pemaquid; F2 (1-57).

Bull, Henry (Gov.); Newport, R. I.; T4 (No. 81); F4 (4-250).
Bull, Stephen; Ashley Hall, S. C.; J (1-76, 265; 17-175).
Bullitt; Bible records, Md.; M (10-94).
Bullitt; Va.; N2 (4-213).
Bullock, Richard; Rehoboth; M (5-49; 6-23).
Bullock; Family record; A1 (61-275).
Bunce; New Haven; B4 (2-358).
Bunker, George; Charlestown; A1 (62-67).
Bunker; Bible records, Durham, N. H.; A1 (75-80).
Bunnell, William; New Haven; B4 (2-358, 511, 944; 6-1528).
Burbank, John; Suffield; A1 (61-139, 307).
Burchard, see Birchard.
Burd, James (Col.); Tinian; Q3 (2-214).
Burden; Bible records, S. C.; J (26-173).
Burdick, Robert; Newport, R. I.; U (19-62, 127, 166; 20-127, 172; 21-29).
Burdick; Bible record; A2 (50-156).
Burford, Thomas (Att'y-Gen.); Md.; X1 (15-65).
Burgess; Smithfield, R. I.; M (17-63).
Burgis, Thomas; Guilford; A1 (57-404).
Burk; Bible records; P (11-187).
Burkhart; Swiss data; M (18-81).
Burley; Family record, Maine; A1 (62-201).
Burnap, Robert; Roxbury, Reading, with English ancestry; Y1 (56-225, 265; 57-105, 177, 321; 58-209; 59-153, 265, 385; 60-81, 177, 257, 333; 61-49, 185, 265).
Burnham, Robert; Dover; F3 (5-190).
Burns, John; Milford; S2 (9-1).
Burnside, James; Savannah; Northampton County, Pa.; Q1 (21-117).
Burr, Benjamin; Hartford; S1 (16-394).
Burr, Jehu; Roxbury, Springfield, Fairfield; A1 (84-62); A2 (51-164; 54-181); (Ohio branch); E (6-174); (Lt. Stephen); B3 (10-359).
Burr; Hartford; B4 (2-369).
Burr; Torringford, Conn.; Pa.; Q3 (1-157).
Burrell, John; A1 (60-209).
Burrill, George; Lynn; Y1 (51-271; 52-54); English ancestry; A1 (83-117).
Burrill; New Haven; B4 (2-370).
Burritt; New Haven; B4 (2-370).
Burrough; Bible records, N. J.; Q1 (16-122).
Burroughs; New Haven; B4 (2-371).
Burrowes; Marshfield; D (17-186).
Burrows; Rahway, N. J.; Q1 (34-419).
Burt, Hugh; Lynn; A1 (58-406).
Burt, Richard; Taunton; A1 (54-91).

Burt; Bible record, N. J.; P (5-260).
Burtis [Pietro Caesare Alberti]; Venetian ancestry; B1 (1-29).
Burton, John; Salem; C2 (7-302).
Burton, Robert; Accomac County, Va.; P (10-84).
Burton, Stephen; Bristol, R. I.; A1 (60-28); D (10-56).
Burton; Pa.; P (11-200).
Burton; Mecklenburg County, Va.; V1 (2-273).
Burton; Manchester, Eng.; E (6-13).
Burwell, John; Milford; B4 (2-371).
Burwell, Lewis (Maj.); York County, Va.; N2 (2-4-54).
Burwell; Va., N. J.; V1 (2-327).
Bury, William; English clue; A1 (61-69).
Busby, Nicholas; Watertown; English clue; A1 (66-87).
Bush, Reynold; Cambridge; English clue; A1 (63-98).
Bushnell, Francis; Guilford; A1 (52-446; 53-208; 59-109); E (7-137).
Bushrod, Thomas; York County, Va.; V1 (3-300).
Butler, James; Va.; S. C.; J (4-296).
Butler, John; Branford, New Haven; B4 (2-372).
Butler, Thomas C.; New York; A2 (52-108, 258; 53-34).
Butler, William; Va.; English clue; A1 (61-92).
Butler; Ipswich; A1 (59-216).
Butter; English data; A1 (76-278).
Buttles; E (6-191; 7-61); Bible records, Vt., Pa.; M (8-48).
Buttolph, Thomas; Boston; E (6-191).
Button; North Haven; B4 (2-373).
Butz; Pa.; S1 (15-373).
Buys, Jan Cornelise; New York, Brooklyn; A2 (56-264).
Bye; Bucks County, Pa.; P (6-320).
Byfield; English data; A1 (52-135 ff.).
Byington, John; Branford; B4 (2-374).
Byles, Josias; Boston; A1 (69-101, 285).
Byley, Christopher; Salisbury; English ancestry; A1 (51-181, 348; 52-44).
Byram; Bible record, Me.; B5 (15-256).
Byrd; Va.; Ohio; E (11-1).
Cabell; Bible record, Va.; Z (45-345).
Cadle; English data; C4 (3-55).
Cadman; Dartmouth; D (22-2).
Cadmus [Thomas Fredericksen or Cuyper]; New York, Bergen; B1 (1-54).
Cadwell; Durham; B4 (2-374).
Cady, Nicholas; English data; A1 (68-61).
Caffinch; New Haven; B4 (2-375).
Cail; Family record, Del.; Q1 (43-273).
Caile, John and Hall; Dorchester County, Md.; X1 (11-79).

Cain; Hopewell, N. J.; M (17-64).
Caldwell, Charles; Guilford; A1 (58-36).
Caldwell, David; Pa.; Irish origin; Q1 (37-83).
Caldwell, John; Pa., Va.; G2 (3-89).
Caldwell, John; Somerset County, Md.; Kent County, Del., branch; P (6-190).
Caldwell; M (2-25; 3-12; 3-2-9).
Calendar; A1 (61-94).
Calhoun, Andrew; Concord, N. H.; B2 (3-184, 198, 207; 4-245, 252).
Calhoun, David; Stratford, Washington; B2 (2-144).
Calhoun; Va.; S. C.; J (2-248; 7-81, 153).
Calkins, Hugh; New London; A2 (49-17); B2 (2-146).
Calkins; Family records (Stephen); D (4-17).
Call, Thomas; Charlestown, Mass.; B2 (5-26, 45).
Callaghan, Dennis; Va.; G2 (26-45).
Callicott, Richard; Dorchester; English clue; A1 (66-87).
Callis, Robert; Gloucester County; V1 (8-275).
Calvert; Md.; X1 (1-363; 2-141, 369; 3-184, 191, 283; 10-372; 11-282; 16-50, 189, 313, 386, 389; 24-126; 25-30; 26-283, 315); English wills; X1 (21-303; 22-1, 115, 211, 307).
Calvert; Bible records, Va.; M (19-17).
Cameron, John (Dr.); Norfolk, Va.; N2 (2-4-57).
Cammock, Thomas (Capt.); Scarboro, with English data; C4 (4-7).
Camp, Nicholas, Edward; Milford; B4 (2-375).
Camp; Nazing, co. Essex, Eng.; A1 (54-346).
Campbell, Alexander; Washington County, Pa.; N2 (2-4-65).
Campbell, Archibald (Dr.); Bermuda; V1 (1-70).
Campbell, Francis; Shippensburg; Q1 (28-62).
Campbell, John; Perth Amboy, N. J.; A2 (16-6).
Campbell; Prince Edward's County, Va.; M (17-64).
Canaga; see Gnaegi.
Candee, Zaccheus; West Haven; B4 (2-376).
Canner, Henry; New Haven; B4 (2-380).
Canney, Thomas; Bible record; A1 (66-188).
Canney; English clue; F3 (5-102).
Cannon; English data; A2 (40-229).
Cantey, Teige; S. C.; J (11-203).
Capehart; see Kebhart.

Capers, William (Capt.); Berkeley County, S. C.; J (2-273; 3-242).
Card, Richard; Newport; A1 (83-89).
Carder, Richard; New London; A2 (52-87).
Carewe; see Cooke alias Carewe.
Carey; Wyoming, Pa.; Pw (12-117).
Cargill, Hugh; Concord; G2 (3-110).
Carleton; Boston; A1 (55-52).
Carley; see Kerly.
Carlisle, Andrew; Pa., Va., Ohio; E (8-1).
Carman, John; Roxbury, Hempstead; A2 (13-48).
Carman; Bible records; P (9-154).
Carmer; see Kermer.
Carnes, Thomas; New Haven; B4 (2-380).
Carney; Me.; G2 (14-201).
Carpenter, William; Rehoboth; S1 (18-186).
Carpenter, William; Providence; A2 (12-200).
Carpenter; England; American settlers; U (16-60).
Carpenter; Harford, Pa.; A2 (58-56); Attleboro, Mass.; A2 (58-67).
Carpenter; Minisink, N. Y.; M (17-65).
Carpenter; Bible record, Pa.; Q1 (31-371).
Carrington, Paul; Charlotte County, Va.; R1 (4-228).
Carrington, Peter; New Haven; B4 (2-380, 511; 7-1788).
Carroll; Prince George's County, Md.; X2 (1-26; 2-6).
Carroll; Md.; G2 (9-258; 17-99).
Carroll; N. Y.; G2 (26-84).
Carroll; Bible records, Md.; X1 (25-302).
Carstang, Gideon; New York; A2 (58-221).
Carter, John; Philadelphia; T6 (2-246).
Carter, John; Norfolk County, Va.; N2 (2-4-56).
Carter, Joseph; English clue; A1 (61-92.)
Carter, Thomas; Charlestown; Y1 (65-499; 66-124, 257, 330, 464).
Carter; (Hebron and Kent); A1 (55-223).
Carter; Wallingford; B4 (2-388).
Carter; Williamsburg; V1 (6-212).
Carter; Inscription, Clarke County, Va.; M (11-51).
Carter; Bible record, Pa.; Q1 (16-248).
Carter; Bible records, Lancaster County, Va.; P (7-265).
Carter; Bible record, Va.; V1 (10-205; 11-49, 178).
Carter; Bible records, Nomini Hall, Va.; A1 (79-330).
Carter; Bible records; B2 (4-300, 309); Q1 (40-370).

Carter; English clue; X1 (5-294).

Cartwright; Md.; Va.; S3 (8-2-12; 8-3-9; 8-4-7; 8-5-8; 8-6-10; 9-1-14; 9-2-10).

Carver, John (Gov.); Plymouth; A1 (67-382).

Carver, John; Philadelphia; E (11-46).

Carver, Richard; Watertown, Mass.; A1 (69-342).

Carver; Marshfield, Weymouth; A1 (55-221).

Carwithy, David; Salem, Southold; B2 (2-138).

Cary, Miles; Warwick County, Va.; N2 (2-4-53); A1 (55-334); English data; A2 (41-78).

Cary; Abingdon; V1 (1-71).

Casady; Bible records; B1 (6-31).

Case, John; Simsbury; E (7-49).

Case; Ohio branch; E (6-181).

Cass, John; Boston, Hampton; A1 (56-305, 410).

Cass; Exeter, N. H.; S2 (4-501).

Casswall, John; Boston; English origin; A1 (62-92).

Castle; Waterbury; B4 (2-388).

Castor; Bible records, Germantown; P (7-43).

Catlin; Deerfield; B4 (2-389).

Caton, Richard; Catonsville, Md.; X1 (16-299; 17-74; 17-292).

Caudebec, Jacques; Kingston, Minisink; A2 (55-364).

Caulfield; Bible record, Va.; V2 (1-52).

Chadsey, William; North Kingston, R. I.; A2 (32-67, 153, 217).

Chadwick; Brookfield, Malden, Falmouth; C3 (5-96).

Chaffee, Matthew; Boston; A1 (70-184).

Chalker, Alexander; Guilford, Saybrook; A1 (59-133; 63-196).

Chamberlin; Bible records; P (9-315).

Chamberlin; Family records; A1 (84-348).

Champlin, Geoffrey; Newport, R. I.; A2 (46-324); English clue; A1 (82-70).

Chandler, Edmund; Scituate, Duxbury; D (12-108; 14-65).

Chandler, Roger; Plymouth; A1 (63-201); D (11-129).

Chandler, William; Roxbury; English ancestry; A1 (85-133); S2 (4-129, 239; 7-5).

Chandler; Bible records, N. J.; B1 (1-96).

Chandler; Bible records; Q1 (40-370).

Chandler; Family records; P (5-119).

Chandler; (Joshua, Tory); B3 (10-287).

Chapin, Samuel; English ancestry; A1 (83-351).

Chapin; Bible records, Wilbraham; A1 (85-440).

Chapin; (Seth, Revolution); A1 (64-289).

Chaplin, Clement; Wethersfield; English clue; A1 (56-184).

Chapman, Edward; S1 (14-404).

Chapman; Ashford, Bolton; A2 (46-155).

Chapman; Norwich; A2 (52-89).

Chapman; Bucks County, Pa.; Q1 (27-112).

Charles, John; Branford; B4 (2-391).

Chase, Thomas; Hampton, N. H.; E (13-43).

Chase; Freetown; D (21-142).

Chase; Family records, Mass.; Y2 (1-16).

Chase; Bible record, N. H.; B5 (6-222).

Chatfield, Francis, Thomas and George; Guilford, Easthampton; English ancestry; A1 (70-55, 125).

Chatfield, George; Guilford (Derby branch); A1 (78-259).

Chatterton, William; New Haven; B4 (2-392).

Chaucer, Geoffrey; Maternal ancestry; A1 (83-391).

Chauncy, Charles; English data; A1 (55-337, 432; 64-138).

Checkley; Providence; T6 (2-207).

Checkley; co. Northampton, Eng.; A1 (61-66).

Cheever, Ezekiel; New Haven, Boston; A1 (57-40); S2 (9-223).

Chenoweth, John; Md.; Va.; V1 (3-186).

Chester, Leonard; Wethersfield; E (10-154).

Chetwood; England; A2 (53-259).

Chevalier; Bible record, Phila.; Q1 (32-120); P (9-153).

Chickering, Henry and Francis; Dedham; English ancestry; A1 (61-69, 189; 63-282; 64-137; 68-105; 69-226).

Chidsey, John; East Haven; A1 (60-268, 307); B4 (2-396).

Child, James; S. C.; Bible record; J (15-111).

Childs; Barnstable; Dx (2-47).

Chilson; Wallingford; B4 (2-402).

Chilton, James; Plymouth; A1 (63-201); D (1-65; 10-52, 106; 11-129); M (4-54).

Chipman, John (Elder); Barnstable, Sandwich; D (3-181; 16-65; 24-129); Y2 (13-38).

Chisman, John (Lt.); Elizabeth City, Va.; A2 (42-430).

Chittenden, William (Maj.); Guilford; B4 (2-402).

Chittester; Wallingford; B4 (2-403).

Choate; Family record, Vt.; C4 (3-41, 210).

Christian; New Kent County; V1 (10-60).

Christianson, Peter; Newton, Ia.; B2 (1-55).
Christie; Londonderry; S2 (10-52).
Christison, Winlock; Boston; Md.; Q1 (17-88).
Christophers, Jeffrey and Christopher; New London, Southold; A2 (42-210, 337; 50-110, 211, 318; 51-8, 148, 206, 329; 52-55, 175, 231).
Christophers; Family records; A2 (54-253).
Church, Edward; Bristol; D (10-56; 22-153).
Church, Richard; Plymouth, Hingham; D (4-152; 5-118; 7-100, 135; 8-54, 119; 22-22; 24-130); Dx (2-47); English ancestry; C4 (3-192).
Church; Bible records, N. Y., Vt.; M (17-35).
Churchill, John; Plymouth; D (18-40).
Claas; Bible record; P (4-22).
Claesen, Bartel; Flatbush; A2 (55-317).
Claesen, Peter; B6 (8-49).
Claiborne, William; Va.; Md.; X1 (2-160).
Claiborne; Windsor, Va.; V1 (5-127).
Clapp; Scituate; D (22-17).
Clarke, Christopher; Lovisa County, Va.; E (1-1).
Clark, Daniel; Windsor; A2 (28-65); E (11-289; 12-5).
Clark, Edward; Haverhill; A2 (45-287).
Clark, George; Milford; A1 (54-384; 55-108); B4 (2-419).
Clark, Hugh; Roxbury; S2 (27-47).
Clark, James; New Haven; B4 (2-407; 5-1242).
Clarke, Jeremiah; Newport; English ancestry; see also Weston; A1 (74-68, 130).
Clarke, John (Dr.); Newport; English ancestry; see also Cooke alias Carewe and Kerrich; A1 (75-273).
Clark, John; Farmington; U (22-113).
Clark, John; New Haven; B4 (2-403).
Clarke, Joseph; Newport, Westerly (Block Island branch); A1 (85-417; see also 63-198).
Clark, Joseph; Windsor; A2 (59-214).
Clarke, Latham; R. I.; B3 (12-429).
Clarke, Richard; Rowley (Rockingham branch); A1 (58-267).
Clarke, Thomas; Ipswich; A1 (69-89).
Clark, Thomas; Guilford; A1 (59-132); A2 (19-176).
Clark, Thomas; Lyme branch; A2 (47-198).
Clark, Thomas; Pa.; English origin; Q1 (22-250).
Clarke, Thurston; Plymouth, Duxbury; English ancestry; A1 (69-252).
Clark; East Haddam; M (17-65).
Clark; Bible record, Mass.; A1 (51-34).
Clark; Bible records, N. J.; P (7-26).

Clark; Hopkinton, R. I.; M (17-66).
Clark; Lebanon; A2 (61-180); M (17-67).
Clark; Dobbs County, N. C.; M (17-65).
Clark; Orange County, Va.; M (17-66).
Clark; Stafford County, Va.; M (17-67).
Clarke; Bible record; Q1 (32-252).
Clarkson, Matthew; New York, Philadelphia; A2 (30-77).
Clason, Stephen; Stamford; B5 (12-200).
Clawson, John; Bible record, Md.; P (11-78).
Clay, Joseph; Guilford; A1 (62-303).
Clay; Va.; V1 (2-139).
Claypole, James; Pa.; M (2-23).
Clayton, John; Va.; V1 (8-140, 207; 10-285).
Clayton; Monmouth County, N. J.; M (17-67).
Clayton; Monongalia County, Va.; M (17-68).
Cleator, Joseph; Rye; English clue; A1 (59-219).
Cleaves, William; Lyman, Me.; Beverly, Mass.; M (11-2).
Cleaveland; Frederick County, Va.; M (17-68).
Clements; Haverhill; English ancestry; Y1 (53-250).
Clements; Bible records, Caroline County, Md.; X1 (12-387).
Clendinen; Baltimore; N2 (4-189; 5-157).
Cleveland; N. Y.; M (17-69).
Cleveland; Ancestry of Pres. Grover; C2 (1-153).
Clinton, Charles; New York; A2 (12-195; 13-5, 139, 173; 51-360).
Clinton, Lawrence; Ipswich, Providence, Newport; A1 (69-50, 159, 198); B4 (2-423).
Clitz; Family record; B5 (5-105).
Clogston; Nashua, Goffstown, N. H.; A1 (52-25).
Clopper, Cornelius; New York; A2 (36-138).
Clopton, John; English data; A2 (40-240).
Clopton, William; Va.; English clue; A1 (59-219, 327).
Close; Inscriptions, Auburn, N. Y.; B2 (8-28).
Cloud, William; Pa.; M (1-22).
Cloud; S. Carolina; M (1-23).
Clough; Bible records, Boston; A1 (71-188).
Clowes, Samuel; Jamaica; A2 (50-157); Family record (Del); Q1 (29-489; 32-252).
Clutch; N. J.; Q1 (22-131).
Coate; Family record; M (19-13).

Cobb, Henry; Plymouth, Barnstable; A1 (62-96).

Cobb; Middleborough; D (24-35).

Cobb; Bible records, Middleborough; D (2-44).

Cobham; Salisbury; D (20-39).

Coburn; Meriden; B4 (2-427).

Cock; (L. I. family; Penn. branches); A2 (4-188; 8-9).

Cocke, Oliver; Salisbury; English origin; A1 (63-281).

Cocke; Va.; V1 (7-212).

Cocke; co. Bucks, Eng.; A1 (78-147).

Cockever, Alexander; Bushwick; A2 (58-209).

Coddington; Woodbridge, N. J.; A2 (23-190); B6 (2-125).

Coe, Robert; Stamford, Hempstead; S1 (14-251).

Coerten, Guert and Harmen; New York, Bergen; A2 (56-266).

Coffin, Tristram; Salisbury, Haverhill, Nantucket; A2 (17-1); B2 (5-26, 49, 61; 6-5); S1 (13-61); S2 (8-99); English data; A1 (52-66); Y1 (52-49).

Coffin; Philadelphia; P (8-102).

Coggeshall, John; Newport; English ancestry; A1 (73-19; 76-278; 79-84).

Coggeshall; R. I.; A1 (63-362).

Cohen, Jacob I. and Israel I.; Pa.; Md.; X1 (18-357; 19-54).

Coker, Robert; Newbury; English clue; A1 (61-278).

Colby, Anthony; Salisbury; U (20-53).

Colcock, John (Capt.); Charleston; J (3-216; 4-76, 192).

Colcord; Stratham, N. H.; A1 (73-79).

Colden, Cadwallader (Lt.-Gov.); Philadelphia, New York; A2 (4-161).

Cole, Henry; Wethersfield; B4 (2-428).

Cole, Isaac; Woburn; A1 (59-417).

Cole, James; Hartford; A2 (62-116 ff.); E (9-65).

Cole, John; English clue; A2 (42-295).

Cole; Plymouth; D (27-41).

Cole; English data; A1 (61-67).

Coleman, Robert; Lancaster, Pa.; Q1 (36-226).

Coleman; Bible records, Va.; V1 (4-440).

Coleman; Family records, Va., Ala.; M (17-16).

Coles, Robert; Warwick, R. I., Oyster Bay, N. Y.; A2 (27-214; 36-58, 135; 43-197).

Colladay, Jacob; Germantown; P (10-195).

Collamore; Scituate; D (11-65; 16-193).

Colles, Christopher; Philadelphia; Irish ancestry; G2 (29-67).

Colleton, John; Barbadoes; (S. C.); J (1-325; 2-244).

Collett, Richard; Md.; English data; X1 (1-191).

Collier, Isaac; York County; V1 (6-52; 10-52).

Collier; English clue; V1 (4-445).

Collins, Edward; Cambridge, Charlestown; A1 (61-281, 304); U (22-23).

Collins, John; Guilford; A1 (69-209).

Collins, Joseph; Woodbridge; B4 (2-433).

Collins, Tillinghast; Providence, Philadelphia; C2 (3-30).

Collins, William; New Haven; B4 (2-432).

Collins; Eastham; A1 (69-91).

Collins; Guilford; B4 (2-433, 511).

Collins; Bible records, Pa.; P (6-130).

Collins; Bible records; A1 (80-224).

Collis; Gloucester, New Haven; B4 (2-511).

Colson, John; Weymouth; C2 (6-121).

Colton, George; Springfield; E (1-180; 2-9).

Comer, John; English clue; A1 (57-110).

Comstock, William; Wethersfield, New London; A2 (50-76).

Conant, Christopher and Roger; English data; F2 (2-189); Y1 (52-51).

Conant, Roger; Salem; S1 (13-181).

Conde, Adam; Albany; A2 (59-143).

Coney, Nathaniel; Boston; English ancestry; A1 (61-47).

Coney; English data; A2 (40-184).

Congdon; Family record; B5 (6-199).

Conklin; Bible records; A2 (56-111, 115).

Conkling, Ananias and John; Salem, Southold, Huntington; A2 (27-152; 28-171; 29-117; 33-107); English origin; A1 (61-386).

Conley; Kittery; A1 (70-185).

Conn, John; Groton; A1 (81-23).

Connolly; New York; A2 (56-301).

Conover [Wolfert Gerritsen Van Kouwenhoven]; Albany; S1 (16-88); M (1-13, 42, 68).

Conrad, Frederick; Winchester, Va.; N2 (5-140).

Conrad; Bible record, Va.; M (15-22).

Constable, David; English clue; A1 (59-109).

Converse, Edward; Charlestown; English data; A1 (59-172).

Conwell, Yeates; Sussex County, Del.; B5 (3-50).

Conwell; Bible records, Del.; P (11-188).

Conwell; Bible records; P (3-256, 271).

Conyers, Edward; Woburn; A2 (26-24).

Conyngham, Redmond; Philadelphia; Pw (8-183).

Cooke, Aaron; Northampton; B3 (6-440).

Cooke, Francis; Plymouth; D (2-24; 3-33, 95, 236; 8-48; 10-44; 15-136; 16-148; 17-55; 18-147; 21-42; 22-13; 27-145); Bible record; Dx (3-63; 4-39); M (4-54).

Cooke, George; Cambridge; arms; A1 (52-185).

Cook, Henry; Salem; B4 (2-435; 4-944; 5-1243).

Cooke, John; English clue; A1 (61-68).

Cooke, Joseph; Cambridge; English clue; A1 (56-185).

Cooke, Josiah; Plymouth, Eastham; D (5-185; 15-34; 23-76); A2 (39-66).

Cooke, Peter; Chester, Pa.; A1 (52-478).

Cooke, Thomas; Taunton, Portsmouth; B2 (5-15).

Cooke, Thomas; Guilford; A1 (62-218; 63-195).

Cook; Bible record, Provincetown; D (28-130).

Cook; Middletown; A1 (60-315).

Cook; Norwich, Conn.; C2 (6-35).

Cook; Dorchester County, Md.; X1 (3-183).

Cook; Bible record, Mass.; A1 (51-34).

Cooke; Bible record (Hercules); Q1 (23-125).

Cook; Bible record (Josiah); M (15-21).

Cooke; Malden; C4 (4-42).

Cooke alias Carewe; English data; A1 (75-280).

Coolidge, John; Watertown; A1 (77-270; 78-29, 334); English data; A1 (80-401).

Cooper, James; Philadelphia; A2 (15-1).

Cooper, John; Cambridge; B5 (14-115).

Cooper, John; New Haven; B4 (2-451; 5-1243).

Cooper; Bible record; B5 (14-153).

Cope, Oliver; New Castle County, Del.; P (10-242).

Copeland; Family record, Scituate; Dx (5-40).

Copley, Thomas; Springfield, Suffield; A1 (64-248).

Copp, Jonathan; Bible records, Lebanon, Me.; A2 (56-51).

Copp, William; Boston; A2 (62-338).

Corbet; Bible records, Boston; A1 (71-284).

Corbin; Dudley; A1 (61-305).

Corey, John; Southold; A2 (31-225; 32-30; 50-115).

Corey; Branford; B4 (2-462; 3-764).

Cornelise; see Egmont.

Cornell, Thomas; Boston; Portsmouth, R. I.; New York; A2 (42-438); A1 (51-218); T6 (2-244).

Cornell; Inscriptions, Portsmouth, R. I.; A2 (31-180).

Cornell; Bible record, Westchester County, N. Y.; B5 (12-165).

Cornell; Family record; A2 (54-68).

Cornell; B6 (2-178).

Cornwell, William; New Haven branch; B4 (2-461).

Corson; Staten Island; B6 (2-129).

Cortelyou, Jacques; Dutch origin; B6 (1-103).

Cortelyou; Bible records, Ten Mile Run, N. J.; M (18-84).

Corwin, George (Capt.); Salem; D (1-238); Y1 (64-22).

Cory, Giles; Salem; M (11-2).

Cory; Westfield, N. J.; S1 (17-111).

Cossart, Jacob; Brooklyn; B6 (8-236).

Cossart; Holland; A2 (28-111, 131, 241; 29-114).

Cossart; Bridgewater, N. J.; A2 (29-244).

Cotter, Derby; Hamden; B4 (2-462).

Cotton, John (Rev.); Dorchester; A2 (49-87).

Cotton, William; Portsmouth, N. H.; A1 (58-294, 337; 59-34, 186); U (20-104).

Cottringer, John; Philadelphia; G1 (18-71).

Couch, Robert (Dr.); Boston; Virginia; A1 (51-219).

Couch; Wallingford branch; B4 (2-462).

Coulston; Bible records, Pa.; P (6-246; 7-96).

Coultas; Philadelphia; P (9-51).

Covenhoven; Bible records, N. J.; P (7-267).

Covert, Dennis; New Haven; B4 (2-463; 3-764).

Covert, Theunis Janssen; New York; A2 (37-117, 197, 267).

Cowdery; Family records, Montagu, Sandisfield; A1 (79-106).

Cowes, Giles and Christopher; Ipswich; English ancestry; A1 (85-385).

Cowing; Bible record, Rochester, Mass., Seneca, N. Y.; Dx (1-35).

Cowles, John; Hartford, Farmington, Hatfield; B3 (10-77); B4 (2-429; 5-1242).

Cox, John (Dr.); Philadelphia; Q1 (52-168).

Cox; Early New England settlers; K (1-81).

Coy, Richard; Ipswich; C2 (2-177).

Craddock, Matthew, George; English data; A2 (41-78; 64-84).

Craig, Isaac (Maj.); Philadelphia; Q3 (1-289).

Craig, Moses; Somerset County, N. J.; B6 (7-158).

Craig; Family record; C4 (3-210).

Cram, John; Exeter, Hampton; English ancestry; A1 (68-64).

Dean; Bible records, Vt.; B2 (6-57).
Dean; Bible records, Francestown, N. H.; A1 (82-512).
Dean; Bible records; P (5-262, 263).
Dearborn, Godfrey; Exeter, Hampton; English ancestry; A1 (60-308; 68-68); S2 (7-124).
Death, John; Sudbury; U (21-16).
De Bardeleben; S. C.; M (15-27).
De Bevoise [Carel de Beauvois]; Ancestry of wife, Sophia Van Lodensteyn; B1 (3-3).
De Bevoise [Carel de Beauvois]; Dutch ancestry; B1 (3-9).
De Blois, Stephen, etc.; Boston, Newport, Halifax; A1 (67-6, 186).
DeBruyn, Francoys; New York, New Utrecht; A2 (10-35, 85).
Decker, Cornelius; Bible records; A2 (27-131).
DeCow; Bible records; M (4-43).
De Decker, Johannes; New York; A2 (54-357).
Deering, Henry; Salisbury, Boston; A2 (52-40).
Defenbaugh; Bible records, Ohio; M (19-107).
DeGrove; New York; A2 (37-224; 47-88).
De Haven; P (9-92).
Delafield, John; New York; A2 (7-91; 17-245).
De La Mare, Philip; Utah; ancestry in Isle of Jersey; U (21-113, 177; 23-11).
De Lamater [Glan de Le Maistre]; Flatbush, Harlem; A2 (20-131).
De Lancey, Stephen; New York; A2 (4-181; 5-192).
De Lange, Jacob Jansen; Kingston; A2 (53-70).
Delano, Philip; Plymouth, Duxbury; D (6-22; 11-249; 20-31; 23-148); M (17-39); S1 (13-300).
De Long; Brazil; M (16-40, 43).
De Long; Origin; P (8-207).
De Marees [Demarest]; Holland; A2 (57-376).
De Meyer, Nicholas; New York; A2 (9-13).
De Mille, Anthony; Dutch ancestry; B1 (3-58).
Deming, John; Wethersfield; S1 (13-285).
Deming; Bible records; B3 (10-179).
Demott; Bible records; B1 (6-95).
Denise, Tunis; Freehold, N. J., ancestry and children; A2 (49-353).
Denison, John; Ipswich; A1 (56-207).
Denison, Robert; Milford, Newark; East Haven branch; B4 (3-532).
Dennet, William; Va.; English clue; A1 (61-199).

Denning, William; New York; A2 (30-133).
Dennis; New Haven; B4 (3-534, 765).
Dennis; Woodbridge, N. J.; A2 (28-172).
Denny, Samuel; Arrowsic Island; F2 (1-187).
Denny, William (Gov.); Pa.; Q1 (44-97; 45-391).
Denslow, William; New Haven; B4 (3-534, 765; 5-1243).
Dent, John; St. Mary's County, Md.; X1 (19-193).
Dent, Thomas (Judge); St. Mary's County, Md.; M (19-3, 87).
Dent; Monongalia County, Va.; M (17-39).
Denton; England; A2 (29-240).
De Nys, Pieter; New York; A2 (59-9).
Depew, see Dupuis.
De Peyster; Bible record, Albany; A1 (51-334).
Derby, John and Richard (Roger); Plymouth, Yarmouth (Salem); English ancestry (Derby, Symondes, Moone, Hyde, Leachland, Jones); A1 (79-410; 80-343; 81-91, 178, 314, 486, 488; 82-55, 63, 65, 66).
Derby, John; Marblehead; E (13-36).
Derby, Roger; Ipswich; Y1 (65-243, 451; 66-65).
Derby; Weymouth; A1 (68-107).
De Riemer, Isaac; New York; A2 (7-61; 36-5; 40-207).
De Sadelaer; Holland; A2 (57-378).
De Sille, Nicasius; New Utrecht; A2 (34-24, 146).
De Sille; Bible records; A2 (20-190); P (7-127).
De Veau; Ga.; M (1-52).
Devereux, John; Salem, Marblehead; A1 (74-114, 199, 293).
Devereux; Bible record; Q1 (43-257).
De Vries, Titus Syrachs; New Utrecht; A2 (39-5).
Dewees; Ky.; Q1 (28-251).
Dewey, Thomas; Dorchester, Windsor; A2 (6-63, 129, 166; 8-108, 153; 59-214).
Dewing, Andrew; Dedham; A1 (57-101).
De Witt, Tjerck Claessen; New York, Albany; A2 (5-161; 17-251; 18-13; 21-185; 22-3).
Dexter; Newburyport; ("Lord" Timothy); Y2 (7-97).
Dey, Dirck Janse; New York; A2 (7-57).
Dey; Bible records; A1 (85-347).
Diamond; Lynn; Y2 (3-33).
Dibble; Wallingford, New Haven; B4 (3-535).
Dickenson; Bible record, Amherst, Mass.; M(19-104).

Dickerman, Thomas; Dorchester (New Haven branch); B4 (3-536, 765).
Dickerson, Philemon; Salem, Southold; A2 (22-21; 30-180, 247).
Dickerson; N. J., Md.; E (10-55).
Dickinson, Adam; Augusta County, Va.; N2 (2-2-54).
Dickinson; Bible record; A1 (51-359).
Dieffendorff; Family record, Pa.; Q1 (17-375).
Diggins, Jeremiah; Windsor; A1 (61-142; 62-98).
Diggs, Edward (Gov.); Va.; English data; A2 (42-433).
Dillenback, Martin; Livingston Manor, N. Y., and Stone Arabia, Montgomery Co., N. Y.; A2 (29-115).
Dillon; Bible records, Ky.; M (16-18).
Dillwyn, William; Philadelphia; Q1 (28-248).
Dimock, Thomas; Hingham, Barnstable; B3 (9-927; 11-662); S1 (13-282).
Dimon; see Dymont.
Disborough; English data; A1 (54-95).
Disbrow; Rye; A2 (49-297).
Ditmas; Bible records; A2 (54-333).
Dix, Leonard; Watertown, Wethersfield; S1 (18-442).
Dix, Ralph and John; Reading; C4 (4-83).
Dixwell, John; New Haven; T2 (6-337); B4 (3-544).
Doane; Bible records; A1 (59-160).
Dobbin, Alexander (Rev.); Gettysburg, Pa.; Q1 (1-109).
Dobbins; Bible records; P (11-186).
Dodd; New Haven; B4 (3-544).
Dodd; Bible records; Q1 (35-380). .
Doddridge, John; N. J.; (Pa.; Va.); N2 (2-1-54).
Dodge, William; Salem; Z (62-233).
Dodge; New London, New Haven; B4 (3-545).
Dodson; Greenfield, Bedford County, Pa.; B2 (9-34).
Dolbear; Family records; A1 (83-511).
Dolliver; Families; C2 (4-157).
Donbavand; Bible record; B5 (7-63).
Donnally, Andrew (Col.); Va.; N2 (1-3-52).
Doolittle, Abraham; New Haven, Wallingford; B4 (3-546).
Dooly, John; Ga.; G2 (26-179).
Dorchester, Anthony; Windsor, Springfield; B4 (3-562).
Dorman, Edmund; New Haven; B4 (3-563, 765; 5-1243).
Dorman; Bible record; Q1 (32-252).
Dorr, Edward; Roxbury; S1 (17-465).
Dorrance, George; R. I.; G2 (2-152).
Dorsey; Anne Arundel County, Md.; X1 (25-397).

Dorsey; Prince George's County, Md.; M (6-45).
Dorsey; Bible records, Ky.; M (16-17).
Dorsey; Bible record; M (5-46).
Doten; see Doty.
Dotter; Bible record, Va.; M (14-47).
Doty, Edward; Plymouth; D (3-87; 4-65, 233; 5-111, 210; 6-77; 19-176; 20-27; 25-164); M (4-55).
Dougal; New Haven; B4 (3-571).
Doughty, Francis (Rev.); Taunton, Mass., Newtown, New York; A2 (43-273, 312).
Doughty; Burlington County, N. J.; A2 (30-122); Bible records; A2 (30-254).
Doughty; Bible records; X2 (2-6).
Douglas; Wallingford; B4 (3-571).
Douglas; Mercer County, N. J.; B2 (4-228).
Douglas; Bible records; V1 (12-257).
Douglas; arms; M (6-36).
Douw, Volkest Janse; Albany; A2 (3-82).
Douw; Bible records; A1 (51-340, 341).
Dow, Henry; Hampton; A1 (69-342).
Downe; Md.; English clue; X1 (3-183).
Downer; Bible records, Preston, Conn.; A1 (85-449).
Downes, Edward; Dorchester; A1 (64-370; 65-36).
Downes, Thomas; Dover; F3 (6-145; 7-49).
Downing; Kittery; A1 (61-254).
Downs, John; New Haven; B4 (3-572).
Downton; Va.; V1 (9-134).
Dowsett; English data; A1 (76-75).
Doxy, Thomas; New London; English data; A2 (42-175).
Doyle; Boston; G2 (15-395).
Doyle; Lancaster, Pa.; G1 (18-66).
Drake, John; Windsor; (royal ancestry); A2 (27-176).
Drake; East Greenwich, R. I.; C1 (1-74).
Drake; N. H.; Z (64-561).
Drake; N. J.; P (10-185).
Drake; Bible records; B1 (6-32).
Draper; Bible record; Q1 (32-253).
Drayton, Thomas; Barbados; S. C.; P (8-1); J (14-16).
Drew; Plymouth; D (7-114).
Drew; Bible records, Mass.; A1 (66-84).
Dreyer, Andreas; Albany; A2 (51-194).
Dring; Bible record, Little Compton, R. I.; C3 (3-106).
Drinker; Family record, Pa.; Q1 (22-373).
Drowne, Leonard; Kittery, Me., Boston; A2 (17-215; 35-171; 42-438; 48-390).
Drown; Family record; A1 (54-449).

Drumheller, Dewalt; Berks County, Pa.; S1 (14-175).

Drummond, Alexander; Georgetown; A1 (57-241).

Drummond, Robert; New York; A2 (17-35).

Drury; Bible records, Landaff, N. H.; A1 (83-254).

Du Bois, Jacques and Louis; Kingston; A2 (24-153; 27-190; 28-13).

Du Bois; New York; N2 (3-49).

Dubs, Jacob; Milford, Pa.; Q1 (18-367).

Duda, Philip; Dover, N. H.; C1 (1-75).

Dudley, Gamaliel; English data; A1 (61-66).

Dudley, Thomas (Gov.); Roxbury, Mass.; A2 (43-94; 49-88); S2 (11-153); English data; A1 (56-206; 65-189; 80-447); Maternal ancestry; A1 (66-340).

Dudley, William; Saybrook, Guilford; A1 (54-95; 62-200); Wallingford; B4 (3-581).

Dudley; Gloucester County; V1 (12-266).

Duer, William; New York; S1 (13-292).

Duer; Bible record, Bucks County, Pa.; Q1 (39-218).

Duffield; Bible records, Pa.; B2 (6-59).

Duke, John; Frederick County, Va.; N2 (4-70).

Duke; James City County; V1 (7-213).

Dulany, Daniel; Annapolis; X1 (13-20, 143).

Dulany; Md.; Z (57-18).

Dummer, Edward; New Haven; B4 (3-582).

Dummer, Richard; Newbury; (Rev. Shubael of York); F2 (9-33).

Dumont, Wallerand; Kingston, N. Y.; A2 (29-103, 161, 237; 30-36; 34-191); (N. J. branch); B6 (1-106, 208).

Dunbar, John; Fairfield, New Haven; B4 (3-583).

Dunbar; N. H.; S2 (4-263).

Duncan; Berkeley County, Va.; N2 (2-2-74).

Dungan; Bible record, Pa.; Q1 (24-118); P (7-285).

Dunham, John; Plymouth; A2 (27-94).

Dunkerly; Family record; P (10-87).

Dunlap; Me.; F2 (4-69, 174).

Dunlap; Augusta County, Va.; N2 (3-255).

Dunn, Hugh; Dover, Piscataway; F3 (1-149).

Dunn, Robert; Kent Island, Md.; X1 (7-329).

Dunning, Andrew; Brunswick, Me.; A1 (74-97).

Dunning, Theophilus; Salem; S1 (18-457); Conn. branch; A1 (52-38; 55-345); A2 (45-188, 288; 52-213).

Dunscomb, Daniel; Family records; A2 (56-64).

Dunster, Henry (Rev.); Cambridge, Scituate; English ancestry; A1 (61-186; 64-186; 80-86).

Dunton, Robert and Samuel; Reading; A1 (54-286).

Dunton; Philadelphia; Q1 (24-116).

Dupuis [De Puy, Depew], Nicholas and Francois; Kingston; A2 (32-53, 77, 141, 231).

Durand, John (Dr.); Milford; B4 (3-585).

Durand; Family records, New Orleans; C3 (3-25).

Durant, George; Malden, Middletown; A2 (43-289).

Durbin; Loretto, Pa.; B2 (1-56).

Duryea, Joost; New Utrecht, Bushwick; A2 (11-62).

Dustin, Thomas; Me.; B2 (2-135); F2 (3-37).

Dutcher, Wilhelm; Albany, Brooklyn, Kingston; A2 (40-185, 249; 41-44, 109, 240).

Dutrieux, Philippe; see Truax.

Dutton, Thomas; Reading, Woburn; U (20-62); Lyme, Wallingford branch; B4 (3-586).

Dutton; Bible records; P (3-265).

Duty, William; Rowley; U (20-28).

Du Vall; Bible records, N. J.; A2 (22-105).

Duyckinck, Evert; New York; A2 (23-33); Dutch ancestry; B1 (1-64).

Dwight, John; Watertown, Mass.; A2 (42-445).

Dwight; English records; A2 (17-23).

Dyckman, Jan; Harlem; A2 (34-23).

Dyer, George; Dorchester; English clue; A1 (61-280).

Dyer, William; Dorchester; English data; A1 (61-199; 65-189).

Dyer, William; Boston, Providence; F4 (3-77).

Dyer, William (Dr.); Truro; C4 (4-20).

Dyer; Boston; C4 (1-129).

Dymont, Thomas; East Hampton, L. I.; B5 (13-54).

Eager, William; Marlboro; S1 (18-191).

Eames, Anthony; Hingham, Marshfield; A1 (56-409).

Eames, Robert; Woburn; A1 (62-58, 150; 69-90).

Eames, William; English clue; A1 (61-199).

Eames; Boxford, Mass.; Northumberland, N. H.; S2 (26-240).

Earle; Tiverton; D (17-60, 253).

Eastabrooks, Thomas; Swansea; A1 (83-464).

Eastman, Roger; Salisbury; English ancestry; A1 (54-343); A2 (46-58).

Eastman; Ashford, North Haven; B4 (3-591).

Easton; Morristown, N. J.; B1 (1-23).

Easton; Barbados; A1 (54-346).

Eaton, Francis; Plymouth; D (2-172; 12-226; 18-125); M (4-57).

Eaton, Jonas; Lynn, Reading; B5 (15-233).

Eaton, Martha (Jenkin); English ancestry; A1 (76-54).

Eaton, Nathaniel; Cambridge; T2 (4-185).

Eaton, Theophilus (Gov.); New Haven; B4 (3-591, 765); English data; A1 (53-432; 64-88); T2 (7-1).

Eaton, William; Watertown, Reading; wife's ancestry; A1 (76-54).

Eaton; Family record; A1 (85-349).

Eberly; Bible record, Franklin County, Pa.; M (12-28).

Eckerson, Jan Thomaszen; New York; A2 (7-119).

Eddy; Middleborough; Dx (5-104).

Edenden; see Iddenden.

Edes, John; Charlestown; A1 (77-83); S1 (13-290).

Edes; Bible records, Boston; A1 (85-460).

Edgar, Thomas; Rahway, N. J.; S1 (16-260).

Edgar; Bible records; M (16-7).

Edmands, Walter; Concord; C4 (4-58); Bible record, Mass.; C4 (4-62).

Edmonds; Bible record, Fauquier County, Va.; Q1 (33-253).

Edmundson, Thomas; Rappahannock County; V1 (7-185, 263).

Edsall, Samuel; Boston, New York, Bergen, Brookhaven; A2 (13-191).

Edwards, James; English clue; A1 (61-92).

Edwards; Surry County; V1 (10-38, 130).

Edwards, John (Dr.); Charlestown; A1 (67-297).

Edwards, Rice; Salem, Wenham; A1 (56-60).

Edwards, William; Hartford; English ancestry; A1 (58-202); A2 (62-116); New Haven branch; B4 (3-591).

Edwards; Bucks County, Pa.; E (11-46).

Edwards; Phila.; Q1 (36-126).

Eells; Milford; B3 (4-110).

Eggleston, Bigod; Dorchester, Windsor; A2 (23-99).

Eggleston; East Haven; B4 (3-593).

Eggleton; Woburn; A1 (59-417).

Egmont, Cornelis Segerse; Albany; A2 (46-343; 47-3).

Eigenbrodt, Lewis - Ernest - Andrew; New York; A2 (18-122).

Ela; Haverhill, Sanbornton; S2 (27-303).

Elbridge, Giles; Pemaquid; English ancestry; A2 (42-92).

Elbridge, Thomas; Pemaquid; A1 (52-361).

Elcock, Anthony; New Haven; B4 (3-593).

Eld; New Haven; B4 (3-593).

Elder; Franklin County, Pa.; Q1 (29-378).

Eldred [Eldredge], William; Yarmouth; A1 (51-46; 62-202); U (4-145, 181).

Eldridge; Va., Conn., N. Y.; G1 (7-24).

Elfreth; Family record, Pa.; P (2-215).

Eliot, Andrew; Beverly; A1 (81-3).

Eliot, John (Rev.); Roxbury; A2 (25-42).

Eliot, Philip, (Rev.) John, and Jacob; Roxbury; C4 (1-37).

Eliot; Roxbury; A1 (51-70).

Eliot; New Haven, Leicester; B4 (3-594).

Ella; Bible records, N. Y.; P (6-132).

Ellicott, Joseph; Bucks County, Pa.; with English data; X1 (26-362).

Ellington; Va.; V1 (10-207; 12-71).

Elliott, Thomas; S. C.; J (11-57).

Ellis, John; Bible records, Franklin; A1 (66-85).

Ellison; Bible record, N. J.; B5 (15-197).

Ellyson, Robert (Capt.); New Kent County; V1 (10-32).

Ellot; Bible records, Pa.; P (10-77).

Ellwood, Richard; Minden, N. Y.; A2 (53-2, 147, 261, 367; 54-85).

Elmendorf, Jacobus Conradt (van); Kingston; A2 (20-101); B6 (6-194).

Elser, Henry; Frankford, Pa.; Q1 (17-375).

Elsey, Nicholas; New Haven; B4 (3-594); English data; A1 (64-347).

Elting, Jan; Flatbush, Kingston; A2 (16-25; 21-46); N2 (3-122).

Elton; Bible record, Harwinton, Canaan, Conn.; B5 (4-15).

Elwell, Robert; Dorchester, Salem; A1 (53-25); Branford; B4 (3-594).

Elwell; N. J.; P (6-243).

Ely; Lyme; A1 (66-284).

Ely; Bible records, Md.; P (10-82).

Ely; B3 (10-177).

Emerson; Bible record; A1 (51-359); Q1 (32-253).

Emery; Bible records, Maine; D (9-52).

Emery, John and Anthony; English data; A1 (54-313).

Emley, William; Burlington County, N. J.; English origin; Q1 (36-319).

Emmert; Hagerstown, Md.; M (12-11).

Emory, Arthur; Md.; X1 (23-363; 26-199).
Emory; Bible record, Md.; P (11-80); X1 (12-164).
Endecott, John (Gov.); English data; C2 (7-111, 176, 251).
Endicott; Bible records, Danvers; A1 (85-110).
Endicot; Boston; A1 (56-91).
Engle; Shenandoah Valley, Va.; N2 (5-153).
English, Clement; Salem*(New Haven branch) B4 (3-594).
English, Philip; Salem; Y1 (66-273).
Enloe; Bible records; P (9-148).
Eno; Bible record, Onondaga County, N. Y.; C3 (3-97).
Enoch; Hampshire County, Va.; V1 (4-442).
Ensign, Thomas; Scituate; English data; A2 (42-97); A1 (66-87; 72-3).
Ent; Bible record, New York, Germantown; B5 (14-185).
Eoff, Jacob; Pluckemin, N. J.; B6 (7-240, 284).
Epps, Daniel; English data; A1 (71-91).
Erskine, Alexander; Bristol, Me.; A1 (74-16, 87).
Erving; Boston; A2 (30-209).
Erwin, Arthur; Bucks County; Q1 (19-397).
Esling, Johan George; Philadelphia; G1 (2-333).
Esterbrook, Thomas; Swansea; S1 (13-189).
Estes; Italian theory; C2 (2-248; 3-105).
Estey, Jeffrey; Salem, Southold, Huntington; A2 (49-90).
Estow, William; Newbury, Hampton; A1 (69-342).
Estrey, Edward; English data; A2 (40-229).
Evance, John; New Haven; B4 (3-596).
Evans, John; Pa.; P (3-142).
Evans, Nicholas; English clue; A1 (61-92).
Evans; Bible record; M (12-27).
Evarts, John; Concord, Guilford; A1 (61-25, 307); A2 (47-313); B2 (2-96).
Everard, Richard (Sir); N. C.; R1 (2-328).
Everest, Isaac; Guilford; A1 (61-395).
Everton; East Haven; B4 (3-596, 765).
Evetts, James; New York; A2 (12-145).
Ewer, Thomas; Charlestown; English data; A1 (69-357).
Ewing, Thomas; Lancaster; Q3 (2-206).
Ewing; Culpepper County, Va.; N2 (4-203).
Ewing; Family record, Va.; M (18-13).

Eyre; see Aires.
Fadre; Boston; A1 (72-246).
Failor; Bible record; M (16-52, 65).
Fairbanks, Jonathan; Dedham; English data; A1 (60-152).
Fairchild, Thomas; Stratford (New Fairfield branch); B3 (3-352).
Fairfax; Charles County, Md.; X1 (26-320).
Fairfield; Woodstock, Conn.; A2 (29-102).
Falconer, Patrick; New Haven, Newark; A1 (60-21).
Faneuil, Benjamin; New York; French ancestry; A2 (47-123).
Fanning; New Haven; B4 (3-597).
Farley; Antigua, Va.; V1 (1-70; 2-322); R2 (1-428).
Farnes, Samuel; New Haven; B4 (3-597).
Farnham, John; Dorchester; A1 (62-15).
Farrar, Thomas; Lynn; English origin; A1 (61-386).
Farrel, Benjamin; Waterbury; B4 (3-601).
Farren; East Haven; B4 (3-597).
Fassouer, Henry; New York; A2 (16-41).
Fauconnier, Pierre; New York, Hackensack, N. J.; A2 (43-89).
Faulkner, Patrick; New Haven, Newark; B4 (3-597).
Fawcett, Thomas; Pa.; G2 (3-118).
Faxon; Correction of genealogy; M (1-10).
Fayson, Henry; Va.; V1 (6-270).
Feake, Henry; Lynn, Sandwich, Newtown, L. I.; A2 (11-70).
Feake, Robert; Watertown, Greenwich; A2 (11-13).
Feake, Tobias; Yarmouth, Greenwich, Flushing; A2 (11-71, 168).
Feering, John; Hingham; English data; A2 (41-7).
Felch, Henry; Boston; A2 (50-85); Y1 (56-148); S1 (17-207).
Fellows; Poplin, N. H.; S2 (8-316).
Felton, Benjamin and Nathaniel; Salem; English data; A1 (52-234 ff.).
Felton; Bible record, Marblehead; Y1 (57-339).
Femell; co. Somerset, Eng.; A1 (80-368).
Fenimore; Bible records, N. J.; P (7-34); Q1 (16-377).
Fenn, Benjamin; Milford; B2 (2-133).
Fenn, Edward; Wallingford; B4 (3-598; 5-1243).
Fenner, Arthur, John, and William; Providence, Saybrook; English clue; A1 (62-200; 63-99).
Fenno, John; Milton; A1 (52-448).
Fenton; New Haven; B4 (3-600).

Fenwick, John (Maj.); Salem, N. J.; English ancestry; Q1 (49-151, 256; 50-267).

Fenwick; S. C.; J (8-222; 14-3).

Ferebee, John; Lower Norfolk County; V2 (1-193).

Ferguson [Vergison]; New Haven; B4 (3-601).

Fernald; Kittery; A1 (65-85).

Ferne; Va.; English data; A1 (54-192).

Ferns, Samuel; New Haven; A1 (66-310).

Ferson; see MacPherson.

Fessenden; Sandwich; D (20-58).

Fick, Adolph C.; Lancaster, Pa.; G1 (2-367).

Ficklin; Bible records, Ky.; M (16-19).

Field, John; Providence; A1 (51-359).

Field, Robert; Dedham, Newport, Flushing; A2 (6-193; 42-205).

Field, Zachariah; Dorchester, Hartford, Northampton; A2 (32-7).

Fielding; Va.; A1 (53-24).

Fields; East Haven; B4 (3-602).

Fifield, William; Family records; A1 (65-382).

Filkin; Records, Dutchess County; Bible record; A2 (34-108, 216; 35-15).

Fillmore; English clue; A1 (65-87).

Finch, Daniel; Fairfield; B4 (3-602).

Finch; Kent County, Md.; X2 (1-30).

Finch; Md.; X1 (4-197).

Fine [Finie, Finney], John; New York; A2 (37-317).

Finney, John; Barnstable; D (20-97).

Finney, Robert and John; Plymouth; (Bristol branch); A1 (60-67, 155).

Finney; Pa.; English clue; P (9-187).

Firman, Josiah; Boston; English clue; A1 (56-182).

Fischel; York County, Pa.; Q1 (31-508).

Fish, John and Jonathan; Boston; English data; A2 (41-284).

Fish, Jonathan, John, and Nathaniel; Sandwich, Newtown, L. I.; A2 (25-1; 54-329).

Fish; Portsmouth, R. I.; A1 (56-121).

Fish; Great Bowden, Leicester, Eng.; A2 (53-53).

Fishels; York County, Pa.; Q1 (44-287).

Fisher, Hendrick; Somerset County, N. J.; B6 (8-1, 154).

Fisher; Va.; N. C.; R2 (1-134, 350).

Fisher; Berks County, Pa.; M (17-40).

Fisher; English data; A1 (53-126).

Fisk; Bible record (Gen. John); C4 (3-186).

Fiske; Milford, Wallingford; B4 (3-604).

Fiske; English data; A1 (53-125).

Fitch, James (Rev.); Saybrook, Norwich, Conn.; A2 (34-155; 43-92).

Fitch, Zachary; Reading; English ancestry; A1 (55-288, 400; 56-41; 57-415; 63-162; 69-88, 189).

Fitch; Wallingford, New Haven; B4 (3-604).

Fitch; Lebanon inscription; A1 (51-72).

Fitch; Bible records, Newton, N. J.; P (9-161).

Fitch; Diary of Jabez, see Norwich.

Fitzgerald, Edward; Cumberland County, N. J.; M (4-34).

Fitzgerald, John; Alexandria; G2 (18-233).

Fitzgerald; Va.; G2 (27-229).

Fitz-Randolph; New Jersey; A2 (30-106).

Flagg; Bible records, Watertown; A1 (66-185).

Flanagan, Christopher; Bedford, N.Y.; A2 (23-62).

Fletcher, John; N. Car.; B2 (7-8).

Fletcher; Bible records, Va.; B2 (8-67).

Flint, Thomas and Henry; Concord and Braintree; English ancestry; A1 (56-312; 61-198).

Flint, William; Salem; Y1 (57-19).

Flood; Gorham, Me.; B5 (10-31).

Floyd, John (Capt.) Rumney Marsh; A1 (63-245).

Floyd; Setauket inscriptions; A2 (15-41).

Floyd; Bible records; A2 (27-110).

Flucker, James; Charlestown; C2 (2-201).

Fobes; Family records; Dx (2-152).

Focken, Jan; see Jan Heermans.

Follett; Harford, Pa.; A2 (58-59).

Folsom, John (Dea.); Hingham, Exeter; English data; A1 (61-185).

Fooks; Bible records; P (5-111).

Foos; Ohio; E (14-87).

Foote, Joshua; Boston, Providence; English data; A2 (41-8).

Foote, Nathaniel; Watertown, Wethersfield; Branford, North Haven, branches; B4 (3-606, 765).

Foote; English data; A1 (51-135 ff., 249 ff.).

Forbes, Alexander; Perth Amboy; A2 (21-159).

Forbes; Hartford, East Haven; B4 (3-607; 4-944; 5-1244).

Forbes; (Rev. Eli, Westborough); S1 (13-62).

Ford, John; Woodbridge; A2 (53-162).

Ford, Timothy; New Haven; B4 (3-611, 765; 4-944).

Ford, Widow; Marshfield; C4 (1-199).

Ford, William; Duxbury; A2 (53-160).

Ford; Morristown, N. J.; Charleston, S. C.; J (13-132).

Ford; Bible record; Hebron, Conn.; B5 (6-170).

Forde; Bible records, Philadelphia; P (4-321).

Fordham, Robert (Rev.); Southampton, L. I.; English origin; A1 (57-298).

Fordham; Bible record, N. J.; B5 (15-197).

Forgerson; Bible records, Goshen, N. Y.; P (9-160).

Forman, Robert; Flushing, Oyster Bay; B6 (6-262); A2 (50-392).

Formicula, Serafina; Eltham, Va.; V1 (2-194).

Forrester; Family records, S. C., Texas; M (17-50).

Forsyth, Matthew; Chester, N. H.; S2 (8-251).

Foster, Christopher; Bible records, Southampton, L. I.; A2 (34-282).

Foster, Edward; Scituate; A1 (52-339).

Foster, Hopestill (Capt.); Dorchester; A1 (52-194, 336); English ancestry; A1 (67-36).

Foster, Reginald; Ipswich; S1 (14-401); U (21-18).

Foster, Thomas; Weymouth; Kingston branch; A1 (75-123).

Foster, Thomas; Braintree, Billerica; S1 (18-450).

Foster; Plymouth; D (24-24); Family record, Marshfield; Dx (4-36).

Foster; Gloucester, Wallingford; B4 (3-620).

Foster; Family records, Topsfield; Y2 (3-13).

Foster; English clue; A2 (42-300).

Foulke; Bible record, N. J.; Q1 (11-207).

Fountain; Families; B3 (3-106, 235, 351, 353, 480, 481; 4-218, 220; 5-121).

Fowke, Gerard (Col.); Va., Md.; X1 (16-1).

Fowle; English data; A1 (75-226).

Fowler, Henry; Providence, Mamaroneck; A2 (49-197, 199; 58-257, 340; 59-166, 328).

Fowler, John; Guilford; A1 (53-310).

Fowler, Philip; Ipswich; S2 (4-1).

Fowler, William; Milford; E (5-133); English clue; A1 (54-352).

Fowler; Rye; A2 (49-384).

Fowler; Bible records; A2 (54-266); Q1 (32-253).

Fowler; Family records, Mass.; Y2 (1-16).

Fox; Cheshire; B4 (3-622).

Fox; Bible records; P (6-248).

Foxworthy; Prince William County, Va.; X1 (26-315).

Francis; Wethersfield, Wallingford; B4 (3-624).

Franklin, John; Canaan, Conn.; Pw (10-139).

Franklin; Family account, N. Y.; A2 (23-127).

Franklin; Bible records, Flushing, L. I.; P (5-257).

Franklin; Pa.; Q1 (23-1).

Franklin; Family record; Q1 (21-129).

Franklin; (Benjamin); Q1 (35-308).

Franks, Jacob; New York; Q1 (34-253).

Fraser, John; Charleston; J (5-56).

Frederick, William; Wallingford; B4 (3-623).

Fredericksen, Thomas; see Cadmus.

Freeland; Bible records; P (5-110).

Freeman, Edmond; Lynn, Sandwich; D (12-248); S1 (18-454).

Freeman, John; Eastham; D (3-65; 5-143; 8-65; 13-19; 14-40).

Freeman, Samuel; English clue; A1 (64-84).

Freeman; Newark; M (17-40).

Freeman; Woodbridge, N. J.; P (5-268).

Freeman; Bible record, Morris County, N. J.; S3 (4-3-6).

Freeman; Bible record; P (5-260, 261).

Freer, Hugo; Kingston, New Palz; A2 (33-31; 34-11, 132, 171, 273; 35-24, 123, 172, 241).

Freestone; Horncastle, co. Lincoln, Eng.; A1 (72-51; 74-140; 79-170).

Freeze; Bible record; A1 (51-344).

Frelinghuysen, Theodorus Jacobus (Rev.); N. J., Pa.; Dutch ancestry; B1 (2-11).

French, Francis; Derby; B4 (3-624, 765).

French, John; English origin; A1 (61-393).

French, Philip; New York; A2 (9-118); B6 (7-318).

French, Thomas; Ipswich; U (20-18).

French, William; English data; A1 (65-284).

Frey; Germantown, Pa.; P (7-282).

Frierson; Bible records, Ga.; M (17-14).

Fries; Bible records, Pa.; P (10-169, 170).

Frink; Stonington; A1 (56-153).

Frisbie, Edward; Branford; A1 (58-178; 59-218); B4 (3-626).

Frost, John; New Haven; B4 (3-631).

Frost, Roger; Va.; English data; A1 (54-194).

Frost, William; Oyster Bay; A2 (11-169).

Frost; Bible records, Kittery; A1 (61-222).

Frost; Bible records; A1 (53-242); Family records; A1 (55-441).

Fryer; Hamden; B4 (3-635).

Fugill, Thomas; New Haven; B4 (3-635).

Fuller, Edward and Matthew; Plymouth; A2 (33-171, 211, 227; 34-17, 124, 182, 267; 35-48, 112, 159, 244; 36-33); D (2-237; 13-7; 16-129); M (4-57); U (20-65, 70).

Fuller, John; Ipswich; A1 (53-335; 56-206).

Fuller, Samuel (Dr.); Plymouth; D (5-65; 8-129; 22-65; 23-76; 25-55); Dx (5-71); M (5-6).

Fuller, Thomas; Dedham; English data; A1 (52-241; 59-327); a line of descent; S1 (13-288).

Fuller; Early settlers; English data; A1 (55-192, 410).

Fuller; East Haven; B4 (3-635).

Fuller; English data; A1 (53-125).

Fuller; Bible record, New Haven; M (16-11).

Fuller; Bible records, Plympton; D (2-44).

Fullerton, Humphrey; Donigal, Pa.; E (14-44).

Fullerton; Marshfield; A1 (59-221, 419).

Furman; Philadelphia; P (9-70).

Futcher; Bible record, Del.; Q1 (29-467).

Fyfe, James; Berlin, Mass.; A1 (56-167).

Gabitas; N. J.; P (5-168).

Gage, John; Rowley; A1 (54-260).

Gage, John; Ipswich; A1 (62-254); S2 (6-62).

Gage, Thomas; Yarmouth, Harwich; A1 (53-201; 54-354).

Gage; Bible records, Westchester County, N. Y.; A1 (83-252).

Gage; Beverly, Milford; C2 (6-240).

Gaines, Henry; Lynn; A1 (85-30).

Gale, Christopher (Justice); Edenton, Car.; C2 (4-81).

Gallaudet, Pierre Eliseé (Dr.); New Rochelle; A2 (19-118).

Gallison, Joseph; Marblehead; Y1 (58-313).

Gallop, Hannah (Lake); English ancestry; A1 (84-304).

Gallop, John; Taunton; A1 (54-89).

Galpin, Philip; New Haven, Stratford, Rye; A2 (49-299); B4 (3-636).

Gamage; A1 (59-215).

Gansevoort, Harmen Harmense; Albany; A2 (3-84).

Ganson; Salem; E (12-75).

Garde, Roger; York, Me.; A1 (82-69, 185).

Gardiner, Lion; Saybrook, Gardiner's Island; A2 (17-32; 23-159; 30-1; 31-47; 42-212, 335; 50-17).

Gardiner, Luke (Capt.); Md.; X1 (16-19).

Gardiner, Rebecca (Crooke); Roxbury; English data; A1 (63-279).

Gardiner; Inscriptions, Eaton Neck, L. I.; A2 (27-213).

Gardiner; N. J.; P (9-318).

Gardiner; Bible records; A1 (60-270); P (9-160).

Gardner, George; Family records, R. I.; A1 (65-347); M (2-32).

Gardner; Nantucket; D (20-170).

Gardner; Bible records; Q1 (38-253).

Garfield, Edward; Watertown; S2 (4-13); U (21-16).

Garis; Northampton County, Pa.; S1 (15-375).

Garnock, Duncan; New Haven; B4 (3-636).

Garret; English clue; A1 (61-69).

Garrett; Bible records; B5 (7-13).

Garson; Bible records; P (7-42).

Garwood; Bible records, Philadelphia; P (7-33).

Gascoyne, Thomas; Hewlett's Point, Va.; V1 (11-28).

Gaskell, Samuel; New Haven; B4 (3-636).

Gaskill; Burlington County, N. J.; P (9-190).

Gaskill; Bible records; P (9-314).

Gaston, Alexander (Dr.); Newbern, N. C.; G1 (6-225); G2 (10-253).

Gaston, Hugh and Joseph; Somerset County, N. J.; B6 (5-33, 125, 198).

Gates, George; Hartford, Haddam; U (20-56).

Gates, Stephen; Hingham, Lancaster; C2 (7-173).

Gaudey; English clue; Y1 (52-52).

Gautier, Jacques; New York; A2 (3-1).

Gavet, Philip; Salem; A1 (77-34).

Gavit; Westerly; E (8-393).

Gaylord [Gayler], William, John, Alice; English ancestry; A2 (41-183).

Gaylord, William; B2 (3-212, 241, 244).

Gaylord; Bible records; B2 (5-86).

Gaylord; Bible record; A1 (53-450).

Gaylord; B4 (3-636).

Gee; Martha's Vineyard, Ipswich; Y2 (8-164).

Gelston, Hugh; Southampton, L. I.; A2 (2-131, 208).

Gent, Thomas; Me., Boston; A1 (59-324).

George, Peter; Braintree, Block Island; wife's ancestry; A1 (63-360).

George; Bible records; P (3-275).

Gereardy, Philip; New York; A1 (52-313).

Gerhard, Frederick; Heidelberg; Q1 (24-117).

Gernaut; Bible records; M (19-63).

Gerould; N. H., Ohio; E (9-255).

Gerretse, see Blauvelt.

Gerrish, William (Capt.); Newbury; A1 (67-105).

Gerrish; Bible record, Dover; A1 (51-67).

Gerrits, Guert; New York; A2 (56-266).

Gerrodette, William; New York; A2 (58-238).

Getchell, Samuel; Salem, Hampton, Salisbury; A1 (63-265); A2 (49-190).

Geynes, Henry; Lynn; English origin; A1 (63-283).

Gibb, Andrew; Oyster Bay, Brookhaven; A2 (13-197).

Gibbard, William; New Haven; B4 (3-641).

Gibbes, Robert (Gov.); S. C.; J (12-78; 22-99).

Gibbon; Philadelphia; P (9-72).

Gibbons, Henry and William; New Haven; B4 (3-641).

Gibbs, Francis; English clue; A1 (61-92).

Gibbs, James; Md.; X2 (2-2).

Gibbs, Matthew; B2 (9-4).

Gibbs, Thomas; Sandwich; D (23-123).

Gibbs, William; English origin; A1 (63-277).

Gibbs; Bible records, Providence; A1 (71-285).

Gibbud; Naugatuck; B4 (3-641).

Gibson, Christopher; Boston; English data; A1 (65-63).

Gibson, Samuel; Hillsborough; S2 (5-328).

Giddings, George; Ipswich, Mass.; A1 (59-216); A2 (42-442).

Giffin; Hardwick, Wethersfield, Bennington; A2 (44-286).

Gifford; English data; A1 (71-170; 74-231, 267; 75-57, 129).

Gifford; Family record; A1 (72-321); B5 (3-32; 4-32).

Gifford; Family record, Westport, Mass.; B5 (4-31).

Gilbert, Matthew (Dep.-Gov.); New Haven; B4 (3-642, 765; 4-944; 8-2045).

Gilbert; Bible records, Westchester County, N. Y.; A1 (83-251).

Gilbert; Family records, Boston; A1 (72-159).

Gilbert; Ceres Town, McKean County, Pa.; B5 (9-210).

Gilbert; Taunton; D (21-117).

Gilbert; Bible records, Conn.; B2 (1-79).

Gilbert; Bible records; B3 (10-179).

Gildersleeve; Bible records; B2 (5-5).

Gill; North Haven; B4 (3-658).

Gillespie; Family record, Md., Pa.; P (11-73).

Gillett, Jonathan and Nathan; Dorchester, Windsor; English ancestry; A2 (41-282); B2 (1-7).

Gillet; Derby; B4 (3-659).

Gillingham; Family record; Q1 (24-224).

Gillon; Charleston; J (9-189); Bible records; J (19-146).

Gillpatrick, Thomas; Wells, Me.; A1 (54-100).

Gilman; Bible records; A1 (83-382).

Gilmer; Bible records, Va.; V1 (2-132).

Gilpin, Joseph; Pa., with English ancestry; Q1 (49-289; 50-97).

Gist, Christopher; Baltimore County, Md.; X1 (8-373).

Glazier; Bible records, New Braintree, Virgil; A1 (81-492).

Gleason, Thomas; Watertown, Charlestown; E (3-23, 68, 109, 161; 4-7; 5-82, 130).

Gleason, Thomas; (Westmoreland, N. H., branch); E (11-217); (Sharon, Austerlitz); E (12-61).

Glen, Alexander Lindsay; New York, Albany, Schenectady; A1 (52-475).

Glen; Scotland; Ireland; Q1 (36-480).

Glover, Henry; New Haven; B4 (3-660, 765; 4-945; 5-1244).

Glover, John; Dorchester; S1 (15-182).

Glover; Boston; G2 (5-16).

Gnaegi [Canaga], Christian; Pa., Ohio; B2 (6-63).

Gobrecht, John Christopher; Philadelphia; Q1 (30-355).

Goddard, William; Watertown; with English ancestry; U (21-59).

Goddard; Bible records, Watertown, A1 (53-242).

Goddin; Bible records, Richmond; V1 (1-172).

Godfrey, William; Watertown; English clue; A1 (63-32).

Godfrey; Charleston; J (16-134).

Godfrey; Bible records, Newport; A1 (67-158).

Godfrey; Family record, Pa.; Q1 (18-124).

Goff; Family record, R. I.; M (18-33).

Going; Vt.; E (7-240).

Gold, Nathan; Fairfield; A2 (47-205; 50-229; 54-177).

Goldsmith; New Haven; B4 (3-663; 4-945).

Goldthwaite, Thomas; English data; C2 (4-124, 280).

Goodell, David; Amherst; S2 (6-273).

Goodenow, Edmund; Sudbury; U (20-109).

Goodgame, Anthony; English clue; A1 (61-199).

Gooding, Daniel (Gen.); Newport News, Va., Roxbury, Cambridge, Mass.; A2 (43-297).

Goodrich, Bartholomew; Branford; B4 (3-663).

Goodrich, John; Isle of Wight County; V1 (2-130; 12-66).

Goodsell, Thomas; Branford, East Haven; A2 (54-188); B4 (3-664; 6-1528).

Goodspeed; Barnstable, Mass.; A2 (39-92); A1 (82-443; 84-236).

Goodwin, Ozias; Hartford; S1 (13-55).

Goodwin, Samuel; Pownalborough, Me.; A1 (67-27).

Goodwin; New Haven; B4 (3-668).

Goodwin; Bible records; Q1 (40-370).

Goodyear, Stephen (Dep.-Gov.); New Haven; B4 (3-668); English data; A1 (61-189).

Gordon, James and John; Va.; E (2-49).

Gordon; Northumberland; V1 (6-283).

Gordon; Kent County, Del.; X1 (25-405).

Gordon; New Haven; B4 (3-674).

Gordon; York County, Pa.; M (15-55).

Gordon; Bible record, Lancaster County; V1 (11-41).

Gordon; Bible records; P (3-257); M (15-57).

Gordon; Tillyangus, Scotland; V1 (6-175).

Gorges; English data; A1 (54-190).

Gorham, John (Capt.); Plymouth, Yarmouth; A1 (52-229; 53-207; 54-167; 59-91, 108; 69-242); A2 (28-133, 197); D (4-153, 217; 5-28, 172; 6-181; 13-50; 17-66, 251; 22-171); No. Carolina branch; A1 (82-426); (Yarmouth branches); A1 (52-357, 445); (Hardwick branch); A1 (56-75); (Fairfield branch); A1 (57-325); Bible records (Col. John); A2 (29-45,52); Joseph of Stratford; A2 (29-91); New Haven branch; B4 (3-674; 4-945; 6-1528).

Gorham; Family records; A1 (52-186).

Gorton, Mary (Maplet); English ancestry; A1 (70-115, 282).

Gorton, Samuel; Warwick; English ancestry; A1 (51-199; 82-185, 333); F4 (6-91); T6 (7-203).

Gorton, Samuel; R. I.; wife's ancestry; A1 (70-115, 282).

Gosnold, Bartholomew; English data; A1 (56-402; 57-93, 216; 58-311, 396; 59-101; 83-373).

Gough; Bible records, Md.; X1 (25-302).

Gould, Alexander; New Harbor, Me.; A2 (51-30).

Gould, John; Elizabeth, N. J.; A2 (37-90; 43-98).

Gould, Zaccheus; Topsfield; U (20-22).

Gould; Hanover, N. H.; B5 (7-19).

Gould; Family records, Topsfield; Y2 (4-92).

Gould; Bible records; A2 (51-28).

Gourley; New Haven; B4 (3-679).

Gouverneur, Nicolaes; New York; A2 (60-221).

Gower; Family records; B2 (1-71).

Grafton, Joseph; Salem; Y1 (64-49, 145, 209, 333).

Graham; Northumberland; V1 (6-280).

Graham; New Haven; B4 (3-679).

Graham; Bible records, Lancaster County, Pa.; P (9-150).

Graham; Family records; Q1 (42-184).

Graisbery; Family records; P (10-192).

Granger; East Haven; B4 (3-680).

Grannis, Edward; New Haven; B4 (3-680; 5-1244).

Grant, Matthew; English data; C4 (3-63).

Grant, Seth; Cambridge, Hartford; A1 (64-83).

Grant; Bible record; A2 (54-67).

Grant; New Haven; B4 (3-687).

Gravenraet; Dutch records; A2 (46-290); see Grevenraet.

Gravenraet; A2 (56-207 ff.; 58-189, 393).

Graves, George; Hartford; A1 (56-260, 409).

Graves, John; Concord, Mass.; B2 (5-21; 6-12).

Graves, Thomas; Charlestown; English data; A1 (52-113).

Graves; Killingly; B3 (1-409; 2-288).

Graves; Sudbury; B3 (3-114).

Graves; Bible records; M (8-48).

Gray, Henry and John; Fairfield; English origin; arms; A1 (61-386).

Gray, John; Yarmouth; S1 (18-433).

Gray, Mary (Westcott); Md.; English clue; X1 (2-180).

Gray, William; Lynn; Y1 (52-113).

Gray; Plymouth; D (21-62, 84, 156; 23-76; 28-105).

Gray; Philadelphia; P (9-50).

Gray; Salem; Y1 (56-145).

Gray; Bible record; Q1 (32-253).

Grayson; Va.; V1 (5-195, 261; 6-201; 7-54; 8-119; 12-181).

Greene, John (Dr.); Warwick, R. I.; T6 (4-171); royal ancestry; B2 (1-81).

Greene, John; Salem, Mass.; A2 (30-69).

Greene, John; Kittery; C2 (1-238).

Green, Percival; Cambridge; A1 (74-243).

Green, Thomas; James City County; V1 (5-135; 6-37).

Green, Thomas; Malden, Mass.; A2 (35-77; 46-272); S1 (13-65).

Green, William; Charlestown, Woburn; English clue; A1 (61-65).

Green, William; Smyrna, Del.; A1 (66-366).

Green, William; Plymouth; A1 (57-17); A2 (39-109, 199; 54-293).

Greene, William of Barnstable; A2 (30-54).

Green; Dover, N. H.; F3 (2-7).

Green; Malden; Family record; A1 (54-211).

Green; New London; K (4-51); B4 (3-687; 4-945).

Green; Va.; V1 (7-199, 287).

Green; Bible records, S. C.; A1 (57-328).

Greene; Bible records; B2 (3-166, 176, 221).

Greene; Green's Norton, Northampton, Eng.; A2 (53-258).

Greenberry; Anne Arundel County, Md.; X1 (2-185).

Greenleaf, Edmund; Newbury, Boston; A2 (43-300); English data; A1 (69-358).

Greenough; Boston; B4 (3-688).

Greenway, James (Dr.); Dinwiddie; V1 (8-65).

Greenwood; Family records; B2 (1-72).

Gregg; Bible records; B2 (7-6).

Gregory; Bible record, Me.; A1 (55-343).

Gregory; Va.; V2 (2-58, 59).

Gregory; Family record; V1 (8-264).

Gregson, Thomas; New Haven; B4 (3-689).

Grevenraet, Isaac; New York; A2 (7-60; 60-202; 61-41, 127, 232); see Gravenraet.

Grey; Early English records; A1 (76-295).

Gridley, Richard; Boston; A1 (76-240).

Gridley, Thomas; Hartford; C2 (4-46).

Griffen, Edward; Flushing, L. I.; A2 (37-54).

Griffin, Jasper; Marblehead, Southold; A2 (22-192).

Griffin, John (Sergt.); Simsbury; A2 (49-23).

Griffen, Richard; Flushing; C3 (5-190).

Griffen; Bible records, Marblehead; Y1 (52-112).

Griffen; Flushing, L. I.; A2 (36-197).

Griffin; Harrison, Flushing; A2 (49-386).

Griffin; Bible records; A2 (54-267).

Griffith, Thomas (Rev.); New Castle County, Del.; Q1 (20-574).

Griffith; Philadelphia; E (11-120).

Griffith; Bible records, Md.; M (17-51).

Griffith; Bible records; P (9-155).

Griggs, Humphrey; Braintree; English origin; A1 (56-183; 63-285).

Griggs, Robert; Lancaster County; V1 (11-166).

Griggs; Cheshire, Plymouth; B4 (3-690).

Grimball, Paul; Edisto Island, S. C.; J (23-1, 39, 94; 28-256; 29-231).

Grimes; Bible record, Va.; M (15-23).

Grimké; S. C.; J (13-42).

Grinnell; Derby; B4 (3-690).

Griswold; Windsor; B3 (12-323).

Griswold; New Haven; B4 (3-691).

Griswold; Ohio; E (6-171).

Groesbeck; Baptisms at Schaghticoke, N. Y.; A2 (29-109, 140, 210).

Groff; Bible records, Amwell, N. J.; B1 (6-124).

Groom; Md.; English clue; X1 (1-381).

Groot, Symon Symonse; Albany, Schenectady; A2 (4-8).

Gross, Daniel; Pa.; B2 (2-136).

Grosse, Isaac; Boston; A1 (73-238; 76-79).

Grosvenor, John; Roxbury; English ancestry; A1 (72-131).

Grove; Winchester, Frederick County, Pa.; M (19-68).

Groves; New Haven; B4 (3-691).

Grow; Bible records; P (3-271).

Grozier; Bible records, Truro; D (9-64).

Guest, Henry; New Brunswick, N. J.; A2 (29-100).

Guest; Bible records, Brunswick, N. J.; P (7-43).

Guier; Philadelphia; P (9-59).

Guion, Isaac; New Rochelle; Bible records; A2 (51-26).

Guitteau; Wallingford, Bethlehem; B4 (3-691).

Gumfield; English clue; A1 (59-109, 326); A2 (42-295).

Gunn, Jasper; Milford; B4 (3-691).

Gunne; co. Gloucester, Eng.; A1 (84-290).

Gunnell; Fairfax County, Va.; V1 (1-166).

Gushee; Raynham; D (21-81).

Guttridge, John; Watertown; A1 (57-332).

Hack, George (Dr.); Northampton County; V1 (7-253; 9-64).

Haddock; Bucks County, Pa.; Q1 (22-377).

Haffield, Richard; Ipswich; English clue; A1 (56-181).

Hafte, Jacob Hendrickse; Flatbush; A2 (55-317).

Haige, William; N. J.; Q1 (24-81).

Haigh; Bible records, England; A2 (54-63).

Hairston, Peter; Va.; V1 (6-66).

Halbidge, Arthur; New Haven; B4 (3-692).

Hale, Gershom; Concord; B4 (3-692).

Hale, Samuel; Wethersfield; A1 (61-177).

Hale, Thomas; Newbury; English data; A1 (52-65; 64-186); wife's ancestry; A1 (76-75).

Hale, Thomasine (Dowsett); English ancestry; A1 (76-75).
Hale; Stow, Mass.; C4 (1-31).
Halenbake; Albany; A2 (30-123).
Haliburton, Andrew; Boston; A1 (71-57).
Hall, Jacob; Bucks County, Pa.; X1 (8-217).
Hall, John; Boston, Hartford, New Haven, Wallingford; B4 (3-693, 765; 5-1244).
Hall, John; Yarmouth; K (3-97).
Hall, John; English data; A1 (53-23).
Hall, Richard; Calvert County, Md.; X1 (8-291, 381).
Hall; Boston; A1 (73-236).
Hall; Bible record, Mass.; A1 (51-34).
Hall; Bible records; A2 (56-116); Q1 (17-113).
Hallet, William; Hellgate; A2 (22-128).
Hallett, William; Newtown, L. I.; A2 (6-28).
Hallett; (New York); A2 (7-91).
Hallett; Bible records; A2 (54-64).
Halley, Edmund (Dr.); English astronomer, family; A2 (29-13, 164; 34-52, 106; 38-151).
Hallock; Bible record, Quogue, L. I.; A2 (37-55).
Halsey, Thomas; Bible records, Southampton, L. I.; A2 (34-282).
Halsey; Bible records, Morristown; P (9-161).
Halstead; New Windsor, N. Y.; B2 (5-4, 27, 37, 65, 70).
Halsted; Bible records, N. J.; B1 (2-63).
Ham, William; Portsmouth, N. H.; U (20-105).
Ham; Bible records, Me.; B5 (7-25).
Hamer; Md., Ohio; B2 (4-227).
Hamilton, Alexander; A2 (45-111).
Hamilton, David; Charleston, S. C.; G2(2-176).
Hamilton, Francis; English clue; A1 (55-441; 61-189).
Hamilton, John; North Yarmouth, Me.; A1 (63-14).
Hamilton; Pa.; Q1 (17-175).
Hamilton; Bible records, New York; A2 (46-122).
Hamilton; Bible records (Andrew); M (15-27).
Hamlin; Barnstable; Dx (2-47).
Hammock; New Haven; B4 (3-718).
Hammond, John; Watertown; English data; A2 (41-278).
Hammond, Richard; Marblehead; English data; A1 (54-104, 288).
Hammond, William and Thomas; Watertown, Hingham; English clue; A1 (56-184).
Hammond; Family record, Mansfield, Conn.; M (18-34).

Hanbury, Peter; English clue; A1 (60-312).
Hance, John; Dover, N. H., Shrewsbury, N. J.; A2 (27-165; 35-6, 127, 184, 249; 36-17, 102; 43-90).
Hance; Bible records, Shrewsbury, N. J.; B2 (1-42).
Hancock; Bible records; M (16-20).
Hand, John; Easthampton (Guilford branch); A1 (55-31, 222).
Hand; Bible records, Philadelphia; P (8-100).
Hanford; Bible records, N. Y.; M (7-8).
Hanna; N. J.; Harrisburg, Pa.; Q3 (1-81).
Hanna; Md.; X2 (2-8).
Hansell; Bible record, inscriptions, Philadelphia; P (4-318).
Hansen; Bible records, Albany; A1 (53-118).
Hansford, William; Culpeper County, Va.; N2 (4-49).
Harbeson; Philadelphia; P (9-71).
Harcourt, Richard; Warwick, R. I., Oyster Bay, L. I.; A2 (37-155).
Hardcastle; Bible records, Caroline County, Md.; P (8-289, 292).
Harding; Family record, Northumberland County, Va.; M (8-32); V1 (2-104).
Harding, Stephen; Providence; Pw (21-1).
Hardy, Thomas; Y1 (51-197).
Hardy; Bedford County, Va.; Z (46-349).
Haring; Bible records; B1 (6-29).
Harker, Adam; Middletown, Bucks County, Pa.; S3 (6-1-2, 4, 6; 6-2-2).
Harlakenden; English data; A1 (56-40, 319); B3 (8-545).
Harleston, John; S. C.; J (3-151, 243).
Harley; Bible record, Pa.; M (17-71).
Harlow, William; D (12-193; 20-163).
Harned, Edward; Salem, Huntington; A2 (61-14).
Harper; Norfolk, Va.; V2 (2-102).
Harriman, John; New Haven; B4 (3-719).
Harriman; Family record, New Castle, Me.; M (18-36).
Harrington, Henry; English clue; A1 (59-109).
Harrington; Bible records, Mass.; A1 (82-512).
Harrington; Bible record, Hartford; A1 (66-84).
Harris, John; Boston; English clue; A1 (55-333).
Harris, Martha (Lake); English ancestry; A1 (84-304).
Harris, William; Charleston; J (27-30).
Harris; Ipswich, Ashburnham; S2 (17-367).
Harris; New Haven; B4 (3-719).

Harris; Bible record, Minot, Me.; B5 (14-147).
Harris; Family record, Del.; Q1 (43-273).
Harris; Bible records; A2 (56-112); M (12-28); B5 (10-228).
Harris; E (1-53).
Harrison, Burr; Prince William County, Va.; X1 (26-321).
Harrison, Jeremiah (Dr.); Va.; V1 (6-202; 7-286).
Harrison, Richard; New Haven, Branford; A1 (70-69); B4 (3-720).
Harrison, Robert; Dorchester County, Md., with English ancestry; X1 (10-376).
Harrison; Family record, Pa.; P (10-183).
Harrison; Calvert County, Md.; Q1 (13-447).
Harrison; Bible records, Caroline County, Md.; X1 (12-386).
Harrison; Bible records, Va.; V1 (2-132).
Harrison; Bible records, N. C.; H (3-472).
Hart, Edward; Hopewell; A2 (21-36).
Hart, John; Salem, Marblehead; C3 (3-67).
Hart, John (Gov.); Md.; P (1-28).
Hart, John; Newtown, L. I.; A2 (26-170); M (7-18).
Hart, Stephen (Deacon); Hartford, Farmington; A2 (15-108); U (23-62); Ohio branch; E (6-180); see also B4 (3-720).
Hart; Stratford, co. Warwick, Eng.; U (22-132).
Hartaffel, Robert; Warwick, Pa.; Q1 (32-511).
Hartley; Bible records, Pa.; B2 (8-65).
Hartshorn, Richard; Middletown, N. J.; A2 (14-95).
Hartshorn; Bible record, N. J.; B5 (15-196).
Hartshorn; Bible records, Providence, R. I.; A1 (84-345).
Harvey, Jacob; English clue; A1 (59-327).
Harvey, William; Taunton; English clue; A1 (61-279).
Harvey; Family records, Pa.; B5 (8-82).
Harvey; Chester County, Pa.; P (8-105).
Harvey; Perquimans County, N. C.; H (3-476).
Harvey; Bible record, S. C.; M (18-19).
Harvie; Va.; N2 (2-4-44).
Harwood, James; Nashua, N. H.; A1 (52-25).
Harwood, John; Boston; A1 (70-183).
Harwood; Md.; English data; X1 (4-193).

Harwood; New Haven; B4 (3-722).
Hasbrouck; New York, Esopus; A2 (17-261).
Hasbrouck; Family record, N. J.; A2 (54-64).
Hasell, Thomas (Rev.); St. Thomas and St. Dennis, S. C.; A2 (23-147).
Hasey, William (Lieut.); Puling Point, Rumney Marsh; A1 (54-211).
Hasey; Family records, Cambridge; A1 (71-187).
Haskell, John; Middleborough; D (6-6).
Haskell; Gloucester, Falmouth; F2 (7-235).
Haskell; D (20-190; 27-39).
Haskens; N. H.; A1 (64-376).
Haskett, Stephen (Capt.); Salem; Y1 (51-1, 97); English ancestry; A1 (53-13 ff.; 77-71, 110; 78-54; 84-273, 433).
Haskins, Thomas; Dorchester County, Md.; X1 (11-76).
Hassing [Hassinck]; Holland; A2 (57-374).
Hastings, Thomas; (Charlestown, N. H., branch); A1 (54-406).
Hastings; Bible records; P (10-174).
Hatch, Thomas and William; Scituate; English ancestry; A1 (70-245).
Hatch, William; Scituate; D (5-111; 7-29; 10-38; 21-97; 22-155; 27-97); A1 (51-34).
Hatch; New Haven; B4 (3-722).
Hatfield, Matthias and Thomas; Elizabethtown, Mamaroneck; A2 (48-388; 49-195).
Hatfield; Pa.; Ohio; P (9-90).
Hatfield; Bible records; A2 (54-267).
Hathaway; Dartmouth; D (16-110; 17-76).
Hathaway; Bible record; P (5-264; 7-98).
Hatherly, Timothy; Scituate; A1 (52-76).
Hathorne, William (Maj.) and John; Salem; English ancestry; A1 (67-248; 79-311); C2 (1-41); S1 (14-255).
Hathorne; English data; notes; A1 (56-204, 409).
Hathorn; Wilmington, Del.; Warwick, N. Y.; A2 (20-169).
Hatton, Thomas and Richard; Md.; X1 (1-191).
Haugh, Atherton; Boston; English data; A1 (70-185).
Haughwout [Lefferts], Pieter Janse; Flatbush; A2 (33-49, 167, 235).
Hauser; see Howser.
Hausil, Bernhardt Michael (Rev.); Fredericktown, Md.; X1 (10-57).
Hawarden, Thomas; New York; A2 (59-193).
Hawes, Edmund; Duxbury, Yarmouth; A1 (65-160); D (20-73).
Hawes, Edward; Dedham; S1 (14-143).

Hawes, Richard; Dorchester; English ancestry; A1 (83-312; 84-335).
Hawes; A1 (61-200).
Hawes; B4 (4-945).
Hawkes, Adam; Lynn; D (17-222).
Hawkins; B3 (11-498).
Hawksworth, Peter; Hatfield, Pa.; Q1 (10-100).
Hawxhurst, Christopher; Salem, Oyster Bay, Matinecock; A2 (26-19; 32-172, 221; 33-24).
Hay, Anthony; Williamsburg; V1 (8-277).
Hayden, John; Braintree; U (20-107).
Haydon; Family record, Franklin County, Ky.; M (18-36).
Hayes; New Haven; B4 (3-723).
Hayes; Bible records, Lebanon, Me.; A1 (69-281).
Haymond, William (Maj.); Md.; Harrison County, Va.; N2 (4-232).
Hayne, John; Colleton County; J (5-168).
Haynes, Mabel (Harlakenden); Royal ancestry; A1 (56-40).
Haynes, Walter; Sudbury; A1 (65-295).
Haynes; Warwick County, Va.; V1 (1-68).
Hays; Bible record; X2 (1-17).
Hayward, William; English data; A2 (43-71).
Hayward; Boston; B4 (3-725).
Hayward; Family record; X2 (2-28).
Hayward; English data; A1 (51-128).
Haywood, Judith (Phippen); English origin; A1 (66-87).
Hazard, Thomas; Boston, Portsmouth, Newport, R. I.; A2 (42-206); S1 (14-158).
Hazard; South Kingston, R. I. (Diary of Thomas B.); F4 (1-7, 28, 91, 167, 277).
Hazelrigg; Prince William County, Va.; Bath County, Ky.; B2 (9-38).
Hazelrigg; Bible records, Va.; B2 (8-67).
Hazlewood; Philadelphia; P (9-45).
Hazzard, Richard; Port Royal, S. C.; M (3-4).
Heale; Lancaster County, Va.; V1 (7-287).
Heard, John; Kittery, Me.; A1 (70-185).
Hearle, William; Portsmouth, N. H.; U (20-105).
Hearn; Philadelphia; Bible record; A2 (5-45).
Hearne, Peter; Jamestown, S. C.; J (22-101).
Hearsey; Bible records, Hingham, Milton; A1 (58-115).
Heath; Amesbury, Haverhill, Hampstead; A2 (57-400).

Heath; Bible records, Mendon; A1 (66-85).
Heath; Bible record; Q1 (31-118).
Heaton, James; New Haven; B4 (3-725; 4-945; 5-1244).
Hebert [Hebard], Robert; Salem, Beverly; A1 (51-316).
Heckedorn, John; York, Pa.; Q1 (32-511).
Hedden, Edward; Newark, N. J.; A2 (42-332).
Hedge; English data; A1 (53-18).
Heermans, Jan; Kingston; A2 (21-58).
Heffner, John; Cumberland County, Pa.; B2 (9-27).
Heiskell; Family records, Va.; P (8-293).
Helder, Edmund (Dr.); Stafford County, Va.; V1 (4-19).
Hellakers, Jacob; New York; A2 (59-7).
Helms; New Haven; B4 (3-731).
Hemingway, Ralph; Roxbury (East Haven branch); B4 (3-731; 5-1244; 8-2045).
Hempstead, Robert; New London; A2 (51-259).
Henderson, James (Lieut.); Concord, Rutland; A2 (53-28).
Henderson, John, James, and Samuel; Augusta County, Va.; N2 (5-108).
Henderson; Va.; V1 (10-60).
Henderson; S. C. (Gen. Wm.); J (28-108).
Henderson; Bible records; M (19-12).
Hendrick; Wallingford; B4 (3-737).
Hendrick; Family record, Amsterdam, N. Y.; B5 (10-44).
Hendricks; Westmoreland County, Pa.; P (8-106).
Henning; Bible records, Pa.; P (10-80).
Henry, Frederick; Westmoreland County, Pa.; Q1 (39-120).
Henry, John; Chester County, Pa.; Q1 (27-91).
Henry, Michael; Readington; B6 (7-98; 8-327).
Henry; Bible records, Colrain; A1 (84-462).
Henry; Bible record, Pa.; M (19-106).
Henry; Bible records; P (10-176).
Hensel; Bible record, Lancaster, Pa.; B5 (14-186).
Henshaw, Joshua; Dorchester; N2 (4-149).
Henshaw; Bible record, Boston; P (7-267).
Herbert, Francis; Elizabeth, N. J.; A2 (21-41).
Herbert, John and Buller; Petersburg, Va.; A2 (26-30); V2 (2-45, 48).
Herbert, John; Lower Norfolk County; V2 (1-249).

Hereford; Loudoun County, Va.; N2 (5-114).
Heritage; Bible records; P (9-312).
Herman, Augustine; New York; Cecil County, Md.; X1 (15-395); A2 (9-57, 190; 22-1); Q1 (15-321).
Herrick, Henry; Salem, Wenham, Beverly; A1 (83-387).
Herster, Andrew; Easton, Pa.; S1 (15-379).
Hertzler; Bible records, Berks County, Pa.; M (19-64).
Hesselius, Gustavus; Philadelphia; Q1 (29-129, 367).
Hesselius; Bible records; X1 (21-277).
Hessels, Pieter; Bergen, Hackensack; A2 (56-269).
Het, René; New York; A2 (11-145).
Hett, Thomas; Cambridge; A1 (64-239).
Hewes; C4 (3-201).
Hews; Norfolk County, Va.; C4 (4-47).
Hewson, John; Philadelphia; Q1 (37-118).
Hext, Hugh; Colleton County; J (6-29, 126).
Heyward; S. Car.; E (7-257).
Hibbard; Windham; A1 (71-367).
Hickling; Family record, Boston; P (7-88).
Hickman; Bible records; P (3-270).
Hickox; Wallingford; B4 (3-738).
Hicks, Samuel; New Haven; B4 (3-739).
Hidden, Andrew; Rowley; U (20-29).
Hide; see Hyde.
Hiester, John, Joseph, and Daniel; Berks County, Pa.; Q2 (vol. 16); Q3 (1-156).
Higby, Edward; Middletown; B3 (7-189).
Higginbotham; Conn.; B4 (3-739).
Higginbotham; Tazewell County, Va.; U (7-189).
Higgins, Richard; Plymouth, Eastham, Piscataway; A2 (46-387; 47-20; 57-298); D (18-189); Dx (1-21).
Higgins; Eastham, Hardwick, Bennington; A2 (44-285, 338).
Higgins; East Haven, West Haven; B4 (3-739).
Higginson, Francis (Rev.); Salem; English data; C2 (6-1, 36, 81, 117, 157, 187; 7-1, 66, 157); A1 (64-88; 66-87).
Higginson, Humphrey and Christopher; Va.; English data; A2 (43-69).
Higginson, Robert (Col.); York County, Va.; N2 (2-4-55).
Higginson; Family records, Salem; A1 (76-312).
Hiland, George; Guilford; A1 (62-384).
Hiland, Thomas; Scituate; English ancestry; A1 (66-61).

Hill, Adam; Talbot County, Md.; X1 (3-184).
Hill, Charles; New London; C2 (3-257).
Hill, Frances (Freestone); English ancestry; A1 (72-51; 74-140).
Hill, John; Dorchester; A1 (58-157, 237; 59-105); English clue; A1 (61-278).
Hill, John; Guilford; A1 (57-87, 250).
Hill, John and William; Oyster River; F3 (5-97).
Hill, Luke; Windsor, Simsbury; A1 (57-87); B4 (3-743).
Hill, Robert and John; New Haven; B4 (3-741); S1 (13-367, line in error).
Hill, Robert; Isle of Wight County, Va.; M (16-66).
Hill, William; Fairfield; wife's ancestry; A1 (51-358); A2 (44-184); a line of descent; S1 (13-69).
Hill; Guilford; B4 (3-744).
Hill; Sussex County; Q1 (35-381).
Hill; Berks County, Pa.; Q1 (20-278).
Hill; N. C.; H (2-472).
Hill; Bible record; Q1 (31-374).
Hillegas, John Frederick; Montgomery County, Pa.; Q1 (18-85).
Hills, Hercules; Scituate; English data; A1 (66-87).
Hills, Joseph; Malden; C4 (1-123).
Hilton, Edward; Dover; S1 (16-168); English clue; A1 (61-199).
Hinchman; Bible records; B2 (4-293).
Hinckley, Samuel; Scituate, Barnstable; English ancestry; A1 (65-287, 314; 68-186; 75-238); D (5-237; 10-11; 12-203).
Hinds, James; Salem, Southold; B5 (14-171).
Hine, Thomas; Milford; B4 (3-745).
Hines; Essex County, Mass.; C1 (2-47).
Hitch; Bible records; P (5-112).
Hitchborn; Boston; A1 (72-246).
Hitchcock, Matthias and Edward; New Haven; B4 (3-749; 4-773; 8-2045).
Hitcheson; New Haven; B4 (4-780).
Hite [Heydt], Hans Jost; Kingston; N2 (3-51, 99).
Hoar, Leonard, etc.; Braintree; English ancestry; A1 (53-92, 186, 289; 54-149).
Hoar; Braintree, Concord; E (11-128).
Hobart, Peter (Rev.); Family records; A1 (85-441).
Hobart; Hingham; D (19-187).
Hobart; English clue; A1 (57-224).
Hobbes; English data; A1 (64-185).
Hobbs, Thomas; English clue; A1 (59-418).
Hobby; Bible records, Mass.; A1 (59-253).

Hobson, Thomas; Northumberland County; V1 (8-127).

Hobson; Cambridge, Eng.; A1 (52-487).

Hobson; see Hopson.

Hoch; Bible records, Berks County, Pa.; M (14-11).

Hockaday, William; New Kent, Va.; V2 (1-191).

Hocker; Bible record, Pa., Ohio; M (19-67).

Hodge; Windsor (New Haven branch); B4 (4-780, 946).

Hodges; Taunton; D (21-96).

Hodges; Lyme, East Haven; B4 (4-782).

Hodson, John; New Haven; B4 (4-783).

Hodgkin; see Hotchkin.

Hoe, Robert; New York; A2 (41-1; 45-89).

Hoes, Jan Tyssen; Albany; A2 (31-52, 89, 133).

Holbrook, Richard; Milford (East Haven branch); B4 (5-1244).

Holbrook, Thomas; Weymouth; A1 (58-305; 59-324).

Holcomb, John and Jacob; Buckingham, Pa.; Q1 (44-158; 47-277).

Holcomb; Wallingford; B4 (4-784).

Holden, James; English clue; A1 (66-358).

Holden, Richard and Justinian; English data; C4 (3-23).

Holden; Levi (Revolutionary); A2 (30-109, 141).

Holden; Cranbrook, co. Kent, Eng.; A1 (51-214).

Holladay; Bible records, Va.; V1 (2-257).

Holland, Henry (Capt.); Albany; A2 (9-129, 190).

Holland; Bible records; Q1 (35-380).

Hollard, Angell; Weymouth, Boston; English ancestry; A1 (63-381; 64-346; 68-61).

Hollinshead; Burlington County, N. J.; Q1 (16-121).

Hollinshead; Bible record; M (12-27).

Holloway, William; Marshfield; A1 (58-404).

Hollyday; Md.; X1 (26-159); Bible records; X2 (1-9).

Holman, John; Dorchester; A1 (72-185, 286); English data; A1 (63-33; 67-260).

Holme, Thomas; Pa.; Q1 (19-413; 20-128, 248).

Holmes, George; Roxbury; A1 (58-21, 143, 254).

Holmes, Obadiah (Rev.); Newport; (English ancestry); A1 (64-237; 67-21); F4 (4-294); S1 (16-91).

Holmes, Richard; Norwalk; A1 (64-83).

Holmes; Plymouth, Pembroke, Halifax; D (18-227, 232; 20-166, 168); Family record; D (23-172); Bible record; Dx (1-60).

Holmes; Marshfield; D (4-173).

Holmes; New Haven; B4 (4-784).

Holmes; N. J., Va.; E (10-55).

Holmes; Bible records; M (16-21).

Holt, Randall; Hog Island; V1 (7-277).

Holt, William; New Haven, Wallingford; B4 (4-784, 946).

Holt; (John, printer, b. 1721); A2 (30-49).

Holyoke, Edward; Lynn; Y1 (66-441).

Homans; Dorchester; A1 (51-69).

Hood, John; Cambridge; English clue; A1 (56-184).

Hood; New Haven; B4 (4-791).

Hood; Bible records; X2 (2-10).

Hooe; Stafford County; V1 (9-204).

Hooglant; Family record, N. Y.; P (9-150).

Hooke, Humphrey; Me.; A1 (52-441).

Hooke, William (Gov.); Me.; English data; A1 (54-410).

Hooke; Bible records; P (3-268).

Hooker, Thomas (Rev.); Hartford; A2 (18-74); E (7-12); S1 (13-381); English ancestry; A2 (48-393).

Hooper, Daniel; Barbadoes; Q1 (36-60).

Hooper; Barbadoes; English clue; A1 (59-326).

Hoover; Pa.; M (15-2; 17-1, 19, 53).

Hoover; Bible records, Ohio; B2 (8-25).

Hopkins, Garrard and William; Anne Arundel County; R1 (4-395).

Hopkins, Stephen; Plymouth; D (1-110; 2-12; 4-114; 5-47; 8-240; 12-112, 236; 15-115, 175; 16-35, 105; 20-67; 23-76); Dx (4-41); M (5-6).

Hopkins; N. J.; P (5-168).

Hoppe, Hoppen, Hopper; A2 (39-269).

Hopper, Andries; New York; A2 (39-269; 40-9, 123, 168, 258; 41-54, 287; 43-195; 50-391).

Hopper; Families; C2 (4-1).

Hopson, John; Guilford; A1 (59-46).

Hopton; Charlestown, S. C.; A1 (54-196).

Horn; N. H.; M (13-55, 72).

Horne; see Orne.

Horner; N. J.; English ancestry; Q1 (36-322).

Horner; Chesterfield, N. J.; A2 (29-137).

Hort; Vital entries from Journal; S. C.; J.(24-40).

Horton, Barnabas; Southold, L. I.; A2 (36-38, 104); B2 (1-73).

Horton; Springfield, New Haven; B4 (4-792; 7-1789).

Horton; White Plains; A2 (49-295).

Horton; Bible records; A2 (54-263, 264); P (8-201).

Hosford; Wallingford; B4 (4-794).

Hoskins, Richard; Pa.; A1 (51-117; 54-189).

Hoskins, Thomas; Edenton, N. C.; H (2-310; 3-116, 300).

Hosmer, James; English connections; A1 (68-187).

Hossington; Wallingford; B4 (4-794).

Hotchkin, John; Guilford; A1 (58-281).

Hotchkiss, Samuel; New Haven; A1 (58-283; 66-327; 67-48, 123, 223); B3 (11-409); B4 (4-795, 946; 5-1245; 8-2046).

Houck, John; Berks County, Pa.; S1 (14-177).

Hough, Richard; Bucks County; Q1 (18-20).

Hough, William; New London (Wallingford branch); B4 (4-845).

Hough; Bozrah; N. H.; S2 (12-110).

Hough; Boston; C4 (1-129).

Houghton, John; Lancaster; A1 (79-392).

House, Samuel and Thomas; Scituate, Barnstable, Yarmouth; English data; A1 (66-356).

Houston; Somerset County, Md.; N2 (3-281).

Hovey, Dorcas (Ivory); English ancestry; A1 (67-330).

Howard; Bible records; M (16-22).

Howard; Bible records; X2 (2-18).

Howe, Abraham; Roxbury, Dorchester; A1 (85-355); Y1 (56-50).

How, Abraham; Marlborough; M (7-12); U (22-20).

Howe, Edward; Watertown; English clue; A1 (63-285; 65-295); Y2 (2-187); New Haven branches; B4 (4-854; 5-1245).

Howe, James; Ipswich; Y1 (54-33, 145, 257, 353).

Howe, John; Sudbury, Marlborough; U (11-183; 20-153; 21-16).

Howell, Edward; Lynn, Southampton, L. I.; New Haven branch; B4 (4-860).

Howell; Bible records; B2 (3-192).

Howell; English records; A2 (28-50, 83).

Howes, Thomas; A1 (59-217).

Howes, Thomas; Yarmouth; D (6-157).

Howett, John; Va.; A1 (63-363).

Howland, John; Plymouth; D (2-70; 3-54; 6-86, 147; 7-198; 10-86; 11-32, 82; 13-65, 17-187, 219; 20-131; 21-145, 179; 23-76; 27-41, 81); M (5-7); S1 (12-265); U (20-72).

Howland; Bible record, Barnstable; M (19-106).

Howse, Samuel; Scituate; English data; A1 (66-356; 67-260; 69-284).

Howser, Jacob and Christopher; New York; A2 (60-79, 172).

Hoy; New Haven; B4 (4-864).

Hoyle; Bible records; P (9-163).

Hubbard, George; Wethersfield, Milford, Guilford; C2 (5-237; 6-49).

Hubbard, Samuel; Newport; F4 (5-289); English data; A1 (70-183).

Hubbard; Jamaica, Huntington, L. I.; A2 (33-107); New Haven branch; B4 (4-864).

Hubbard; Philadelphia; P (10-89).

Hubbard; Salisbury; A1 (66-88, 89).

Huber [Hoover]; Pa.; M (15-2; 17-1, 19, 53).

Hubley; Lancaster County, Pa.; Q3 (1-75).

Huckins, Robert; Dover; A1 (67-81, 180, 270, 348; 68-93, 150, 249, 328; 69-28, 136, 255, 319); F3 (5-190).

Huckens, Thomas; Barnstable; D (24-179); Dx (2-47).

Huckstep; English data; A1 (67-44).

Hudson, Ralph; English data; A1 (64-284).

Hudson, William; Philadelphia; Q1 (15-336; 16-108); English origin; Q1 (36-320).

Hudson; Wallingford; B4 (4-868).

Huggins, John; Branford; B4 (4-869; 8-2046).

Hughes, Barnabas; Lancaster; Q1 (17-124).

Hughes, Richard; Guilford; A1 (62-229).

Hughes; East Haven; B4 (4-870).

Hughes; Va.; B2 (8-64).

Hughes; Bible record, Pa.; M (19-65).

Hughes; C4 (3-201).

Hull, Joseph (Rev.); Weymouth, Dover; E (12-86, 134; 13-26, 138; 14-51; 15-13); S1 (14-159).

Hull, Richard and Andrew; New Haven; B4 (4-872; 8-2047).

Hulme; Bible records, Pa.; P (7-131).

Hulme; see Holmes.

Hulse; New Haven; B4 (4-891).

Humfry, John; Y1 (65-293).

Humiston, Henry; New Haven; B3 (11-161); B4 (4-892).

Humphreville, John; West Haven; B4 (4-902).

Humphrey, Daniel; Haverford; P (8-121).

Humphrey, John; Lynn; English clue; A1 (61-280); 65-86).

Humphrey, Jonas; Barrington branch; C1 (2-123).

Humphrey, Jonas; Dorchester; English origin; A1 (63-278); a line of descent; B5 (12-198).

Humphrey, Michael; Windsor, Simsbury; A1 (61-278).

Humphrey; Haverford; Q1 (17-115).

Humphrey; Bible record; C4 (4-53).

Hungerford, Thomas; Hartford, New London; English clue; A1 (55-333).

Hungerford, William; Charles County, Md.; X1 (5-381).

Hunnewell, Ambrose; Me., Boston; A1 (54-140).

Hunnewell; New Haven; B4 (4-907).

Hunsicker; Bible record, Pa.; Q1 (16-247).

Hunt, John; East Haven; B4 (4-907).

Hunt, Ralph; Newtown, L. I.; N. J. branch; B1 (2-5, 39, 79, 129).

Hunt, Thomas; Stamford, Conn., Westchester, N. Y.; A2 (43-115).

Hunt, William; Concord; U (20-30).

Hunt, William; Charles City County, Va.; V1 (2-277).

Hunt; Chilmark; D (28-105).

Hunt; Bible record, Falmouth; M (16-9).

Hunt; Bible records, Tarrytown, N. Y.; A2 (54-252).

Hunt; Bible record, Westchester County, N. Y.; B5 (12-165).

Hunt; Bible records; A1 (64-284; 84-462).

Hunt; English data; A1 (63-286).

Hunt; London, Eng.; A1 (54-216).

Hunter, David and Nicholas; York, Pa.; N2 (5-151).

Hunter, Newberry, Va.; E (8-73).

Hunter; Bible records; A1 (63-196).

Hunting, Esther (Seaborn); English origin; A1 (63-361).

Huntington; Woodbridge; B4 (4-908).

Huntley, John; Boston; U (20-54).

Huntress, George; Portsmouth, Newington; F3 (6-177).

Huntress; Strafford, Vt.; A1 (76-313).

Hurd, John; Boston; D (8-111).

Hurd; Stratford; B5 (14-149).

Hurd; Bible records, Killingworth; B2 (8-22).

Hurford, John; Abington; Buckingham; Q1 (44-158; 47-277).

Hurlbut; Note, Cayuga County, N. Y.; A2 (54-88).

Hurry, Samuel; Philadelphia; A2 (35-198).

Hurst; Fairfax County, Va.; V1 (1-170).

Hussey, Richard; Dover; F3 (5-179; 6-97; 7-1); S2 (27-257).

Husted; Bible records; A2 (32-52).

Huston; Bible record, Pa.; M (19-107).

Hutchinson, Anne (Marbury); English ancestry; A2 (45-17, 164); Massacre; A2 (60-120).

Hutchinson, Richard; Salem; S2 (9-2).

Hutchinson, William; Boston, Newport; A2 (45-17, 164; 47-318); English ancestry; A1 (51-118 ff.; 79-170).

Hutchinson; (Gov. Thomas); A1 (51-473).

Hutson, William (Rev.); Charleston; J (9-127).

Hutton; Bible record, N. Y.; Q1 (43-257).

Hyde, Humphrey; Windsor, Fairfield; English origin; A1 (59-418); a Utah branch; U (4-59).

Hyde, Jonathan; Newton; A1 (71-257, 342).

Hyde, Joseph and Edmund; English clue; A1 (59-418).

Hyde, Samuel; Newton; A1 (71-144).

Hyde; Family record, Conn., Vt.; M (18-37).

Hyde; Family records; A1 (85-444).

Hyde; co. Dorset, Eng.; A1 (81-318).

Hyland, John and Nicholas; Cecil County, Md.; X1 (25-401).

Hynes; Family record; Q1 (37-118).

Hynson, Thomas (Col.); Md.; X1 (15-242; 18-186).

Hyrne, Edward; S. C.; J (22-101; 26-172).

Iddenden, Edmond; Scituate, Boston; A1 (67-37; 68-186; 70-349).

Iggleden, Stephen and John; Roxbury and Fairfield; English ancestry; A1 (65-174).

Ince, Jonathan; New Haven; B4 (4-908).

Ingersoll, Richard; Y1 (52-192).

Ingersoll; New Haven; B4 (4-908).

Ingersoll; English data; A1 (54-94, 343).

Ingraham; New Haven; B4 (4-909).

Ingraham, Joseph and Edward; English data; A2 (42-296, 431).

Inman, Edward; Warwick; F4 (6-78).

Innis; N. J.; S3 (5-3-5).

Iredell; Edenton, N. C.; H (2-163).

Ireland; Gloucester County, N. J.; Q1 (25-417).

Irish, Nathaniel; Bucks County, Pa., Q1 (22-506).

Irish; Falmouth; F2 (7-235).

Isaacs; New Haven; B4 (4-909).

Iverson; Bible records, Boston; A1 (71-284).

Ives, John; Va.; English origin; A1 (63-285).

Ives, William; New Haven; B4 (4-910; 5-1245; 8-2047).

Ives; Bible record, Conn., Pa.; M (18-81).

Ivory, William; Lynn; English data; A1 (67-330).

Izard, Ralph; Berkeley County, S. C.; J (2-205).

Jackson, Abraham; Plymouth; S3 (6-3-2, 4; 6-4-5; 7-1-10; 7-2-9; 7-5-11).

Jackson, John and Edward; Cambridge and Newton; English data; A1 (66-84).

Jackson, John; New Haven, Derby; B4 (4-935).

Jackson, Nicholas; Rowley; A1 (62-372).

Jackson, Stephen; Providence; G2 (7-33); T6 (2-206).

Jackson, William; New York, N. Y.; A2 (37-83).

Jackson; S. C.; J (11-190).

Jackson; Richmond, Vt.; B5 (12-174).

Jackson; Bible records, Conn.; A2 (53-135).

Jackson; Bible records, N. H.; B2 (6-57).

Jackson; Bible records; B2 (5-24); C4 (4-53).

Jackson; Inscriptions, Jerusalem, L. I.; A2(26-79).

Jacob, Nicholas; English clue; A1 (57-224).

Jacobs, Bartholomew; New Haven; B4 (4-936).

Jacobs; Family record; Q1 (31-374).

Jacobsen, Cornelis; see Stille.

Jacocks; N. Carolina, New Haven; B4 (4-941).

Jacquelin, Edward; Jamestown, Va.; N2 (2-4-53).

Jaggard; N. J.; P (5-168).

James, Thomas; Salem; English origin; A1 (63-164).

James, Thomas (Rev.); Charlestown; English data; A1 (51-423).

James, William; Albany; A2 (55-101, 222, 301).

James; Scituate; D (19-97; 20-153).

James; Bible record, East Greenwich; A1 (64-284).

James; Bible records; M (16-22).

Janeway, James; Ohio; E (13-187).

Janeway; English data; A2 (44-378).

Janney, Thomas; Bucks County, Pa.; Q1 (27-212); R1 (8-119, 196, 275).

Jans, Anneke; New York; A2 (56-201; 57-11, 27, 81, 119).

Jansen, Roelof; New York; A2 (56-204).

Janszen, Sybrant; New York; A2 (57-19).

Janszen, Thymen; New York; A2 (7-123).

Jaques, Henry; Newbury; English data; A1 (52-68); family record; A1 (63-376; 64-157).

Jarrett, Robert; New Kent County; V1 (9-122).

Jasper; co. Suffolk, Eng.; A1 (83-293).

Jay, Augustus; New York; A2 (7-110).

Jay, Thomas; Boston; N. J. branch; S3 (2-4-5).

Jebine; New Haven; B4 (4-941).

Jefferis; Bible records; P (3-262).

Jefferson, Thomas; Henrico County, Va.; V2 (1-33); V1 (6-199, 264; 7-49, 119, 214; 8-39; 10-174).

Jeffries, David; Boston; English data; A1 (53-23).

Jeffries, Thomas; New Haven; B4 (4-941).

Jellison, Nicholas; Kittery; C2 (1-238).

Jenckes; Bible record, Providence; D (20-175).

Jenkin; English data; A1 (76-54).

Jenkins, Joel; Braintree, Malden; A1 (66-268, 315; 67-89).

Jenkins, John; Colleton County; J (20-223).

Jenkins; Barnstable; D (22-156).

Jenkins; Sandwich, West Greenwich; F4 (4-251).

Jenkins; Philadelphia; P (9-50).

Jenkins; Private record; A1 (68-108).

Jenney, John; Plymouth; D (6-169; 8-171; 10-129).

Jennings, Charles; Elizabeth City County, Va.; V1 (4-425).

Jennings, Joshua; Fairfield; A2 (54-179).

Jennings; Family record, Prince Edward County, Va.; M (18-41).

Jennings; Bible records; A1 (83-381).

Jennings; Bible records; X2 (2-9).

Jennings; N. J.; E (1-148; 8-185); P (9-90, 319).

Jennings; Estate in England; M (1-41).

Jentilman; English ancestry; A2 (45-114).

Jerome; Wallingford; B4 (4-941).

Jerrill; M (4-34).

Jervey, David; Charleston; J (7-31, 109).

Jett; Bible record, Culpeper County, Va.; M (19-18).

Jewell, Mark; Sandwich, N. H.; S2 (5-245).

John, Evan; Chester County, Pa.; Welsh origin; Q1 (37-84).

Johns, Richard; Calvert County; R1 (4-416).

Johnson, Edward (Capt.); Woburn; A1 (59-79, 143, 275; 68-142); K (4-50); English ancestry [see also Porredge]; A1 (67-169).

Johnson, Francis; Pa.; English origin; Q1 (22-250).

Johnson, George; Stratford; B4 (5-1057).

Keen; Family record, Marshfield; D (28-1).
Keen; Bible record; P (5-265, 267); Q1 (29-116).
Keen; Family records; P (5-119).
Keffer; E (9-142).
Kellogg, Joseph; Hadley; S1 (16-269).
Kellogg; Braintree, Eng.; A1 (52-271).
Kellogg; Wallingford; B4 (5-1070).
Kelly, Torrance; Wheeling, W. Va.; G1 (2-369).
Kelly; N. H.; G2 (5-32).
Kemball, Richard; Ipswich; wife's ancestry; A1 (52-248); see Kimball.
Kemp, William; Duxbury, Mass.; A2 (35-101).
Kempe, Richard; Va.; A2 (42-434).
Kendall, Francis; Woburn; A1 (55-443); E (11-124).
Kendall; Bible record, Hollis, N. H.; B5 (2-70).
Kenly; Md.; Pa.; Q1 (31-503).
Kenney; Bible record; Y1 (53-288).
Kennon, Richard (Col.); Henrico County; V1 (11-176).
Kenrick; G1 (9-459).
Kent, Joseph; Dedham; S1 (18-190).
Kent, Stephen; English data; A1 (68-107).
Kent, Thomas; Gloucester; A2 (4-83).
Kent; Family record, Suffield, Conn.; B5 (3-35).
Kenyon, Roger; Block Island; A1 (67-296).
Kenyon; Family record, Richmond, R. I.; B5 (3-37).
Kerly, William; Lunenburg County, Va.; A1 (78-39).
Kermer, Abraham; New York; A2 (61-356).
Kern, Nicholas; Lehigh County, Pa.; M (1-7).
Kerr; Philadelphia; Ohio; E (13-75).
Kerr; Bible record, Williamsburg; V1 (4-39).
Kerrich; English data; A1 (75-290).
Keteltas, Jan Evertszen; A2 (36-140; 37-236).
Keteltas; New York; family records; A2 (28-172).
Kettell, John; Lancaster, Stow; A1 (51-294; 52-37).
Key, Philip; St. Mary's County, Md.; X1 (5-194).
Keyes, Robert; Sudbury; A1 (61-303).
Kierstede, Hans (Dr.); New York; A2 (13-24).
Kilbourne, Thomas; Wethersfield: E (6-111, 123, 182; 10-81).
Kilby; New Haven; B4 (5-1070).
Killam, Austen; Salem; English data; A1 (52-238; 56-344).
Kimball, Caleb and Thomas; York County, Me.; C2 (4-131).

Kimball, Richard; Ipswich; S2 (4-435); see Kemball.
Kimball; Family records, Mass.; Y2 (1-16).
Kimberly, Thomas; New Haven, Stratford; B4 (5-1070).
King, Ann (Evans); Pa.; Welsh origin; Q1 (22-249).
King, Clement; Marshfield, Mass., Providence, R. I.; A2 (39-77; 43-295).
King, Daniel; Lynn; English data; A1 (65-84; 66-125).
King, James; Suffield; English ancestry; A1 (58-347).
King, John; Palmer; S1 (13-411).
King, Peter; Boston; A1 (51-168).
King, Thomas; Sudbury; A1 (63-281).
King, William; Salem; A2 (33-71, 145).
King; Bath, Me.; F2 (2-50).
King; East Haven; B4 (5-1076).
King; Mansfield, Conn.; A2 (39-139).
King; Philadelphia; P (7-281).
King; Bible record, Suffield, Conn.; M (14-46).
King; Bible records; B5 (7-45); P (3-272); Q1 (43-277).
King; English data; A2 (31-8, 70, 135, 198; 36-222, 263; 38-139, 213; 41-263; 42-7).
King; Southold, N. Y.; A2 (32-89).
King; Columbia County, N. Y.; A2 (42-342).
Kingsbury, Henry; Rowley; A1 (54-260).
Kingsley; Wallingford; B4 (5-1077).
Kinsey, Hugh; Anne Arundel County; R1 (4-432; 5-300).
Kinsey; Woodbridge, N. J.; P (11-91).
Kinsman, Robert; Ipswich; U (18-113).
Kip [De-Kuype], Hendrick Hendrickszen; New York; A2 (8-67, 124; 12-29; 20-12).
Kip, Hendrick; Dutch notes; B1 (2-118).
Kirby, John; Lynn, Sandwich, Middletown; A2 (42-444); B4 (5-1077).
Kirby; N. J.; P (6-244).
Kirby; Family record, Hanover, N. J.; M (18-50).
Kirby; Bible records, Va.; V1 (1-282).
Kirkham, Thomas; Wethersfield; A1 (59-254).
Kirkpatrick, Alexander; Somerset County, N. J.; B6 (3-268; 5-171, 316).
Kirkwood; Boston; A1 (61-257).
Kirtland; Wallingford; B4 (5-1078).
Kitchen, John; Salem; Y1 (51-126).
Kline, Jacob; Hunterdon County, N. J.; B6 (7-26).
Knapp; Taunton; E (9-258).
Knapp; Danbury; C4 (1-68).
Knapp; White Plains; A2 (49-174).

Kneass, Johan Christian; Philadelphia; P (7-107).
Knickerbocker, Harmen Jansen; Albany; A2 (39-33, 116, 179, 277; 40-55, 100).
Kniffen; Rye; A2 (49-297).
Knight, Alexander, Philip and Robert; English data; A2 (40-238).
Knight; Family record; B5 (4-37, 78).
Knollys, Hansard; Piscataqua; A1 (70-184).
Knowles, John and Francis; Oxford, Pa.; Q1 (18-255).
Knowles, Richard; Plymouth, Eastham; A1 (79-286, 379; 80-6, 119, 265); D (25-109).
Knowles; Family record, Haddam, Conn.; M (18-51).
Knox; Ashford; M (17-40).
Knox; Bible record; B5 (1-15).
Kock; Holland; A2 (57-371).
Kollock, Jacob; Sussex Co., Del.; A2 (8-184).
Krebs; Bible records; P (11-191).
Kuhn, Jacob; Boston; A1 (51-441).
Lacey, Edward; Shippen, Pa.; R2 (1-41).
Lake, John; English ancestry; A1 (84-304).
Lake, Thomas and John; Boston; A1 (52-275).
Lake; Bible record (Dutch); Q1 (31-118).
Lake; Bible record, N. J.; Q1 (37-253).
Lakin, William; Reading, Groton; A1 (63-318).
Lamar, Thomas; Calvert County, Md.; R1 (1-203).
Lambert; Salem, Lynn; Y1 (54-49, 187).
Lambert; Milford; B4 (5-1078).
Lambert; N. J.; Q1 (17-371).
Lamberton, George (Capt.); New Haven; English data; A1 (61-189; 68-283); B4 (5-1078).
Lambson; Niagara County, N. Y.; Utah; U (6-145).
Lampo, Jean; New York; Dutch ancestry; A2 (61-174).
Lampson, Thomas; New Haven; B4 (5-1079).
Lamson, William; Ipswich, Mass.; A2 (42-441).
Lancraft; East Haven; B4 (5-1079).
Landon, Nathan; Southold, L. I.; A2 (28-24).
Lane, John; Hingham, Norton; A1 (83-466).
Lane, John; Milford; B4 (5-1079).
Lane [Matthys Jansen Laenen] New Utrecht; B6 (2-113, 194, 281; 3-43, 124, 211, 280; 4-41).
Lane, Richard; Jamestown; (Halifax, N. C., branch); V1 (3-166).

Lane; Rye; A2 (49-300).
Lanfair; East Haven; B4 (5-1080).
Langdell-Langdon; Beverly; B2 (4-225).
Langdon, Thomas; Lynn, New Haven, Hempstead; B4 (5-1080).
Langdon; Bible records, Boston; A1 (67-379).
Langley, John; Boston; A1 (51-168).
Lanier; Va.; V1 (3-126, 210).
Laning; Bible records, N. J.; N. Y.; P (7-268).
Lank; Bible records; P (3-263).
Lansing, Gerrit; Albany; A2 (3-84).
Larabee; West Haven; B4 (5-1080).
Larcom, Mordecai; Ipswich; Y1 (58-41, 129).
Larkham; English data; A1 (51-115).
La Serre, Octave; Ohio; E (3-39; 4-43).
La Serre; Guernsey; E (8-40; 9-86).
Latham, Cary; Cambridge, Mass.; New London, Conn.; A2 (35-293); English origin; A1 (61-385).
Latham; Bridgewater; D (21-40; 22-118); Dx (1-10).
Lathrop; see Lothrop.
Latimer, Robert; New London; A2 (52-6, 374).
Latimer; Bible record, New London; A1 (75-78).
Lattin, Latting, Richard; Concord, Fairfield, Oyster Bay; A2 (2-8, 54).
Lawrence, John, William and Thomas; Flushing, Newtown, L. I.; A2 (3-26, 121, 178; 13-62); A1 (51-452).
Lawrence, William; Monmouth; A2 (16-141, 185).
Lawrence; Boston; A1 (63-278).
Lawrence; Groton; A1 (61-276).
Lawrence; N. J.; P (5-168).
Lawrence; Bible records, N. J.; P (7-129).
Lawrence; Bible records; A2 (54-258).
Lawrence; Bible records; A1 (74-238).
Lawrence [Popinga]; A2 (59-314, 317).
Lawton; Bible records, Rehoboth; A1 (69-91).
Lawton; Bible record; P (5-262).
Lay, John; Lyme; A2 (52-93; 56-85).
Lay, Robert; Saybrook; A1 (62-172, 238).
Lay; see Ley.
Lea, John; Pa., with English data; X1 (25-403).
Lea; Wilmington, Del.; Q1 (52-90).
Leach, Lawrence; Salem; S1 (13-177).
Leach; Kingsessing; Q1 (35-343).
Leachland; A1 (81-320, 486; 82-63).
Leager, Jacob; Boston; English ancestry; A1 (69-355).
Leak; see Lake.
Leaming, Christopher; Southampton, L. I.; A2 (24-92, 148; 26-150).

Lear, Tobias; Portsmouth, N. H.; S2 (6-5, 66).
Leary; N. Y.; G2 (15-112).
Leavenworth, Thomas; Stratford; A1 (72-77).
Leavit; Branford; B4 (5-1082).
Lechford; English data; A1 (54-215).
LeCompte, Anthony; Dorchester County, Md.; X1 (12-46).
Ledyard, John; Southold,* Hartford; A2 (7-10).
Lee, Edward and John; Guilford; A1 (53-53).
Lee, Henry; Manchester; Y1 (52-33, 145, 225, 329; 53-65, 153, 257).
Lee, John; Charlestown; A1 (54-194).
Lee, Thomas, William and John; Boston; A1 (76-197).
Lee, Thomas; Saybrook, Lyme; A1 (61-116).
Lee; Lyme; A2 (52-91).
Lee; Conway, Mass.; E (9-309).
Lee; Frederick, Md.; N2 (4-290).
Lee; Va.; V1 (7-136).
Leeds, Thomas; Shrewsbury; A2 (48-310).
Leek, Philip; New Haven; B4 (5-1082).
Leeman, Samuel; Charlestown; S2 (14-375).
Leet; Pa.; M (15-53).
Lefferts; see Haughwout.
Le Forge, Henry; Hamden; B4 (5-1085, 1245).
Legare; Bible records, S. C.; J (26-174).
Leggett, Gabriel; Westchester; A2 (44-236, 313; 45-74, 127, 279, 373; 46-69, 177, 292, 394; 47-82, 185).
Leib; Family record, Pa.; P (10-184).
Leipham, Peter; Russell Hill, Pa.; Pw (20-1).
Leisler, Jacob; New York; A2 (7-145).
Leland; Grafton, Mass. (Elder John); S2 (8-226).
Lenox, Robert; New York; Scots ancestry; A2 (44-218).
Leonard; N. J.; P (5-168).
Leonard; English ancestry; A2 (18-34).
Leoser; Bible record; Q1 (42-183).
Le Roux, Pierre; New York; A2 (50-151).
Le Roy, Francois Caesar; New York; C2 (2-163).
Leslie; Essex County; Y1 (51-356).
Lesslie, James; Topsfield; Y1 (51-233, 329).
Lespinard, Anthony; Albany; A2 (2-70; 8-185; 24-97); S1 (14-262).
Lester, Bryant; Lunenburg County, Va.; R1 (1-127).
Lester; Bible records; A2 (56-108, 111).
L'Estrange, Daniel; see Strang.

Le Sueur, François; New York; A2 (55-360).
Leverett, Thomas (Elder); Boston; English data; A1 (70-184).
Levering; Bible records, Pa.; P (6-246).
Levet, Thomas; Exeter, Hampton; English data; A1 (67-66).
Levett; Prince George's County, Md.; X1 (1-380).
Levy; Richmond County; V1 (10-33).
Levy; Bible records, New York, Philadelphia; X1 (21-201).
Lewin, Philip; Prince George's, Md.; X2 (2-2).
Lewis, David; Schenectady, N. Y.; A2 (41-22, 121, 168).
Lewis, John; Augusta County, Va.; N2 (4-81, 116, 136, 142).
Lewis, John (Maj.); Va.; V1 (1-285).
Lewis, Samuel; Va.; M (1-66).
Lewis, Sarah (Meed); Scituate; English ancestry; A1 (66-356).
Lewis, Thomas; Albany; A2 (34-111; 40-131, 245).
Lewis, Thomas; English data; A1 (62-92).
Lewis, William; Farmington; B4 (5-1085).
Lewis; (Various, New Haven); B4 (5-1089).
Lewis; Somerset County, N. J.; B6 (6-118).
Lewis; Loudoun County, Va.; P (9-191).
Lewis; Patrick County, Va.; V1 (9-64).
Lewis; Bible record, R. I.; A1 (73-320).
Lewis; Gwynedd, Pa.; Q1 (24-203).
Lewis; Ga.; M (3-4-11).
Ley, Stephen (Dr.); Staunton, Va.; N2 (5-139).
Ley, Thomas; English clue; A1 (61-67).
L'Hommedieu, Benjamin; Shelter Island; A2 (2-1, 208).
Libbey, John; Scarborough; S1 (14-390).
Lightfoot; Family record, Va.; V1 (11-111).
Lillibridge, Thomas; Newport; A1 (63-43).
Lilly; English wills; E (2-16).
Lincoln, Thomas, Daniel and Samuel; Hingham; A2 (60-115).
Lincoln, Samuel; Salem; Hingham; (Gov. Enoch of Me.); F2 (3-139).
Lincoln; Taunton; S1 (16-398).
Lincoln; Hingham (Lt.-Gov. Levi); A1 (51-425).
Lincoln; Abraham's father; A1 (84-389).
Lindon, Henry; New Haven; B4 (5-1090).

Lindsly; Bible records, Morristown; A2 (46-412).
Lines, Ralph and Henry; New Haven; B3 (9-420, 659); B4 (5-1090).
Ling, Benjamin; New Haven; B4 (5-1105).
Linsford, Thomas; Boston; English data; A1 (71-91).
Linsley, John; Branford; B3 (11-664).
Linthicum, Thomas; Md.; X1 (25-275, 406).
Linzee; English data; A1 (53-20).
Liscome; Bible record, Stoughton; A1 (75-79).
Lispenard; see Lespinard.
Lithgow, Robert; Topsham, Brunswick, Me.; A2 (29-1).
Littell, William; Georgia; English data; A2 (43-68).
Little, James; Stamford; S1 (13-313).
Little, Richard; New Haven; B4 (5-1105; 6-1528).
Little, Thomas; Plymouth, Marshfield; D (4-161; 17-82; 19-158, 165; 24-1, 7, 165; 28-1).
Little; Edenton, N. C.; H (3-159).
Little; Bible record; B5 (14-173).
Little; (Justice Wm., Car.); C2 (4-81).
Littlefield, Edmond; Exeter, Wells; English ancestry; A1 (67-343).
Littlejohn, William; Edenton; H (1-268).
Livermore; Holderness; S2 (4-175).
Livingston, Robert; Albany; A2 (32-129, 193; 42-446; 43-91).
Livingston; Bible records, N. Y. family; A2 (10-98; 14-113); Scotland; A2 (15-15, 105, 159; 18-137); Heraldry; A2 (18-83).
Livingston; N. Y.; Z (57-602).
Livingston; Revolutionary records; A2 (41-192, 299); Notes; A2 (46-230).
Livingston; Wallingford; B4 (5-1106).
Lloyd, Cornelius (Col.) and Edward (Col.); Va.; Md.; A2 (40-177; 41-75); X1 (7-420; 8-85).
Lloyd, James; Huntington, L. I.; T7 (Vol. 60, 1927, p. 879).
Lloyd, John and Thomas; Richmond County, Va.; English clue; A1 (59-219, 327).
Lloyd; Pa.; Q1 (17-118).
Lloyd; Inscriptions, Md.; X1 (17-20).
Lloyd; arms; M (6-40).
Lobdell; English notes; A2 (54-103).
Lockington, William; English clue; A1 (61-92).
Lockwood, Robert; Watertown, Fairfield; A1 (62-97); A2 (43-191; 58-395); S1 (13-202).
Lodge; N. J.; P (5-168).
Lomas; Annapolis, Md.; X1 (4-196).
Lombard; Bible record; M (16-10).
London; Wallingford; B4 (5-1107).

Long, Robert; Charlestown; English origin; A1 (57-415).
Long, William; Boston; A1 (63-381).
Long; Family record, Abbeville, S. C.; M (18-57).
Long; Bible record; B5 (14-173).
Longfield [Van Langevelt], Cornelis; New York; A2 (59-306).
Loockermans, Govert, Jacob, Pieter Janse, and Balthus; New York; A2 (8-11, 91); Bible records; A2 (5-69); Md. branch; X1 (11-193, 295).
Looker, Henry and John; Sudbury; A1 (63-280; 64-136).
Loomis, Joseph; Windsor; B3 (10-361); with English ancestry; U (20-58).
Loomis; Ohio soldiers, 1861-65; E (7-46).
Loomis; Wisconsin soldiers, 1861-65; E (7-194).
Lord, Nathan; Kittery; S2 (26-227).
Lord, Theodorus; Pa.; English clue; P (9-188).
Lord, Thomas; Hartford; Y1 (54-94); Lyme branch; A2 (52-91).
Lord; Lyme, West Haven; B4 (5-1107).
Lord; Bible record, Falmouth; M (16-10).
Loree; Bible records; A2 (53-136).
Lorillard; New York; A2 (8-89).
Loring; Duxbury; D (21-126).
Loten; Holland; A2 (57-376).
Lothrop, John (Rev.); Boston, Barnstable; A1 (67-261; 69-284; 84-437); B4 (5-1081); D (11-42); A2 (48-305); U (20-66; 23-60); English data; A1 (54-92; 66-356).
Lotshaw; Bible records, Ohio; B2 (9-14).
Lott; Bible record; A2 (36-205).
Lounsbury, Richard; Rye, N. Y.; A2 (49-300).
Lounsbury; Dutchess County; A2 (17-280).
Lounsbury; New Haven branch; B4 (5-1107, 1247).
Love; New Haven; B4 (5-1110, 1247).
Lovelace, Francis (Gov.); New York; A2 (51-175).
Lovell, Alexander; Westfield, Mass.; English data; A2 (42-294).
Lovell, Joseph (Col.); Richmond, Va.; N2 (4-295).
Lovering, Thomas; Watertown; A1 (56-184).
Loving; Amherst County, Va.; E (6-192).
Low, Andrew; New Haven; B4 (5-1110).
Lowe, Henry (Col.); Md.; English data; X1 (2-180, 280).

Lowe, Thomas; Ipswich; English data; A1 (52-67).

Lowe [Jan Bastiaensen]; Harlem; B6 (6-203).

Lowe; co. Derby, Eng.; X1 (9-115).

Lowell, Percival; A1 (54-315; 63-300).

Lowell; Family record, Cambridge, Mass.; M (18-58).

Lowndes, Christopher; Prince George's County, Md.; X1 (2-276).

Loxley; Family record; Q1 (23-265).

Lozier; see Le Sueur.

Lucas; Plymouth; D (27-21).

Lucas; Del.; S. C.; J (27-212).

Lucken, Jan; Bible record, Pa.; Q1 (23-270, 408).

Luddington, William; Malden, East Haven; A1 (58-72); B4 (5-1111; 8-2048).

Ludlam, William; Southampton, Huntington; A2 (15-93; 47-308).

Ludlow, Gabriel; New York; A2 (50-34, 134).

Ludlow; Bible records; A2 (56-30).

Ludwell; Va.; English clue; A1 (57-110).

Lumas, Edward; Ipswich; Y1 (53-137, 305).

Lumpkin, William; Yarmouth; D (12-139).

Lumsdon; New Haven; B4 (5-1118).

Lundy; N. J.; Q1 (19-340).

Lupher; Bible records, Pa.; P (10-178).

Lupton, Thomas; Norwalk; B4 (5-1118).

Lyddall, George (Col.); New Kent County, Va.; A2 (43-194).

Lyford, John (Rev.); Plymouth, Nantasket; A2 (60-117).

Lyman, Richard; Roxbury, Hartford; New Haven, Wallingford, branches; B4 (5-1118).

Lyman; R. I.; T4 (No. 33, p. 42).

Lynch, Charles; Albemarle County, Va; E (1-1).

Lynch, Gabriel; Newtown, L. I., Rye; A2 (49-173).

Lynde; Boston deed; A1 (51-64).

Lynes, Philip; Charles County, Md.; X1 (2-184).

Lynn; Philadelphia; Bible record; A2 (5-45).

Lynn; Family record; Q1 (17-376).

Lynus, Nathaniel; New York, Stratford; B4 (5-1119).

Lyon, David; New Kent County; V1 (9-275).

Lyon, Ephraim; Ashford branch; A2 (28-75).

Lyon, Matthew; Wallingford, Vt.; G2 (16-37).

Lyon, William; Roxbury; A2 (28-235; 29-98).

Lyon, William; New Haven; B4 (5-1119).

Lyon; Bible record, Essex County, N. J.; M (14-58).

Lyons, Peter; Va.; V1 (8-184).

McCalla; Bucks County, Pa.; Q1 (39-378).

McCalla, David; S. C.; P (9-318).

McCalla; Bible records, Jenkintown; P (8-193).

McCarthy; Bible records, Boston; A1 (85-350).

McCarty; Va.; G2 (15-118).

McClary; Springfield; S1 (13-401).

McCleave; Wallingford; B4 (5-1156).

McClellan; Bible records, Pa.; P (10-175, 176).

McClintick; Cumberland County, Pa.; E (7-73).

McClure; Chester County, Pa.; B2 (6-22).

M'Connell; Bible records; A2 (56-116).

McConnaughhay; Bible record, Ky., Pa.; M (15-14).

McConnelly; New Haven; B4 (5-1157).

McCoy; New Haven; B4 (5-1157).

McCrackan; New Haven; B4 (5-1157).

McCrea, William; Newark, Del.; (N. J. branch); B6 (4-248; 7-81).

McCullen; New York; A2 (31-120).

McCulloch, John; Philadelphia; Q1 (22-245).

McDonald, William (Col.); Somerset County, N. J.; B6 (5-70; 6-149).

McDonald, William; Pa.; Ohio; E (8-13).

McDonald; Hamden; B4 (5-1158).

McDougal; Bible records; M (16-22).

McElvain; Ky.; Ohio; E (15-167).

McFeely, Robert; Lancaster County, Pa.; B5 (13-70).

McIlvain; Bible records; P (3-268).

McKain; Chester County, Pa.; Q1 (39-120).

McKay; Wethersfield, Wallingford; B4 (5-1158).

McKee, Andrew; East Hartford; B2 (2-102).

McKee; Derby; B4 (5-1159).

McKeehan; Bible records, Pa.; P (7-270).

McKeinzie; Gairloch; E (12-201).

McKelvey, Matthew; Pa. and Ohio; E (1-20).

McKenzie; Suffolk, Va.; H (2-603).

MacKenzie; Scotland; E (8-33); U (7-148); arms; E (10-167).

McKeun; Pa.; P (11-89).

Mackie, Alexander (Col.); S. C.; V2 (2-58).

Mackie, Peter; Bible record, Philadelphia; P (11-76).

Mackie; Talbot County, Md.; X1 (2-375).

McLene; Chester County, Pa.; Q3 (1-218).

McMichael; Bible record, Del.; P (8-204).

McNeil, Archibald; Branford, New Haven; B4 (5-1159).

Macpherson, John (Capt.); Philadelphia; Q1 (23-51).

MacPherson, Paul; Chester; E (8-27).

McPherson; Family record, Md., Ky.; M (19-74).

Macpherson; Pa.; P (7-199).

Macpherson-MacNeal; Bible records, Philadelphia; P (8-294).

McPike, James; Baltimore, Md.; A2 (29-13); Baltimore and Ky.; E (7-267).

MacSparran, James (Rev.) and Archibald; R. I.; G2 (3-52).

MacSweeny; G2 (29-72).

McVickar, John; New York; S1 (13-306).

McWhorter; N. Y.; W. Va.; N2 (1-3-64; 2-1-68).

McWilliams, Andrew; Mt. Carbon, Pa.; S1 (14-172).

Mabie [Pieter Casparzen Van Naerden]; New York; A2 (38-100; 52-251).

Machell, Alason; English clue; A1 (61-199).

Mack, John; Salisbury, Lyme; U (20-52).

Macock, Thomas; Milford, Guilford; A1 (83-127).

Macomber; Marshfield; D (19-16).

Macomber; Dartmouth, New Haven; B4 (5-1120).

Mahony; G2 (14-165).

Makepeace; Taunton; D (21-135).

Makernes; English data; A1 (71-324).

Mallett, John; Fairfield; S1 (13-75).

Mallet, Thomas; Newport; A1 (60-400).

Mallory, Peter; New Haven; A1 (54-320); B4 (5-1121, 1247); Family record, Conn., Mass.; M (19-74).

Mallory, Philip (Rev.); Virginia; A2 (40-181).

Malone; New Haven; B4 (5-1136).

Maltby, William; Branford; E (9-314).

Maltby; Pa.; Sullivan County, N. Y.; A2 (52-168).

Man, William; Cambridge; S1 (14-148).

Man; Bible records, New York; A2 (21-92).

Man; Bible records; A1 (61-395).

Manchester; Family records; Dx (1-97).

Mandeville, Yellis Jansen; New York; A2 (28-244; 38-284).

Manlove; Bible records, Va.; P (9-146); Q1 (31-251).

Manney; Bible records, Malta, N. Y.; B2 (4-289).

Manning; Cambridge; A1 (57-110).

Manross; Meriden, Bristol; B4 (5-1136).

Mansfield, Richard; New Haven; A1 (66-308); B4 (5-1137, 1248; 6-1528).

Mansfield; Bible records, Stoddard, N. H.; A1 (84-346).

Mansor, William; Medford, New Haven; B4 (5-1147).

Mansur, Robert; Charlestown; C3 (2-29, 105, 185).

Mansur; Bible records, Temple, N. H.; M (14-45).

Manton, Edward; F4 (4-296).

Manwaring, Oliver; Salem, New London; A2 (51-307; 56-84); English ancestry; A1 (79-110).

Manwaring, Peter; New London; A2 (51-300).

Manwaring, Thomas; New London, Lyme; A2 (51-303).

Mapes; Bible record; A2 (33-52).

Maplet; English data; A1 (70-115, 282).

Maps; Bible records; B1 (6-93).

March, Hugh; Newbury; A1 (53-121).

Marchant; Milford, Wallingford; B4 (5-1148).

Mareen; Virginia; English clue; A2 (43-70).

Marion; Inscriptions; J (26-158).

Maris, Jury; see George Morris.

Maris; Bible records; P (8-190).

Marks, William; Middletown, Wallingford; B4 (5-1148; 7-1789).

Marll; Bible record; M (15-19).

Marquand, Henry; Fairfield; S1 (14-68).

Marr; Md.; X2 (2-27).

Marsh, Jonathan and Samuel; New Haven; B4 (5-1149).

Marsh; Pa.; E (11-120).

Marsh; Bible record, Stowe, Vt.; M (16-11).

Marshall, Abraham; West Bradford, Pa.; A1 (55-341).

Marshall, Thomas; English data; A2 (40-230).

Marshall, William; Marshall Hall, Md.; M (19-1).

Marshall; Philadelphia; P (9-67).

Marshall; N. J.; P (5-168).

Marshall; Md.; M (15-11); Inscriptions, Marshall Hall, Md.; X1 (24-172).

Marshall; Milford; B4 (5-1149).

Marshall; Va.; N2 (2-4-47).

Marshall; Bible record, Lewes, Del.; Q1 (29-331; 30-245).

Marshall; Bible records, Md.; M (15-36).

Marshfield; Springfield; A1 (65-382).

Marsteller, Frederick; Trappe, Pa.; Q3 (1-27).

Marston, John and William; Salem; A1 (69-342).

Marston, John; Flushing; A2 (60-274); see Maston.

Marston, Robert and William; Hampton; A1 (69-342).

Martense [Adriaen Reyersz]; Flatbush; A2 (8-62).

Martiau, Nicholas; Va.; V1 (1-52).

Martin, John; Dover, N. H.; Piscataway, N. J.; Q1 (34-480; 36-143).

Martin, Samuel; Antigua; L. I.; Mass.; A1 (54-27).

Martin; Boston; A1 (83-383).

Martin; Wallingford; B4 (5-1150).

Martin; English data; A1 (51-116); Portsmouth, Boston; A1 (51-118).

Martin; Bible record, Pa.; M (19-76).

Martin; Family record, Va.; M (18-59).

Mârtonson, Mârton; Chester County; Q1 (36-362).

Marvin, Matthew; Hartford, Norwalk; A1 (51-330).

Mason, Edward; Wethersfield; A1 (61-93).

Mason, Hugh (Capt.); Watertown; English data; A1 (54-189; 78-256).

Mason, John (Capt.); N. H.; English data; A1 (56-308; 59-141).

Mason, John; Norfolk; English clue; A1 (55-333).

Mason; Bible records; P (5-110); Q1 (22-373; 31-251).

Massie; New Kent County, Va.; V1 (1-58).

Masten; Bible record; Q1 (31-251).

Maston [Marston], John; New York; A2 (20-171).

Mather, Jeremiah; English data; A1 (53-22).

Mather; Boston; A1 (52-366).

Mather; English data; A1 (54-348).

Mathews; King George County; V1 (5-143).

Matteson; Bible records, Newton, Mass.; A2 (54-260).

Matthews, William; New Haven; B4 (5-1151, 1248; 8-2048).

Matthews; Note; A2 (45-364).

Mattoon; Deerfield, Wallingford; B4 (5-1155).

Mattox; Colleton, S. C.; M (13-39).

Maull; Bible records; P (3-255, 257, 262, 269).

Maverick, John (Rev.) and Samuel; Dorchester; English ancestry; A1 (69-146, 382; 78-448).

Maverick, Moses; Marblehead; D (5-129).

Maverick; Marblehead; A1 (62-384).

Mawry, Roger; Plymouth, Salem, Providence; F4 (6-79).

Maxey; Bible records; M (16-22).

Maxfield, John; Salisbury, Mass.; B2 (6-52; 7-20, 42, 61, 87; 8-15).

May; Bible records, Roxbury; A1 (85-462).

Mayer, Christopher Bartholomew; Fredericktown, Md.; X1 (10-57).

Mayhew, John; A2 (50-113 ff.).

Mayhew, Thomas (Gov.); English ancestry; K (4-1).

Mayhew; A1 (52-203).

Maynard, John; Sudbury; U (20-112).

Mayo, John (Rev.); Yarmouth; D (9-119); Private record; Dx (2-78).

Mayo; Eastham, Mass., Middletown, Conn.; A1 (70-365).

Mayrant, Nicholas; Berkeley County, S. C.; J (27-81, 231).

Meacham, Jeremiah; S3 (6-2-3).

Meacham; Family record, Salem, Mass.; B5 (1-47).

Meade, Andrew; N. Y.; N. C.; G2 (25-90).

Meade, Robert; Philadelphia; G1 (3-193); Q1 (24-242).

Meade; Nansemond, Va.; R1 (2-335).

Meadows, Elizabeth (Iggleden); English ancestry; A1 (65-174 ff.).

Means; Boston; S. C.; J (7-204).

Meed; English data; A1 (66-353).

Meek; Bible records; P (8-304).

Meeker; New Haven; B4 (5-1160).

Meigs, Vincent; Guilford; B3 (10-372).

Melick; Bible records; B5 (11-85).

Mellowes, Abraham; Charlestown, Mass.; C4 (1-123); A1 (76-198).

Meloy; New Haven; B4 (5-1160).

Melvin; Bible records, Caroline County, Md.; P (8-298).

Melyn, Cornelius; Staten Island; B4 (5-1161).

Mendall; Marshfield; Dx (2-55).

Menefie, George; Buckland, Va.; A2 (40-239; 41-74).

Meng, John Christopher; Germantown; German origin; Q1 (22-379).

Mercein; Bible records; A2 (44-339).

Mercer, John; Marlborough, Va.; X1 (2-191).

Mercier, Bartholomew; Boston, New York; A1 (45-364; 46-414).

Meredith; Warwick, Bucks County, Pa.; P (11-91).

Meriwether, Nicholas; Surry County; V1 (11-171).

Merriam, Joseph; Concord; E (12-148); U (20-63).

Merriam, Thomas; English clue; A1 (61-199).

Merriam; Lynn, Wallingford; B4 (5-1161).

Merrill, Nathaniel; Newbury; A2 (59-215); B2 (4-250).

Merrill; Bible record; A1 (51-72).

Merriman, Nathaniel (Capt.); New Haven, Wallingford; B4 (5-1167; 6-1528); English data; A1 (53-21).

Merritt; Rye; A2 (49-301).

Merryman, John; Lancaster County, Va.; X1 (10-176, 286; 11-85).

Mersereau, Joshua and Daniel; Staten Island; A2 (27-195; 28-17, 71, 125).

Mertz; Bible records; M (16-37).

Merwin, Miles; Milford; B4 (5-1178, 1248).

Mesier, Pieter Jansen; New York, Wappingers Falls; A2 (58-172; 59-77).

Messenger; Family records; A1 (64-286).

Messler; Corrections to printed genealogy; B6 (5-263).

Metcalf, Michael; Dedham; English ancestry; A1 (80-312).

Metcalf; Philadelphia; P (7-195).

Metcalf; co. Norfolk, Eng.; A1 (78-63).

Metters; co. Cornwall, Eng.; Columbus, Ohio; E (1-62).

Mettler, Johann George; Rockaway, N. J.; B6 (6-124).

Mew, Ellis; New Haven; B4 (5-1181; 8-2048).

Meyer, Christian; Saugerties; Z (58-28).

Meyer, Jan Dirckszen; New York; A2 (61-42).

Meyer [Jillis Pieterszen]; New York; A2 (9-3).

Michie; Charleston; J (21-36).

Mickle, James; New York; A2 (28-161, 211).

Middagh, Aert Anthonize; Brooklyn; B6 (6-112).

Middlecott; Boston; D (21-1).

Middleton, Alexander; Boston; A1 (52-13).

Middleton, Arthur; Carolina; J (1-228; 2-155).

Middleton, Edward; Charleston, S. C.; A2 (28-167, 239).

Middleton; N. J.; P (5-168).

Mikell; Va.; S. C.; J (27-212).

Miles, James; Philadelphia; Q1 (37-240).

Miles, Richard (Dea.); New Haven; B4 (5-1182, 1248, 1267); English clue; A1 (54-352).

Miles; Wallingford, Conn.; G1 (10-423).

Millard, Humphrey; Reading; A2 (46-189).

Millard, Thomas and John; Boston, Newbury, Rehoboth; A2 (47-245).

Millen; Bible records; A2 (55-61).

Miller, Adam; Lancaster County, Pa.; Va.; N2 (4-9, 172, 185).

Miller, Alexander; Conn., Pa.; Pw (7-171).

Miller, Christian; Philadelphia, Pa.; B2 (3-195, 216).

Miller, James; Va.; V1 (1-285).

Miller, James; Norwalk, Rye; A2 (27-141).

Miller, Simon (Capt.); Essex County; V1 (12-237).

Miller; Middleborough; D (6-127; 25-101).

Miller; New Haven; B4 (5-1193).

Miller; Pa.; Md.; Va.; N2 (2-2-38).

Miller; Bible records, South Salem, N. Y.; B2 (1-11).

Miller; Bible records, Mass.; A1 (51-33).

Miller; Bible records, Port Royal, Va.; M (11-44).

Miller; Family records; A2 (54-68); M (16-24); Q1 (37-382).

Mills, Thomas; Saco, Wells; A1 (69-189).

Mills; Family record, Va. and Me.; A1 (79-218).

Mills; Prince George's County, Md.; Q1 (39-242).

Mills; Va., N. H.; V2 (1-105).

Mills; Family records, Salem, N. Y.; M (19-75).

Mills; Bible records, S. C.; M (9-40).

Mills; Va.; E (7-93).

Miner, Thomas; Charlestown, Hingham, New London, Stonington; A1 (72-304); Pw (14-57); Trumbull branch; B4 (5-1193).

Minot; Boston; A1 (52-469).

Minot; Concord, New Haven; B4 (5-1194).

Minuit, Peter; New York; A2 (59-58).

Mitchell, Experience; Duxbury, Bridgewater; D (4-150; 7-1; 20-140; 21-185); Dx (3-101).

Mitchell, Michael; Wallingford; B4 (5-1194).

Mitchell, Richard; Newport; S1 (12-443).

Mitchell, Thomas; New Haven; B4 (5-1194).

Mitchell, Thomas; Block Island; A1 (82-456).

Mitchell, William; Va.; S1 (16-390).

Mitchell; Bethel, N. Y.; A2 (52-169).

Mitchell; Kittery, Me.; A1 (54-351).

Mitchell; Philadelphia; Q1 (37-384).

Mix, Thomas; New Haven; B4 (5-1195; 7-1789).

Mixer, Isaac; Watertown; English origin; A1 (63-277; 65-380; 66-178); U (21-15).

Mixsell; Lancaster and Northampton Counties, Pa.; S1 (15-370).

Mohun; see Moone.

Monfoort, Pieter (and Jans); New York; A2 (7-152).

Moss, John; New Haven, Wallingford; B4 (5-1219).

Mott, Adam; New York, Hempstead; A2 (25-49; 36-279; 43-198; 45-117).

Mott, Nathaniel; Scituate; A1 (67-23).

Mott; Wallingford; B4 (5-1233).

Mott; Bible records; P (9-146).

Mottrom, John (Col.); York, Va.; V1 (11-163).

Moulder, Nicholas; Boston, Newport, Barbados; A1 (61-198).

Moulte, William; Va.; A2 (41-76).

Moulthrop, Matthew; New Haven; B4 (5-1234).

Moulton, John, Thomas and William; Hampton; A1 (69-342).

Moulton, John; Hampton; B2 (4-265, 274).

Moulton, Thomas; York; A2 (45-90, 189, 393).

Moultrie, John (Dr.); Charleston, with Scots ancestry; J (5-229).

Mountain; Pa.; P (10-185).

Mousall, Ralph (Dea.); Charlestown; A1 (61-94).

Mowatt; New Haven; B4 (5-1241).

Mowry, Roger; Plymouth, Salem, Providence; A1 (52-207); E (2-101).

Moxley; Fairfax County, Va.; V1 (1-166).

Moye, John; Virginia; English data; A2 (40-86).

Mudge, Thomas; Malden; English data; A1 (53-432).

Mudge; New Haven; B4 (6-1285).

Mueller; Pa.; Md.; Va.; N2 (2-2-38).

Mühlenberg, Henry Melchoir, D.D.; Trappe, Pa.; M (2-41; 3-10; 3-2-6; 3-3-6; 3-4-9; 4-32); Q2 (Vol. 10).

Muirson; Brookhaven; B4 (6-1285).

Mulford; New Haven; B4 (6-1285).

Mulford; Bible records; A2 (43-61).

Mullanphy, John; Frankford; G2 (29-173).

Mullett; Md.; English clue; X1 (1-379).

Mullett; Bible records; P (7-269).

Mullinor, Thomas; New Haven; B4 (6-1285); English data; A1 (51-421).

Mullins, William; Plymouth; D (1-230; 7-37, 179).

Mumford, Thomas; Portsmouth, Kingston; A2 (43-299).

Mumford; Va.; V1 (3-66, 174); see Munford.

Mumford; Bible records, Salem, New London; A2 (54-254).

Muncy, Francis; Brookhaven; A1 (60-314).

Munford; Prince George County; V1 (11-175; 12-88, 279); see Mumford.

Munger, Nicholas; Guilford; A1 (54-46).

Munning, George; Watertown; English ancestry; A1 (57-331).

Munro, Harry (Rev.); New York; A2 (4-113).

Munroe; Bible records; P (11-187).

Munsell, Thomas; New London; A2 (11-53).

Munson, Thomas; New Haven; B4 (6-1285); A1 (66-310); English clue; A1 (57-331).

Murdaugh; Nansemond County, Va.; V2 (1-46).

Murdock, Jeremiah and John; Va., Md.; X1 (25-262).

Murdock, Robert; Roxbury; U (13-17, 78, 119, 158; 14-42, 87, 136, 187; 15-43, 93, 139, 187; 16-46, 93).

Murphy; Va.; G2 (21-103; 24-154).

Murphy; N. C.; G2 (10-137; 14-260).

Murphy; S. C., Ohio; E (10-233).

Murphy; Bible records; Q1 (39-119).

Murray, Jonathan; East Guilford, Conn.; A1 (55-255); B2 (6-29, 67; 7-11, 31, 51, 79; 8-6, 35).

Murray; Newtown, New Milford; B4 (6-1310).

Murray; Bible records; P (7-40).

Murrell; Va.; R1 (2-84; 3-177).

Mussey, John and Abraham; Ipswich; A1 (60-94).

Myers; Saugerties; S1 (16-176).

Myhill, John; Elizabeth City County; V1 (10-138).

Nails, Henry; East Haven; B4 (6-1311).

Nance; Va.; V2 (1-257).

Nance; Bible records; B2 (1-4).

Nash, Francis; Braintree; A1 (54-404).

Nash, Thomas; New Haven; B4 (6-1312, 1528).

Nash; Duxbury; A1 (52-76; 56-205).

Nay; Bible records; B2 (8-27).

Naylor; Bucks County, Pa.; E (11-38, 112).

Naylor; Philadelphia; E (11-190).

Naylor; English notes; E (12-128).

Neal; Portsmouth, N. H.; S2 (4-266).

Neale, James; Charles County, Md.; X1 (7-201).

Neale, Walter; Me.; English clue; A1 (65-299).

Need, Joseph; Darby, Pa.; English ancestry; Q1 (37-86).

Needler, Benjamin; Va.; V1 (1-69).

Nees; Bible records; B2 (6-4).

Neibaur, Alexander; Alsace; Utah; U (5-53).

Nelson; Middleborough, Plymouth; D (19-190).

Nelson; Lancaster County, Pa.; Columbus, Ohio; E (11-77).

Nelson; Family record; A1 (74-158).

Nelson; Bible records; A1 (66-185).

Nesbit; New Haven; B4 (6-1313).

Nesmith, James; Londonderry; S2 (4-259).
Nestell; Bible records; A2 (8-44).
Nettleton, Samuel; Branford; B3 (11-491; 12-146, 305).
Nevius, Johannes; New York; A2 (5-158); B6 (2-29).
Newby, Robert; Poughkeepsie; A2 (52-162).
Newby; Bible records; A2 (52-157).
Newcomb; Sandwich; D (20-58).
Newcomb; Bible record; B5 (13-3).
Newdigate; English data; A1 (51-132).
Newell, Thomas; Farmington; U (22-118).
Newell; Family records; A1 (76-157).
Newgate, John; Boston; English clue; A1 (56-183).
Newhall, Thomas; Lynn; B5 (12-173).
Newhall; Salem, New Haven; B4 (6-1313).
Newman, Francis and Robert; New Haven; B4 (6-1313).
Newman, Richard; New Haven; B4 (6-1313).
Newman, Thomas; Va.; V1 (9-211).
Newman; Yorktown; V1 (6-277).
Newton, Bryan; New York; A2 (7-97).
Newton, George; Norfolk; English clue; A1 (55, 332, 338).
Newton, Roger (Rev.); Hartford, Farmington, Milford; A1 (63-195).
Newton, Thomas; Boston; A1 (68-101).
Newton; Milford; B4 (6-1313).
Nichols; Bolton, Mass.; C3 (2-90).
Nichols; New Haven; B4 (6-1319).
Nichols; Bible record, Thompson, Conn.; A1 (58-203).
Nicholson, Francis (Gov.); Md.; X1 (4-101, 201).
Nicholson, Robert; English data; A1 (64-138).
Nicoll; Family records; A2 (12-50).
Niles, John; Braintree; A1 (85-145).
Nisbett, Alexander; Dean, Scotland; Dean Hall, S. C.; J (24-17).
Nobles; New Haven; B4 (6-1319).
Noland; Loudoun County, Va.; B2 (9-40).
Noland; Bible records, Va.; V1 (2-132).
Norcross, Jeremiah; English data; A2 (40-183).
Norfleet, Marmaduke, Elisha and James; Nansemond County, Va.; Chowan County, N. C.; H (2-313).
Norman, Hugh; Plymouth, Yarmouth; English data; A1 (68-62).
Norman, William; Kittery; A1 (65-85).
Norman; Family record, Newport; D (22-123).
Norman; Marblehead; A1 (62-384).
Norman; Bible record; Q1 (31-500).
Norris; Family record, N. H., N. Y.; M (15-19).

Norris; Family record, Phila.; Q1 (32-104, 255).
Norris; Bible records; M (15-47).
North, John; Farmington; U (23-19).
North, Thomas; New Haven; B4 (6-1319).
North; Boston; English data; A1 (62-92).
Northend, Jeremiah and Ezekiel; English data; A1 (66-352).
Northrop; New Milford; B4 (6-1319; 8-2048).
Norton, George; New York; A2 (49-63).
Norton, John; Branford, Farmington; A1 (53-87; 54-451); S1 (13-387).
Norton, Thomas; Guilford; A1 (51-221; 54-269).
Norton, William; Boston; A2 (29-91).
Norton; Yorktown, Va.; V1 (3-287; 4-64).
Norton; Inscriptions, Edgartown; A1 (75-239).
Norwood, John (Capt.); Md.; X1 (25-409).
Nott, John; Wethersfield; B3 (9-549).
Nott; Wallingford; B4 (6-1320).
Noyes, James; A2 (20-66).
Noyes, Nicholas; Newbury; A1 (53-35; 55-196).
Noyes; Stonington, New Haven; B4 (6-1320).
Nudd, Thomas; Hampton; A1 (69-342).
Nurse, Francis; Salem; C2 (1-96).
Nutter; Bible records, Portland, Me.; A1 (79-217).
Nutter; Bible records, Rochester, N. H.; A1 (85-445).
Nyce; Bible records, Pa.; P (7-274).
Nys; see De Nys.
Nyssen, Theunis; New York; A2 (49-356).
Oakes; New Haven; B4 (6-1322).
Oakley, Richard; English clue; A1 (59-109).
Oakley; Westchester; A2 (49-387).
Oakman; Marshfield; D (22-36); Family records, Marshfield; Dx (4-110).
Ober, Richard; Beverly; English ancestry; C3 (3-93).
O'Brian, Brian; Berks County, Pa.; G2 (27-17).
O'Brien; Ga.; G2 (14-193).
Ochterloney, David; Boston; Scots ancestry; A1 (56-187).
Odell, William; Concord, Fairfield; A1 (60-91); F2 (3-58); Rye branch; A2 (49-299); English ancestry; A2 (34-99; 44-118; 55-201).
Odenheimer, John; Philadelphia; P (9-57).
Odiorne; Bible records; P (6-16).
Odlin; Bible record; Y1 (51-200).

Offley, David; Boston; P (9-188).
Offley; Bible records, Pa.; P (6-130).
Ogden; Rye branch; A2 (49-381).
Ogden; Conn.; N. J.; M (5-46).
Olcott; B3 (10-177).
Olds; New Haven; B4 (6-1322).
Oliver, Evan; Philadelphia; A2 (19-137; 20-1).
Oliver; Georgetown, Me.; M (14-31).
Oliver; Bible records, Philadelphia; P (7-274).
Oliver; Bible records; P (10-303).
Olmsted, James and Richard; Hartford, Norwalk; U (20-57; 22-119); A1 (59-355).
Onderdonk; Bible records; A2 (6-183).
O'Neal; see Nails.
Oothout, Jan Janse; Albany; A2 (2-69).
Opie; Family record, Del.; Q1 (43-273).
Orcutt, William; Bridgewater; A1 (59-108).
Ordway, James and Abner; Watertown; C1 (1-185; 2-146).
Ormsby; Family record; Q1 (24-119).
Orne, John (Dea.); Salem; Y1 (60-219, 293).
Orr, John; Leedstown, Va., with Scots origin; V1 (4-47).
Orr, William; Rostraver, Pa.; B2 (1-48).
Orser; see Aert Willemszen.
Orshall; New Haven; B4 (6-1322).
Osborn, Richard; Hingham, Windsor, New Haven, Fairfield, Eastchester; A2 (62-379); E (9-150, 190).
Osborn, Thomas and William; New Haven, Easthampton; B4 (6-1322, 1528; 7-1789).
Osborn; Monmouth County, N. J.; M (17-41).
Osborne; Pembroke, Mass.; Revolutionary service; A1 (54-283).
Osborn; Bible record, Phila.; Q1 (32-120).
Osborn; Family record, Antigua; P (9-152).
Osgood, Christopher; Ipswich; A1 (74-306).
Osgood, John; Andover, Mass.; A2 (42-207).
Otis, John; Hingham; A1 (51-328).
Otis; Scituate; A1 (63-299); D (20-103).
Ottee; East Haven; B4 (6-1334).
Oudewater, Frans Jacobsen; Albany; A2 (55-349).
Oulton, John; Boston; A1 (53-391).
Oursler; Bible records, Md.; M (6-32).
Outen, Bogart Gysbert; New York; A2 (53-68, 272; 54-88).
Overington; Bible records, Pa.; P (10-169).

Owen, John; Windsor; A1 (83-39).
Owen; Lebanon, Salisbury; P (9-317).
Owens; Md.; X1 (25-392).
Owens; Bible record, Md.; M (19-109).
Owens; Bible records; M (18-68).
Owings; Md.; M (4-62); Bible record; M (5-63).
Owings; Md.; X1 (25-392).
Oxenbridge, John (Rev.); Boston; English data; A1 (53-116); A2 (42-98).
Pabodie, John; Duxbury; C2 (5-1, 79, 205; 6-9, 45, 69, 102, 144, 191, 224, 260, 306; 7-3, 77, 165, 225, 262); D (6-129; 17-129; 23-105); U (21-18).
Packard, Samuel; Bridgewater; A1 (59-107, 325); D (15-253).
Paddock; Duxbury, Plymouth; S1 (18-448).
Page, George; Branford; B4 (6-1334).
Page, Robert; Salem, Hampton; English data; A1 (66-180; 69-342).
Page; Watertown, Lunenburg; A1 (65-297).
Page; Gloucester, Va.; Q1 (39-496).
Page; Va.; Z (57-451).
Page; co. Suffolk, Eng.; A1 (69-252).
Paige, Nicholas (Col.); Rumney Marsh; English data; A1 (64-185).
Paine, Moses; Braintree; E (13-9); English data; A1 (65-290).
Paine, Tobias; Boston; A2 (42-168).
Paine, William; Watertown, Ipswich, Boston; A1 (56-184).
Paine; Private records, Truro; A1 (54-87).
Paine; Eastham; D (15-189; 19-93; 25-115, 124; 28-160).
Paine; Journal of Dea. John, Eastham, Mass., 1695-; D (8-180, 227; 9-49, 97, 136).
Paine; see Payne.
Painter, Thomas; Hingham, Charlestown, Rowley, Newport, Westerly; A1 (68-273); B4 (6-1336, 1345).
Painter, William; English clue; A1 (61-199).
Painter; Kent County, Del.; Q1 (42-170).
Palmer, John (Sergt.); Rowley; U (20-30).
Palmer, Walter; Charlestown, Rehoboth, Stonington; A2 (43-193).
Palmer, William; Watertown, Hampton; A1 (68-259; 69-342; 75-79, 158, 318); A2 (47-202).
Palmer; Inscriptions, Santee, S. C.; J (26-61).
Palmer; Bible records, Burlington, Otsego County, N. Y.; A1 (81-365).
Palmes, Edward; New London; A1 (65-379).
Palmes; New London, notes; A2 (40-140).

Pardee, George; New Haven; B4 (6-1345; 8-2048).
Pardoe, Thomas; Lewisburg, Pa.; P (8-304).
Parish, John; Braintree, Mendon, Groton; A1 (63-364).
Parke, Arthur; Chester County, Pa.; M (1-36, 61).
Park, Richard; Cambridge, Newton; A2 (51-87).
Parke, Robert; B2 (7-1, 37, 50).
Park, William; Boston; A1 (79-3).
Park; Plainfield, Franklin; M (5-33).
Parker, Edward; New Haven; B4 (6-1362, 1529; 8-2049).
Parker, Elisha; Woodbridge, N. J.; A2 (29-190; 30-31, 176).
Parker, James (Rev.); Dorchester; A1 (68-202).
Parker, Nahum; Kittery, Me.; A1 (54-387).
Parker, Robert; Wethersfield; English clue; A1 (56-184).
Parker, Thomas and George; Isle of Wight County and Accomac; Z (61-15).
Parker, Thomas; English data; A1 (52-66).
Parker; Hollis, Harvard; A1 (67-87).
Parker; Bible records, Newton, Mass.; A1 (85-445).
Parker; Bible records, Castleton, Vt.; P (8-95).
Parker; Diary of James, see Shirley, Mass.
Parkhill; Bible records, Williamstown, Mass.; C2 (5-110).
Parkhurst, George; Watertown, Boston; English data; A1 (68-370).
Parkinson, William; Londonderry; S2 (3-161; 5-215).
Parkinson; Somerset County, N. J.; B6 (6-258).
Parkman, Elias; A1 (55-322).
Parkman; Boston; E (10-343).
Parkman; Bible records; A1 (63-197).
Parmelee, John; Guilford; A1 (53-405); B5 (15-209); New Haven branches; B4 (6-1376).
Parmenter, John (Dea.); Sudbury; English clue; A1 (63-281; 68-262).
Parmenter, Robert; Braintree; English ancestry; A1 (66-167).
Parrett, John; English clue; A1 (61-92).
Parris; S. C.; J (26-137).
Parrish; Philadelphia; P (9-58).
Parrot; Lynn, New Haven; B4 (6-1378).
Parsons, William; Philadelphia; Q1 (33-340).
Partlow; Spotsylvania County; V2 (1-256).

Partridge, John; Medfield; A1 (57-50, 184, 281, 389).
Partridge, Ralph (Rev.); Duxbury; A1 (57-416).
Partridge, William; Lynn, Salisbury; English origin; A1 (63-283); Medfield; A1 (63-90); U (7-122).
Paschall; Bible record; Q1 (29-216).
Patch, Nicholas; Salem, Beverly; A1 (56-198); English ancestry; A1 (71-166).
Paterson, James; Wethersfield; A2 (21-99).
Paterson, Richard; B6 (1-161, 241).
Paterson, William; Philadelphia; A2 (23-81).
Pattan; Bible records; A1 (84-463).
Pattee; Alexandria, N. H., branch; A2 (57-326).
Patterson, Edward; New Haven; B4 (6-1379).
Patterson, John; Bucks County, Pa.; P (8-197).
Patterson; N. Car.; B2 (4-277).
Patterson; Bible records, Pendleton County, Va.; P (8-99).
Patteshall, Edmund; Kennebec; English ancestry; A1 (72-153).
Paul, John; Virginia; A2 (23-51).
Paul; Family records, Pa.; P (10-83).
Pawling, Henry; N. Y., Pa.; P (7-1).
Payne, John; Block Island; A1 (83-84; 85-347).
Payne, John; Lancaster County; V1 (11-239).
Payne, William; New Haven; B4 (6-1379).
Payne; Preston; A1 (56-93).
Payne; Boston; D (21-1).
Payne; Westmoreland County; V1 (10-206).
Payne; Bible records; X2 (2-13).
Payne; co. Suffolk, Eng.; A1 (69-251; 79-82).
Payne; see Paine.
Paynter; Bible records; P (3-256, 266); Q1 (29-340; 30-345).
Peabody; Boxford; (Rev. Oliver); Y2 (9-23).
Peabody; see Pabodie.
Peach, John; Marblehead; English data; A1 (54-104, 276).
Peacock; English data; A1 (53-17).
Pearce, Susanna (Wright); English ancestry; A1 (84-427).
Pearce; Muscongus; K (1-95; 2-26).
Pearce; Yarmouth; D (9-162).
Pearce; New Fairfield; B3 (3-481; 4-220).
Pearce; Bible records, Cecil County, Md.; X1 (21-201).
Pearsall; Bible records, Flushing, L. I.; P (5-257).

Pearson, Henry; Southampton; English clue; A1 (65-298); S1 (17-110).

Pearson, John; Ipswich; Y1 (61-345; 62-65).

Pearson, Thomas; Pa.; Q1 (21-506).

Pearson; Philadelphia; P (9-56).

Pearson; Family records; A1 (52-371).

Pease; New Haven, Derby; B4 (6-1383).

Peck, Henry; New Haven; B4 (6-1389; 8-2049).

Peck, Joseph; Milford; B4 (6-1409; 1529; 7-1789).

Peck, William (Dea.); New Haven; B4 (6-1383).

Peck; Bristol; B4 (6-1409).

Peckham, John; Newport; A1 (57-31, 154; 63-198); B2 (1-75).

Peckham; Hamden; B4 (6-1416).

Peek; Bible records; A2 (56-117).

Peery; Virginia; U (8-21, 69, 122, 177; 9-31, 65, 106, 169; 10-17).

Peirce, John (Capt.); London, Eng.; A1 (67-147); Y1 (66-237, 360).

Peirce; Boston; A1 (56-90).

Peirce; Family records, Boston; A1 (78-333).

Peirce; Family record, Pa.; P (2-214).

Pelham, Thomas; English clue; A1 (61-199).

Pell, John; Family record, Mt. Vernon, N. Y.; A2 (60-239).

Pemberton, James; Newbury, Boston; A2 (50-236; 54-220); E (1-113).

Pemberton; Bible records, Md.; P (10-70).

Pemberton; English data; A1 (54-195, 214).

Pendleton; Bible records, Va.; M (19-16).

Pendleton; R1 (4-256).

Penfield, Samuel; Lynn, Mass., Bristol, R. I.; A2 (42-332); B4 (6-1417).

Pengelly; co. Cornwall, Eng.; E (1-163).

Penington; Bordentown, N. J.; Q1 (21-504).

Penington; Bible records, N. J.; P (7-129).

Penn, William; Pa.; A1 (54-325); Q1 (14-50, 160, 281; 16-330; 17-55; 19-274; 20-1, 158, 370, 435; 21-1, 137, 324, 421; 22-71, 171, 326; 23-60, 224, 329, 464).

Pennington, Ephraim; New Haven; B4 (6-1419).

Pennock, Christopher; Chester County, Pa.; X1 (25-404).

Penrose, Bartholomew; Philadelphia; English origin; Q1 (25-285).

Penrose; England; Utah; U (16-138, 188; 17-140).

Penruddock; Md.; English clue; X1 (4-194).

Pepper, Henry; Philadelphia; P (9-63).

Pepperrell, William; Maine; A2 (18-97); S2 (9-263).

Percival; Bible records, Chatham, Conn., Campton, N. H.; A1 (74-239).

Percival; Bible record; A1 (61-397).

Perit, Peter; Milford; B4 (6-1419).

Perkins, Abraham; Hampton, N. H.; P (7-165).

Perkins, Edward; New Haven; B3 (9-196, 666); B4 (6-1420; 7-1790; 8-2049).

Perkins, Isaac; Hampton, N. H.; Del. branch; P (7-170).

Perkins, John; Ipswich; Norwich branch; P (7-173).

Perkins, William (Rev.); Ipswich, Roxbury, Weymouth, Gloucester, Topsfield; English ancestry; A1 (76-223); P (7-163); Y2 (3-54).

Perkins; Ipswich; C2 (3-90).

Perkins; Topsfield; A1 (85-237).

Perkins; Enfield, Derby; B4 (6-1438).

Perkins; Maine; M (7-43).

Perkins; Bible records; P (7-41).

Perkins; English records; C2 (2-85, 119, 128, 191, 222, 261; 3-21, 115, 151).

Perley; Bible record, Boxford; Dx (2-43).

Perrin, Daniel; Elizabeth; A2 (20-92).

Perrin; English clue; X1 (5-293).

Perry, Edward; Sandwich; A2 (43-296).

Perry, Ezra; Sandwich; B3 (3-109, 237, 352, 480; 4-219).

Perry; Sandwich, Norwich, Shaftsbury; A2 (44-334).

Perry; Family record, Del.; Q1 (43-273).

Peter, Hugh; English data; A2 (48-68, 180).

Peter; Family record, Pa.; Q1 (31-125).

Peterman; Bible records; B5 (7-13).

Peters; Hebron; M (17-41).

Peters; English data; A1 (54-339).

Peterson, John; Duxbury; A1 (70-161, 266, 349).

Peterson; Bible records; A2 (56-105).

Petoe, Henry; English clue; A1 (59-418).

Pettegrew, Alexander; Woodbury; U (4-175).

Pettingell, Richard; Salem, Newbury; A2 (49-194, 307); S1 (17-203); U (9-100, 160; 10-74).

Pettit; Woodbridge; B4 (6-1439).

Petty, Edward; Southold; A2 (13-145).

Peverly, Thomas; Portsmouth, N. H.; A1 (81-138, 248, 496; 84-345).

Phelps, Henry; Salem; S1 (13-58).

Phelps; Rutland; E (7-104).

Phelps; New Haven; B4 (6-1439).

Phile; Philadelphia; P (9-69).

Philipse, Frederick; New York; A2 (9-119).

Phillips, George (Rev.); E (13-119).

Phillips, Hannah (Salter); English ancestry; A1 (73-238).

Phillips, Michael; Newport; E (2-100).

Phillips, Nicholas; Weymouth; A1 (63-298).

Phillips, Nicholas; Boston; A1 (73-238); English data; A2 (41-278).

Phillips; D (14-161).

Phillips; Bible records; A1 (79-107).

Phillips; Bible records; A2 (56-104).

Phinney; Barnstable; D (20-142; 23-165); Dx (5-81).

Phippen; English data; A1 (66-87).

Phipps, Danforth; Falmouth, New Haven; B4 (6-1439).

Pickens; Bible records, Pa.; A1 (63-196).

Pickering; Salem; Y1 (56-281).

Pickett; Bible records, Marblehead; Y1 (52-112).

Pierce, Michael (Capt.); Hingham, Scituate; A1 (56-409); S1 (18-181).

Pierce; Woburn; A1 (52-52).

Pierman; Bermuda; English data; A1 (54-196).

Pierpont, James; Roxbury; New Haven branch; A1 (75-89); B4 (6-1440); T2 (7-258); S1 (13-379).

Pierpont; Catonsville, Md.; M (7-25).

Pierson; Bible record; Q1 (38-252).

Pierson; see Pearson.

Pieterszen, Adriaen; see Van Alcmaer.

Pike, John; Newbury; English ancestry; A1 (66-257); Ipswich, Salisbury; Y2 (4-113).

Pike, John; (Dover, N. H.); F3 (3-77, 97, 145).

Pike; Barkhamsted; B3 (2-398).

Pike; Woodbridge, N. J.; B6 (8-241).

Pillsbury, Joshua; Newbury; N. H. branch; S2 (3-333).

Pillsbury, William; Newbury; S2 (5-377).

Pillsbury; Family record, Bradford (Maine branch); A1 (63-373; 64-75, 156).

Pine, Charles; Scarborough; F2 (8-207).

Pine, James; Stamford, Conn., Hempstead, L. I.; A2 (43-1).

Pingree; England; Utah; U (21-25, 171).

Pinion, Nicholas; Lynn, East Haven; B4 (6-1449).

Pinkethman, Timothy; York County, Va.; V1 (6-120).

Pinney, Humphrey; Dorchester, Windsor; A1 (59-328); E (6-186; 7-165).

Pinney, Thomas and Sarah; English data; A1 (63-36).

Pinto; Stratford, New Haven; B4 (6-1450).

Pitkin, William; Hartford; English ancestry; A1 (66-160).

Pitts; Family record, Me.; B5 (8-139).

Plaisted, Roger; N. H.; A1 (67-188).

Plasse, William; Salem; English data; A1 (51-407).

Plasto; Kent County, Md.; X1 (3-182).

Plater, George; St. Mary's County, Md.; X1 (2-370; 15-168).

Platt, Francis; English clue; A1 (61-67).

Platt, Richard; New Haven, Milford; A2 (62-140); B4 (6-1450).

Platt, Thomas; N. J.; P (2-226).

Platts; Bible record, N. J.; Q1 (29-115).

Plowden, Edmund (Sir); Virginia; A2 (40-81).

Plumb, John; Dorchester, Wethersfield, Branford; B4 (6-1451, 1529); Hartford, Milford; S1 (15-75).

Plumer, Francis; Ipswich; Y1 (50-17, 169, 265, 337; 51-81, 161, 217, 313; 52-17, 209, 313; 53-33).

Plumsted; Bible record; Q1 (43-257).

Pluymert; New Haven; B4 (6-1453).

Plympton, Thomas; Sudbury, Mass.; A2 (43-89).

Poe, David; Baltimore; R2 (1-281).

Poe; Ancestry of Edgar Allen; A2 (38-55).

Poinier; Bible records; B1 (4-183).

Pole, William; Taunton, Dorchester; A1 (52-185).

Polhemus, Johannes (Rev.); German ancestry; B1 (3-102).

Polk; see Pollock.

Pollard; Boston; A1 (62-384).

Pollard; Va.; V1 (10-58); Bible record; V1 (12-189).

Pollard; Bible record, Morris County, N. J.; S3 (4-2-4; 4-3-6).

Pollock, Robert (Capt.); Somerset County, Md. (No. Car. and Tenn. branch, spelling Polk); A1 (77-133, 213, 250; 78-33, 159, 318).

Pollock; Carolina; H (3-156).

Pomeroy, Eltweed; Dorchester, Windsor, Northampton; English data; A1 (57-208, 268; 67-261; 68-47; 70-55); U (4-19).

Pond, Samuel; Windsor, Branford, Milford; B3 (10-161, 234); B4 (6-1453).

Poole, Edward; Weymouth; A1 (59-328).

Poole, William and Elizabeth; Taunton; English data; A1 (61-280).

Pope, Matthew; Yorktown, Va.; A1 (58-406).

Pope, Thomas; Plymouth, Dartmouth; D (18-129; 19-24).

Popinga, Thomas Laurenszen; New York; A2 (59-306).

Porredge; English data; A1 (67-173).

Porter, Francis; English clue; A1 (61-199).

Porter, John; Hingham, Danvers; C2 (3-270); N. J. branch; B5 (11-108, 127, 148; 12-173, 198, 228).

Porter; (West Haven); B4 (6-1458).

Porter; Bible records; X2 (2-18).

Post, Lodewyck Corneliszen; New York; B6 (7-64, 159).

Post, Richard; Lynn, Southampton; S1 (13-81).

Post, Richard and Thomas; Woburn and Cambridge; English data; A1 (66-350, 351).

Potter, John; Cumberland County, Pa.; B2 (9-27).

Potter, Robert; Lynn; S2 (6-323).

Potter, William and John; New Haven; A1 (54-20); B4 (6-1459).

Powell, Thomas; New Haven; B4 (6-1476).

Powell, William; Jamestown; V1 (2-268).

Powell; Philadelphia; Q1 (22-121).

Powell; Bible record, Philadelphia; Q1 (21-121).

Powell; Bible record, Md.; P (8-163).

Powell; Family record; B5 (5-146).

Powers; New Haven, Farmington; B4 (6-1477).

Pratt, Phineas; Charlestown; D (3-1; 4-87, 129; 6-1, 127); C3 (3-48).

Pratt, William; Hartford; U (15-6).

Pratt; Philadelphia; Q1 (19-460).

Pratt; Boston; A1 (56-408).

Pratt; West Haven; B4 (6-1477).

Pray, Quinton; Lynn, Braintree; A1 (55-280).

Predmore; Bible records; B1 (6-31).

Prence, Thomas (Gov.); Plymouth, Duxbury, Eastham; A1 (59-217); D (3-203; 6-157, 230; 24-129).

Prendergast, William; Pawlings; G2 (5-59).

Prentice; New Haven; B4 (6-1477).

Prentiss, Thomas; Newtown, Mass.; A2 (20-145).

Prentis; New London; A1 (62-93).

Prescott, John; Lancaster; A1 (69-189).

Prescott; Corrections of printed genealogy; P (7-98).

Prescott; New Haven; B4 (6-1477).

Presley; Northumberland County; V1 (9-265).

Preston, Elizabeth (Sale); English ancestry; A1 (65-63).

Preston, Richard; Md.; Q1 (16-207).

Preston, Roger; Ipswich, Salem, Mass.; A2 (42-329; 44-187; 52-326; 53-41, 103, 206, 336; 54-3, 88, 150, 268, 320); Y1 (61-425; 62-17, 161, 273, 369; 63-81, 161, 253, 333; 64-177, 381; 65-153, 371; 66-129, 379, 537; 67-65, 177).

Preston, William; New Haven; B4 (6-1478; 7-1790); A1 (69-254); wife's ancestry; A1 (65-63).

Preston, William; Philadelphia, with English ancestry; P (11-103).

Preston; England; Virginia; U (1-33, 71).

Preston; Danvers; A1 (56-80).

Preston; Bible records, Pa.; P (7-38).

Prevost, James-Marcus (Col.); Paramus, N. J.; A2 (13-27; 25-43).

Price, John; English clue; A1 (59-109).

Price, William; Kent County, Md.; X1 (25-399; 26-198).

Price; Inscriptions, Pa.; Q1 (15-125).

Price; Greenbrier; N2 (5-135).

Price; Bible records, Newport, R. I.; A1 (52-371).

Price; Bible record, Elizabethtown, N. J.; B5 (1-32).

Price; Family record, Del.; Q1 (30-247).

Price; Bible record, Pa.; C4 (4-53).

Price; Bible record; B5 (12-226).

Prichard, Roger; Springfield, Milford; B4 (6-1491).

Prickett; Bible record, N. J.; Q1 (18-512).

Priest, Degory; Plymouth; A2 (28-168); D (7-129; 22-15); M (5-9).

Prime, James; Milford; A2 (17-197).

Primrose; Bible record; B5 (15-224).

Prince; Bible records, Newport; A1 (67-158).

Prince; Bible records, North Yarmouth, Me.; D (1-34).

Prince; Bible records, Candia, N. H.; B5 (15-298).

Prindle, William; New Haven; B4 (6-1487).

Pringle, Robert; Bible record, S. C.; J (22-25).

Pritchett, John; Dorchester County, Md.; X1 (6-71).

Probasco, Jurryen;. Brooklyn; B6 (6-213).

Proctor, John; Ipswich; English data; A1 (51-409; 60-208).

Proctor, Robert; Concord, Chelmsford; English clue; A1 (57-416).

Proud; Bible records, Burlington County, N. J.; P (7-34).

Proudfit, James (Rev.); Pequea, Lancaster Co., Pa., and Salem, N. Y.; A2 (29-121).

Prout, Timothy; Boston; English ancestry; A1 (55-95).

Prout; Boston, New Haven; B4 (6-1492).
Prouty; Bible records, Brattleborough, Vt.; A1 (59-417).
Provoost, David; New York; A2 (6-1; 18-1; 25-96; 55-366).
Prudden, Peter (Rev.); Milford; A1 (84-62).
Pruyn, Jacques, Francis; New York, Albany; A2 (13-11, 71, 156; 14-25, 53, 101; 15-17, 97; 17-208; 21-8, 124, 178; 22-15; 27-159, 206; 29-69, 128, 224).
Pryer, Thomas; Bergen, N. J.; A2 (41-295; 43-289).
Pryor; Bible records; V1 (8-138).
Puddington; see Purrington.
Punchard; Salem, New Haven; A1 (75-309); B4 (6-1493).
Punderford; New Haven; B4 (6-1494).
Punderson, John; New Haven; B4 (6-1494).
Purchase, Thomas; Lynn; Y2 (10-132, 167); B4 (6-1498); English origin; A1 (61-279).
Purdy, Francis; Rye; A2 (49-302).
Purdy; Family record, Md.; X1 (7-432).
Purdy; Bible records; A2 (51-24).
Purdy; Family records, White Plains; A2 (54-257).
Purnell; Bible records; P (3-261).
Purrington; American settlers; English data; C2 (7-47, 140, 191).
Pusey; Family records; B5 (8-82).
Putnam; Holland; C2 (7-95, 125).
Putnam, John; Salem; English data; arms; C2 (6-65); C4 (4-23, 49); (Gen. Israel); C2 (1-3, 45).
Putnam; Bible records; C4 (3-47; 4-66).
Pyle, Robert and Nicholas; Pa.; English origin; Q1 (37-85).
Pynchon, William; Roxbury, Springfield; E (3-15).
Quackenbos, Pieter; New York, Albany; A2 (24-173; 25-17, 77, 133).
Quarles; Family records, Va.; M (19-38).
Quilter, Mark; Ipswich; English ancestry; A1 (68-189).
Quinby; Bible records; A2 (50-82).
Quintard; Stamford; B4 (6-1498).
Raber, John and Samuel; Ohio, Ind.; B2 (6-62).
Rabone, George; Exeter, Hampton; English data; A1 (68-72).
Rachel, John; Boston; C4 (4-33).
Radcliffe; Talbott County, Md.; X2 (1-3).
Radford, Henry; Boston; C4 (4-31).
Raguet, James Michael; Pa.; Q1 (31-503).
Raithbeck; Horncastle, co. Lincoln, Eng.; A1 (72-51; 74-143).

Ralph; North Haven; B4 (6-1499).
Ramsay; Hunterdon County, N. J.; B6 (6-239).
Ramsdale; Lynn, New Haven; B4 (6-1499).
Ramsden, Joseph; Plymouth; D (8-18).
Ramsey, William; Bucks County, Pa.; A2 (43-388).
Randall, Robert; A1 (63-98).
Randall; Bible record, Westmoreland County, Va.; M (11-49).
Randall; Md.; X1 (25-396).
Randolph, William (Col.); Va.; N2 (2-4-51).
Rankin; Cumberland County, Pa.; M (17-42).
Rapalje, Joris Jansen; New York; Dutch ancestry; B1 (4-1).
Rathbun; Bible records, Block Island; A1 (67-184).
Ratliff [Radcliffe], William; Elizabeth City, N. C.; B2 (7-25).
Rawdon; Tolland, Conn.; S1 (16-268).
Rawson, Edward; A1 (59-105).
Rawson, Keating; Lansingburgh, N.Y.; G1 (7-1).
Ray, Mary (Rowning); English origin; A1 (63-360, 68-322; 69-17).
Ray, Simon; Braintree; English origin; A1 (63-360; 64-51; 66-178).
Ray, William; Chester County, Pa.; B2 (1-32).
Ray; New Haven; B4 (6-1499).
Ray; Bible records; M (16-25).
Raymond, Richard; Salem, Saybrook; C4 (3-52).
Raynor, Thurston; Southampton, L. I.; A2 (37-187); English ancestry; A1 (66-164).
Raysor; Bible record, Pa.; M (18-27).
Read, Charles; Philadelphia; Q1 (9-339).
Reade, Esdras; Boston; A1 (60-137).
Reade, Thomas (Col.); Salem; English ancestry; A1 (84-113).
Reade, Thomas; Sudbury; English clue; A1 (56-184).
Read, Thomas; Petersham; English clue; A1 (59-327).
Read; Corrections of printed genealogy; A1 (63-200).
Read; Weymouth; D (23-72).
Read; New Haven; B4 (6-1502).
Read; Norwich; A1 (58-404).
Read; Gloucester County, Va.; English data; A1 (54-193).
Read; Halifax, N. S.; P (11-200).
Reading, John; Family record, N. J.; P (11-72).
Reddick; Bible records, S. C.; M (9-40).
Reddough, Henry; Providence, Oyster Bay; A2 (26-20).

Redington, John; Topsfield; A1 (61-225).

Redman, John; Philadelphia; Q1 (43-279).

Reed, Thomas; (Woburn, Medford); C3 (3-231).

Reed, William; A1 (52-52).

Reed; Frederick County, Md.; Q1 (35-120).

Reed; Family record, Mass., N. Y.; M (18-58).

Reed; Bible records, Taunton; A1 (84-237).

Reed; Bible records, Rockland County; A2 (31-185).

Reed; Bible records, Pa.; P (8-98).

Reed; Bible records; P (8-200).

Reepmaecker; Holland; A2 (57-378).

Reeve, William; Salem; English data; A2 (42-174).

Register; S. C.; Ga.; M (12-32; 13-39).

Reichel, Richard Lorenz; New York; A2 (30-177).

Reidhead, William; Penobscot; F1 (5-226).

Reilly, Paul; Lancaster, Pa.; G1 (22-160).

Reinhold; Bible records; P (6-18).

Relyea, Dene; Kingston; A2 (55-62).

Remington, John; Rowley; S1 (14-165).

Remington, Thomas; Windsor, Suffield; A1 (63-178; 64-72).

Renaudet; Family record, N. Y.; P (9-150).

Renew [Reneau]; Miscellaneous; A2 31-121).

Renick; Va.; R1 (3-221).

Rescoe; see Ruscoe.

Revere; (bells made by Paul); A1 (58-151).

Rexford, Arthur; New Haven; B4 (6-1503).

Reyerson, Marten; Flatbush; A2 (8-62).

Reyersz, Adriaen; Flatbush; A2 (8-62).

Reynolds, William; Providence; Pw (4-20).

Reynolds; Philadelphia; P (9-58).

Reynolds; West Haven; B4 (6-1505).

Reynolds; Family record; Q1 (16-250).

Reynolds; Bible records, South Salem, N. Y.; M (7-7).

Rhett, William (Col.); S. C.; J (4-37, 110, 258, 312).

Rhett; S. C.; J (30-257).

Rhinelander, Philip Jacob; New Rochelle; S1 (14-267).

Rhinelander; Bible records; A2 (54-334).

Rhoads, John; Darby, Pa.; Q1 (19-64).

Rhodes; New Haven; B4 (6-1506).

Rice, Edmund; Sudbury; A1 (61-308; 64-79).

Rice, John Christopher; York, Pa.; Pw (21-181).

Rice, Zachariah; Chester County, Pa.; Q1 (24-524).

Rice; Bible record (Charles); A2 (54-68).

Rice; see Royce.

Rich, Richard; Dover, N. H., Eastham, Mass.; A1 (83-261, 394; 84-34, 117, 294); Conn. branch; A2 (51-222, 380, 381).

Rich; Wallingford; B4 (6-1506).

Richards, Richard; Lynn; U (1-5, 54, 111, 149).

Richards, Thomas; Weymouth; D (9-89).

Richards; West Haven; B4 (6-1508).

Richards; Bible record, Pa.; Q1 (22-254).

Richards; A1 (59-327).

Richardson, Ezekiel, Samuel and Thomas; English origin; A1 (57-298).

Richardson, Samuel; Charlestown; A1 (61-94); Pa. branch; A2 (55-171).

Richardson, Stephen and Hugh; Gloucester; M (4-21).

Richardson; Wallingford; B4 (6-1509).

Richardson; Phila.; Q1 (33-371).

Richardson; S. C. (Gen. Richard); J (8-173).

Riché; Bible records, Pa.; P (10-81).

Richmond, John; Taunton; D (9-58; 21-44, 186).

Richmond, Robert; Princess Anne County, Va.; V2 (2-147).

Richmond; Little Compton; D (21-12, 54).

Ricketson; Dartmouth; C4 (3-191).

Rider; see Ryder.

Ridgely; Bible records, Md.; X1 (11-376).

Ridgway, John; Boston, Pemaquid; A1 (66-332).

Ridgway; Burlington, N. J.; E (5-5, 39).

Ridgway, Samuel; Pa.; E (5-40).

Ridgway; Bible record, Pa.; Q1 (16-248; 17-381, 516); P (11-186).

Rigby; co. Lancaster, Eng.; F2 (2-1, 65, 145).

Riker [Abraham de Rycke]; New York; A2 (20-175).

Ring, Andrew; Plymouth; D (4-193; 6-95; 17-150; 22-38, 160, 169).

Ringgold, Thomas (Col.); Md.; X1 (15-245).

Ripley, John; Hingham; D (28-97).

Rising, James; Boston, Bermuda, Salem, Windsor, Suffield; A1 (63-333; 85-288).

Ritter; New Haven; B4 (6-1509).

Ritzema, Joannes (Rev.); New York; A2 (9-192).

Rives, Surry County, Va.; V1 (5-138).
Robbins; Bible record, N. J.; Q1 (37-253).
Roberts, Giles; Scarboro; C4 (4-14).
Roberts, Hugh; Utah; with Welsh ancestry; U(17-186, 235, 284; 18-44, 93, 187; 19-45).
Roberts, John; Merion, Pa.; Q1 (19-262).
Roberts, John; Family record, Montgomery County, Pa.; B5 (14-136).
Roberts, Mark; Pa.; English origin; Q1(37-83).
Roberts, Thomas; English clue; A1 (61-199).
Roberts, William; Milford; B4 (6-1510; 7-1790).
Roberts; East Haven, West Haven; B4 (6-1510).
Robertson, Archibald; New York; A2 (51-130).
Robins, Edward; English clue; A1 (61-92).
Robins, John; Branford; B4 (6-1514).
Robins; Bible records, Pa.; P (10-179).
Robinson, Jacob; East Haven; B4 (6-1515).
Robinson, John (Rev.); Duxbury; English ancestry; A1 (53-198; 67-381).
Robinson, John; Haverhill; English origin; A1 (63-34).
Robinson, John; Oyster Bay; A2 (52-201).
Robinson, Thomas; Guilford; A1 (56-57, 206).
Robinson; Wallingford; B4 (6-1518).
Robinson; King William County, Va.; V1 (4-42).
Robinson; Bible records, Portland, Me.; A1 (79-217).
Roby; Bible record, N. H. and Boston; A1 (60-92; 65-293).
Rockwell, William; Windsor; A2 (2-99; 4-46).
Rockwell; Bible record, Pa.; B5 (10-65).
Rodgers; Tatnall County, Ga.; M (13-40).
Rodney, William; Kent County, Del.; A1 (55-335).
Rogers, Giles; New Kent County; V1 (10-169).
Rogers, Hope; Mansfield, Conn.; A1 (55-47).
Rogers, James; Milford, New London (Norwalk branch); A2 (15-150; 16-10, 72, 157; 19-37).
Rogers, John (Rev.) "martyr"; England; A1 (53-433; 63-285); A2 (8-97, 145).
Rogers, Nathaniel (Rev.); Ipswich; maternal English ancestry; A1 (63-356; 64-51).

Rogers, Thomas; Plymouth; D (3-67, 254; 5-205; 8-63; 11-178; 15-165; 18-46; 20-1, 19, 39; 23-76; 25-30); Dx (4-70); M (5-9).
Rogers, William; Wethersfield, Hempstead, Huntington, L. I.; A2 (60-102); Branford branch; B4 (6-1519).
Rogers; Lancaster; A1 (60-313).
Rogers; Bible records, Dutchess Co., N. Y.; B2 (4-289).
Rogers; Bible records; P (7-134).
Rohrer, John; Family record, Lancaster County, Pa.; Q1 (34-484).
Rolfe, Henry and John; English ancestry; A1 (66-244).
Rolfe; Mecklenburg County, Va.; V1 (3-301).
Rolle; Md.; X1 (4-197).
Rollins, James; Dover, N. H.; S2 (5-73).
Roman, John Cornelius; Pa.; German origin; Q1 (22-250).
Romine; Bible records; A2 (27-108).
Roosa, Allard Heymansen; Kingston; A2 (58-149).
Roosa; Ulster and Dutchess Counties, N. Y.; A2 (31-163, 235).
Root; New Haven; B4 (6-1519).
Rose, Robert; Wethersfield, Branford; B4 (6-1519).
Rose, Robert and Charles; Va.; Z (59-221).
Rose, Thomas; Burlington; family record; Q1 (28-102).
Rose; N. J.; P (6-243).
Rose; Family records, Pittsgrove, N. J.; P (7-35).
Rosecrans; Pa., Ohio; E (9-311).
Rosewell, William (Capt.); New Haven; B4 (6-1521).
Ross, John; Annapolis; X1 (9-118; 11-378).
Ross, John; Philadelphia; Q1 (23-77).
Ross, William; Narragansett; A2 (52-89).
Ross; Philadelphia; P (11-90).
Ross; Martin County, N. C.; R2 (1-207).
Ross; Chester and York Counties, Pa.; C4 (1-66).
Ross; New Haven; B4 (6-1521).
Ross; Washington, D. C.; A2 (58-181).
Ross; New Castle, Del.; Q1 (50-94).
Ross; Bible record, Wilkes-Barre; Pw (11-222).
Rösser; Bible record, Pa.; M (18-27).
Rossiter, Bryan; Dorchester, Windsor, Guilford; A1 (55-149).
Rothrock, Philip; Philadelphia and York Counties; Q1 (21-498).
Round, James; Md.; wife's English paternity; X1 (4-295).
Rousby, Christopher and John; Md.; X1 (15-292).

Rouse; Family record, Newport; A1 (69-380).

Row; English item; A1 (55-441).

Rowand; S. C.; J (11-57).

Rowe, Matthew; New Haven; B4 (6-1521).

Rowland; Bible records; P (3-261).

Rowlandson, Thomas; Marblehead; C2 (7-123).

Rowley, Henry; Plymouth, Scituate; A2 (37-57, 97, 203, 251; 38-136); U (20-69).

Rowning; English data; A1 (68-322; 69-17).

Roy, Joseph; Woodbridge, N. J.; B6 (6-319). •

Royce, Evan; Wallingford; B4 (7-1570).

Royce, Robert; Stratford, New London; A1 (80-107; 83-127); B2 (1-30, 44, 52, 80; 2-99, 139, 149; 3-168, 219); B4 (7-1549, 1790; 8-2050); U (23-23).

Royster; Charles City County; V2 (1-188).

Ruck, Thomas; English clue; A1 (66-358).

Rudd; Bible records; B2 (1-23).

Rudderow, John; Chester, Burlington County, N. J.; A2 (29-112).

Ruddock; see Reddough.

Ruffner, Peter; Lancaster County, Pa.; Frederick County, Va.; N2 (1-2-31; 1-3-33; 1-4-46; 2-1-45; 2-2-60; 2-3-36; 2-4-33).

Ruggles, Jeffrey, George and John; English data; A2 (41-279).

Ruggles, Thomas and John; Roxbury; A2 (25-164; 28-214; 43-290; 44-188); E (1-59); English data; arms; A1 (54-219); C2 (6-173); C4 (3-233).

Ruggles; Cambridge; A2 (56-101).

Ruggles; New Haven; B4 (7-1571).

Rule; Bible record, N. J.; M (18-29).

Rumsey, Charles; Cecil County, Md.; N2 (3-187).

Ruscoe, William; Hartford, Norwalk, Jamaica; A1 (71-113).

Russell, Giles (Capt.); Marblehead; A1 (52-360).

Russell, James and William; New Haven; B4 (7-1572; 8-2050).

Russell, John; Dartmouth; A1 (58-364; 59-22; 79-109).

Russell, John; Cambridge, Wethersfield, Hadley; A1 (60-383; 61-94).

Russell, Ralph; Lynn, East Haven; B4 (7-1572).

Russell, William; New Haven; B4 (7-1577).

Russell; Bible records, Pa.; P (10-175).

Rutgers [Rutger Jacobsen Van Schoenderwoerdt]; New York; see Van Woert; A2 (2-23; 17-82).

Rutgers; Bible record; A2 (30-253).

Rutherford, Henry; New Haven; B4 (7-1582).

Rutherford, Thomas and Robert; Burks [?] County, Pa.; Va.; N2 (1-4-54).

Ryckert [Riker]; Holland; A2 (57-375).

Ryder, Samuel; Plymouth, Yarmouth; D (11-49, 170, 182; 12-256; 15-64); English clue; A1 (79-316).

Ryder; Bible record; Dx (2-58).

Ryerson; Bible record; B6 (5-320).

Rynearson [Arent Theunissen Van Hengel]; Staten Island; B6 (5-285; 6-55, 126).

Sabin; New Haven; B4 (7-1582).

Sackett, John; New Haven; B4 (7-1583).

Safford, Thomas; Ipswich; English data; A1 (52-67).

Sage; Bible record, Salem; C4 (3-211).

St. Clair; Boston; E (9-33, 166).

St. John; English data; A1 (54-341 ff.).

Sale, Edward; Marblehead, Weymouth; English ancestry; A1 (65-63).

Sale; Family record, Boston; P (7-88).

Salisbury; Bible record, Bristol; A1 (65-379).

Salter, Edward; English data; A1 (64-140).

Salter, Theophilus; Ipswich; English origin; A1 (55-107; 57-331); A2 (41-278).

Saltonstall, Richard; Watertown, Ipswich; A2 (25-75; 42-213, 330, 339; 48-206); English data; A1 (69-380).

Saltonstall; Letter, 1636; A1 (51-65).

Saltonstall, English ancestry; A1 (53-114, 250).

Salvador, Francis; S. C.; J (3-59).

Salway; Arundel County, Md.; X1 (1-380).

Samborne; see Sanborn.

Sammans, Johannes Thomaszen; New York; A2 (7-121).

Sampson [Samson], Henry; Duxbury; D (2-142; 6-114, 184; 7-225, 254; 8-31; 9-109; 20-96; 22-109; 23-42, 161, 173); A1 (59-221); M (5-9).

Sampson; Duxbury; A1 (52-76; 56-205).

Sampson; Dartmouth; K (4-83).

Sampson; Bible records, Plympton; D (2-44).

Sampson; Plymouth; B2 (2-131).

Samson; Inscriptions, Brattleboro; A1 (74-238).

Sanborn, John, William and Stephen; Hampton, N. H.; A1 (51-57); M (2-18); with English data; S2 (19-440; 20-32; 23-321).

Sanders, Martin; Braintree; English data; A1 (66-176).

Sanders; Gloucester County, N. J.; Q1 (25-585).
Sanderson, Edward; Watertown; English clue; A1 (61-65).
Sanderson; Cheshire; B4 (7-1588).
Sandford; Va.; X1 (5-293).
Sands, James (Capt.); Block Island, R. I.; A2 (43-293).
Sands, Stephen; Pa.; Q1 (16-462).
Sands; Prince George County, Md.; R2 (1-352).
Sands; Family record, Brooklyn; A2 (39-219).
Sands; Bible records, Amity, Pa.; P (7-274).
Sanford, Thomas; Milford (New Haven branches); B4 (7-1588).
Sanford; Portsmouth, R. I.; A1 (56-294, 409; 58-200).
Sanford; Bible records, Dartmouth; A1 (60-94).
Sanford; Bible records, Medway; A1 (62-335).
Sankey, Robert; English clue; A1 (61-92).
Santvoort, Jacob Abrahamsen; New York; A2 (7-118).
Sanxay, Jacques (Rev.); Corrections of printed genealogy; A2 (50-78).
Sargeant; Barnstable, Malden; D (24-9).
Sargent, Digory; Boston, Worcester; A1 (58-377).
Sargent, William; Gifford ancestry in Eng.; A1 (71-170; 74-231, 267; 75-57, 129); Makernes ancestry in Eng.; A1 (71-324); Grey ancestry in Eng.; A1 (76-295); Royal ancestry; A1 (79-358).
Sargent; see Sergeant.
Saughier; Bible records, Va.; X1 (14-76).
Sault; Bible record, N. Y.; B5 (13-41).
Saunders, Tobias; Westerly; A1 (63-198).
Saunders; Braintree; A1 (70-181).
Saunders; Va.; V2 (1-195).
Saunders; Bible records; B2 (3-185, 214).
Saunderson, Robert; Boston; A1 (52-23).
Sava; New Haven; B4 (7-1597).
Savage, James; Newton, Mass.; G2 (6-55).
Savage, Thomas; Boston; A1 (67-198, 309; 68-18, 119).
Savery; Plymouth County; A1 (54-102).
Savory, Anthony and Thomas; Plymouth; A1 (66-367).
Sawyer; Bible record, Thetford, Vt.; B5 (2-52).
Saxton; Md., Pa.; B2 (8-68).
Say; Bible record; Q1 (29-216).

Sayer, John; English clue; A1 (59-327).
Sayles, John; Providence; S1 (17-192; 18-328).
Scales, William; Rowley; A1 (66-42).
Scammon, Humphrey; Saco; C2 (1-119, 187, 214).
Scammon; Kittery; A1 (65-293).
Scarborough, John; Bucks County, Pa.; P (11-194).
Scarborough; Bible records, N. C.; H (3-473).
Scarlet; Inscriptions, Va.; M (15-10).
Scarlett, John; Springfield; English data; A1 (63-278).
Schall; Bible records, Pa.; M (19-65).
Schenck, Roelof Marstense; New York; B6 (5-89); S1 (16-96).
Schenck; Bible record, Waldoboro; S3 (4-4-5).
Schermerhorn, Jacob Jansen; Albany, Schenectady; A2 (2-22; 36-141, 200, 254).
Schieffelin, Jacob; Philadelphia; A1 (51-449).
Scholl, Pieter Jansen; New York, Hempstead; P (10-213).
Schoonmaker, Hendrick Jochemse; Albany, Esopus; A2 (19-22).
Schrick, Paulus; Hartford, New York; A2 (9-115).
Schuerman, Frederick; New Rochelle; A2 (21-61; 24-132; 25-82); see Shuerman.
Schulthess, Rudolph Arnold; Utah; with Swiss ancestry; U (3-145).
Schuyler, David Pieterse; Albany; A2 (1-28; 5-60; 43-195).
Schuyler, Philip Pieterson; Albany; A2 (1: 3, 18; 2-190; 5-60; 6-73; 45-111).
Schuyler; Albany; A2 (5-4); Bible records; A2 (5-75; 8-164; 10-99); Miscellaneous; A2 (5-110).
Schuyler; N. J.; Q1 (37-120).
Scot; Mattox, Va.; X1 (5-295).
Scott, Edward; Hadley, New Haven; B4 (7-1597).
Scott, James; Bible record, Va.; V1 (10-213).
Scott, John; Springfield; C2 (4-293; 5-115).
Scott, John; English data; A2 (40-183).
Scott, Richard; Boston, Providence; A1 (60-168); A2 (2-174); English clue; A1 (66-87).
Scott, Thomas; Ipswich; English data; A1 (52-248).
Scott, William; New Haven; B4 (7-1598).
Scott; Bible records, Lunenburg; D (8-80).
Scott; Bible records, Watertown, Conn.; P (9-156).

Scott; Bible records, Nova Scotia; P (8-96).
Scott; Bible records; A2 (55-71); M (11-44).
Scovil, Arthur; Boston, Middletown, Conn.; A2 (45-177, 211, 393).
Scovill; Middletown, Wallingford; B4 (7-1599).
Screven, William (Rev.); Kittery, Me.; Georgetown, S. C.; J (9-230; 16-93).
Scrivener; Md.; English clue; X1 (2-185).
Scruggs, Thomas; Salem; English ancestry; A1 (85-388).
Scudder; Bible record; Q1 (15-243).
Scull; Family record; Q1 (15-377).
Scull; see Scholl.
Seaborn, John; Boston; English clue; A1 (63-360).
Seabrook, Robert (Capt.); Colleton County; J (17-14, 58, 175).
Seabrook; St. Paul's, Stono; J (11-72).
Sealis, Richard; Scituate; A1 (70-349); D (13-94); English ancestry; A1 (65-321).
Sealy; Isle of Shoals; English ancestry; A1 (85-74).
Seaman, John (Capt.); Hempstead; A2 (11-150; 16-95).
Seamans; Rehoboth; Dx (1-38).
Searl; New Haven; B4 (7-1600).
Searle; Coventry; E (8-80).
Sears; New Haven; B4 (7-1600).
Sears; Bible records; D (7-255).
Sears; Bible record, Halifax; Dx (1-23).
Sebring, Jacob; Somerville; B6 (3-118).
Seckel, George David; Philadelphia; P (9-60).
Sedgwick, Joan (Blake); English ancestry; A1 (70-366).
Sedgwick, Robert (Maj.-Gen.); Charlestown; A2 (32-104); Hartford branch; B4 (7-1601); wife's ancestry; A1 (70-366).
Seeley, Robert; Watertown, Wethersfield, New Haven, Huntington; A2 (48-385); B2 (3-210).
Seeley; North Haven; B4 (7-1601).
Segers, Gerrit and Johannes; Albany, Schenectady; A2 (47-10).
Sehner [Söhner], Gottlieb; Lancaster, Pa.; G1 (2-367).
Seidle; Bible records, Berks County, Pa.; M (19-66).
Selden; V1 (10-52).
Selden; Bible record, Conn.; B5 (9-155).
Selden; Bible records; Q1 (27-111).
Selkirk, Alexander; co. Devon, Eng.; A1 (51-150).
Selleck, David; Boston; English ancestry; A2 (42-299).

Sellivant, Daniel; New Haven; B4 (7-1602).
Selyns, Henricus (Rev.); New York; A2 (57-119, 365, 369; 58-184).
Semple; Family record; V1 (8-142).
Senguerdius [Sengwerd]; Holland; A2 (57-379).
Sergeant; Charlestown; Y1 (64-22); see Sargent.
Sewall, Henry; Newbury, Rowley; A1 (66-283).
Sewall, Henry; Md.; X1 (1-190; 4-290).
Sewall, Jane (Lowe); Md.; English ancestry; X1 (9-115).
Sewall; Bible records, Newbury, York; A1 (66-86).
Seward, Obadiah; N. J.; B6 (7-155).
Seward, William (Lieut.); Guilford; A1 (52-323).
Seward; New Haven; B4 (7-1602).
Sewell; English data; A1 (67-262).
Sewill; English clue; A1 (61-66).
Sexton; Enfield; B4 (7-1602).
Sexton; see Saxton.
Seymour, Richard; Hartford, Norwalk; A1 (72-209, 312; 73-6); A2 (11-116); English ancestry; A1 (71-105).
Seymour; Md.; X1 (2-183).
Shakespeare; Stratford, co. Warwick, Eng.; U (22-132).
Shares; Hamden; B4 (7-1602).
Sharp, Isaac; Sharpstown, N. J.; Q1 (20-134).
Sharp; New Haven; B4 (7-1603).
Sharp; B3 (9-513).
Sharpe, John; English clue; A1 (61-68).
Sharples; Bible record; P (5-257).
Shattuck, William; Watertown; B4 (7-1603).
Shaw, Abraham; Dedham; A1 (51-191).
Shaw, John; Plymouth; D (10-33; 20-44).
Shaw, Roger; Hampton; S2 (12-77).
Shaw; Woolwich; S2 (12-217).
Shead; Brookline; S1 (14-382).
Sheaffe; Boston, Guilford; A1 (55-208; 61-393).
Sheaffe; English maternal ancestry (Juxon); A1 (52-105 ff. to 129).
Shearer, James; Union, Palmer; S1 (13-410).
Sheather, John; Guilford; A1 (59-45).
Sheers; Va.; English data; A2 (42-172).
Sheffield, Edmund; Portsmouth, R. I.; A1 (74-83).
Sheffield, Edmund, William, Amos and Ichabod; English ancestry; A1 (77-190).
Shehy, Daniel; Pa., Ohio; S1 (16-184).
Sheldon, Isaac; Windsor, Northampton; A1 (80-378).

Shelly, Robert; Scituate, Barnstable; A1 (60-332).

Shepard, Thomas; Charlestown, East Haven; B4 (7-1603, 1609); Ohio; E (9-51).

Shepard, Thomas (Rev.); Cambridge; English ancestry; A2 (42-94).

Shepard, William; Taunton; Y1 (64-236).

Shepard; Coventry, Conn.; S2 (2-299).

Shepardson, Daniel; Charlestown; E (9-59).

Shepherd, Giles; Pa.; English origin; Q1 (22-250).

Shepherd, Thomas; Shepherdstown, Va.; N2 (2-2-31; 2-4-28; 3-67, 125, 190, 288).

Shepley, John; Salem, Chelmsford; A2 (57-307).

Sherburne, Henry; Portsmouth, N. H.; A1 (58-227; 59-104).

Sherburne, John; Portsmouth, N. H.; A1 (58-391; 59-56).

Sherburne; Family record, Newbury; A1 (61-82, 201).

Sherman, Henry; R. I.; A1 (59-221).

Sherman, John (Capt.); Watertown, Mass.; A2 (42-209).

Sherman, John (Rev.); New Haven branch; B4 (7-1611).

Sherman, Philip; Providence; A1 (61-271; 64-284; 65-343, 346); S1 (12-255).

Sherman, William; Marshfield; D (4-171; 25-133).

Sherman; Bible record, Boston; M (17-43).

Sherman; English ancestry; A1 (51-309, 357; 54-62, 152; 59-397; 66-322; 67-154; 68-146; 69-284).

Sherwood; Va.; V1 (2-207).

Sherwood; Talbot County, Md.; Guilford County, N. C.; M (12-27).

Shipley; see Shepley.

Shipman; New Haven; B4 (7-1618).

Shippen, Edward (Dep. Gov.); Boston, Philadelphia; A1 (76-79); A2 (55-131); English ancestry; Q1 (28-385).

Shippen; Mass.; Pa.; P (7-283).

Shockley; Bible record; Q1 (33-377).

Shores; Philadelphia; P (8-206).

Short; Derby; B4 (7-1618).

Shove; Bible records; A1 (80-223).

Shryock, Johannes; Manchester, Pa.; A2 (61-410).

Shuerman, Jacobus; New Brunswick, N. J.; A2 (23-201); see Schuerman.

Shurger [Shurrager]; Bible records; A2 (54-258).

Shute; Bible record; Q1 (24-118).

Sibthorp; English data; A1 (54-344).

Siecken, Dirck Janszen; New York; A2 (7-57).

Sill, John; Cambridge; S1 (13-397).

Sille; see de Sille.

Silsbee; Bible records, Lynn; C1 (1-78).

Silsby, Henry; Lynn; Y1 (61-1, 113, 241).

Silver, Thomas; Ipswich, Newbury; B2 (3-159; 4-223).

Silvester, Richard; Weymouth, Marshfield; A1 (85-247, 357).

Silvester; Plymouth; D (19-122).

Simmons, Simon; New Haven, Wallingford; B4 (7-1619).

Simmons; Duxbury; D (19-51; 21-142).

Simonson; Philadelphia, Baltimore; X2 (2-26).

Simpson, Robert; New Haven; B4 (7-1619).

Sinclair, Robert; New York; A2 (10-170; 50-47).

Singleton; Va.; S. C.; J (7-101).

Skellenger; Bible records; B1 (6-30).

Skelton, Samuel (Rev.); Salem; English data; A1 (52-347; 53-64).

Skiles; Lancaster, Pa.; N2 (3-188).

Skillman; New York, Newtown, L. I.; A2 (37-22, 91, 167, 277; 38-29, 103, 193, 294; 39-51, 84, 158, 285).

Skinker; Family record, Va.; V1 (10-167).

Skinner, Thomas; Malden; A1 (53-401; 54-450).

Skinner; Bible records, Marblehead; A1 (54-413).

Skipwith; Mecklenburg County, Va.; V1 (7-58).

Skirm; Bible records; Q1 (11-207).

Slade, William; Newport; S1 (12-119).

Slade; Chelsea, Mass.; Troy, N. Y.; U (6-118).

Slade; Bible records; A1 (83-381).

Slaughter; East Haven; B4 (7-1619).

Slaughter; Va.; V1 (9-122, 124).

Sloan, William; Lamington; B6 (7-276).

Sloan; New Haven; B4 (7-1619).

Slocomb; Templeton; E (10-76).

Slocum, Anthony; Taunton, Mass.; Albemarle County, N. C.; E (12-1).

Slocum, Giles; Portsmouth, R. I.; English ancestry; A1 (70-283; 78-395).

Slosson, George; Nathaniel[3] of Norwalk and Kent; A2 (3-108, 165).

Smalley; Piscataway; Q1 (21-126).

Smallwood, James; Charles County, Md.; X1 (22-139).

Smith, Abel; Hempstead; A2 (53-12).

Smith, Abraham; Rye; A2 (49-171).

Smith, Alexander; N. C.; Va.; V1 (2-196).

Smith, Charles; Pa.; B2 (5-91).

Smith, Christopher; Providence (Walpole branch); A1 (62-281).

Smith, George; West Haven; B4 (7-1619, 1791).
Smith, Henry; Dorchester, Springfield; English clue; A1 (61-280; 65-382).
Smith, Henry; Rehoboth; D (10-172).
Smith, John (Capt.); Jamestown; V1 (7-118).
Smith, John; Beverly; M (11-4).
Smith, John; Dorchester, Providence; S1 (14-169).
Smith, John, Rock; Hempstead; A2 (30-200).
Smith, John; Milford, Conn.; B2 (1-46).
Smith, John; Taunton; A1 (59-107, 325).
Smith, John and Alexander; Va.; M (3-3-5).
Smith, Nehemiah; New London; P (8-103).
Smith, Nicholas; Petsworth Parish, Va.; V1 (11-177).
Smith, Richard; Lancaster; A1 (56-182).
Smith, Richard; Calvert County, Md.; X1 (3-66, 384; 4-65).
Smith, Robert; Boxford; A1 (55-267); line of Joseph, "Prophet"; U (20-1).
Smith, Samuel; Eastham; D (12-112, 236).
Smith, Samuel; Topsfield; B2 (4-267).
Smith, Thomas; S. C.; J (6-135, 179; 22-60; 28-169; 30-255); Bible records; J (20-72).
Smith, Thomas; East Haven; B4 (7-1645).
Smith, William "Tangier"; Brookhaven; A2 (1:4, 20).
Smith, William; Wrightstown, Pa.; P (7-131).
Smith, William; S. C.; J (4-239, 312).
Smith, William (Capt.); New York A2 (11-145, 146).
Smith, William (Judge); New York; A2 (11-98).
Smith, William; Port Royal, New York; A2 (10-32).
Smith, William; Farmington; U (22-121).
Smith, William; Peterborough; S2 (27-223).
Smith, William; East Haven; B4 (7-1661).
Smith; Boston; D (20-107).
Smith; Chatham, Mass.; A1 (64-187).
Smith; Watertown; A1 (62-305).
Smith; Hampton, N. H.; A2 (45-92).
Smith; Milford, Woodbridge; B4 (7-1661, 1663).
Smith; Westchester; A2 (25-153).
Smith; Paxtang, Pa.; Q3 (1-230).
Smith; N. J.; P (5-168).
Smith; Philadelphia; P (9-68).

Smith; N. Y. City; Wyoming, Pa.; Pw (12-114).
Smith; Hanover County, Va.; V1 (4-150).
Smith; New York; Bible records; A2 (27-100).
Smith; Bible records, Smithtown, L. I.; A1 (84-347).
Smith; Inscriptions, White Plains, N. Y.; M (16-6).
Smith; Bible records, Westchester County, N. Y.; A1 (83-251).
Smith; Bible record, Mass.; C4 (4-62).
Smith; Bible records; A2 (56-110); P (10-76); Y1 (51-200); B5 (1-15).
Smith; Bramham, co. York, Eng.; Q1 (22-368).
Smoot; La Plata, Md.; M (8-31).
Smyser, Matthias; York County, Pa.; Q3 (1-154).
Snead; Bible records, Va.; X1 (11-279).
Snell; Va.; V1 (11-265).
Snelling, William and John; Boston; A1 (52-342).
Snelson; Md.; English clue; X1 (3-182).
Snoddy; Rowan County, N. C.; M (17-42).
Snow, Nicholas; Plymouth, Eastham; D (3-167; 5-1; 8-101; 18-193; 22-47, 99, 165); A1 (51-76, 204; 64-284).
Snow, Richard; Woburn; U (2-101; 3-30, 33, 64; 14-104, 161).
Snow; Bible record; Q1 (33-379).
Snyder; Bible records; B2 (4-293).
Soan, William; Scituate; D (19-143); English data; A1 (70-260).
Solendine, John; Dunstable; A1 (60-366).
Somerindike; Bible record, Williamsburgh, N. Y.; A2 (48-315).
Somers, John; Upper Dublin, Pa.; M (7-64).
Somes, Morris; Gloucester; C4 (2-18).
Soper; Taunton; D (21-10); Bible record; Dx (2-77).
Soole; English data; A1 (68-186).
Sortore; E (7-48).
Sotcher, John; Pennsbury, Pa.; P (4-264).
Soule, George; Plymouth, Duxbury; D (2-81; 4-98, 159; 5-46, 110; 6-120; 7-72, 210; 8-184; 9-246; 10-107, 133; 14-129; 15-193; 18-233; 19-136; 20-145; 23-49; 24-104; 25-72; 26-1; 27-39); A1 (76-101); M (5-20); Family records; Dx (1-97).
Soule, Joseph; Fairfield, Vt.; A1 (76-85).
Southall; Bible record; V1 (8-133).
Southard; Basking Ridge; B6 (3-253).
Southcott, Richard and Thomas; Dorchester; English clue; A1 (61-280).

Southworth, Thomas and Constant; Plymouth; D (3-144; 10-1; 18-244; 19-25, 112; 21-24, 73).

Spader; Bible record; B6 (5-319).

Span, John (Rev.); Va.; English clue; A1 (59-219).

Sparhawk, Nathaniel; English data; C4 (3-145).

Sparks, James; Philadelphia; P (9-67).

Sparrow, Richard; Plymouth, Eastham; D (11-1, 231; 12-57; 14-1, 193, 255).

Sparrow, Thomas; Md.; R1 (4-428).

Sparrow; Bible records; X1 (11-281).

Spaulding, Edward; (Chelmsford, Plainfield); A1 (63-379; 64-79).

Spear; Bible records; B2 (6-23).

Specht; Holland; A2 (57-380).

Spelman, Richard; Middletown; E (10-246).

Spence, Keith; Portsmouth, N. H., with Scots ancestry; F3 (4-4).

Spencer, [Gerard]; Bible records, Hadlyme; A2 (57-160).

Spencer; New Haven; B4 (7-1665).

Spencer; Bible records, Portage, N. Y.; B2 (6-18).

Sperry, Richard; New Haven; B4 (7-1665, 1673; 8-2051).

Spickerman; Bible record; C4 (3-39).

Spier, Hendrick Jansen; New York; A2 (55-314).

Spink; East Haven; B4 (7-1697).

Spinney, Thomas; Kittery; A1 (65-85).

Spinning, Humphrey; New Haven; A1 (59-267; 80-107; 83-127); B4 (7-1697).

Spooner; Dartmouth; D (23-192).

Spoor; Bible record; A1 (51-345).

Sprague, Ralph and William; Salem, Charlestown, Hingham; A1 (63-147); D (18-220; 20-100, 190); E (9-77); English clue; A1 (66-87).

Sprague; Johnston, R. I.; A1 (68-301).

Sprague; English data; A1 (51-105).

Spranckhuysen; Holland; A2 (57-374).

Sprat, John; New York; A2 (12-174).

Sprigg, Thomas; Prince George's County, Md.; X1 (8-74).

Sprong, Jan; New York, Flushing, Bushwick; A2 (37-270).

Sprout, Robert; Middleborough; D (6-8; 25-9, 101, 126).

Squier; Bible records; Q1 (40-370).

Staats, Abram; New York; A2 (2-140).

Stacy, Simon; Ipswich; English data; A1 (54-346; 58-91).

Stacey; Boston, New Haven; B4 (7-1697).

Stacey; Marblehead; Y1 (56-81).

Stafford, Thomas; Newport, Portsmouth, Warwick, R. I.; A2 (42-440).

Stagg; New York; A2 (9-85, 131).

Stanborough, Josiah; Southampton; English origin; A1 (63-166).

Standish, Myles (Capt.); Plymouth, Duxbury; A1 (51-71); A2 (47-312); D (3-153; 12-48, 99, 176; 15-123, 190; 20-16; 21-1, 71; 23-133); M (5-21); English ancestry; A1 (68-339).

Standish; Bible records, Plympton; D (2-44).

Standley; Philadelphia; P (9-54).

Stanes, John; English data; A2 (40-236).

Stanley; Vt. and Conn.; B2 (1-9).

Stanley; Waterbury, Wallingford; B4 (7-1698).

Stanley; arms; M (6-38).

Stansbury [Detmar Sternberg]; Md.; X1 (9-72; 10-62).

Stanton, Thomas; Stonington; A1 (56-153); A2 (60-31).

Stanton; Meriden; B4 (7-1699).

Stanwood, Philip; Gloucester; A1 (52-75).

Staple; Taunton; D (19-34; 21-96).

Stark, Aaron; New London; E (12-190).

Stark; Lebanon, Meriden; B4 (7-1699).

Stark; (Gen. John); S2 (10-121).

Starr, Comfort (Dr.); Boston; English data; A1 (64-73).

Stauffer, Hans; Valley Forge, Pa.; P (10-296).

Stayner; Bible records, Boston; B2 (5-88).

Stead, (Thomas); England; Utah; U (5-83, 134, 173).

Stearns, Isaac; Watertown; A1 (56-183); chart; U(19-facing p. 97; 20-147).

Stebbing; English data; A1(53-433).

Stebbins John; New London; S1 (18-445).

Stedman, Isaac; Scituate, Boston; A1 (66-67).

Steed; see Stead.

Steel, John; New York; A2 (26-203).

Steele; Bible records, N. J.; A2 (21-40).

Steelman, Charles; Burlington County, N. J.; Q1 (36-464).

Steelman; Md.; N. J.; M (19-38).

Steene; Family record, Carlisle, Pa.; P (11-75).

Steenwyck, Cornelis; New York; A2 (57-137).

Steere, John; Providence; F4 (6-86).

Steinmetz; Philadelphia; P (9-51).

Stelle, Poncet; St. Christopher, Boston, New York, Shrewsbury; A2 (44-61, 107); B1 (2-93).

Stelwagon; Bible records, Chester County, Pa.; P (7-36).

Stent, Eleazer; Branford; B4 (7-1699).

Stephens; Plymouth; Dx (5-97).

Stephenson, Hugh W.; Lawrence County, Ala.; M (17-34).

Sternberg, Detmar; see Stansbury.

Stevens, Henry; New Haven; B4 (7-1704).
Stevens, John; Newbury, Andover; English ancestry; A1 (85-396).
Stevens, John; New London, West Haven; B4 (7-1700, 1791; 8-2050).
Stevens, John; Guilford; A1 (56-356).
Stevens, John; Family records, Newport; A1 (61-93).
Stevens, John; English clue; A1 (61-68).
Stevens; Bible records; B2 (5-75).
Stevenson, Thomas; Southold, Flushing, Newtown; A2 (13-117, 144; 48-78).
Stevenson; see Stimpson.
Stever, Baltis; Columbia County, N. Y.; C4 (3-37).
Steward; Bible records, Rutland, Vt., Ohio; A1 (82-127).
Stewart, Charles; Hunterdon County, N. J.; S1 (14-266).
Stewart, Edward; Kent County, Md.; X1 (12-390).
Stewart; Colrain; S1 (16-272).
Stewart; Middletown, Conn.; A2 (52-168).
Stewart; Bible records (Gen. Walter); Q1 (22-381).
Stewart; see Stuart.
Steynmets, Casper; New York; A2 (56-255).
Stickney, William; Rowley; S2 (5-328); U (20-31).
Stileman, Elias; Salem; A1 (51-346).
Stiles; Windsor, North Haven; B4 (7-1704).
Stiles; Sampler record; B5 (10-243).
Stille, Cornelis Jacobsen [see Woetendyk]; New York; A2 (7-49).
Stillman; Wethersfield, New Haven; B4 (7-1706).
Stillwell; New Haven; B4 (7-1707).
Stilson, Vincent; Milford, Marblehead; A2 (51-30).
Stimpson, Andrew; Cambridge, Charlestown; A1 (59-242, 365; 60-209).
Stimpson, Jonathan; Cambridge, Watertown; A1 (85-446).
Stites, John; Hempstead, L. I.; A2 (28-165, 237; 29-93).
Stites; Bible record, N. J., Del.; P (6-249).
Stith; Campbell County, Va.; V1 (4-143).
Stockbridge, John; Scituate; A1 (70-260; 71-367).
Stocking, George; Cambridge, Hartford, Middletown; A1 (79-332).
Stockton; Bible records; A2 (55-70).
Stoddard, Anthony; English clue; A1 (61-92).
Stoddard; Pa.; P (7-196).
Stoddart; Philadelphia; S1 (15-286).

Stoffelsen, Jacob; New York; A2 (56-252).
Stokes, Jonathan; Branford; A1 (62-364).
Stokes; Md., Va., S. C.; V1 (10-44).
Stoll; Bible records, S. C.; M (17-13).
Stone, Gregory; Watertown, Cambridge; E (2-51, 103).
Stone, Simon (Dea.); Watertown; A1 (53-345); A2 (27-90); E (14-1); U (22-15); English clue; A1 (63-285).
Stone, William (Gov.); Md.; E (4-45, 124); M (2-1, 13, 34, 51; 3-5; 3-2-9; 3-4-6).
Stone; Andover, Shrewsbury; A1 (66-266).
Storer; Charlestown, New Haven; B4 (7-1707).
Storrs; Note, Mansfield, Conn.; A1 (51-76).
Story, Elisha; Boston; Y1 (50-297; 51-41).
Stout, John (Capt.); Freehold, Wilmington; P (7-195).
Stout; Bible records; B5 (11-104); A2 (54-65).
Stoutenburg, Pieter; New York; S1 (16-90).
Stoutenburg; Dutchess County, N. Y.; E (13-67).
Stover, Silvester; A1 (74-301; 85-300).
Stow; Roxbury; English clue; A1 (66-358).
Stowe, John; Roxbury; English ancestry; A1 (70-347); A2 (44-116).
Stowers, Hannah (Frost); Charlestown; English data; A1 (63-278).
Strang, Daniel; New Rochelle; A2 (2-179; 21-130; 41-146).
Stratenmaker, Dirck; New York; A2 (56-262).
Stratton, Bartholomew; Boston; B4 (5-1267).
Stratton, Samuel; Watertown; S1 (13-193).
Stratton; Salem; C2 (4-209).
Stratton; Bible records; B2 (7-6).
Stratton; English ancestry; Y1 (54-177).
Street, Nicholas (Rev.); Taunton, New Haven; B4 (7-1709; 8-2050).
Street; English records; C2 (1-19, 128, 210, 255, 323).
Streeter, Stephen; A1 (83-512; 85-382).
Strengthfield; Narragansett; A1 (54-309).
Stribling; Berryville, Va.; N2 (5-114).
Strider; Bible record, Va., Ohio; B5 (15-304).
Stridles, Gabriel Thomaszen; Albany, New York; A2 (7-122).
Strijcker, Jan and Jacobus; New York, Flatbush; A2 (32-65; 38-1; 43-196; 50-296).

Strong; Bible record, Pawlet, Vt.; M (18-24).
Strother, William; Va., with English data; V1 (11-113, 182, 251; 12-42, 196, 262); R1 (2-149).
Strowshour; Bible record, Tuscaloosa; M (15-63).
Strycker; Bible records; A2 (54-334).
Stryker; Bible records; M (18-86).
Stryker; see Strijcker.
Stuart, David (Rev.); Va.; M (7-47).
Stuart, Hugh; Family record, Carlisle, Pa.; P (11-75).
Stuart, John and Charles; Carolina; A2 (41-282).
Stuart; Augusta County, Va.; N2 (5-119).
Stuart; Scarboro, Me.; B5 (10-33).
Stuart; Bible records; A2 (60-42).
Stuart; see Stewart.
Stubblefield; Gloucester County; V2 (1-53).
Sturdivant; Family record, Va.; V1 (10-51).
Sturges, John; Fairfield; A2 (50-234, 235).
Sturtevant, Samuel; Plymouth; Dx (5-123).
Sturtevant; Family record, Halifax, Mass.; A1 (55-78); Family record; A1 (55-441).
Stuyvesant; Bible records; A2 (9-150).
Styer; Bible records, Pa., Ohio; M (19-108).
Sullivan, Daniel; Va.; G2 (25-90).
Sullivan, John; Berwick, Me.; A2 (45-110).
Sullivan; Dover, Berwick; G2 (5-63).
Sullivan; (Gen. John); S2 (5-18).
Summers; Ind.; M (14-48).
Summers; Fairfax County, Va.; N2 (3-228).
Summers; Va.; Ky.; M (9-42, 43).
Sunderland; Boston, Eastham; D (17-99).
Sutliff; Durham; B4 (7-1713).
Sutton, Daniel; Burlington, N. J.; A2 (5-159).
Sutton, John; Va.; English data; A2 (40-237).
Sutton; Bible record, Newport, Del.; P (4-316).
Suydam [Hendrick Rycken]; New York; S1 (13-294).
Suydam; Bible records; A2 (54-332).
Swan, Richard; Boston, Rowley; A2 (29-213; 30-10, 118); B2 (1-57; 4-229).
Swart, Teunis Cornelissen; Schenectady, N. Y.; A2 (37-72).
Swarts, George; Abingdon, Mass.; B2 (6-58).
Swayne; Newfoundland; A1 (59-418).
Sweet; Bible record; B5 (4-125).

Sweeting, Lewis and Henry; Rehoboth; A1 (74-146).
Swift; Sandwich, Wareham; D (23-39).
Swift; Philadelphia; Q1 (30-129).
Swiggett; Family records; M (16-6).
Swords, Thomas; Ireland; New York; A2 (1: 10).
Swords; Conn.; B3 (1-409).
Sybrants [Sybrant Janszen]; New York; A2 (57-12).
Sydnor, Fortunatus; Bible record, Va.; V1 (3-282; 4-45).
Sylvester, Constant; Barbados; English clue; A1 (59-418).
Symes, Lancaster; New York; A2 (5-1).
Symonds, Samuel; Boston; A2 (43-96).
Symonds; cos. Somerset and Dorset, Eng.; A1 (80-343).
Taber; Dartmouth; D (16-226).
Tades, Michiel; New York; A2 (56-254).
Talbot, Peter; Dorchester; E (12-65).
Talbot; Settlers; C4 (1-139).
Talbott, Christopher; Boston; A1 (55-334).
Talbot; Bible records; B2 (1-24).
Talcott, John; Cambridge, Hartford; A2 (54-180); A1 (64-81); English data; A1 (51-496).
Taliaferro, Robert; York County, Va.; V1 (11-12, 179).
Tallman, Peter; Barbados, Portsmouth; German ancestry; A1 (69-90; 85-69).
Talmadge, Robert; New Haven; B4 (7-1714, 1791).
Talmadge, Thomas; Lynn, Southampton, with English clues; B6 (3-32, 99; 7-259; 8-18, 81, 251).
Talmadge; Morris County, N. J.; M (17-42).
Talmadge; Easthampton, Branford; B4 (7-1721).
Talmage, Enos; Bible records, N. J. branch; A2 (55-54).
Tandy, William; Va.; G2 (29-132).
Tapley; Bible record, Cambridge; C4 (4-62).
Tapp, Edmund; Milford; English clue; A1 (54-352).
Tarbell, Thomas; Watertown, Groton, Charlestown; A1 (61-70, 165, 299, 307, 394).
Tasker, Thomas (Capt.); Calvert County, Md.; X1 (4-191; 16-179).
Tatem; Bible records, Del.; P (11-188, 189).
Tatham, John; Burlington, N. J.; G1 (6-61).
Tattnall; S. C.; J (14-3).
Tayer; see Thayer.
Tayloe; Va.; V1 (1-212).
Taylor, John; England; Utah; U (21-49, 105, 158; 22-68, 136, 165; 23-71).

Thorne, William; Lynn, Flushing, Gravesend; A2 (19-153; 20-77; 22-174; 47-413; 53-18).

Thornton, Thomas (Rev.); Yarmouth; A1 (63-383).

Thornton, William; Va.; V1 (3-181; 4-123).

Thorpe, William; New Haven; B4 (7-1776); Fairfield branch; A1 (59-392).

Thrall, William; Windsor; E (9-169).

Thrall; Vt., Ohio; E (10-83).

Thresher, Henry; Salem, Mass., Falmouth, Me.; C3 (3-143).

Thrift; Va.; V1 (9-135).

Throckmorton; Middletown; English clue; A1 (59-327).

Throckmorton; Va.; English ancestry; V1 (6-207).

Throope, William; Barnstable, Mass., Bristol, R. I.; A2 (36-118, 207, 302; 37-35, 103).

Throop; Bristol; B4 (7-1786).

Thurmer; Calvert County, Md.; X1 (3-181).

Thwing; Bible records; A1 (51-219).

Tibbitts [Tippett], George; Flushing, Yonkers; A2 (50-354; 51-63, 103, 266, 346; 52-79, 375).

Tichenor; New Haven, Newark; B4 (7-1787).

Tiffany, Humphrey; Pa. branch; A2 (55-39).

Tilden, Lydia (Huckstep); English ancestry; A1 (67-44).

Tilden, Marmaduke; Kent County, Md.; X1 (1-75).

Tilden, Nathaniel; Scituate; English ancestry; A1 (65-322).

Tilden; English ancestry (Bigge line); A1 (66-54).

Tileston; A1 (61-308).

Tilghman, Richard (Dr.); Queen Anne County, Md., with English ancestry; X1 (1-181, 280, 290, 369; 2-65; 15-410); family letters; X1 (21-20, 123, 219).

Tilley, John; Plymouth; D (10-65; 23-76); A2 (27-162, 215; 60-14).

Tillinghast, Pardon; Newport; T6 (4-126).

Tilly, William; Boston, Kittery; A1 (59-215).

Tilton, William; Lynn; S2 (12-29).

Tilton; Sanbornton, N. H.; S2 (6-65).

Tilton; Monmouth County, N. J.; U (1-191).

Timberlake, Henry; Newport; English data; A2 (40-233).

Tingley, Samuel; Malden; C3 (2-214).

Tinker, John; Hartford, Conn.; A2 (39-111).

Tinker; New Haven; B4 (7-1787).

Tinkham, Ephraim; Plymouth; D (4-122; 12-145; 17-162, 186; 21-97).

Tisdall, John; Taunton; D (21-29).

Tisinger; Bible records, Va.; M (17-36).

Titcomb; Bible records, Boston; B5 (15-297).

Titus, Ezekiel; Harford, Pa.; A2 (56-369).

Titus, Robert; Weymouth, Rehoboth, Huntington, L. I.; A2 (12-92; 51-74; 52-32).

Titus [Titus Syrachs De Vries]; New Utrecht; A2 (39-5).

Todd, Adam; New York; A2 (23-15).

Todd, Christopher; New Haven; A1 (62-48, 203); B4 (8-1817, 2051).

Todd, Thomas; Anne Arundel County, Md.; X1 (9-298).

Toers [Arent Laurensen]; New York, Bergen; B1 (1-50, 76).

Tolles, Henry; West Haven; B4 (8-1841).

Tolles; Vt.; A1 (75-40).

Tomes; co. Gloucester, Eng.; A1 (84-286).

Tomlinson; New Haven; B4 (8-1847).

Tompkins; Bible records; A2 (48-67).

Tomson, John (Lieut.); Barnstable, Middleborough, Halifax; D (4-22; 19-95, 135; 20-159; 22-135; 24-167; 25-20, 56, 175).

Toplife; English clue; A1 (66-358).

Topliff, Clement; Dorchester; A1 (58-117; 61-201).

Topliffe; Dorchester; C4 (2-18).

Toppan, Abraham; English data; Y1 (52-53).

Topping; Simsbury, Worthington; E (7-56).

Torrence; Bible records, Allegheny County, Pa.; P (8-101).

Torrey, William, James, Philip and Joseph; English data; A1 (61-189); B5 (12-228).

Torsey, Gideon (Dr.); Gilmanton, N. H.; A1 (61-375).

Totten; New Haven; B4 (8-1847).

Tourneur; Amiens, France; A2 (41-151).

Towle; Bible records, N. H.; A1 (79-326).

Towles; Bible records, Va.; M (7-12).

Town; Bible records, Woodbury, Vt.; A1 (78-334).

Towne, William; Topsfield; Y1 (61-438).

Towner; Branford, Wallingford; B4 (8-1848).

Townsend; Boston, New Haven; B4 (8-1849).

Townsend; (L. I. family; Penn. branches); A2 (4-189; 8-10).

Towson; Bible records, Baltimore; A1 (79-327).

Tracy, Patrick (Capt.); Newburyport; Y1 (57-57).
Tracy, Thomas (Lt.); Norwich; A1 (61-93).
Tracy; Md.; Ohio; X1 (7-431).
Traill, Robert; Portsmouth, N. H., with Scots ancestry; F3 (4-1).
Traill, Robert; Northampton; Q3 (2-256).
Trask; Rochester; Dx (3-11).
Traske, William (Capt.); Salem; A1 (53-43; 55-321, 385; 56-69, 199, 397; 57-65, 384).
Traske; East Coker, co. Somerset, Eng.; A1 (54-279).
Travis, Garratt; Rye; A2 (49-298).
Treadway, Nathaniel; Sudbury; A1 (65-295).
Treat, Richard; Wethersfield, Milford; B2 (7-49).
Treat; English records; C2 (1-19, 128, 210, 255, 323).
Tredwell, Edward; Ipswich, Branford, Southold, Huntington, L. I.; A2 (42-177, 301, 417; 43-73, 127, 211, 373).
Treadwell, Thomas; Ipswich; A1 (60-48, 191, 291, 386).
Trenholm, William; Charleston; J (16-151).
Trevelyan; arms; M (6-39).
Trezevant, Daniel; S. C.; J (3-24, 179).
Trickey; New Haven; B4 (8-1853).
Trickey; Bible record; A1 (63-195).
Triggs; English data; A1 (68-59).
Triglandus; Holland; A2 (57-377).
Trimble, John; Pa.; (Ohio); E (9-195, 275; 10-1, 110; 11-106; 12-16).
Triplett; Fauquier County; V1 (11-37).
Tripp; Bible records; A1 (70-92).
Tromper, Jacob; Dutch ancestry; A2 (45-218).
Trotter; Family record, Pa.; P (2-213).
Trowbridge, Thomas; New Haven; English data; A1 (59-291).
Truax [Philippe du Trieux]; New York; A2 (45-51, 392; 57-208, 336; 58-76, 111, 267, 326; 59-17, 182, 284, 386).
True, Henry; Salem, Mass.; S3 (7-2-11).
Truesdale; Family records, Boston; A1 (72-159; 76-312).
Trumbull; North Haven; B4 (8-1865).
Trumbull; Bible record, North Haven; M (15-10).
Trumbull; Bible record; M (9-39).
Trussell; West Haven; B4 (8-1866).
Tryon; Bible records, New Fairfield; A2 (58-183).
Tucker, Morris; Salisbury; C2 (3-1).
Tucker, Richard; Portland, Me.; A1 (53-84).
Tucker; co. Kent, Eng.; A1 (76-232).
Tuers; see Toers.

Tufts, Peter; Charlestown, Malden; A1 (51-299).
Tullock, William (Capt.); Portsmouth; S2 (3-311).
Tunison; Somerset County, N. J.; B6 (7-225).
Turhand, Thomas; Guilford; B4 (8-1866).
Turner, Edward; Boston, Milford, Middletown; A2 (13-124; 24-148).
Turner, Elizabeth (Freestone); English ancestry; A1 (72-51; 74-140).
Turner, Humphrey; Scituate; D (5-41; 20-84; 21-97; 24-42); Dx (2-158); A2 (48-83; 60-388).
Turner, Nathaniel (Capt.); New Haven; B4 (8-1866, 1877, 2051).
Turner; Bible records, Boston; A1 (83-380).
Tuthill, John; Southold, N. Y.; A2 (29-123, 215).
Tuttle, William; New Haven; A2 (43-97); B4 (8-1881, 2052); S1 (13-371).
Twells, Godfrey; Philadelphia; P (9-54).
Twigg, George; English clue; A1 (61-199).
Twiss, Thomas; Wallingford; B4 (8-1920).
Twitchell; Bible records; A1 (84-463).
Tyler, Charles; Westmoreland County; V1 (5-252).
Tyler, Henry; York County, Va.; V1 (8-209).
Tyler, Roger; New Haven (Branford); B4 (8-1921, 1928, 2052).
Tyler, William; Milford; B4 (8-1922).
Tyley, Thomas; Boston; B4 (5-1267).
Tymens; see Thymen Janszen.
Tyng, Edward and William; Boston; English parentage; C4 (1-134).
Tynte, Edward (Gov.); S. C.; J (12-219).
Tyson; Bible records, Elizabeth, N. J.; A2 (21-40).
Udall, Lionel (Dr.); Bible records, Stonington; A1 (60-330).
Ufford, Thomas; Roxbury, Milford; A2 (43-299); B2 (6-16).
Uhl, John; Beekman, N. Y.; B2 (4-263).
Umberfield; see Humphreville.
Underhill, Humphrey; Jamaica, Rye; A2 (49-172).
Underhill, John (Capt.); A2 (58-352); S1 (13-297).
Underhill; Bible records; A2 (32-52).
Ungrich, Henry; New York; S1 (13-311).
Unthank, John; N. Car.; B2 (4-297).
Upson; Wolcott; B3 (2-398).
Urie; Bible records; P (6-17).
Urin, William; Isle of Shoals; A1 (64-7, 116).

Usher, Hezekiah and Robert; Boston, Stamford; A1 (54-76).

Utter; East Haven; B4 (8-1929).

Utter; Family records, Warwick; A2 (49-379).

Utge; Va.; Md.; X1 (1-191).

Vail, Christopher; Boston; A1 (58-310).

Vail, Jeremiah; Southold; A2 (2-151).

Vail, Thomas; Southampton, L. I., Eastchester, N. Y.; A2 (27-218; 43-99).

Valentine; N. C.; H (2-123, 309).

Vallotton; Family record, Savannah; A1 (64-287).

Van Alcmaer, Adriaen Pieterszen; New York; A2 (7-117).

Van Arsdale, Symon Jansen; Flatlands; B2 (3-171, 179, 201); B6 (8-96, 238).

Van Beeck [Isaac]; New York; A2 (9-114).

Van Beuren, Johannes (Dr.); New York; A2 (9-9).

Van Bibber; Bottetourt County, Va.; N2 (3-213).

Van Borsum, Egbert; New York; A2 (26-192; 27-50, 101; 55-362).

Van Breestede, Jan Janszen; New York; A2 (7-117; 55-358).

Van Brugh, Johannes Pieterse; New York, Albany; A2 (13-201; 14-142).

Van Brunt, Rutger Joesten; New Utrecht; Monmouth County, N. J., branch; A2 (35-33, 83).

Van Buren [Maessen], Cornelis; Albany; A2 (28-121, 207).

Van Bursum; Will of Cornelis; A2 (35-202).

Van Buskirk, Laurens Andriesen; New York; E (11-45).

Van Cortlandt, Olaf Stevense; New York; A2 (49-369); Bible records; A2 (5-70, 168).

Van Cott, Claes Cornelius; New York; U (17-215).

Van Couwenhoven, Wolfert Gerretsen; New York; M (1-13, 42, 68).

Van Dam, Claas Ripse; Albany; A2 (2-24; 13-201).

Van den Berg, Gerrit; Albany; A2 (8-131).

Vanderheyden; Family records, N. Y.; P (10-179).

Vanderheyden, Matthys; New York; A2 (45-308; 46-9, 301); S1 (12-455).

Vandermark; New Haven; B4 (8-1929).

Van der Poel, Wynant Gerritse; Albany; A2 (2-192).

Van der Zee, Storm; Albany; A2 (35-45).

Van der Veen, Pieter Corn; New York; A2 (7-123).

Van der Volgen; Bible records; A2 (56-117).

Vander Voort, Michael Pauluszen; Brooklyn; A2 (22-157).

Van Deursen [Deusen], Abraham Pietersen; New York; A2 (30-46, 101, 152, 205; 31-55; 28-233); B5 (12-194, 217, 242; 13-5).

Van Deursen; New Haven; B4 (8-1930).

Van Deusen; Inscriptions; A2 (26-90).

Van Deusen; Inscriptions, Great Barrington; A2 (29-42).

Van de Water, Benjamin; Dutch ancestry; B1 (4-145).

Van Dusen; Documents; A2 (50-68).

Van Duyn, Gerret Cornellissen; New York, Brooklyn, New Utrecht; A2 (10-155).

Van Dyck, Hendrick, Franz; New York; A2 (9-52; 30-57).

Van Dyck, Jan Thomasse; New Utrecht; B6 (4-262; 8-235, 323); A2 (37-114).

Van Dyck; Bible records; P (10-176).

Van Elmendorf, Jacobus; Kingston; Dutch ancestry; B1 (1-73).

Van Etten, Jacob Jansen; Kingston; N. Y.; A2 (30-52, 183, 229; 53-70).

Van Fleet; Bible records, Hunterdon County, N. J.; B1 (6-125).

Van Gaasbeek, Laurentius (Rev.); Kingston; A2 (25-28, 56); Dutch ancestry; B1 (2-33).

Van Goodenhausen, Samuel; New Haven; B4 (8-1930).

Van Harlingen, Johannes Martinus; Harlem, New Brunswick; Dutch ancestry; B1 (2-88).

Van Hengel; see Rynearson.

Van Hook, Laurence; New York, N. Y., Freehold, N. J.; A2 (39-67).

Van Hoorn, Jan Cornelius; New York; Q1 (20-424).

Van Horne; New York; B6 (4-244).

Van Houten [Roelofse], Helmigh, Cornelis and Tonis; Bergen, N. J.; A2 (27-183; 28-9).

Van Husen, Jan Franse; Albany; A2 (51-285).

Van Huyse, Theunis; New York; A2 (59-7).

Vanhyst; Bible records, N. J.; P (7-128).

Van Leuvenigh, Hendrick; New Castle County, Del.; P (7-207).

Van Liew [Frederick Hendricksen Van Leeuwen]; N. J.; B6 (8-41, 93).

Van Meter, Jan Gysbertsen; New Utrecht; N2 (2-2-5).

Van Meter, Joost Jan; Kingston; N2 (3-45; 4-224).

Van Meter; Bible records; B3 (3-484).

Van Nest, Pieter Pietersen; New York, Brooklyn; B1 (1-58); B6 (6-211).
Van Nuyse, Aucke Jansen; Brooklyn; B6 (6-210).
Van Pelt; B6 (4-81).
Van Ranst, Gerret and Pieter; New York; A2 (58-302).
Van Rensselaer, Kiliaen; Rensselaerswyck; A2 (57-220); S1 (14-274).
Van Rensselaer; Bible records; A2 (5-72).
Van Salee, Anthony Jansen; New York; A2 (42-443).
Van Santvoord, Cornelius (Rev.); Staten Island, Schenectady; Dutch ancestry; A2 (61-218).
Van Schaick, Adriaen Corneliszen; New York; A2 (59-8).
Van Schaick, Cornelis Aertszen; New York; A2 (7-53).
Van Schaick, Goosen Gerritse (and Claas); Albany; A2 (2-191).
Van Schelluynen, Dirck; New York; A2 (59-61).
Van Sickle; Bible record; A2 (49-84).
Van Sysen, Joost Carelsen; Dutch ancestry; B1 (4-57, 144).
Van Thienhoven; New York; M (7-44).
Van Tilburg, Barent Jansen; New York; A2 (61-254).
Van Valkenburgh; Bible records; B2 (2-155).
Van Vlierden, Petrus (Rev.); Catskill, N. Y.; A2 (35-69).
Van Vliet; B6 (7-152).
Van Volkenburgh; Bible records; A1 (85-456).
Van Voorhees, Steven Coerte; Flatlands; S1 (16-94).
Van Vorst, Cornelis; New York; A2 (56-260).
Van Vredenburgh; see Vredenburgh.
Van Wagenen [Jacob Aertse]; Albany, Kingston; A2 (10-86, 107, 182; 21-118; 22-151; 23-64).
Van Wickle; Bible records; P (7-127).
Van Winkle, Jacob Walings; New York; A2 (56-244).
Van Woert (see Rutgers); Teunis Jacobsen Van Schoenderwoert; Albany; A2 (2-24).
Van Wyck, Cornelius Barentsen; Flatbush, L. I.; A2 (43-100).
Van Yderstein; see Tades.
Van Zandt, Adam Wensel; New York; A2 (61-317; 62-160).
Varick, Rudolphus (Rev.); Flatbush; A2 (8-16); Dutch ancestry; B1 (4-99).
Varleth, Casper; Hartford, New York; A2 (9-54, 113, 153; 10-35).
Vassall, William; Roxbury, Scituate; A1 (51-152).
Vassall; English data; A1 (51-280 ff.).

Vaughan, George; Middleborough; D (18-115).
Vaughan, Howell; Va.; English clue; A1 (59-109).
Vaughan, Robert; Md.; X1 (15-230).
Veacock; Philadelphia; P (9-57).
Veasie, William; Braintree; English data; A1 (66-352).
Veghte, Klaes Arents; Brooklyn; A2 (9-180).
Veghte; Bible records; B2 (3-164).
Ventrus; New Haven; B4 (8-1930).
Verbrugge; see Van Brugh.
Vernon; Md.; X1 (2-183).
Vernoy, Cornelis Cornelissen; Kingston; B1 (4-102).
Ver Planck, Abraham Isaacse; New York; A2 (24-39, 60).
Verschuur, Wouter Gysbertsen; Bushwick, Paramus; A2 (48-352).
Vesey, George; Lancaster County; V1 (11-31).
Viall; Family record, Newport; A1 (55-184).
Vickery; English records; B2 (4-276, 312; 5-1).
Vielé Cornelis Cornelison; Schenectady; A2 (34-1).
Viele, [Cornelis Volkertszen]; New York; A2 (44-232).
Villiers; England; E (5-1, 38).
Vincent, John; Sandwich; English clue; A1 (61-280).
Vincent, John; New Haven; B4 (8-1930).
Vines, Richard (Gov.); Me.; A1 (54-146).
Vining, John; English origin; A1 (66-187).
Vinton, John; Lynn, New Haven; A1 (85-109); B4 (8-1930).
Vliet; see Van Vliet.
Vogt, William; Wheeling, W. Va.; S1 (18-75).
Volck, Andrew; Newburgh, N. Y.; Lynn, Pa.; Q1 (23-127).
Vollume; New Haven; B4 (8-1930).
Voorhees; B6 (8-237).
Vosburgh, Abraham Pietersen; A2 (46-192).
Vosseller, Jacob; Somerset County, N. J.; B6 (3-26, 112, 206, 292; 4-123).
Vredenburgh, Willem Isaacsen; New York, Kingston; B6 (7-69); A2 (9-62; 21-164).
Vroom, Cornelius Pieterse; New York; B6 (2-129; 6-216).
Waddell, William; Bethel, N. Y.; A2 (52-169).
Wade; New Haven; B4 (8-1930).
Wade; Bible records; P (7-43).
Wadsworth, Christopher; Duxbury; S1 (14-373).

Wadsworth, William; Hartford; A1 (64-81).

Wadsworth; Duxbury; D (9-246; 21-89).

Wagener, Casper; Pa.; S1 (15-377).

Wainwright, Philippa (Sewell); English ancestry; A1 (67-262).

Wainwright; Wallingford; B4 (8-1931).

Waite, Thomas; Portsmouth, R. I.; A1 (73-291)..

Waite; Bible records, Exeter, R. I.; P (8-191).

Waits; Bible records, Pa.; P (9-311).

Wakefield, John; New Haven; B4 (8-1931).

Wakelee, Henry; Stratford; S1 (15-81).

Wakeman, John; New Haven, Hartford; A2 (47-314; 54-186).

Waldo, Cornelius; Ipswich, Chelmsford; A1 (52-213).

Waldo; Family record, R. I.; M (18-33).

Waldo; Family records, Conn.; Z (45-347).

Waldo; Bible records; A1 (70-92).

Waldron, Isaac; Boston; English ancestry; C4 (3-154).

Waldron; Bible record; A2 (54-66).

Walke, John; Salem; C2 (1-349).

Walker, Adam; Pa.; S1 (18-464).

Walker, Benjamin; Boston; A1 (67-297).

Walker, Francis; D (27-39).

Walker, John; New Haven; B4 (8-1931).

Walker, John; Northumberland County, Pa.; Q1 (28-118).

Walker, John; St. Joseph, Mo.; U (10-108, 152).

Walker, Samuel; Reading, Woburn; A1 (57-350; 67-99).

Walker (Widow); Rehoboth, Mass.; A2 (43-190).

Walker; East Haven; B4 (8-1931).

Wall, John; Goshen, Pa.; English clue; A2 (43-70).

Wallace, John; Londonderry; A1 (56-185).

Wallace; New Haven; B4 (8-1932).

Waller, Thomas; Boston; A1 (56-410).

Walley, William; Charlestown; English clue; A1 (61-199).

Walling; Bible records; B2 (7-6).

Walpole, Caesar; Prince George County; V1 (8-272).

Walrath; B2 (1-88).

Walstone, John; Guilford; A1 (59-385).

Walter, Richard; Boston; A1 (66-87).

Walter, William; North Haven; B4 (8-1932).

Walter; Bible record, Pa.; C4 (4-53).

Walton; Va.; R2 (2-116).

Walton; Family record;. Q1 (21-500).

Wampler; Bible records; X2 (2-18).

Wandell; Bible records; B1 (4-183).

Wanshaer, Jan; New York; A2 (7-122).

Wantwood; East Haven; B4 (8-1941).

Ward, Andrew; Watertown, Wethersfield, Stamford, Fairfield; A2 (50-231; 51-162); Wallingford branch; B4 (8-1941); English ancestry; A2 (44-119).

Ward, Cornelius; Somerset County, Md.; V1 (11-51, 241).

Ward, John; Newport; A2 (6-123).

Ward, John; West Haven; B4 (8-1945).

Ward, Joyce (widow of Richard); Wethersfield; A2 (49-262).

Ward; Bible records, Gloucester County, N. J.; P (8-297).

Ward; Cumberland County, Pa.; N2 (4-278).

Ward; English pedigrees; E (2-129).

Ward; co. Norfolk, Eng.; Columbus, Ohio; E (1-109).

Wardlow, James; Pawtucket; S1 (14-150).

Wardrop; Calvert County, Md.; X1 (4-195).

Wardwell, William; Boston; S1 (12-128).

Ware, Joseph; Salem; B5 (10-72).

Ware; Bible records, Wrentham; A1 (66-89).

Waring, Benjamin; S. C.; J (24-81).

Waring, Richard; Brookhaven, L. I.; A2 (34-272; 52-37).

Waring; Inscriptions, S. C.; J (20-220).

Warland; New Haven; B4 (8-1946).

Warner, Robert; Middletown; A1 (64-83).

Warner; Boston; A1 (62-93).

Warner; New Haven; B4 (8-1946).

Warner; Md.; English clue; X1 (4-197).

Warren, John; Watertown; English ancestry; A1 (64-348).

Warren, Richard; Plymouth; D (2-36; 3-45, 105; 4-14; 7-143; 14-256; 21-76, 104; 22-43; 23-152; 25-3); A1 (55-70, 161; 57-247); M (5-21, 11-2); B4 (8-1954).

Washburn, John; Duxbury; Pw (21-47).

Washburn; Bridgewater, Plymouth; D (15-247; 16-47, 248; 21-40; 24-44); Dx (5-1); Bible record, Bridgewater; Dx (2-76).

Washburn; Family records, Leicester; D (2-65).

Washburn; Bridgewater; P (9-91; 10-194).

Washburn; Family record; B5 (3-37).

Washington, John (Capt.) and Lawrence; Westmoreland County, Va.; Q1 (45-320; 47-58); V1 (4-315; 8-73, 111, 217; 9-34); English data; V1 (4-359; 6-61; 8-104, 117); A1 (78-387; 81-135); C2 (6-277); royal line; M (3-2).

Washington, John; Surry County, Va.; A2 (47-60); V1 (7-45, 124); M (17-17).

Washington; St. Paul's, S. C.; J (10-245).

Washington; Pedigree; A2 (33-200).

Washington; Austrian branch; V1 (6-158).

Wass; Bible records; P (7-42).

Wasse; Philadelphia; P (10-197).

Waterbury, William; Boston; English clue; A1 (64-135; 66-177).

Waterman, Richard; Salem; S1 (12-243).

Waterman, Robert; Marshfield, Halifax; D (11-100; 22-126; 24-145); Family record; Dx (5-90).

Waterman; Wallingford; B4 (8-1955).

Waters, Edward; Elizabeth City, Va.; A2 (41-281).

Waters, Richard; Salem; English data; A1 (51-407).

Waters; Somerset County, Md.; X1 (3-182).

Waters; Bible records; A1 (73-155).

Watrous; Derby; B4 (8-1956).

Watson, Edward; New Haven; B4 (8-1956).

Watson, Luke; Kent County, Del.; Q1 (42-170).

Watson, Matthew; Barrington; G2 (3-130).

Watson; Calvert County, Md.; E (12-165).

Watson; Family record, Va.; M (19-40).

Watson; Bible record; Y1 (53-288).

Wattell; Chelmsford; A1 (60-314).

Watts, Henry; English clue; A1 (61-199).

Watts, Richard; Hartford; English clue; A1 (61-278).

Watts, William; Va.; English clue; A1 (61-199).

Wattson; Bible records, Md., Pa.; P (10-180).

Way, George; Dorchester; English clue; A1 (61-278).

Way; New London (East Haven, Wallingford, branches); B4 (8-1957).

Wayman; English wills; E (2-5).

Wayne, Anthony; P (9-318).

Wayte, Thomas; Portsmouth, R. I.; A1 (69-188).

Weare, Nathaniel; Newbury, Nantucket; English data; arms; C2 (6-245).

Weare, Peter; York; A1 (55-55; 63-296; 64-180; 66-77).

Weaver, Clement; Newtown; S1 (14-90).

Webb, Christopher; Braintree; A2 (29-241); Dx (2-49).

Webb, Giles; Nansemond; V1 (11-177).

Webb, Richard; Cambridge, Hartford, Norwalk; A1 (64-83); A2 (26-190).

Webb; Me.; K (4-28).

Webb; Va.; V1 (7-191, 269; 8-52; 9-136; 12-277).

Webber, Wolfert; New York; A2 (56-203; 57-20, 372; 58-186).

Webber; Settlers; C2 (7-57; 115).

Webber; Milford, New Haven; B4 (8-1963).

Webly, Walter; Barbadoes, New York, Morrisania; A2 (13-196).

Webster, John (Gov.); Hartford, Hadley; A2 (46-305); English ancestry; A2 (62-232).

Webster, John; Ipswich; A1 (51-360).

Webster, William; Prince George's, Md.; X2 (2-1).

Webster; Early families; C3 (5-89, 139, 183, 196); C4 (1-97).

Webster; Family records; A1 (84-348).

Webster; (Ebenezer of Kingston); S2 (6-145).

Weed; Derby; B4 (8-1963).

Weeden, James; Newport, Portsmouth; English ancestry; A1 (76-115).

Weeden, Philip (Cocke); English ancestry; A1 (61-199; 78-147).

Weekes, Francis; Providence, Oyster Bay; A2 (53-280).

Weeks; Bible records; A1 (85-457).

Weiser, John Conrad; N. Y.; Pa.; Q2 (Vol. 32).

Welch, Thomas; Milford; English clue; A1 (54-352).

Weld, Thomas (Rev.); Roxbury; A1 (54-442).

Welles, Alice (Tomes); English ancestry; A1 (84-286).

Welles, Thomas (Gov.); Cambridge, Hartford, Wethersfield; A2 (42-439; 54-189); U (6-1); English ancestry; A1 (80-279, 446; 84-343).

Welles; Bible records; A2 (53-133).

Wells; New Haven; B4 (8-1964, 2052).

Wells; Bible records; A1 (67-380); B5 (12-234).

Welsh; Va.; Ill.; V1 (7-90).

Wemple, Jan Barentsen; Albany; A2 (35-191, 234; 36-47, 91, 191, 248; 44-5, 99, 265, 365).

Wendel, Evert Jansen; New York, Fort Orange, Albany; A2 (48-80, 309).

Wendover [Windeford], John; New York; A2 (26-178).

Wessels, Warnaer; New York; A2 (44-322).

West, Francis; Duxbury; A1 (60-142); D (26-1, 53, 103, 171); S1 (16-399); U (1-75, 123, 134, 174; 2-7; English line in error).

West, John (Capt.); West Point, Va.; V1 (6-116).

West, Joseph (Gov.); S. C.; J (19-189; 20-147).

West, Thomas (Dr.); Tisbury; A1 (52-271).

West, William, Thomas and John; Chester County, Pa.; Q1 (32-1, 377, 508).

West; Family records, Yarmouth; A1 (78-266).

West; Tolland; A2 (61-162).

West; Sussex County, Del.; P (3-139).

West; Bible records, Va.; X1 (11-278).

West; Frederick County, Md.; M (17-43).

West; Bible record; Q1 (32-118).

Westbrook, Jonathan; Rochester, N. Y.; A2 (37-89).

Westbrook; Ulster County, N. Y.; A2 (18-41).

Westcote, Stukeley; F4 (5-1).

Westcott; Bible record; B2 (9-6).

Westfall [Westvael], Juriaen; Kingston; A2 (33-10, 87).

Weston, Edmund; Duxbury; D (15-186; 24-19, 81).

Weston; co. Essex, Eng.; A1 (74-134).

Wetherburne; Williamsburg; V1 (4-30).

Wetherby; Bible record; Q1 (39-487).

Wetmore; East Haven; B4 (8-1965).

Whale, Philemon; Sudbury; English data; A2 (41-5); A1 (63-35).

Whaples; Wethersfield; B4 (8-1966).

Wharton; Bible records; P (5-111).

Wheadon, Thomas; New Haven, Branford; B4 (8-1966).

Wheeler, Moses; Stratford; S1 (15-83).

Wheeler, Thomas and William; Milford, Stratford; English clue; B3 (12-253).

Wheeler, Thomas, Sr.; Concord, Fairfield; U (20-146).

Wheeler; Concord, Mass.; C1 (1-186).

Wheeler; New Haven, Cheshire; B4 (8-1967).

Wheeler; Royalston, Mass.; E (11-52).

Wheeler; Bible records, Palatine, N. Y.; A1 (85-449).

Wheelwright, John (Rev.); Exeter, Hampton; English ancestry; A1 (68-73); mother's ancestry; A1 (74-51).

Whipple, Matthew and John; Ipswich; C2 (2-5, 63; 3-183; 5-217, 235; 6-125); U (22-16); English records; C2 (3-256).

Whipple; N. H.; F3 (2-96).

Whistler, John; Hagerstown; G2 (2-167).

Whitakar; Bible record; B5 (3-75; 5-97).

Whitaker, Jonathan; L. I., N. J.; B6 (2-98).

Whitcomb, John; Dorchester, Lancaster; English ancestry; A1 (61-279; 68-63).

White, Gawen; Scituate; English data; A2 (41-282).

White, John; Cambridge, Hartford; English ancestry; A1 (55-22); New Haven branch; B4 (8-1968).

White, John; Watertown, Brookline; A1 (52-421).

White, John; Newbury; S2 (4-49).

White, John; Nequasset, Me.; A1 (73-237).

White, John Campbell (Dr.); Baltimore; M (3-3-3).

White, Thomas; Weymouth; A1 (53-392).

White, William; Plymouth; D (1-129; 3-119; 7-193; 8-165; 9-122, 218; 10-25; 12-97, 117; 13-2; 17-1; 20-61; 22-7, 16; 23-76; 24-128; 28-27); Dx (1-1; 5-83); B2 (4-231, 255, 279, 301; 5-7, 29, 53, 77); M (5-23).

White; Salisbury, Conn.; B2 (5-41).

White; Shrewsbury, N. J.; A2 (36-220).

White; Md., Pa.; B2 (9-26).

White; Philadelphia; P (9-70).

White; Bible and gravestone records, Dartmouth, Mass., Guilford, N. Y.; B2 (7-10).

White; Bible records, Calvert, Md.; M (2-6).

White; Pittsfield, N. H.; S2 (9-275).

White; Family record, St. Croix; P (9-152).

White; Bible records; B3 (10-179); P (3-265, 267; 5-110).

Whitfield, William; Nansemond County, Va.; H (1-567).

Whitehead, Daniel; Hempstead, Smithtown, Huntington, Newtown; A2 (33-101; 47-311; 48-78).

Whitehead, John and Thomas; New Haven, Branford; A1 (55-180).

Whitehead, Samuel; New Haven; B4 (8-1970).

Whitehill; Lancaster County, Pa.; Q3 (2-158).

Whiteside; Bible records, Harrisburg, Pa.; B5 (7-46).

Whitfield, Henry (Rev.); Guilford, Conn.; A2 (43-94); English ancestry; A1 (51-410 ff.; 52-130; 53-10 ff.).

Whiting, Henry (Dr.); Gloucester County; V1 (12-259).

Whiting, William (Maj.); Hartford; E (2-106; 3-19); B4 (8-1971).

Whiting; Westford, Mass.; E (7-81).
Whiting; Family record, New Britain; M (15-59).
Whitman, Robert; Ipswich; English data; A1 (58-310); A2 (42-99).
Whitmore, Thomas; English clue; A1 (59-109).
Whitney, John; Watertown; B2 (6-10); B3 (2-196); S1 (16-402); Correction to printed genealogy; A1 (61-395).
Whitney; Bible record; A2 (54-67).
Whitney; Bible records, Marlborough, Mass.; B2 (5-72).
Whiton, Thomas; English clue; A1 (57-224).
Whittier, Thomas; Haverhill; S2 (4-336); English data; A1 (66-252).
Whittier; Pownalboro, Me.; F2 (5-43).
Whittingham, John; Ipswich; English data; A1 (70-185).
Whittlesey; Wallingford; B4 (8-1975).
Wiard; Bible records, Boston, Hartford; A1 (62-56).
Wiatt; Bible records, Va.; V1 (10-12).
Wickes, Joseph; Md.; X1 (15-236).
Wickham; Bible records, Southold; A2 (32-135).
Wiggin, Thomas (Gov.); N. H.; S3 (3-4-5).
Wiggins, John; Southold; A2 (59-120, 277).
Wight, Thomas; Exeter; English data; A1 (68-77).
Wightman; Bible records; F4 (4-158).
Wikoff; Bible record; Q1 (15-244).
Wilcox, Daniel; A1 (60-400).
Wilcox; Tiverton; D (16-239; 20-150).
Wilcox; Middletown, letters 1775-76; A1 (54-440).
Wilcox; Bible records, Killingworth; B2 (8-22).
Wilcoxon, Thomas; Prince George's County, Md.; M (6-44).
Wilcoxson, William; Stratford; A1 (66-309); S1 (13-391).
Wilder, Thomas; Mass.; M (2-42).
Wilder; Bible record, Vt., N. Y., Pa.; M (15-13).
Wildes; Topsfield; A1 (85-237).
Wilen; Bible records; P (10-172).
Wiles; Hamden; B4 (8-1977).
Wilfong; Bible record; B5 (11-124).
Wilkinson, John; English data; A1 (51-116).
Wilkinson, William (Rev.); Md.; X1 (14-384).
Wilkinson; Bible records, Md.; M (10-94).
Willard, Simon (Maj.); Cambridge, Concord, Lancaster; A2 (54-191).
Willcox, Thomas; Concord, Chester County, Pa.; G1 (8-28).

Willemse, Willem; Gravesend; A2 (12-154).
Willemszen, Aert; New York; A2 (26-134).
Willet; English records; A2 (33-106).
Willett, Thomas (Capt.); Plymouth, New York; A2 (18-74, 126; 19-174; 20-44; 28-190; 60-7); A1 (61-157).
Willett, Thomas; Flushing; A2 (27-171; 47-119).
Willett; Notes and corrections; A2 (46-415).
Willett; North Kingstown, R. I.; F4 (2-121).
Willetts; Bible records; A2 (27-109, 164).
Williams, Emmanuel; Taunton; A1 (57-75).
Williams, John; Newbury, Haverhill; A1 (62-184); C4 (3-1).
Williams, John; Norwich; U (1-181).
Williams, Marmaduke; Md.; English clue; A1 (55-334).
Williams, Richard; Taunton; English data; A1 (51-209); M (15-46).
Williams, Robert; Roxbury, Mass.; A1 (54-226); A2 (43-292).
Williams, Roger (Rev.); Providence; A1 (53-60; 54-212); Y1 (66-291); T6 (8-67); English ancestry; A1 (67-90; 75-234; 78-272).
Williams, Samuel; Groton; A1 (57-198).
Williams, Thomas; Philadelphia; Q1 (18-239).
Williams; Groton; A1 (54-106).
Williams; Taunton; D (22-60; 23-1); A1 (60-313).
Williams; Raynham; D (23-33).
Williams; Wallingford; B4 (8-1977).
Williams; Plainfield, Conn.; C3 (4-111).
Williams; Guilford County, N. C.; E (1-1).
Williams; Bible records, Boston; A1 (62-66).
Williams; Bible records, Taunton; A1 (56-363).
Williams; Family record, Va.; M (18-12).
Williams; Chester County, Pa.; Winchester, Va.; N2 (2-1-36).
Williams; Bible records, Pa.; P (7-272).
Williams; Bible records; P (7-40).
Williamson, John; Chester County, Pa.; E (7-148).
Williamson, Roger; Virginia; English data; A2 (43-69).
Williamson, Timothy; Marshfield; A1 (81-72, 292, 379; 82-8, 169, 264, 395); F2 (5-73).
Willis, Henry; Oyster Bay, Hempstead; A2 (15-170).

Willis; Bible records, Boston; D (8-104).

Willis; Bible records; A2 (16-186).

Willix, Balthazar; Exeter; English ancestry; A1 (68-79, 81).

Willoughby, Joseph; New London, Conn.; A2 (41-339).

Willoughby; West Haven; B4 (8-1981).

Wills; Bible record, Va.; V1 (6-146, 208).

Wilmer, Simon; Md.; X1 (15-414).

Wilmot, Benjamin; New Haven; A1 (59-67); B4 (8-1981).

Wilmot; Md.; Ky.; X1 (6-352).

Willson, Benjamin; Rehoboth; E (9-257).

Wilson, Anthony; Fairfield; A1 (52-83).

Wilson, John (Rev.); Boston, with English ancestry; A1 (61-36, 127, 397); A2 (43-199).

Wilson; Greenwich and Bolton, Mass.; A1 (54-351).

Wilson; Townsend, Mass.; Keene, N. H.; S2 (7-339).

Wilson; New Haven; B4 (8-1993).

Wilson; Family record, Newport; A1 (69-380).

Wilson; Bible records, Thompson, Conn.; A1 (65-349).

Wilson; Bible records, Plainfield; A1 (60-401).

Wilson; Family records, Montgomery County, Md.; M (6-27).

Wilson; Amwell, N. J.; B6 (8-53).

Wilson; Bible records; B2 (6-41).

Wilson; Ulster, Ireland; Q1 (38-346; 40-351).

Wilson; arms; M (6-35).

Wiltbank; Bible records, inscriptions; P (3-274).

Wiltbank; Bible record, Del.; Q1 (29-339).

Wiltshire, Thomas; Wallingford; B4 (8-2005).

Winchester, John; Hingham; A1 (78-7, 123, 230, 343; 79-11, 119).

Winchester, William; Westminster, Md.; X1 (25-385).

Winfree; Va.; R2 (2-196).

Wing, John; Lynn, Sandwich; E (5-73).

Wingate; Bible record; A1 (66-188).

Winsatt; St. Mary's County, Md.; X2 (2-5).

Winship; Cambridge; A1 (57-110).

Winslow, Edward (Gov.); Plymouth; D (1-65, 238; 3-129; 4-1; 5-82, 224; 8-100; 22-66; 24-30; 26-97; 27-49); Dx (4-70); A1 (82-136); A2 (27-121); B2 (2-108); M (5-23).

Winslow, John; Plymouth; D (1-65; 3-129; 10-52, 106; 12-129; 21-1; 24-165).

Winslow, Kenelm; Plymouth, Marshfield; A2 (45-2; 46-306).

Winslow; Warren, Ohio; M (15-55).

Winslow; Family record, Marshfield; A1 (68-107).

Winslow; Bible record; A1 (51-33).

Winslow; English ancestry; A2 (31-35).

Winsor; Bible records; B2 (8-24).

Winston, John; New Haven; B4 (8-2005).

Winter, Christopher; English clue; A1 (61-199).

Winthrop, John (Rev.); A2 (45-110).

Winthrop; English data; A1 (53-20; 69-188).

Winus, John; New Haven; B4 (8-2007).

Wischmeier, Henry; Burlington, Ia.; B2 (1-53).

Wise, Thomas; Sydenham, Va.; Z (61-263, 577).

Wise, New Haven; B4 (8-2007).

Wise; Bible records; X1 (11-281).

Wiser; Bible record; B5 (15-304).

Wistar; Bible record; P (5-257).

Wiswall; Duxbury; D (19-1).

Witham; Va., Mass.; Y1 (67-289).

Witherbee, John; Marlborough; S1 (14-269).

Witherell, William (Rev.); Scituate; English data; K (1-21).

Witheridge; Family record; Q1 (22-120).

Withers; M (19-11).

Witherspoon; Inscriptions, S. C.; J (13-65).

Witherspoon; Alleged Knox ancestry; A1 (64-80).

Withington, Henry; Dorchester; A1 (75-142, 196, 246; 76-6); S1 (13-66).

Withington; Bible record, Stoughton; A1 (75-79).

Withington; English data; A1 (52-68; 54-219).

Witman, John; Reading, Pa.; Q3 (2-76).

Witter; Family record, Lynn, Stonington; A1 (81-357).

Wittich, Immanuel Frederick; Ohio; E (7-228; 8-195; 9-134).

Wodhull, see Woodhull.

Woertendyk [Cornelis Jacobsen] [see Stille]; New York; A2 (28-244).

Woertman, Dirck Janse; Brooklyn; A2 (4-42).

Wolcott, Henry; Windsor; B4 (8-2011).

Wolcott, John; New Haven; B4 (8-2008).

Wolcott; English data; A1 (68-62).

Wolfer; E (9-141).

Wolseley; co. Stafford, Eng.; X1 (9-113, 116).

Womack, Ashley; Va.; (Ga. and Ala. branch); R2 (2-288).

Womack; Bible record, Ga., Ala., Texas; M (17-48).

Wood, George; English clue; Q1 (26-408).

Wood, John; Portsmouth; A1 (60-400; 69-188).

Wood, William; Concord; A1 (56-312).

Wood; Bible records, Newport; A1 (67-158).

Wood; Middleborough; D (18-227); Bible record, Middleborough; Dx (2-42).

Wood; Norwalk, Wallingford; B4 (8-2012).

Wood; Ipswich; Y2 (8-164).

Wood; Family record, Beverly; A1 (64-156).

Wood; Bible records; A1 (85-458); A2 (56-113); M (1-33; 19-68).

Woodbridge; Corrections to printed genealogy; A1 (54-401); Woodbridge branch; B4 (8-2013).

Woodbury; English data; A1 (54-224).

Woodcock; Family records, Pa.; P (6-242).

Woodford, Thomas; Hartford, Northampton; U (22-114).

Woodhouse, Henry; Va.; with English data; V2 (2-108, 153).

Woodhull, Richard; Jamaica, Setauket, L. I.; A2 (1-25; 3-10; 4-54, 124; 13-189); English records; A2 (27-52, 94).

Wooding, William; New Haven; B4 (8-2013).

Woodman, Archelaus and Edward; Newbury; English data; A1 (54-345); A2 (44-121); S2 (6-238).

Woodruff, Matthew; Farmington; (lineage of Wilford); U (22-54; chart facing p. 49).

Woodruff; Conn.; E (7-35).

Woods, George; Bedford, Pa.; Q1 (32-335).

Woods, Samuel; Watertown, Cambridge, Groton; A1 (64-34, 144, 205, 285, 309).

Woods; Family record, Marlborough, New Braintree); A1 (75-239).

Woods; Groton; A1 (61-396).

Woods; New Braintree; A1 (61-200).

Woodward, Henry (Dr.); S. C.; J (8-29, 173).

Woodward, John (Rev.); Norwich; A1 (62-136); East Haven branch; B4 (8-2026).

Woodward, John; Hector, Schuyler County, N. Y.; A2 (37-136, 218).

Woodward, Nathaniel; Boston; A1 (51-169).

Woodward, Richard; Watertown, Cambridge, Mass.; A2 (43-192); C4 (4-91).

Woodward; Plainfield, Conn.; C3 (4-114).

Woodward; Bible records; X1 (21-277).

Woolasten; New Castle, Pa.; E (11-46).

Woolley, Christopher; Concord; A1 (75-29, 320).

Woolley, Edmund; Newport, R. I.; A2 (42-204).

Woolley; Bible records; Q1 (11-207).

Woolsey, George; New York, Flushing, Jamaica; A2 (4-143; 5-12, 76, 139; 6-24).

Wooster, Edward; Derby; A1 (75-175); A2 (30-242; 31-39); B4 (8-2029).

Worcester, William (Rev.); Salisbury; (Hollis branch); S2 (3-245; 25-300).

Workman; Pa.; M (15-51).

Works; M (15-27).

Worthing [Worthen], George; Vermont branch; A2 (56-333).

Worthington; Bible records; X1 (14-79); Q1 (36-254).

Worthington; E (5-33, 121; 6-1, 33).

Wotton; Calvert County, Md.; X1 (1-380).

Wouters, Jan; New York, Flatbush, Branford; A1 (66-15).

Wouterszen, Egbert; New York; A2 (7-117).

Wragg, Samuel and Joseph; S. C.; J (19-121).

Wrenshall, John; Pittsburgh, Pa.; A2 (34-97).

Wright, John; Woburn; C2 (3-230, 291).

Wright, Peter, Anthony and Nicholas; Oyster Bay; A2 (3-35).

Wright, Richard; Plymouth; D (4-165, 239; 11-242; 21-53; 24-83); B2 (2-123).

Wright, Richard; Northumberland County; V1 (1-127, 177; 8-194; 11-165).

Wright, Richard (Capt.); Westmoreland County, Va.; V1 (4-153).

Wright, Samuel; Northampton; E (7-1; 12-161).

Wright; Lebanon, Hartland, Conn., Mayfield, N. Y.; A2 (52-302; 54-86).

Wright; Family record, Berkshire County, Mass.; M (18-17).

Wright; Bible record, N. J.; Q1 (30-379).

Wright; Bible record; Q1 (39-487).

Wright; C4 (1-227).

Wright; English clue; A2 (42-176).

Wroe; Bible records, Va.; M (11-40).

Wyatt; Va.; M (5-4).

PLACE AND SUBJECT INDEX

Abbeville County, S. C.
Vital entries, Calhoun Journal; R1 (8-192).
Abington, Conn.
Cong. Church records; B3 (3-354, 482; 4-329; 5-188, 246, 440).
Abington, Mass.
Vital records; D (8-9).
Diary of John Burrell, 1759-60; A1 (59-352).
Inscriptions; A1 (57-416).
Abington, Luzerne County, Pa.
Marriages, 1802-1856; Pw (7-178).
Adams County, Pa.
First settlers, Manor of Maske; Q3 (2-153).
Adams, Mass.
Quaker records, East Hoosuck; A1 (71-360; 72-16, 107).
Adams, N. Y.
Revolutionary soldiers buried; Z (31-731).
Addison, Me.
Residents, Pleasant River, 1778; F1 (1-173).
Aged residents, 1890; F1 (5-169).
First settlers, 1794; F1 (2-18).
Alabama
Revolutionary Pensions; Z (18-132).
Albany County, N. Y.
Cedar Hill (Bethlehem) Inscriptions; A2 (85-151).
Residents, 1674; A2 (48-236).
Miscellanea; A2 (21-170).
Albany, N. Y.
Mayors, 1686-1888; A2 (20-42).
Soldiers at Fort Albany and Half Moon, 1689; A2 (22-106).
Albemarle County, N. C.
Miscellaneous records; H (1-609; 2-146; 3-139, 243).
Petition, 1680; H (3-51).
Albemarle County, Va.
Inscriptions; M (19-96).
Alexandria County, D. C.
Marriages, 1801-1803; Z (49-121).
Alexandria, Licking County, Ohio
Inscriptions; E (15-182, 191).
Alexandria, Va.
Newspaper vital items; Z (48-434; 49-277; 50-55); M (5-17).
First Pres. Church, marriages, 1789-1825; Z (50-195, 240, 411; 54-454, 586).
Alfred, Me.
Vital records, 1796-1881; F2 (4-56, 133, 203, 266; 8-135).

Algiers
American prisoners, 1793; F2 (1-124).
Allegheny County, Pa.
History; G1 (4-194).
Abstract of wills; P (7-44, 136, 226).
Revolutionary soldiers buried; Z (45-343; 46-383).
Allen, Cumberland County, Pa.
Marriages, 1828-1830; P (11-88).
All-Saints Waccamaw, S. C.
Inscriptions; J (13-163).
Almanacs
New England; F4 (4-27).
Alverton, Westmoreland County, Pa.
Inscriptions; M (19-61).
Amanda, Fairfield County, Ohio
Baptisms, 1811-1813; M (18-83).
Amenia, N. Y.
Marriage Records, 1759-1785; A2 (33-46, 90).
Baptisms, 1749-1782; A2 (35-61, 107, 203, 282; 36-15).
Amesbury, Mass.
Church admissions, dismissions; Y1 (64-19).
Inscriptions; Y2 (1-28, 51, 119, 143, 164, 167, 190; 2-10, 30).
Vital records (from County records); Y2 (11-32, 33).
Amherst, N. H.
Marriages, 1780-1829; A1 (61-235, 378).
Amsterdam, Montgomery County, N. Y.
Census 1800; A2 (50-281).
Andover, Eng.
Y2 (11-49).
Andover, Mass.
Church admissions, dismissions; Y1 (58-225).
Deaths of men at Louisburg, 1745-46; W (1-177).
Genealogical notes, 1863; Y1 (continued; 50-41, 253; 51-306; 52-84, 281; 53-54, 187; 54-138, 246; 55-75).
Inscriptions; Y2 (2-39, 119, 143).
Andover, N. H.
Marriages, 1782-1828; A1 (58-16; 61-307).
Sketch; S2 (21-187).
Annapolis, Md.
St. Ann's Parish, vestry records, 1712-1762; X1 (6-325; 7-59, 166, 268, 395; 8-66, 149, 270, 353; 9-47, 162, 280, 336; 10-37, 127).

Ann Arundel County, Md.
Record sources; X1 (22-62).
Marriages, 1778-1781; Z (42-132; 43-612).
Oath of Fidelity, 1778; Z (51-49, 84).
Anson, Me.
Revolutionary soldiers buried; Z (36-409).
Antrim, Hillsborough County, N. H.
Revolutionary soldiers buried; Z (46-341; 50-243).
Revolutionary soldiers; Z (48-363).
Antwerp, N. Y.
Marriages, 1828-1844; A1 (81-272).
Archer, Richardson County, Neb.
Inscriptions; B2 (9-36).
Arkansas
Revolutionary pensioners; Z (18-256).
Arrowsic Island, Me.
Notes; F1 (3-41).
Inscriptions; F2 (2-54).
Ashburnham, Mass.; Corrections, vital records; A1 (64-375).
Ashby, Mass.
Revolutionary soldiers; C2 (4-80, 111, 289).
Ashford, Conn.
Cong. Church records; B3 (10-381, 735; 11-150).
Inscriptions; A1 (66-38; 69-276, 334; 70-239).
Ashley Ferry Town, S. C.
Notes; J (14-203).
Ashley River, S. C.
Settlements; J (20-3, 75).
Upper Ashley; J (20-151).
Athens, Pa.
Revolutionary soldiers buried; Z (30-200).
Athol, Mass.
First settlers; A1 (60-356).
Atlantic County, N. J.
See Smithfield, May's Landing, Galloway, Estelville, Tuckahoe, Linwood, Somers Point, Port Republic, Landisville, Oceanville.
Attleborough, Mass.
Baptisms and Marriages, 1774-1781; Dx (1-39, 64, 80).
Auburn, Me.
Inscriptions; A1 (73-233).
Auburn, Cayuga County, N. Y.
Church list, 1807; B6 (6-200).
Augusta County, W. Va.
Early Court officers; N2 (2-1-5).
Augusta, Me.
Inscriptions; F1 (6-65).
Austerlitz, Columbia County, N. Y.
Inscriptions; A2 (31-229).
Bainbridge, Geauga County, Ohio
Inscriptions; E (7-278, 282).

Bakersfield, Vt.
Inscriptions; A1 (74-150, 167, 310; 75-12, 98).
Baltimore County, Md.
Record sources; X1 (22-245).
Abstract of early records, to 1670; X1 (18-1; 24-151, 342; 25-255; 26-228).
Place names; X1 (25-321).
Tax list, 1699; X1 (12-1).
Militia, 1779; X1 (7-90).
Baltimore, Md.
Marriage records, 1777-1779; Z (42-24; 43-404, 559).
Revolutionary pensioners, 1840; X2 (2-28).
Artificers Co., 1777; X1 (2-367).
Independent Cadets, 1774; X1 (4-372).
St. Patrick's (Catholic) Church; G1 (1-374).
Old St. Peter's (Catholic) Church; G1 (1-372).
Bangall, Dutchess County, N. Y.
First Stanford (Baptist) Church, marriages 1776-1805; A2 (37-174, 314; 38-95, 206; 40-46; 41-181).
Bangor, Me.
First Cong. Church; F1 (3-101).
First Meth. Society; F1 (3-129).
Graveyards; F1 (4-84).
Parole of inhabitants, 1814; F1 (4-177).
Early settlers; F1 (1-2, 62, 118; 3-169, 233; 4-192; 9-1).
Marriages, 1796-1832; F1 (1-39, 83, 158; 2-63, 79).
Intentions, 1806-1833; F1 (1-198; 2-61; 3-93, 194; 5-37).
Deaths, 1777-1850; F1 (2-138, 180, 217, 243; 3-17, 238; 4-37, 80).
Marriages, 1791-1802; see Eddy Family, by J. W. Porter, 1877, p. 56.
Family records; F1 (6-293; 7-172; 8-37, 86, 148; 9-71).
Masonic Lodge; F1 (7-1).
Military Co., 1805; F1 (7-143).
Revolutionary soldiers buried; Z (30-304, 496; 31-546; 32-24, 122).
Barbados
Records pertaining to New Eng. and Va.; A1 (67-360; 68-177).
Inhabitants, 1638; F4 (3-230, 282).
Bar Harbor, Me.
Inscriptions; F1 (3-19).
Lots; F1 (3-30).
Barnstable County, Mass.
Probate records, beginning 1685; D (2-176; 3-176, 201; 4-179; 10-6, 100; 11-26; 12-38, 88, 187; 14-116; 15-76; 16-58; 18-58, 134; 19-43; 22-185; 23-61; 24-59; 27-35).

Barnstable County, Mass.—Cont.
Original unrecorded deeds; D (8-155;
9-239; 10-238; 11-225; 13-107; 14-
76, 175, 210; 15-92, 154, 201; 16-1,
90, 172, 218; 17-10, 124, 173, 203;
18-23, 98, 132, 217; 19-10, 84, 119,
152; 20-46; 21-133; 22-142, 167; 24-
69; 26-184).
Barnstable, Mass.
Vital records, earliest to 1823; D (2-
212; 3-51, 71, 149; 4-120, 221; 5-72,
171; 6-97, 135, 236; 10-249; 11-95,
130; 12-153; 14-86, 225; 19-77, 125,
154; 20-41; 23-125; 25-129, 147; 27-
5).
Inscriptions; F2 (6-311).
Barnstaple, Eng.
A1 (57-59).
Barnstead, N. H.
History; S2 (22-11).
Barre, Mass.
First Church records, baptisms 1767-
1831; A1 (57-410; 58-54).
Inscriptions; A1 (63-98).
Barrington, Nova Scotia
Vital records, beginning 1761; D (8-
138, 221; 9-27, 78, 142, 199).
Mass. settlers, 1776; A1 (60-364).
Basin Harbor, Vt.
Inscriptions; A2 (25-191).
Basking Ridge, Somerset County, N. J.
Pres. Church, 1769-1776; 1783-1786;
B1 (5-97, 106).
Inscriptions; B6 (1-123, 214).
In Revolution; B6 (2-241).
Bath County, N. C.
Miscellaneous records; H (1-441).
Bath, Me.
Inscriptions; F1 (6-165).
Notes; F1 (9-157).
Marriages, 1813-1853; F2 (6-478).
Revolutionary soldiers buried; Z (43-
480; 48-112).
Bath, Steuben County, N. Y.
Census 1800; A2 (60-49).
Beatrice, Neb.
Inscriptions; B2 (2-152; 3-169, 177,
240).
Beaufort, S. C.
Early settlers; J (9-141).
Beaver County, Pa.
Revolutionary soldiers buried; Z (37-
129).
Bedford County, Pa.
Abstract of wills; P (10-66, 164, 268;
11-39, 168).
Bedford County, Va.
Deeds; C2 (6-174).
Marriages, 1780-1783; C2 (6-67).
Probate Records; C2 (6-138).
Revolutionary records; Z (27-707;
30-104, 200).

Bedford, Mass.
Marriage intentions, 1748-1776; A1
(63-73).
Deaths, 1808-1834; A1 (62-69, 157).
Bedford, N. H.
Sketch; S2 (24-1).
Bedford, Westchester County, N. Y.
Census, 1710; A2 (38-219).
Census, 1800; A2 (58-10).
Bedminster, Somerset County, N. J.
Inscriptions; B6 (2-62, 131, 225, 294).
Inhabitants, 1760; B6 (7-51).
Old records; B6 (6-35).
Voters, 1797-1803; B6 (6-267).
Bedminster, Bucks County, Pa.
Church records (Tohickon), 1745-
1869; Q2 (vol. 31).
Beemerville, Sussex County, N. J.
Inscriptions; B1 (6-117).
Belfast, Me.
Marriages, 1774-1840; F1 (2-102, 195;
3-111, 130; 4-179).
Petition, 1816; F1 (5-233).
Belknap County, N. H.
See Centre Harbor.
Belleville, N. J.
Dutch Reformed Church, marriages,
1727-1794; B1 (3-41, 123, 155; 4-34,
90, 134).
Bellevue, Neb.
Pres. Church records, 1850-1864; B2
(8-1, 29).
Bellevue Precinct, Neb.
Inscriptions; B2 (8-57).
Belpre, Ohio
Residents, 1792; E (13-22).
Beltsville, Prince Georges County, Md.
Inscriptions; M (9-39).
Bennington, Vt.
Declaration, 1775, with list; Z (61-
277).
Bensalem, Bucks County, Pa.
Dutch Reformed Church records; P
(5-24).
Berkeley County, W. Va.
Abstracts, early probate; V1 (3-44);
see Z (49-39).
Berkeley, Mass.
Vital records; C3 (1-234).
Berkeley, N. C.
See Perquimans Precinct.
Berks County, Pa.
Inscriptions; M (15-33, 34).
St. Paul's (Catholic) registers, 1741-
1800; G1 (2-316; 3-295; 8-330).
Administrations, 1792-1795; Q1 (47-
178).
In Revolution; Z (26-1).
Roll, Capt. Reiff's Co., 1777; Q1 (34-
491).
Militia, 3rd Batt., Rev. War; Z (34-
500).

Berkshire County, Mass.
Deeds to Conn. men; B3 (2-289, 396).
Berlin, Hartford County, Conn.
Revolutionary soldiers buried; Z (37-99).
Berlin, N. H.
Vital records; S2 (12-132).
Sketch; S2 (20-184).
Berlin, Vt.
Marriages, 1791-1830; C3 (3-221).
Bermuda
History; S2 (8-107).
Bermuda, S. C.
Notes; J (14-136).
Bern, Berks County, Pa.
Church records, 1739-1835; P (5-38).
Bernville, Berks County, Pa.
Inscriptions; M (15-32).
Bertie County, N. C.
Abstract of wills; H (2-324, 496).
Court records; genealogical items; H (3-443).
Marriage bonds, 1762-1834; H (2-314, 364, 589).
Berwick, Me.
First Church records, 1701-1829; A1 (82-71, 204, 312, 500; 83-9, 147).
Inscriptions; F2 (2-55).
Marriages, 1710-1828; A1 (55-309, 372).
Quaker records; A1 (72-253; 73-43, 124; 75-5).
Second Church records, 1755-1857; A1 (74-211, 246).
Marriages, 1822-1845; Z (59-243).
Capt. Hill's Co., 1740; F2 (2-203).
Bethany, Conn.
Deaths, 1788-1793; B4 (5-1272).
Bethel, Me.
Marriage intentions, 1801-1813; C2 (2-217).
Bethlehem, Conn.
Vital entries, 1813-14; A1 (77-158).
Bethlehem, N. H.
Notes; S2 (7-29).
Sketch; S2 (17-16).
Bethlehem, Pa.
Old Moravian Cemetery, 1742-1910; Q2 (vol. 21).
In Revolution; Q1 (12-385; 13-71).
Beverly, Essex County, Mass.
Y1 (55-81, 209, 273; 56-33, 98, 209).
Vital records, early; C4 (1-107, 155, 187, 203, 257, 299, 319, 343; 2-50, 53).
First Church Baptisms, 1667-1710; C2 (5-161; 6-17, 56, 86, 127, 161, 183, 272, 297; 7-25).
Revolutionary document; C2 (7-36).
Inscriptions; Y2 (3-1, 31, 38, 56, 77, 90, 105, 122, 129, 150, 171, 182).

Biddeford, Me.
First Church records, 1730-1777; F2 (5-202; 6-293, 333, 492; 7-8, 82, 130, 181).
1st Co., 1778; F2 (8-35).
See Saco.
Binghamton, N. Y.
Revolutionary soldiers buried; Z (20-18).
Blackstone, Mass.
Inscriptions; G2 (29-145).
Blendon, Franklin County, Ohio
Early settlers; inscriptions; E (6-17, 40; 8-215; 10-127, 175).
Bloomfield, Conn.
Wintonbury Church records, 1738-1837; A1 (71-74, 153, 271, 295; 72-29, 87, 166).
Bloomfield, Essex County, N. J.
Inscriptions; B1 (2-109; 5-99).
Blount County, Tenn.
Index to Probate Records, 1795-1800; Z (58-99).
Blue Hill, Me.
Families, 1807; F1 (1-93).
Notes; F1 (1-148).
Cong. Church; F1 (2-113).
Militia, 1815; F1 (3-158).
Representatives before 1820; F1 (3-191).
Inhabitants, 1777; F1 (4-199).
Family records; F1 (5-181).
Early settlers; F1 (8-17).
Assessment, 1790; F1 (9-108).
Petition, 1785; F1 (9-129).
Boardville, Passaic County, N. J.
Inscriptions; B1 (2-107).
Bohemia Manor, Md.
Labadists; X1 (1-337).
Bolton, Conn.
Church records, 1725-1812; A1 (52-180, 307, 408; 53-447; 54-80, 253; 55-34, 281; 56-162, 347).
Inscriptions; A1 (83-93, 156).
Boston, Mass.
Almanac notes (Parkman); E (10-343).
Banks, 1681-1740; A1 (57-274).
Boyle's Journal, 1759-1778; A1 (84-142, 248, 357; 85-5, 117).
Christ Church bells; A1 (58-63).
Marriages, 1704, 1711; Q1 (31-493).
Deaths, 1799-1815; A1 (77-227, 312; 78-65, 177, 299, 396; 79-35).
Diary of Rev. Samuel Cooper, 1764-1769; A1 (55-145).
Marriages, 1702; A1 (63-379).
Revolutionary Co., 1777; M (18-3).
Tax list, 1687; A1 (55-139).
Vital entries, Williston diary, 1808-1814; A1 (65-366).
Irish settlers; G2 (6-75; 15-397).
Botetourt County, Va.
Abstracts of wills; V1 (9-272).

Bound Brook, Somerset County, N. J.
Inscriptions; B6 (1-304; 4-207).
Bowdoinham, Me.
Vital records; C1 (2-12).
Bowers, Berks County, Pa.
Inscriptions; P (9-74).
Boxborough, Mass.
Town records, 1784-1793; A1 (69-244).
Boxford
Parishes in England; Y2 (6-104).
Boxford, Mass.
Inscriptions; Y2 (4-8, 24, 40, 49, 70, 86).
Tax rate, 1687; Y1 (56-297).
Tax lists, 1711-1748; Y1 (57-242, 337).
Bradford County, Pa.
Notes; Pw (10-119).
French Catholics, 1794-1800; G1 (18-245).
Revolutionary soldiers buried; Z (38-208).
Bradford, Mass.
Church admissions, dismissions; Y1 (57-173).
Inscriptions; Y2 (5-17, 41, 58, 72, 92, 104, 150).
Braintree, Mass.
Early items; A1 (62-93).
First Church records, 1672-1708; A1 (59-87, 153, 269, 360).
Inscriptions; A1 (60-313).
Marriages, 1739-1762; A1 (60-41).
Braintree, co. Essex, Eng.
A1 (56-271).
Branchburg, Somerset County, N. J.
Inscriptions; B1 (1-14, 44, 69).
Voters, 1866; B6 (8-37).
Brandywine Manor, Pa.
Inscriptions; P (7-223).
Branford, Conn.
Early settlers; T2 (3-249; 4-299).
Inscriptions; A1 (62-143).
Brattleboro, Mass.
Revolutionary soldiers buried; Z (37-131).
Brattleboro, Windham County, Vt.
Vital records; C4 (4-60).
Bremen, Me.
Families; K (2-45, 77, 107; 3-12, 36, 70, 123; 4-52, 73, 104).
Brewer, Me.
Family records; F1 (6-78; 9-92).
Petition, 1811; F1 (2-211).
Cong. Church admissions, 1813-1834; F1 (3-153).
Marriages and intentions, 1812-1823; F1 (5-34; 9-39).
Inscriptions; F1 (5-142).
See Orrington, New Worcester.
Brewster, Mass.
See Harwich.

Bridgeport, Conn.
Revolutionary soldiers buried; Z(47-260).
Bridgewater, Mass.
Marriages, 1777; A1 (53-246).
Military roll, 1754; A1 (51-159).
Vital records; D (2-90, 144, 241; 3-8, 142; 5-247; 6-7; 7-55; 14-45, 180, 203; 15-45, 84, 168, 195; 16-39, 97, 185).
Vital entries (Fobes book); Dx (2-152).
See Brocton.
Bridgewater, Somerset County, N. J.
Voters, 1866; B6 (6-272).
Bristol, Me.
See Harrington.
Bristol County, Mass.
Probate records, 1687-1698; K (3-118; 4-58, 123); A1 (62-179, 231, 345; 63-77, 126, 227, 327; 64-26).
Miscellaneous wills; T6 (5-89, 132, 190, 228; 6-137).
Deeds, 1700; C3 (3-179).
Marriages from Court records; C4 (3-190).
Bristol County, R. I.
Revolutionary pensioners; F4 (2-128).
Bristol, Eng.
Records relating to emigrants; A1 (55-331).
Bristol, Me.
Families; K (2-45, 77, 107; 3-12, 36, 70, 123; 4-52, 73, 104).
Revolutionary soldiers; K (4-155).
Marriages, 1758-1847; K (1-9, 65, 102; 2-9).
Marriage intentions to 1800; K (4-153).
Revolutionary soldiers; K (4-155).
Tax list, 1798; K (3-65, 113, 152).
Bristol, N. H.
Sketch; S2 (5-262).
Bristol, R. I.
Early records; F4 (3-59, 157, 205, 276).
Broadalbin, Montgomery [now Fulton] County, N. Y.
Census 1800; A2 (50-30).
Brocton, Mass.
Revolutionary soldiers buried; Z (36-539, 722).
Brookfield, Conn.
Inscriptions; B3 (2-288).
Brookhaven, Suffolk County, N. Y.
Census 1800; A2 (56-277, 323).
Inscriptions; A2 (10-48; 16-131; 17-259; 21-73).
Wills (from N. Y. Surrogate's office); A2 (11-24; 12-46, 198; 14-140; 24-88, 142).

Brooklyn, Windham County, Conn.
Vital records; Z (47-254, 320; 48-50).
Marriages, 1800-1823; Z (47-261, 338).
Brooklyn, Kings County, N. Y.
Census 1800; A2 (55-124).
Early settlers; A2 (46-219).
Brooksville, Me.
Early settlers; F1 (8-10).
Brunswick County, Va.
Patriots, 1782; V1 (6-106).
Brunswick, Cumberland County, Me.
Maire Point settlers; C2 (4-5, 37, 128, 181).
Early settlers; F2(8-224; 9-5, 100, 132, 163, 196).
Marriage intentions, 1738-1769; C2 (3-251, 287; 4-21, 76, 245).
Inscriptions; F1 (2-17; 6-107).
Marriage intentions, 1740-1764; F1 (4-92).
Soldiers, 1732-35; C2 (1-137).
Buckland, Mass.
Marriage intentions, 1793-1820; A1 (75-302).
Bucks County, Pa.
Marriages, 1773-1824; P (3-201).
Marriages, 1768-1793; baptisms, 1768-1772; Q1 (12-222).
Inscriptions; Q1 (34-233).
Residents, 1677-1687; Q1 (9-223).
Committee of Safety, records 1774-1776; Q1 (15-257).
Wills; A2 (24-81).
Abstract of wills, 1684-1697; P (1-198; 2-7).
See Plumstead.
Bucksport, Me.
History; F1 (1-65, 85, 103).
Petition, 1805; F1 (6-238).
Inscriptions; F1 (2-80; 3-50).
Marriages, 1793-1811; F1 (3-178; 5-179; 7-16).
Intentions, 1793-1802; F1 (5-235).
In 1827; F1 (6-42).
Buffalo Valley, Pa.
Revolutionary soldiers buried; Z (21-301).
Burlington County, N. J.
Justices, 1682-1709; Q1 (16-250).
Marriages, 1787-1800; Q1 (16-380).
Tax list, 1684; Q1 (15-346).
Swedish settlers; Q1 (23-110).
Poll list, 1739; Q1 (18-185).
Freeholders, 1745; Q1 (29-421).
In Revolution; Z (43-591).
Marriages at Mansfield, 1806-1817; B5 (11-90).
Marriages, 1782-1794; B1 (3-12).
See Chairville, Lower Springfield.
Burlington, Me.
Vital records; F2 (8-44).
Civil War soldiers; F1 (7-43).

Burlington, N. J.
Register, St. Mary's Church, before 1700-1836; P (2-241).
Family notes; Q1 (19-124).
Interments, Friends' Graveyard; Q1 (24-48, 149).
Members, Quaker Society, 1776; Q1 (17-116).
Poll list, 1787; Q1 (44-77).
Burlington, Otsego County, N. Y.
Marriage register, 1812-1822; A2 (61-39).
Burlington, Vt.
Marriages; C3 (1-279).
First Church Baptisms, 1811-1820; C3 (2-44).
Church records, 1822-1848; C3 (3-206).
Bush River, Md.
Early inhabitants; X2 (1-23).
Bushwick, Kings County, N. Y.
Census 1800; A2 (55-129).
Butler County, Pa.; Irish settlers; G2 (18-198).
Butler, Pa.
Inscriptions; Pw (19-236).
Buxton, Me.
Inscriptions; F2 (1-199).
Byfield Parish, Mass.
See Newbury.
Cabell County, W. Va.
Early settlers; N2 (1-4-1).
Caldwell, Essex County, N. J.
Inscriptions; B1 (2-14, 55).
Calendar
Old and New Style; D (1-17); Y2 (4-65); Q1 (2-394; 3-65); U (10-158).
Calhoun County, S. C.
Inscriptions, Belleville; J (27-37).
California
Spanish missions; A2 (53-118).
Calvert County, Md.
Early landholders (names A-H); X2 (1-6; 2-29).
Cambridge, Mass.
First Church records; C3 (4-47, 121, 209, 265; 5-33, 65, 123, 167); C4 (1-22, 53, 73, 115, 163, 179, 211, 242, 273, 287, 323, 347).
Cambridge, Guernsey County, Ohio
Inscriptions; E (4-12, 50; 5-127).
Camden County, Ga.
Index to Probate Records, 1795-1829; Z (60-251).
Camden, S. C.
Inscriptions; J (25-47).
Camillus, Onondaga County, N. Y.
Census 1800; A2 (53-365).
Campbell County, Va.
Tax list, 1782; V2 (2-96).
Canaan, N. H.
Sketch; S2 (22-65).
Canaan, Columbia County, N. Y.
Inscriptions; M (18-65).

Canada
Noblesse; E (11-9, 102).
Canajoharie, Montgomery County, N. Y.
Census 1800; A2 (49-280).
Canal Winchester, Franklin County, Ohio
Inscriptions; E (8-58).
Candia, N. H.
Notes; S2 (4-404).
Canisteo, Steuben County, N. Y.
Census 1800; A2(60-118).
Canopus Hollow, Putnam County, N. Y.
Inscriptions; A2 (56-289).
Canterbury, Conn.
B3 (10-65).
Inscriptions; A1 (70-43, 153, 342).
Marriage records; C2 (1-272).
Canterbury, N. H.
Vital records, early; Z (46-266, 348; 47-79); S2 (4-391, 431, 507; 5-163, 195).
Canton, Conn.
Inscriptions; A1 (81-275, 404).
Canton, Penn.
Marriages, 1828-1841; Z (47-386; 48-52).
Cape Elizabeth, Cumberland County, Me.
Garrison, 1820; M (16-15).
Cape Elizabeth, Me.
Inscriptions; F2 (4-227; 5-52).
Cape May County, N. J.
Earmarks, 1690-1730; Q1 (15-370).
Early vital records; Q1 (15-493).
Court records, 1758; Q1 (37-224).
Cold Spring Pres. Church records, 1804-1815; D (8-5, 95, 134, 211).
Cape May Court House, N. J.
Inscriptions; Q1 (35-356, 506; 36-110, 231).
Carlisle, Mass.
Vital records, 1752-1758; A1 (54-50; 62-32).
Carlisle, Cumberland County, Pa.
Inscriptions; M (6-63).
St. Patrick's (Catholic) Church, sketch; G1 (6-266, 353).
Carmel, Me.
Vital records; A1 (83-136).
Carmel, N. Y.
See Southeast.
Caroline County, Md.
Record sources; X1 (26-135).
Marriage licenses, 1774-1815; Q1 (28-209, 320, 428).
Caroline, Tompkins County, N. Y.
Inscriptions; A2 (52-132, 268; 54-389).
Carthage, N. Y.
Catholic church; G1 (10-17, 138).
Castine, Me.
Inscriptions; F1 (1-47).
Inhabitants, 1786; F1 (1-57).

Castine—Cont.
Marriages, 1787-1788; F1 (1-102).
Early settlers; F1 (8-8).
Castletown, Richmond County, N. Y.
Census 1800; A2 (60-317).
Catharines, Tioga County, N. Y.
Census 1800; A2 (59-339).
Cayuga County, N. Y.
Marriages, 1830-1843 (Baptist); A1 (76-262).
See Venice, Locke, Port Byron, Genoa.
Cazenovia, N. Y.
Revolutionary soldiers buried; Z (37-33).
Cecil County, Md.
Record sources; X1 (23-20).
Oath of Allegiance, list, 1778; Z (62-561).
North Elk Parish; X1 (9-315).
Cedar Hill, Albany County, N. Y.
Inscriptions; A2 (58-151).
Centerburg, Knox County, Ohio
Inscriptions; E (9-186).
Center County, Pa.
Revolutionary soldiers buried; Z (33-997).
Central College, Ohio
E (9-294).
Centre Harbor, Belknap County, N. H.
Inscriptions, Garnet Hill; A2 (58-154).
Chairville, Burlington County, N. J.
Inscriptions; B1 (4-28).
Chambersburg, Pa.
Marriages, 1801-1844; P (8-67).
Charles City County, Va.
Militia, 1661; V1 (12-190).
Militia, 1776; V1 (5-58).
Tax list, 1787; V2 (2-43).
Notes; V1 (6-275).
Charles County, Md.
Record sources; X1 (21-261).
Early settlers, list from court records; X1 (23-344).
Vital records, 1654-1726 (names A-H); X2 (1-15, 23, 28; 2-3, 14, 17).
Marriages, 1777-1801; Z (61-233, 453).
Trinity Parish, history; X1 (1-324).
Charleston, S. C.
Early settlers; J (9-12; 19-3).
Congregational (Circular) Church, register 1732-1738; J (12-27, 53, 135).
St. Philip's Parish, extracts 1720-1758; G2 (12-144).
Quaker records; J (28-22, 94, 176).
Inscriptions, Cong. Churchyard; J (29-55, 133, 238, 306).
Notes; J (16-1, 49).
Hog Island and Shute's Folly; J (19-87).
Members, Library Society, 1750; J (23-169).

Charlestown, Mass.
Mill Pond; A1 (56-235).
Charlestown, Montgomery County, N. Y.
Marriages, 1796-1800; Z (49-37).
Census 1800; A2 (50-274).
Charlestown, R. I.
Marriages; F4 (1-257).
Births and Deaths; F4 (2-52, 145).
Charles Town, Jefferson County, W. Va.
Academy, subscription list, 1796; N2 (5-18).
Charlotte County, Va.
Marriage Bonds, 1765-1780; V1 (5-67).
Chatham, Mass.
Vital records; D (4-182, 198; 5-120, 141; 7-137; 9-33, 179, 221; 10-194; 11-39, 119; 12-171, 215; 13-27; 15-130; 16-212; 17-87; 24-64, 101).
Deaths, 1836; A1 (62-382).
Inscriptions; A1 (62-203, 303); D (8-236; 13-76, 175; 19-49).
Chautauqua County, N. Y.
See Mayville.
Chelmsford, Mass.
Marriages, 1656-1692; A1 (51-307, 447).
Warnings, 1790, 1794; A1 (83-164).
Chelmsford, Eng.
A1 (56-375).
Chelsea, Mass.
Marriage intentions, 1739-1760; C2 (3-277, 317).
Chemung, Tioga County, N. Y.
Census 1800; A2 (59-340).
Chenango, Tioga County, N. Y.
Census 1800; A2 (59-234).
Cherryfield, Me.
Inscriptions; F1 (3-59).
Family records; F1 (7-176).
Cheshire, Delaware County, Ohio
Inscriptions; E (9-261).
Chester County, Pa.
Early settlers; P (4-281).
Vital records (Dutton), 1770-1870; P (4-23).
Marriages, 1795-1832; P (4-101).
Inscriptions; M (14-39); P (7-224).
Inscriptions, Great Valley, East Whiteland; Q1 (15-440).
Chester, N. H.
Notes; S2 (4-139).
Chester, Morris County, N. J.
Inscriptions; B1 (2-29).
Chester, Lunenburg County, N. S.
Settlers, 1759; A1 (54-44).
Chesterfield, Burlington County, N. J.
Town records, 1692-1712; Q1 (35-211).
Quaker marriages, 1685-1730; Q1 (9-347).

Chestnut Hill, Pa.
Tax list, 1809; Q1 (15-449; 16-42).
Childsbury, S. C.
Notes; J (14-198; 15-107).
Chillicothe, Ohio
Inscriptions; E (3-32, 75; 5-50).
Chilmark, Mass.
Cong. Church records, 1787-1820; A1 (59-195, 257, 378).
China, Me.
Quaker records, Harlem; A1 (70-268, 318).
Chittenden County, Vt.
Probate records; C3 (1-150).
Chowan County, N. C.
Location of first church; H (1-256).
Land grants; H (1-1).
Abstract of deeds; H (1-85, 284, 615; 2-135, 283, 443, 607).
Abstract of wills; H (1-132, 516; 2-1).
Marriage bonds, 1741-1870; H (1-235, 392, 558; 2-89, 227, 415).
Superior Court records, beginning 1670; H (1-135).
Chowan Precinct, N. C.
Miscellaneous Court records; H (1-443).
Court records, 1711; H (3-441).
Christ Church Parish, S. C.
Church register, 1694-1833; J (18-50, 70, 124, 168; 19-80, 114, 124; 20-64, 123, 199, 252; 21-31, 52, 105, 144; 22-12).
Inscriptions; J (21-73, 132).
Inscriptions, Wappetaw; J (25-136).
Claiborne, Ala.
Inscriptions; M (15-42).
Claremont, N. H.
Grantees; S2 (15-206, 241, 282, 318).
Epis. Church marriages, 1781-1835; Z (45-31).
Sketch; S2 (14-112; 16-103).
Clarendon County, S. C.
Inscriptions, St. Mark's Parish; J (28-55).
Clark County, Ind.
Voters, 1802; M (3-4-6).
Clarkesboro, N. J.
Marriages, 1792-1798; P (9-183).
Clarkstown, Rockland County, N. Y.
Census 1800; A2 (61-350).
Claverack, N. Y.
Inscriptions; A2 (26-90).
Clay County, Mo.
Marriages, 1821-1826; Z (44-393).
Sketches; Z (44-393; 45-243, 330; 46-24).
Clinton, Me.
Tax list, 1780; F1 (7-45).
Clinton, Franklin County, Ohio
Inscriptions; E (7-284).

Clovesville, N. Y.
Revolutionary soldiers buried; Z (34-609).
Coalsmouth, Kanawha County, W. Va.
Historical; N2 (5-35).
Colebrook, Conn.
Notes, residents who moved west; A2 (54-69).
Colestown, N. J.
St. Mary's Church records, 1781-1815; P (3-237).
Colleges, American
Check list of biographical directories and catalogues; A2 (46-51).
Colleton County, S. C.
Volunteers, 1775; M (18-3).
Colonial Governors
A2 (30-184, 230).
Colrain, Franklin County, Mass.
Vital records; A1 (73-246; 74-7).
Columbia County, N. Y.
Inscriptions; A2 (26-118).
Livingston Manor, records 1776-; A2 (60-239, 325).
Columbia, Conn.
Inscriptions; A1 (60-370).
Columbia, Me.
Sketches; F2 (9-84).
Marriages and intentions, 1796-1806; F1 (4-117).
Columbia Falls, Me.
Inscriptions; F1 (3-156).
F1 (1-136).
Columbus, Ohio
Settlement; E (15-36).
Early settlers; E (15-96).
Borough; E (15-107).
Inscriptions; E (1-67; 9-187; 10-248, 353; 11-53, 223).
Concord, Me.
Revolutionary soldiers buried; Z (36-409).
Concord, Mass.
See Carlisle.
Concord, N. H.
First Cong. Church records, 1732-1844; F3 (6-9, 49, 104, 161; 7-17, 65).
Marriages and intentions; C1 (2-107).
Vital records, 1780 (Walker Diary); S2 (4-101).
First Cong. Church, history; S2 (2-261).
Sketch; S2 (8-263).
East Cong. Church; S2 (14-133).
Marriage Intentions, 1732-1739; S2 (14-50).
Conewago, Pa.
Settlers from N. J.; B6 (4-161).
Dutch Church baptisms, 1769-1793; B6 (4-267).
Marriages, 1789-1793; B6 (5-78).

Connecticut
Census 1790, errors; A1 (77-80).
Deaths and marriages, record kept by Hartford man, 1819-1834; A1 (79-150).
Newspaper items, 1805-06, '19; M (5-41).
Probate Files, at State Library in 1924; A1 (78-222).
Pensioners, K. Philip's War; F4 (1-144).
Court records, 1639-1663; T3 (vol. 22).
French and Indian War Rolls; T3 (vols. 9, 10).
Muster rolls, 1745, 1747; T3 (13-66, 272; 15-111).
Revolutionary War Rolls; T3 (vols. 8, 12); T7 (vol. 47, 1914, p. 48).
Orderly books and journals, Rev. War; T3 (vol. 7).
Irish settlers; G2 (24-125).
Colonial services, 1636-1665; B4 (4-961).
Conway, N. H.
Sketch; S2 (20-347).
Cooper, Me.
Marriages, 1822-1827; A1 (85-349).
Coos County, N. H.
History; S2 (3-25).
Cornish, N. H.
Church and marriage records, 1768-1805; A1 (72-279).
Death records, 1811-1815; A1 (71-338).
Cornwall, Conn.
Revolutionary deaths; A1 (51-70).
Cortlandt, Westchester County, N. Y.
Census 1800; A2 (58-137).
Coventry, R. I.
Oath of Fidelity, list, 1776; Z (61-47).
Coxsackie, N. Y.
Revolutionary Declaration, 1775, list; Z (59-35).
Cranberry Islands, Me.
Early settlers; F1 (4-22).
Cumberland County, Me.
Officers, Col. Waldo's Regt., 1762-67; F2 (9-151).
Cumberland County, N. J.
Marriages, 1794-1799; M (10-91).
Place names; B5 (9-156).
Court records, 1752-58; Q1 (37-361).
Inscriptions, West Creek Bapt. Churchyard; B5 (14-93).
Manumission of slaves, 1789-1829; B5 (2-72).
Cumberland County, Pa.
Inscriptions; M (3-3-8; 4-7, 30).
Marriages, 1761-1800; P (9-297; 10-25).
Petitioners, 1760, 1761, 1770; M (7-1).

Cuyahoga County, Ohio
Revolutionary soldiers buried; Z (22-22).

Dallas, Pa.
Early settlers; Pw (6-143).

Danbury, Conn.
Vital records; B3 (4-115, 331; 5-189, 296).

Danby, Tompkins County, N. Y.
Inscriptions; A2 (52-269; 54-388).

Danvers, Essex County, Mass.
Early history; C2 (5-141).
Church records; C2 (6-231).
Inscriptions; Y2 (6-19, 75, 112, 156).
Diary, 1753; C3 (2-51).
Diary of John Preston, 1744-1760; A1 (56-80).
Diary excerpts, 1816-1871; C1 (2-111, 171); C2 (1-28, 61, 125, 250).
Muster roll, 1775; C2 (2-221).

Danville, Me.
History; F2 (5-12).

Danville, N. H.
See Hawke.

Darby, Chester County, Pa.
Settlers; Q1 (24-182).

Daretown, Salem County, N. J.
Inscriptions; B1 (6-71, 97); B5 (10-236, 35, 56).

Dartmouth, Mass.
Vital records; D (3-216).
Purchasers, 1660; D (4-185).

Davidson County, Tenn.
Elderly residents, Census 1850; M (12-11).

Decatur, Ind.
Revolutionary soldiers buried; Z (39-91).

Dedham, Mass.
Diary of John Whiting, 1743-1784; A1 (63-185, 261).

Deerfield, N. J.
Inscriptions; B5 (11-91, 113, 133, 155; 12-176, 206).

Deerfield, Ross County, Ohio
Inscriptions; E (6-97).

Deering, N. H.
Inscriptions; A1 (85-448).

Deer Island, Me.
Petition, 1762; F1 (1-195).
Petition, 1775; F1 (2-103).
Marriages, 1832-1852; F1 (5-156).
Early settlers; F1 (8-13).

Deerpark, Orange County, N. Y.
Reformed Dutch Church records, 1716-1827; A2 (42-229, 369; 43-12, 141, 225, 349; 44-37, 156).
Census 1800; A2 (62-406).

Delaware
Dutch passenger list, 1661; A2 (60-68).
Miscellaneous vital records; Q1 (43-273).

Delaware—Cont.
Members of the Colonial Assembly; P (5-245).
Baptists; Q1 (9-45, 197).
Irish settlers; G2 (18-187).
Wills; Q1 (22-102).

Delaware County, N. Y.
See Walton.

Delaware County, Ohio
Pioneers; E (2-7).
Classes, Meth. Epis. Churches, 1839-1840; E (11-181).

Delaware County, Pa.
Marriages, 1798-1809; P (5-323).

Denmark
See Scandinavia.

Dennis, Mass.
Vital records; D (6-2, 91, 165, 251; 7-3, 66, 159; 8-50; 10-36, 116, 209; 11-211; 12-40; 13-14, 120, 254).
East Yarmouth Church records, 1727-1806; K (2-33, 71; 3-17, 85; 4-47, 118, 129).

Dennysville, Washington County, Me.
Settlement; F2 (8-218; 9-11).
Marriages, 1787-1830; F2 (9-17).
Marriages, 1791-1830; F1 (6-168).
Births before 1820; F1 (6-258).
Early settlers; F1 (6-269).
Intentions; F1 (6-272).

Denver, Col.
Marriages, 1859-1862; Z (42-195, 271).

Deptford, Baltimore County, Md.
Census, 1776; X1 (25-271).

Derby, Conn.
Inscriptions; A1 (84-134).
St. James's (Epis.) Church records, 1740-1796; A1 (76-130, 170).

Derry, Westmoreland County, Pa.
Inscriptions, Salem Churchyard; M (9-30).

Dinwiddie County, Va.
Inscriptions; V1 (9-65).
Order book, 1789; V2 (2-142).

District of Columbia
Marriage licenses, 1801-1820; M (7-33, 49; 8-27, 55).
Revolutionary soldier burials; M (7-27, 40).

Dobbs Ferry, N. Y.
Inscriptions; M (2-34).

Dorchester County, Md.
Record sources; X1 (23-243).
Marriage Licenses, 1790-1802; P (8-252; 9-85, 130).

Dorchester, Mass.
First Church, baptisms, 1748-1792; A1 (68-215, 309).
New residents, 1767-1789; A1 (60, 387; 61-42).
Petition, early; A1 (58-404; 59-104).
Religious society of young men, 1698; A1 (60-30).

East Harwich, Mass.
Inscriptions; D (19-157; 21-49).
East Lyme, Conn.
Inscriptions; A1 (79-66).
East Machias, Me.
Inscriptions; F1 (4-196).
Church members, 1836; F1 (5-40).
East Middleborough, Mass.
Inscriptions; D (12-256).
Easton, Conn.
Inscriptions; T1 (1891-92, p. 63).
Easton, Talbot County, Md.
Quaker records; M (11-9).
Easton, N. Y.
Inscriptions; A2 (47-385; 48-4, 104, 299, 399; 49-22, 120).
East Pembroke, Mass.
Inscriptions; D (11-63, 219).
Eastport, Me.
Early settlers; F1 (1-115, 173; 3-95; 9-230).
Inscriptions; F1 (2-150).
Marriages, 1790-1812; F1 (3-80, 99).
East Vincent, Pa.
See Vincent.
Eaton Neck, Suffolk County, L. I.
Inscriptions; A2 (27-213).
Eddington, Me.
Marriages, 1791-1802; F1 (1-56).
Rate bill, 1791; F1 (3-60).
Family records; F1 (9-54).
Eden, Me.
Tax list, 1797; F1 (5-180).
Edenton, N. C.
Abstract of deeds, 1710-; H (1-120).
St. Paul's Church; H (1-600).
Riot, 1728; H (1-439).
Edgartown, Mass.
Church; A1 (60-159).
Deaths, 1761-1827; A1 (52-230, 368; 53-102; 59-202, 297, 400).
Inscriptions; A1 (51-196).
Vital records; B3 (3-353, 482).
Officers, 1776; Z (34-537).
Edgecomb, Me.
Vital records, 1775-1823, diary of Moses Davis; A1 (83-414).
Edmunds, Washington County, Me.
Early settlers; F1 (1-49).
Edmundsbury, S. C.
Sketch; J (11-42).
Elizabeth, N. J.
St. John's Church, baptisms, 1750-1775, 1792-1819; B1 (3-14, 80, 119, 151; 6-1, 37, 113).
St. John's Church, marriages, 1751-; B1 (5-33).
Elizabeth City County, Va.
Tax list, 1787; V2 (1-177).
Quit Rent Roll, 1704; V2 (1-179).
Elizabethtown, N. Y.
Settlement; A2 (31-193).
Ellicott City, Md.
Inscriptions; X1 (19-200).

Ellsworth, Me.
Inscriptions; F1 (3-38; 6-262).
Unrecorded deeds; F1 (3-70, 219).
Settlement; F1 (3-125; 5-106).
Petition, 1798; F1 (3-127).
Names, 1793; F1 (3-232).
Marriage intentions, 1800-1810; F1 (8-115).
History, settlers; F1 (8-181).
Emporia, Greensville County, Va.
Marriages, 1785-1795; Z (43-509).
Enfield, Conn.
Inscriptions; A1 (60-306).
Enfield, N. H.
Shaker records, 1793-1895; A1 (62-119).
Enfield, Tompkins County, N. Y.
Inscriptions; A2 (52-372; 53-75; 54-386).
England
Record sources, location, etc.; A1 (58-184, 285, 349; 59-48); C3 (1-188); U (6-55; 7-78; 8-113; 11-93; 12-169; 13-23; 16-153).
Admiralty and Port records; C4 (3-69); A2 (47-73, 109, 251, 330).
Regnal years, English rulers; C3 (1-148).
Channel Islands, records; U (6-87, 136; 7-34).
Isle of Man, records; U (8-106, 170; 9-61).
Origin of New Eng. settlers; A2 (61-3).
Marriage; U (1-75, 101).
Domesday Book; U (2-107).
Heraldic Visitations; U (5-148).
English settlers before 1800
A1 (60-399); see also Passenger Lists.
English Parish Registers
C1 (2-51).
List of those printed prior to 1898; E (1-74).
Hessett, co. Suffolk, excerpts; A1 (52-42).
Leek, co. Stafford; C2 (4-186, 262).
London, St. Mary le Strand, marriages 1605-1625; A2 (18-36, 68, 107, 153).
London, St. Mary Whitechapel, marriages 1605-1625; A2 (19-103; 20-132, 181; 21-87; 22-52, 75, 204; 23-42, 151; 24-37).
London, St. Dunstan in the East, 1605-1625; A2 (25-194; 26-21, 110).
London, St. Saviour's, Southwark, marriages 1605-1625; A2 (27-47, 81, 161; 28-43, 79; 29-171).
Melford, co. Suffolk, 1600; C4 (3-33).
Much Haddam, co. Herts; C2 (4-264).
Raynham, co. Norfolk; A1 (52-318).

English Parish Registers—Cont.
Stewkley, co. Bucks, 1545-1653; C2 (4-10, 33, 65, 106, 176, 220; 5-37, 57, 97).
co. Suffolk, transcripts, 1588-91; C4 (3-93, 160, 219).
English Probate Records*
A1 (51-105, 249, 297, 389; 52-105, 234; 53-9, 301; 54-91, 188, 214, 325, 341; 55-95, 331, 432; 56-84, 308, 402; 57-93, 216; 58-311, 396; 59-101, 172); A2(34-288; 35-119, 179, 271; 36-22, 114, 172, 260; 37-49, 184; 38-205; 39-46, 217; 40-4, 80, 108, 155, 177, 229, 276; 41-4, 56, 72, 142, 175, 183, 278, 367; 42-50, 92, 168, 193, 294, 319, 430; 43-67; 44-116); C1 (1-67); C2 (3-59, 96, 127, 253; 4-51, 183; 7-167); C3 (4-36, 137, 177; 241; 5-1, 99); C4 (1-45, 313).
Epping, N. H.
Vital records; F3 (3-113, 177; 4-83, 131, 165; 5-9, 65, 180; 6-6, 92).
Erie County, Ohio
Revolutionary soldiers buried; Z (22-22).
Erie County, Pa.
Abstract of wills; Z (62-482, 706; 63-688).
Revolutionary soldiers buried; Z (36-311).
Erie, Pa.
Revolutionary soldiers; Z (38-12).
Essex County, Mass.
Court of Sessions, records 1699; C4 (4-36).
County Court Records; C1 (2-95, 190); C2 (1-134; 2-169, 173; 5-11, 195, 202); C3 (1-282; 2-1, 128, 203; 3-26, 83, 161).
Deeds; C2 (2-165; 3-110, 228; 4-302; 5-22, 128, 190, 230; 6-110, 141, 257; 7-135, 289); C3 (1-47).
Probate Records; C2 (5-27; 6-58, 78, 113, 152, 180, 313; 7-6, 119, 298); C3 (1-118); Y1 (50-217, 313; 51-57, 137).
Miscellaneous items; C4 (3-188).
Names legally changed; Y2 (4-90).
Indentures of apprentices; Y1 (58-263).
Newspaper items, 1765-1768; Y1 (51-131, 290; 52-141, 273; 53-133, 297; 54-188, 251).
Revolutionary soldiers; Y2 (1-7, 31, 63, 101, 130, 157, 195; 2-23, 67, 97, 128, 165; 3-28; 4-105; 5-10, 174; 6-31, 80, 116, 164; 7-84, 126; 8-133, 179; 9-178; 10-182; 11-38, 86; 12-86, 130, 185; 13-126).
Revolutionary roll; C2 (7-184).

Essex County, N. J.
See Bloomfield, Millburn, Caldwell, Orange.
Essex, Mass.
Inscriptions; Y2(7-49).
Essex, Va.
Militia, 1781; V2 (1-237).
Estelville, Atlantic County, N. J.
Inscriptions; B1 (5-17).
Esther Institute (Columbus, Ohio)
E (9-143).
Etna, Licking County, Ohio
Inscriptions; E (11-65).
Exeter, Mass.
Vital records (from County records); Y2 (5-14, 46; 11-33).
Exeter, N. H.
Revolutionary soldiers buried; Z (48-353).
In Revolution; S2 (3-410).
Sketch; S2 (16-16).
Exeter, Pa.
Inscriptions; Pw (18-134).
Exeter, R. I.
Baptist Church; F4 (2-1).
Inscriptions; A1 (74-13).
Fabius, Onondaga County, N. Y.
Census 1800; A2 (53-358).
Fairfax County, Va.
Abstracts of wills, 1742-1751; M (10-65).
Committee of Safety, 1774-1775; Z (49-239).
Court records, 1756-63, location; M (10-86).
Land records, 1742-1746; M (10-97, 113).
Poll tax, list, 1744; M (10-103).
Fairfield, Conn.
Greenfield Hill Church records; A1 (68-169, 286, 375; 69-39, 127, 230, 364; 70-33).
Marriages, 1692-1832; P (8-164, 275).
Fairfield, Cumberland County, N. J.
Data from Bateman Journal (starts 1799); B5 (13-55, 80; 14-106, 127, 154, 174; 15-210, 235).
Male inhabitants, with ages, 1800; B5 (14-128).
Fairfield, Essex County, N. J.
Baptisms, 1741-1748; B1 (6-7).
Fairmont, Neb.
Inscriptions; B2 (1-24, 70).
Fairview, Ill.
Settlers from N. J., 1845; B6 (2-255; 3-109, 278).
Fall River, Mass.
Vital records, 1804-1829; Z (43-666, 743).

---

* Many others are not listed here, because they will be found under specific surnames in the Name Index.

Falmouth, Mass.
Vital records; K (3-57, 81; 4-19, 81, 111).
3d Co., 1759; Z (52-82).

Falmouth, Me.
Agreement, 1769; F2 (1-9).
Capt. Berry's Guard, 1754; F2 (3-98).
Capt. Knight's Co., 1776; F2 (3-210).
Deserters, 1765; F2 (2-60).
French War, 1757; F2 (1-11).
Inscriptions; F2 (3-91; 5-125, 171).
Killed and wounded, 1689; F2 (1-196).
Marriages, Second Parish, 1756-1797; F2 (3-101, 185).
Willis Papers; F2 (1-9, 41, 110, 160).

Farmers Mills, Putnam County, N. Y.
Inscriptions; A2 (56-187, 288).

Farmington, Conn.
Inscriptions; A1 (60-372).

Farmington, Me.
Inscriptions; F1 (5-42).

Farmington, N. H.
Sketch; S2 (19-259).

Farnham, Richmond County, Va.
Marriages, 1672-1800; Z (58-620).

Fauquier County, Va.
Oath of Allegiance, list, 1778; Z (62-776).

Fayette County, Ky.
Tax lists, 1787, 1788; V2 (1-239; 2-38).

Fayette County, Pa.
Inscriptions; M (19-62, 63).

Fishkill, N. Y.
Historical Sketch; A2 (21-51).
Inscriptions; A2 (23-212; 24-26).
Revolutionary soldiers buried; Z (46-334; 48-433).

Fitchburg, Mass.
Revolutionary soldiers; C2 (7-245); Z (19-166).

Fitzwilliam, N. H.
Sketch; S2 (24-311).

Flanders, Morris County, N. J.
Inscriptions; B1 (3-101).

Flatbush, Kings County, N. Y.
Census 1800; A2 (55-23).

Flatlands, Kings County, N. Y.
Census 1800; A2 (55-25).

Fleetwood, Berks County, Pa.
Inscriptions; M (15-31).

Florida
Census 1850, persons of New England birth; A1 (76-44).

Florida, Montgomery County, N. Y.
Census 1800; A2 (50-307).

Flushing, Queens County, N. Y.
Census 1800; A2 (54-213).

Fluvanna County, Va.
Abstracts of wills, 1777-1784; V1 (11-60).

Fonda, Montgomery County, N. Y.
Marriages, 1772-1795; Z (50-338).

Fordham, Westchester County, N. Y.
Census, 1698; A2 (38-218).
Census, 1800; A2 (59-35).

Fort Ann, Washington County, N. Y.
Inscriptions; A2 (46-277).

Fort Pownal, Me.
F1 (7-61; 9-23); Muster roll, 1759; F1 (9-33).
Garrison, 1774; F1 (6-106).

Foster, R. I.
Diary of Elisha Fish, 1785-1799; A1 (56-121).

Foxborough, Mass.
Warnings, 1779-1796; A1 (65-39).

Framingham, Mass.
Deaths, 1757-1803; A1 (65-356).

Framlingham, Eng.
A1 (57-193).

France
Nobility; E (10-219).

Francestown, N. H.
Sketch; S2 (23-85).

Franconia, N. H.
Sketch; S2 (21-148).

Frankfort, Me.
Petition, 1807; F1 (3-150).
Settlers, 1793; F1 (6-243).
Inscriptions; F1 (8-224).

Franklin County, Ga.
Abstract of Deeds, 1784-1802; M (13-68; 14-1).

Franklin County, Ohio
Organization; E (15-57).
County officers; E (15-65).
Land patents; E (3-183).
Marriages, 1803-1830; E (1-36, 91, 119, 183; 2-20, 61, 113, 139; 3-36, 84, 134, 188; 4-18; 7-114; 8-56; 9-184).
Commissioners' records, 1803-1807; E (7-186).
Classes, Meth. Epis. Churches, 1839-1840; E (11-181).
Revolutionary soldiers buried; Z (42-104).

Franklin County, Pa.
Inscriptions, Welsh Run; M (12-10).
Pew holders, Lower West Conococheague Church, c. 1780; P (8-203).
Revolutionary burials, Brown's Mill; M (18-64).

Franklin County, Va.
Marriages, 1786-1837; B2 (5-24).

Franklin, N. H.
Notes; S2 (3-132).
Sketch; S2 (18-153).

Franklin, Sussex County, N. J.
Notes; B6 (4-25, 108, 175, 256; 5-25, 115, 182, 256; 6-23, 85, 184).
Six-Mile Run Church, baptisms 1743-1805; B6 (8-123, 211, 264).
Inscriptions; B1 (6-53).
Inhabitants, 1825; B6 (7-47, 128).

Franklin, Licking County, Ohio
Inscriptions; E (15-178).
Franklin, Williamson County, Tenn.
Marriages, 1807; Z (57-677).
Franklin Park, N. J.
Inscriptions; B6 (3-135, 221, 298).
Franklinton, Ohio
Settlement; E (15-36).
Frederick County, Md.
Record sources; X1 (25-206).
All Saints Parish records; P (7-245).
List, oath of fidelity, 1778; M (6-33).
Revolutionary soldiers, 1778; X1 (6-256).
Journal of Committee of Observation, 1775-1776; with list of Associators; X1 (10-301; 11-50, 157, 237, 304; 12-10).
Frederick County, Va.
Notes; V1 (6-272).
Marriages, 1782-1788; Z (47-80).
Frederick, Frederick County, Md.
Inscriptions; M (8-19).
Fredericktown, Steuben County, N. Y.
Census 1800; A2 (60-53).
Freeport, Me.
Marriage intentions, 1789-1801; C1 (1-59).
Freetown, Mass.
Vital records; K (4-33).
French and Indian Wars
Tuscarora Expedition, 1711; J (9-28; 10-33).
Capitulation of Louisbourg, 1745; A1 (57-214).
Roll of artificers and laborers, Louisbourg, 1745; A1 (55-65).
Soldiers, Me., 1745; K (2-62).
Sailors, Louisbourg Expedition, 1745; A1 (59-192).
Louisbourg Expedition, 1745, New England naval participation; A1 (77-59, 95).
Louisbourg expedition, 1745 (Cleaves Journal); A1 (66-113).
Redeemed captives, 1747; A1 (70-260).
Letters and papers, 1723-1750; P (9-141).
Journal, Crown Point, 1759; A1 (60-236).
Officers, 1754-1763; A1 (77-239).
Va., Augusta County troops; N2 (3-127).
Diary of Capt. Charles Lewis, Va., 1755; M (1-17).
Officers, Va. Regt., 1762; M (1-20).
Capt. Thomas Hobby's company, Conn., 1761; B3 (3-106).
Maine prisoners, 1754-58; F1 (2-58).
Me., Petition of soldiers, 1762; F1 (8-174).

French and Indian Wars—Cont.
Me., Capt. Berry's Co., Fort Pownal, 1759; F1 (9-33).
Roll, Maj. Richard Godfrey's Mass. Regt., 1758; A1 (58-141).
Roll of Capt. Timothy Hamant's Mass. Co., 1762; A1 (56-74).
Orderly book of Sergt. Josiah Perry, Dudley, Mass., 1759-60; A1 (54-70, 164).
Diary of Capt. Asa Foster, Andover, Mass., 1758; A1 (54-183).
Diary, 1759; C4 (1-307, 339).
Maine soldiers; C2 (2-157, 215).
Newbury company, 1755; C2 (3-89).
Mass. company, 1755; C2 (4-266).
Military roll, Bridgewater, Mass.; A1 (51-159).
Roster of Md. troops, 1757-1759; X1 (5-271).
Md. soldiers, lists; X1 (9-260, 348).
Muster-Roll, Capt. Theo. Terry's N. Y. Company; A2 (26-73).
Wounded, Col. Titcomb's Regt., 1755; Y1 (58-176).
Dwight Journal (1755); A2 (33-3, 65, 164).
Westchester County Muster Roll; A2 (37-201, 266; 38-15, 87).
Maxatawney Volunteers, 1756, Pa.; P (8-201).
Soldiers from Warren and Barrington, R. I.; A1 (56-362).
Va. soldiers; V2 (1-208).
Seafaring, Md.; X1 (10-1).
List, killed and wounded with Braddock, 1755; Q1 (27-499).
Letters of Col. Whiting; T2 (6-133).
French Spoliation Claims
History; R. I. claimants; F4 (4-202).
Friedensburg
See Oley.
Friends
See Quakers.
Friendship, Me.
Tax list, 1798; K (4-150).
Poll list, 1817; A1 (83-375).
Funeral Rings
(Deaths records); C1 (1-45, 102); C2 (1-221).
Gahanna, Ohio
Inscriptions; E (11-152).
Galena, Ill.
Catholic Parish Registers, 1827-1833; G1 (22-164).
Gallipolis, Ohio
Inscriptions; E (7-178).
Galloway, Atlantic County, N. J.
B1 (5-17).
Gambier, Knox County, Ohio
Inscriptions; E (4-134; 5-13).
Gates County, N. C.
Abstract of wills; H (2-39).

Glastonbury, Conn.
Inscriptions; A1 (60-139; 85-57, 159, 305, 401).
Eastbury [Buckingham] Parish records, 1767-1826; A1 (60-376; 61-84, 190, 293, 387; 62-83, 192, 291, 375; 63-67).

Glastonbury, co. Somerset, Eng.
Lay subsidy; C4 (1-30).

Gloucester County, N. J.
Marriages, 1799-1801; Q1 (25-594).
Early Vital records; Q1 (27-80).
Swedish settlers; Q1 (17-83).
Court records, 1752-62; Q1 (37-207).
Court records, extracts, 1781-83; Q1 (42-69).
Revolutionary records; P (10-198).

Gloucester County, Va.
Marriage licenses, 1777-1778; V1 (5-57).

Gloucester, Mass.
Inscriptions; Y2 (9-1, 68, 106, 152).
Marriages, 1761-1764; A1 (56-318).
See also Rockport.

Goffstown, N. H.
Sketch; S2 (24-249).

Goochland County, Va.
Marriage Bonds, 1787-1823; Z (55-50).

Goose Creek, S. C.
Members of Club, 1740; J (27-187).
Settlers and history; J (29-1, 71, 167, 265).
Vital records, 1807-1830; J (29-164).

Gorham, Me.
Inscriptions; F2 (1-129, 197).
Tax list, 1799; F2 (1-200).

Goschenhoppen, Montgomery County, Pa.
Reformed Church, history and records, 1731-1833; Q2 (vols. 27, 28).
Catholic registers, 1741-1819; G1 (2-316; 3-295; 8-330; 11-43, 196, 303).
Marriages, 1731-1790; Q3 (2-137, 179).

Gosport, N. H.
Church records; A1 (66-141, 209, 294).
Town records; A1 (67-56, 132, 231, 354; 68-32, 127).

Gouldsborough, Me.
Marriages and intentions, 1789-1806; F1 (6-248).
History; F1 (7-67).

Granby, Conn.
Inscriptions; A1 (70-91).

Granville, Licking County, Ohio
E (8-235, 245, 255).
Baptist Church records, 1819-1833; E (8-260).
St. Luke's (Epis.) records, 1827-1861; E (8-283).
Presbyterian Church records, 1805-1822; E (8-382).

Granville—Cont.
Inscriptions; E (8-405, 416, 429, 435).
Soldiers, all wars; E (8-398).

Granville Female College
With list of graduates; E (8-317).

Gravesend, Kings County, N. Y.
Census 1800; A2 (55-121).
Quaker Records; A2 (4-39).
Vital Records; A2 (4-199).
Historical; A2 (16-97).

Gray, Me.
Petition, 1777; F2 (8-185).

Great Barrington, Mass.
St. James's Epis. Church records; C2 (7-152, 169, 199); C3 (1-53, 126, 179, 227; 2-16).
Inscriptions; A1 (53-396; 54-69; 76-174).
Inscriptions (Van Deusen); A2 (29-42).

Green County, Ohio
Aged residents, 1820; M (5-47, 7-43).

Green Bay, Wis.
Early memoirs; E (7-160).

Greene County, Ga.
Index to wills, 1786-1806; M (19-14).

Greene County, Tenn.
Tax list, 1783; Z (53-199).

Greenfield, Mass.
Church records, 1761-1812; A1 (62-263).
New settlers, 1767-1770; A1 (64-188).
Town records, 1775-1780; C2 (4-25).

Greenfield, Saratoga County, N. Y.
Church Records, 1792-1814; A2 (34-141, 212, 284; 35-29).

Greenland, N. H.
Marriages, 1710-1737; A1(65-351).

Greensburgh, Westchester County, N. Y.
Census 1800; A2 (58-249).

Greensburg, Westmoreland County, Pa.
Inscriptions; M (19-59); P (6-26, 29).
Father Helbron's Bapt. Register, 1799-1822; G1 (26-250, 371; 27-65, 161, 346; 28-85, 135, 266, 297).

Greensville County, Va.
Court's Valuation of impressed property, 1782; V1 (5-269).
Marriage Bonds, 1781-1827; V1 (2-248; 3-58, 194; 6-177, 285; 7-57).

Greenville County, S. C.
Abstracts of Court of Ordinary records, 1787-1789; J (26-214).

Greenville, Monmouth County, N. J.
Inscriptions; B1 (5-44).

Greenwich, Conn.
Vital Records; A2(36-196).
Marriages, 1681-1730; Z (44-322).
Revolutionary soldiers buried; Z (44-384).
St. John's (Epis.) Church records; B3 (4-115, 332).
Inscriptions; A1 (58-405).

Greenwich, N. Y.
Inscriptions; A2 (47-385; 48-4, 104, 299, 399; 49-22, 120).
Groton, Conn.
Inscriptions; A2 (7-14).
Soldiers and Patriots, Rev. War; Z (27-705, 782).
Groton, N. H.
History; S2 (7-278; 9-52, 142, 195, 230, 272).
Groton, Tompkins County, N. Y.
Inscriptions; A2 (53-401; 54-73, 167).
Groveland, Mass.
Genealogical notes, 1863; Y1 (55-241).
Church admissions, dismissions; Y1 (59-81).
Inscriptions; Y2 (10-1).
Groveport, Franklin County, Ohio
Inscriptions; E (8-152).
Guilford County, N. C.
Abstracts of wills; M (17-44).
Guilford, Conn.
Fourth Church records, 1743-1788; A1 (58-299, 360; 59-61).
Inscriptions; T2 (4-405).
Hackensack, N. J.
Early settlers; A2 (7-133).
Haddonfield, N. J.
Inscriptions; B1 (5-45).
See Newton.
Hadley, Mass.
Deaths 1748, from diary; A1 (55-442).
Soldiers, 1695; A1 (55-343).
Hagerstown, Washington County, Md.
Inscriptions; M (8-1).
Probate distributions; M (18-31).
Halifax County, Va.
Marriage Bonds, 1754-1830; V1 (4-58).
Halifax, Mass.
Church records, from 1734; D (26-176; 27-24, 117, 179).
Inscriptions; D (9-151; 10-8, 103; 12-239; 13-11, 150, 217; 14-5).
Vital records; D (3-30, 157; 4-20, 103; 5-151; 6-49; 7-48, 110).
Hamburg, Sussex County, N. J.
Inscriptions; A2 (56-43).
Hamden, Conn.
Deaths, 1801-1847; B4 (4-1015; 5-1249; 6-1529).
Burials, 1789-1850; B4 (6-1792).
Pay roll, Goodyear's Co., 1777; M (9-45).
Hamden, Vinton County, Ohio
Inscriptions; E (7-179, 180).
Hamilton, Mass.
Inscriptions; Y2 (11-7).
Hampden, Me.
Early settlers; F1 (2-25).

Hampden—Cont.
Inscriptions; F1 (4-96).
First Cong. Church; F1 (4-113).
Family records; F1 (6-181, 245).
Hampshire County, W. Va.
Records; M (15-49).
County records; V1 (5-247).
Hampton, Mass.
Vital records (from County records); Y2 (5-46, 77, 133; 11-32, 34).
Hampton, N. H.
Grantees, settlers, genealogical; Y1 (53-228).
Vital records; F3 (2-81, 105).
Deaths, 1727-1755; A1 (58-29, 136).
Sketch; S2 (21-1).
Marriages by Samuel Perley, 1767-1782; A1 (51-460).
Hampton Falls, N. H.
Baptisms, 1735; A1 (66-151).
First Church Records, 1712-1736; C2 (5-93, 112; 6-234).
Hampton, Sussex County, N. J.
Inscriptions; B1 (1-71).
Hancock County, Me.
Lawyers; F1 (2-173).
Representatives before 1820; F1 (3-138).
Probate before 1800; F1 (3-157; 4-65; 7-96).
Early deeds; F1 (4-72; 5-141; 6-257).
Rev. pensioners; F1 (7-98).
Handwriting
Colonial; Y2 (1-175).
Hanover, N. H.
Vital records (Rev. John Smith); A1 (70-150).
Hanover, Morris County, N. J.
Pres. Church, baptisms, 1796-1819; B1 (6-33, 77, 101).
First Church, marriages 1746-1796; Z (56-535).
Revolutionary soldiers buried; Z (35-993).
Hanover, Licking County, Ohio
Inscriptions; E (12-216).
Hanover, Va.
Petition, 1783; Z (56-209).
Hanson, Mass.
Inscriptions; D (9-140).
Hardy County, W. Va.
County records, 1786-1811; V1 (5-240).
Hardyston, Sussex County, N. J.
Inscriptions; B1 (1-99).
Harford County, Md.
Record sources; X1 (26-135).
Place names; X1 (25-321).
Marriage Licenses, 1779-1838; P (8-151).
Muster rolls, Rev. War; Z (31-543, 544; 32-277).
Harford, Susquehanna County, Pa.
Settlers, 1790; A2 (55-37).

Harlem, Me.
See China, Me.
Harlem, N. Y.
Reformed Dutch Church, marriages
1816-1836; A2 (8-41).
Harlingen, N. J.
Church records, 1727-1734; A2 (40-
281).
Harpswell, Cumberland County, Me.
Vital records; C3 (2-179; 3-19, 71,
151; 4-21, 205); C4 (1-89; 2-87).
Harpswell Centre, Me.
Inscriptions; F2 (9-324).
Harpswell District, Me.
Petition, 1768; F1 (2-120).
Harrington, Me.
Inscriptions; F1 (3-152; 4-91).
Early settlers; F1 (8-222).
Harrison County, W. Va.
Marriages, early; Z (48-190).
Harrison, Westchester County, N. Y.
Census 1800; A2 (57-116).
Quaker Records; A2 (3-45).
Hartford, Conn.
Early vital and land records; T3
(vol. 14).
Church controversy, 1656-59; T3 (2-
51).
Town votes, 1635-1716; T 3(vol. 6).
Census, 1670; T3 (21-195).
Inscriptions; A2 (7-14).
Sexton's list, Center Church Grave-
yard; B3 (4-180, 264, 417; 5-118,
186, 242, 290, 336, 382, 426, 481,
520).
Diary of William Watson, 1819-1836;
A1 (79-298, 401; 80-54).
Hartford, Trumbull County, Ohio
Inscriptions; E (2-152).
Hartford, Vt.
Revolutionary history; C3 (3-115).
Hartland, Conn.
Church records, beginning 1768; A1
(60-392; 61-31).
Harvard, Mass.
Shaker records; A1 (61-341).
Harvard College
A1 (51-26).
Bells, A1 (65-275).
Harwich, Mass.
Vital records; D (3-174; 4-175, 207;
5-86, 202; 6-54, 82; 7-194; 8-34, 105,
159, 217; 11-173, 248; 13-55, 66,
147; 19-55, 116; 20-24; 23-55, 117;
24-110, 150; 25-60, 100).
First Church (now in Brewster)
records; D (4-242; 5-17; 6-152, 215;
7-33, 93, 146; 8-119, 247; 9-207; 10-
123, 130, 251; 12-52, 156, 252; 13-
36, 98, 135).
Inscriptions; D (12-256; 13-2, 235;
14-27).

Haverhill, Mass.
Church admissions, dismissions; Y1
(57-141).
Captives, 1701; Y2 (3-61).
Vital records (from County rec-
ords); Y2 (4-139, 175; 5-12).
In 1700; Y2 (3-161).
Inscriptions; Y2 (12-1, 62, 78, 108,
152, 155).
Haverstraw, Rockland County, N. Y.
Census 1800; A2 (62-81).
Havre de Grace, Md.
Early settlers; X1 (13-197).
Hawke, N. H.
Church records, 1764-1781; A1 (58-
41, 121).
Hebron, Licking County, Ohio
Inscriptions; E (13-52).
Heidelberg, Davie County, N. C.
Lutheran Church records; M (19-4).
Heidelberg, Berks County, Pa.
Church records, 1745-1805; P (5-53).
Inscriptions; M (9-33).
Hempstead, Queens County, N. Y.
Census 1698; A2 (45-54).
Census 1800; A2 (54-27, 112).
First Presbyterian Church Records,
1805-1893; A2 (53-235, 381; 54-30,
138).
Inscriptions; A2 (54-201, 335; 55-72,
154, 243).
Proprietors, 1647; A2 (10-9).
Quaker records, Westbury; A2 (16-
171; 17-218).
St. George's Church Records, 1725-;
A2 (9-182; 10-16, 89, 133; 11-47, 88,
133; 12-45, 78, 141; 13-93, 140; 14-
43, 70, 116; 15-77, 111, 176; 24-79).
Vital records; A2 (54-42; 55-270, 368;
56-19).
Hempstead, Rockland County, N. Y.
Census 1800; A2 (62-76).
Henniker, N. H.
Sketch; S2 (17-287).
Heraldry
A1 (60-94; 72-147); A2 (49-4; 50-338;
52-229; 56-143, 296); B1 (3-95); C2
(3-113, 214, 306; 4-101, 133); C3
(5-155); C4 (2-19); D (2-160); E
(2-110; 7-38); M (2-21, 48; 3-2-2);
F2 (8-121); S1 (15-54); U (5-32).
Arms of American families; A1 (82-
146).
Herkimer County, N. Y.
Revolutionary soldiers buried; Z (61-
697).
Hillsborough County, N. H.
Organization; S2 (29-236).
Hillsborough, N. H.
Vital records, 1772-1795; C2 (2-206).
Sketch; S2 (22-154).
Hillsborough, Somerset County, N. Y.
Millstone Church records, 1767-1825;
B6 (7-199, 306; 8-132, 184).

Hinsdale, Mass.
Cong. Church, baptisms 1797-1850;
A1 (57-288, 357).
Hinsdale, N. H.
Inscriptions; A1 (52-478).
Holden, Me.
Church members, 1813-1821; F1 (5-91).
Family records; F1 (6-78).
Holden, Mass.
First Church records, 1743-1822; A1
(58-274, 371).
Holderness, N. H.
Sketch; S2 (23-279).
Holland
Records; M (16-33); U (23-76).
Noble and titled surnames; A2 (15-69).
See also Dutch genealogy, Genealogy
and New York, N. Y.
Hollis, Hillsborough County, N. H.
Revolutionary soldiers buried; Z (37-240).
Sketch; S2 (24-95).
Homer, Mich.
Revolutionary soldiers buried; Z (49-275).
Homer, Onondaga County, N. Y.
Census 1800; A2 (53-362).
Hoosick, Rensselaer County, N. Y.
Vital records, 1782-1844; A1 (82-255).
Hopewell, Dutchess County, N. Y.
Inscriptions; A2 (39-242).
Hopewell, Mercer County, N. J.
Inscriptions; B1(6-41).
Hopewell, York County, Pa.
Church register (Lutheran), 1761-1831; Q2 (8-155).
Hopkinton, N. H.
Notes; C2 (7-25).
Churches; S2 (2-22).
Hopkinton, R. I.
List of patriots, 1776; F4 (4-138).
Hornellsville, N. Y.
Revolutionary soldiers buried; Z (20-222; 22-650, 971).
Horseneck, Conn.
Troops, 1778-1782; Z (17-570).
Horton, Neb.
Inscriptions; B2 (1-55).
Houlton, Me.
Early settlers; F1 (3-14).
Inscriptions; F1 (4-109).
Huguenots
N. J.; (24-49).
Hull, Mass.
A1 (59-177).
Hunterdon County, N. J.
Marriages, 1778-1780; B1 (4-27).
Marriages, 1768-1793; baptisms,
1768-1772; Q1 (12-222).
Hunter's Point, Va.
Inscriptions; M (16-7).

Huntingdon County, Pa.
Inscriptions; M (15-28).
Huntington, Mass.
Marriages, 1785-1797; Z (61-588).
Huntington, Suffolk County, N. Y.
Census 1800; A2 (55-339; 56-9).
Inscriptions; A2 (31-113, 142, 247;
32-47, 93, 176, 228; 33-97; 60-264).
Vital records; A2 (50-72, 127).
Inscriptions; A1 (66-226).
Miscellaneous records; T7 (vols. 59-60, 1926-1927; *in particular*, vol. 59,
pp. 319-334).
Huntington, Ross County, Ohio
Inscriptions; E (6-96).
**Hunt's Point, Westchester County,
N. Y.**
Inscriptions; A2 (15-42).
Huron County, Ohio
Revolutionary soldiers buried; Z (22-23).
Hyde Precinct, N. C.
Freeholders, 1715; H (3-425).
Illinois
Irish settlers; G2 (9-331).
List of Episcopal records; E (1-81).
Revolutionary officers; M (16-52).
Indian Wars
See Pequot War; King Philip's
War; French and Indian Wars.
Indiana
List of Episcopal records; E (1-80).
See Post Vincennes.
Inscriptions
New York, New Jersey, Conn.; A2
(45-182, 270).
Iowa
Revolutionary soldiers buried in; P
(8-202); Z (27-27).
Ipswich, Essex County, Mass.
Petitioners, 1658; C2(5-135).
Roll, minute men, 1775; A1 (56-83).
Church records, 1749-1849; Y1 (55-33, 129).
Division of land, 1720; Y1 (58-151).
Church admissions; Y1 (58-233).
Capt. Burnham's Co., 1775; F2 (8-244).
Capt. Dodge's Co., 1775; F2 (9-310).
Capt. Parker's Co., 1776; F2 (9-312).
Col. Wade's Co., 1776; F2 (9-314).
Vital records, 1657-1659; F2 (9-355).
Miscellaneous records; F2 (8-242; 9-18, 37, 67, 120, 144, 173, 209, 229,
270, 309, 346, 355).
Soldiers, 1724; Y2 (1-149).
In 1700; Y2 (6-14).
Pequot War soldiers; Y2 (3-119).
Inscriptions; Y2 (13-1, 58, 114, 156).
Ireland
Record sources, with extracts; U (8-11, 15, 86; 9-75).
Muster roll, Ulster, 1630; Q1 (36-257).

Kinderhook, N. Y.
Marriages, 1735-1774; Z (58-95).
Baptisms, 1725-1728; Z (59-246).
King and Queen County, Va.
Tax list, 1787; V2 (2-144).
King George County, Va.
Recruits, 1781; V1 (9-202).
Patriots, 1782; V1 (5-54).
Tax list, 1782; V2 (1-238).
King Philip's War
Great Swamp Fight; F4 (5-331).
Me. petition, 1676; F2 (6-357).
King's College
Alumni, 1758-1774; A2 (25-123, 174; 26-5, 83, 120, 185; 27-35, 106).
Kings County, N. Y.
Abstracts of deeds; A2 (48-110, 291, 355; 54-105, 241, 303).
Abstracts of wills; A2 (47-161, 227; 48-79).
See Flatbush, Flatlands, Gravesend, New Utrecht, Brooklyn, Bushwick.
Kings County, R. I.
Slaves enlisted, Continental Army; F4 (1-313).
Kingston, Mass.
Inscriptions; D (7-20, 82, 167, 221).
Vital records; K (2-1, 39, 119; 3-22, 77; 4-14, 68).
Kingston, N. H.
Church record, 1725; C3 (1-37).
First Church Records, 1725-1755; F3 (2-43, 65, 129; 3-37, 86, 129, 167; 4-173; 5-17, 103, 153; 6-26).
Sketch; S2 (17-351).
Kingston, N. Y.
Inscriptions; A2 (58-319).
Kinsman, Trumbull County, Ohio
Inscriptions; E (2-155).
Kirkersville, Licking County, Ohio
Inscriptions; E (11-69).
Kittery, Me.
Early history; A1 (71-89).
Marriage intentions, 1717-1723; F2 (1-47).
Ear marks, 1702-1712; F2 (6-422).
Military lists, 1722, 1754-62; F2 (3-160; 8-115).
Land division, 1744; F2 (7-122).
Miscellaneous records; F2 (1-21, 65, 133; 3-159; 4-50; 5-122; 7-207).
Early settlers; F2 (9-252).
Remonstrance, 1784; A1 (54-444).
Petition, 1799; F2 (1-146).
Tax lists, 1756-1770; A1 (55-249).
Quakers, 1734; F2 (1-65).
Knox County, Tenn.
Index to Probate Records, 1792-1803; Z (58-98).
Laconia, N. H.
Sketch; S2 (17-62).
Lafayette, Sussex County, N. J.
Inscriptions; B1 (6-17).

Lake Mahopac, Putnam County, N. Y.
Inscriptions; A2 (56-68, 289, 290, 308).
Lamington, Somerset County, N. J.
Church petition, 1792; B6 (6-179).
Inscriptions; B6 (2-310; 3-132; 225, 295; 4-61, 134).
Lampeter, Lancaster County, Pa.
Inscriptions; P (10-63).
Lancaster County, Neb.
Marriage records, 1866-1869; B2 (9-50).
Probate records, 1869-1872; B2 (9-36).
School census, 1875; B2 (9-41).
Lancaster County, Pa.
German pioneers; S1 (18-34).
Swiss settlers; M (8-36, 39).
Ephrata registers, 1728-1813; Q1 (14-297, 387).
Inscriptions; M (14-33).
Revolutionary soldiers, 1781; Q1 (19-125).
Lancaster County, Va.
Inscriptions, Christ Church; M (7-30).
Lancaster, Mass.
Loyalists; S2 (9-40).
History; S2 (9-351).
Lancaster, Neb.
Inscriptions; B2 (1-9).
Lancaster, N. H.
Sketch; S2 (16-329).
Lancaster, Seneca County, N. Y.
Inscriptions; A2 (35-200).
Lancaster, Ohio
Inscriptions; E (3-28, 71; 6-46).
Lancaster, Pa.
First Reformed Church, births and baptisms, 1736-1800; Q2 (4-249; 5-203).
Burials, Moravian Church, 1744-1821; P (10-140, 259; 11-55).
Trinity Lutheran Church, births and baptisms, 1747-1799; Q2 (3-191; 4-189; 5-173; 6-251).
St. Mary's (Cath.) Church, registers, 1795-1804; G1 (25-259, 342).
Furnishers of forage, 1778-1779; M (16-28, 41).
Lists of firemen, 1766; Q1 (3-469).
Inscriptions; M (19-79, 98, 99); P (11-89).
Catholic Church, sketch; G1 (5-305).
Land
Transferring title; A1 (65-265).
Landisville, Atlantic County, N. J.
Inscriptions; B1 (6-14, 54).
Lanesborough, Mass.
Inscriptions; B2 (3-187).
Lansing, Tompkins County, N. Y.
Inscriptions; A2 (54-173, 285, 358; 55-15).

Laurens County, S. C.
Probate records and deeds; M (17-45).
Lawrence County, Pa.
Epitaphs, Neshannock; Q1 (29-370).
Lebanon, Conn.
Inscriptions; A1 (60-370; 74-53, 108).
Lebanon, Me.
Vital records; A1 (69-281).
Lebanon, N. H.
Vital records, 1765-1789; C3 (2-233).
Inscriptions; C3 (2-248; 3-147, 187).
Settlers and history; S2 (12-114, 117, 145).
Sketch; S2 (16-227).
Lebanon, Pa.
Furnishers of forage, 1778-1779; M (16-42).
Lee, Penobscot County, Me.
Civil War soldiers; F1 (9-159).
Lee, N. H.
Marriages, from 1801; F3 (4-75, 125, 181).
Lehigh County, Pa.
St. Paul's Evang. Lutheran Congregation, records 1750-1764; Q1 (35-188).
Marriages and burials, 1790-1810; P (5-6).
Great Swamp Reformed Church, Lower Milford Tp., records 1736-1833; Q2 (28-437).
School children, Allentown, 1815; Q1 (21-413).
Lempster, N. H.
Notes; S2 (3-465).
Lenora, Kans.
Inscriptions; B2 (1-43).
Lenox, Mass.
Early deeds; B3 (2-289, 396).
Non-consumption agreement, 1774, with list; Z (61-691).
Lenox, Madison County, N. Y.
Vital Records, 1848-1849; B2 (1-31, 49, 65).
Leominster, Mass.
Revolutionary soldiers; Z (47-180).
Lewes, Del.
Inscriptions; Q1 (31-372).
Lewis County, N. Y.
Revolutionary soldiers buried; Z (48-435).
Lewisburg, Pa.
Revolutionary soldiers buried; Z (25-864).
Licking County, Ohio
Inscriptions; E (15-26, 28, 29, 181, 193, 194, 195, 199, 200, 203).
Marriages, 1808-1821; E (12-206; 13-47, 194).
Revolutionary soldiers buried; Z (33-898; 35-31, 399, 620, 994).

Limington, Me.
Marriage intentions, 1814-1822; A1 (85-447).
Lincoln County, Me.
Organization; F1 (3-121).
Marriages, 1759-1777; F1 (4-140, 159; 9-135).
Deeds, F1 (5-24; 6-34; 7-144, 202; 8-93; 9-102, 131).
Early Probate; F1 (6-265; 7-38).
Petitions, 1752; K (3-1).
Lincoln, Me.
Notes; F1 (1-89).
Masonic Lodge; F1 (8-25).
Lincolnville, Me.
Early settlers; F1 (5-166; 6-243).
Lindsley, Steuben County, N. Y.
Census 1800; A2 (60-50).
Linwood, Atlantic County, N. J.
Inscriptions; B1 (5-85; 6-86, 119).
Lisbon, Conn.
Separatist Church; C4 (1-232).
Lisbon, N. H.
Notes; S2 (10-95).
Lisle, Tioga County, N. Y.
Census 1800; A2 (59-232).
Litchfield County, Conn.
Pension Applications, Rev. War; Z (24-415, 515).
Litchfield, Me.
Early items; F2 (3-14).
Little Compton, R. I.
Inscriptions; F4 (7-425).
Little Falls, Me.
Militia roll, 1778; F2 (8-232).
Littleton, N. H.
Sketch; S2 (5-292; 17-165).
Livingston, Columbia County, N. Y.
Committee of Safety, Revolutionary War; A2 (60-239, 325).
Locke, Cayuga County, N. Y.
Inscriptions; A2 (53-323).
London, Eng.
See English Parish Registers.
Londonderry, co. Ulster, Ireland
Muster rolls, 1630, 1663; Q1 (38-355).
Londonderry, N. H.
Early settlers; A1 (51-467).
Londontown, Anne Arundel County, Md.
Historical; X1 (19-134).
Long Island, N. Y.
Printed records of towns; A2 (48-75).
Settlers from New England; A1 (55-297, 377).
Suffolk County Marriages; see Suffolk County.
Inventories, Suffolk County, 1670-1692; A2 (12-132).
Revolutionary soldiers buried; Z (49-340).

Long Pond, Putnam County, N. Y.
Inscriptions; A2 (56-290).
Lorain County, Ohio
Revolutionary soldiers buried; Z (22-22).
Loretto, Cambria County, Pa.
Paschal Confessions, Communions, and Confirmations; G1 (3-399).
Lost Creek, Pa.
Marriages, 1806-1844; P (11-66, 163).
Loudoun County, Va.
Marriages, 1793-1796; Z (45-152); M (9-47).
Louisiana
Sources; Q1 (39-110).
Louisville, Ky.
Revolutionary soldiers buried; Z (44-258).
Lowell, Me.
Civil War soldiers; F1 (9-98).
Lowell, Mass.
Sketch; S2 (9-299).
Lower Dublin, Pa.
Pennypack Baptist Church records, 1689-1732; Q1 (11-58).
Lower Merion, Pa.
Revolutionary soldiers buried; Z (21-299).
Lower Providence, Montgomery County, Pa.
Inscriptions; P (8-27).
Lower Salford, Montgomery County, Pa.
Inscriptions; M (8-62; 9-14).
Lower Springfield, Burlington County, N. J.
Inscriptions; B1 (4-71).
Loyalists
Military organizations; Q1 (39-493).
Annapolis County, N. S., 1784; A2 (33-214, 34-38).
Disbanded Officers and Loyalists, N. S.; A2 (34-259).
Digby, Annapolis County, Nova Scotia; A2 (28-81; 34-118, 192).
New Brunswick; A2 (35-38, 87, 165, 277; 36-27, 185, 286; 37-11, 131, 209, 303; 38-10, 140, 171, 251; 39-14, 187, 243; 40-23, 115).
N. J. Company; A2 (52-256).
Georgia; A1 (62-300).
Lancaster, Mass.; S2 (9-40).
Penobscot, Me.; F1 (1-97; 5-89; 8-11).
Md.; X1 (1-316; 2-133; 4-287).
North Carolina; H (2-208, 390, 566).
Pa. Dragoons, 1777; Q1 (34-1).
Rhode Island; F4 (3-52, 132, 202, 263; 4-77).
So. Car.; J (14-36).
In South Wales; S1 (13-146).

Lubec, Me.
Inscriptions; F1 (3-196).
Early settlers; F1 (9-231).
See Eastport.
Lunenburg County, Va.
Marriage Bonds, 1763-1810; V1 (8-35).
Lunenburg, Mass.
Revolutionary soldiers; C2 (7-245).
Luzerne County, Pa.
Early history; Pw (13-93).
See Wyoming Valley.
Lycoming County, Pa.
Marriages, 1808-1847; Z (46-114).
Lyme, Conn.
Inscriptions; A1 (61-75).
Marriages, 1825-1826; A1 (81-272).
Inscriptions; A1 (78-365).
See Old Lyme, East Lyme.
Lyme, N. H.
Note on records; C4 (3-31).
Lynn, Mass.
Vital records; C3 (4-1).
First Church, history; Y2 (1-151).
Lyons, Berks County, Pa.
Inscriptions; M (12-21).
Lysander, Onondaga County, N. Y.
Census 1800; A2 (53-366).
Machackemeck, N. Y.
See Port Jervis, Deerpark.
Machias, Me.
Early settlers; F1 (8-70).
Early deeds; F1 (4-163).
Muster roll, 1777; F1 (6-105).
Marriages, 1776-1797; F1 (9-35).
Marriage intentions, 1796-1810; F1 (6-143; 9-74).
Inscriptions; F1 (2-44, 89).
Petition; F1 (3-5).
Naval battle, 1775; F1 (3-161).
Enlistments, 1777; F1 (4-78).
Madison County, Ill.
Revolutionary soldiers buried; Z (41-203).
Madison County, N. Y.
Revolutionary soldiers buried; Z (37-314).
Madison County, Ohio
4th Co., 1st Brig., 1st Regt., 13th Div., 1843; E (8-146).
Madison, Licking County, Ohio
Inscriptions; E (13-97).
Mahoning County, Ohio
Revolutionary soldiers buried; Z (22-22).
Maine
Town and County Records, location, condition; C2 (2-31, 72, 109; 4-113).
Towns, incorporated before 1820; F1 (9-133, 214).
Names of towns, modern, ancient; F1 (5-28).
Settlements before 1620; F2 (2-207).
Wills, list to 1760; F2 (9-109).

Maine—Cont.
Early probate items; F2 (2-129, 197, 258; 3-52, 128, 200, 273).
Abstracts of deeds; A1 (62-94).
Land grants, east of Penobscot River; F1 (1-29).
Petition, 1752; F1 (3-187).
Early marriages, eastern Me.; F1 (6-235).
Eastern Claims; F2 (4-105, 278; 5-33, 106, 151, 209; 6-276, 433, 469; 7-15, 73, 146, 186; 8-19, 77, 177, 198).
Depositions; F2 (5-161).
Marriages from newspaper, 1800; F2 (1-15, 45).
"Founders"; F2 (1-86, 149, 211).
French Spoliation Claims; F2 (9-297).
Royalists, 1665; F2 (1-145).
Garrisons, 1711; F2 (2-113).
Garrisons and forts; F2 (5-173).
Soldiers, Canada Expedition, 1690; F2 (4-245).
Early Irish records; G2 (12-129).
Colleges and Academies; F1 (3-137).
Col. McCobb's Regt., 1777; F1 (4-119).
Presidential Electors, 1789-1816; F1 (4-127).
Attorneys; F1 (7-31).
Inscriptions, miscellaneous; F1 (5-19; 9-99, 219); F2 (4-113).
Ministers, East Me. Conference, 1848-88; F1 (5-35).
Governors, 1820-1892; F1 (7-121).
Maj. Treat's Day Book, names 1786-90; F1 (5-93).
Mills, eastern Me.; F1 (6-18).
Deaths, from newspapers, 1815-1830; F1 (6-156).
Early settlers, eastern Me.; F1 (8-1).
Revolutionary soldiers buried; F1 (8-239); Z (36-409; 41-169).
Land grants, 1785-1820; F1 (9-48, 72).
Islands under Contract, before 1820; F1 (9-73).
Letters in Post-Offices, 1786-1804; F2 (1-22, 141).
Officers, Aroostook War, 1839; F1 (2-121; 6-118).
Majorbiguaduce, Me.
Settlers, 1761-1784; F1 (8-55).
Maldon, Eng.
A1 (62-162).
Mamaroneck, Westchester County, N. Y.
Oaths of Allegiance, 1698; A2 (59-68).
Census 1698; A2 (59-103).
Census 1800; A2 (57-112).
Inscriptions; A2 (56-33).
Manheim, Montgomery County, N. Y.
Census 1800; A2 (49-288).

Manlius, Onondaga County, N. Y.
Census 1800; A2 (53-355).
Mansfield, Mass.
Revolutionary records; A1 (55-170).
Mansfield, Warren County, N. J.
Inscriptions; B1 (3-154).
Mantua, Portage County, Ohio
Inscriptions; E (2-12; 3-124, 178).
Marblehead, Mass.
Church members, 1684; C3 (4-31).
Early documents; Y1 (54-22, 181, 276, 317; 55-78, 229; 56-70, 156, 202; 62-113, 201, 364; 64-122, 199; 65-369, 558; 66-21).
In 1700; Y2 (13-132, 175).
Marbletown, Ulster County, N. Y.
Inscriptions; A2 (61-114).
Marcellus, Onondaga County, N. Y.
Census 1800; A2 (53-352).
Marietta, Ohio
St. Luke's Church records, 1820-; E (2-28, 54, 141; 3-87).
Marion County, Ohio
Marriages, 1824-; E (7-176).
Revolutionary soldiers buried; Z (19-388).
Marion, Marion County, Ohio
Genealogical Notes and St. Paul's records; E (8-50, 206).
Marlborough, Conn.
Death of aged persons, 1856-1873; M (15-14).
Marlboro, Prince George's County, Md.
Marriage licenses, 1777-1850; Z (42-332; 43-403).
Marlborough, Mass.
Colonial records, 1656-1729; A1 (62-220, 336; 63-59, 117, 217).
Marlborough, N. H.
Sketch; S2 (21-311).
Marriages, U. S.
From newspaper *Centinel*, 1785-1794; C2 (2-229, 251; 3-16, 99, 135, 145, 283, 318; 4-58, 71, 120, 141, 188, 210, 249; 5-87, 178; 6-25, 90, 130, 166, 202, 267, 302; 7-16, 130, 187, 274, 301); C3 (1-3).
Marshall County, Kans.
Early settlers; B2 (5-89).
Marshall Hall, Md.
Inscriptions; M (15-11, 40).
Marshalton, Pa.
Marriages, 1796-1813; P (3-190).
Marshfield, Mass.
Vital records; D (2-3, 110, 179, 249; 3-41, 187; 4-125; 5-233; 6-18, 67; 7-118, 131; 8-42, 176; 9-183).
First Church records, beginning 1696; D (11-36, 121).
Census, 1765; Dx (5-41).
Inscriptions; D (8-196; 10-47, 246; 11-70; 12-54, 148, 251; 13-46, 109, 129, 241; 14-48).
Revolutionary patriots; Z (17-30).

Marshfield Hills, Mass.
Inscriptions; D (9-92, 167, 203).
Marsh Island, Me.
Early settlers; F1 (9-149).
Martha's Vineyard
Stock delivered to British, 1778; A1 (66-80).
Maryland
Parish registers; X1 (2-126).
Acadians transported to; X1 (3-1).
Accounts of ship *Rumney and Long*, 1747-61; M (6-45, 48).
Baltimore County militia, 1779; X1 (7-90).
Catholic Clergy, Diocese of Baltimore, 1819; G1 (22-238).
Chancery Depositions, index, 1668-1789; X1 (23-101, 197, 293).
Commissions, 1733-1770; X1 (26-138, 244, 342).
County marriage licenses in print; X2 (1-21).
Depositions, from land records; X1 (19-261; 20-42).
Early clergy; X1 (5-289).
Early genealogical notes; X1 (16-279, 369).
Early settlers (names Aa—Ar); X2 (1-3, 15, 21, 25; 2-3, 14, 21, 31).
Early Quaker records; P (3-197).
German settlers, with muster rolls; Q2 (vol. 22).
Governors, 1631-1692; Q1 (22-98).
Irish settlers; G2 (14-207).
Garrison at Fort Mifflin, list, 1777; X1 (5-218).
Items from Del. records; X1 (18-52, 184).
Judges, Court of Appeals, 1778-1924; X1 (20-375).
Land grants, 1633-1657; X1 (3-158).
Land records, 1634-1655; X1 (5-166, 261, 365; 6-60, 195, 262, 365; 7-183, 307, 385; 8-51, 186, 257, 332; 9-38, 170, 290).
Marriages, 1707-1712; Q1 (23-105).
Militia, lists, 1740, 1748; X1 (6-44, 180).
Militia Officers, 1776-1783; Q1 (25-583).
Rolls, Revolutionary War; T7 (vol. 47, 1914, p. 138).
Roll, Capt. Hindman's Co., 1776; Q1 (21-503).
Newspaper deaths, etc., beginning 1728; X1 (17-364; 18-22, 150, 273).
Physicians, list, 1775-1783; X1 (24-1).
Provincial Executive Officers, 1631-1776; X1 (7-321).
Rent rolls; X1 (19-341; 20-23, 183, 273; 21-285, 336; 22-259, 380; 23-26, 182, 265, 373; 24-43, 132, 228; 25-209; 26-33, 171, 264).

Maryland—Cont.
Revolutionary Associations, with lists; X1 (6-241, 305).
Capt. Price's Co., roll 1775; X1 (22-275).
Roll of 33d Batt., Md. Militia, 1777; X1 (4-379).
Roster of troops, 1757-1759; X1 (5-271).
Soldiers, French and Indian War; X1 (9-260, 348).
Tax Commissioners, 1777; M (6-21).
Tax and County Commissioners, 1777; X2 (1-5).
Cabinet makers, 1746-1820; X1 (25-1).
Wills of early Catholics; G1 (13-22).
See Montgomery County, Washington County, Frederick County, Prince George's County.
Maryville, Blount County, Tenn.
Marriages, 1791-1802; Z (57-90).
Massachusetts
Town vital records, printed; A1 (73-52).
Adventurers, Mass. Bay Colony; C4 (1-126).
Voting qualifications; Y2 (12-145).
Marriage bonds, 1687-1688; A1 (64-188).
Miscellaneous marriage records, 1727-1750; A1 (63-300).
Irish settlers; G2 (15-172; 18-145; 26-137; 29-164).
Probate, list of estates, Mass. Archives, 1666-1697; C3 (2-49).
Co., Port Royal, 1710; C4 (1-366).
Capt. Wheelock's Co., 1723; A1 (62-381).
Capt. Lovewell's Co., 1724; A1 (63-288).
Military Co., 1725; C2 (3-129).
2d Regt., 1779; Z (17-145, 252; 18-118, 131).
Rolls, Revolutionary War; T7 (vol. 47, 1914, p. 154).
Prisoners of War, 1812-15; Y1 (63-135, 217, 323).
Massachusetts, Western
Marriages, 1795-1823, Colrain, Charlemont, etc.; A1 (52-340).
Matinicus Isle, Me.
Settlers; F1 (7-113).
Mattituck, L. I.
Corrections of printed records; A2 (49-309).
Mayfield, Montgomery [now Fulton] County, N. Y.
Census 1800; A2 (50-311).
"Mayflower"
D (18-1; 22-67).
"Mayflower" Compact
D (22-53).

"Mayflower" passengers
D (6-243; 20-57; 23-13; 29-83); M (6-56).
See Plymouth.
May's Landing, Atlantic County, N. J.
Inscriptions; B1 (4-157; 5-17).
Mayville, Chautauqua County, N. Y.
Inscriptions; A2 (58-371).
Meads Corners, Putnam County, N. Y.
Inscriptions; A2 (56-310).
Mecklenburg County, N. C.
Militia, Rev. War; Z (31-7, 363, 763; 61-547).
Medfield, Mass.
Deaths, 1746-1844; A1 (62-368).
Inscriptions; A1 (58-343).
Medina County, Ohio
Marriages, 1853-1856 (Baptist); A1 (76-262).
Revolutionary soldiers buried; Z (22-23).
Medumcook, Me.
See Friendship.
Mekeels Corners, Putnam County, N. Y.
Inscriptions; A2 (55-240).
Mendham, Morris County, N. J.
Hilltop Pres. Church, baptisms, 1805-1832; B1 (5-39, 77).
Mendon, Mass.
Marriages, 1819-1831; A1 (63-273).
Mercer County, N. J.
See Hopewell, Washington.
Mercer County, Pa.
Marriages, 1842-1844; Z (50-72).
Revolutionary soldiers buried; Z (45-343; 46-113).
Mercersburg, Franklin County, Pa.
Inscriptions; P (10-161).
Meredith, N. H.
Notes; S2 (3-437).
Merion, Pa.
Settlers; Q1 (26-42).
Merryall, Bradford County, Pa.
Revolutionary soldiers buried; Z (38-208).
Michigan
List of Episcopal records; E (1-82).
Middleborough, Plymouth County, Mass.
Proprietors, 1690; C2 (5-136).
Inscriptions; C3 (4-116, 169); C4 (1-81, 152, 195, 219, 250, 269, 283); D (12-65, 142, 198; 13-23, 117; 14-80, 130, 214; 15-1, 100).
Vital records; D (1-219; 2-41, 103, 157, 201; 3-83, 232; 4-67; 5-37; 6-179, 226; 7-239; 8-28, 248; 9-46; 12-130, 230; 13-3, 249; 14-243; 15-24, 120, 217; 16-13, 106, 132, 244; 17-19; 18-77, 151; 19-46, 141, 173; 20-34; 22-146; 23-43, 69; 24-38, 55, 131, 185; 25-87, 104; 26-24, 131).

Middleborough—Cont.
Revolutionary soldiers buried; Z (36-311; 37-312).
Middleburg, Loudoun County, Va.
Inscriptions; M (19-37).
Middlebury, Addison County, Vt.
Marriages, 1785-1806; Z (48-362).
Death record, 1820-1874; A1 (71-44, 115).
Middlebush, Somerset County, N. J.
Inscriptions; B6 (6-58, 141).
Middlesex County, Mass.
Oath of fidelity, 1652; A1 (66-186).
Ages from depositions, 1675-1695; A1 (85-453).
Cautions, 1692-1700; C4 (1-263).
Court files, depositions, 1657-59; K (1-90; 4-8).
Miscellaneous early items; C4 (3-122).
Middlesex County, N. J.
Record sources; B6 (5-181).
See Raritan.
Middlesex County, Va.
Extracts, church records; G2 (12-149).
Patriots, 1782; V1 (7-109).
Middleton, Mass.
Church records, deaths 1765-1773; C2 (3-155).
Middletown, Conn.
Inscriptions; B3 (2-375; 4-329).
Revolutionary soldiers buried, Upper Houses; Z (31-807).
Middletown, Steuben County, N. Y.
Census 1800; A2 (60-51).
Middletown Springs, Vt.
Revolutionary soldiers buried; Z (37-475).
Mifflintown, Pa.
Marriages, 1806-1844; P (11-66, 163).
Milan, N. H.
Inscriptions; S2 (5-220).
Milan, Dutchess County, N. Y.
Inscriptions; A2 (40-128).
Milford, Conn.
Inscriptions; B3 (5-430, 484); T2 (5-1).
Milford, Me.
Inscriptions; F1 (9-84).
Milford, N. H.
Revolutionary soldiers buried; Z (18-131, 254).
Sketch; S2 (16-389).
Military Rolls
Bibliography, New England soldiers, all wars; A1 (64-61, 128, 228, 327; 65-11, 151).
Muster roll, *Province Galley*, 1711; Y1 (58-162).
Officers, West Jersey Militia, c. 1721; P (8-205).
Petersburg Cavalry, Chesapeake War, 1807; Y2 (2-138).
Wayne's Legion, 1792; Q1 (16-423).

Military Rolls—Cont.
Officers, Provisional Army, U. S., 1798; Q1 (38-129).
Crew of *Chesapeake*, 1813; A1 (66-32).
Brig *General Armstrong*, 1814; M (4-8).
Millbridge, Me.
Early settlers; F1 (9-223).
Millburn, Essex County, N. J.
Inscriptions; B1 (2-106).
Millfield, Athens County, Ohio
Inscriptions; E (7-285).
Millstone, Somerset County, N. J.
Inscriptions; B6 (4-204, 288).
Milltown, N. Y.
See Southeast.
Milton, Del.
St. John Church register; P (4-312).
Milton, N. Y.
Vital entries from a diary, 1822-1852; A2 (54-265).
Milton, Jackson County, Ohio
Inscriptions; E (7-270).
Milwaukee, Wis.
Irish settlers; G2 (29-103).
Minaville, Montgomery County, N. Y.
Inscriptions; B2 (2-96, 126).
Minden, Montgomery County, N. Y.
Census 1800; A2 (49-107).
Minisink, Orange County, N. Y.
Census 1800; A2 (62-409).
Minot [Poland], Me.
Marriages, 1795-1819; D (10-83, 134).
Mississippi
Revolutionary soldiers buried; Z (35-995).
Missouri
Revolutionary soldiers buried; Z (22-115, 341; 32-499).
See St. Genevieve.
Moncks Corner, S. C.
Notes; J (14-138).
Money
Value in Revolution; A1 (57-163).
Monhegan Island, Me.
F1 (3-141).
Monmouth County, N. J.
Record sources; B6 (5-180).
Early settlers; A2 (20-30).
See West Farms, Greenville, West Long Branch.
Monongahella County, W. Va.
Marriages, 1795-1799; M (14-26).
Monongalia County, W. Va.
Early record sources; N1 (1-209).
Pioneer settlers; N1 (1-62, 169, 240, 261, 284; 2-1).
Marriage licenses, 1794-1802; N1 (2-56).
Marriage Bonds, 1796-1850; Z (62-310, 418, 565; 63-22, 88, 240, 557, 612; 64-295, 363, 512, 703, 741).
Inscriptions, Morgantown; M (12-6).

Monson, Me.
Marriage intentions, 1823-1832; F1 (8-96).
Montague, Sussex County, N. J.
Inscriptions; B1 (5-103).
Montgomery County, Md.
List, oath of fidelity, 1778; M (6-1).
Vital entries, Wilson diary, 1777-1803; M (6-27).
Irish residents, 1778; G2 (24-157).
Marriages, 1798-1800; Z (46-34).
Quaker records, 1883-1891; M (7-58).
Revolutionary soldiers ' buried; Z (51-205).
Montgomery County, N. Y.
Abstracts of wills and administrations; A2 (56-145, 380; 57-163, 264; 59-83).
Inscriptions; A2 (56-376; 57-75, 186, 286, 387; 58-82, 155; 59-85, 171, 267, 380; 60-54, 185, 285, 374; 61-88, 190, 304, 403; 62-85, 318, 427).
See Palatine, Minden, Canajoharie, Manheim, Johnstown, Northampton, Broadalbin, Charlestown, Amsterdam, Florida, Mayfield, Salsbury.
Montgomery County, Ohio
Early settlers; Z (60-682).
Montgomery County, Pa.
Church records, New Goshenhoppen Cong., 1731-1761; Z (42-128, 182, 257, 324).
Marriages, 1812-1839; P (4-305); Q1 (30-437).
Old Goshenhoppen Church; M (16-12).
Montgomery, Hampden County, Mass.
Census 1800; M (12-14).
Montgomery, Orange County, N. Y.
Census 1800; A2 (62-313, 401).
Montpelier, Vt.
Vital records, 1791-1829; C3 (3-194).
Morgantown, W. Va.
Inscriptions; M (14-58; 19-37).
Mormons
Settlements in western States; U (10-6, 81, 120, 181; 11-34, 82, 141, 170; 12-41, 104, 125, 188; 13-38).
Morris County, N. J.
Marriages, 1795-1823; B1 (4-30, 83, 119, 171; 5-20, 57, 94, 117; 6-21, 59, 83, 108).
See Hanover, Pompton Plains, Mendham, Chester, Flanders, Pequannock.
Morrisania, Westchester County, N. Y.
Census 1800; A2 (59-36).
Census 1698; A2 (59-104).
Morristown, N. J.
In Revolution; S1 (12-210).
Morristown, Lamoille County, Vt.
Vital records; C4 (3-13, 179).

Moultonborough, N. H.
Marriages, 1779-1833; A1 (59-283).
Mount Desert Island, Me.
Early settlers; F1 (1-179; 2-81, 218; 7-223; 8-19).
Marriage intentions, 1789-1809; F1 (5-143).
Mount Desert, Me.
First Church records, 1792-1867; A1 (73-279).
Mount Holly, S. C.
Inscriptions; J (13-67).
Mount Pleasant, Westchester County, N. Y.
Census 1800; A2 (58-253, 333).
Mount Pleasant, Westmoreland County, Pa.
Marriages, 1794-1823; P (10-293).
Tax list, 1785; M (19-49).
Inscriptions; M (19-61).
Murfreesboro, Rutherford County, Tenn.
Marriages, 1808-1819; Z (57-466).
Muscongus, Me.
Petition, 1767; F1 (2-158).
Nantucket
Churches and pastors; A1 (56-17).
Marriages, 1717-1777; A1 (51-54, 161).
Narragansett, R. I.
Inhabitants, 1663; F4 (3-170).
Nashua, N. H.
Early settlers (Dunstable); A1 (55-186).
Marriages, 1853-1855 (Universalist); A1 (77-145, 175).
Nashville, Davidson County, Tenn.
Marriages, 1789-1805; Z (57-465; 58-158; 59-124).
Nassau, New Providence
Records relating to Americans; A1 (68-238).
Natick, Mass.
Deaths, 1757-1803; A1 (65-356).
Nauvoo, Ill.
Inscriptions; U (9-133).
Needham, Mass.
Historical data; A1 (53-33).
First Church records, marriages 1738-1811; A1 (55-258, 391).
Church records (baptisms, 1720-1849); A1 (57-21, 144, 252, 370).
Church records, 1802-1808; A1 (66-10).
Vital records (marriages, 1720-1798); A1 (56-30).
Vital records (births, 1749-1762); A1 (56-141).
Vital records (deaths, 1749-1762); A1 (56-265).
Deaths, 1757-1803; A1 (65-356).
Newark, N. J.
Revolutionary soldiers; B1 (1-33).

Newark, Ohio
Inscriptions; E (11-302; 12-93; 13-106).
New Boston, Me.
See Gray.
New Braintree, Mass.
Deaths, 1810-1872; A1 (62-17, 128).
New Brunswick
Index of wills and administrations, 1785-1850; A2 (62-182, 304).
New Brunswick, N. J.
In Revolution; B6 (4-167).
Taverns; B6 (3-9).
Newburgh, Orange County, N. Y.
Census 1800; A2 (62-174).
Inscriptions; A2 (27-45).
Newbury, Essex County, Mass.
Soldiers, 1775; C2 (3-7).
Church admissions, dismissions; Y1 (56-222; 58-20; 59-85).
Vital records, Goodhue diary, 1742-1763; Y1 (67-401).
Byfield Parish, baptisms, 1709-1783; Y2 (2-51; 6-49); deaths, 1748-1802; Y2 (7-145).
Revolutionary soldiers buried; Z (18-255).
Newburyport, Essex County, Mass.
Soldiers, 1775; C2 (3-7).
Newcastle County, Del.
Probate records, extracts; G2 (14-187).
New Castle, Del.
Tax list, 1677; P (1-29); Q1 (3-352).
Early Justices; P (1-35).
New Castle, Rockingham County, N. H.
Revolutionary soldiers buried; Z (50-309).
Vital records; F3 (1-23; 2-33).
Tax list, 1720; F3 (1-21).
Records, 1693-1694; S2 (24-50).
Notes; S2 (13-73).
New Castle, Westchester County, N. Y.
Census 1800; A2 (57-260).
New Connaught, Md.
Petition with list, 1779; X1 (5-58).
New Durham, N. H.
Inscriptions; A1 (85-440).
Town records, 1749-1769; A1 (61-359).
Newfoundland
Refugees in Boston, 1762; C4 (4-31).
New England
Original sources; E (12-21).
List of subscribers, Prince's Annals; E (13-108; 14-47).
New England ministers
Deaths, 1760-1765; A1 (62-273).
New Fairfield, Conn.
Marriages, 1746-1791; A2 (39-213).
Cong. Church records; B3 (3-486).
Inscriptions; B3 (3-236).
Families; B3 (3-352, 481; 4-220).

Newfield, Tompkins County, N. Y.
Inscriptions; A2 (52-282, 350).

New Germantown, N. J.
Church records, 1769-1800; A2 (31-107, 139, 232; 32-36, 97, 138, 200; 33-27, 108, 141, 220; 34-56, 100, 197, 248).

New Gloucester, Me.
Petition, 1762; F2 (1-107).

New Hampshire
Counties and Towns; S2 (1-120).
Early Baptists; S2 (1-156).
David Thompson's Indenture, 1622; F3 (2-1).
Marriages from Provincial Court Records, Exeter, 1673-1680; C2 (5-133).
Vital records from *N. H. Gazette*, 1765-1790; C3 (4-16, 193, 289; 5-57); C4 (1-15, 61, 93, 191, 223, 237, 267, 295, 327, 362; 2-37, 82).
Rolls, Revolutionary War; T7 (vol. 47, 1914, p. 312).
Men at Bunker Hill and Bennington; S2 (1-209, 241; 2-266).
Men at Saratoga; S2 (1-228).
Men at Hubbarton; S2 (1-279).
Members of Continental Congress; S2 (6-275).
Revolutionary pensioners; M (11-28, 43, 52; 12-4, 21; 13-41; 14-60, 64; 15-17; 18-77).
Cincinnati, members; S2 (15-123, 238).
Naval services, Rev. War: F3 (2-177; 3-19, 65; 4-25; 5-161).
Inscriptions; S2 (5-115).
Irish settlers; G2 (3-122; 9-247; 18-176; 25-62).
Scots-Irish settlers; S2 (11-17, 50, 85; 12-69).
Miscellaneous; C2 (4-259).

New Hanover, Montgomery County, Pa.
Lutheran Church records, 1740-1825; Q2 (20-198).

New Hartford, Conn.
Inscriptions; A1 (82-375, 453).

New Haven Colony
Colonial services, 1638-1665; B4 (4-961).

New Haven County, Conn.
Physicians; T2 (2-239).

New Haven, Conn.
Inscriptions; T2 (3-471; 8-351).
Probate records, 1647-1687; A1 (91-121).
Second Congregational Church records, 1749-1796; A2 (42-28).
Errors in vital records; B4 (2-504).
Division of lands, 1704; B4 (4-1011; 6-1805).
Census, 1704; B4 (6-1531).
Town poor, 1786; B4 (6-1535).

New Haven—Cont.
Pequot War soldiers; B4 (1-238).
K. Philip's War soldiers; B4 (1-238).
Revolutionary War soldiers; B4 (1-248; 2-497).
French and Indian War; B4 (1-242; 2-485).
Revolutionary soldiers buried; Z (19-264; 25-670).

Newington, Conn.
Residents 1776; C2 (7-145, 205, 233, 294); C3 (1-28).

Newington, N. H.
Sketch, 1713-1810; A1 (58-247).
Church records, beginning 1716; F3 (2-167; 3-1, 57, 105, 154; 4-14, 59, 105, 153; 5-73).
Vital records (private), 1824-1865; A1 (73-188).

New Ipswich, N. H.
Church records, 1764-1773; A1 (71-357).

New Jersey
Records, location; C3 (1-167).
Abstracts of Commissions, 1703-1769; P (6-181, 286; 7-62, 147, 236; 8-60, 139, 237; 9-17, 112, 227; 10-51, 133, 250).
Persons naturalized, 1702-1776; A2 (28-86).
Dutch settlers; B1 (4-49); P (4-125).
Huguenots; A2 (24-49).
Settlers in West N. J.; A2 (30-114, 175).
Rolls, Revolutionary War; T7 (vol. 47, 1914, p. 332).
Corrections of Whitehead's Contributions to East Jersey History; A2 (34-50).

New Kent County, Va.
Inscriptions, Cedar Grove Farm; V1 (12-194).
Military Classes, 1782; V1 (10-177).

New London, Conn.
Vital records, 1644-1667; C3 (2-282).
Inscriptions; M (16-25).
Irish settlers; G2 (26-182, 192).
Capt. Pease's Co.; Z (29-264).

New London, N. H.
Baptisms and Marriages, 1788-1824; Dx (1-41, 62, 81, 90).
Sketch; S2 (19-93).

New London, S. C.
See Wiltown.

New Marblehead, Me.
See Windham.

Newmarket, N. H.
Vital records; F3 (6-59, 133, 151; 7-37, 55).

New Munster, New Ireland County, Md.
G2 (26-30).

Newport, N. H.
History; S2 (3-228, 269).
Sketch; S2 (20-1).

Newport, R. I.
Cemeteries; T4 (No. 10).
Births and deaths, 1760-1764; A2 (62-283, 352; 63-51).
Wills; F4 (7-302).
Second Baptist Church, Members 1729; A1 (69-91).
New Portland, Me.
Revolutionary soldiers buried; Z (36-409).
New Providence, Union County, N. J.
Revolutionary soldiers; B1 (2-113; 3-25, 50).
New Providence, Montgomery County, Pa.
Trappe Church records, 1729-1777; Q2 (6-159; 7-477).
New Rochelle, Westchester County, N. Y.
Census 1800; A2 (58-338).
Oaths of Allegiance, 1698; A2 (59-68).
Census 1698; A2 (59-105).
Newton and Haddonfield, N. J.
Quaker church records, 1684-1813; B1 (3-20, 63, 109, 145; 4-11, 79, 128, 179; 5-23, 63, 95, 110).
Newtown, Queens County, N. Y.
Census 1800; A2 (54-218, 346).
Presbyterian Church records, 1652-1882; A2 (55-162, 281, 393; 56-73, 173, 353).
Church records; C2 (2-115).
Newtown, Tioga County, N. Y.
Census 1800; A2 (60-45).
New Utrecht, Kings County, N. Y.
Census 1800; A2 (55-122).
New Windsor, Orange County, N. Y.
Census 1800; A2 (62-308).
New Eng. items in church marriages, 1781-1788; A1 (63-194).
Extracts, church records; G2 (12-139).
New Worcester, Me.
Petition, 1783; F1 (1-14).
Marriage intentions, 1785-1788; F1 (3-88).
Petition, 1788; F1 (5-240).
New Yarmouth, Kent County, Md.
History; X1 (3-273).
New York State
Record sources; M (18-69).
Archives; A2 (20-106).
Central lake section (Military Tract), historical; A2 (40-15).
Copy of records; list of those (Burhans Collection) in possession of N. Y. Gen. & Biog. Society; A2 (33-180).
Counties, organization, county seats; A2 (54-18).
Settlement of New Netherland, 1624-1626; A2 (55-3, 211).

New York State—Cont.
Newspaper vital records; A2 (47-393; 48-304, 411; 49-343, 345).
Muster rolls, French and Indian War; T7 (vol. 24, 1891).
Rolls, Revolutionary War; T7 (vol. 48, 1915, p. 338).
Committee records, Revolutionary period; T7 (vols. 57-58, 1924-1925).
Revolutionary Officers; A2 (21-91, 140).
Revolutionary War Records; A2 (46-330; 47-172, 283, 336; 48-57).
Revolutionary soldiers buried, small cemeteries; Z (36-408; 37-33).
Loyalists; A2 (21-180).
Sales of forfeited lands; A2 (59-108, 247, 342; 60-64, 164).
Lords of Manors; A2 (39-292).
Irish settlers; G2 (14-238).
New York County, N. Y.
Probate records; T7 (vol. 25-41, 1892-1908).
New York, N. Y.
Early immigrants; A2 (14-181; 15-34, 72; 45-387).
Dutch aliases; A2 (10-38).
Church records; list of those copied by N. Y. Gen. and Biog. Society; A2 (49-11; 52-152).
Reformed Dutch Church records, 1639-1800; admissions to 1830; A2 (5-26, 84, 148, 175; 6-32, 81, 141, 183, 184; 7-19, 69, 125, 161; 8-25, 80, 116, 168; 9-20, 38, 72, 132, 161; 10-24, 77, 111, 162; 11-34, 75, 125, 137, 172; 12-37, 84, 124, 187; 13-16, 29, 63, 77, 131, 165; 14-32, 74, 124, 173; 15-23, 81, 114, 162; 16-32, 87, 115, 176; 17-40, 101, 224, 268; 18-26, 75, 114, 162; 19-13, 77, 110, 165; 20-15, 69, 114, 161; 21-28, 65, 113, 151; 22-7, 81, 141, 183; 23-18, 73, 131, 193; 24-18, 71, 117, 162; 25-9, 67, 115, 166; 26-11, 59, 126, 162; 27-27, 73, 133, 198; 28-27, 93, 137, 217; 29-22, 75, 145, 194; 30-15, 85, 159, 213; 31-19, 91, 145, 209; 32-17, 81, 145, 207; 59-69, 158, 259, 372; 60-71, 156, 279, 343; 61-72, 165, 264, 373; 62-40, 191, 288, 391).
Marriages Licenses (Lord Cornbury), 1702-1705; A2 (1-3, 13; 2-25).
Marriage Licenses (Surrogate's Office), 1692-1701; A2 (2-141; 3-91, 192; 4-31).
Marriage Licenses, 1756 and 1758; A2 (2-194).
Marriage Licenses, 1686-1688; A2 (5-174).
Marriage Licenses; A2 (46-279, 337; 47-68, 176, 286).
First Presbyterian Church records, 1728-1783; A2 (4-98, 140, 195; 5-35,

New York, N. Y.—Cont.
    100, 183; 6-48; 7-35, 65, 135, 169; 8-
    20, 74; 9-16, 80, 169; 10-44, 93, 127,
    177; 11-29).
First and Second Presbyterian
    Church records, 1756-; A2 (11-83,
    120; 12-32, 134; 13-43, 87; 14-40,
    90, 118, 169; 15-31, 89, 132; 16-40,
    86, 114, 138; 17-50, 232, 277; 18-
    170; 19-59; 20-35, 177).
Marriages, 1849-1853 (Universalist);
    A1 (77-145).
Quaker Records; A2 (3-51).
Trinity Church Records, 1746-1778;
    A2 (19-147).
Trinity Church marriages, 1771-1783;
    A2 (46-167).
Christ Church records, beginning
    1794; A2 (42-322).
Tax List, 1676; A2 (2-36).
Freemen, 1675-1866; T7 (vol. 18,
    1886).
Tax lists, 1695-1699; T7 (vols. 43, 44,
    1910-1911).
Assessment, East Ward, 1791; T7
    (vol. 44, 1911, p. 317).
Court records, 1680-1682; 1693-1701;
    T7 (vol. 45, 1912).
Land records, 1673-1675; T7 (vol. 46,
    1913).
Indentures of Apprentices; T7 (vol.
    42, 1909, p. 111).
Militia 1776; A2 (2-156, 208).
List of those at funeral 1723; A2 (49-
    369).
Dutch records relative to R. I.
    people; F4 (8-241).
Inscriptions; A2 (17-39, 279; 21-81;
    25-143; 60-8).
Rope-Makers and Rope-Walks; A2
    (57-233).
Irish residents; G2 (15-243).
Miscellanea; A2 (21-171).
Nobleborough, Me.
Marriages, 1796-1820; A1 (84-421).
Marriages, 1808, 1851; A1 (63-376;
    64-75, 154, 374; 66-274, 359).
Tax list, 1798; K (4-148).
Nomenclature
See Genealogy.
Nonesuch Point, Me.
F2 (6-378).
Norfolk County, Mass.
Abstracts of deeds, 1649-1684; Y2
    (1-19, 49, 84, 113, 147, 178; 2-11, 47,
    81, 114, 148, 181; 3-10, 42, 75, 108,
    138, 171; 4-9, 43, 77, 108, 138, 175;
    5-12, 46, 77, 133, 179; 6-41, 83, 131,
    171; 7-30, 87, 136; 8-38, 126, 175;
    9-137; 10-89, 109; 11-30, 172; 12-81,
    178; 13-105); Y1 (56-298; 57-75,
    155, 313; 58-101, 234; 59-90, 281;
    60-147, 229, 303; 61-177, 353; 62-
    12, 121, 298; 63-45, 328; 64-329; 65-
    240, 448; 66-182; 67-170).

Norridgewock, Me.
Marriages, 1814-1816; F2 (7-63).
Norriton, Montgomery County, Pa.
Inscriptions; P (7-218).
Northampton County, Pa.
Capt. Shoemaker's Co., Rangers,
    1781; Pw (10-118).
Roster, Capt. Jennings' Co.; Q1 (22-
    249).
Moravians; S1 (14-1).
Settlers, "Irish Settlement"; Q3 (1-
    34, 122, 208).
Northampton County, Va.
Marriage Bonds, 1706-1800; V1 (1-
    192, 338).
**Northampton, Montgomery [now Ful-
    ton] County, N. Y.**
Census 1800; A2 (50-26).
North Anson, Me.
Revolutionary soldiers buried; Z (36-
    408).
North Berwick, Me.
Inscriptions; A1 (59-107).
Northbridge, Mass.
Marriage intentions, 1772-1783; Z
    (49-194).
Warnings, 1775-1783; A1 (70-283).
North Bucksport, Me.
Inscriptions; F1 (7-27).
North Carolina
Records, location; C2 (6-317).
Territorial divisions; H (3-304).
Abstract of wills to 1760; H (1-26,
    163, 323, 483).
Division of estates; H (2-256).
Deeds; H (3-125, 423).
English gleanings; H (3-463).
Early Baptists; H (1-283).
Indian war, 1711; H (1-437).
Miscellaneous records; H (1-117,
    301; 2-296, 465, 620).
Orders of nobility; H (1-584).
Mecklenburg County Court records,
    1775-1776; R1 (11-329).
Mecklenburg Declaration; R1 (11-
    261).
Rolls, Revolutionary War; T7 (vol.
    48, 1915, p. 512).
Land warrants for Rev. service; Z
    (60-37).
Women in Revolution; Z (45-145).
Loyalists; H (2-208, 390, 566).
Convention, 1788, members; R1 (3-
    122).
Stockholders, Dismal Swamp Canal,
    1791; H (1-430).
Company roll, 1813; M (7-4).
**North Castle, Westchester County,
    N. Y.**
Census 1800; A2 (57-113).
North Duxbury, Mass.
Inscriptions; D (11-55).
Northfield, N. H.
Notes; S2 (30-22).

Oldham County, Ky.
Inscriptions; M (15-16).
Old Hurley, Ulster County, N. Y.
Inscriptions; A2 (61-226).
Old Laporte, Neb.
Inscriptions; B2 (9-15).
Old Lyme, Conn.
Inscriptions; A1 (77-194; 78-250).
Old Town, Me.
Sketches; F2 (9-183).
Inscriptions; F1 (6-72).
Olean, Cattaraugus County, N. Y.
Marriages, 1809-1820; Z (48-362).
Oley, Berks County, Pa.
Inscriptions; M (11-8; 15-30; 16-38).
Oneonta, N. Y.
Revolutionary soldiers; A2 (54-69).
Onondaga County, N. Y.
Revolutionary soldiers (bounty land);
A2 (30-237; 31-36, 79, 170, 242; 32-
25, 108, 156, 204; 33-17, 76, 156,
242; 34-44, 93, 206, 263; 35-17);
see also Z (57-94).
See Pompey, Pompey Hill, Onon-
daga, Marcellus, Manlius, Fabius,
Homer, Solon, Camillus, Lysander.
Onondaga, Onondaga County, N. Y.
Census 1800; A2 (53-232).
Ontario County, N. Y.
Marriages, 1834-1838 (Baptist); A1
(76-262).
Orange County, N. Y.
See Newburgh, New Windsor, Mont-
gomery, Deerpark, Minisink, Port
Jervis.
Orange County, Va.
Early Germans; N2 (4-61).
Orange, Essex County, N. J.
Inscriptions; B1 (4-46, 65, 112, 143,
159).
Orange, Rockland County, N. Y.
Census 1800; A2 (61-347).
Orange, Delaware County, Ohio
Inscriptions; E (9-267).
Orangeburgh, S. C.
Petition, 1749; J (24-48).
Orient, L. I.
Inscriptions; A2 (6-107).
Orleans County, Vt.
Probate records, 1797-1830; A1 (65-
374; 66-19).
Orleans, Mass.
First Church records, beginning
1772; D (10-165, 230; 11-252; 12-
151; 13-90, 162; 14-53, 123, 137; 15-
13).
Inscriptions; D (7-77).
See Eastham.
Orono, Me.
Sketches; F2 (9-183).
Marriage intentions, 1806-1817; F1
(3-177).
Petition, 1804; F1 (4-157).

Orphan's Island, Me.
Early settlers; F1 (8-67).
Orrington, Me.
Settlement, early history; F1 (1-17;
6-27; 7-183).
Methodist church, members; F1 (1-
22).
Congregational Church; F1 (1-139).
Marriages, 1787-1808; F1 (1-108,
135).
Intentions, 1787-1812; F1 (1-176).
Petition, 1812; F1 (4-101).
Family records; F1 (4-211, 236; 5-4).
Otisfield, Me.
Tax list, 1809; F2 (8-229).
Overwharton, Stafford County, Va.
Extracts, Ep. Church records, 1720-
1758; G2 (12-156).
Owego, Tioga County, N. Y.
Census 1800; A2 (59-333).
Revolutionary soldiers buried; Z (21-
300).
Oyster Bay, Queens County, N. Y.
Census 1800; A2 (54-350; 55-16).
Baptist Church Marriages, 1802-
1815; A2 (29-174).
Inscriptions; A2 (31-111).
Painesville, Ohio
Newspaper, deaths of Revolutionary
soldiers; Z (31-547).
Painted Post, Steuben County, N. Y.
Census 1800; A2 (60-52).
Palatine, Montgomery County, N. Y.
Census 1800; A2 (49-51).
Palatine settlers
See Germany.
Paris, France
American inscriptions; Q1 (43-251).
Paris, Ky.
Deaths of Revolutionary soldiers,
1831-1865; Z (47-25, 88).
Revolutionary soldiers buried; Z (46-
36).
Parkersburg, Wood County, West Va.
Revolutionary soldiers buried; Z (34-
304).
Parsonsfield, Me.
Inscriptions; F2 (7-174).
Passadumkeag, Me.
Census, 1835, with births; F1 (2-52).
Inscriptions; F1 (3-92).
Passaic County, N. J.
See Boardville.
Passenger Lists
To Mass., 1635-1637; A1 (75-217; 79-
107).
Winthrop Fleet, 1630; A1 (75-236).
To Virginia; V2 (1-180, 226).
1697-1707; A1 (64-158, 252, 336; 65-
43, 165).
Hannah and Elizabeth, 1679; Y2 (4-
137).
To New England, 1687; Y2 (11-65).

Passenger Lists—Cont.
Immigrants to New England, 1700-1775; Y1 (63-177, 269, 365; 64-25, 257; 65-57, 113, 531; 66-411, 521; 67-89, 201, 305).
To Penn.; Q2 (vol. 39).
To Philadelphia, 1682-1687; Q1 (8-328).
Swedes, 1641; Q1 (3-462).
Swedes, 1649; Q1 (8-107).
1773-1776; A1 (62-242, 320; 63-16, 134, 234, 342; 64-18, 106, 214, 314; 65-20, 116, 232).
Submission, to Md. 1682; P (1-7).
Dutch to Delaware, 1661; A2 (60-68).
Moravians to Pa., 1734-1765; Q1 (33-228).
Germans to Phila., 1758; Q1 (33-501).
From Zürich to Car. and Pa.; M (8-17, 33).
Boston; G2 (13-177).
Irish apprentices, Phila., 1745; Q1 (30-348, 427).
Philadelphia apprenticeships, 1745-1746; 1772-1773; Q1 (30-348, 427; 31-83, 195, 351, 461; 32-88, 237, 351; 33-475; 34-99, 213).
From Ireland, 1811, 1815-16; G2 (28-65; 29-183).
To Philadelphia, 1775; Q1 (18-379).
To Philadelphia, 1791-1792; Q1 (24-187, 334).
Elizabeth, to Phila., 1819; Q1 (25-255).
Euryal, Dublin to Phila., 1747; Q1 (26-287).
1803-1804; A1 (60-23, 160, 240, 346; 61-133, 265, 347; 62-78, 168; 66-30, 306).
C4 (3-139, 217; 4-1, 73).
Path Valley, Pa.
Marriages, 1794-1800; P (8-65).
Pawtucket, R. I.
Purchasers; T6 (1-185).
Pawtuxet Valley, R. I.
Sketches; F4 (8-97).
Peekskill, Putnam County, N. Y.
Inscriptions; A2 (49-76, 177, 303, 363).
Pelham, Mass.
Irish settlers; G2 (3-114).
Pelham, Westchester County, N. Y.
Census 1800; A2 (57-258).
Pemaquid Fort, Me.
Inscriptions; F1 (3-15).
Pembroke, Mass.
Revolutionary soldiers, 1775; C2 (4-23).
Vital records, early; K (1-25, 57).
Vital records, 1742; A1 (69-283).
Pembroke Center, Mass.
Inscriptions; D (9-3, 112, 235; 10-97, 155, 234; 11-28).

Pendleton County, W. Va.
Marriage Bonds, 1791-92; M (9-14).
Pennsylvania
Records, location; C3 (1-155).
Counties, organization; M (1-59).
List, Reformed Church records; M (6-57).
German settlement; Q2 (9-47; 10-1).
Migration, N. Y. to Pa.; Q2 (9-347).
Lutheran and Reformed Churches; Q2 (vols. 11, 12).
English settlers; Q1 (52-317).
French settlers; Q1 (53-322).
Irish settlers; G2 (6-37).
Welsh Tract purchases; Q1 (16-457; 17-117, 372, 385).
Apprentice papers, 1745-1746, 1772-1773; Q1 (30-348, 427; 31-83, 195, 351, 461; 32-88, 237, 351; 33-475; 34-99, 213).
Moravian settlers; Q1 (33-228).
First Provincial Council, members, 1681; P (6-1).
Schwenkfelders; Q2 (vol. 13).
French and Indian War, with rolls; Q2 (vol. 15).
Indentures of apprentices, Philadelphia, 1771-1773; Q2 (vol. 16).
Marriage Licenses, 1742-1748; Q1 (39-176, 364, 434).
Marriage Licenses, 1762-1776; Q1 (40-104, 208, 319, 436; 41-224, 334, 489).
Marriage Licenses, 1748-1752; Q1 (32-71, 233, 345, 471).
Marriage Licenses, 1772-1774; P (11-194).
Marriages, German Reformed, 1763-1769; Q1 (26-375).
Vital entries, Sproat Journal, 1778-1780; Q1 (27-505).
Abstracts of Marriage Certificates, Friends; P (2-60; 7-92).
Marriages and deaths, from Bedford newspaper, 1832-1834; P (11-175).
Marriages, "Schwenkfelders," 1735-1804; Q1 (5-470).
Divorces, Supreme Court, 1785-1801; P (1-185).
Probate Records; B2 (1-28).
Petition, 1692; Q1 (38-495).
Petition of Swedes, 1722; Q1 (38-427).
Abstract of General Loan Office Mortgages, 1723-1724; P (6-266).
Licenses to settle on Susquehanna River, 1733-1734; P (11-180).
Settlers killed by Indians, 1755-56; Q1 (32-309; 38-380).
Captives taken by Indians, 1764; Q1 (20-571).
Old mills in eastern Pa.; Q2 (vol. 39).
Revolutionary soldiers; P (11-81,

Philadelphia, Pa.—Cont.
St. Mary's (Catholic) Church, minute book, 1782-1811; G1 (4-245).
Pew Registers, 1787-1791;G1 (5-357).
St. Augustine's (Catholic) Church; G1 (1-351); marriages, 1801-1830; G1 (13-165); baptisms, 1801-1810; G1 (13-334, 497).
Deaths, miscellaneous; Q1 (31-508).
Burials, 1806-1807; P (1-225; 2-34).
Deaths, from newspaper, 1810-1811; P (11-160).
Inscriptions; P (1-14; 2-303, 340; 3-135; 5-135; 9-248; 10-279; 11-21, 137).
Inscriptions, St. Mary's Graveyard; G1 (3-253); interments, 1788-1800; G1 (5-19).
Interments in vaults, St. John's Churchyard; G1 (23-212).
Marriages, from newspaper, 1810-1811; P (11-50).
Minutes, Quaker Meetings, 1682-1759; P (1-251; 2-93; 4-141; 6-64, 201, 295; 7-70, 179, 251; 8-76, 174, 261; 9-35, 164, 236; 10-56, 123, 238; 11-9, 127).
Quaker residents, 1757-60; Q1 (16-219).
Catholic deaths, yellow fever, 1798; G1 (23-129).
St. Peter's Church, history; Q1 (47-328; 48-39, 181, 251, 354).
Members, Moravian Congregation, 1757; Q1 (35-254).
Early landowners, list; M (14-49).
French residents, 1756; Q1 (24-248).
Welsh settlers, 1698; Q1 (1-330).
Welsh settlers; Q1 (40-362).
Record of families of Middle Ferry; P (9-38).
San Domingo Refugees; G1 (28-97, 213, 356; 29-68, 140, 262; 30-177, 227, 309).
Tax list, 1754; Q1 (14-414).
Masonic Lodge, list, 1749; Q1 (20-116).
Roster, Masonic Lodge No. 2, 1749-1763; Q1 (31-19).
Members, fire co., 1738-45; Q1 (27-472).
Public House keepers, 1771; Q1 (22-126).
Patriotic Association, list, 1778; Q1 (23-356).
Roll, Capt. Peters' Militia Co., 1775; Q1 (23-394).
2d Troop, Cavalry; Q1 (45-257, 364; 46-57, 154, 262, 346; 47-67, 147, 262, 357; 48-270, 372; 49-75, 163, 367; 50-79, 179; 52-372; 53-283, 375; 54-65, 175, 374).
List of patients, Marine Hospital, 1784; Q1 (26-92).
State Guard, 1814; Q1 (35-369).

Philadelphia, College of
Graduates, 1752-63; Q1 (15-238).
Philipsborough, Cortland & Rikes Patent
Census, 1710; A2 (38-221).
Philipsburgh, N. Y.
Town records, ear marks, beginning 1742; A2(59-203).
Philipstown, Putnam County, N. Y.
Inscriptions, Garrisons village; A2 (55-78, 168).
Phoenix, Ariz.
Inscriptions; B2 (2-153; 3-163, 202, 220).
Pickaway County, Ohio
Marriage Licenses, 1810-1814; E (7-116, 288; 8-227).
Pike County, Pa.
Marriages, 1808-1809; Q1 (28-251).
Revolutionary pensioners, 1835; Pw (11-224).
Piscataway, Md.
Parish records, early; M (3-2).
Piscataway, N. J.
Settlers, 1666-1716; A2 (29-38).
Pittsburgh, Pa.
Residents, 1760, 1761; Q1 (2-303, 469; 6-344).
Unclaimed letters, 1794; P (8-299).
Pittsgrove (Daretown), Salem County, N. J.
Baptist Church Marriages, 1772-1793; B1 (2-100, 122).
Militia Co.; P (9-186).
Pittston, Me.
Early settlers; F2 (7-165).
Capt. Jewett's Co., 1799; F2 (1-80).
Pittston, Pa.
Marriages, 1832-1885; Pw (11-211).
Pittstown, Rensselaer County, N. Y.
Inscriptions; A2 (31-230; 62-285).
Plain Township, Franklin County, Ohio
First settlers; E (7-16).
Inscriptions; E (7-22).
Plainfield, Conn.
First Cong. Church records, 1747-1819; A1 (70-171, 220, 309).
Inscriptions; A1 (71-33).
Death record, 1799-1818; A1 (71-133).
Revolutionary records; Z (27-353).
Black Hill Boarding School; scholars, 1817-24; F4 (8-22).
Plainfield, N. H.
Sketch; S2 (24-221).
Plattsmouth, Cass County, Neb.
Methodist Church records, 1873-1885; B2 (9-44).
Pleasant Ridge Plantations, Me.
Revolutionary soldiers buried; Z (36-409).
Pleasantville, Berks County, Pa.
Inscriptions; M (11-7; 15-30, 33).

Pluckemin, Somerset County, N. J.
Residents, 1768-1798; B6 (2-265).

Plumstead, Bucks County, Pa.
Vital entries, Dyer diary, 1763-1805;
P (3-38).

Plymouth Colony
Probate records, beginning 1633; D
(1-23, 79, 154, 197; 2-8, 87, 147,
209; 3-74, 160, 220; 4-75, 168; 5-
153; 6-169, 248; 8-84, 143, 207; 9-30,
81, 155, 224; 10-21, 159, 198; 11-6,
87, 152, 198; 12-244; 14-21, 112, 150,
227; 15-58, 234; 16-21, 123, 156; 17-
22, 109, 155, 214; 18-63, 71, 185,
248; 19-30, 60, 132, 162; 24-41, 71,
133; 25-37, 89, 119; 26-80).
Deeds; D (1-91, 131, 213; 2-27, 93,
166, 245; 3-39, 78, 138, 225; 4-35,
82; 5-90; 6-99, 245; 7-107; 8-72, 130,
200; 9-44, 104, 163, 232; 10-16, 71,
140, 213; 11-15, 165, 209; 12-6, 80,
132, 212; 13-39, 87, 141, 228; 14-12,
89, 142, 234; 15-29, 178, 243; 16-76,
178, 205; 17-38, 100, 166, 239; 18-
33, 86, 171; 19-64, 106; 25-64, 135;
26-32, 101; 27-87).
Vital records; D (13-83; 15-25; 16-
120, 235; 17-70, 181, 199; 18-55, 68,
166, 171; 19-21, 68, 108; 20-51; 21-
36, 56, 107, 152; 22-92, 114).

Plymouth County, Mass.
Marriages, 1692-1746; K (1-1, 33,
105; 2-17, 49, 81; 3-49, 125).
Unrecorded deeds; D (15-214; 16-
138; 17-117; 18-43).
Marriage records, 1693-94; D (26-
35); Dx (3-120).
Deeds; Dx (4-7, 91; 5-5, 62, 66, 87,
99, 119).
Probate records, 1686-1696; K (1-17,
41, 73, 113; 2-25, 59, 89, 104; 3-26,
89, 109; 4-25, 88); Dx (4-1, 107,
123; 5-13, 19, 61, 90, 108, 114).

Plymouth, Conn.
Inscriptions; C1 (1-121).

Plymouth, Mass.
Bradford's Mayflower list; D (1-9,
161).
Depositions; D (2-45, 178, 248); Dx
(2-133; 4-5).
Census (division of land) 1623; D
(1-227).
Census (division of cattle) 1627; D
(1-148).
First Church records; D (4-212; 5-
214; 8-214; 12-26; 13-72, 152; 14-
101, 188; 15-21, 223; 16-53).
Mayflower Compact; D (1-77).
Vital records; D (1-139, 206; 2-17,
77, 163, 224; 3-12, 121; 4-110; 5-53,
99; 7-176, 208; 12-10, 84, 222; 13-
32, 111, 165, 199; 14-34, 70, 156,
239; 15-38, 110, 159, 209; 16-62, 84,
164, 254; 17-3, 123, 131; 18-28, 117,

Plymouth, Mass.—Cont.
139, 211; 19-5, 90, 149; 20-70; 21-
19, 94, 162; 22-31, 105, 178; 23-8,
186; 24-14; 25-51, 139, 187; 26-39,
84, 139, 189; 27-44, 175; 28-34, 70;
29-90).

Plymouth, Eng.
Inhabitants, 1625; C4 (1-235).

Plympton, Mass.
Inscriptions; D (8-150; 9-117, 214;
10-111, 144, 217; 11-64, 115, 127,
161, 194).
Vital records; D (1-174, 245; 2-50,
121, 138, 234; 3-91, 163; 5-180, 206).

Pocahontas County, W. Va.
Early settlers; N2 (2-2-76).

Point Pleasant, W. Va.
Historical; N2 (5-92).

Pomfret, Conn.
Cong. Church records; B3 (3-354,
482; 4-329; 5-188, 246, 440).
Inscriptions; A1 (73-105).
Marriages, 1706-1753; A1 (67-371).

Pompey, Onondaga County, N. Y.
Census 1800; A2 (53-225).
Settlers, Military Tract; Z (33-901).

Pompey Hill, Onondaga County, N. Y.
Inscriptions; A2 (44-69).

Pompion Hill, S. C.
Inscriptions; J (14-112).

Pompton Plains, Morris County, N. J.
Church records, marriages 1736-
1809; B1 (1-20, 40, 71, 98).

Pondstown, Me.
Petition, 1770; F2 (8-175).

Poplarneck, Berks County, Pa.
Inscriptions; M (15-35).

Portage County, Ohio
Revolutionary soldiers buried; Z (19-
589; 22-21).

Port Byron, Cayuga County, N. Y.
Inscriptions; A2 (54-59).

Port Elizabeth, N. J.
Inscriptions; B5 (12-249; 13-20, 45,
68).

Port Jervis, Orange County, N. Y.
Inscriptions; A2 (44-379).

Portland, Me.
Poor widows, 1806; F2 (1-55).
Marriages, 1804; F2 (9-284).
Deaths, 1804; F2 (9-319).
St. Paul's Church records, extracts
1763-1829; F2 (2-243; 3-33).
Rifle Co., 1810; F2 (7-42).
Tax list, 1798; F2 (1-126).

Port Republic, Atlantic County, N. J.
Inscriptions; B1 (5-87, 111; 6-10).

Port Richmond, N. Y.
See Staten Island.

Portsmouth, Me.
Inscriptions; F2 (3-44).

Portsmouth, N. H.
Strawberry Bank grants and deeds;
F3 (1-1).
Lists, 1658-1671; F3 (1-9).

Portsmouth, N. H.—Cont.
Land grants; F3 (2-22, 59).
Town officers, 1652-1849; F3 (2-97, 157).
Church members, 1693; F3 (3-172).
Church members, 1707; C2 (4-193).
Inhabitants, 1711; A1 (51-43).
Notarial records, 1692-1708; A1 (69-359).
North Church records, 1671-1796; F3 (3-49; 4-49, 97; 5-38, 86, 129, 183; 6-41, 76; 7-11, 73).
South Church records, 1714-1921; A1 (81-419; 82-25, 138, 281, 410; 83-21, 168, 295, 421; 84-17, 439).
1752-1760; C2 (6-176).
Methodist Church; S2 (6-209, 229, 314, 347).
Inscriptions; F3 (1-13; 2-17); A1 (67-89).
Revolutionary soldiers; Z (26-14).
Records of Irish; G2 (13-187).

Post Vincennes, Ind.
St. Francis Xavier (Cath.) Parish Records, 1749-1773; G1 (12-41, 193, 322).

Poughkeepsie, N. Y.
Poll List, 1783; A2 (2-149).

Poundridge, Westchester County, N. Y.
Census 1800; A2 (58-246).

Pownalborough, Me.
Marriage intentions, 1760-1802; F1 (4-26; 7-17, 215; 8-60).
Marriages, 1760-1801; F1 (7-81; 9-43).
Pew owners, 1771; F2 (5-167).
Vital records; F2 (7-229; 9-241).

Prairie-du-Chien, Wis.
Catholic Parish Registers, 1827-1833; G1 (22-164).

Preston, Conn.
Inscriptions; A1 (60-121).
Marriages, 1769-1811; A1 (55-176).
Vital records; C2 (6-42, 94, 134, 169, 198, 299; 7-10).

Prince Frederick Winyah, S. C.
Inscriptions; J (18-91).

Prince Georges County, Md.
Record sources; X1 (24-17).
Marriage licenses, 1777-1824; A1 (73-134, 217, 261).
St. John's Parish records, 1697-1794; C3 (1-39, 246).

Prince William County, Va.
Tax list, 1784; V2 (2-40).

Prince William Parish, Beaufort County, S. C.
Inscriptions; J (18-180).

Prospect, Me.
Petition, 1789; F1 (2-209).
Marriages and intentions, 1789-1818; F1 (9-166, 189).

Prosperity, Pa.
Inscriptions; B2 (1-52, 67; 2-113).

Providence, R. I.
Proprietors; T6 (3-143, 199; 4-75, 139, 203).
Militia lists, 1687; T6 (7-232).
Tax list, 1679 (*not* 1649); T6 (1-231).
Inscriptions; F4 (4-70, 116, 178, 283; 5-67, 166, 268).
Vital Records (Drowne); A2 (46-80).
Marriages, 1859-1869 (Universalist); A1 (77-175).
Tax list, 1798; T6 (8-161).
Yellow fever victims, 1800; F4 (3-136).
Revolutionary fortifications; F4 (5-209).
Taverns; F4 (8-53).

Provincetown, Mass.
Vital records; D (9-100; 11-47, 187, 216; 12-21, 76; 14-146; 15-149; 22-101; 23-92, 141, 168; 26-112; 27-123).
Inscriptions; D (8-20, 225; 9-222; 10-29, 67; 14-128).

Purrysburgh, S. C.
Early settlers; J (10-187).

Putnam County, Ind.
Revolutionary soldiers buried; Z (48-165).

Putnam County, N. Y.
See Peekskill, Southeast, Tilley Foster, Philipstown, Lake Mahopac, Farmers Mills, Kent Cliffs, Long Pond, Meads Corners.

Putnam, Luzerne County, Pa.
Town records, 1772-1802; Pw (7-157).

Quakers
Index to biographical sketches published in "The Friend," vols. 27-36; P (3-109).
U (2-145).
Cecil County, Md., 1696; X1 (7-328).
Essex County, Mass.; Y2 (1-135; 13-145); C2 (2-179).
Frederick County, Va.; N2 (3-55).

Quaker Records
Location, etc.; Q1 (27-249).
England; P (3-226).
Harrison, N. Y.; A2 (3-45).
New York City; A2 (3-51).
Long Island; A2 (3-184; 4-32, 94, 190; 5-38, 102, 186; 6-97, 192; 7-39, 85).
Gravesend; A2 (4-39).
Rahway, N. J.; A2 (8-176; 9-28, 64, 174; 10-20, 139; 11-42).
Hempstead (Westbury); A2 (16-171).
New York State, location; A2 (45-263, 366).
Washington County; A2 (46-122).
Nansemond and Isle of Wight Counties, Va.; R1 (6-220, 304, 408, 499; 7-17, 96, 207).

Revolutionary War and Soldiers—Cont.

Conn., Capt. Blackman's Co., 1777; Z (46-257; 48-363).

Conn., Soldiers from Tolland County; A1 (59-21).

Conn., Capt. Joseph Stebbins' Co., 1781; A1 (60-331).

Ga.; King's Mountain Volunteers; Z (17-541; 45-154).

Soldiers, Battle of Kettle Creek, Ga.; Z (19-30; 30-493).

Ill. officers; M (16-52).

Buried in Iowa; B2 (2-98); P (8-202).

Ky. roll, 1779; M (16-52).

Maine; C2 (2-153).

Me., Capt. Sullivan's Co., 1777; F1 (3-39).

Me., Orderly Book (Lawrence), Castine, 1779-80; F1 (5-146).

Me., Penobscot River, 1779; F1 (5-226).

Me., Capt. Darby's Co., Old York, 1775; F2 (3-108).

Me., Col. Francis' Regt., 1776; F2 (5-168; 9-72).

Me., pay roll, Capt. Leighton's Co., Col. Francis' Regt.; F2 (5-170).

Me., Capt. Fernald's Co., Kittery, 1775; F2 (3-283).

Me., Capt. Bragdon's Co., Col. Scammon's Regt., 1775; F2 (6-431).

Me., Muster roll, Capt. Dorman's Co., Col. Scammon's Regt., 1775; F2 (6-381).

Me., Col. Cutt's Regt., 1778; F2 (7-219).

Me., Soldiers, York County; A1 (65-76, 107, 254, 333).

Maryland, oath of fidelity, 1778; M (6-1, 33).

Md. Troops, Battle of Long Island; X1 (14-110).

Md., Roll of Capt. Price's Co., 1775; X1 (22-275).

Md., Baltimore County, militia, 1779; X1 (7-90).

Md., Baltimore Co., 1777; X1 (2-367).

Md., Frederick County, soldiers, 1778; X1 (6-256).

Md., Frederick County, Committee of Observation; X1 (10-301; 11-50, 157, 237, 304; 12-10).

Md., Washington County, Committee of Observation, 1775-1776; X1 (12-142, 261, 324; 13-28, 227).

Md., garrison list, 1777; X1 (5-218).

Md., 33d Batt., Militia, 1777; X1 (4-379).

Mass. soldiers; C2 (1-32, 88, 117, 190; 2-93, 153, 168, 221); A1 (58-235).

Newburyport, Mass.; C3 (3-220).

Waggoners, Mass., 1782-1783; A1 (51-39).

Revolutionary War and Soldiers—Cont.

Mass., Capt. Lowell's Co. of Matrosses, 1778; A1 (78-110).

Mass., orderly book of Capt. Putnam of Danvers, 1776; Y1 (67-49, 119, 249, 361).

Mass., Capt. Simeon Brown's Co., Col. Wade's Regt., 1778; Y1 (58-245).

Mass., drafted men, Taunton, 1776; Z (33-1126).

Mass., Muster roll, Capt. Joseph Pray's Co., Col. Nathaniel Wade's Regt.; A1 (54-98).

Mass., Capt. Pierce's Co., Siege of Quebec, 1776; A1 (76-155).

Siege of Boston; A1 (56-48).

Boston Co., 1777; M (18-3).

Boston prisoners; A1 (52-311).

Concord, Mass., soldiers; A1 (61-353; 62-98).

Orderly book, Concord, Mass., company; C2 (1-306, 335; 2-25, 75, 104).

Essex County, Mass.; C2 (7-184).

List 1777 of those driven from Mass. towns since the blockade; A1 (55-388).

N. H. pensioners; M (11-28, 43, 52; 12-4, 21; 13-41; 14-60, 64; 15-17).

N. H., Capt. Enoch Page's Co., 1775; A1 (60-44).

Newark Minute Men, 1776; B1 (1-33).

New Providence soldiers; B1 (2-113; 3-25, 50).

N. J. pensioned widows; B1 (3-129, 159; 4-40, 73, 96, 143).

N. J. Flotilla-men; A2 (22-89).

N. J., diary of a Quaker, 1776; M (2-31, 50; 3-3-1; 3-4-2; 4-58).

Gloucester County, N. J., rolls; P (10-198).

American prisoners on L. I.; A2 (7-175).

American prisoners, N. Y.; A2 (24-85).

Mess Account, 2d N. Y. Regt.; A2 (19-126, 173).

New York Officers; A2 (21-91, 140).

N. Y., Muster-Roll, 8th Co., 1st Regt.; A2 (26-56).

N. Y., Account of arms, 10th Co., 1st Regt.; A2 (27-209).

N. Y. Discharges; A2 (30-235).

Onondaga County (bounty land); A2 (30-237).

Roster of Butler's Rangers; A2 (31-12).

N. Y., 4th Regt., Dutchess County; A2 (46-269).

N. Y. Records; A2 (46-330; 47-172, 283, 336; 48-57).

Roll of Schenectady Company; A2 (48-156).

Revolutionary War and Soldiers—Cont.
Prisoners in Mill Prison, Eng.; Z (28-59).
American prisoners at Quebec, 1776; Q1 (32-119).
Prisoners in Philadelphia, 1778; Q1 (42-173).
American prisoners, Mill Prison, Plymouth, 1782; J (10-116).
Prisoners taken by British; Z (20-1035).
American Prisoners at Quebec; C3 (2-149, 183; 3-43).
Prisoners captured with Ethan Allen; Z (20-163).
Prison Ship Martyrs; Z (17-34, 148, 254, 364, 455; 18-24, 131; 19-29, 503; 23-170, 175, 364; 33-961).
Prisoners, 1778; Q1 (17-159, 316).
Sick at Lititz Hospital, 1778; Q1 (36-379).
Prize money to John Paul Jones' men; Z (29-761; 30-16).
Pay-Roll, Hospital Dept., 1782; Q1 (25-580).
Continental Hospital Returns, 1777-1780; Q1 (23-35, 210).
Naval, list armed vessels, Phila., 1776-77; Q1 (26-145).
Sailors; Q1 (27-115).
Marine Officers; Z (56-23; 57-409).
Marines in Battles of Trenton and Princeton; Z (55-303).
Officers of *Putnam*, 1776; F2 (9-165).
Letters of Daniel Wilcox, 1775-76; A1 (54-440).
Journal, Ingalls of Andover, 1775-1776; Y1 (53-81).
Journal of Dr. Daniel Shute of Hingham, 1781-1782; A1 (84-383).
Correspondence of Col. Aylett, Com. Gen., Va.; V1 (1-87, 145).
Col. John Lamb's 2d Regt., Continental Artillery, roll-book of Capt. Joseph Thomas; A2 (62-245).
Officers under Washington, 1778; Q1 (18-64).
Rhode Island
Town records, location and condition; T6 (1-99).
Miscellaneous early items; C4 (3-119).
Early Magistrates, 1636-1686; F4 (3-87, 249).
Presidential Electors, 1788-1880; F4 (3-144; 6-301).
Judiciary; F4 (7-57).
Baptist Churches; F4 (1-203).
R. I. people in early N. Y. records; F4 (8-241).
Jews; F4 (4-301).
Quaker records; F4 (7-65, 164).
Emigrants to Nova Scotia; F4 (7-89).

Rhode Island—Cont.
Irish settlers; G2 (4-109; 9-365; 15-156).
Revolutionary War rolls; T6 (2-180, 215; 3-248); T7 (vol. 48, 1915, p. 572).
Richardson County, Neb.
Marriages, 1855-1857; B2 (9-35).
See Archer.
Richmond County, N. Y.
See Northfield, Castletown, Southfield, Westfield.
Richmond County, Va.
Marriages, 1709-1716; Z (57-675).
Patriots, 1782; V1 (7-108).
Richmond, Me.
Inscriptions; C1 (1-76).
Richmond, N. H.
Marriages, 1770-1784; A1 (79-244).
Richmond, N. Y.
Inscriptions; A2 (32-40).
Richmond, R. I.
Vital records; F4 (5-74, 181, 259; 6-272, 331).
Richville, N. Y.
Marriages; A2 (50-55).
Ridgebury, Conn.
Cong. Church records; B3 (4-330).
Rising Sun, Md.
Inscriptions; X1 (18-55).
River Edge, N. J.
Huguenot Inscriptions; A2 (41-291).
Riverhead, Suffolk County, N. Y.
Census 1800; A2 (56-330; 57-55).
Roanoke Island, N. C.
H (2-101).
Rochester, Mass.
Vital records, early; K (4-65).
Rochester, N. H.
First Cong. Church records, 1737-1853; F3 (4-145; 5-1, 49, 113, 145; 6-33, 65, 113, 171; 7-27, 85).
Inscriptions; A1 (80-306).
Vital records, 1858-1862; A1 (68-203, 382).
Sketch; S2 (18-358).
Rock Bluff, Neb.
Inscriptions; B2 (8-52).
Rockbridge County, Va.
Inscriptions, Lexington and Timber Ridge; M (11-35).
Rockingham County, N. H.
Deeds; C3 (1-250).
Rockingham County, Va.
Notes; V1 (6-274).
Rockingham, Vt.
First Church records, 1773-1839; A1 (54-197, 289, 435; 55-58, 425; 56-248, 384).
Rockland County, N. Y.
See Orange, Clarkstown, Hempstead, Haverstraw.
Rockport, Mass.
Church records, baptisms, 1755-1808; Y2 (2-151, 189).

Rockville, Montgomery County, Md.
Inscriptions; M (6-32).
Rome, Franklin County, Ohio
Inscriptions; E (7-283).
Ross County, Ohio
Marriages, 1803-; E (6-95, 194; 8-149).
Rowan County, N. C.
Early settlers; M (3-3-14).
Marriage Bonds, 1762-1799; Z (43-547, 654; 45-129; 46-33, 105).
Rowley, Eng.
Y2 (11-36).
Roxbury, Conn.
Inscriptions; A1 (72-77).
Roxbury, Mass.
Marriages, 1841-1849 (Universalist); A1 (77-145).
Royalty
Seize Quartiers of English sovereigns; C2 (1-258).
Russell, Hampden County, Mass.
Census 1800; M (12-13).
Rutland, Worcester County, Mass.
Inscriptions; E (5-85).
Rutland, Vt.
Cong. Church marriages, 1797-1821; Z (46-165).
Rye, N. H.
Baptisms; A1 (66-150, 301).
Vital records; F3 (1-33, 81, 129; 2-135, 191).
Rye, Westchester County, N. Y.
Early families; A2 (49-170, 292, 381).
Baptisms, 1709; Q1 (23-105).
Christ's Church Records, 1790-1879; A2 (37-4, 146, 257; 38-17, 145, 208, 278; 46-234, 403; 47-14, 128, 297, 395; 48-63, 124, 228, 330).
Marriages, 1772-1776; A2 (33-54).
Inscriptions; A2 (16-137).
Census 1800; A2 (57-109).
Saccarappa, Me.
Inscriptions; F2 (1-199).
Saco, Me.
Vital records, earliest to 1780; A1 (71-123, 211).
Deaths, 1765-1803; A1 (52-77).
Sag Harbor
Inscriptions; A2 (2-30).
St. Andrews, N. B.
Inscriptions; F1 (4-167).
St. Andrews, Berkeley County, S. C.
Church register, 1719-1774; J (12-172; 13-21, 104, 154, 213; 14-20, 81, 147, 209; 15-39, 97).
Inscriptions; J (13-113).
St. Andrews Town, S. C.
Notes; J (14-206).
St. Clair, Allegheny County, Pa.
Inscriptions; P (6-24, 25).
St. Clairsville, Ohio
Revolutionary soldiers buried; Z (50-194).

St. Genevieve, Mo.
Church records, 1759-1837; M (5-1, 24, 38, 55; 10-121, 128; 11-17, 57, 64).
Inscriptions; M (10-111, 121).
St. Helena's Parish, S. C.
Church register; J (23-8, 46, 102, 171).
St. James, Santee, S. C.
Church register, 1758-1788; J (15-133, 197; 16-16, 68, 109, 164; 17-34, 73, 103).
Inscriptions; J (12-153).
St. John, N. B.
Settlers; S2 (10-109).
Inscriptions; F2 (7-66, 225; 8-96, 151, 204).
Family notes; F2 (9-49, 81).
St. John's Parish, S. C.
Militia List, 1756; J (23-92).
Inscriptions; J (11-171).
St. Louisville, Ohio
Inscriptions; E (12-155).
St. Mark's Parish, S. C.
Petition, 1758; J (26-122).
St. Mary's County, Md.
Record sources; X1 (26-58).
Justices, 1777; X2 (1-3).
St. Lawrence County, N. Y.
Marriages, 1823-1828 (Baptist); A1 (76-262).
St. Louis, Mo.
Early Irish; G2 (6-46; 9-206).
St. Stephen's Parish, Berkeley County, S. C.
Inscriptions; J (26-113, 158; 27-215).
Salem County, N. J.
Marriages, 1793-1813; B1 (2-23, 45; 4-106, 165; 5-25).
Notes on a few families; A2 (49-117).
Capt. Dubois' Co., Col. Dick's Regt., Pittsgrove, 1775; P (9-186).
Court records, 1751-62; Q1 (37-215).
Resolutions, 1774, with list; M (14-24).
Patriots, 1775; Z (22-232).
See Daretown.
Salem, Conn.
Inscriptions; A1 (80-186).
Salem, Essex County, Mass.
Deaths and departures, c. 1690; C2 (4-146).
Early planters; C3 (3-3).
Inscriptions; C1 (2-19, 54).
Marriage intentions, 1709-1759; C1 (1-5, 51, 105, 153).
Marriages; C2 (6-212; 7-30, 242); C3 (1-14).
Petition, 1667; Y2 (2-27).
Tax lists, 1683, 1700; C3 (2-167; 4-9).
Town records, 1659-1682; C3 (2-153).

Salem, Mass.
Town records, 1680-1686; Y1 (62-81, 177, 257; 63-65; 64-65, 201; 65-25; 66-209, 505; 67-233, 385).
Town records, 1775; C2 (3-219).
Diary entries, 1719-1721; Y1 (51-282).
English origin of settlers; Y1 (66-317).
Essex Guards, 1814; Y1 (57-249; 58-25).
Houses built, 1750-1773; Y1 (58-292).
In 1700; Y2 (2-167; 3-65; 4-17, 97, 161; 5-33, 145; 6-97, 148; 7-18, 67, 116, 160; 8-20, 66, 113, 152; 9-37, 72, 114, 162; 10-21, 60, 114, 152; 11-12, 66, 108, 158; 12-31, 59, 113, 177; 13-35, 80, 132).
Notes; Y1 (51-23, 177, 257, 361; 52-177; 53-332; 54-115, 225, 289; 55-49).

Salem, Washington County, N. Y.
Church; A2 (34-158, 235).
Inscriptions; A2 (37-179, 271; 38-23, 89, 200).
Assessment Roll, 1794; A2 (43-8).

Salem, Westchester County, N. Y.
Census 1800; A2 (58-16, 135).
Church records; A2 (31-82, 174, 238; 32-12, 71, 164, 241; 33-38, 113, 161, 208; 34-47, 89, 221, 295; 35-20, 136).

Saline County, Neb.
Inscriptions; B2 (1-4, 15).

Salisbury, Conn.
Revolutionary soldiers buried; Z (48-51).

Salisbury, Mass.
Inscriptions; A1 (66-88).
Grantees; Y2 (4-154).
Vital records (from County records); Y2 (4-12, 43, 77, 108, 138; 11-32).

Salisbury, Me.
Muster roll, Crown Point, 1756; F2 (1-147).

Salmon Records
See Southold.

Salsbury, Montgomery [now Herkimer] County, N. Y.
Census 1800; A2 (50-314).

Salt Lake City, Utah
Burials, 1848-1861; U (2-86, 132, 182; 3-38; 19-39, 89, 188; 20-191).

Sandwich, Me.
Capt. Nye's Co., 1813-1831; F2 (5-65).

Sandwich, Mass.
Vital records, early; K (3-33, 73; 4-9, 99); D (14-106, 166; 29-21, 68).
Vital entries (Percival Diary), 1777-1817; Dx (1-53, 73, 87, 112; 2-27, 36).

Sanford, York County, Me.
Marriages, 1786-1822; F2 (2-56, 108).
Revolutionary soldiers, 1775; C2 (4-144).

Sangamon County, Ill.
Revolutionary soldiers buried; Z (40-42).

Sangerfield, Oneida County, N. Y
Aged persons, 1871; A2 (2-201).

Santa Barbara, Calif.
Inscriptions; A1 (80-110).

Saratoga County, N. Y.
See Saratoga Springs, Stillwater.

Saratoga Springs, Saratoga County, N. Y.
Inscriptions; A2 (44-177, 289, 389; 45-126; 47-233, 403).
Revolutionary soldiers buried; Z (24-118).

Scaghticoke, Rensselaer County, N. Y.
Dutch Church Records (Groesbeck name); A2 (29-109, 140, 210).

Scandinavia
Research: location of records; U (2-19; 4-75; 6-173; 11-191; 19-1; 20-177, 179; 21-41).
Emigration from Sweden; Q2 (vol. 18); Q1 (2-224).

Scarborough, Me.
First Cong. Church records, 1728-1842; F2 (1-51, 112, 163; 2-29, 78, 162, 230; 3-8, 83, 144, 238; 4-29, 87, 195, 256).
Inscriptions; F2 (7-223).
Land grants, 1663; F2 (1-193).
Miscellaneous records; F2 (3-268; 4-137).
Vital records; F2 (5-56, 114, 134, 214; 6-302, 367, 396; 7-46).

Scarsdale, Westchester County, N. Y.
Census 1800; A2 (57-259).

Schaghticoke, Rensselaer County, N. Y.
Dutch Reformed Church records, 1750-1789; A2 (59-318; 60-15, 124, 267, 358; 61-80, 182, 296, 395; 62-23, 203, 296, 411).

Schenectady, N. Y.
Early Freeholders; A2 (3-71, 104).
Inscriptions; A1 (73-128).
Revolutionary Roll; A2 (48-156).
Agreement, 1776; Z (43-414).

Scituate, Mass.
Vital records; D (1-42, 106, 164, 233; 2-32, 84, 169; 3-117; 5-114; 8-204; 9-85; 10-74).
Inscriptions; D (8-115; 10-27).
First Church records; D (10-90, 175, 225; 11-44, 138, 207).
Second Church (now Norwell) records, 1645-1834; A1 (57-82, 178, 318, 398; 58-82, 168, 260, 387; 59-74, 134, 308, 387; 60-61, 175, 271, 335; 61-56, 172, 288, 372).

Scituate, Mass.—Cont.
 Marriages, 1762-1767; A1 (82-383).
 Universalist Church members, 1827;
  A1 (62-383).
Scituate, R. I.
 Census 1779; M (14-30).
 Revolutionary pensioners; M (14-29).
Scotland [includes Orkneys and Hebrides]
 Records, research, etc., with extracts; U (1-159; 3-41, 84, 135, 178; 4-28, 113, 163; 5-36, 77, 140, 180; 6-26, 74; 7-49, 83, 141; 9-136; 10-35, 191); C2 (6-205).
 Emigrants to N. J.; B6 (6-1).
 Clans; S1 (17-315, 436; 18-313).
 American students in; A1 (78-221).
Seabrook, N. H.
 Sketches; S2 (15-335, 373).
Sedgwick, Me.
 Early settlers; F1 (8-16).
 Census 1785; F1 (9-158).
Setauket, L. I.
 Inscriptions; A2 (15-41).
Sewall's Falls, N. H.
 S2 (20-138).
Shaftesbury, Bennington County, Vt.
 Marriages to 1802; Z (49-344).
 Revolutionary soldiers buried; Z (33-710).
Sheepscot, Me.
 Refugees, 1676; F1 (5-217).
Sheffield, Mass.
 Petition, 1757; C4 (1-65).
 Revolutionary soldiers buried; Z (48-51).
Shelby County, Ky.
 Inscriptions; M (15-16).
Shelbyville, Ky.
 Revolutionary soldiers buried; Z (19-263; 25-8).
Sheldon, Beaufort County, S. C.
 See Prince William.
Shelter Island, Suffolk County, N. Y.
 Census 1800; A2 (56-271).
 Inscriptions; A1 (54-53).
Shepardson College
 With list of graduates; E (8-359).
Shepherdstown, W. Va.
 St. Peter's Lutheran Church, marriages, 1801-1822; Z (61-589); baptisms, 1786-1801; Z (61-371).
Sherman, Conn.
 Inscriptions; B3 (4-114, 333).
 See New Fairfield.
Shiloh, Cumberland County, N. J.
 Inscriptions; B5 (14-138, 163, 190; 15-217, 246, 272, 300).
Shipmasters, 1799
 A1 (61-145).
Shipmasters
 Port of Roanoke, N. C.; H (1-433).

Shirley, Mass.
 Diary of James Parker, 1770-; A1 (69-8, 117, 211, 294; 70-9, 137, 210, 294).
 Inscriptions; A1 (57-68, 200).
 Residents received and refused, 1767-1785; A1 (66-100).
 Capt. Haskell's Co.; Z (17-253).
Shoreham, Vt.
 Inscriptions; M (4-53).
Shrewsbury, Mass.
 North Parish church records, 1743-1791; A1 (77-17).
Shrewsbury, Monmouth County, N. J.
 Inscriptions; A2 (28-55; 34-28, 103, 217).
Skippack, Pa.
 Q2 (35-123).
Smithfield, Atlantic County, N. J.
 Inscriptions; B1 (4-152).
Smithfield, Pa.
 Reformed Dutch Church records, 1742-1807; A2 (57-63, 142).
 Presbyterian Church records, 1832-1852; A2 (57-153).
Smithfield, R. I.
 Marriages, 1730-1850; F4 (3-33, 116, 236, 301; 4-57, 105, 110, 189, 193, 196, 257; 5-54, 55, 173, 176, 240; 6-286, 369, 371; 7-41, 158, 357, 369; 8-33, 201, 210, 211, 217, 230).
 Births and Deaths, 1730-1850; F4 (3-119, 307; 4-100, 108, 112, 192, 196, 264; 5-55, 59, 175, 179; 6-289, 371; 7-50, 162; 8-38, 208, 224, 230).
 Notes; T6 (5-125).
Smithtown, Suffolk County, N. Y.
 Census 1800; A2 (56-10).
 Church records, 1774-1822; A2 (42-128, 272).
 Church records, 1751-1867; A2 (44-279, 384; 45-8).
 Freeholders; A2 (56-102).
Soldiers
 See Revolutionary War, French and Indian War, etc.
 At Fort Albany and Half Moon, 1689; A2 (22-106).
Solon, Onondaga County, N. Y.
 Census 1800; A2 (53-364).
Somers, Conn.
 Inscriptions; A1 (60-307).
 Soldiers, 1762 Expedition; A1 (55-109).
Somers Point, Atlantic County, N. J.
 Inscriptions; B1 (5-86).
Somerset County, Md.
 Record sources; X1 (22-349).
 Vital records, early; M (6-74; 18-30).
 Militia, 1780; X2 (2-25).
Somerset County, N. J.
 Court records; B6 (3-6, 81).
 Origin of early settlers; B6 (5-119, 188, 272; 6-38, 81).

Somerset County, N. J.—Cont.
Marriage licenses, 1795-1879; B6 (1-128, 292; 2-51, 221; 3-64, 311; 4-46, 230, 309; 5-51, 150, 223; 6-232, 281; 7-146, 191, 301; 8-56, 193, 283).
Wills, 1804-1812; B6 (6-303; 7-135, 187, 298; 8-62, 180).
Inscriptions, small graveyards; B6 (1-118, 119, 121, 274; 3-52, 138, 301, 303; 4-64, 136; 5-49, 140, 218, 294, 298, 299; 6-222).
Church records, list; B6 (6-182).
Petition, 1767; B6 (7-28).
Roll, Col. Frelinghuysen's Recruits, 1778; B6 (8-171).
Neshanic Dutch Church records, 1762-1878; B6 (1-133, 221, 286; 2-58, 145, 218, 306; 3-61, 143, 233, 304; 4-57, 148).
Neshanic Church, subscriptions, list; B6 (7-171, 263).
Unrecorded deeds; B6 (7-183).
Roll of Somerset Lodge, No. 1, F. and A. M., 1787-1829; B6 (8-165).
Inhabitants, 1765-1772; B6 (6-92).
Civil List, 1688-1799; B6 (8-33, 119).
Low papers; B6 (8-87, 175).
Johnston Journals, 1743-1763; B6 (1-190, 262; 2-35, 120, 186, 277; 3-19, 106, 193, 261; 4-35, 113, 198).
Journal, with deaths 1823-1864; B6 (7-55, 123).
Manumissions of slaves, 1805-1844; B6 (1-275; 2-46; 6-95, 201).
Losses in Revolution; B6 (1-279; 3-256).
Miscellaneous records; B6 (4-251).
In Revolution; B6 (5-15, 97, 241).
Revolutionary pensioners; B6 (5-45, 197).
Innholders, 1778-1799; B6 (8-277).
Militia roll, 1808; Q1 (29-373).
Kerke op de Millstone; A2 (26-67).

Somersworth, N. H.
Vital records (Tate diary); A1 (73-304; 74-34, 124, 179).

Somerton, S. C.
Notes; J (14-134).

Somerville, Somerset County, N. J.
First Reformed Church records, 1699-1839; B6 (2-38, 138, 209, 298; 3-56, 139, 228, 307; 4-54, 145, 227, 291; 5-64, 147, 228, 306; 6-71, 224, 284; 7-76).
In 1812; B6 (7-241).
Inscriptions; B1 (3-31, 72, 115, 140; 4-20, 60).
Lutheran Church; B6 (2-87, 161).

South Amboy, N. J.
Inscriptions; A2 (21-112).

South Carolina
Deaths, from newspapers, 1766-1782; J (16-34, 86, 129, 184; 17-46, 87, 121, 147).

South Carolina—Cont.
Marriages and deaths from newspapers, 1782-1807; J (18-37, 85, 143, 184; 19-77, 105, 136, 170; 20-52, 142, 213, 260; 21-24, 77, 121, 153; 22-19, 65, 89, 119; 23-26, 72, 152, 205; 24-30, 69; 25-36, 101, 148, 179; 26-45, 128, 162, 228; 27-42, 95, 172, 219; 28-44, 132, 198, 236; 29-49, 151, 258, 329; 30-60, 117, 185, 241).
Deaths, from newspapers, 1732-1781; M (2-47; 3-2-4; 3-3-9; 3-4-5; 4-12, 48, 67; 5-15, 47).
Marriages, S. C. Gazette, 1786, 1788; J (5-119, 192).
Vital items, newspapers, 1797, 1781-1785; M (11-47, 53).
Marriage Bonds, 1743-1744; J (19-95, 130, 162).
Marriage Licenses, 1765-1766; J (22-34).
Early marriage licenses; Z (45-208).
Vital records, Hayne Journal, 1750-1779; J (10-145, 220; 11-27, 92, 160).
Plantation memoranda, Hayne Journal; J (12-14).
Abstracts of Court of Ordinary records, 1692-1712; J (8-164, 195; 9-73, 118, 187; 10-10, 83, 136, 236; 11-50, 123; 12-70, 146, 207; 13-56, 84; 14-58); 1764-1768; J (22-94, 124; 23-34, 77, 158, 213; 24-101; 25-143; 26-124; 27-91; 30-236).
Cattle marks, 1695-1721; J (13-126, 224).
Members of Assembly, 1702-1711; J (27-170).
Inscriptions, miscellaneous; J (27-36, 181; 30-256).
Census 1870, note; J (28-139).
Justices, 1734, 1737; J (11-186).
Justices, 1756; J (20-73).
French settlers; J (18-101).
Swiss settlers; J (21-93; 23-85).
Baronies; J (11-75, 193; 12-5, 43, 109; 13-3, 71, 119; 14-61; 15-3, 63, 149; 18-3).
Manigault Diary, 1754-1781; J (20-57, 128, 204, 256; 21-10, 59, 112).
Revolutionary Association, list, 1775; M (18-1).
Members of 2d Provincial Congress, 1775; J (7-103).
Declaration, 1775, with list; Z (61-909).
Muster rolls, Rev. War; J (5-15, 59, 82, 94, 117, 144, 209; 6-15, 53, 99, 111, 161; 7-20, 69); T7 (vol. 48, 1915, p. 578).
Revolutionary soldiers; J (7-51, 99, 171; 10-128, 184).
Bounty grants to Rev. Soldiers; J (7-173, 217).

Stephentown [Somers], Westchester County, N. Y.
Census 1800; A2 (57-352; 58-9).
Steuben County, N. Y.
Marriages, 1847-1849 (Baptist); A1 (76-262).
See Bath, Lindsley, Middletown, Painted Post, Fredericktown, Canisteo.
Steuben, Me.
Marriages, 1812-1824; F1 (7-182).
Early settlers; F1 (8-221).
Family records; F1 (8-233).
Stillwater, Saratoga County, N. Y.
Inscriptions; A2 (45-81).
Stockbridge, Mass.
Early deeds; B3 (2-289, 396).
Stogumber, co. Somerset, Eng.
Lay subsidy rolls; C3 (4-175).
Stoneham, Mass.
Church records, 1729-1832; A1 (54-392; 55-142; 56-63, 289).
Stonington, Conn.
Revolutionary soldiers buried; Z (42-6).
Stow, Mass.
Inscriptions; K (1-49; 2-57; 3-55; 4-73).
Strafford, N. H.
Marriage records, 1813-1864; A1 (76-27).
Strasburg, Lancaster County, Pa.
Inscriptions; P (10-61).
Stratford, Conn.
Baptisms, 1710; Q1 (23-105).
Stratham, N. H.
Vital records; F3 (1-183; 2-9, 49, 113, 151; 3-11, 121, 161; 4-20, 71, 113; 5-35).
Deaths, 1777-1826; A1 (73-62).
In Revolution; S2 (25-11).
Sketch; S2 (26-133).
Strausbury, Lancaster County, Pa.
Men in Rev. service, 1776; Q1 (25-591).
Strawberry Chapel, S. C.
Inscriptions; J (21-161).
Stroudsburg, Pa.
Inscriptions; Q1 (32-372).
Stroudwater, Me.
Inscriptions; F2 (2-190, 252; 3-267).
Sturbridge, Mass.
Deaths, 1779-1786; A1 (51-188).
Stuyvesant, Columbia County, N. Y.
Inscriptions; A2 (27-42).
Sudbury, Eng.
A1 (56-179).
List of inhabitants, 1592; C4 (3-207).
Sudbury, Mass.
Deaths, 1757-1803; A1 (65-356).
Inscriptions; A1 (61-14, 120).
Settlers, with English origin; A1 (60-357).

Suffield, Conn.
Inscriptions; A1 (60-305).
Suffolk County, Mass.
Superior Court Files; Dx (3-67, 115).
County Court records relating to Essex County; Y2 (9-97; 10-134; 11-83, 182; 12-122, 167; 13-41, 83, 112, 162).
Suffolk County, N. Y.
Marriages, 1804-; A2 (24-86, 159; 25-6, 89, 137, 161).
See Huntington, Smithtown, Islip, South Hampton, Shelter Island, East Hampton, Brookhaven, Riverhead, Southold; also Long Island.
Sullivan, Me.
Early settlers; F1 (1-146).
Pay Rolls, 1777-80; F1 (6-66, 124).
Petition, 1797; F1 (6-155).
Summit County, Ohio
Revolutionary soldiers buried; Z (21-22).
Surnames
See Genealogy.
Surry County, Va.
Marriage Bonds, 1768-1791; V1 (7-111).
Susquehanna County, Pa.
Revolutionary soldiers; Z (39-16).
Revolutionary pensioners, 1835; Pw (11-225).
Susquehanna Purchase
R. I. purchasers; F4 (4-150).
Susquehannah Manor, Md.
Petition with list, 1779; X1 (5-58).
Sussex County, Del.
Gleanings; P (4-5).
Roll, 4th Co., 8th Regt., 1803, 1807; Q1 (30-249).
Sussex County, N. J.
Marriages, 1777-1810; B1 (6-65).
See Sparta, Montague, Lafayette, Sussex, Wantage, Franklin, Hardyston, Hampton, Hamburg, Beemerville.
Sussex County, Va.
Vital entries, 1739-1775; V1 (7-178).
Sussex, Sussex County, N. J.
Inscriptions; B1 (6-20, 47).
Swansea, Mass.
Deaths, King Philip's War; A1 (52-145).
Sweden
See Scandinavia.
Talbot County, Md.
Record sources; X1 (22-186).
St. Michael's Parish, register 1672-1704; Q1 (29-427).
Tamworth, N. H.
Marriages, 1792-1836; S2 (19-217).
Taneytown, Md.
Early settlers; X1 (11-74).

Vermont
Founding; S1 (12-147).
Revolutionary soldiers buried; Z (35-995).
Vernon, Conn.
Church records, 1762-1824; A1 (58-193, 400; 59-95, 208, 412; 60-73, 199, 262).
Inscriptions; A1 (83-357, 496; 84-84).
Vernon, Sussex County, N. J.
Inscriptions; B1 (2-108).
Vincent, Chester County, Pa.
Q1 (34-74, 194, 361).
Vineland, N. J.
Early settlers, 1861-65; B5 (1-11, 24, 41, 54; 2-5, 21, 30, 41, 61); list (3-26, 46, 65; 4-25, 45).
Inscriptions; B5 (2-13, 33, 53, 73; 3-17, 39, 60, 76; 4-5, 18, 39; 5-98, 119, 139, 160; 6-175, 192, 204, 223; 7-14, 31, 46, 63; 8-84, 102, 123).
First Pres. Church records, 1863-1887; B5 (7-5, 20, 40, 61; 8-68).
Inscriptions, Old Soldiers' Home; B5 (14-166, 187).
Vital records, 1863-1888; B5 (3-72; 4-7, 28, 49, 68; 5-90, 110, 131, 150; 6-164, 183, 195, 210; 7-11, 28, 37, 53; 8-76, 88, 109, 130; 9-149, 169, 194, 211; 10-232, 23, 45, 68; 11-88, 107, 126, 144; 12-170, 188, 210, 239; 13-17, 43, 64, 76; 14-116, 123, 150, 183; 15-206, 226, 257, 294).
Members of Lyon Post, G. A. R. [Civil War]; B5 (10-78; 11-97, 119, 139, 159; 12-183, 208, 231, 255; 13-24, 47, 71, 95; 14-118, 143).
Virginia
State Library material; M (19-25).
Bibliographies; M (19-33).
Organization of Counties; M (6-46).
Early Land Patents; V2 (1-85, 109, 144, 210; 2-19, 83, 130).
Marriages, 1792-1796; M (9-46; 12-30).
Vital items, Leesburg newspaper, 1820-21; M (7-31, 54).
Passenger ships, 1607-1624; M (14-23).
Irish settlers; G2 (2-161; 4-30; 13-209; 15-366; 24-87; 26-70).
Wills (miscellaneous); V2 (2-61, 101).
Index, Probate Records, 1772-1776, extinct Fincastle County; Z (61-49).
Legislative Assembly, 1619; M (14-17).
Abstracts, Court cases, 1728-1743; V1 (1-60, 115).
Miscellaneous County records; V1 (7-59, 208).

Virginia—Cont.
District of West Augusta; Court records; N2 (4-21).
Chancery Court abstracts, 1818-21; V2 (2-114).
Military expedition, 1645; C4 (4-21).
Indian captives, 1755-62; Q1 (38-380).
Captives taken by Indians, 1764; Q1 (20-570).
Revolutionary officers and volunteers; M (10-76, 80, 85).
Battle of Point Pleasant, 1774; lists; N2 (2-1-19).
Soldiers, 1775; M (14-24).
Rolls, Revolutionary War; T7 (vol. 48, 1915, p. 588).
Capt. Muhlenberg's German Regt.; Z (42-265).
Col. Penn's Co.; Z (45-206).
Commissioners, Revolutionary War; Z (21-207).
Land warrants issued to soldiers; E (7-109).
Light Dragoon, 1779; M (16-5).
Scots prisoners, 1776; V1 (5-59).
Officers, 9th Regt., 1777; Q1 (22-122).
Society of the Cincinnati; N2 (5-5); V2 (1-29); R1 (4-344).
Women in the Revolution; Z (1-252).
Navy in Revolution; V2 (1-9, 62, 129, 197; 2-3, 65, 117, 123).
Notes from English records; V1 (9-271).
Waldo County, Me.
Inhabitants, 1804; F1 (2-159).
Representatives before 1820; F1 (3-155).
Waldoborough, Me.
Tax list, 1798; K (3-116; 4-43, 147, 152).
Wallingford, Conn.
Sketch; T2 (7-298).
K. Philip's War soldiers; B4 (1-241).
Wallkill, Ulster County, N. Y.
Inscriptions; A2 (27-46).
Walpeck, N. Y.
Church Records, 1741-1830; A2 (40-193, 264; 41-28, 83, 200, 345).
Walpole, Mass.
Warnings, 1779-1807; A1 (57-141).
Walpole, N. H.
Births, 1759-; C3 (2-47).
Walton, Delaware County, N. Y.
Inscriptions; A2 (62-199).
Walworth County, Wis.
Marriages, 1857-1874 (Baptist); A1 (76-262).
Wantage, Sussex County, N. J.
Clove Dutch Reformed Church records, 1785-1819; A2 (57-355; 58-45).
Inscriptions; B1 (6-51).

Westchester County, N. Y.—Cont.
Revolutionary soldiers buried, Middle Patent; Z (44-389).
See Rye, Mamaroneck, North Castle, Harrison, White Plains, Pelham, Scarsdale, New Castle, Yorktown, North Salem, Stephentown [Somers], West Farms, Bedford, Salem, Cortlandt, Poundridge, Greensburgh, Mount Pleasant, New Rochelle, Westchester, Fordham, Morrisania, Yonkers, Eastchester.

Westchester, Westchester County, N. Y.
Census 1698; A2 (38-129).
Census 1800; A2 (59-33).
Oaths of Allegiance, 1698; A2 (59-66).

Westchester, N. Y.
Town records; A2 (60-105, 256, 303).

West Dunstable, N. H.
Settlers; S2 (15-346).
Notes; S2 (10-165).

West Eden, Me.
Early settlers; F1 (7-57).

Westerly, R. I.
Settlement; F4 (1-125; 2-34).
Marriages; F4 (1-50, 128, 182).
Births and Deaths; F4 (1-61, 135, 190).
Signers of Test Act, 1776; Z (28-124).

Western Reserve
See Ohio.

Western Reserve College
E (12-29).

West Farms, Monmouth County, N. J.
Inscriptions; B1 (5-44).

West Farms, Westchester County, N. Y.
Early settlers; A2 (44-236, 313; 45-74, 127, 279, 373).

Westfield, Richmond County, N. Y.
Census 1800; A2 (60-321).

Westfield, Union County, N. J.
Inscriptions; B1 (2-128).

Westford, Conn.
Church records; B3 (11-177).

West Greenwich, R. I.
Early landowners; F4 (3-1).

West Jefferson, Madison County, Ohio
Inscriptions; E (11-62).

West Long Branch, Monmouth County, N. J.
Inscriptions; B1 (6-44).

Westmoreland County, Conn. [Pa.]
Probate records, 1777-1783; Pw (18-139).
Tax lists, 1776-1780; Pw (5-205).

Westmoreland County, Pa.
Abstract of wills; P (5-326; 6-31; 8-46; 11-151).
Abstract of administrations; P (6-251).
Rev. Pay Roll; Z (20-330).

Westmoreland County, Pa.—Cont.
Revolutionary pension applications; M (19-54); Z (21-115; 23-119, 195, 292, 364).
Revolutionary petitions; M (16-60).

Westmoreland County, Va.
Tax list, 1782; V2 (2-98).

Westmoreland, Pa.
Deeds, 1772; Pw (12-205).

West Neck, L. I.
Inscriptions; A2 (26-45).

Weston, Conn.
Inscriptions; T1 (1896-97, pp. 103, 105).

Weston, Somerset County, N. J.
Inscriptions; B6 (1-219).

West Point Pleasant, Ocean County, N. J.
Inscriptions; B1 (1-22).

Westport, Conn.
Inscriptions; T1 (1896-97, p. 77).

West Virginia
Record sources; M (19-69).
Frontier counties; N2 (3-8).
Names of towns; N2 (3-255).
Pioneers; N2 (3-289).

West Yarmouth, Mass.
Inscriptions; D (11-223; 12-44, 90).

Wethersfield, Conn.
Census 1670; T3 (21-197).
Church records (Mix); B3 (7-100, 189, 400; 8-156).

Weymouth, Mass.
Second Church of Christ, records 1723-1818; K (2-65, 113; 3-41, 101; 4-37).
Those slain 1675-1676; A1 (64-186).

White Plains, Westchester County, N. Y.
Census 1800; A2 (57-257).
Early families; A2 (49-170, 292, 381).
Map 1797; A2 (60-130).

Wicacoa, Pa.
Church subscription list, 1684; Q1 (2-342).

Wilkes-Barre, Pa.
First Presbyterian Church, history; Pw (4-45).
Records, 1803-1829; Pw (6-295).
St. Stephen's (Epis.) Church records, 1814-1866; Pw (12-155; 14-251; 15-191).

Williams, Pa.
(Lutheran) Congregation, records, 1733-1831; Q2 (vol. 18).

Williamsburg, Blair County, Pa.
Inscriptions; B2 (3-165).

Williamsport, Pickaway County, Ohio
Inscriptions; E (13-83).

Willington, Conn.
Cong. Church records, 1759-1803; A1 (67-115, 215).
Inscriptions; A1 (67-63, 290, 376; 68-198, 334; 69-82, 183, 274; 70-242).

Willington, S. C.
Inscriptions; J (28-246).
Willtown, S. C.
Early settlers; J (10-20).
Wilmington, Del.
St. Peter's (Catholic) Church; G1
(1-368).
Wilmington, Mass.
Revolutionary soldiers, 1775; C2 (4-
130, 145).
Wilton, N. H.
Sketch; S2 (12-252).
Wiltown Bluff, S. C.
Inscriptions; J (27-104).
Winchester, Conn.
Revolutionary soldiers buried; Z (31-
807).
Winchester, N. H.
Inscriptions; B5 (15-234).
Sketch; S2 (21-268).
Windham, Conn.
Inscriptions; A1 (71-176, 200, 337;
72-78).
Windham, Me.
Vital records, 1744-1762; F2 (3-284).
Settlement and history; F2 (4-35, 98,
197, 248; 5-44, 90, 178, 225; 6-270,
486; 7-32, 108, 156, 210; 8-8, 108,
168; 9-22, 53, 103, 138, 167, 214,
333).
Vital (miscellaneous); F2 (5-139).
Church records, early; F2 (7-33, 161,
210; 8-8; 9-29, 53).
Inscriptions; F2 (5-242; 6-379).
Revolutionary soldiers; B2 (5-23).
Windham, N. H.
Sketch; S2 (5-213; 7-118; 10-86, 248,
280, 296).
Windsor, Conn.
Census, 1670; T3 (21-190).
Revolutionary soldiers buried; Z (19-
589).
Winslow, Me.
Tax list, 1780; F1 (7-44).
Winsted, Conn.
Revolutionary soldiers buried; Z (31-
733; 35-399).
Winthrop, Kennebec County, Me.
Marriages, 1788-1789; M (19-42).
Wintonbury, Conn.
See Bloomfield.
Wiscasset, Me.
Marriages and intentions (selected);
F2 (5-43).
Vital records and inscriptions; F2
(8-74).
Inscriptions; A1 (72-240, 273); F1
(2-235; 3-26).
Militia roll, 1757; F1 (3-109).
See Pownalborough.
Wiscasset (District), Me.
Soldiers, 1757; C2 (2-215).

Wisconsin
List of Episcopal records; E (1-83).
Revolutionary soldiers buried; Z (35-
401).
Irish settlers; G2 (13-237).
Witchcraft
C1 (2-151, 168).
Records relating to, Mass.; A1 (70-
65).
Conn. witches; B4 (4-951).
Woburn, Mass.
Military company, 1649; C3 (5-150).
Wood County, West Va.
Revolutionary soldiers buried; Z (34-
304).
Volunteers, 1806; N2 (4-325).
Woodbridge, Conn.
Sketch; T2 (6-101).
Church records; B3 (10-724; 11-330;
12-157, 313).
Woodbury, Conn.
Militia company, 1795; B3 (4-107).
Woodstock, N. H.
Sketch; S2 (23-11).
Woolwich, Me.
Marriages, 1817-1831; F1 (5-218).
Worcester County, Md.
Record sources; X1 (25-28).
Probate, list of estates, 1667-1742; P
(7-192).
Marriages, 1795-1797; Z (45-249).
Marriage licenses, 1795-1801; X2 (1-
1, 13, 18, 29; 2-4).
Militia, 1794; X1 (21-149).
Worcester, Mass.
Sketch; S1 (13-1).
Worthington, Franklin County, Ohio
Inscriptions; E (1-15, 64, 165; 7-23).
Muster roll, 1808; E (6-153).
Female seminary; E (6-154).
Medical college; E (6-157).
Worthington, Ohio
St. John's (Epis.) Church records,
1833-1844; E (1-125, 176; 2-11; 6-
147).
Methodist Epis. Church; E (7-28).
Presbyterian Church; E (7-33).
Wyoming County, Pa.
Revolutionary soldiers buried; Z (27-
801).
Wyoming Valley, Pa.
Marriages, 1850-1894; Pw (8-292).
Marriage certificates; Pw (12-154;
13-72).
Marriages and deaths, from news-
papers, 1828-1836; Pw (4-133);
same, 1797-1809; Pw (7-204); same,
1810-1818; Pw (10-167).
Massacre, Revolutionary documents;
Pw (7-78; 9-189; 12-69; 13-124).
Sullivan Expedition, 1779; Pw (19-
219).
See Westmoreland County, Conn.

Yarmouth, Mass.
Vital records; D (2-207; 3-36, 245; 4-188; 5-27, 159; 7-246; 9-251; 10-24, 242; 11-111; 13-220; 23-108).
Marriage records; B3 (3-109, 258).
See Dennis.

Yarmouth, Nova Scotia
Marriages, 1772-1795; D (9-40, 124, 132, 197; 10-3, 83).

Yonkers, Westchester County, N. Y.
Census 1800; A2 (59-36).
Oaths of Allegiance, 1698; A2 (59-68).

York County, Me.
Early marriages from Court files; F2 (4-60, 293).
Miscellaneous items; F2 (4-142, 218, 289; 6-427).
Wills, list to 1774; F2 (9-109).
Court records, miscellaneous; F2 (9-233, 262, 343, 383).
Marriages, 1771-1794; A1 (63-167).
Registers of Deeds, 1642-1872; F2 (3-136).
2d Regt., 1776; F2 (8-186).
Revolutionary soldiers; A1 (65-76, 107, 254, 333).

York County, Pa.
German settlement; Q2 (vol. 24).
Recruits, 1778; Q1 (25-420).

York County, Va.
Miscellaneous records; V1 (2-204, 270).
Clerks, 1638-1919; V1 (8-264).
Presbyterians, 1765; V1 (5-66).
Notes; V1 (5-208, 256; 6-60, 276).

York, Me.
Early families; F1 (7-14).
Inscriptions; M (7-43).
Militia lists, 1696, 1720; F2 (3-109).
Diary of Jeremiah Weare; A1 (55-55; 63-296; 64-180; 66-77, 155, 261, 311).

York, Pa.
Moravian Church records; P (4-324).

York, Va.
Notes; V1 (9-95).

York-Hampton, York County, Va.
Tax list, 1763; V1 (7-179).

Yorktown, Westchester County, N. Y.
Census 1800; A2 (57-345).
Marriages, 1783-1824; see Journal of Rev. Silas Constant, 1903; p. 369.
Baptisms; same, p. 386.
Church Meetings; same, p. 390.

Zanesville, Ohio
Marriages, Putnam Pres. Church, 1841-1898; E (4-52).

INDEX

TO

GENEALOGICAL PERIODICALS

BY

DONALD LINES JACOBUS, M.A.

Volume II

HOW TO USE THIS INDEX

For Inexperienced Searchers

Preliminary

Genealogical sources are of two kinds. Primary sources are original records in which contemporary mention of your ancestors was made. Among these are probate, court and land records, vital statistics kept by towns or churches, cemetery inscriptions, pension files and census schedules.

The information you want may not be in print. Even if it is, verification in primary sources is often desirable. Nevertheless, much can be accomplished by the use of secondary sources in libraries. These are, in general: family genealogies; town and county histories; published vital statistics of towns or churches; and digests of probate or other records.

The first step is to try your library catalogue for a genealogy of your family. Consult also American and English Genealogies in the Library of Congress, and Munsell's Genealogical Index (1900, Supplement 1908) for the surnames in which you are interested. If your own library does not have some of the books listed which you wish to consult, join a society which has a lending library, such as the New England Historic Genealogical Society in Boston, and borrow the books.

Use also this Index and the first volume (1932) which preceded it. The two index volumes cover nearly all the genealogical data which has appeared in American periodicals since 1900 and much before that date. Even if there is a printed family history of the surname in which you are interested, there may have been more recent discoveries or important corrections published in magazine articles.

Use of this Index

Turn first to the Name Index and look for the surname you seek. Following the surname is the first name of the original American settler and his earliest or chief place of residence. When the name of the first settler is not given in the article listed, the index places in parentheses the Christian name of the earliest known member of the family or the name of the individual with whom the account begins.

In a separate index will be found, alphabetically arranged, Family and Bible Records. Here, under the surname, is given in parentheses the earliest male member of each family. The earliest known residence is also given if mentioned in the family record. When name and place are given, the consultant can often determine without looking up the article whether it is likely to relate to his family.

Following this, Revolutionary Pensions are indexed separately. If the pension application of your ancestor has appeared in print, the reference should appear here. If you do not find here the name of your own ancestor, it may pay at times to look up the pension records of others of the surname who lived in the same region, for sometimes a great deal of collateral information is included in the pension files, and a pensioner may have been a near relative of your ancestor. The same observation applies to the index of Family Records.

The Place Index is arranged by states alphabetically arranged and foreign countries are also included. Under the state look for both the county and the township (or village) where your ancestors lived. If records of these places are in print, follow up the references; in a magazine article you may find one or more items of importance to you, perhaps the marriage bond of your ancestor or the record from his gravestone.

A final section, the Topic Index, is a catch-all for items which do not fall under the preceding categories. The student with plenty of time at his disposal may find it rewarding to read through the titles in this index. Here he will be referred to articles on heraldry, on methods of research, on the interpretation of records, and on many allied subjects.

In the first volume, all name references (including family and pension records) were listed under a single Name Index, and topics were (inadequately) listed in the Place and Subject Index under such headings as Genealogy, Heraldry, and Passenger Lists.

Other Indexes

In addition to Munsell's Index, already mentioned, try the four index volumes covering Volumes 1 to 50 of The New England Historic Genealogical Register and index volumes of the Collections of the Essex Institute for New England ancestry; and Swem's Virginia Index for southern ancestry. Most of the genealogical magazines provide full-name indexes for the individual volumes, and as a last resort these can be consulted. The purpose of the present Index is to save time and effort by indicating where any substantial amount of material on

specific families or places may be found. This may
lead you to just what you want. But it sometimes hap-
pens that the single item you seek is buried so deeply
that no general index can indicate its location; and
then the searcher, if he possess the leisure and the re-
quisite patience, has no recourse except to plod through
the indexes of perhaps hundreds of individual volumes
or even to read through unindexed volumes. Patience is
sometimes rewarded, as the author discovered when he
once found precisely what he sought in the eighth volume of a seventeen-volume set of unindexed books after
fruitless page-by-page inspection of the first seven
volumes.

Reference Symbols

In this Index, each periodical is assigned a reference symbol, such as A2, M, WF, etc. A key is provided
and for convenience is printed twice, in the front and
back of the book.
Following the symbol, the first figures refer to
volume, the second to page. Thus, A1 (94-308) means
Volume 94, page 308, of The New England Historical and
Genealogical Register. In a few cases three sets of figures have to be given, because each issue of a volume is
separately paged. Here the first numeral indicates the
volume, the second the issue (quarter or month), the
third the page.

THE BIRTH OF AN INDEX

To the hasty searcher who casually makes use of the Index, it may seem to have sprung, like Athena, full-grown from the brow of Jove. Its real genesis was far different and far more laborious.

From year to year the compiler indexed genealogical magazines as they appeared, and these were published annually in The American Genealogist. It might be supposed it would be a simple matter to combine the fifteen annual indexes and presto, the book! The actual processes are complex and involved.

The problem was to combine fifteen separate indexes into a single unit with alphabetical arrangement. At first it was thought that each index could be cut into strips and each item pasted on a slip, and the slips alphabetically arranged, This was tried with one issue, but the strips were narrow and hard to handle, and it was feared that after pasting, constant handling of the slips would cause the pasted strips to rub and tear or come loose.

Pasting was abandoned, and it was decided to type all entries on separate slips. This was done an issue at a time, the typed entries read back and verified, and then each set of slips was distributed in alphabetical order through the main body of slips already organized.

This involved employing an assistant who typed the slips; the verifying was done by typist and compiler together, and the compiler arranged the slips. Frequently entries had to be combined, when articles were continued from volume to volume.

A printing estimate had been obtained, and it was figured that the sales during the first year would cover printing costs and the assistant's time. Thereafter, it was hoped that occasional sales would compensate the compiler for some portion of his own time.

The printing house closed after the Index was started, and new estimates were three times higher. At such prices, the Index could be produced only if the compiler donated all of his time and was prepared to absorb a money loss of from $1,500.00 to $2,000.00. The choice was between abandoning the project or turning to lithoprinting.

Lithoprinting is cheaper than ordinary printing, and it might be supposed that by use of this process the cost of the Index might be reduced from the $12.00 per copy which it was estimated would have to be charged to cover the costs of ordinary composition and printing.

However, the saving in one direction was offset by increased costs in another direction.

It must be understood that in ordinary printing the contract price includes the setting up of the type (composition), the actual printing or press work, and binding. In lithoprinting only the second of these three processes is covered by the price.

In the place of composition, the author has to provide a perfect typescript or master copy which the lithoprinters reproduce by their process. In the case of ordinary printing, the compositors do this work, and they could have set up the book from the typed slips which had been prepared. Instead of that, the services of a typist was required for many weeks, to prepare the typescript, and each typed page had to be checked and verified by the compiler. Slight errors had to be painted out and typed over, while a more serious error might involve cutting the typed columns and pasting with rubber cement.

Hire of a typist and the additional time the compiler had to spend, and the cost of binding the books at a binding establishment after they had been lithoprinted, made the total cost as high as had originally been estimated. That would not be true of most books done by the lithoprinting process, but because of the nature of the Index, the entire work had to be typed and verified twice.

Useful though the Index is in its field, the sale of such a book is very limited. Only 300 copies are printed. The sales of the first year, it is estimated, will cover the money cost of production (typing, printing, binding, mailing, circularizing). Sales in future years, it is hoped, will bring the compiler some small return on his large donation of personal time and labor. To speak of a commercial profit on a publication of this type, would be laughable.

Despite great care, perfection in a work of this kind is not likely to be attained. The compiler will welcome the information if errors or omissions are noted.

Acknowledgments

The earlier volumes of Proceedings of the New Jersey Historical Society were indexed by Mr. Philip Mack Smith of Washington, D. C.; and The Journal of American Genealogy was indexed by Mr. Herbert F. Seversmith of Washington, D. C. Mr. Richard B. Sealock, Curator of the Queens Borough Library, Jamaica, N. Y., kindly supplied the items from The Jerseyman.

KEY TO PERIODICALS

A1 The New England Historical and Genealogical Regis-
    ter. Vols. 86-100. 1932-1946.
A2 The New York Genealogical and Biographical Record.
    Vols. 63-77. 1932-1946.
B1 The Genealogical Magazine of New Jersey. Vols. 7-
    20. 1931-1945.
B2 The Nebraska and Midwest Genealogical Record. Vols.
    10-18. 1932-1943.
B4 The American Genealogist. Vols. 9-23. 1932-1947.
B5 The Vineland Historical Magazine. Vols. 17-30.
    1932-1946.
B7 Cape May County New Jersey Magazine of History and
    Genealogy. Vols. 1-2 (Nos. 1-5). 1931-1943.
C5 The Grafton Magazine of History and Genealogy. Vols.
    1-2. 1908-1910.
Col The Colorado Genealogist. Vols. 1-7. 1939-1946.
D   The Mayflower Descendant. Vols. 29 (Nos. 3 and 4)-
    34. 1931 (July)-1937.
Dt The Detroit Society for Genealogical Research Maga-
    zine. Vols. 2-10. 1938-1947. [Vol. I contained
    no genealogical data.]
E1 The County Court Note-Book. Vol. 10. 1931. [Final
    volume.]
E2 The Delaware Historical and Genealogical Recall.
    Vol. 1. 1933. [All published.]
E3 Early Settlers of New York State. Vols. 1-8. 1934-
    1942.
G1 Records of the American Catholic Historical Society
    of Philadelphia. Vols. 43-44. 1932-1933.
H1 North Carolina Historical and Genealogical Record.
    Vols. 1-2 (Nos. 1 and 2). 1932-1933. [All pub-
    lished.]
H2 The North Carolina Historical Review. Vols. 9-13.
    1932-1936.
J   South Carolina Historical and Genealogical Magazine
    Vols. 31-47. 1930-1946.
JM The Jerseyman. Vols. 1-10.
K2 The Filson Club History Quarterly. Vols. 15-20.
    1941-1946.
L1 Year Book, Church of the Advent: Cape May, N. J.
    Nos. 1-6. 1927-1932.
LI The Long Island Historical Society Quarterly. Vols.
    1-4 (No. 1). 1939-1942. [All published.]
M   National Genealogical Society Quarterly. Vols. 20-
    34. 1932-1946.
N3 Register of Kentucky State Historical Society. Vols.

30-44. 1932-1946.
N4 East Tennessee Historical Society Publications.
Vols. 1-14. 1929-1942.
Ng The Niagara Frontier Genealogical Magazine. Vols.
1-6. 1941-1946.
NE Magazine of New England History. Vols. 1-3. 1891-
1893.
NH Historical New Hampshire. [Occasional publication.]
O The Ohio Genealogical Quarterly. Vols. 1-8 (Nos. 1
and 2). 1937-1944 (Apr.).
OU Olde Ulster. Vols. 1-10. 1905-1914.
P Publications of The Genealogical Society of Pennsyl-
vania. Vols. 11 (No. 3)—15 (No. 1). 1932-1945.
Pw Wyoming Historical and Geological Society. Vols.
21-22. 1930, 1938.
Q1 Pennsylvania Magazine of History and Biography.
Vol. 55-63. 1931-1939. [Recent volumes, 1940-
46, contain virtually no genealogy.]
S1 Americana-Illustrated. Vols. 1-11 (called American
Historical Magazine, vols. 1-3). 1906-1916.
Vols 19-37. 1925-1943. [Vols. 12-18 were includ-
ed in the first volume of the Index.]
S3 The Bulletin of the California State Society Sons
of the Revolution. Vols. 9-17. 1932-1938. [La-
ter volumes have no genealogical data.]
S4 The Journal of American Genealogy. Vols. 1-5.
1921-1925.
T8 Bulletin of Connecticut Historical Society. Vols.
1-11. 1934-1944.
T9 New York Historical Society Quarterly Bulletins.
Vols. 21-30. 1937-1946.
U The Utah Genealogical and Historical Magazine. Vols.
23-30. 1932-1939.
V1 Tyler's Quarterly Historical and Genealogical Maga-
zine. Vols. 13-28. 1931-1947.
V3 The Virginia Magazine of History and Biography.
Vols. 40-54. 1932-1946.
W2 William and Mary College Quarterly Historical Maga-
zine. Second Series, Vols. 12-24. 1932-1944.
[Subsequent volumes contain no genealogy.]
WF Wisconsin Families. Vol. 1. 1940-41. [All pub-
lished.]
X1 Maryland Historical Magazine. Vols. 27-41. 1932-
1946.
X2 Maryland Genealogical Bulletin. Vols. 3-17. 1932-
1946.
Y1 The Essex Institute Historical Collections. Vols.
68-82. 1932-1946.
Z Daughters of the American Revolution Magazine.
Vols. 65-80. 1932-1946.
Z1 The Hyde Park Historical Record. Vols. 1-9. 1891-
1913.

Z2 The Register of the Lynn Historical Society. Vols.
    1-24. 1897-1929.
Z3 Proceedings of the New Jersey Historical Society.
    Series I, Vol. 1-Series IV, Vol. 16. 1845-1931.
    [Indexed by three numbers indicating Series, Vol.
    and page, and covering the first 49 vols.]. Vols.
    50-64. 1932-1946.

ALEXANDER; N. J.; Bl (14-25, 49).
ALEXANDER; St. Paul's, King George
Co., Ga.; M (29-67, 69).
ALEXANDER; (will of John), Va.,
1677; Vl (21-122).
ALEXANDER; (Solomon), Newton, Mass.;
Sl (25-430).
ALFORD, BENJAMIN; Boston, Mass.; Bl
(14-49).
ALFORD, DAVID; Woodbridge, N. J.;
Bl (14-51).
ALFREE, THOMAS; Shrewsbury, N. J.;
Bl (14-51).
ALGER, TRISTRAM; Me.; English ori-
gin; Al (96-91).
ALGER [AUGUR], THOMAS; New Haven,
Conn.; Woodbridge, N. J.; Bl (14-
52).
ALGORE; co. Essex, Eng.; U (24-13).
ALISEA, LOUIS SANTO; Baltimore, Md.;
X2 (9-28).
ALLABEN, JOHN; Braintree, Mass.; S4
(3-37).
ALLCOTT, WILLIAM; Northampton, N. J.;
Bl (14-54).
ALLEN, BENNET (REV.); Md.; Xl (38-
299).
ALLEN, CHARLES; Elizabethtown, N. J.;
Bl (15-32).
ALLEN, EDWARD; Ipswich, Mass.; N. J.
branch; Bl (15-34); (Sylvanus3);
Nantucket, Mass.; NE (3-146).
ALLEN, GEORGE; Sandwich, Mass.; Bl
(16-1, 25).
ALLEN, JAMES; Kerr's Creek, Ky.; N3
(43-345).
ALLEN, JOHN; Marblehead, Mass.; Z2
(14-41).
ALLEN, JOHN; Sandwich, Mass.; Bl
(16-49).
ALLEN, MATTHEW; Burlington Co., N.
J.; Bl (16-32).
ALLEN, RALPH; Sandwich, Mass.; N. J.
branches; Bl (16-73; 17-7, 25, 49).
ALLEN; Martha's Vineyard, Mass.; Al
(91-170).
ALLEN; miscellaneous, N. J.; Bl (17-
50, 73; 18-16, 25, 50, 73).
ALLEN; Augusta County, Va.; W2 (13-
187).
ALLEN; (will of William, Sandwich,
Mass., 1705); D (32-26).
ALLEN; (Jedediah), Shrewsbury, N. J.;
M (29-65).
ALLEN; (John), Argyle, N. Y.; A2 (73-
83).
ALLEN; (Paschal), Seekonk, Mass.; M
(32-76).

ALLEN; (will of Ursula L.), Fauquier
Co., Va., 1793; Dt (4-55).
ALLEN; (will of William), Elizabeth
Co., Va., 1731; Vl (19-110).
ALLER; New Jersey; Bl (19-1).
ALLERTON, ISAAC; Plymouth, Mass.;
Sl (33-282); Bl (19-4).
ALLERTON; Gift to Dr. Giles Heale;
D (34-1).
ALLES, JOHAN-JACOB; Lancaster Co.,
Pa.; M (29-91).
ALLEY, HUGH; Lynn, Mass.; Z2 (10
[1906]-88 ff.).
ALLIN, JOHN (REV.); Dedham, Mass.;
English ancestry of wife Katha-
rine Deighton; B4 (9-212).
ALLINDER; New Jersey; Bl (19-9).
ALLING, ROGER; New Haven; N. J.
branches; Bl (19-25).
ALLINSON, JAMES; Burlington Co., N.
J.; Z3 (2-8-71).
ALLINSON, JOSEPH; Burlington, N. J.;
Bl (19-30).
ALLISON, RICHARD (CAPT.); Burling-
ton, N. J.; Bl (19-53).
ALLISON; Vl (17-190).
ALLMON, JOSEPH; Newcastle Co., Del.;
Bl (19-56).
ALLOWAY, JOHN; Northampton, N. J.;
Bl (19-57).
ALLSEBROOK, GEORGE-SAMUEL; Col.;
English ancestry; Col (3-69).
ALLYN, MATTHEW; Hartford, Conn.; M
(26-56).
ALLYN, ROBERT; New London; M (26-
55).
ALLYN, THOMAS; Barnstable, Mass.;
Ng (2-117).
ALLYN; (estate of Thomas of Barn-
stable, 1697); D (31-185).
ALMY, WILLIAM; Portsmouth, R. I.;
Bl (19-58); English data; Al (100-
217).
ALMY; Portsmouth, R. I.; NE (2-182).
ALPAUGH; New Jersey; Bl (19-73).
ALSTON, JOHN: Woodbridge, N. J.; Bl
(19-77).
ALSTON, WILLIAM; N. C. and Ga.; Hl
(2-3).
ALSTON; N. C.; J (39-145).
ALTON, ERASMUS; Westchester, N. Y.;
Rahway, N. J.; Bl (20-1).
ALWARD, (WIDOW) ANNE; Woodbridge,
N. J.; Bl (20-3, 25).
ALYEA, ALICE, JAN; Hackensack, N.J.;
Bl (20-26, 31).
AMBLER, JOSEPH; Philadelphia, Pa.;
Bl (20-30).

AVERY, CHRISTOPHER; New London,
Conn.; S1 (20-415).
AXSON; S. C.; Ga.; A1 (95-203).
AXTELL, THOMAS; Sudbury, Mass.; S1
(26-164).
AXTELL; Shenley, Herts, Eng.; B4
(13-205).
AYER, JOHN; Haverhill, Mass.; S1
(32-152).
AYRES, RICHARD; Stamford, Conn.; S1
(27-326).

BABCOCK, JAMES; Stonington, Conn.;
S1 (21-241).
BACKER, JACOB; New York; M (30-7).
BACKERT, ANTON; Cleveland, Ohio; S1
(22-81).
BACKUS, WILLIAM; Norwich, Conn.; B4
(14-242).
BACON, MICHAEL; Dedham, Mass.; S1
(26-139).
BACON, NATHANIEL; Barnstable, Mass.;
English origin; B4 (22-187).
BACON, SAMUEL; Salem, N. J.; Z3 (4-
6-188, 255).
BACON, WILLIAM AND MICHAEL; Salem
and Dedham, Mass.; English ances-
try; A1 (90-300).
BACON; notes; S4 (2-270).
BADDIE, THOMAS; New York; A2 (65-
234).
BADGER; Utah; U (24-19).
BADIE, THOMAS; A2 (64-107).
BAGG, JOHN; Springfield, Mass.; S1
(20-145).
BAGGERLY, JOHN; Md.; family records
(Isaac3), Va.; M (31-40).
BAGNALL, ANTHONY (DR.), JAMES AND
ROGER: Va.; W2 (18-350).
BAILEY, JOHN; Hartford, Haddam,
Conn.; S1 (36-479).
BAILEY, JOHN; Cleveland, Ohio; S1
(24-103).
BAILEY; notes; S4 (2-347).
BAILEY; Louisa Co., Va.; W2 (14-
241).
BAIRD, JOHN; Tapenamus, N. J.; S4
(1-351).
BAKER, RICHARD; Dorchester, Mass.;
A1 (86-3).
BAKER, RICHARD; S. C.; J (34-62).
BAKER, THOMAS; East Hampton, N. Y.;
B4 (9-201).
BAKER; Lancaster Co., Pa.; Prince
Edward Co., Va.; V3 (49-311; 50-
181).
BAKER; (will of Francis, 1693); D
(31-107).

BALDWIN, JOSEPH; Milford, Conn.;
S1 (20-152); wife identified; B4
(16-64).
BALDWIN, SYLVESTER; Milford, Conn.;
S1 (32-221; 34-668).
BALDWIN; notes; S4 (2-343).
BALDWIN; Litchfield Co., Conn.; B4
(16-239).
BALE, BENJAMIN; Dorchester, Boston;
A1 (86-456).
BALFOUR; (will of James), Charles
City County, Va., 1742; V1 (19-
218).
BALIOL; baronial family; S1 (36-
772).
BALL, ALLING; New Haven, Conn.; B4
(10-208).
BALL, JOHN; Watertown, Mass.; S1
(34-615, 655).
BALL; Immigrants; S4 (1-183).
BALL; Va.; W2 (14-46, 47).
BALL; Bayside, Talbot Co., Md.; X1
(40-154).
BALL; Identity of Mary (Johnson);
W2 (15-176).
BALL; (Esther, Mrs. Chinn); W2 (18-
294).
BALL; (Frank-Daniel), Spencer, Mass.;
Col.; Col (2-68).
BALLARD; (Col. Thomas), Williams-
burg, Va.; V1 (28-125).
BALLOU, MATURIN; Providence, R. I.;
S1 (29-447).
BANCKER, GERRIT; Albany, N. Y.; S1
(26-293); arms; A2 (65-60).
BANCROFT, JOHN; Lynn, Mass.; B4 (17-
21); Reading line; S1 (34-624).
BANCROFT, THOMAS; Reading, Mass.;
A1 (94-215, 311; 95-56, 109, 276,
363; 96-49, 126, 284, 327; 97-
65, 124, 214; 100-256).
BANCROFT; notes; S4 (2-355).
BANGS, EDWARD; Plymouth, Eastham,
Mass.; S1 (26-545; 27-125);
English origin; S1 (36-518).
BANISTER; notes; V1 (18-245).
BANKHEAD; Caroline Co., Va.; V1
(18-249).
BANKS, ADAM; Stafford County, Va.;
V1 (15-116, 236).
BANKS, RICHARD; York, Me.; A2 (63-
22).
BANKS, WILLIAM; King and Queen Co.,
Va.; V1 (16-20, 114).
BANKS; Stafford Co., Va.; addenda;
V1 (17-179).
BANNING, PHINEAS; Dover, Del.; S1
(19-221).

BANNING, SAMUEL; Lyme, Conn.; S1 (22-88; 26-516).

BANTON, ANDREW; Boston, Mass.; English clue; A1 (100-220).

BARADALL; Williamsburg, Va.; V3 (44-180).

BARBER, PATRICK; N. Y.; A2 (71-42).

BARCLAY, JOHN; Perth Amboy, N. J.; origin and royal ancestry; Z3 (58-202, 254).

BARDENS; Walpole, Mass.; A1 (88-211).

BAREFOOTE, WALTER; York, Maine; Dover, N. H.; A1 (95-213).

BARHAM, CHARLES (CAPT.); Surry Co., Va.; V3 (48-276, 358).

BARKER; (will of Robert, 1692); D (31-102).

BARKER; (Jonathan of Middleborough); D (31-18).

BARLOW, JOHN; Fairfield, Conn.; Dt (8-105).

BARNARD, RICHARD; Middletown, Pa.; Dt (4-95).

BARNARD, THOMAS; Salisbury, Mass.; S1 (25-271; 31-165; 36-807).

BARNE; London, Eng.; ancestral to Lovelace; S1 (36-245; 37-199).

BARNES, THOMAS; Farmington, Conn.; B4 (9-40).

BARNES; (will of Richard), 1687; B4 (14-187).

BARNES; (Quaker marriage, Trenton, N. J.); B5 (21-227).

BARNET, JOHN; Goochland County, Va.; W2 (16-272).

BARNETT; Va.; Ga.; W2 (12-202).

BARNEY, WILLIAM; Baltimore, Md.; X2 (14-55).

BARNUM, THOMAS; Danbury, Conn.; S1 (19-391).

BARRINGTON; Baronets, Hatfield-Broad-Oak, Essex, Eng.; A1 (91-68).

BARRINGTON; notes; S4 (4-69).

BARRON, ELLIS; Watertown, Mass.; B4 (20-135; 21-177).

BARROWS; (will of John, 1692); D (31-159).

BARTHOLOMEW, WILLIAM; Branford branch, corrections; B4 (10-129).

BARTLETT, THOMAS; Talbot, Md.; X1 (41-236).

BARTON, THOMAS (REV.); Philadelphia, Pa.; origin; M (30-1).

BARTON, WILLIAM (CAPT.); St. Mary's County, Md.; U (24-152).

BARTON; notes; S4 (3-238).

BARTOO [BARTEAU], Francis; Flushing, N. Y.; branch of Silas4; E3 (1-6, 18, 29, 55, 67, 78, 91, 106, 114).

BASS, SAMUEL; Braintree, Mass.; S1 (34-684).

BASS; (John), Va., Ky.; S1 (19-211).

BASSETT, MICHAEL; New York, N. Y.; A2 (72-42); S1 (26-29).

BASSETT, WILLIAM; Lynn, Mass.; Z2 (10 [1906]-85).

BASSETT; Uley, co. Gloucester, Eng.; B4 (10-20).

BATCHELDER, STEPHEN (REV.); Hampton, N. H.; S1 (25-276).

BATCHELDER; (wife of Capt. Edmund, Wenham, Mass.); A1 (100-69).

BATES, EDWARD; Weymouth, Mass.; Ng (4-111).

BATES, JAMES; Dorchester, Mass.; Z (74-11-53).

BATES, JOHN; York Co., Va.; (Benjamin?); V3 (51-87).

BATES; notes; S4 (5-37).

BATTAILE, JOHN; Essex County, Va.; V3 (41-175, 257, 356).

BATTE, JOHN; Va.; M (32-43).

BATTISCOMBE, PETER; English data; A1 (100-217).

BATTON; (Henry), Chester Co., Pa.; Ind.; Dt (8-130).

BAXTER, FRANCIS; Enfield, Conn.; S1 (22-449).

BAXTER, GEORGE and THOMAS; New York; A2 (70-3).

BAYARD, SAMUEL and JUDITH; origin; arms; A2 (65-345; 72-310).

BAYFORD; Fornham, co. Essex, Eng.; A1 (96-301).

BAYLEY, JOSEPH; Huntington, N. Y.; B4 (10-46, 202).

BAYLOR, JOHN; Caroline County, Va.; S1 (28-564).

BAYLOR; (will of Gregory), King & Queen Co., Va.; V1 (19-161).

BEAL, JOHN; Hingham, Mass.; B4 (13-262).

BEALE; (family of Benjamin3, Braintree, Mass.); A1 (91-372).

BEANE; London, England; B4 (15-143).

BEAR; Elkton, Va.; W2 (21-177).

BEARD; Va., Md.; W2 (18-351).

BEARDSLEY, WILLIAM; Stratford, Conn.; S3 (14-3-7); Dt (5-129).

BEARDSLEY; notes; S4 (4-28).

BEARSE, AUSTIN; Plymouth, Mass.; U (26-99); B4 (15-111).

BEASMAN; (William), Baltimore Co., Md.; X2 (10-26).

BEATTY, GEORGE; Pa., Va.; M (30-94).
BEAUCHAMP, EDMUND; Md.; English data;
Z (66-234).
BEAUVOIS, DE, CAREL; New York; A2
(66-376).
BEBOUT, JAN; New York; with ances-
try in Flanders; A2 (66-102, 237;
76-34).
BECK; Charles Co., Md.; X2 (16-14).
BECKWITH, MARMADUKE (SIR); Richmond
Co., Va.; V3 (44-182).
BECKWITH, MATTHEW; wife of Joseph[2],
Lyme, Conn.; B4 (18-15); correc-
tions of Genealogy; B4 (21-259;
22-49).
BEDELL, ROBERT; Hempstead, N. Y.;
A2 (71-3, 144, 245, 368; 72-62,
143).
BEDFORD; (Stephen), Cumberland Co.,
Va.; W2 (17-116).
BEDLE; England; B4 (23-149).
BEDLO, ISAAC; New York, N. Y.; ori-
gin of family; A2 (72-221).
BEEBE, JOHN; New London, Conn.; S1
(34-150); Bible records (Roder-
ick); E3 (5-377).
BEECHE, THOMAS; New York; A2 (68-
104).
BEECHER, ISAAC; New Haven, Conn.;
S1 (26-566).
BEECK; (will of William, Kingston,
N. Y., 1684); OU (3-274).
BEEKMAN, MARTIN; Albany, N. Y.; Ng
(5-232).
BEEKMAN, WILLIAM; coat-of-arms; A2
(64-358).
BEHEATHLAND, ROBERT; Jamestown, Va.;
W2 (12-26).
BEHETHLAND; St. Paul's Parish, K.
George County, Va.; W2 (13-28).
BELCHER, GREGORY; Braintree, Mass.;
A2 (73-chart opp. 172); S1 (34-
690).
BELDEN, RICHARD; Wethersfield, Conn.;
B4 (10-51, 191); probate of des-
cendants; B4 (23-117).
BELL; Rowan County, N. C.; U (24-78).
BELL; (estate of John, 1700), Yar-
mouth, Mass.; D (34-130).
BELLMAN, CONRAD CORNELIUS (DR.);
Berks Co., Pa.; P (13-277).
BENEDICT, THOMAS; Norwalk, Conn.; S1
(29-98;30-157, 192); (Abraham),
New Lisbon, N. Y.; Ng (4-86).
BENFIELD, DAVID; Md.; X1 (37-193).
BENJAMIN, JOHN; Watertown; A1 (86-
238); C5 (1-3-46; 1-4-34).
BENNETT, EDWARD; London, Eng.; V1

(16-239).
BENNETT, EDWARD; Isle of Wight County,
Va.; W2 (13-117).
BENNETT, HENRY; Ipswich, Mass.; B2
(18-13).
BENNETT, MARY (BOURNE); Isle of
Wight County, Va.; English ances-
try; W2 (13-131).
BENNETT, RICHARD (GOV.); Va.; W2 (13-
5); English data; W2 (16-316).
BENNETT; (Thomas of Loudoun County,
Va.); W2 (13-272).
BENNETT; Wyvelscombe, Somerset, Eng.;
W2 (16-493).
BENNETT; (Abraham of Cape May, N.
J.); B7 (1-108).
BENNET; (William of Flatbush); A2
(66-58, 191).
BENSLEY; (William), Smithfield, R.
I.; Smithfield, Pa.; A1 (93-204).
BENSON, DIRCK; New York, Albany; Dt
(3-170).
BENTON, ANDREW; Hartford, Conn.; S1
(31-182).
BERESFORD; S. C.; J (32-317).
BERGER, HENRY; Bethel, Berks Co.,
Pa.; S1 (37-218).
BERKELEY, EDMUND; Md. and Va.; V3
(41-289).
BERKELEY, WILLIAM (SIR); Va.; Eng-
lish ancestry; W2 (16-302, 315).
BERKELEY; Purton, Gloucester County,
Va.; V3 (43-150).
BERKELEY; (Carter), Hanover Co.,
Va.; B3 (47-1).
BERNARD; Va.; V3 (42-70); M (28-123).
BERTHOLFF, GUILLIAM (REV.); Dutch
ancestry and heraldry; A2 (68-111).
BETTIES, HUGH; Rehoboth, Mass.; A1
(97-33).
BETTS, THOMAS; Guilford and Norwalk,
Conn.; English ancestry; A1 (92-
296).
BEVELL, ESSEX; Henrico Co., Va.; Eng-
lish ancestry; W2 (19-69).
BEVERLEY, ROBERT (MAJ.); Middlesex
Co., Va.; S1 (37-719).
BEVERLEY; Blanfield, Va.; V1 (18-
104, 181).
BEVIER, LOUIS; New Paltz, N. Y.; OU
(1-151).
BEWITT; (will of George, 1675),
Sandwich, Mass.; D (34-114).
BEYER, ANDREAS; Philadelphia, Pa.;
S1 (36-112).
BIBAU, see Bebout.
BICKER, GERRIT; New York; Dt (3-148).
BICKNELL; Barrington, R. I.; NE (2-

66).

BIDAMAN; (Henry, Sharpsburg, Va.); Sl (31-349).

BIDWELL; (Joseph), East Hartford, Conn.; York, N. Y.; Dt (5-219).

BIGG; Co. Suffolk, Eng.; Dt (4-214).

BIGGE, JOHN; Cranbrook, Kent; Dorchester, Mass.; English data; Al (92-395).

BIGGERSTAFF, SAMUEL; Mecklenburg and Rutherford counties; Hl (1-101).

BIGHAM, HUGH; Bible records, Baltimore Co., Md.; X2 (12-53).

BILL, JOHN; Boston, Mass.; Sl (36-491).

BILLINGS, NATHANIEL; Concord, Mass.; Saco, Me., branches; Al (96-176); (John5), Deer Isle, Me.; others, Me.; Al (97-347; 98-5, 106).

BILLINGS, ROGER; Milton, Mass.; Al (92-261, 371; 93-67, 154, 264, 341; 94-48, 298).

BILLINGS; (Ebenezer), Milton, Mass.; Al (91-234).

BILLINGSLEA; Md.; X2 (5-8).

BIRCHARD, THOMAS; Norwich, Conn.; B4 (16-157, 221; 17-35, 177).

BIRD, GEORGE; Freeland, Pa.; Ng (3-125).

BIRD, THOMAS; Hartford, Conn.; Sl (19-241; 22-111; 25-585; 26-546).

BIRD, WILLIAM; Charles City County, Va.; V3 (41-189, 323; 42-41, 123, 247).

BISHOP, EDWARD; Beverly, Mass.; (John3 of Rehoboth); Al (97-33).

BISHOP, JAMES (DEP.-GOV.); New Haven; B4 (12-77, 185); Sl (26-569); Ng (6-260).

BISHOP, JOHN (REV.); Stamford, Conn.; B4 (16-196).

BISHOP, JOHN; Guilford, Conn.; B4 (10-17).

BISHOP; (Deed of Townsend), Salem, Mass., 1641; Yl (72-350).

BITTING; (Anthony, of Md., Va., N. C.); M (20-31).

BLACK, JOHN; Salem, Mass.; B4 (17-136).

BLACKBURN; (Benjamin), Va., Tenn.; N4 (6-12).

BLACKINTON, PENTECOST; Marblehead, Mass.; Sl (26-105).

BLACKMAN, ADAM (REV.); Stratford, Conn.; B4 (10-260).

BLACKWELL, MICHAEL; Sandwich, Mass.; Sl (25-569).

BLAKE, BENJAMIN; S. C.; English data; J (39-103); correction, ancestry of Gov.; J (40-42).

BLAKE, RICHARD; Boston, Mass.; Bible record; J(36-14, 42, 89, 113).

BLAKE, WILLIAM; Dorchester, Mass.; family record; Al (89-284); English origin; Sl (31-357).

BLAKE; notes; S4 (5-49).

BLANCHARD, JOHN; Kingston, N. Y.; Newcastle, Del.; Elizabeth, N. J.; A2 (75-145).

BLANCHARD, JOSEPH; Boston, Mass.; Al (93-162, 229).

BLANCHARD; (Richard), Canterbury, N. H.; Sl (31-154).

BLAND; notes; Vl (18-245).

BLATCHLY, THOMAS; Guilford, Conn.; (Ebenezer3, Huntington, L. I.); M (25-36).

BLEDSOE, GEORGE; Northumberland County, Va.; S3 (10-2-12; 10-3-12; 10-4-12).

BLEECKER, JAN JANSE; Albany, N. Y.; arms; A2 (65-353; 72-226).

BLENKINSOPP; Eng.; Al (94-206).

BLENNERHASSET; Suffolk, Eng.; Al (98-271).

BLISS, THOMAS; Hartford, Conn.; Sl (20-542; 23-471).

BLODGET, THOMAS; English origin; S3 (14-2-16).

BLOOD, JAMES; Concord, Mass.; Sl (23-220).

BLOOMER, ROBERT; Setauket, Rye, New Rochelle, N. Y.; A2 (69-323; 71-33).

BLOOMFIELD, THOMAS; Woodbridge, N. J.; A2 (68-58).

BLOSSOM, THOMAS; Plymouth; ancestry of wife (Anne Helsdon); Al (99-336); family notes; Dt (9-27).

BLOUNT; (Gov. William), N. C., Tenn.; N4 (4-122).

BLOWER, JOHN; Boston, Mass.; B4 (21-238).

BLUNT, WILLIAM; Andover, Mass.; (Samuel3, Plainfield, Conn., Oxford, Mass.); Al (97-53).

BOARDMAN; (Jonas), Norwich, Vt.; Sl (20-572).

BOBBY, THOMAS; Charles City County, Va.; Vl (19-221).

BOCKIUS; Germantown, Pa.; Richmond, Va.; W2 (13-189).

BODDIE, WILLIAM; Isle of Wight County, Va.; with English ancestry; W2

(14-114).
BODET; Bushwick, N. Y.; A2 (67-82).
BODINE; Inscriptions, Sandy Ridge
Cemetery, Stockton, N. J.; P (13-
275).
BODWELL, HENRY; Mass.; (line of
Joshua, Ohio and Ky.); Al (86-
460).
BOEL, HENDRICUS (DOMINE); New York,
N. Y.; A2 (72-294).
BOELEN [BOELE ROELOFFSZ JONGERMAN];
New York; A2 (67-344; 72-265).
BOGAERT, JANS LAURENS; New Nether-
land; Dutch ancestry; A2 (67-
56); Dt (3-57, 79, 147, 169, 216).
BOGARDUS, EVERARDUS (REV.); New
York; origin; arms; A2 (65-349);
Sl (25-118).
BOGARDUS; (will of Rachel, Kingston,
N. Y., 1781); OU (9-15).
BOGART, TUNIS GYSBERT; Brooklyn, N.
Y.; M (29-89).
BOHN; will of Han Deal (Frederick
Co., Md., 1761); estate of Abra-
ham (Augusta Co., Va., 1834); Ng
(5-187).
BOHUN, EDMUND (CHIEF JUSTICE); S. C.;
J (34-62).
BOLAN, RICHARD; Beaufort, S. C.;
family records; J (41-162).
BOLLING, ROBERT; Vl (14-25); (Diary
of Col. William), Va.; the home-
stead; V3 (43-237, 330, 343; 44-
15, 120, 238, 323; 45-29; 47-27);
(John); V3 (45-48); notes; Vl (18-
244).
BOLLING; Bollingbrook, Petersburg,
Va.; W2 (16-545).
BOLLING; (Diary of Col. William); V3
(46-44, 146, 234, 321).
BOLTON; notes; S4 (3-212).
BONAPARTE; American marriages; Sl
(26-408).
BOND, ROBERT; East Hampton, N. Y.;
Sl.(36-463).
BOND; (Richard), Albany County, N.
Y.; Sl (26-266).
BONNEY, THOMAS; Duxbury, Mass.; Al
(89-220); (will, 1693); D (34-182).
BONREPOS, DAVID (REV.) and ELIAS;
Boston; New Rochelle, N. Y.; Dt
(7-95).
BOOKER, EDWARD; York Co., Va.; Vl
(16-257).
BOOKER; (wills of Richard, 1743,
and Martha, 1742), York Co., Va.;
Vl (18-169).
BOOMER, MATTHEW; Newport, R. I.; Sl

(26-97).
BOONE, SQUIRE; Berks Co., Pa.; K2
(16-141).
BOONE; (Daniel); Ky.; N3 (32-187).
BOONE; will (Squire), Logan County,
Ky.; Z (80-189).
BOONE; Wills of Robert (1759) and
Thomas (1774), Md.; O (5-433).
BOOTH, RICHARD; Stratford, Conn.;
English origin; Sl (32-204).
BOOTH, ROBERT; York County, Va.; Vl
(14-181).
BOOTH; Stratford, Conn.; B4 (11-
190).
BOOTHBY; (will of Edward, 1698); X2
(4-9).
BORDEN, RICHARD; Portsmouth, R. I.;
Sl (23-341); NE (2-247); with Eng-
lish ancestry; Sl (26-111).
BORDET; (Daniel of Boswick); A2 (66-
191).
BORDINGH, CLAES CLAESEN; New York;
M (21-96).
BORTON, JOHN; Bible records (Wil-
liam); N. J.; P (13-102).
BOSE; (William, 1796-1875); Xl (28-
1).
BOSTWICK, ARTHUR; Stratford, Conn.;
English ancestry; B4 (14-216).
BOTELER; arms; Al (95-394).
BOTSFORD, HENRY; Milford, Conn.;
English ancestry; B4 (14-58); Sl
(36-454).
BOTT; Petersburg, Va.; Vl (16-244).
BOULTON, WILLIAM; Queen Anne's Co.,
Md.; Sl (32-574).
BOULWARE, BOWLER; Lancaster Co., Va.;
V3 (47-257).
BOURDOUX; St. Thomas, W. I.; S4 (1-
74).
BOURNE, THOMAS; Pw (21-52).
BOURNE; Somerset and London, Eng.;
W2 (13-131).
BOURNE; Barnstable County, Mass.; D
(33-50).
BOUTON, JOHN; Norwalk, Conn.; B4 (11-
114).
BOWDEN, AMBROSE; Me.; English origin;
Al (96-91).
BOWDITCH, WILLIAM; Salem, Mass.; Eng-
lish data; Al (100-215); (Joseph3);
Yl (80-322).
BOWERS; (Jonathan), Salem, Somerset,
Mass.; M (32-77).
BOWES-LYON; Elizabeth, Queen of Eng-
land, relationship to Washington
and Lee; A2 (70-201).
BOWIE, JOHN; Prince George's Co.,

Md.; X1 (38-141).
BOWLER; (wife of Col. Thomas), Va.;
W2 (16-469).
BOWLES, JOHN; Roxbury, Mass.; (first
wife); B4 (23-149).
BOWLES, JOHN; Jamestown, Va.; W2
(16-602).
BOWMAN, EDMUND; Accomack County,
Va.; V3 (44-97).
BOWNE, JOHN; Bucks Co., Pa.; B4
(19-166).
BOWNE, THOMAS; Flushing, N. Y.; S1
(20-89).
BOWNE, WILLIAM; Middletown, N. J.;
Dt (4-94).
BOWNE; JM (7-1-1; 7-2-12; 7-3-20;
8-2-13; 8-3-24; 8-4-25).
BOXLEY; King William Co., Va.; W2
(16-474).
BOYD, HUGH; Indiana; Dt (5-41).
BOYD; (Alexander), Mecklenburg Co.,
Va.; V3 (50-119).
BOYD; (William), Bedford Co., Va.;
W2 (22-65).
BOYER, see Beyer.
BOYNTON, JOHN; Rowley, Mass.; Z2
(18-30).
BOYNTON, WILLIAM; (Eliphalet4),
Bradford, Mass.; U (28-97).
BOYSE; Halifax, co. York; B4 (19-
135, 232).
BRACE; (Stephen), Swansea, Mass.;
Z (77-116).
BRACKETT, ANTHONY; Portsmouth, N.
H.; S1 (31-504).
BRADBURY, THOMAS; Salisbury, Mass.;
B4 (18-220; 19-36; 21-218).
BRADFORD, JOHN; Fauquier County,
Va.; V1 (27-114).
BRADFORD, WILLIAM (GOV.); Plymouth;
his first wife; D (29-27); Life
by Mather; D (29-114); D (31-105);
wife of Thomas3; B4 (11-12); S1
(19-521; 32-372); S4 (1-271).
BRADLEY, NATHAN; Dorchester, Mass.;
S1 (19-517).
BRADLEY, WILLIAM; New Haven, Conn.;
S1 (19-231; 22-98; 26-524).
BRADLEY; (William R.), Cumberland
Co., Va.; V3 (48-362).
BRADSHAW, JAMES; Princeton, N. Y.;
S1 (26-282).
BRADSTREET, SIMON; Salem, Mass.; S1
(21-304).
BRAGG, HENRY; (wife of Nicholas3,
Mass., Vt.); B4 (23-255).
BRAINARD, DANIEL; Haddam, Conn.;
Col (3-66); Dt (7-115).

BRANCH; Marshfield, Mass.; D (32-
116, 120).
BRAND; Va.; N. C.; W2 (12-130).
BRANDRETH, TIMOTHY; Burlington Co.,
N. J.; B7 (2-191).
BRANNON, JOHN; Cumberland Co., Pa.;
V1 (19-94).
BRANSFORD, JOHN; Va.; W2 (14-93).
BRAS [HENDRICK PIETERSZ]; New York;
B4 (20-140, 215).
BRAT, ARENT ANDRIESE; Schenectady,
N. Y.; S1 (26-280).
BRAXTON; Amherst Co., Va.; W2 (19-
318).
BRAY, WILLIAM; Androscoggin Co.,
Me.; S1 (35-53).
BRAZELTON; (William, Guilford Co.,
N. C.); B2 (12-23).
BRAZIER [BRESSER], HENRY; Graves-
end, New York; B4 (21-155).
BREAZEALE; Inscriptions, S. C.; A1
(93-200); Bible records (Kenon),
Anderson Co., S. C.; A1 (93-201).
BREED, ALLEN; Lynn, Mass.; S1 (34-
159); wife identified; B4 (14-2);
Z2 (10 [1906]-89 ff.; 15-42, 69);
Ng (3-180).
BRENNER, HANS CASPAR; Lancaster Co.,
Pa.; (Philip, Ohio); M (28-104).
BRENT, GILES; Md.; Indian blood; X1
(29-212, 259).
BRENT; Lancaster County, Va.; W2
(12-130). (William, Md.); X2 (3-
28).
BRENTON; (will of William, 1674); D
(34-75).
BREWER, JOHN; Sudbury, Mass.; S1
(34-658).
BREWER, JOHN; Family record (Josi-
ah4), Hopkinton, R. I.; B4 (12-
58).
BREWSTER, FRANCIS and NATHANIEL;
New Haven, Conn.; Brookhaven, N.
Y.; B4 (12-199; 13-8, 113, 154,
221; 14-105; 21-210); A1 (90-
202); (Sir Francis), Dublin, Ireland; B4 (21-208).
BREWSTER, WILLIAM; Plymouth; D (30-
97); S1 (27-364); (Jonathan2); D
(32-1); (Jabez6 and Stephen6); Dt
(3-83); corrections, Genealogy; Dt
(3-173).
BRIDGER; (inventory, Col. Joseph),
Isle of Wight Co., Va.; 1686; W2
(22-187).
BRIDGES, ROBERT (CAPT.); Lynn, Mass.;
Z2 (14-85).
BRIES, HENDRICK; Albany, N. Y.; A2

(67-6, 8); B4 (21-153).
BRIES, HENDRICK VOLCKERTSZ; Brook-
  lyn, N. Y.; B4 (21-147; 23-55).
BRIGGS, CLEMENT; (line to Geo. Ly-
  man7); Dt (2-189).
BRIGGS, HENRY; Surry Co., Va.; V3
  (44-232).
BRIGHAM, THOMAS; Cambridge, Mass.;
  S1 (23-234).
BRIGHAM; notes; S4 (4-31).
BRIMMER, JOHN-GEORGE; Petersburg,
  N. Y.; S3 (13-4-8).
BRINK, LAMBERT HUYBERTSE; Kingston,
  N. Y.; OU (2-113, 145, 250; 9-
  250); (will of Lambert Huybertse,
  1702); OU (8-143).
BRISCOE, JOHN; Md.; M (21-73).
BRISTOW, JOHN; Va.; V1 (23-64, 118,
  202, 260; 24—147).
BRISTOW, BRISTOL; American settlers;
  English data; V1 (22-45, 110, 176,
  234).
BROADHURST, JONATHAN; Albany, N. Y.;
  Dt (3-169, 215).
BROCK, HENRY; Dedham, Mass.; S1 (26-
  170).
BROCK; (John of Gloucester, Mass.);
  S1 (31-501).
BROCK; co Essex, Eng.; U (24-14).
BROCKETT, JOHN; New Haven, Conn.;
  S1 (32-171).
BROMBACH, MELCHIOR; Spottsylvania
  Co., Va.; Dt (7-123).
BROMLEY, THOMAS; Charleston, S. C.;
  J (35-40).
BRONSON, JOHN; Farmington, Conn.;
  S1 (26-304; 32-122).
BRONSON; (Enos, Conn. and Pa.); Q1
  (57-355).
BRONSON, see Brownson.
BROOKE, ROBERT; Charles County, Md.;
  X1 (29-152); W2 (13-3).
BROOKE, ROBERT; Essex Co., Va.; V3
  (43-65).
BROOKS, HENRY; Woburn, Mass.; Z3 (4-
  9-40).
BROOKS; Frederick Co., Md.; X1 (32-
  52).
BROQUIN [BROOKINGS], Charles; Cecil
  County, Md.; A1 (88-3).
BROUSE, ADAM; Penn Township, Pa.;
  S1 (27-251).
BROUWER, ADAM; New York; B4 (23-
  193); A2 (67-103, 217); branch of
  Adolphus3; A2 (64-110); correc-
  tions; A2 (69-172; 72-332).
BROWN, ADAM; Cumberland Co., Pa.;
  S1 (23-309).

BROWN, CHARLES; Rowley, Mass.; S1
  (25-431).
BROWN, DAVID; Bible records; Tenn.,
  Ky.; A1 (100-256).
BROWN, EDWARD; Newbury, Mass.; A1
  (97-260, 353).
BROWN, GAWEN; Boston, Mass.; A2 (64-
  317).
BROWN, HENRY; Salisbury, Mass.; S1
  (24-255).
BROWN, JOHN; New Castle, Pa.; S1
  (23-343).
BROWN, JOHN (REV.), Va., Ky.; ori-
  gin abroad; (Dr. Preston W.2,
  Frankfort, Ky.); K2 (19-3).
BROWNE, JOHN; Charles City Co., Va.;
  V3 (51-387).
BROWNE, NATHANIEL; Middletown, Conn.;
  B4 (22-157, 240; 23-101).
BROWN, NICHOLAS; (William4, Reho-
  both, Mass.); B4 (22-153, 248);
  (Edward), Newburyport, Mass.;. Y1
  (80-55).
BROWN, THOMAS; Lynn, Mass.; S1 (20-
  555; 23-483; 25-411).
BROWN, THOMAS ; Indiana; Dt (5-42).
BROWNE, WILLIAM; Saybrook, Conn.;
  N. Y.; B4 (15-84).
BROWN; notes; S4 (2-265).
BROWN; Franklin Co., Va.; S4 (4-53).
BROWN; Virginia; B2 (13-37).
BROWN; Cambridge and Reading; B4
  (12-25).
BROWN; (Charles), Buxton, Me.; A1
  (96-89).
BROWN; (Rev. John), Augusta Co.,
  Va.; N3 (35-99).
BROWN; (John), Frankfort, Ky.; N3
  (35-1).
BROWN; (John), Liberty Hall, Ky.;
  K2 (16-75).
BROWN; (Mather), Boston, painter;
  Z (65-725).
BROWN; (Letter, 1834, Cincinnati,
  Ohio, to Bridgeton, N. J.); B5
  (19-90).
BROWNELL, THOMAS; Portsmouth, R. I.;
  S1 (26-147); A2 (68-1).
BROWNING, JOHN (CAPT.); Elizabeth
  City, Va.; S1 (36-744).
BROWNSON, RICHARD; Bible record
  (E115), Manchester, Vt.; A1 (98-
  283); (Timothy4); A1 (98-284).
BRUCE; Scotland; S1 (2-525; 3-50,
  158, 263, 389, 494, 597; 4-72,
  198, 301).
BRUEN, OBADIAH; New London, Conn.;
  Newark, N. J.; B1 (17-30).

BRUMBACK [BROMBACH], MELCHIOR; Va.;
German ancestry; V3 (40-325).
BRUNDISH, JOHN; Fairfield, Conn.;
NE (1-193, 195).
BRUSH; Thomas and Richard; Hunting-
ton, N. Y.; A2 (66-201, 353; 67-
16, 124, 269, 321); English clues;
B4 (10-264); (Zophar), Southeast,
N. Y.; S1 (29-114; 30-185).
BRUYN, JACOBUS; Shawangunk, N. Y.;
OU (6-82).
BRUYN; (Jacobus-Severyn, Rev. War
Officer); OU (9-275).
BRYAN, ALEXANDER; Milford, Conn.;
English data; B4 (9-89; 10-90).
BRYAN, WILLIAM and MORGAN; Roanoke,
Va.; and Rowan Co., N. C.; origin;
N3 (40-318); K2 (20-37).
BRYAN; (Alexander), Saratoga Springs,
N. Y.; Mich.; Dt (5-199).
BRYAN; (Frederick), York Co., Va.;
W2 (17-116).
BRYAN; (Richard), King George Co.,
Va.; V3 (51-377).
BRYAN; (William), Kent Island, Md.;
X2 (13-6).
BRYAN; (will of George, 1815); M
(21-71).
BRYAN; Papers of Ky. family; N3 (34-
196).
BRYANT, ABRAHAM; Reading, Mass.; S1
(21-312).
BRYANT, STEPHEN; Duxbury, Mass.;
(ancestry of William-Cullen); S1
(22-408).
BRYANT, WILLIAM; Boston, Mass.; A1
(96-321; 97-43, 117, 391).
BRYANT; Bertie Co., N. C.; W2 (18-
352).
BRYANT; (Samuel), Scituate, Mass.;
B4 (14-271).
BUCHANAN; Carbeth, Blairlusk, Scot-
land; M (24-85; 25-14).
BUCHANAN; (James); Q1 (55-289; 56-
15).
BUCHANAN; Ancestry in Ireland of
Pres. James; M (25-67).
BUCHANAN; (William), Pa.; Baltimore,
Md.; X1 (35-262).
BUCK, EMANUEL; Wethersfield, Conn.;
B4 (10-51).
BUCK, HENRY; Wethersfield, Conn.;
B4 (23-114).
BUCK, RICHARD (REV.); Jamestown,
Va.; V1 (14-172).
BUCKINGHAM, THOMAS; Milford, Conn.;
English clue; B4 (13-205).
BUCKNER, JOHN; Va.; V3 (44-56).

BUCKNER; Caroline County, Va.; V1
(21-174).
BUELL, WILLIAM; (William3), Lebanon,
Conn.; B4 (23-190).
BULKELEY, GRACE (CHETWODE); Concord,
Mass.; English ancestry; B4 (21-
69).
BULKELEY, PETER (REV.); Concord,
Mass.; B4 (9-227); (Joseph), Weth-
ersfield, Conn.; B2 (17-8); (Pe-
ter2), Fairfield, Conn.; B4 (20-
252; 22-259).
BULL, STEPHEN and BARNABY; S. C.;
English ancestry; J (36-36).
BULL, THOMAS; Hartford, Conn.; WF
(1-78).
BULL; (wife of John), S. C.; J (33-
174).
BULL; Charleston, S. C.; J (47-70).
BULLOCK; (David), Louisa Co., Va.;
V3 (46-349).
BULLUS; Sheffield, York, Eng.; S1
(33-430).
BUNKER, GEORGE; Topsfield, Mass.; S1
(25-283).
BUNNELL, WILLIAM; New Haven, Conn.;
S1 (32-97; 34-659).
BURBANK, JOHN; Rowley, Mass.; A1
(94-393).
BURCH; Inscriptions, St. Mary's Co.,
Md.; X2 (12-61, 62).
BURD, EDWARD; Philadelphia, Pa.; P
(13-173).
BURDEN, BURDET, ROBERT; Malden,
Mass.; A1 (97-306).
BURDICK, ROBERT; Westerly, R. I.;
S1 (20-549; 23-478).
BURGE, JOHN; Weymouth, Mass.; B4
(10-71).
BURGESS, THOMAS; Sandwich, Mass.;
S4 (2-63).
BURKE; (Thomas, Gov. of N. C.); H2
(9-22).
BURLEY, GILES; Ipswich, Mass.; B4
(20-236).
BURNAP, ROBERT; Reading, Mass.; A2
(70-139).
BURNETT, JAMES; Rev. soldier; M (22-
17).
BURR; (Aaron, papers); B5 (19-95,
114).
BURRALL; (Thomas-Davies), Geneva,
N. Y.; Dt (7-46).
BURRIDGE, WILLIAM; Bible record,
Devonshire, Eng., and Ohio; Dt
(4-152).
BURRILL, GEORGE; Lynn, Mass.; Z2
(11-64).

BURRITT; (ancestry of Elihu); M (31-1).
BURROWS; Greene Co., Ohio; O (5-432).
BURROWS; Inscriptions, Stonington, Conn.; A1 (88-205).
BURRUSS; Va., Ky.; V1 (18-59).
BURRUS; (will of Jacob), Caroline Co., Va., 1742; V1 (20-105).
BURT, HENRY; Springfield; English ancestry; A1 (86-77, 216); S4 (4-34); S1 (19-394; 20-163).
BURT, HUGH; Lynn, Mass.; English data; A1 (100-218).
BURT, ULALIA (MARCH); Springfield; English ancestry; A1 (86-77, 247).
BURT; Caundlemershe, co. Dorset, England; A1 (100-223).
BURTIS, see Albertis.
BURTON, JOHN; Danvers, Sutton, Mass.; Ng (2-75, 98).
BURTON; Gloucester County, Va.; W2 (14-361).
BURWELL; (John, Va.); W2 (15-304).
BURWELL; (Lewis), Va.; W2 (21-172).
BUSHI, JOHAN NICOLAUS; Pa.; M (21-15).
BUSHNELL, FRANCIS; Guilford, Conn.; English ancestry; B4 (16-45; 17-31); S1 (35-122).
BUSHNELL; (Daniel, Litchfield, N. Y.); E3 (2-96).
BUSHROD, THOMAS and RICHARD; Va.; English data; W2 (16-319).
BUTLER, JAMES; Boston, Mass.; B4 (23-16).
BUTLER, RICHARD; Hartford, Conn.; WF (1-5, 63, 136, 191); (Joseph2), Wethersfield, Conn.; B4 (13-218).
BUTLER, THOMAS; Carlisle, Pa.; W2 (14-363).
BUTLER; Frederick County, Va.; V1 (13-272).
BUTLER; Madison, N. J.; B1 (9-118).
BUTLER; Westmoreland County, Va.; V3 (40-259, 362; 43-262).
BUTTER; Dedham, co. Essex, England; additions; A1 (100-224).
BUTTERWORTH, JOHN; Swansea, Mass.; S1 (26-144).
BUTTOLPH; (George), Wethersfield, Conn.; B4 (19-153).
BUTZ, JOHN; Berks Co., Pa.; S1 (36-117).
BUYS, JAN CORNELIS; Brooklyn, N. Y.; A2 (66-225).
BYE, THOMAS; Bucks Co., Pa.; C5 (1-2-8).
BYE; English data; S4 (1-162).

BYRD, WILLIAM; Charles City County, Va.; V1 (16-36, 93, 100, 198); V3 (47-285); S1 (37-721).

CABELL; Winton, Amherst County, Va.; V3 (41-229).
CABLE, JOHN; Fairfield, Conn.; NE (3-135).
CADMAN, WILLIAM; Portsmouth, R. I.; B4 (19-126, 230).
CADY, NICHOLAS; (Daniel2), Canterbury, Conn.; B4 (14-272).
CALDWELL, JOHN; Charlotte Co., Va.; (Rev. James, N. J.); Z3 (1-3-80).
CALEF, ROBERT; Roxbury, Mass.; Y1 (74-251, 373; 75-73, 175, 291, 393; 76-177).
CALHOUN; Va.; S. C.; J (39-50).
CALKINS; (will of Stephen); B4 (10-52). See Caulkins.
CALL, PHILIP; Ipswich, Mass.; S1 (30-175).
CALVERT, GEORGE; Md.; S1 (26-355); English data; X1 (27-335; 29-330).
CALVERT; Virginia; W2 (20-411).
CALVERT; (Christopher), Accomack Co., Va.; V3 (50-264); S1 (25-231).
CAMERON, WILLIAM; Tenn.; Ill.; S3 (10-3-13).
CAMP, NICHOLAS; Milford, Conn.; co. Essex records; B4 (15-125).
CAMP, NICHOLAS; Rehoboth, Mass.; A1 (97-35).
CAMPAU, ETIENNE; Montreal, P. Q.; S1 (22-485).
CAMPBELL, ARCHIBALD; Mecklenburg Co., N. C.; (George-Washington2); N4 (10-3).
CAMPBELL, NEIL (LORD); N. J.; B4 (14-146).
CAMPBELL, WILLIAM; King & Queen Co., Va.; V1 (17-171, 256).
CAMPBELL; Campbeltown, Scotland; M (23-73, 105).
CAMPBELL; (Charles), Rockbridge Co., Va.; N3 (34-289).
CAMPBELL; (Dr. Francis-Watkins), S. C.; W2 (14-358).
CAMVILLE; feudal English house; B4 (21-95).
CANFIELD; Norwalk, Conn.; B4 (23-238).
CANNON; notes; S4 (4-89).
CANNY, THOMAS; Dover, N. H.; B4 (16-238).
CANTELOU, LOUIS; Edgefield, S. C.; W2 (18-353).
CAPEHART, see Gebhardt.

CAPRON, BANFIELD; Attleboro, Mass.;
S1 (33-249).
CARD; (Joseph), Lebanon, Conn.; S1
(20-540; 23-469).
CARLL, JOHN; East Hampton, N. Y.;
Salem Co., N. J., branch; L1 (5-
24).
CARLL; (John), Long Island; M (32-
59).
CARLTON, EDWARD; Rowley, Mass.;
English ancestry; A1 (93-3); B4
(17-105); see also Strickland.
CARLTON, ELLEN (NEWTON); Rowley,
Mass.; English ancestry; A1 (94-
1).
CARMAN, JOHN; Roxbury, Lynn, Sand-
wich, Hempstead; A2 (70-332).
CARNEGIE; Scotland; S1 (19-405).
CARPENTER, ALICE; S1 (19-526).
CARPENTER, JONATHAN; King & Queen
Co., Va.; W2 (16-95).
CARPENTER, WILLIAM; Rehoboth, Mass.;
S1 (31-142; 33-241); (Josiah3),
Rehoboth; A1 (97-37); (Samuel2),
Rehoboth; A1 (98-172); (John3),
Woodstock, Conn.; A1 (98-176).
CARPENTER, WILLIAM; Weymouth, Mass.;
S1 (26-135; 31-381).
CARPENTER, WILLIAM; Providence, R.
I.; S1 (20-83).
CARR, GEORGE; Salisbury, Mass.; S1
(22-345).
CARR, JAMES; Newbury, Mass.; A1 (98-
284).
CARRINGTON, PAUL (DR.); Barbadoes;
(Va. branch); M (27-33); (Edward
of Va.); S1 (34-458).
CARROLL, CHARLES; Carrollton, Md.;
S1 (26-359). Letter books; cont.;
X1 (27-215, 314; 31-298; 32-35,
174, 193; 33-187, 371).
CARROLL; (David), Anne Arundel Co.,
Md.; X2 (17-69).
CARTER, JOHN; Woburn, Mass.; S1 (24-
431).
CARTER, ROBERT; (Ann-Hill, Shirley,
Va.); W2 (16-417).
CARTER, THOMAS; Barford, Lancaster
Co., Va.; V3 (43-153); V1 (18-
236).
CARTER, THOMAS; Charlestown, Mass.;
family records; A1 (91-300).
CARTER, WILLIAM; Surry Co., Va.; V3
(48-75).
CARTER, WILLIAM; James City, Va.;
V3 (48-74).
CARTER; Va.; V3 (40-372); Va.; N.
C.; V1 (13-60).

CARTER; Pampatike, King William Co.,
Va.; V3 (41-223).
CARTER; (John), Albemarle Co., Va.;
W2 (18-506).
CARTER; (Landon), "Cleve," King
George Co., Va.; V3 (44-343; 45-
52); V1 (13-246).
CARTER; (Robert); Jefferson Co., W.
Va.; W2 (22-426).
CARTERET, GEORGE; will; Z3 (3-5-1).
CARTERET, PHILLIP; English ancestry;
Z3 (2-1-31).
CARTWRIGHT; N. C.; Amherst County,
Va.; Ky.; S3 (9-1-14; 9-2-10; 9-
3-8; 9-4-4; 10-3-11).
CARUTHERS; (William), Va.; Dt (7-
39, 59, 103).
CARVER, ROBERT; Marshfield, Mass.;
A1 (88-215, 311; 89-34); (Robert5,
Isaac6), Mass.; A1 (96-304).
CARY, MILES; Warwick Co., Va.; W2
(15-256).
CARY, THOMAS; Warwick Co., Va.; V1
(25-54).
CARY; (William-Myles), Va.; S4 (1-
81).
CASE; Norwich, Conn.; B4 (17-175).
CASEY; R. I.; NE (3-83).
CASS; (Ebenezer), Norwich, Conn.;
B4 (19-46).
CASSIER, PHILIP; Harlem, N. Y.; S1
(35-144).
CASWELL, THOMAS; Taunton, Mass.; S1
(22-352).
CATE, JAMES; Portsmouth, N. H.; B1
(21-33).
CATHCART, JOHN and HUGH; Rockville,
S. C.; W2 (18-506).
CATIN; (Henry), Quebec; S1 (22-509).
CATLIN, THOMAS; Hartford, Conn.; Pw
(21-82); (George, Indian artist);
Pw (21-68).
CAULKINS, HUGH; New London, Conn.;
S1 (25-588). See Calkins.
CAULKINS; (Elijah), Sharon, Conn.;
E3 (3-15).
CENTER, JOHN; Chelsea, Mass.; B4
(20-109; 21-94).
CHADBOURNE; corrections to Geneal-
ogy; M (28-126; 31-97).
CHAMBER; Bray, co. Berks, Eng.; A1
(95-318).
CHAMBERLAIN, HENRY; Hingham, Mass.;
S1 (19-124); (Henry5), Westmore-
land, N. H.; Dt (2-63, 91, 113,
141, 169, 182, 213).
CHAMBERLAIN, JACOB; Chelsea, Mass.;
B2 (21-35).

CHAMBERLAIN, THOMAS; Woburn, Chelmsford, Mass.; S1 (27-254); (Benjamin5), Mass., Vt., N. Y.; E3 (4-153, 169).
CHAMBERLAIN; (Thomas), Westmoreland, N. H.; Dt (5-86).
CHAMBERLAIN; Bible and other records (Joshua); Richmond, Mass.; Quebec branch; Dt (7-68).
CHAMBERS, THOMAS; Ulster Co., N. Y.; A2 (72-308); arms; A1 (96-94); Inscriptions, Rondout, N. Y.; OU (1-117).
CHAMPE, JOHN; Stafford County, Va.; V3 (44-80, 174, 269, 349); (Sergt. John); W2 (18-322).
CHAMPE; Prince William and King George Counties, Va.; W2 (17-145).
CHAMPE; Lamb's Creek, Va.; V3 (45-94).
CHAMPION, THOMAS; Hempstead, N. Y.; B4 (20-43; 23-32).
CHAMPLIN, JOHN and Jeffrey; Newport, R. I.; B4 (20-106); (John3), Lyme, Conn.; B4 (17-109).
CHANCELLOR, JOHN (CAPT.); Somerset Co., Md.; W2 (15-178).
CHANDLER, WILLIAM; Roxbury, Mass.; ancestry of wife Agnes (Bayford); A1 (96-301).
CHANDLER; Caroline Co., Va.; V1 (22-50).
CHAPIN, SAMUEL; Springfield, Mass.; English data; S1 (22-450; 24-527).
CHAPIN; (children of Dr. Benjamin, Va.); A1 (100-74).
CHAPPLE, JOHN (REV.); Chagrin Falls, Ohio; S1 (24-91).
CHASE, AQUILA; Newbury, Mass.; B2 (22-1).
CHASE, WILLIAM; Yarmouth, Mass.; A1 (87-46, 127, 242, 314; 88-7, 105); B5 (19-121); (Family of Nathan6); A1 (90-302).
CHASE; (Samuel), New Brunswick, Canada; Dt (6-84).
CHATTERTON, WILLIAM; New Haven, Conn.; S1 (32-181).
CHAUVIN, RENE; Montreal, Canada; M (26-1).
CHEADLE; (Thomas); N3 (36-30).
CHEEVER; Canterbury, co. Kent, Eng.; Boston, Mass.; B4 (11-118).
CHENEY, WILLIAM; Roxbury, Mass.; S1 (21-460).
CHENEY; (John3), Newton, Mass.; wife identified; B4 (16-144).

CHENOWETH; Baltimore Co., Md.; X2 (12-24).
CHERINGTON; (Thomas), Exeter, Pa.; P (13-277).
CHETWODE; family, England; B4 (21-69).
CHETWOOD, THOMAS; Lancaster Co., Va.; W2 (18-507).
CHEVES, ALEXANDER; S. C.; J (35-79, 130).
CHEW, JOHN; Jamestown, Va.; X1 (30-157).
CHEW, RICHARD; Gloucester Co., N. J.; Z3 (3-6-20).
CHICK, RICHARD; Roxbury, Mass.; English ancestry; B4 (16-205).
CHICKERING, FRANCIS; Dedham, Mass.; B4 (17-70).
CHICKERING, HENRY; Dedham, Mass.; S1 (26-127).
CHICKERING; (Deed to John), Salem, Mass., 1641; Y1 (72-350).
CHILD; notes; S4 (5-40).
CHILD; (Seth), Woodstock, Conn.; E3 (4-89).
CHILD; (probate of Richard, 1691); D (31-60).
CHILES, WALTER (COL.); (Henry5), Caroline Co., Va.; N3 (36-30 to 32, 43 to 45, 47 to 53, 128 to 130, 131 to 137, 150 to 157, 376).
CHILES; Hanover Co., Va.; V3 (45-51).
CHILTON, JAMES; Plymouth; S1 (19-543).
CHINN; Kentucky; N3 (34-365).
CHINN; (Rawleigh), Lancaster Co., Va.; W2 (18-294).
CHIPMAN, JOHN; Barnstable, Mass.; A1 (91-159); (Rev. John of Barnstable); D (29-145).
CHISHOLM; Va., Ky.; V3 (51-95).
CHISHOLM; (John), N. C., Tenn.; N4 (1-60).
CHITTENDEN, WILLIAM; Guilford, Conn.; S1 (35-96).
CHOATE; (Letters of Rufus); Y1 (69-81).
CHRISTENSON, JOHN; Utah; ancestry in Sweden; U (28-145); wife's ancestry; U (29-19).
CHRISTISON, WENLOCKE; New Eng.; Md.; X1 (34-223; 37-320).
CHRISTOPHER; Md.; War of 1812; X2 (16-18).
CHRISTOPHER; (John); X2 (3-30).
CHRISTOPHERS, CHRISTOPHER; John2, New London, Conn.; B4 (18-103);

English clue; A2 (63-51).
CHUBBUCK, THOMAS; Hingham, Mass.; B4 (13-117).
CHURCH, RICHARD; Hingham, Mass.; S1 (26-108).
CHURCH; Ky.; M (28-87).
CHURCH; (Jonathan), Brattleboro, Vt.; Ng (3-129).
CHURCHILL; maternal ancestry of Winston; A2 (73-163, 219, 227).
CHURCHILL; (Armistead), Va., Ky.; W2 (22-65).
CLACK; (John S.), Mecklenburg Co., Va.; V3 (48-355).
CLAIBORNE, WILLIAM (SEC.); Va.; V1 (27-287); English origin; W2 (19-474). See Maryland, Admiralty Court records.
CLAPP; (John), Westchester Co., N. Y.; S1 (20-87).
CLARKE, BENJAMIN; Amboy, N. J.; Z3 (4-16-463).
CLARK, DANIEL; Topsfield, Mass.; ancestry of wife; B4 (15-143).
CLARK, JAMES; New Haven, Conn.; S1 (32-100).
CLARK, JOHN; Wethersfield, New Haven, Conn.; B4 (10-51).
CLARK, JOHN; Saybrook, Conn.; A1 (91-174).
CLARK, JONAS; Cambridge, Mass.; S1 (32-145).
CLARKE, JOSEPH; Newport, R. I.; branch of Christopher4; A1 (91-249); (Thomas6), Hopkinton, R. I.; A1 (92-61); Bible record; English ancestry; NE (1-202).
CLARKE, JOSEPH; Medfield, Mass.; S1 (19-122); (Timothy3), Medway, Mass.; Dt (6-27).
CLARK, NICHOLAS; Hartford, Conn.; B4 (12-129).
CLARK, RICHARD; Southold, L. I.; B4 (10-201).
CLARK, RICHARD; Brookhaven, L. I.; B4 (10-201).
CLARK, RICHARD; (Family of Abraham, "Signer"); B1 (7-89); Z3 (4-10-107); A2 (63-96).
CLARKE, SAMUEL; Marlborough, Pa.; S4 (1-144).
CLARKE, THOMAS; Clarkesboro, N. J.; Z3 (3-6-17).
CLARK, THOMAS; Gloucester Co., N. J.; Z3 (3-6-19).
CLARK, THOMAS; Essex Co., N. J.; Z3 (4-7-78).
CLARK, WILLIAM (LIEUT.); Northampton,

Mass.; S1 (20-136; 31-203); wife of William2; B4 (12-255).
CLARK, WILLIAM; Hartford, Haddam, Conn.; S1 (36-478); B4 (17-19).
CLARK, WILLIAM; Hampshire County, Va.; U (24-151).
CLARKE; Lebanon, Conn.; Z (73-3-86).
CLARK; Rappahannock, Va.; family of Wm. Sr.; V1 (13-31).
CLARK; Hingham, Eng.; B4 (13-151).
CLARK; (Christopher), Winchester, Montgomery County, Va.; W2 (12-202).
CLARK; (David), Bedford, Penn Yan, N. Y.; Dt (2-211).
CLARK; (Edmund), Wallingford, Conn.; S3 (17-3-9).
CLARK; (John), Madison Co., Ky.; Co1 (7-115).
CLARK; (Samuel), York Co., Pa.; W2 (19-117).
CLARKE; (William, Loyalist, Dunmore Co., Va.); W2 (15-78).
CLAY, JOHN; Charles City Co., Va.; V3 (52-59).
CLAY; (Sir John), Hanover Co., Va.; W2 (21-61).
CLAY; (will of John, 1782); W2 (14-174).
CLAYBROOKE; (Thomas W., travels from Va. to Tenn., 1832); W2 (13-163).
CLAYPOLE; (Joseph), Hardy Co., Va.; Dt (7-9).
CLAYPOOLE, JAMES; Philadelphia, Pa.; identity of wife, Helena Mercer; B4 (18-201).
CLAYTON, JOHN (REV.); Virginia; W2 (19-1).
CLELAND, ARTHUR; Family records, Pittsburgh, Pa.; Ohio; M (20-114).
CLEMENS: Family of "Mark Twain"; Va.; W2 (15-294).
CLEMENTS, ELIZABETH (FULLER); Surry Co., Va.; V1 (17-125, 250).
CLEMENTS, ROBERT; Haverhill, Mass.; S1 (24-258).
CLEMENTS; Surry Co., Va.; V1 (18-111).
CLEVELAND, MOSES; Woburn, Mass.; S1 (22-353); (wife of Benjamin3), Canterbury, Conn.; B4 (12-129).
CLINTON, CHARLES; New York; English ancestry; A2 (66-330); OU (1-52; 10-275); (descendants of DeWitt); S1 (6-950).
CLINTON, EARLS OF LINCOLN, see Fiennes.

CLORE; Va.; W2 (12-132).
CLOSE, "GOODMAN"; Stamford, Conn.;
  S1 (34-157).
CLOUD; (will of Joseph, 1838), Con-
  cord, Pa.; M (30-18).
CLUVERIUS, JOHN (REV.); York County,
  Va.; V1 (13-189).
COALE, WILLIAM; Warwick Co., Va.;
  Anne Arundel Co., Md.; W2 (21-62).
COATS, ROBERT; Lynn, Mass.; Stoning-
  ton, Conn.; B4 (18-218).
COBB, HENRY; (Samuel3, Ebenezer4),
  Falmouth, Me.; Dt (10-9, 31).
COBB; (James of Barnstable); D (31-
  33).
COBB; (Capt. James, Rev. soldier,
  Va.); V1 (14-174).
COBB; (estate of Gershom, 1675),
  Middleboro, Mass.; D (34-112).
COCKE, RICHARD; Henrico County, Va.;
  W2 (13-143, 209); V3 (43-74; 44-
  136; 51-387); identity of wife;
  W2 (21-180); V3 (50-74).
COCKE; Pickthorne, Shropshire, Eng.;
  W2 (16-313).
COCKROFT, WILLIAM; Lower Norfolk Co.,
  Va.; English origin; A1 (100-96
  and chart).
COCQ, BEATRIX (OUSEEL); New York; A2
  (74-96).
CODDINGTON, WILLIAM (GOV.); R. I.;
  English origin; A2 (72-5).
CODY; Md.; Va.; V1 (13-64, 133).
COFFIN, TRISTRAM; Nantucket, Mass.;
  English ancestry; S1 (21-289; 25-
  261; 36-823).
COGAN; co. Somerset, England; A1
  (100-223).
COGGESHALL, JOHN; R. I.; English an-
  cestry; A1 (86-257; 99-315; 100-
  14); (Family of William4); A1 (90-
  296); see also NE (2-99).
COGSWELL, JOHN; Ipswich, Mass.; Y1
  (76-152).
COLCORD, EDWARD; N. H.; B4 (16-65;
  17-216; 18-34).
COLE, SAMUEL, ISAAC and JOHN; Boston,
  Mass.; R. I.; A1 (97-194).
COLE, SOLOMON; Beverly; (Stark, N.
  H., branch); A1 (86-60, 143, 299,
  359).
COLEMAN, HENRY; Rev. Pension (John),
  Va.; M (24-56).
COLEMAN, ROBERT; Essex Co., Va.; V3
  (54-258).
COLEMAN, THOMAS; Branch of Jethro,
  Stanfordville, N. Y.; A1 (87-86).
COLEMAN [KOHLMAN], Valentine; Bible

records; B2 (10-66).
COLEMAN; Ky.; N3 (36-138 to 150).
COLEMAN; (will of Joseph, 1675);
  D (34-73).
COLGIN; Charles City County, Va.;
  V1 (16-249).
COLLETT, JOHN and JAMES; Md.; Va.;
  V3 (47-80).
COLLIER, THOMAS; Hull, Mass.; B4
  (19-43).
COLLINS, EDWARD; Cambridge, Mass.;
  English ancestry; A1 (89-73,
  148; B4 (23-149).
COLLINS; Halifax County, Va.; Lex-
  ington, Ky.; N3 (30-93).
COLLINS; Sheffield and Rotherham,
  York, Eng.; S1 (33-452).
COLLINS; (Spencer), Ky.; N3 (40-
  423).
COLMAN, LASSE ANDRIESSEN; Glouces-
  ter Co., N. J.; B1 (13-18).
COLQUITT, JOHN; Cumberland Co., Va.;
  V1 (17-247; 18-54, 106).
COLT, JOHN; Hartford, Conn.; S1 (9-
  883).
COLTON, GEORGE; Springfield, Mass.;
  S1 (25-575).
COLVE, ANTHONY; New York, N. Y.;
  A2 (72-186).
COLVER, see Kolfs.
COLYER [CALJER], JOCHEM; New York;
  B4 (20-97).
COMBS; (Joseph), Stafford Co., Va.;
  V3 (54-341).
COMER, JOHN; Boston, Mass.; Eng-
  lish origin; A1 (100-223).
COMPTON, WILLIAM; N. J.; (Abraham5),
  Botetourt Co., Va.; W2 (23-212).
COMPTON; (John), N. J.; Dt (9-138).
COMSTOCK, WILLIAM; New London,
  Conn.; S1 (29-444).
COMYN, CUMMING; arms; A1 (96-206).
CONEY; N. J.; B5 (19-84).
CONKLIN, ANANIAS; East Hampton, N.
  Y.; B4 (11-139); S1 (32-105);
  genealogy; B4 (21-48, 133).
CONKLIN, JOHN; Southold, Hunting-
  ton, N. Y.; B4 (21-210, 247; 22-
  111, 226).
CONKWRIGHT [KRANKHEIT]; Clark Co.,
  Ky.; N3 (32-274).
CONLEY, NICHOLAS; Bible record; Dt
  (2-205).
CONN, JOHN; Branch of Emery, Ashby,
  Mass.; A1 (87-88).
CONOVER, see Van Kouwenhoven, Van
  Couwenhoven.
CONSTANT; (John of Ky.); N3 (32-

23).
CONSTANT; (will of John, 1811),
  Fleming Co., Ky.; N3 (43-351).
CONVERSE, EDWARD; Woburn, Mass.; S1
  (28-153).
CONYERS; Sockburn, co. Durham; S1
  (36-755).
COOKE, AARON (MAJOR); Northampton,
  Mass.; B4 (11-179).
COOK, ARTHUR; (Joseph[2]), Philadel-
  phia, Pa.; B4 (20-193).
COOK, ELLIS; Hanover, Morris Co.,
  N. J.; Z3 (2-11-55; 3-5-100).
COOKE, FRANCIS; Plymouth, Mass.; Pw
  (21-49).
COOK, HENRY; (Capt. David[3]), Wall-
  ingford, Conn.; B4 (14-163).
COOK, THOMAS; Portsmouth, R. I.; M
  (29-120).
COOK; (Andrew); U (23-122).
COOL, CORNELIS LAMBERTSZEN; A2 (64-
  107; 65-15, 122, 234).
COOLEY, BENJAMIN; Springfield,
  Mass.; M (26-122).
COOLEY; (Col. Benjamin), Pittsford,
  Vt.; Dt (3-203).
COOPER, ANTHONY; Hingham, Mass.;
  English records; B4 (13-151).
COOPER, JOHN; New Haven, Conn.; S1
  (32-178).
COOPER, JOHN-BAPTIST-HENRY; Monte-
  rey, Calif.; S1 (29-663).
COOPER, ROBERT (REV.); Charleston,
  S. C.; J (38-120).
COOPER, THOMAS; Boston, Mass.; A1
  (100-221).
COOPER, THOMAS; Hingham, Rehoboth,
  Mass.; English records; B4 (13-
  151).
COOPER, THOMAS; Springfield, Mass.;
  B4 (23-95); S1 (20-157).
COOPER; Washington, Westmoreland Co.,
  Va.; W2 (15-195).
COOP, WILLIAM; Boston; cont.; A2
  (63-60; 64-150, 205); (Canadian
  branch, Samuel4); A2 (65-30, 132,
  251, 373); (Line of John4); A2
  (68-34, 119, 251, 345); (David),
  New London; B4 (14-45); (Capt.
  John), New York; A2 (72-210).
CORBIN; (Gawin and Richard), Middle-
  sex Co., Va.; V3 (46-38).
CORBLY, JOHN (REV.); Greene Co., Pa.;
  S1 (37-382).
CORDES, ANTHONY (DR.); Berkeley Co.,
  S. C.; French origin; J (43-133,
  219; 44-17, 115, 184).
CORLISS, GEORGE; Haverhill, Mass.;

S1 (20-443; 31-205).
CORN, GEORGE; Pa., Ky.; N3 (44-70).
CORNBURY, VISCOUNT, see Hyde.
CORNELL, THOMAS; Boston, Mass.;
  Portsmouth, R. I.; Westchester Co.,
  N. Y.; Dt (5-173, 191).
CORSON; Origins of American families;
  A2 (66-221).
CORSON; (Daniel), Clinton twp., On-
  tario; Ng (4-80-98).
CORTELYOU, JACQUES; N. Y.; S1 (7-
  721).
CORY, JOHN; Southold, N. Y.; S1 (36-
  455).
CORYELL; (Daniel), N. Y., Ohio, Ill.,
  Iowa; B2 (21-11).
COTTON, JOHN (REV.); Boston, Mass.;
  English ancestry; S1 (21-301, 440).
COTTON, JOHN; York County, Va.; V1
  (14-61).
COTTON, WILLIAM (REV.); Northampton
  Co., Va.; W2 (19-34, 299).
COUILLARD, JOHN; Mass., Me.; B4 (23-
  255).
COULSON; (Joseph), Stoughton, Mass.;
  S1 (21-239).
COULTAS, JAMES (CAPT.); Bible rec-
  ord; P (13-109).
COUNTRYMAN; Ingham Co., Mich.; Dt
  (10-26).
COVENHOVEN; Bible record; B1 (13-72).
COVERT; Inscriptions, Lodi, N. Y.;
  Dt (4-9, 29).
COVEY; (Family of Walter); U (26-
  156).
COWAN; (Edgar, U. S. Sen.), Pa.; S1
  (26-247).
COWDREY, WILLIAM; Reading, Mass.;
  English data; B4 (10-14); (Family
  of Oliver7); U (26-106).
COWES, MICHAEL; Marblehead, Mass.;
  English ancestry; B4 (18-67).
COWLES, JOHN; Farmington, Conn.;
  WF (1-80); (John), Sheffield,
  Mass.; B4 (18-192).
COX, WILLIAM; Henrico Co., Va.; S1
  (25-233); V3 (52-214).
COX; (will of John, 1695), Old Rap-
  pahannock Co., Va.; V1 (23-115).
CRAIG; (Toliver), Ky.; N3 (31-179,
  181).
CRANSON, SAMUEL; Marlboro, Mass.;
  B4 (23-75).
CRANSTON, JOHN (GOV.); R. I.; A1
  (87-74, 75).
CRARY, PETER; New London, Conn.; S1
  (28-262).
CRAWFORD, JOHN; Va.; N3 (36-42).

CRAWFORD, ROBERT; Beaver Co., Pa.;
Z (69-765).
CRAWFORD; Surry Co., Va.; V3 (48-
74).
CRAWFORD; (Alexander), Augusta Co.,
Va.; N3 (34-281).
CREAL; (Philip, Harford Co., Md.);
X2 (4-18).
CRICHTON; V1 (16-250).
CRITTON, CRIGHTON, etc.; Va.; W2
(18-509).
CROCKER, WILLIAM; Barnstable, Mass.;
(branch of Eleazer3); B4 (16-207);
(estate of Jabez, 1700); D (34-56).
CROCKETT, SAMUEL; Wythe Co., Va.; V3
(48-304).
CROCKETT; Deer Isle, Maine; B4 (17-
138).
CROESEN, see Kroesen.
CROFT; Brunswick County, Va.; V1
(14-185).
CROLLIUS; Marburg, Hesse; (ances-
tral to Rubincam); B4 (21-225).
CROOKE, JOHN; New York, N. Y.; A2
(67-77).
CROOPER, JOHN (GEN.); Accomack
County, Va.; V3 (44-97).
CROSBY, ANN (BRIGHAM); English an-
cestry; M (21-100).
CROSBY, RICHARD; Chester Co., Pa.;
Q1 (62-12).
CROSBY, SIMON; English ancestry; M
(21-101); maternal ancestry; M
(21-100); (Thomas2), Barnstable
Co., Mass.; A2 (71-232, 375; 72-
48, 156).
CROSBY, THOMAS; Rowley, Mass.; S1
(30-188).
CROSBY; Billerica, Mass.; A2 (72-
159).
CROSHAW, RALEIGH (CAPT.); Elizabeth
City Co., Va.; W2 (21-265).
CROSS, PETER; Windham, Conn.; S1
(31-215).
CROSS; (Robert), New Windsor, N. Y.;
Dt (6-83).
CROSS; (Stephen), Newbury, Mass.;
Canadian journal, 1756; Y1 (75-
334; 76-14).
CROWFOOT, JOSEPH; Springfield, Mass.;
B4 (16-145; 17-23, 30, 120).
CROWLEY; (will of William, 1779),
Amelia Co., Va.; W2 (17-94).
CRUTCHER; (will of Thomas, 1786),
Caroline Co., Va.; V1 (27-280).
CUDDINGTON; (Zechariah), Washington
Co., Ohio; Dt (5-49).
CUE, ROBERT; Salem, Mass.; B4 (14-

150).
CULBERTSON, ALEXANDER (CAPT.); Lan-
caster Co., Pa.; N3 (39-313).
CULBERTSON; Campbeltown, Scotland;
M (23-105).
CULPEPPER; (William and Daniel),
Warren County, Ga.; Z (80-507).
CULVER, EDWARD; New London, Conn.;
S1 (19-475); (wives of John2 and
John3); Conn.; B4 (22-107).
CULVER, NATHANIEL; Boston, Mass.;
WF (1-153).
CULVERWELL; Md.; X2 (7-51).
CUNNINGHAM, ANDREW and THOMAS; Lan-
caster Co., Pa.; V3 (52-135, 205,
281).
CUNNINGHAM; Augusta Co., Va.; W2
(17-301).
CUNNINGHAM; (Alexander), Prince Ed-
ward Co., Va.; V3 (46-82).
CURD, JOHN; Va.; V3 (45-409).
CURRIER, RICHARD; Salisbury, Mass.;
S1 (21-308).
CURRY; (Lewis), Putnam Co., N. Y.;
Dt (5-53).
CURTICE, RICHARD; Southold, N. Y.;
Z3 (56-207).
CURTIS, BENJAMIN; Bible records;
Bristol, Eng.; Colo.; M (30-147).
CURTIS, ELIZABETH; Stratford, Conn.;
S1 (35-82).
CURTIS, HENRY; Sudbury, Mass.; S1
(28-126).
CURTIS, THOMAS; Wethersfield, Conn.;
Thomas3, Elnathan4; A2 (71-163).
CURTIS, WILLIAM; Stratford, Conn.;
S1 (32-201).
CUSHING, MATTHEW; (Line of Benjamin6,
Camden, Me.); A1 (89-339).
CUSHING; Hanover, Mass.; Camden, Me.·
A1 (88-400).
CUSHMAN, ROBERT; Plymouth, Mass.; S1
(33-276).
CUSHMAN; notes; S4 (3-216).
CUSTIS; Arlington, Va.; S1 (28-449);
W2 (23-209).
CUSTIS; Holland, Belgium; M (30-75);
V3 (52-15).
CUTHBERTSON, JOHN (REV.); Lancaster
County, Pa.; M (21-17).
CUTHBERTSON, Campbeltown, Scot-
land; M (23-73).
CUTLER, JOHN; Hingham; English clue;
A1 (86-257).
CUTTS, JOHN; Family record (Samuel);
A1 (91-300).
CUYLER; arms; A2 (65-102).
CUYLER; note on English branch; A2

(72-229).

DABNEY, CORNELIUS; Virginia; origin;
V3 (45-121, 273; 46-161));
(Charles4); V3 (51-186).
DADE, FRANCIS; St. Paul's Parish,
King George Co., Va.; V1 (16-47);
Norfolk Co., Eng.; Stafford Co.,
Va.; V1 (16-157, 243; 17-49); W2
(12-26; 13-29).
DAGGETT, JOHN; Watertown, Mass.; S1
(26-85).
DAHLGREN; (Col. Ulric, Civil War);
W2 (12-1).
DAINS, ABRAHAM; New London, Norwich,
Conn.; Dt (8-95, 121; 9-3, 53,
100).
DALBO, PETER-MATSCN and WOOLA; Pa.,
N. J.; Bl (13-13, 15).
DALE, EDWARD; Racine Co., Wis.; Eng-
lish ancestry; B1 (21-13).
DALLAS; (Alexander C. P.), Prince
Wm. Co., Va.; S1 (21-234).
DALRYMPLE, WILLIAM; Calvert County,
Md.; S1 (32-391).
DALTON; (Letters of Samuel M.),
Salem, 1803-14; Y1 (68-321); (fam-
ily letters), Newbury, Mass.; Y1
(71-7).
DAME [DAM], JOHN; Dover, N. H.; Bi-
ble records; Al (89-192); (line
of John7, Nottingham, N. H.); Al
(89-385); additions and branch
of Joseph6; Al (91-203, 304, 389;
100-225); (line of William2); Al
(92-101, 220, 359); additions,
line of John2; Al (92-203); (Rich-
ard6); Al (94-392); inscriptions,
Dover, N. H.; Al (92-95).
DAMEN, JAN; Brooklyn, N. Y.; A2 (66-
225).
DAMON, JOHN; Scituate, Mass.; Ng (2-
87); (Dedham branch); Z1 (5-29).
DAMON, THOMAS; Reading, Mass.; Ng
(4-17).
DANA, RICHARD; Cambridge, Mass.; S1
(1-461).
DANFORTH, NICHOLAS; Cambridge,
Mass.; M (21-98).
DANIEL, ROBERT; Cambridge, Mass.;
Al (88-383; 89-154).
DANIEL; Middlesex County, Va.; W2
(14-93); V1 (15-265); V3 (42-161).
DANIEL; Revolutionary War soldiers;
V1 (14-154).
DANIEL; Va.; cont.; V1 (13-84).
Halifax, N. C.; V1 (13-107).
DANSEY; King William County, Va.;

W2 (13-139).
DARCY; English mediaeval family;
B4 (21-171).
DARLING, DENICE; (Branch of Arte-
mus of Norwich, N. Y.); B5 (17-
20).
DARLING; (wife of Joseph), Fair-
field, Conn.; B4 (20-252).
DARNALL; marriages, Md.; X2 (8-21).
DARROW, GEORGE; (Norwalk branch);
B4 (10-123).
D'ARSSENS, JOHN; Medway, S. C.; J
(34-218).
DAUGHERTY; Virginia; N3 (37-10).
DAVENANT, WILLIAM (SIR); X1 (28-
101).
DAVENPORT, JOHN (REV.); New Haven,
Conn.; B4 (10-33); (will of uncle
Christopher); B4 (15-65).
DAVENPORT, THOMAS; Boston, Mass.;
line of Wm.4 of Newburyport; Y1
(73-258).
DAVIDSON, ROBERT; Pa., N. C.; S1
(25-444).
DAVIE, HUMPHREY; Boston, Mass.; B4
(23-206).
DAVIES, JOHN; Litchfield, Conn.;
English origin; S1 (32-49, 154).
DAVIS, CHRISTOPHER; Kingston, N. Y.;
OU (10-97).
DAVIS, JOHN; Pilesgrove, N. J.; P
(14-76).
DAVIS, JOHN; Philadelphia; Hagers-
town, Md.; X1 (30-11).
DAVIS, THOMAS; Haverhill, Mass.; S1
(31-206).
DAVIS, THOMAS; Middletown, Conn.;
English ancestry; B4 (15-30).
DAVIS, THOMAS; Reading, Pa.; S1 (24-
85).
DAVIS; (Rev. Thomas), Charles City
Co., Va.; S1 (37-175).
DAVIS; (Journal of Hannah, 1830);
B5 (17-164).
DAVOL, WILLIAM; Duxbury, Mass.; Dt
(3-115).
DAY, JAMES; Isle of Wight Co., Va.;
V1 (16-239); V3 (45-195).
DAY, NICHOLAS; Ann Arundel Co., Md.;
X2 (12-7).
DAY; (Nicholas), Baltimore Co., Md.;
X2 (9-16).
DAYTON, RALPH; East Hampton, N. Y.;
N. J. branches; B4 (22-129); S1
(32-103).
DEAN, JOHN; Taunton, Mass.; S1 (22-
354).
DEAN, WALTER; Taunton, Mass.; wife's

family; Al (100-223); deeds; B4
(23-174).
DEAN, see Dains.
DEANE; Cumberland Co., Va.; W2 (14-
181).
DE BAUN, JOOST; Bushwick, N. Y.; A2
(66-12); Dutch origin; A2 (70-
115).
DECKER, JAN BROERSEN; Kingston, N.
Y.; OU (2-244; 3-27; 5-120, 155,
181).
DECKER; Inscriptions, Bruynswick,
Ulster Co., N. Y.; A2 (72-220).
DE CLERCQ, HENDRIK; Cazenovia, N. Y.;
arms; A2 (66-179).
DE FRIES; (Ancestry of Hyrum), Ha-
waii; U (24-1).
DE GARMO, PIERRE; Albany, N. Y.; Dt
(5-73, 93, 115, 137).
DEGGE, JOHN; Gloucester Co., Va.;
W2 (16-101).
DE GRAUW, LEENDERT ARENTSZEN; New
York; Dt (3-147).
DE GRAUW; Albany, N. Y.; correction;
A2 (65-88).
DE GROOT, STAES JANSZ; Dutch origin
and arms; A2 (69-224).
DE HOGGES, ANTHONY; Albany, N. Y.;
A2 (67-4).
DE HONEUR, GUILLAUME; New York; A2
(63-169, 414).
DE HUBERT, HERMAN ANTHONISZ; New
York; Dutch ancestry; A2 (71-241).
DE HULTER, JOHANNES; Rensselaers-
wyck; ancestry of self and wife;
A2 (69-339; 70-55).
DEIGHTON; English ancestry of Fran-
ces (Deighton) Williams, Jane
(Deighton) (Lugg) Negus and Kath-
arine (Deighton) (Hagburn) (Dud-
ley) Allin; B4 (9-212).
DE JONGH; (ancestry of wife of Aldert
Hymansen Roosa); A2 (70-33); Hol-
land; arms; A2 (72-30).
DE LA MAR, PHILIP; U (26-173; 27-
138).
DELAMATER, CLAUDE; Flatbush, N. Y.;
S1 (22-355).
DE LA MONTAGNE; Kingston, N. Y.; A2
(67-8, 14, 15).
DELANO, PHILIP; Duxbury, Mass.; B4
(15-165).
DEMAREST [DE MAREES]; Holland; A2
(72-310).
DE MILL; (Family of Garret); U (26-
149).
DEMING, JOHN; Wethersfield, Conn.,
S1 (34-264); (correction, Henry,

1752); S3 (10-1-7).
DEMING, THOMAS; East Hampton, N. Y.;
(Moses5, Conn., Ohio); O (7-577).
DENISON, JOHN; Ipswich, Mass.; S1
(32-150).
DENISON, WILLIAM; Roxbury, Mass.;
English ancestry; A2 (67-46); S1
(33-105; 36-487); Ng (5-182).
DENISON; Thorley, Herts, Eng.; A2
(68-399).
DENNISTON, JOHN; Philadelphia, Pa.;
S1 (22-381).
DENNY; (Simon), Harford Co., Md.;
X2 (7-23).
DENSLOW, BENJAMIN; Harpswell, Me.;
A2 (77-110).
DENSLOW, NICHOLAS; Windsor, Conn.;
English ancestry; A2 (77-49).
DENSLOW; (Philander, N. Y., Ohio);
A2 (77-175).
DENT, THOMAS; (Thomas-Marshall5),
Md.; M (25-104).
DE PEYSTER, ABRAHAM; New York; Flem-
ish ancestry; A2 (70-210, 313);
origin; see Société de l'Histoire
de Protestantisme français, Bul-
letin, vol. 82 (1933).
DE PEYSTER, JOHANNES; arms; A2 (65-
58).
DE RASIÈRE, ISAAC; New York, N. Y.;
S1 (26-394).
DERBY, ROGER; Salem, Mass.; mother's
family; Al (93-175).
DERBY; (Benjamin of Ellington,
Conn.); S1 (27-344).
DE RIEMER, ISAAC; New York; A2 (63-
4, 7, 14); Bible record; A2 (63-
285); Z3 (4-12-451); arms; A2 (64-
147); Dutch ancestry; A2 (72-227).
DE RUYTER, CLAES JANSEN; New York;
A2 (66-89).
DESELLEM; (Moses), Montgomery Co.,
Md.; S1 (37-158).
DE SILLE, NICASIUS; coat-of-arms;
A2 (64-13).
DESPENCER; English pedigree; S4
(3-86).
DESTOUCHES, CHARLES-ADRIAN-GRAVILLE-
CESAIRE; Philadelphia, Pa.; M
(25-77).
DEURCANT; arms; A2 (66-73).
DE VEAUX [DEVOL], Frederick; Mor-
risania, N. Y.; Dt (2-185, 201;
3-6, 35, 139, 161, 183, 205).
DEVENISH, JOHN; Virginia; English
clue; Al (100-217).
DEVENPECK, CHRISTIAN; Albany, N.
Y.; S1 (26-261).

DE VRIES, PIETER RUDOLPHUS; New York; A2 (70-19).

DEW; Dewsville, Va.; V3 (46-112).

DEW; Baltimore County, Md.; X2 (4-4).

DEWEY, THOMAS; Windsor, Conn.; S1 (32-193).

DEWEY; additions to Genealogy; Dt (6-137).

DEWEY; (Miles[6]), Canandaigua, N. Y.; additions to Genealogy; Dt (8-139).

DEWITT, TJERCK CLAESEN; Kingston, N. Y.; OU (1-313, 345, 380; 2-25, 58, 88, 280); (will of Tjerck Claesen, 1710); OU (8-18).

DEWITT; Inscriptions, Ellenville, Ulster Co., N. Y.; A2 (72-209).

DEXTER; ("Lord" Timothy), Newburyport, Mass.; NH (Feb. 1946).

DEY [DUYTSZEN], DERRIK; New York; WF (1-30).

d'Eyncourt; England; A1 (96-307).

DEYO, CHRISTIAN; family record (Jacob5), New Paltz, N. Y.; Dt (9-55).

D'HINIOSSA, ALEXANDER; Dutch origin; A2 (73-246).

DIBBLE; Danbury, Conn.; B4 (13-249).

DICKENS, NATHANIEL; Providence, Newport, Block Island; A1 (86-174).

DICKERSON; (will of Charles, 1823), Ovid, N. Y.; Dt (7-139).

DICKIE; marriage contract (Rev. Adam, 1735), King and Queen Co., Va.; V1 (27-285).

DICKINSON, CHARLES; South Kingstown, R. I.; B4 (21-258).

DICKINSON, JOHN; Talbot Co., Md.; S3 (17-2-8).

DICKINSON, JOHN; Oyster Bay, N. Y.; B4 (21-256).

DICKINSON, JONATHAN; Philadelphia, Pa.; Q1 (59-420).

DICKINSON, NATHANIEL; Wethersfield, Hadley; M (32-23); (Thomas3), Glastonbury, Conn.; B4 (20-166; 21-92); (John5), Amherst, Mass.; A1 (92-99).

DICKINSON; Emigrant list; S4 (1-85).

DICKINSON; (Charles), Caroline Co., Md.; S3 (17-1-8).

DICKINSON; (David), Caroline Co., Va.; V3 (54-260).

DICKINSON; (John), Md.; Q1 (60-1).

DIEFFENDERFER, JOHN and ALEXANDER; Berks and Lancaster Counties, Pa.; M (21-30).

DIGGES, EDWARD; Va.; Z (67-617).

DIGGS, see Degge.

DIKE, ANTHONY (CAPT.); (Jonathan3), Newton, Mass.; B4 (17-163).

DIMSDALE, ROBERT (DR.); Lumberton, N. J.; English origin; Z3 (57-98).

DINGLEY; (probate of Jacob, 1691); D (31-61).

DINWIDDIE, WILLIAM; Pa.; Campbell Co., Va.; Tenn.; V1 (15-30, 125, 189; 16-48).

DINWIDDIE; (Campbell and Bedford Counties, Va.; V1 (14-176).

DINWIDDIE; (Robert), Bath County, Va., will 1796; V1 (14-243).

DISNEY; Marriage Licenses, Md.; X2 (10-23).

DIXON; Calvert and Talbot Cos., Md.; S1 (37-311).

DOANE; (will of Ephraim, 1700); D (34-56).

DOBBINS, JACOB; Caswell Co., N. C.; Z (79-111).

DODGE, WILLIAM; Salem, Mass.; S1 (23-246).

DODMAN, JOHN (COL.); Warwick Co., Va.; V1 (25-52).

DOLBERE; family, Colyton, co. Devon; Eng.; B4 (15-208).

DONALDSON; Fairfax County, Va.; W2 (13-59).

DONIPHAN, ALEXANDER (CAPT.); Richmond Co., Va.; V1 (28-238).

DONIPHAN; (will of Alexander), Stafford Co., Va.; 1768; V1 (26-275).

DOOLITTLE, ABRAHAM; Wallingford, Conn.; NE (3-151).

DOORN, DIDLOF; New York, N. Y.; A2 (72-226).

DORCHESTER, ANTHONY; Springfield, Mass.; B4 (17-206).

DORSEY, EDWARD; Anne Arundel Co., Md.; X1 (32-47; 33-27).

DORSEY; Md.; X1 (31-254).

DOTY, EDWARD; (Family of John2 of Plymouth); D (33-114).

DOTY; (probate of Edward, 1695); D (31-65).

DOUGHTY, FRANCES (REV.); Taunton, Mass.; New York; Northampton Co., Va.; W2 (19-38, 300).

DOUGLAS; Charles County, Md.; X2 (16-23, 47).

DOUGLASS; (William), Cape May, N. J.; L1 (6-21).

DOW, HENRY; Hampton, N. H.; English ancestry; S1 (23-251; 34-604).

DOWNEY; (Samuel), Pa.; Augusta Co., Va.; N3 (34-281).

DOWNING, WILLIAM; Northumberland

County, Va.; W2 (14-94).
DOWNING; (James), Brooks Co., W.
  Va.; Col (2-69).
DOWNMAN, WILLIAM; Lancaster Co.,
  Va.; V1 (16-188).
DRAKE, FRANCIS; Portsmouth, N. H.;
  M (32-21).
DRAKE, JOHN; Windsor, Conn.; Dt (8-
  101).
DRAKE [DRAAK], JOHANNES; N. Y., N.
  J.; S1 (25-117).
DRAKE, THOMAS; Weymouth, Mass.; Eng-
  lish origin; A1 (98-280).
DRAPER, JAMES; Roxbury, Mass.; Eng-
  lish ancestry; B4 (15-236; 17-19).
DRESSER, JOHN; Rowley, Mass.; Dt (6-
  13, 136).
DROWN, LEONARD; Boston, Mass.; M
  (32-77).
DRUMMOND; Scotland; S1 (19-400).
DRUSE, STEPHEN, ANDREW and JOHN;
  Scituate, R. I.; N. Y.; Ill.; A2
  (69-24, 114, 230, 346; 70-61).
DUBBS; Pa.; American families; Dt
  (9-59, 93, 117; 10-21, 48).
DU BOIS, GUALTHERUS (REV.); arms; A2
  (64-144).
DUBOIS, LOUIS and JACQUES; Kingston,
  N. Y.; S4 (1-189).
DUBOIS; Inscriptions, Fishkill, N.
  Y.; OU (1-142).
DUDLEY, AMBROSE; Gloucester Co., Va.;
  S1 (37-718).
DUDLEY, THOMAS (GOV.); Roxbury,
  Mass.; S1 (20-404; 21-305; 24-272;
  30-179); ancestry of wife; B4 (9-
  212).
DUDLEY, WILLIAM; Guilford, Conn.;
  B4 (10-76).
DUDLEY; Virginia; V1 (15-174).
DUERCANT; arms; A2 (72-313).
DUICKING; arms; A2 (72-308).
DULANEY; Ill., Mo.; Z (75-3-37).
DUMMER, RICHARD; Newbury, Mass.; Y1
  (81-35).
DUMOND, WALLERAND; Kingston, N. Y.;
  OU (4-150).
DUNBAR; origin of English family; A1
  (97-239).
DUNBAR; (James of Bridgewater); D
  (31-15).
DUNCAN, SAMUEL; Newbury, Mass.; S1
  (21-459).
DUNCAN; (Joseph), Orange Co., Va.;
  N3 (37-172).
DUNCAN; Culpeper and Fauquier Cos.,
  Va.; N3 (30-116; 31-281, 354).
DUNGAN, WILLIAM; English data; B4

(23-242).
DUNHAM, JOHN; Plymouth; S1 (25-605);
  (will of John, 1692); D (31-160);
  probate of John, 1697); D (31-108).
DUNLAP, ARCHIBALD; Chester, N. H.;
  S1 (20-418).
DUNLAP, JAMES; Donegal, Pa.; S4 (1-
  131).
DUNLAP, JOHN; Ovid, N. Y.; Dt (7-
  140).
DUNLAP, WILLIAM; Boston, Mass.; S1
  (19-558).
DUNLAP; (Col. Alexander), Va., Ohio;
  V3 (54-321).
DUNLOP, WILLIAM; Mission to St. Au-
  gustine, 1688; J (34-1).
DUNN, RICHARD; Newport, R. I. ; S1
  (20-427).
DUNN (DURM), ROBERT; Md.; X2 (15-54).
DUNNING, THEOPHILUS; Salem, Mass.;
  Fairfield, Conn.; Col (5-3, 37,
  76, 111; 6-14, 48, 76; 7-1-23; 7-
  2-19; 7-82, 105); (David4), New-
  town, Conn.; B4 (19-49); (Josiah),
  Newtown, Conn.; Williamson, N. Y.;
  E3 (6-442).
DURKEE, WILLIAM; Ipswich, Mass.; Ng
  (3-165).
DURRETT; Va.; (Francis), Henry Co.,
  Ky.; S1 (8-1).
DURYEA; (Joost), Oyster Bay, N. Y.;
  A2 (69-83).
DUSHANE; Md.; X2 (9-39).
DU TRIEU, PHILIPPE; New York; note;
  A2 (70-110).
DUVAL, DANIEL; Va.; W2 (12-203).
DUVAL, MARTIN; Prince George Co.,
  Md.; S1 (25-260).
DUVALL; Md.; Ky.; W2 (13-273).
DUYCKINCK; arms; A2 (65-103).
DWELLEY; estate of Richard, 1692,
  Scituate, Mass.; D (34-182).
DWIGHT, JOHN; Dedham, Mass.; S1 (24-
  546).
DYE, DIRK; (William), Ohio, Mo.,
  Iowa, Neb., Col.; Col (1 No. 2).
DYE; (Andrew), Pa., Ohio; M (27-87).
DYER, WILLIAM; Boston, Mass.; A1 (94-
  300).
DYER, WILLIAM; Newport, R. I.; B4
  (22-210); traditional origin of
  wife Mary; A1 (98-25); P (14-310).
DYER; (John of Braintree; Henry of
  Boston); B4 (15-50).
DYER; (Roger), Pendleton Co., W. Va.;
  (35-131).
DYKE, JOHN; Essex Co., Va.; V1 (17-
  107).

EARL, JOHN; Northampton, Mass.;
Southampton, N. Y.; B4 (22-220).
EARLE, RALPH; Portsmouth, R. I.; S1
(26-152); Z2 (17-161); English an-
cestry; A2 (67-390); wife (Joan
Savage); A1 (93-361).
EARLY, JOHN; Germantown, Pa.; M (30-
16).
EAST, BENJAMIN; Oxford, Pa.; B4 (20-
194).
EASTMAN, ROGER; Salisbury, Mass.;
S1 (31-160).
EASTON, JOSEPH; Hartford, Conn.; S1
(30-735).
EASTON [ESTEN], THOMAS; Providence,
R. I.; S1 (31-659).
EATON, JOHN; Dedham, Mass.; S1 (34-
640).
EATON, JONAS; Reading, Mass.; S1 (34-
637).
EATON, NATHANIEL (REV.); Northampton
Co., Va.; W2 (19-35, 300).
EATON, THEOPHILUS (GOV.); New Haven,
Conn.; S1 (20-413).
EATON; Talbot County, Md.; X2 (3-24).
EATON; (Jonathan), Caroline Co., Md.;
X2 (8-11).
EATON; Md.; X2 (11-3).
EATON; (Anson), Duanesburg, N. Y.;
S1 (34-620).
EBBINGH, JERONIMUS; New York; A2
(70-55).
EBERHARDT, FREDERICK; Penn, Pa.; S1
(36-124).
EDDY, SAMUEL; Plymouth; line of des-
cent; Eddy tablet, East Middleboro,
Mass.; M (25-115).
EDDY; (John), Warren Co., Ohio; M
(26-57).
EDGAR, THOMAS; Rahway, N. J.; Z3 (4-
8-56).
EDLOW, MATHEW; Henrico, Va.; W2 (16-
469).
EDMONDS, ELIAS; Lancaster County,
Va.; W2 (16-97; 23-212).
EDMONDS; Fauquier Co., Va.; W2 (17-
292).
EDMONSTON; (will of Archibald,
1801), Clark Co., Ky.; N3 (43-352).
EDMUNDS, HOWELL; Surry Co., Va.; V1
(17-59, 111, 193).
EDSON; note; B4 (12-123).
EDSON; will of Samuel, 1692, Bridge-
water, Mass.; D (34-181).
EDWARDS, WILLIAM; Hartford, Conn.;
English clue; B4 (10-83); English
ancestry and genealogy; A2 (70-
104, 269, 331; 71-217, 323; 72-56,

124, 213, 320; 73-173, 251); S1
(34-286).
EDWARDS; notes; S4 (2-85).
EDWARDS; Westmoreland Co., Va.; W2
(15-197); N3 (32-357).
EDWARDS; (William), Fairfax, Va.;
W2 (18-510).
EGERTON, CHARLES; Lower Norfolk Co.,
Va.; (Md. branch); X1 (35-292).
EGGLESTON, BERNARD; Baltimore Co.,
Md.; (John); S1 (37-170).
EGGLESTON, BYGOD; Windsor, Conn.;
English origin; B4 (10-197).
EGGLESTON; Michigan; Census records;
Dt (8-51, 73).
EISENHOWER, NICHOLAS; Lancaster Co.,
Pa.; A2 (76-49).
ELBERT, HUGH; Baltimore County, Md.;
S1 (27-69).
ELDER; Annapolis, Md.; X1 (32-50).
ELDERT; Long Island; A2 (77-132).
ELDRED, ELDREDGE, SAMUEL; Wickford,
R. I.; Stonington branch; A2 (66-
115).
ELDREDGE; (Ezekiel), Cape May Co.,
N. J.; B7 (2-157); L1 (5-19);
(Samuel), Cape May, N. J.; L1 (4-
25, 30); Bible record (William,
E11); L1 (6-14).
ELDRIDGE, ROBERT; Chatham, Mass.; S1
(19-512).
ELDRIDGE, SAMUEL; Cape May County,
N. J.; B7 (1-12, 59).
ELDRIDGE, THOMAS; Va.; V1 (14-186);
V3 (46-172, 267).
ELFE, THOMAS; see Charleston, S. C.
ELIAS; Inscriptions, Huntingdon Co.,
Pa.; M (20-86).
ELIOT, PHILIP; Roxbury, Mass.; Eng-
lish data; S1 (21-318).
ELKIN; (will of Rev. Robert, 1822),
Clark Co., Ky.; N3 (43-351).
ELKINS, HENRY; Hampton, N. H.; S1
(21-463).
ELKINTON, GEORGE; Burlington Co.,
N. J.; English ancestry; B4 (22-
1).
ELLINGTON; N. C.; W2 (12-44).
ELLINGWOOD, RALPH; Beverly, Mass.;
S1 (23-245).
ELLIOTT, EDWARD; Talbot, Md.; X1 (41-
240).
ELLIOTT, WILLIAM and JOHN; Family
notes, Md.; M (20-116).
ELLIOTT; Westmoreland Co., Va.; V3
(44-151).
ELLIOTT; Middleton, Pa.; Ohio; S1
(21-231).

ELLIOT; (Will of William of Brandy-
wine, Del., 1778); B2 (14-10).
ELLIS [JOHAN JACOB ALLES]; Pa., Va.,
Ohio; M (29-91).
ELLIS; (Robert of Pittsburgh, Pa.);
U (27-161).
ELLIS; (Rev. John), Norwich, Conn.;
Sl (32-140).
ELLIS; (Journal, letters, notes, of
Job B.); B5 (20-204, 223, 281).
ELMENDORF, JACOBUS COENRADT; King-
ston, N. Y.; OU (10-27).
ELMER; Inscriptions, Bridgeton, N.
J.;B5 (17-221).
ELSWORTH, THEOPHILUS; New York; A2
(64-154, 255, 410; 65-89).
ELTING, JAN; New Paltz, N. Y.; OU
(3-150, 176, 214).
ELY, RICHARD; Lyme, Conn.; Sl (27-
375).
ELY; New London Co., Conn.; B4 (13-
64).
ELZEY; (will of Thomas, 1698 and
1721), Stafford Co., Va.; Vl (27-
275).
EMERY, JOHN and ANTHONY; Newbury,
Mass., and Kittery, Me.; English
origin; Al (89-376); B4 (17-96);
Sl (37-380).
EMIGH, JOHAN NICHOLAS; Beekman Pre-
cinct, N. Y.; A2 (70-223).
EMISON; general U. S.; N3 (42-139).
EMISON; Va.; S. C.; W2 (18-125, 354).
ENDELL; Michael and Richard; Isles
of Shoals; B4 (18-72).
ENDICOTT; (Samuel), Salem, Mass.; B4
(16-115).
ENGLISH, PHILIP; Salem, Mass.; ances-
try, Island of Jersey; Yl (75-23).
ENLOWS; (will of Hendrick, 1702); X2
(4-29).
ENSIGN, THOMAS; Scituate, Mass.; Sl
(26-130).
ENSLOW, JOHN; Pa.; X2 (5-13).
EPPES, FRANCIS (LT.-COL.); Henrico
Co., Va.; Sl (36-689).
ERNST, AUGUSTUS FREDERICK (REV.);
Milwaukee, Wis.; German ancestry;
Sl (35-736).
ESLEECK; (Isaac), Bristol, R. I.; Sl
(25-550).
ESTEN, THOMAS; Providence, R. I.; Sl
(26-146).
ESTES, MATTHEW; Dover, Salem, Mass.;
Z2 (18-53).
ESTILL, THOMAS, DANIEL and WILLIAM;
N. J.; Va. (Ky.) branch; N3 (43-
121).

EUBANK; (James), Henrico Co., Va.;
Ky.; V3 (50-361).
EURE and VESCI; baronial family;
Sl (36-757, 760).
EVANS, HENRY; Charlestown, Mass.; Sl
(26-448).
EVANS, HUGH; Md., Ohio; M (30-95).
EVANS, JOHN; Portsmouth, N. H.; M (24-
128).
EVANS, REES, LEWIS, and DANIEL;
Chester County, Pa.; W2 (12-173).
EVANS, RICHARD; Dorchester, Mass.);
Sl (19-557).
EVANS, WILLIAM; Burlington, N. J.;
M (24-131).
EVANS; (John), N. Y.; E3 (5-313).
EVERETT, RICHARD; Dedham, Mass.; Sl
(26-124).
EWERS, HENRY; Concord, Mass.; Sl (34-
641).
EWING, WILLIAM; Cape May County, N.
J.; B7 (1-13).
EWING; (Thomas), Newfane, Niagara Co.,
N. Y.; Sl (34-622).
EWING; (William), Cape May, N. J.;
Ll (4-25, 29).

FAIRFAX, LORD; Northern Neck, Va.;
W2 (13-55).
FAIRFAX; Va.; note on English ances-
try; Al (100-78).
FAIRFAX; Family letters; Yl (68-169).
FALES, JAMES; Dedham, Mass.; Sl (26-
142); (wife of Ebenezer2); Al (95-
203).
FANCKBONER, FANGBONER, GRUNADYKE;
Warren Co., N. J.; Dt (6-51, 67,
96; 8-135; 9-17).
FANTON, JONATHAN; Fairfield, Conn.;
Sl (19-479).
FARGESON; Virginia; B2 (13-37).
FARIS, JOHN; Cincinnati, Ohio; Irish
ancestry; Sl (19-110).
FARIS, WILLIAM; Annapolis, Md.; Xl
(37-423).
FARIS; (Diary of William, Annapolis,
Md., 1792-1804); Xl (28-197; 36-
420).
FARNUM; (Philo), N. Y., Mich.; E3
(6-489).
FARNUM; (William), Johnston, R. I.;
Col (6-98).
FARR, STEPHEN; Concord, Mass.; M (25-
96).
FARRAR, JACOB; Woburn, Mass.; Sl (34-
674).
FARRAR, THOMAS; Lynn, Mass.; Z2 (10
[1906]-85).

FARRAR, WILLIAM; Va.; his wife
Cicely; W2 (21-180); English origin; V3 (50-350).

FARRAR; Lunenburg County, Va.; V1
(13-58); additions; V3 (45-302).

FARREL, BENJAMIN; Prospect, Conn.;
S1 (32-750).

FARRER, JACOB; Lancaster, Mass.;
English ancestry; A1 (95-3).

FARRINGTON; (Jacob), Holland, N. Y.;
Ng (6-316).

FARWELL; (Samuel of Westminster,
Vt.); A1 (88-92).

FAY, JOHN; Marlboro, Mass.; S1 (23-
230).

FEAKE, ROBERT (LIEUT.); maternal ancestry, England; B4 (16-95).

FEAKE, TOBIAS; Flushing, L. I.;
wife's ancestry; A2 (66-113).

FEATHERSTON; records, Tenn., Ga.; M
(26-30, 31).

FELLOWS [FELLER], NICHOLAS; Livingston Manor, N. Y.; A2 (63-244,
374; 64-63, 410).

FELLOWS, WILLIAM; Ipswich; A1 (86-
140); B4 (17-159).

FELTON, NATHANIEL; Salem, Mass.; B4
(16-115).

FENDALL, JOSIAH (Gov.); Md.; English
origin; X1 (38-277).

FENNER, ARTHUR and JOHN; Providence,
R. I.; Saybrook, Conn.; English
ancestry; B4 (15-80; 17-19); ancestry of Arthur's wife; B4 (15-
84).

FENWICK, JOHN; Salem, N. J.; Z3 (4-
11-495); English data; Z3 (1-4-
53).

FERGUSON, JOHN; Fauquier Co., Va.;
N3 (36-34).

FERGUSON, JOHN; Princetown, N. Y.;
Dt (4-137; 5-196).

FERGUSON; (John of Fairfax Co., Va.);
W2 (15-304).

FERNISIDE, JOHN; Boston, Mass.; A1
(94-174).

FERRAR, WILLIAM (CAPT.); Henrico
County, Va.; English ancestry; W2
(16-267); V3 (47-78).

FERRIS, RICHARD; Va.; S1 (31-645).

FETTIPLACE; East Shefford, Berks;
B4 (13-58, 268).

FICKES, JOST; Pa.; M (21-15).

FIELD, ROBERT; Flushing, N. Y.; S1
(20-79).

FIELD; notes; S4 (1-364).

FIELDING, WALTER; Cleveland, Ohio;
English data; S1 (22-83).

FIENNES; connection with New England; B4 (15-122).

FIFIELD, WILLIAM; Hampton, N. H.;
B4 (15-218; 16-164; 19-90).

FIGG; Richmond, Va.; W2 (21-65).

FINCH; early records of family,
Mass., Conn., N. Y.; B4 (19-50,
118, 188, 249; 20-60, 188, 240; 21-
158).

FINCH; (Pettis), Franklin Co., N. C.;
W2 (19-117).

FINNEY; Va.; N. C.; W2 (20-148).

FISHER; Medway, Uxbridge, Mass.; B5
(24-214).

FISKE, NATHAN; Watertown, Mass.; S1
(28-122).

FISKE; English ancestry; A1 (86-406;
87-40, 141, 217, 367; 88-142, 265;
92-177, 287).

FITCH, JAMES (REV.); branch of Capt.
James, Lebanon; A2 (64-34).

FITCH, JOSEPH (CAPT.); Windsor,
Conn.; B4 (11-62; 14-87, 172).

FITCH, THOMAS; Norwalk, Conn.; with
English data; U (23-109); (wife of
Thomas3); B4 (17-113).

FITCH; (Diary of Jabez); cont.; D
(30-161; 31-44; 32-167; 33-30, 73,
128, 176; 34-63, 119, 165).

FITCH; (Dr. Peletiah, N. Y.); M (26-
57a).

FITHIAN; see Cumberland County, N.J.

FITZGERALD; Amelia Co., Va.; W2 (17-
95).

FITZHUGH, WILLIAM (COL.); Stafford
Co., Va.; English ancestry, co. Bedford; V3 (40-187, 375); arms; V3
(41-75; 42-66); other data; W2 (14-
96); V1 (15-263; 17-123); V3 (45-
144).

FITZHUGH; baronial family; S1 (36-
769).

FITZRANDOLPH, EDWARD; Piscataway,
N. J.; (James6 and James6, Woodbridge, N. J.); M (29-130); (Nath-
aniel2), Woodbridge, N. J.; A1 (97-
275, 330; 98-42, 124, 227, 331; 99-
37, 77, 328). English ancestry;
A1 (97-295; 99-335, 336).

FLAGG, THOMAS; Watertown, Mass.; S1
(20-121; 24-426; 28-117).

FLEMING, ALEXANDER (CAPT.); Rappahannock Co., Va.; S1 (33-326).

FLEMING, JOHN; New Kent Co., Va.;
N3 (36-28).

FLEMING, THOMAS (SIR); Va.; N3 (37-
266).

FLEMING, WILLIAM (COL.); Botetourt

land; B4 (19-17).
GANTT, THOMAS; Md.; M (25-97).
GARARD, JOHN (REV.); Openquan Creek,
Va.; Greene Co., Pa.; S1 (37-371).
GARDE, JOHN; Newport, R. I.; NE (3-
232).
GARDE; Maine and R. I.; B4 (20-106).
GARDINER, GEORGE; Newport R. I.;
"royal ancestry"; B4 (14-243);
(wife of Nicholas2); B4 (17-50);
(George3), South Kingston, R. I.;
B4 (20-202); English origin; B4
(21-191).
GARDNER, BERNHARD; Dauphin Co., O-
hio; M (28-85).
GARDNER, THOMAS; Salem, Mass.; S1
(25-279; 36-818).
GARFIELD, EDWARD; Watertown, Mass.;
M (27-65); S1 (23-499).
GARLICK, JOSHUA; East Hampton, N.Y.;
B7 (2-168).
GARNETT, JOHN; Gloucester County,
Va.; V3 (42-72); Essex County,
Va.; V3 (42-166, 256, 358; 43-69).
GARNETT, THOMAS; Elizabeth City Co.,
Va.; V1 (20-247).
GARRETT; Louisa County, Va.; W2 (12-
13).
GARRETT; (William), Pisgah, Ky.; N3
(37-315).
GARRETT; (Will of John, 1806), Del.;
X2 (7-2).
GARTH; correspondence, cont.; 1769-
72; J (31-46, 124, 228, 283; 33-
117, 228, 262).
GARY, JOHN; Calvert Co., Md.; X1
(37-316).
GASKILL, EDWARD; Salem, Mass.; S1
(20-116).
GATES, STEPHEN; Hingham, Mass.; B4
(10-199).
GATEWOOD, JOHN; Essex Co., Va.; W2
(22-186).
GAUNT, JOHN; Baltimore, Md.; Eng-
lish ancestry; S1 (32-543). Roy-
al ancestry; S1 (32-581).
GAUTIER, JACQUES; N. Y. City; Dt (3-
5).
GAVET, PHILIP; Salem, Mass.; ances-
try in Island of Jersey; A1 (88-
251).
GAY, JOHN; Dedham, Mass.; S1 (32-
368).
GAYER, WILLIAM; Nantucket, Mass.;
English ancestry; S1 (25-290; 36-
801); royal ancestry; S1 (36-827).
GAYLORD, WILLIAM; Windsor, Conn.;
English origin; B4 (17-71).

GEARHART, JACOB; Lebanon, N. J.; B5
(25-77).
GEBHARDT [KEPHART, CAPEHART]; immi-
grant brothers; Pa.; European an-
cestry; M (31-53).
GEDNEY, JOHN; Salem, Mass.; B4 (14-
83; 21-205).
GEIGER; (will of Valentine), 1777;
P (13-276).
GEORGE, PETER; Block Island, R. I.;
Dt (5-35).
GERARD; Berkeley Co., Va.; Dt (4-19,
64).
GEROW; (John-Light, Ulster Co., N.
Y.); B5 (30-200).
GHISELIN, CESAR; Philadelphia, Pa.;
Q1 (57-24; S1 (27-114).
GIANNINY, ANTHONY; Charlottesville,
Va.; B2 (18-25).
GIBBINS, JUDITH (LEWIS); Saco, Me.;
royal line; B4 (19-10).
GIBSON, JACOB; York Co., Pa.; M (30-
95).
GIBSON, JOHN; Talbot County, Md.; S1
(27-91).
GIBSON; (John), Mayor of Philadel-
phia; P (14-67).
GIFFARD; Dry Drayton, co. Cambridge,
Eng.; A1 (95-240).
GIFFARD; ancestry of Earls Halsbury;
M (30-41).
GILBERT, HUMPHREY; Ipswich, Mass.;
B4 (17-135).
GILBERT, THOMAS; Windsor, Conn.; S1
(20-562); 23-490; 30-728).
GILDART; Miss.; V1 (13-233).
GILFORD, JOHN; Hingham, Mass.; S1
(22-247).
GILL, JOHN; Salisbury, Mass.; S1 (24-
257).
GILLAM, BENJAMIN; Middletown, Conn.;
B4 (14-170; 23-236).
GILLESPIE, ROBERT (DR.); Ind.; S1
(23-365).
GILLESPIE; Inscriptions, Bible rec-
ords, (James), Kollock, S. C.; J
(33-175, 177).
GILLESPY, JOHN (MAJ.); Shawangunk,
N. Y.; OU (7-234).
GILLETT, JONATHAN; Windsor, Conn.;
A1 (100-272); wife's ancestry; B4
(15-208; 17-136).
GILLIAM; (John), Va.; W2 (19-76).
GILMAN, EDWARD; Hingham, Mass.; Eng-
lish ancestry; B4 (11-137, 193).
GILMER, JOHN; Kerr's Creek, Va.; W2
(17-118).
GILMER; Inscriptions, Albemarle Co.,

HANCOCK, RICHARD; Bridgeton, N. J.;
Z3 (54-209).
HAND, NATHANIEL; Cape May County,
N. J.; B7 (1-22, 67).
HANDLEY, THOMAS; Boston, Mass.; A1
(91-165).
HANFORD, THOMAS (REV.); Norwalk,
Conn.; English origin; B4 (17-49).
HANKS, BENJAMIN; Pembroke, Easton;
A1 (86-6).
HANNA, JAMES; Pa., Va., Ky.; (James
S.4); N3 (44-241).
HANNA, THOMAS; Buckingham, Pa.; S1
(19-491; 20-259).
HANNUM, WILLIAM; Northampton, Mass.;
A1 (90-157, 255, 337; 91-36, 103).
HARCUTT, RICHARD; Oyster Bay, N. Y.;
A2 (66-90).
HARDENBERGH, GERRIT JANS; New York;
Dutch ancestry; A2 (70-253, 337;
71-36).
HARDENBROOK, ADOLPH; New York; A2 (70-
128, 373); German origin; A2 (70-
133).
HARDING, RICHARD; Braintree, Mass.;
S1 (24-124; 31-679); ancestry of
Warren G.; Pw (21-1).
HARGRAVE, RICHARD; Lower Norfolk
County, Va.; V3 (40-379).
HARGROVE; Md.; Del.; S1 (32-396).
HARLAKENDEN; claim of royal descent;
B4 (14-209); English ancestry; S4
(1-94).
HARLOW, WILLIAM; Plymouth, Mass.;
B4 (9-228); (William3), Bridgewa-
ter; B4 (23-189).
HARPER; (William, Rev. soldier, Va.,
Ga.); V1 (14-175).
HARRIMAN, LEONARD; (Henry6), Brad-
ford, Mass.; U (28-98, 103).
HARRIMAN; (Oliver); N3 (42-248).
HARRINGTON, JOHN; Boston, Mass.; B4
(20-46).
HARRINGTON, ROBERT; (Joshua of Wor-
cester); A1 (86-112).
HARRIS, JAMES; (Asa3, Nova Scotia);
A1 (97-394).
HARRIS, ROBERT; Roxbury, Mass.; S1
(28-131).
HARRIS, THOMAS; (William and Daniel),
Middletown, Conn.; B4 (23-153).
HARRIS, THOMAS; (Family of Martin6);
U (26-107).
HARRIS, THOMAS; (Col. Joseph5),
Charles Co., Md.; X1 (31-333).
HARRIS, WALTER; New London, Conn.;
(Lt. George5, Canaan, N. H.); M
(33-92).

HARRIS, WILLIAM; Hamilton Co., N.Y.;
Ng (3-246).
HARRIS; (Benjamin), Southam, Cumber-
land Co., Va.; S1 (36-693).
HARRIS; (Benjamin), Chatham, Conn.;
B4 (23-161).
HARRIS; (Ephraim and William), Hart-
ford, Woodbury, Conn.; B4 (23-158).
HARRIS; (John), Queensbury, N. Y.;
Dt (10-6).
HARRIS; (Nathaniel), Stafford Coun-
ty, Va.; V1 (14-22).
HARRIS; (Robert), Wethersfield, Conn.;
B4 (23-161).
HARRIS; (Silas), Orange Co., N. Y.;
Dt (6-83).
HARRIS; (Walter), Wethersfield, Conn.;
B4 (23-159).
HARRISON, BENJAMIN; Va.; V3 (52-115,
183); English origin; V3 (53-21;
54-244, 327).
HARRISON, BURR; Fauquier County, Va.;
V3 (40-79).
HARRISON, ISAIAH; Oyster Bay, N. Y.;
Sussex Co., Del.; S1 (32-413).
HARRISON, THOMAS (REV.); Va.; Ips-
wich, Mass.; Ireland; S1 (32-411);
V3 (53-302).
HARRISON; James River, Va.; cont.;
V3 (40-95, 289, 377; 41-87, 162;
51-160, 326).
HARRISON; Westmoreland Co., Va.; V3
(46-264).
HARRISON; Accomack Co., Va.; V3 (47-
52).
HARRISON; Brunswick Co., Va.; V1 (19-
241).
HARRISON; Tenn.; N3 (30-398).
HARRISON; see Aerson, B1 (12-25).
HART, STEPHEN; Farmington, Conn.; U
(23-102); B4 (11-51).
HART, THOMAS; New Kent Co., Va.; S1
(29-134).
HART; (John), Ky.; W2 (20-149).
HART; (Josiah), Berkley Co., Va.;
Clark Co., Ky.; N3 (42-19).
HARTMAR, JOHANNES; Pikeland, Chester
Co., Pa.; Dt (5-183).
HARTSELL; (Capt. Jacob's Co., East
Tenn., 1813); N4 (11-93; 12-118).
HARTUNG, CHRISTOPHER-WILLIAM; Bible
record, Philadelphia; B5 (17-200).
HARVIE; Oglethorpe County, Ga.; W2
(12-134).
HARWOOD, HENRY; Boston, Mass.; S1
(22-444).
HARWOOD, ROBERT; Anne Arundel and
Kent Cos., Md.; X1 (37-319).

HASBROUCK, ABRAHAM; Kingston, N. Y.;
OU (4-186, 217, 249, 283, 315, 342,
376; 5-18, 54); (will of Jean, New
Paltz, 1712); OU (1-84); Family
record (Abraham); A2 (71-13, 153,
250, 354; 72-34).
HASELTINE, JOHN; Haverhill, Mass.;
B2 (22-10).
HASKELL, WILLIAM; Salem, Mass.; S1
(21-436); English origin; A1 (86-
257).
HASKELL, HASCALL; (will of Mark,
1699); D (34-54).
HASKETT, STEPHEN; Salem, Mass.; mat-
ernal English ancestry; A1 (92-67).
HASKIN; (Benjamin F.), Sheffield,
Mass.; A2 (76-166).
HASTINGS; English origin; A1 (96-
36).
HATCH, THOMAS; Barnstable, Mass.; S1
(20-569; 31-199); (Jeremiah7), Ad-
dison Co., Vt.; U (27-162).
HATCHER, WILLIAM; Henrico, Va.; W2
(16-457).
HATFIELD, MATTHIAS; Elizabeth, N. J.;
A2 (68-134, 223); German origin;
A2 (70-7, 127); (Matthias4); A2
(69-85).
HATFIELD; (John, Oxford, Pa.); Q1
(57-299).
HATHAWAY; (Rufus-Brown); Dt (10-110).
HATHAWAY; Inscriptions, Otego, N.Y.;
A1 (100-72).
HATTEN [HATTON]; (William D.), Nel-
son Co., Va.; B2 (18-25).
HAUGHTON, RICHARD; New London, Conn.;
B4 (11-133); A1 (89-396).
HAUGHWOUT, HAGEWOUT, PIETER JANSE;
New York; A2 (66-302; 67-35; 68-
129).
HAUTZ, PHILIP; Bethel, Pa.; Dt (9-
31, 75).
HAUTZ, PHILIP-PETER; Philadelphia;
Dt (10-28).
HAWES, EDMUND; Yarmouth, Mass.; N3
(34-369); English ancestry; S1
(22-528).
HAWES [HOUSE], JOHN; Providence, R.
I.; A1 (97-23).
HAWES, SAMUEL; Caroline Co., Va.;
W2 (15-143).
HAWK, ISAAC; Va.; O (4-368).
HAWLEY, JOSEPH; Stratford, Conn.; S1
(32-195; 35-77, 108); Bible record
(Jabez); A1 (98-281).
HAWLEY; Virginia; Maryland; X1 (34-
175).
HAWTHORNE; maternal English ancestry;

A1 (95-318).
HAY, WILLIAM (CAPT.); York County,
Va.; V1 (14-62).
HAY alias GRAY, JOHN (DR.); Va.; W2
(13-268).
HAYDEN, JOHN; Boston, Mass.; S1 (22-
230).
HAYDEN; Canada; S1 (19-501; 20-269).
HAYES, GEORGE; Simsbury, Conn.; S1
(30-371).
HAYES, JAMES; Richmond, Va.; V3 (49-
282).
HAYS, HAYES; Maryland; X2 (7-41; 8-
1, 20; 9-35).
HAYES; Items; E1 (10-5, 62).
HAYES; Inscriptions, Frderick, Md.;
X2 (17-52).
HAYNER, JOHN; Charleston, N. Y.; S1
(21-454).
HAYNES, JONATHAN; Newbury, Mass.;
B4 (23-110).
HAYNES; Winchester, Va.; W2 (20-
425).
HAYNES; Bedford Co., Va.; W2 (22-
302).
HAYNIE, RICHARD; Northumberland Co.,
Va.; Md.; X1 (36-202).
HAYWARD, WILLIAM; Braintree, Mass.;
S1 (20-115; 21-326; 26-143).
HAYWARD; (John of Concord, Mass.);
A1 (87-115).
HAYWARD; (will of Samuel, 1784),
Stafford Co., Va.; V1 (28-18);
(will of Martha Washington Hay-
ward, 1697), Stafford Co., Va.;
V1 (28-165).
HAYWOOD; (Col. Wm., Edgecombe Co.,
Va.); V1 (16-59).
HAZARD, THOMAS; Portsmouth, R. I.;
S1 (21-275).
HAZELRIGG; Montgomery and Clark
Counties, Ky.; B2 (10-11; 11-11).
HAZELTINE, ROBERT; Bradford, Mass.;
S1 (31-173).
HAZEN, EDWARD; Rowley, Mass.; S1
(22-214).
HEALD, JOHN; Concord, Mass.; English
data; B4 (10-15).
HEALE, (DR.) GILES; Mayflower sur-
geon; D (34-1).
HEALY; Middlesex Co., Va.; V3 (50-
370).
HEATH, ISAAC and WILLIAM; Roxbury,
Mass.; A2 (70-139, 242, 345).
HECKELI, JOHAN-GEORG; Pa.; M (21-15).
HEDGE, SAMUEL; Salem, N. J.; Eng-
lish ancestry; Q1 (56-270).
HEDGES; pedigree (Joseph), Md.; X2

(13-55).

HEGEMAN, ADRIAEN; N. Y.; S1 (1-170).

HEIFER, ANDREW; Me.; English origin; A1 (96-91).

HELLAKER, JACOB; Gravesend, New York; A2 (72-269, 275, 276).

HELME, CHRISTOPHER; Warwick, R. I.; English origin; A1 (98-11).

HELM, ISRAEL ACKESSON; Gloucester Co., N. J.; B1 (13-14).

HELME, THOMAS; Brookhaven, N. Y.; B4 (14-237).

HEMPINGSTALL; Orange Co., Va.; Ky.; N3 (33-71).

HENCHMAN; Boston; Y1 (70-1).

HENCKEL, ANTHONY-JACOB; Germantown, Pa.; M (25-63).

HENDERSON, THOMAS; Va.; Z (71-360).

HENDRICK; (William), Mecklenburg Co., Va.; V3 (52-216).

HENKEL; New Market, Va.; W2 (16-414).

HENRY, PATRICK (REV.); Hanover, Va.; W2 (21-64).

HENSHAW, THOMAS; Woburn, Mass.; S1 (22-368).

HERBERT, WILLIAM; Queen Anne's Co., Md.; S1 (32-572).

HERBERT; Middletown, N. J.; V3 (50-264).

HERMANN, AUGUSTINE; Cecil Co., Md.; Z3 (2-11-23).

HERNDON, HERENDEEN; six colonial immigrants, Va., Md., R. I.; W2 (23-331).

HERNDON; (James), Goochland Co., Va.; S1 (31-639).

HERRICK, HENRY; Salem, Mass.; B4 (14-96).

HERRING, ALEXANDER; Sussex Co., Del.; Dt (4-96).

HERRIOTT, THOMAS; Pa.; English origin; P (13-273).

HETH, HENRY; Frederick Co., Va.; V3 (42-273).

HEWES, JAMES; Princeton, N. J.; Z3 (4-16-470).

HEWES; (Joseph of N. J. & N. C.; Signer 1776); H1 (1-115).

HEWES; (will of John, 1671); Scituate, Mass.; D (34-112).

HEWET; (will of Martha, 1691); D (31-63).

HEWSON, GEORGE; Schenectady, N. Y.; Dt (4-196).

HEYDEN [HIDEN], FRANCIS; V1 (25-148).

HEYDON, see Hiden.

HEYWARD; Inscriptions, Grahamville, S. C.; J (41-75).

HICKOCK, HICKOX, WILLIAM; Farmington, Conn.; E3 (1-83); S1 (19-479; 32-218).

HICKCOX; Family and account-book records (James); E3 (7-185).

HICKS, JOHN; R. I.; A2 (70-116).

HICKS, ROBERT; Plymouth, Mass.; S1 (36-512).

HICKS, THOMAS and ZACHARIAH; Scituate, Cambridge, Mass.; A1 (88-307).

HIDE, SAMUEL (REV.); Attleboro, Mass.; A1 (96-214).

HIDEN, FRANCIS; St. Mary's Co., Md.; English origin; V1 (24-125).

HIGGINBOTHAM, JOHN; Barbados; Salford, Lancs, Eng.; V3 (52-290).

HIGLEY; (Joel), Conn.; Ohio; M (26-122).

HILL, ABRAHAM; Malden, Mass.; S1 (32-142).

HILL, CHARLES; New London, Conn.; Dt (3-173).

HILL, NATHANIEL; Orange Co., N. Y.; Irish origin; A2 (70-82).

HILL, RALPH; (Daniel A.6), Santa Barbara, Calif.; A1 (100-325).

HILL, ROBERT; New Haven, Conn.; S1 (19-474).

HILL, ROBERT and LEONARD; Essex Co., Va.; W2 (16-490).

HILL; King William Co., Va.; W2 (21-173).

HILL; Malden, Mass.; B4 (20-127).

HILL; (William), Brunswick Co., Va.; V3 (45-86).

HILLHOUSE, JAMES (REV.); New London, Conn.; NE (1-92).

HILLIARD, JOHN; Windsor, Conn.; B4 (17-27).

HINMAN; Conn.; P (11-299); Family record (Justus); P (12-85).

HINSDALE, ROBERT; Dedham, Medfield, Mass.; S1 (35-602).

HINSON, THOMAS; Kent County, Md.; S1 (27-89).

HINTON, WILLIAM; N. C.; H1 (2-4).

HITCHCOCK; New Haven, Conn.; S1 (30-376); Springfield; C5 (1-4-24).

HITE [HEYDT], HANS-JACOB; N. Y., Pa., Va.; W2 (17-119).

HITE, JOIST; Ulster Co., N. Y.; Frederick Co., Va.; Ng (2-102; 3-207).

HITT, PETER; Germana, Orange County, Va.; family records; B2 (11-26).

HOBART, EDMUND; Hingham, Mass.; S1 (36-482).

HOBART, PETER (REV.); Hingham, Mass.;

HOTCHKIN, see Hodgkin.
HOTCHKISS, SAMUEL;, New Haven, Conn.;
S1 (32-174); branch of Caleb; B4
(10-233).
HOTZENPILLER, HOTSENBELER, STEPHEN;
Prince William Co., Va.; M (29-
35); Frederick Co., Va.; M (29-
71); Dt (7-124; 8-3, 39, 59).
HOUGHTON; X2 (3-31).
HOUSEMAN, JOHN; Bible record, [N.
J.?]; M (22-8).
HOWARD, MATTHEW; Va.; English origin;
X1 (34-362).
HOWARD, RICHARD-SEABURY; Kinderhook,
N. Y.; WF (1-152).
HOWARD; (Asbury), Cumberland, Md.;
X2 (11-29).
HOWARD; (Enos), Hillsdale, N. Y.;
Ng (5-178, 196, 222, 238; 6-252,
274, 304); Bible records; Ng (2-
31).
HOWARD; (Vachel D.), Md.; X1 (31-
254).
HOWELL, BENJAMIN; Troy Hills, N. J.;
Z3 (4-6-152).
HOWES; (estate of Thomas, 1700),
Yarmouth, Mass.; D (34-131).
HOWES; Inscriptions, North Dennis,
Mass.; A1 (100-320).
HOWKINS, ANTHONY; Farmington, Conn.;
U (24-17).
HOWLAND, HENRY; Duxbury, Mass.; S1
(28-428).
HOWLAND, JOHN; Plymouth; S1 (19-
532; 20-565; 21-272; 23-493).
HOWLAND, Plymouth; English data; B4
(14-214).
HOWLAND; (Caleb5), Clarendon, Vt.;
A1 (100-288).
HOWLAND; (Estate of Joseph), 1692;
D (34-37).
HOYT, SIMON; Stamford, Conn.; B2
(22-13); S1 (24-557).
HUBBARD, GEORGE; Guilford, Conn.;
wife; B4 (10-17); Mass. branch; B4
(11-47, 121).
HUBBARD, JOHN; (John3, Brooklyn,
Conn.); B4 (23-221).
HUBBARD, SAMUEL; Newport, R. I.;
English origin; extracts from
Letter Book; NE (1-172, 193; 2-58,
170, 243); S1 (20-554; 23-482).
HUBBARD, WILLIAM; Ipswich, Mass.;
English clue; B4 (11-120).
HUBBARD; (Ephraim of Rutland, Mass.);
S1 (28-116).
HUDDE, ANDRIES; New York, N. Y.; A2
(69-128).

HUDSON; (George P.), Providence, R.
I.; S1 (24-114).
HUDSON; Hanover County, Va.; V1 (26-
172).
HUFNER; Inscriptions, Waynesboro,
Pa.; M (24-15).
HUGHES, CORNELIUS; Boone Co., Ky.;
N3 (35-160).
HUGHES, HUMPHREY; Southampton, N. Y.;
Cape May branch; B7 (2-143).
HUGHES, JESSE; Cape May County, N.J.;
B7 (1-20).
HUGHES; Bourbon County, Ky.; S3 (9-
3-11).
HUGHES; (Ellis), Catawissa, Pa.; P
(14-75).
HUGHLETT; (William), Queen Anne Co.,
Md.; X2 (11-54; 12-1; 17-40).
HUIDEKOPER, HARM JAN; arms; A2 (66-
183).
HUME, FRANCIS and GEORGE; Va.; Scots
origin; V1 (21-6, 70).
HUME; (John), Ky.; N3 (35-152).
HUME; (William), Fauquier Co., Va.;
V1 (27-309).
HUMISTON, HENRY; New Haven, Conn.;
S1 (32-126).
HUMPHREY, JOHN (COL.); Salem, Mass.;
B4 (15-122).
HUMPHREY, JONAS; Dorchester, Mass.;
S1 (22-370).
HUNGERFORD, THOMAS; New London, Conn.;
S1 (33-570).
HUNLEY, AMBROSE; Rappahanock, Va.;
V1 (28-104).
HUNT, ENOCH; (Ephraim3 of Rehoboth,
Mass.); A1 (97-39).
HUNT, RALPH; Newtown, N. Y.; line of
descent; M (25-116, 117).
HUNT, RICHARD; Southampton, Bermuda;
B4 (23-110).
HUNT, THOMAS; Westchester, N. Y.; S1
(22-514).
HUNT, WILLIAM; Concord, Mass.; B4
(21-128).
HUNT, WILLIAM; Charles City County,
Va.; V1 (13-18).
HUNT; (estate of Bartholomew), 1687;
B4 (14-187).
HUNT; (Esaias), Burlington Co., N.
J.; with Bible records; B4 (23-97).
HUNTER, WILLIAM; Spotsylvania Co.,
Va.; W2 (19-118).
HUNTINGFIELD; William, Magna Charta
Surety; B4 (14-10).
HUNTLEY, JOHN; Lyme, Conn.; A1 (100-
261).
HURLBUT, THOMAS; (Stephen2), Wethers-

field, Conn.; B4 (20-166).
HURLBUT; notes; S4 (5-43).
HURST; (Abednego), South Bend, Ind.;
Col (1 No. 9).
HUSSEY, CHRISTOPHER; Nantucket,
Mass.; S1 (21-466; 25-268; 36-
813).
HUSSEY, RICHARD; Dover, N. H.; Y1
(70-58).
HUSSEY; (Cayuga County, N. Y.); B2
(12-25).
HUTCHINS; (Samuel, Vt.); Dt (2-206).
HUTCHINS; (Thomas, Sr., Rev. Patri-
ot); H1 (1-10).
HUTCHINSON, RICHARD; Salem, Mass.;
B4 (14-83).
HUTCHINSON, WILLIAM; Boston, Mass.;
Dt (4-103, 117, 143, 165); (Brid-
get2); B4 (14-157).
HUTCHINSON; (Samuel and John), Leb-
anon, Conn.; B4 (23-122).
HYDE; (Alonzo-Eugene); U (23-112).
HYDE; Earl of Clarendon; Lord Corn-
bury; A2 (71-106).
HYER, WALTER; New York; Dt (3-148);
A2 (74-1, 63, 106, 173).

IDE, NICHOLAS; Rehoboth, Mass.; S1
(26-121).
INGE; England, Va., Ala.; W2 (17-
119).
INGELS; (James), Chester Co., Pa.;
P (14-79).
INGERSOLL, RICHARD; Salem, Mass.;
English origin; Al (90-92); S1
(31-509); B4 (9-192).
INGERSOLL; Westfield, Mass.; B4 (11-
43).
INGOLDSBY; Fishtoft, co. Lincoln,
Eng.; B4 (11-26, 98, 143, 208).
INGRAHAM, HENRY; Boston, Mass.; B4
(19-84, 178).
INGRAHAM, RICHARD; Rehoboth, Mass.;
B4 (21-190); Jarrett2; Rehoboth;
B4 (19-77); Benjamin5 and Abijah5,
Loyalists; M (34-35).
INGRAHAM, WILLIAM; Boston, Swansea,
Mass.; B4 (19-89).
IRONMONGER; Virgina; W2 (20-138).
IRVING; Scotland, notes; V (18-240).
IRWIN, EDWARD; Bible record, Chester
Co., Pa.; B5 (27-286).
ISHAM, HENRY; Henrico Co., Va.; Eng-
lish ancestry; S1 (36-694); Royal
line; S1 (36-784).
ISRAEL; (John), Baltimore Co., Md.;
S1 (21-236).
IZARD, RALPH; S. C.; S1 (28-486).

JACKSON, ABRAHAM; Plymouth; S1 (21-
452).
JACKSON, ANDREW; "The Hermitage"; S1
(26-502).
JACKSON, JOHN; Portsmouth, N. H.; Al
(97-3).
JACKSON, NICHOLAS; (Nehemiah4), Wood-
stock, Conn.; Al (93-213).
JACKSON; (Samuel), Kent Island, Md.;
S1 (32-578).
JACKSON; Will (Henry), 1705; X2 (9-
11).
JACKSON; Md.; X2 (10-21).
JACKSON; New Scotland, N. Y.; Dt (2-
89, 111, 137).
JACOB, NICHOLAS; Hingham, Mass.; B4
(11-138).
JACOB, RICHARD; Ipswich, Mass.; Y1
(76-56).
JACOB, ZACHARIAH; Md.; S1 (7-1105).
JACOCKS, FRANCIS; Hempstead, N. Y.;
B4 (21-215; 23-32).
JAGGER, JEREMIAH; Stamford, Conn.;
John; Southampton, N. Y.; Al (100-
331).
JAMES, THOMAS (REV.); Charlestown,
Mass.; East Hampton, N. Y.; Eng-
lish ancestry; B4 (11-26, 98, 143,
208).
JAMES; Md., Ky.; N3 (40-424).
JAMES; (John), Somersworth, N. H.;
Al (92-95).
JANES, WILLIAM; Northampton, Mass.;
S1 (24-550).
JANSE, JAN; Bushwick, N. Y.; A2 (66-
190).
JANSEN, MATTYS; Kingston, N. Y.; A2
(72-308, see also 309).
JAQUES, HENRY; Woodbridge, N. J.;
Z3 (4-16-201).
JAQUITH, ABRAHAM; Charlestown, Mass.;
S1 (24-250).
JARVIS, JOHN; Boston, Mass.; S1 (26-
440).
JARVIS, JOHN; Amherst Co., Va.; Z
(80-377).
JARVIS, WILLIAM; Huntington, N. Y.;
S1 (9-889).
JEFFERIES, MORGAN P.; Newark, Ohio;
Bible record; Dt (9-130).
JEFFERSON, THOMAS; Henrico County,
Va.; V1 (13-15, 58); (John-Robert-
son4), Va.; W2 (20-563).
JEFFERSON; (Thomas, letters); W2
(12-145; 13-98).
JEFFERY; (Vincent) Harford Co., Md.;
S1 (32-525).
JEFFREY, GREGORY; Me.; English an-

cestry; B4 (18-71).
JEFFREY; N. J.; Ohio; M (29-65).
JEFFRIES; (will of Nathaniel, 1795),
Buckingham Co., Va.; V1 (27-57).
JEFFRIES; (Will of Thomas, Va.,
1827); W2 (16-79).
JEFFRY; (Letter of James, Salem,
Mass., 1729); Y1 (74-160).
JEIKE, JOHN-HENRY; Cincinnati, Ohio;
German ancestry; S1 (19-105).
JENNEY, JOHN; Plymouth; S1 (25-560);
will of Samuel, 1692; D (33-79).
JENNINGS, JONATHAN; Norwich, Conn.;
S4 (3-69).
JENNINGS, RICHARD; Bridgewater,
Mass.; S1 (26-161).
JENNINGS, WILLIAM; Hanover Co., Va.;
V3 (44-160).
JEPSON, JOHN; Boston, Mass.; B4 (20-
85, 173; 23-239).
JEPSON, WILLIAM; Wells, Me.; origin
in Ireland and descendants; B4
(18-172).
JEROME, TIMOTHY; Windham, Walling-
ford, Conn.; A2 (73-163); identity
of wife; B4 (19-230).
JETER, JOHN; Port Royal, Caroline
County, Va.; W2 (12-209).
JETT, PETER; Rappahannock County,
Va.; B4 (9-145, 204).
JETT; Virginia; W2 (19-146).
JETT; (Will of Francis, 1794), Staf-
ford Co., Va.; V1 (20-234).
JEWELL, THOMAS; Braintree, Mass.; B4
(10-71, 261).
JEWETT, JOSEPH; Rowley, Mass.; S1
(20-573; 23-205).
JEWETT, MARY (MALINSON); Rowley,
Mass.; English ancestry; A1 (94-
107).
JEWETT, MAXIMILIAN and JOSEPH; Row-
ley, Mass.; English ancestry; A1
(94-99); C5 (1-1-42; 2-199).
JOHNSON, ISAAC; Salem, Mass.; B4 (15-
122).
JOHNSON, JOHN; Roxbury, Mass.; S1
(26-159); B4 (22-47).
JOHNSON, (SIR) NATHANIEL; S. C.; J
(38-109).
JOHNSON, ROBERT; Bible record (Wil-
liam-Samuel), Stratford, Conn.;
A2 (70-217); (William), Guilford,
Conn.; S1 (35-121).
JOHNSON, THOMAS (GOV.); English an-
cestry; X2 (10-25).
JOHNSON, WILLIAM; New Haven, Conn.;
S1 (32-92).
JOHNSON, WILLIAM and JOHN; Va.; M

(27-30).
JOHNSON; Schenectady, N. Y.; Dt (3-
167).
JOHNSON; Daubs, Frederick Co., Md.;
M (28-93).
JOHNSON; Culpeper Co., Va.; W2 (20-
427).
JOHNSON; Fauquier Co., Va.; W2 (23-
214).
JOHNSON; (Claiborne), Albemarle Co.,
Va.; S1 (21-474).
JOHNSON; (Dr. Ebenezer); Buffalo,
N. Y.; Ng (4-60).
JOHNSON; (Elisha), R. I.; S1 (21-
268).
JOHNSON; (Ezekiel, Joel H.), Ux-
bridge, Mass.; U (29-169).
JOHNSON; (Family of Joseph-Watkins);
U (26-150).
JOHNSON; (Thomas H.), Dixon, Ill.,
Col.; Col (1 No. 6).
JOHNSON; (Col. Robert, 1745-1815,
Ky.); N3 (30-21).
JOHNSON; (will of Jacob, 1806); M
(21-71).
JOHNSTON, EDWARD; St. Mary's Parish,
Edgecombe Co., N. C.; W2 (17-122).
JOHNSTON, PETER; (Joseph-Eggleston,
Va. soldier); W2 (13-63).
JOHNSTON, THOMAS (REV.); Md.; Va.;
X1 (34-305).
JOHNSTON; (Laurence), Carlisle, N.
Y.; Dt (5-176).
JOHNSTON; (Peter), Culpeper County,
Va.; Scott County, Ky.; N3 (31-
179).
JOHNSTON; (Capt. William); Buffalo,
N. Y.; Ng (4-42).
JONES, BENJAMIN; Huntington, N. Y.;
(William5), Woodbridge, N. J.; Z3
(64-77).
JONES, CORNELIUS; Stamford, Conn.;
(Cornelius5, Orange Co., N. Y.);
A2 (76-16).
JONES, GRIFFITH; Springfield, Mass.;
(Benjamin5, Coventry, Conn.); Ng
(6-258, 293).
JONES, JOHN; Concord, Mass.; Bible
records (William6); A1 (89-90);
(Joseph3 of Stratford, Conn.); B4
(12-257).
JONES, RICHARD; Haddam, Conn.; B4
(11-190).
JONES, ROWLAND (REV.); Williamsburg,
Va.; V1 (13-264).
JONES, SETH; Mass.; Ohio; M (26-121).
JONES, THOMAS; Hull, Mass.; Dt (4-
93).

LANDON, DANIEL; Stonington, Conn.; N. J.; B1 (10-73).
LANDON; (Abner), Litchfield, Conn.; Brookville, Ontario; B4 (21-218).
LANE, ROBERT; Stratford, Conn.; Ng (3-127).
LANE, SAMUEL; Bible records (Jacob6), Pa.; X2 (17-1); (John); X2 (17-17).
LANE; (Matthias, Somerset Co., N. J.); E3 (2-96).
LANGDON, PHILIP; Salem, Mass.; S1 (24-230).
LANGHORNE, NEEDHAM; English data; Washington connection; W2 (23-336).
LANGHORNE; Bedford and Northants, Eng.; W2 (20-404).
LANGHORNE; Cumberland, Va.; V1 (13-263).
LANGWORTHY, LAWRENCE; Newport, R. I.; B4 (15-1).
LANIER, JOHN; Prince George Co., Va.; V3 (43-160; 44-73, 160).
LANSING, ELIZABETH (HENDRICKS); Albany, N. Y.; arms; A2 (65-56).
LANSING, GERRET FREDERICKSE; Albany, N. Y.; S1 (26-288); Dutch origin; A2 (72-26).
LAPHAM, THOMAS; Scituate, Mass.; Pw (21-52).
LARTIGUE; Inscriptions, Blackville, S. C.; J (40-156).
LATHAM; Orient Point, N. Y.; A2 (66-92).
LATHROP, JOHN (REV.); Bible record (Hubbel6); A1 (98-282); (Benjamin4), Norwich, Conn.; Sunderland, Vt.; A1 (98-92).
LATIMER, ROBERT; New London, Conn.; B4 (19-153); S1 (33-89).
LATROBE, BENJAMIN-HENRY; Philadelphia, Pa.; X1 (33-247).
LAUMAN, BERNHARDT; York, Pa.; Ohio branch; M (28-124).
LAURENS, ANDRÉ; Charleston, S. C.; S1 (27-427).
LAURENS; (John), Charleston, S. C.; S1 (30-341).
LAURENSZEN, THOMAS; New York; A2 (64-306).
LAWRENCE, JOHANNES; (Calvin-Cook), Newark, N. J.; P (14-306; 15-112).
LAWRENCE, JOHN; Groton, Mass.; A1 (89-211); English data; B4 (10-78); (Nathaniel2); B4 (19-66, 231).

LAWRENCE, THOMAS; Newtown, L. I.; B4 (17-74).
LAWRENCE; arms; A2 (65-104).
LAWRENCE; Northampton County, Va.; B4 (10-260).
LAWRENCE; St. James Park, co. Suffolk, Eng.; B4 (23-83, 217).
LAWSON; Virginia; W2 (13-242).
LAWTON, GEORGE; Portsmouth, R. I.; S1 (21-274).
LAZELL, JOHN; Hingham, Mass.; A1 (88-257, 358; 89-10, 102, 224, 309).
LEACHLAND; co. Somerset, Eng.; A1 (93-175).
LEAGER, JACOB; Boston, Mass.; English ancestry; B4 (19-193).
LEAMING, THOMAS; Cape May Co., N. J.; L1 (6-13); B7 (1-11, 69).
LEAVENWORTH, THOMAS; Woodbury, Conn.; S1 (32-89).
LEAVITT, JOHN (DEACON); Hingham, Mass.; S1 (30-177).
LEDERER, JOHN; Va., Md., Conn.; W2 (22-175).
LEE, HENRY; Yorktown, Va.; V1 (13-199).
LEE, JOHN; Farmington, Conn.; B4 (11-51).
LEE, SAMUEL; Watertown, Mass.; NE (3-48).
LEE, THOMAS; Middlesex Co., Va.; V3 (49-75).
LEE, WILLIAM; Burlington, N. J.; B4 (18-110).
LEE; (Arthur, Westmoreland County, Va.); V1 (14-65, 129, 197).
LEE; Blenheim, Md.; X1 (37-199)
LEE; relationship of Gen. Robert E. to Earls Halsbury; M (30-41).
LEE; (Greenberry), Ga.; W2 (18-513).
LEE; (Lancelot), Westmoreland and Jefferson Counties, Va.; W2 (12-207).
LEE; (Thomas), Ditchley, Va.; V3 (47-50).
LEEPER, ALLEN; Pennsborough, Pa.; S4 (2-129, 214, 365).
LEETE, WILLIAM (GOV.); Guilford, Conn.; English ancestry; S1 (20-405).
LEFFEL, BALZAR; Amity, Pa.; B4 (21-253).
LEFFINGWELL, see Leppingwell.
LEGER, PIERRE; Craven County, S. C.; W2 (14-352).
LEGRAND, PIERRE [PETER]; Goochland Co., Va.; V3 (44-257; 45-107).

LEHMAN; Inscriptions (Sharon Springs, N. Y.); B2 (13-7).
LEHMER, HANNES; Pa.; M (21-16).
LEIGH, BENJAMIN; Boston, Mass.; Halifax, N. S.; Al (94-60, 164).
LEIGH; (Joseph), Perth Amboy, N, J.; S1 (25-108).
LEITCH, JOHN; New York, N. Y.; Bible record; A2 (77-106).
LE MASTER, ABRAHAM; Charles Co., Md.; X2 (8-46).
LENT; N. Y.; A2 (67-58).
LENUD; S. C.; W2 (14-353).
LEONARD, JAMES; Taunton, Mass.; B4 (10-162, 200; 11-53); S1 (22-330).
LEPPINGWELL, MICHAEL; Woburn, Mass.; S1 (20-123; 24-430).
LE ROY, SIMEON; Montreal, Kingston; A2 (64-41).
LEVERETT, JOHN (GOV.); not knighted; Al (94-92).
LEWIS, GEORGE; Shelbourne Parish, Loudoun County, Va.; W2 (12-115).
LEWIS, JOHN; Westerly, R. I.; S1 (20-546; 23-475).
LEWIS, THOMAS; Saco, Me.; English data; B4 (17-120).
LEWIS; (David), Philadelphia; P (12-183).
LEWIS; (John), Hagerstown, Md.; X2 (9-30).
LEWIS; (Col. John and Aaron), Albemarle Co., Va.; W2 (21-273).
L'HOMMEDIEU, BENJAMIN; (Ezra of Southold, N. Y.); S1 (27-290).
LICKLIDER [LECHLEIDER], CONRAD; Frederick Co., Md.; M (31-7).
LIDDERDALE, JOHN; Bible records, Williamsburg, Va.; V3 (46-64).
LIGHTFOOT, HENRY; Isle of Wight Co., Va.; V3 (51-201).
LIGHTFOOT, JOHN (COL.); Gloucester Co., Va.; English ancestry; S1 (19-215).
LIGHTFOOT; (Francis), Tedington, Va.; V1 (28-185).
LILLIE, GEORGE; Reading, Mass.; Dt (4-124, 149).
LILLY, OWEN; Ireland; Memphis, Tenn.; M (34-108).
LILLIE; (wife of Edward[2]), Boston; A2 (77-36).
LINCOLN, THOMAS and SAMUEL; Hingham, Mass.; English ancestry; B4 (11-193); (line of Waldo[8]); Al (87-307); (line of Pres. Abraham); Dt (3-97).
LINCOLN, EARLS of; B4 (20-46).

LINDENBERG, CHARLES H.; Family record, Columbus, Ohio; O (3-210).
LINDENBERGER; (Jacob-Hopewell), Baltimore, Md.; N3 (42-244).
LINDERMAN, JACOB; Ulster Co., N. Y.; Z3 (4-8-301).
LINDSAY, DAVID (REV.); Northumberland Co., Va.; arms; Al (94-395).
LINN; (Andrew), N. J., Md., Ky.; K2 (20-18, 137, 220).
LINTHICUM; Anne Arundel County, Md.; X2 (4-14, 23; 10-23).
LISLE; (John), Albemarle Co., Va.; W2 (21-273).
LITTLE, GEORGE; (Dr. Stephen[4]), Newbury, Mass.; Y1 (77-262).
LITTLE, WILLIAM; Jefferson Co., Va.; W2 (23-216).
LITTLE; Family record (Ephraim), Scituate, Mass.; D (34-145); other data; D (34-149, 152, 171).
LITTLEFIELD, EDMUND; Wells (Block Island branch); Al (86-71).
LITTLEPAGE; (will of James, 1766), Hanover Co., Va.; V1 (23-57).
LIVESAY; (George), Greenbrier Co., Va.; Dt (10-110).
LIVINGSTON, WILLIAM; Elizabeth, N. J.; Z3 (4-7-164).
LOCKE, WILLIAM; Woburn, Mass.; S1 (22-443).
LOGAN, WILLIAM; Somerset Co., N. J.; Z3 (4-8-57).
LOGAN; (John), Rockbridge Co., Va.; N3 (34-286).
LOGAN; Wills, Morris Co., N. J.; Z3 (3-8-164).
LOGAN; Va.; Lincoln County, Ky.; N3 (30-173).
LOMAX; (will of Thomas, 1811), Caroline Co., Va.; V1 (23-60).
LONDON; Albemarle County, Va.; W2 (12-265).
LONG, ANTHONY-NEALSON; Gloucester Co., N. J.; B1 (13-17).
LONG, JOSEPH; Dorchester, Mass.; English origin; Al (100-220, 328).
LONG, RICHARD; Salisbury, Mass.; Al (100-254).
LONG; Newbury, Mass.; B4 (19-177).
LONGWELL; (Ralph S.), Pa., Ohio; M (34-39).
LOOMIS, JOSEPH; Windsor, Conn.; Al (90-385); S4 (1-89); (wife of Joseph[2]); Al (92-203, 303); royal ancestry; S4 (2-255).
LOOMIS; (three Ruths), Windsor, Conn.; B4 (21-219, 274).

LOONEY; (will of David, 1802), Sullivan Co., Tenn.; M (34-25).

LOPER, JACOB; New York; A2 (68-132, 217).

LORD, ROBERT; Ipswich, Mass.; Sl (29-109; 30-168).

LORENS alias HALLING, MARKUS; Gloucester Co., N. J.; Bl (13-27).

LORING, THOMAS; Hull, Mass.; Sl (23-223).

LOSSING, PETER; Albany, N. Y.; A2 (70-228).

LOTHROP, JOHN (REV.); Barnstable, Mass.; Al (86-455).

LOVE; (Will of William, Kittery, Me., 1687); B4 (13-192).

LOVEJOY; (Joseph, Westminster, Vt.); S3 (11-4-13; 13-4-8).

LOVELACE, THOMAS and FRANCIS; New York; Anne, m. Gorsuch; English ancestry; Sl (37-191); royal ancestry; Sl (37-230).

LOVELACE; English ancestry of Anne (Barne); Sl (36-245).

LOVELAND; (Revilo), Durham, Conn., Kansas, Col.; Col (1 No. 7, 8, 9).

LOW, PETER CORNELIS; Kingston, N.Y.; X2 (7-15).

LOW, THOMAS; Ipswich, Mass.; N3 (42-249).

LOWLE, ELIZABETH (GOODALE); Newbury, Mass.; B4 (22-21).

LOWMASTER, WENDLE; York, Pa.; Ohio branch; M (27-16).

LOWREY; JM (1-3-21).

LOWTHER; Md.; X2 (4-12).

LUCAS; (John), Antiqua; J (46-185).

LUDLAM, WILLIAM; Southampton, N. Y.; B4 (20-8, 238); (Joseph2), Oyster Bay, N. Y.; B4 (14-5).

LUDLOW, CORNELIUS; Morris Co., N. J.; Z3 (3-3-42).

LUDLOW, GABRIEL; Hill Deverill, co. Wilts, Eng.; V3 (54-255).

LUDLOW, GABRIEL; New York; branch of Cary4; A2 (71-120, 257).

LUDLOW, ROGER and GABRIEL; Fairfield, Conn.; Va.; royal ancestry; B4 (15-129).

LUDLOW; (will of George, 1655); M (24-33).

LUGG, JOHN; Boston, Mass.; English ancestry of wife Jane Deighton; B4 (9-212).

LUM, JOHN; Stamford, Conn.; B4 (11-145); English origin; B4 (18-146).

LUPARDUS, GULIELMUS (REV.); Flatbush, N. Y.; A2 (68-24).

LUPP, JOHN; Bible record, New Brunswick, N. J.; Bl (15-47).

LUX; Maine; English clews; B4 (18-74).

LYERS, URBANUS; New York; A2 (64-113).

LYFORD, FRANCIS; Boston; Exeter, N. H.; Sl (29-106; 30-165).

LYGON, THOMAS; Madresfield, co. Worcester, Eng.; Henrico Co., Va.; W2 (16-289).

LYMAN, RICHARD; Hartford, Conn.; English origin; Sl (36-494).

LYMAN; (Samuel, Springfield, Mass., letters); Yl (68-183).

LYNAH, JAMES (DR.); Charleston, S. C.; J (40-87).

LYNDE, SIMON; royal ancestry; Sl (33-122).

LYNN; Fauquier & Prince Wm. Cos., Va.; V3 (50-264).

LYON, THOMAS; Rye, N. Y.; Sl (24-538).

LYON, WILLIAM; (Ebenezer3 of Rehoboth, Mass.); Al (97-42).

LYON; (Henry, Jefferson County, N. Y.); B2 (12-13).

LYON; (Matthew-Brewer), Hartland, Mich.; Dt (6-109).

LYON; Md.; Falmouth, Va.; W2 (15-198).

MCALLISTER, ALEXANDER; Bible record; Dt (7-70).

MCARTHUR, ARTHUR (GEN.); Scotland; Mass., Wis.; A2 (73-170, 227); ancestral chart of Gen. Douglas McArthur follows; latter's descent from Charlemagne; Al (97-342).

MCCALLUM; court and family records (Daniel), N. C.; Z (80-330).

MCCAMMON; (John), Tenn., Col.; Col (7-96).

MCCARTY; Richmond County, Va.; W2 (13-60).

MCCLANAHAM; (will of William, Greenville, S. C., 1802); V3 (41-353).

MCCLANAHAN; Bourbon County, Ky.; Vl (13-117, 276); W2 (12-216).

MCCLELLAN, JAMES; Worcester, Mass.; Sl (26-119).

MCCLELLAN; (Edwin), Cambridge, N. Y.; Sl (23-29).

MCCLUNG; (James), Rockbridge Co., Va.; Dt (7-41); Bible record (Maj. Andrew); Dt (7-133).

MCCLURE, ANDREW; Augusta Co., Va.; N3 (36-345).

MCCLYMONDS, JOHN; Providence, Pa.;

York; Dutch ancestry and arms; A2 (69-222).
MANGOLD, ADAM; Cincinnati, Ohio; German ancestry; S1 (36-125).
MANIGAULT; (Letters of Peter, 1750-54); J (31-171, 269; 32-46, 115, 175, 270; 33-55, 148, 247).
MANLOVE; (Christopher, Va.); W2 (15-304).
MANNING, WILLIAM; Cambridge, Mass.; WF (1-154).
MANNING; notes; S4 (2-90).
MANVILLE, NICHOLAS; Woodbury, Conn.; B4 (22-53).
MARBURY, ANNE; ancestry; Dt (4-145, 165).
MARCH; co. Devon, Eng.; A1 (86-77, 247).
MARKHAM, JOHN; Chesterfield Co., Va.; V3 (45-96).
MARKS, MORDECAI; Derby, Conn.; B4 (17-225).
MARMADUKE; Westmoreland Co., Va.; W2 (15-151).
MARMION; English feudal lords; B4 (20-255; 21-95).
MARQUART, MARTIN; Amity, Pa.; B4 (22-80).
MARR, JOHN; Stafford Co., Va.; V1 (26-286).
MARRIOTT; Surry Co., Va.; V3 (51-200).
MARSH, JOHN; Windsor, Conn.; Northampton, Mass.; English origin; S1 (36-465).
MARSH, THOMAS; Va.; Kent Island, Md.; X1 (35-190).
MARSH; (James, Acton, Mass.); U (27-28).
MARSHALL, JAMES; Pittsburgh, Pa.; S1 (23-321).
MARSHALL, THOMAS (CAPT.); Lynn, Mass.; Z2 (14-89).
MARSHALL, WILLIAM; Md.; M (25-105).
MARSHALL; notes; S4 (5-46).
MARSHALL; baronial family; S1 (36-766).
MARSHALL; Va.; V1 (13-223).
MARSHALL; Calvert County, Md.; M (21-86).
MARSHALL; (Chief-Justice); W2 (12-67).
MARSHAL; (will of Edmund), Suffield, Conn., 1732; B4 (15-106).
MARTIAU, NICOLAS (CAPT.); Jamestown, Va.; V3 (42-145).
MARTIN, JOHN; Swansea, Mass.; S1 (31-677).
MARTIN, JOHN (CAPT.); Va.; V3 (54-

21).
MARTIN [MERTEN], JOHANN JOST; Va.; German ancestry; V3 (40-324).
MARTIN, RICHARD; Plymouth, Mass.; S1 (26-109).
MARTIN; notes; S4 (2-143).
MARTIN; Md.; X2 (12-19).
MARTIN; (Rev. John), Charleston, S. C.; W2 (22-426).
MARTIN; (William), Pisgah, Ky.; N3 (37-317).
MARTINDELL, JOHN; Bucks Co., Pa.; (William3), S. C., Ohio; Dt (9-87; 10-69, 91).
MARTYN, RICHARD; Portsmouth, N. H.; S1 (37-511).
MARTYN; (Michael), Boston, Mass.; A1 (98-364).
MARVIN, REINOLD and MATTHEW; Lyme and Norwalk, Conn.; English ancestry; B4 (18-1); see also S1 (27-371).
MARYE, JAMES (REV.); Spottsylvania County, Va.; B4 (10-141, 258).
MASON, ANNE (PECK); see Lawrence of St. James Park.
MASON, GEORGE; Stafford Co., Va.; V1 (23-193).
MASON, JOHN (MAJ.); Windsor, Conn.; M (20-73); S1 (19-239; 26-7; 36-473).
MASON, ROBERT; Dedham, Mass.; S1 (34-639).
MASON, SAMPSON; Swansea, Mass.; S1 (25-556; 33-233).
MASON; notes; S4 (5-57).
MASON; (George, Va. statesman); W2 (13-10); V1 (14-217).
MASON; (Richard, Surry Co., Va.); W2 (15-73).
MASON; (will of Francis, 1696), Surry Co., Va.; V1 (24-230).
MASSIE; Fauquier County, Va.; V1 (13-124).
MASSIE; (David), Madison Co., Ky.; W2 (18-514).
MASSEY; St. Paul's Parish, K. George County, Va.; W2 (13-30).
MASTERS, JOHN; Watertown, Mass.; letter, 1631; A1 (91-68); see also S1 (31-373).
MASTERS, NICHOLAS (CAPT.); Woodbury, Conn.; B4 (22-222).
MATHER, RICHARD (REV.); Dorchester; A1 (86-243); S1 (27-320; 29-284); data; B4 (10-33).
MATHEWS, SAMUEL; Va.; W2 (15-299).
MATTHEWS, SAMUEL; Jamaica, N. Y.; B4

46 NAME INDEX

(11-205).
MATTHEWS, JOHN; Marlborough, Mass.;
(Increase of Ohio); A1 (86-32).
MATTHEWS, SAMUEL; Va.; W2 (14-105).
MATTYSEN, see Jansen and Van Keuren.
MAULE, THOMAS; Salem, Mass.; Y1 (72-
1).
MAVERICK, JOHN; Dorchester, Mass.;
English data; A1 (96-232, 358;
97-56).
MAVERICK, SAMUEL; (wife of Nathan-
iel4); A1 (98-93).
MAXCY, ALEXANDER; Attleboro, Mass.;
S1 (26-101).
MAXWELL, JOHN; Greenwich, Warren
Co., N.J.; Z3 (2-13-113).
MAY; Frederick, Md.; X2 (4-13).
MAY; (Henry), Charlotte Co., Va.;
V1 (26-75).
MAY; (probate of Edward, 1691); D
(31-104).
MAYBANK, DAVID; S. C.; J (40-115).
MAYHEW, THOMAS (GOV.); Martha's
Vineyard; S1 (24-1, 157, 327,
486; 26-106).
MAYO, JOHN (REV.); Boston, Mass.;
A1 (95-59, 100).
MAYO; Powhatan Seat, Va.; W2 (14-
20).
MAYO; Goochland Co., Va.; W2 (22-
303).
MEACHAM, JEREMIAH; Salem, Mass.; A2
(65-107, 205, 380; 66-32; 68-397;
69-32, 145).
MEAD, WILLIAM; Greenwich, Conn.; S1
(24-555).
MEADE, ANDREW; N. C., Ky.; W2 (17-
415).
MEADE; Va.; V3 (47-361).
MEANS, JOHN; Family record, Pa.;
M (25-125).
MEANS; Inscriptions, Fairfield Co.,
S. C.; Z (67-749).
MEEKS; (William), Kanawha Co., W.
Va.; B2 (18-25).
MEIGS, VINCENT; Guilford, Conn.; S1
(35-111).
MELLOWES, MARY (JAMES); Boston,
Mass.; English ancestry; B4 (11-
26).
MELYN, CORNELIS; New York; ancestry
in Antwerp; genealogy; A2 (67-
157, 246; 68-3, 132, 217, 357).
MENARD, JACQUES; Quebec; S1 (22-
506).
MENEFEE; Va.; W2 (22-427).
MEREDITH; Bedford Co., Va.; Stokes
Co., N. C.; W2 (15-311).

MEREDITH; (William), West Point,
Va.; V3 (46-39).
MERRIAM, GEORGE; Concord, Mass.; S1
(34-650).
MERIAM, JOSEPH; Concord, Mass.;
English origin; S1 (22-437).
MERRICK, WILLIAM (LIEUT.); Duxbury,
Mass.; S4 (2-237).
MERRILL, NATHANIEL; Newbury, Mass.;
with English data; Dt (2-49, 71);
(Peter6), Vt., Iowa; Col (3-15);
(Augustus8), Me.; Dt (3-187).
MERRIMAN, NATHANIEL (CAPT.); New
Haven, Conn.; B4 (9-91).
MERRIWETHER, NICHOLAS; Surry Co.,
Va.; V3 (50-365); also V3 (45-
329).
MERIWETHER; Abbeville Co., S. C.;
V3 (44-131).
MERWIN, MILES; Milford, Conn.; S1
(36-445).
MESSENGER, EDWARD; Windsor, Conn.;
S1 (20-568).
METCALF, JAMES; Lancaster Co., Pa.;
N3 (34-157).
METCALF, MICHAEL; Dedham, Mass.;
A1 (86-252); (John7), Middlefield,
Mass.; B4 (22-195); English ances-
try; S1 (32-349).
MEUTELAER, CLAES CORNELISSEN; New
York; B4 (22-65).
MEYER, CHRISTIAN; West Camp, Sau-
gerties, N. Y.; OU (2-50, 177,
219, 313, 370; 4-53, 311; 5-378;
6-21, 218, 247, 281, 313, 343,
378; 7-58; 10-243).
MICHAEL, PHILIP-JACOB; Lancaster
Co., Pa.; X2 (8-36, 43).
MICHAEL; (Philip), Firm Rock, Md.;
X2 (7-30).
MICHAUX, ABRAHAM; Va.; V3 (44-365;
45-102, 211, 307, 411; 46-76,
165).
MICHAUX; Cumberland Co., Va.; W2
(16-480).
MICHAUX; (wills of Abraham, 1717,
and Jacob, 1744), Henrico Co.,
Va.; W2 (17-96).
MICKELBOROUGH, EDMUND; Middlesex
Co., Va.; V1 (13-193).
MICOU, PAUL (DR.); Essex Co., Va.;
W2 (16-241); V3 (46-362; 47-66,
163).
MIDDAGH; New York; Z3 (3-9-54).
MIDKIFF; (Isaac), Pa.; M (22-63).
MIGEON, HENRI; Wolcottville, Conn.;
S1 (22-239).
MILBURY, HENRY and RICHARD; York,

Me.; English clews; B4 (18-75).
MILLAR; Shenandoah Valley, Va.; W2
(20-428).
MILLARD, HUMPHREY; Reading, Mass.;
(East Haddam, Conn.); B4 (22-141;
23-45, 177).
MILLER, CHRISTIAN; Lynn, Northampton Co., Pa.; S1 (36-121).
MILLER, GEORGE; Bible records,
Ohio; O (1-80).
MILLER, JOHN; Rehoboth, Mass.; S1
(23-332).
MILLER, JOHN; Tappahannock, Essex
County, Va.; V1 (13-275).
MILLER, JOSEPH; Roxbury, Mass.; ancestry, Bishop's Stortford, co.
Herts, Eng.; A2 (70-139, 242,
345; 71-43, 167, 285).
MILLER, JOST; Salem Co., N. J.; P
(13-63).
MILLER, ROBERT; Albemarle County,
Va.; W2 (13-39).
MILLER; Caroline Co., Va.; V1 (18-
247; 19-102).
MILLER; (George), Baltimore, Md.;
S1 (32-575).
MILLER; (will of Robert), Va.,
1813; V1 (21-121).
MILLER; (Samuel), Reading, Pa.; S1
(24-86).
MILLIKEN, HUGH; (Family of Arthur[6]);
U (26-152).
MILLINGTON; (John of Va., b. 1779);
W2 (13-155).
MILLS, NICHOLAS; Hanover County,
Va.; V1 (14-237).
MILLS, WILLIAM; Charleston, S. C.;
M (23-43).
MILLS; Hanover County, Va.; V1 (15-
38).
MILLSPAUGH, MATTHIAS; Montgomery,
N. Y.; S4 (3-189).
MILTENBERGER, NICHOLAS; Rockingham
Co., Va.; M (30-48).
MINER; notes; S4 (2-359).
MINGE; Surry County, Va.; V1 (14-
185).
MISKELL; Fauquier Co., Va.; V3 (54-
265).
MITCHELL, ADAM; Scotland; B4 (14-
15).
MITCHELL, EXPERIENCE; Plymouth,
Mass.; Pw (21-49); D (32-97, 101).
MITCHELL, EXPERIENCE and THOMAS;
Block Island; B4 (12-193).
MITCHELL, MATTHEW; Stamford, Conn.;
B4 (9-37).
MOHUN; co. Dorset, Eng.; A1 (93-

176).
MOLENAER, JOOST ADRIAENSEN; Kingston,
N. Y.; A2 (65-315); P (13-63).
MONCURE; (Senator Wm. A., Va.); W2
(13-184).
MONK, GEORGE; Isles of Shoals; English origin; B4 (18-71).
MONROE, ANDREW and (REV.) JOHN; Westmoreland County, Pomunkie, Va.; W2
(13-233).
MONROE, JOHN; Bristol, R. I.; S1 (23-
340).
MONTAGU; (Charles-Greville, Gov. of
S. C.); J (33-259).
MONTEITH, WILLIAM; Bible record;
Perth, N. Y.; Dt (10-19); Bible
record (William-John); Dt (10-19).
MONTGOMERY, HENRY; Vt., N. Y.; S1 (24-
269).
MONTGOMERY; Immigrants; S4 (1-178).
MONTGOMERY; (John), Augusta Co., Va.;
W2 (22-65).
MONTRESOR; New York; A2 (75-29).
MOODY; (Lady Deborah); Lynn, Mass.;
Gravesend, N. Y.; LI (1-16, 69).
MOODY; marriage contract (William,
1714), Newbury, Mass.; Y1 (81-385).
MOOR; (will of Edward, 1806), Stafford Co., Va.; V1 (28-107).
MOORE, BENJAMIN; Burlington Co., N.
J.; M (28-1).
MOORE, ISAAC (DEA.); Farmington,
Conn.; S1 (26-557).
MOORE, JAMES (GOV.); S. C.; J (37-1).
MOORE JAMES; Nottingham, Pa.; Walker's Creek, Va.; N3 (34-290, 347,
352).
MOORE, JOHN (REV.); (John[2]), Newtown,
N. Y.; B4 (13-111).
MOORE, SAMUEL; Newbury, Mass.; Woodbridge, N. J.; S1 (33-116).
MOORE, SAMUEL; Middlesex County, N.
J.; Z3 (4-11-53, 544).
MOORE; Northern Virginia; W2 (17-
372); Tidewater; W2 (17-378);
South Carolina; W2 (17-388).
MOORE; Norfolk, Va.; W2 (12-137).
MOORE; (Rev. Jeremiah, Fairfax County, Va.); W2 (13-18).
MOORE; (John), Caroline and King
George Cos., Va.; V3 (52-62); V1
(27-140).
MOORMAN, ZACHARIAH; Nansemond County,
Va.; W2 (12-177); Caroline County,
Va.; W2 (14-85).
MORDECAI, MOSES; Philadelphia, Pa.;
V3 (49-364).
MOREMAN; (Thomas), Bedford Co., Va.;

NASH; Probate and vital records (Thomas and William), Richmond Co., Va.; M (22-95).

NAVARRE, ROBERT; Detroit, Mich.; with Royal lines; S1 (22-492).

NEGUS, JONATHAN; Boston, Mass.; English ancestry of wife Jane Deighton; B4 (9-212).

NEIBERGER, CHRISTIAN; Strasburg, Va.; W2 (21-66).

NELSON, EDWARD; Nelson, Hanover Co., Va.; V1 (27-35).

NELSON, JOHN; Mamaroneck, N. Y.; (Capt. John4, Louisville, Ky.); N3 (42-246).

NELSON, THOMAS and WILLIAM; Yorktown, Va.; English connection; V1 (13-185).

NELSON; (James), Hanover Co., Va.; W2 (21-272); V1 (26-270).

NESBIT, JOHN; Bible record (Allen), Pa.; M (26-131).

NESSLEY, JACOB; Lancaster Co., Pa.; S1 (37-163).

NEUSCHWANGER; Lancaster, Pa.; X2 (6-39).

NEVIUS, JOANNES; Brooklyn, N. Y.; S1 (25-120); origin; arms; A2 (64-250).

NEWBERRY; (diary of Benjamin); Newport, R. I.; NE (3-203).

NEWBURGH, DE; English pedigree; S4 (3-141).

NEWBURY, WALTER; Newport, R. I.; A1 (100-219).

NEWHALL, THOMAS; Lynn, Mass.; S1 (25-442); Z2 (10 [1906]-88, 91 ff.; 17-154).

NEWKIRK [VAN NIEUWKIRK], GERRET and MATTHEUS CORNELISSE; Kingston, N. Y., and Bergen, N. J.; P (Special No., Mar. 1934). See Nieukirk.

NEWLON; (will of William, York Co., Pa., 1769); Col (5-74).

NEWSOM, WILLIAM; Surry Co., Va.; V3 (47-265, 363; 48-74, 175, 274, 358).

NEWSWANGER, CHRISTOPHER; Hempfield, Pa.; X2 (6-32).

NEWTON, GEORGE; (Letters of Thomas, Jr., Norfolk, Va.); W2 (16-38, 192).

NEWTON; Yorkshire; Eng.; see Carlton.

NEWTON; (John3 and Thomas4), Milford, Conn.; B4 (14-99).

NEWTON; (will of William, 1789), Stafford Co., Va.; V1 (23-222).

NICHOLS, FRANCIS; Stratford, Conn.; S1 (32-215); Z3 (4-6-246); English ancestry; B4 (9-9).

NICHOLS, JAMES; Malden, Mass.; Z2 (15-54).

NICHOLS, JOHN; Harvard, Mass.; M (30-86).

NICHOLS; marriages in New England before 1750; M (25-15).

NICHOLSON, GEORGE; Charles City Co., Va.; V1 (17-89).

NICHOLSON, WILLIAM; Va.; Md.; S1 (27-79).

NICHOLSON; Family; Va.; W2 (12-49; 14-98).

NICHOLSON; (Christopher), Perquimans Co., N. C.; S1 (36-798).

NICOLL, MATTHIAS (COL.); New York; Wodhull ancestry; B4 (21-69).

NIEUKIRK [GERRIT CORNELISSE]; Dutch ancestry; P (13-122). See Newkirk.

NIEUWENHUYSEN, WILHELMUS VAN (REV.); A2 (63-12).

NILES; (Ezekiel), Niles, N. Y.; Dt (10-27).

NISHWITZ, JOHANN-PETER; Passaic, N. J.; S1 (27-536).

NOBLE, ARTHUR and JAMES; Boston, Rehoboth, Mass.; Georgetown, Me.; A1 (97-103).

NOBLE, CHRISTOPHER; Portsmouth, N. H.; A1 (94-352; 95-28, 184, 245, 374; 96-202).

NOBLE, THOMAS; Westfield, Mass.; S1 (32-191).

NOBLE; Additions to Genealogy; Dt (4-174).

NORMAN, ISAAC; Spotsylvania Co., Va.; V3 (50-265).

NORSWORTHY, TRISTRAM; Isle of Wight Co., Va.; W2 (18-258).

NORTHCUTT; Bourbon County, Ky.; S3 (9-3-13).

NORTHUP, STEPHEN; (Carr4); North Kingstown, R. I.; A1 (92-32).

NORTON, GEORGE; Salem, Mass.; B4 (15-193).

NORTON, JOHN; Branford, Conn.; S1 (25-596; 26-554); (Selah), Ashfield, Mass.; A1 (98-93).

NORTON, NICHOLAS; Martha's Vineyard; S1 (31-189).

NORTON; Sharpenhoe, Beds, Eng.; B4 (16-101).

NORTON; Brookhaven, N. Y.; B4 (12-116).

NORTON; (Rev. Diary of George), Ipswich, Mass.; Y1 (74-337).

PABODY, JOHN; Plymouth; S1 (19-566); D (34-97).
PAFRAET; Holland; A2 (71-345).
PAGE, FRANCIS (COL.); Va.; N3 (36-46).
PAGE, ROBERT; Hampton, N. H.; S1 (21-465).
PAGE, THOMAS; Athens, Pa.; ancestry, Suffolk, Eng.; B4 (23-230).
PAGE; (Letter of John, Va., 1789); V3 (43-289).
PAGE; (Family of Hiram); U (26-151).
PAINE, MOSES; Braintree, Mass.; English ancestry; B4 (21-181; 23-190). See Payne.
PAINE, STEPHEN; Rehoboth, Mass.; S1 (31-652).
PAINE, THOMAS; Eastham, Mass.; S1 (36-504).
PAINE; (Jonathan), Eastham, Mass., Falmouth, Me.; Dt (10-31, 83).
PALGRAVE, RICHARD (DR.); Charlestown, Mass.; B4 (18-206; 23-238); Dt (5-145).
PALMER, GEORGE; Narragansett, R. I.; B4 (17-50).
PALMER, GEORGE; Philadelphia, Pa.; P (13-112).
PALMER, WALTER; Stonington, Conn.; S1 (34-167); (Stillwater, N. Y., branch); B4 (10-228).
PALMER, WILLIAM; Yarmouth, Mass.; Newtown, N. Y.; A2 (71-362); Dt (7-51, 98).
PALMER; Early settlers, Va.; W2 (14-16).
PALMER; notes; S4 (4-76).
PALMER; Washington and Frederick Cos., Md.; O (7-601).
PALMER; (John), Detriot, Mich.: Dt (10-96).
PALMES, EDWARD (MAJ.); New London, Conn.; English ancestry; A1 (33-560).
PALSSON alias MOLLICKA, ERIC; Gloucester Co., N. J.; B1 (13-25).
PANTRY, WILLIAM; Hartford, Conn.; English origin; A1 (96-370, 371).
PAPEN, HEIVERT; Germantown, Penn.; S1 (7-1123).
PARCELL, NICHOLAS; Flushing, N. Y.; B4 (18-162); Dt (5-218).
PARDEE, GEORGE; New Haven, Conn.; S1 (22-371).
PARISH; (Joshua), Norwich, Conn.; Wethersfield, N. Y.; Ng (6-264).
PARKE, ALICE (FREEMAN) (TOMPSON); English ancestry; B4 (13-1).

PARKE, ROBERT; New London, Conn.; (ancestry of Sylvester Parks); M (20-chart facing p. 136).
PARKE; (wills of Robert, Thomas); B4 (14-16).
PARKER, ABRAHAM; Chelmsford, Mass.; S1 (25-592).
PARKER, JOHN; Boston, Mass.; identity of wife; B4 (18-114).
PARKER, THOMAS; Va.; Z (68-728).
PARKER; Eastern Shore, Va.; V3 (44-261).
PARKER; (Estates of John, Ralph); B4 (14-17).
PARKER; (Jonas), Erie Co., Pa.; Z (78-101).
PARKHURST, GEORGE; Boston, Mass.; S1 (24-558).
PARKMAN, ELIAS; Dorchester, Mass.; S1 (26-447).
PARKS; church records (Joel), Ballston, N. Y.; Z (80-379).
PARMENTER, JOHN; Sudbury, Mass.; A1 (91-213).
PARRY, JOHN; Wales; Utah; U (29-63).
PARRY; (Diary of Needham, 1794), Ky.; N3 (34-379).
PARSELL, JOHN; Newtown, N. Y.; B4 (18-153).
PARSONS, JOHN; East Hampton, N. Y.; B4 (20-159); B7 (2-166).
PARSONS, JOSEPH; Springfield, Mass.; S1 (36-452).
PARSONS, ROBERT; East Hampton, N. Y.; B4 (20-148); (John3), Cape May, N. J.; B4 (21-116).
PARSONS, THOMAS; Windsor, Conn.; (John2), Cape May, N. J.; B4 (21-116).
PARSONS; Stepney Parish, Somerset Co., Md.; X2 (6-16).
PARTRIDGE, WILLIAM; (Edward6, Painesville, Ohio); U (28-38).
PARTRIDGE; (Thaddeus), Roxbury, Mass.; S1 (30-171).
PARVIN; (Thomas), Ky.; N3 (34-395).
PASMORE; (estate of Joseph); B4 (14-17).
PASTORIUS, FRANCIS—DANIEL; Relations with Penn; Q1 (57-66).
PATCH, NICHOLAS; Salem, Mass.; (children of James2); A1 (100-72).
PATRICK, DANIEL; Greenwich, Conn.; wife's ancestry; A2 (66-113).
PATRICK, WILLIAM; Bible record; Dt (7-69).
PATRICK; (John), Augusta Co., Va.; N3 (34-289).

PATTEN, NATHANIEL; Dorchester, Mass.; A1 (87-270).

PATTEN, WILLIAM; (Benoni[6], Norton, Mass.); U (27-30).

PATTERSON, DAVID; Me.; (biography of William-Davis); A1 (86-335).

PATTON; (Capt. John), Augusta Co., Va.; Ky. branch; N3 (35-131, 383); Irish origin; N3 (42-227, 252).

PAUL; PHILIP; Bible record, Gloucester Co., N. J.; B1 (20-42).

PAUL; Pa., Va., Ky.; W2 (15-428).

PAWLING, HENRY; Marbletown, N. Y.; OU (1-339, 373); (Journal of Henry, 1777); OU (1-335).

PAYNE, ELIZABETH (SHEAFE); English ancestry; B4 (22-85).

PAYNE, GEORGE; Goochland Co., Va.; S1 (31-643).

PAYNE, (SIR) JOHN; Fairfield Co., Va.; Z (69-364).

PAYNE, MOSES; (Seth[5]), Lebanon, Conn.; Paines Hollow, N. Y.; A1 (97-134, 396). See Paine.

PAYNE; (Col. Edward), Fairfax Co., Va.; N3 (31-177).

PEABODY, JOHN; Bridgewater, Mass.; S1 (32-382).

PEABODY; (Will of John, Newport, R. I., 1687); B4 (13-55).

PEABODY; Rev. Soldier (Ebenezer), Boxford, Mass.; Y1 (78-23).

PEALE, CHARLES (REV.); Annapolis, Md.; X1 (33-389).

PEALE; (Charles-Willson, engraver); Q1 (57-153).

PEARCE, JOHN; Portsmouth, R. I.; NE (1-129; 2-134).

PEARCE, NATHAN; N. Y.; M (34-111).

PEARCE, RICHARD; Portsmouth, R. I.; S1 (26-149).

PEARCE; (Thomas), Md.; S1 (33-111).

PEARSALL, HENRY; Hempstead, N. Y.; B4 (18-165); Dt (5-216).

PEARSALL; family; B4 (18-78, 153).

PEARSON, GEORGE; Bible record (Albany, N. Y.); E3 (5-234).

PEARSON, JOHN; Rowley, Mass.; Y1 (74-49); S1 (21-288).

PEARSON, THOMAS; Chester Co., Pa.; M (21-93; 26-14).

PEARSON; Thomas and Benjamin; Delaware Co., Pa.; S1 (24-87).

PEARSON; Inscriptions, southern Ohio; M (26-18).

PEASE, widow; Salem, Mass.; WF (1-156).

PEASE; notes; S4 (5-61).

PEASE; Newport, R. I.; A1 (87-74).

PEASLEY, JOSEPH; Salisbury, Mass.;

S1 (31-174).

PECK, HENRY; New Haven, Conn.; S1 (32-164).

PECK, JACOB [JOHANN JAKOB BECK]; Frederick County, Fincastle, Va.; W2 (13-273).

PECK, JOSEPH; Hingham, Mass.; English ancestry; A1 (91-7, 282, 355; 92-71; 93-176, 359; 94-71); (Joseph[3]), Rehoboth, Mass.; A1 (97-114, 251); see also S1 (33-261).

PECK, PAUL; Hartford, Conn.; B4 (9-82, 154).

PECK, (REV.) ROBERT and JOSEPH; Hingham, Mass.; English ancestry; A1 (89-327; 90-58, 194, 263, 371); (Joseph, Attleborough, Mass.); U (27-76).

PECK, WILLIAM; New Haven, Conn.; S1 (32-114); (Joseph[4], New Haven); B4 (13-118); (Jonathan and wife); Greenwich, Conn.; B4 (22-105).

PECKINPAUGH; (George-Peter), Brownsville, Pa.; Col (1 No. 7).

PEEBLES, DAVID; Charles City County, Va.; W2 (13-132).

PEEK; New York, N. Y.; A2 (72-275, 288, 289).

PEELE; Nansemond Co., Va.; W2 (18-252).

PEER; Inscriptions, Montville, N. J.; B1 (12-90).

PEGUES, CLAUDIUS; Charleston, S. C.; J (38-104).

PELHAM, HERBERT; Cambridge, Mass.; English ancestry and descendants; B4 (16-129, 201; 18-137, 211); royal lines; B4 (19-197).

PELHAM, PETER; Boston, Mass.; English data; B4 (20-65); V1 (28-6).

PELL, JOHN; Pelham Manor, N. Y.; English ancestry; Dt (3-171, 191, 213).

PELTON; (John), Saybrook, Conn.; M (29-138).

PEMBERTON; (estate of Joseph); B4 (14-103).

PEMBROKE; Benton, Ontario County, N. Y.; S1 (28-414).

PENDLETON, BRYAN; Portsmouth, N. H.; English data; B4 (10-15); S1 (20-556; 23-484; 25-438).

PENDLETON, PHILIP; New Kent Co., Va.; S1 (36-749); English origin; V1 (28-91).

PENDLETON; Va.; V3 (40-81, 179, 293, 383; 41-80, 166, 263, 362; 42-83, 181, 268, 366; 43-71, 168, 266, 278; 44-68, 264, 346). Continued; see volume I, Index.

PIERCE; (estate of Thomas); B4 (14-104).

PIERSON, ABRAHAM (REV.); Newark, N. J.; B4 (9-37); estate of Abraham[2]; B4 (14-18).

PIKE; (estate of John); B4 (14-104).

PINCKNEY, PHILIP; Eastchester, N. Y.; Dt (3-193).

PINCKNEY, THOMAS; Charleston, S. C.; J (39-15, 174).

PINCKNEY; Diary of Charles-Cotesworth, Beaufort District, S. C.; J (41-135).

PINGREE, JOB; cont.; U (23-121; 24-6).

PINKNEY; Annapolis, Md.; X1 (39-277).

PINNEY, HUMPHREY; Windsor, Conn.; English clue; A1 (100-220).

PITMAN, MARK; Marblehead, Mass.; B4 (18-17).

PITMAN, WILLIAM; Boston, Mass.; A2 (66-336).

PITMAN, WILLIAM; Portsmouth, N. H.; A2 (74-21).

PITTMAN; Manchester, Mass.; B4 (19-177).

PITTS; (Levi), Green, N. Y.; Dt (2-7).

PLATT; (Jesse), Huntington, N. Y.; A2 (70-303; 71-22).

PLAYTER, GEORGE (CAPT.); Philadelphia, Pa.; W2 (19-532).

PLOWDEN, EDMUND (SIR); Va.; X1 (35-398).

PLUMB, JOHN; Branford, Conn.; S1 (34-665).

POE, JOHN; Md. (Edgar-Allan family); X1 (37-421).

POLK, ROBERT-BRUCE; Md.; Scots-Irish ancestry; S1 (25-253).

POMEROY, ELTWEED; Northampton, Mass.; English ancestry; B4 (9-235; 11-52).

POOLE, EDWARD; Weymouth, Mass.; S1 (31-669).

POOLE, ROBERT; Baltimore, Md.; X2 (9-40).

POOLE, WILLIAM and ELIZABETH; Taunton, Mass.; English data; B4 (14-222).

POOLE; Reading, Mass.; A1 (94-397).

POOLE; (Ami C.), Salina, N. Y.; S1 (23-502).

POPE, FRANCIS; Newport, R. I.; A1 (100-219).

POPE, NATHANIEL; Westmoreland Co., Va.; V3 (44-179).

POPE, THOMAS; (will of Luen[4], New Braintree, Mass., 1793); Col (5-55).

POPE; English notes; S4 (3-225; 4-92).

POPE; (Thomas), Va., Ky.; W2 (14-246).

POPINGA, THOMAS LAURENSZEN; New York; A2 (64-306); arms; A2 (65-104).

PORCHER; (Peter), S. C.; J (38-11).

PORTEOUS, JOHN; Detroit; Little Falls, N. Y.; Ng (2-71); Bible record; Ng (3-132).

PORTER, DANIEL; Farmington, Conn.; M (25-117); WF (1-209); S1 (19-481).

PORTER, JAMES; Susquehannah Manor, Md.; M (26-2().

PORTER, JOHN; Windsor, Conn.; English ancestry; B4 (16-49, 122; 17-86; 18-56).

PORTER, JOHN; Salem, Mass.; line of descent; M (25-113).

PORTER, RICHARD (DR.); Talbot County, Md.; S1 (27-94).

PORTER; notes; S4 (4-80).

PORTER; Ridgefield, Conn.; B4 (11-190).

PORTER; (Edward), Boston, Mass.; B4 (23-238).

PORTER; (Hannah Hawley-Nichols-Wolcott); B4 (14-13, 189).

PORTER; (John), N. C.; W2 (18-355).

PORTER; (estate of Nathaniel), 1709; B4 (14-184).

POST, ADRIAN; Bergen, N. J.; B1 (10-1); M (25-117).

POST, RICHARD; Southampton, N. Y.; M (25-118).

POST, STEPHEN; Saybrook, Conn.; A1 (91-173); English ancestry; Ng (2-56); family record (Aaron); Ng (4-36); family record (Bela); Ng (4-38); (Eldad[5]), Thetford, Vt.; Ng (6-318).

POST; (estates of Abraham, Joseph, Obadiah, Sarah, Thomas); B4 (14-185).

POTTER; (Will of John, 1839), Bedford Co., Pa.; B2 (13-8).

POTTER, DE, CORNELIS; New York City; Batavian origin; A2 (72-224).

POTTS, THOMAS; Philadelphia; S1 (27-105).

POTUM, CHARLES; Me.; English origin; B4 (18-72).

POUND; Spotsylvania Co., Va.; W2 (15-198).

POWELL, MICHAEL; Dedham, Mass.;
identity of wife); B4 (23-149),
POWER, NICHOLAS; (line of Arthur6,
Mich.); Dt (3-110).
POWERS, WALTER; Concord, Mass.; WF
(1-154).
POYTHRESS, FRANCIS; Prince George
County, Va.; W2 (14-77, 249; 15-
45, 312).
PRAA, PETER; Brooklyn, N. Y.; A2
(65-308; 66-58, 191; 69-394).
PRATHER; Md.; Z (73-3-87).
PRATT, THOMAS; Watertown, Mass.;
line of descent; M (25-118).
PRATT, WILLIAM; (Jared, Canaan, N.
Y.); U (27-80, 102); (biography
of Orson); U (27-117, 163; 28-42,
92, 118).
PRATT; (estates of Joseph, Samuel),
Saybrook, Conn.; B4 (14-186).
PRATT; (David), Hardwick, Mass.; Dt
(4-42).
PRENCE, THOMAS (GOV.); Plymouth,
Mass.; S1 (26-542; 27-362); D (33-
97).
PRENTICE, HENRY; Cambridge, Mass.;
(line to Narcissa7); A2 (69-365).
PRENTICE, VALENTINE; Roxbury,
Mass.; English data; B4 (10-15).
PRENTISS; (Dr. John H.), Baltimore,
Md.; X2 (15-59).
PRESTON, JOHN; Hadley, Mass.; S1
(20-151).
PRESTON, JOHN; Staunton and "Smith-
field," Va.; V3 (47-109).
PRESTON, WILLIAM; New Haven, Conn.;
English data; B4 (14-134).
PRESTON, WILLIAM (REV.); Va.; V1
(14-107).
PRESTON; (Ezekiel), Ill.; M (24-
29).
PRESTON; Inscriptions, Edgewood,
Iowa; M (24-47).
PREWITT; Campbell County, Va.; Shel-
by County, Ky.; N3 (30-93).
PRICE, DAVID T.; Green Lake County,
Wis.; S1 (28-113).
PRICE, JOHN; Henrico Co., Va.; V3
(45-53); W2 (22-67, 305).
PRICE; account book entries (Ed-
ward), Cape May, N. J.; L1 (1-51).
PRICHARD, ROGER; Springfield, Mass.;
Milford, Conn.; S1 (26-580).
PRIDE; Inventory (Halcott), Dinwid-
die Co., Va., 1774; W2 (18-219).
PRIEST, JOHN; Lancaster, Mass.; M
(30-81).
PRINCE, EDWARD; Petersburg, Va.; V1

(16-50).
PRINCE, ROBERT; Salem, Mass.; B4 (14-
83).
PRIOLEAU; Inscription, Charleston; J
(40-33).
PRIOR, JAMES; Boston, Mass.; S1 (21-
460).
PROBASCO, JURRIAEN; Kings Co., N. Y.;
Z3 (4-12-342).
PROTZMAN; wills, Frederick & Washing-
ton Cos., Md.; M (29-147); Rev.
Pension (Peter), Md., Pa.; M (29-
133).
PRUDDEN, PETER (REV.); Milford, Conn.;
English ancestry; B4 (16-1, 122,
177; 17-52; 18-60); ancestry of
Joanna (Boyse); B4 (19-135, 232).
PULASKI, (COUNT CASIMIR); S1 (26-
474).
PULLEN, NICHOLAS; Rehoboth, Mass.; A1
(97-254).
PULLIAM, EDWARD; Henrico Co., Va.;
W2 (20-566).
PULLMAN, JOHN and JASPER; Me.; Eng-
lish origin; B4 (18-73).
PUMPELLY; S1 (8-865).
PURDY, FRANCIS; Fairfield, Conn.;
Westchester Co., N. Y.; A2 (69-
202).
PURNELL, THOMAS; Somerset County, Md.;
M (21-105).
PURSALL, THOMAS; Md.; B4 (18-80).
PURSELL, THOMAS; Va.; B4 (18-88).
PUTENHAM; cos. Herts and Bucks, Eng-
land; A1 (95-122).
PUTNAM, JOHN; Salem, Mass.; B4 (14-
83); English ancestry; B4 (15-8;
23-93); wife of Lt. James3; B4 (19-
209).
PYNCHON, WILLIAM; Springfield, Mass.;
English data; A1 (87-224); S1 (20-
210).

QUARLES; (Will of Aaron, 1771), St.
John, King Wm. Co., Va.; V3 (45-
191).
QUIGLEY; (Joseph-Murphy); Pa., Ohio;
S1 (36-443).
QUILHOT, JOHN (DR.); Kinderhook, N.
Y.; A2 (77-145).
QUINBY, WILLIAM; Westchester, N. Y.;
S1 (20-92).
QUINCY, EDMUND; English ancestry; A1
(92-30).
QUYAN; (Wm. son of Allen), Annapolis,
Md.; X1 (31-181).
RACE; (Nicholas), Linlothgo, N. Y.;
S1 (20-419).

RICH; English noble house; B4 (21-234; 22-27).
RICH; (estate of Richard of Eastham, 1697); D (31-186).
RICHARD, DANIEL; Flatbush, N. Y.; A2 (66-122).
RICHARD, PAULUS; Flatbush, N. Y.; A2 (66-134, 245).
RICHARDS, THOMAS; Dorchester, Mass.; English ancestry; U (24-92).
RICHARDS, THOMAS; Weymouth, Mass.; S1 (19-554).
RICHARDS, THOMAS; Hartford, Conn.; S1 (32-224).
RICHARDS; notes; S4 (5-9).
RICHARDSON, AMOS; New London, Conn.; S1 (20-560; 23-488).
RICHARDSON, EZEKIEL; Woburn, Mass.; A1 (98-363; 99-172).
RICHARDSON, JOHN; Cumberland Co., Va.; V3 (45-201, 316, 405; 46-65).
RICHARDSON, SAMUEL; (Abiel4, Cambridge, Mass.); A1 (100-128).
RICHARDSON, THOMAS; Woburn, Mass.; S1 (26-451).
RICHARDSON; Baltimore County, Md.; X2 (3-2).
RICHMOND, JOHN; Taunton, Mass.; S1 (9-957).
RICHMOND, JOHN; Saco, Me.; Pw (21-53).
RIDALL, WILLIAM; Wilkes-Barre, Pa.; Ng (3-149).
RIDDLE; Va., Mo.; Z (79-607).
RIDGEWAY, RICHARD; Burlington Co., N. J.; Z3 (4-14-359); (Thomas2); M (29-78).
RIGBY, JAMES; Anne Arundel County, Md.; X1 (36-39; 37-69).
RIGDON, HENRY; (William5 of Allegheny Co., Pa.); U (27-156).
RIGGLES, JOHN; Bible records, Washington, D. C.; M (24-89).
RIKER [ABRAHAM RIJCKEN]; Newtown, N. Y.; A2 (67-58). See Rycken.
RILEY, JOHN; Wethersfield, Conn.; B4 (10-51).
RIMEL; (John), Greene Co., Tenn.; Dt (4-108).
RIND; (Inventory of William, 1773), York Co., Va.; W2 (17-53).
RINER, PETER; Berkeley Co., W. Va.; S1 (24-421).
RING, MARY; Plymouth, Mass.; S1 (33-274).
RISLEY, RICHARD; Hartford, Conn.; S1 (34-279).
RITTENHOUSE, WILLIAM; Germantown,

Pa.; M (26-105).
RITTENHOUSE; (David, colonial scientist); Q1 (56-193).
RITTENHOUSE; (Peter), Cresheim, Pa.; M (31-42).
RITTER, HENRY; Salisbury, Pa.; S1 (36-100).
RIVES, WILLIAM; Southwark, Va.; S4 (3-57, 157; 4-41).
ROANE; King and Queen Co., King William Co., Va.; W2 (18-286).
ROBBINS, JOHN; Wethersfield, Conn.; B4 (10-51).
ROBBINS, NICHOLAS; Duxbury, Mass.; S1 (25-581).
ROBERT, LOUIS; Quebec; French ancestry; S1 (22-507).
ROBERTS, JOHN; Dover, N. H.; Y1 (70-64).
ROBERTS; Md.; X2 (11-3).
ROBERTS; (Robert-Morgan), Md., Pa.; X2 (11-30).
ROBERTSON, CHRISTOPHER; Prince George County, Va.; V3 (44-77).
ROBERTSON; (Grafton), Kingsville, Md.; S1 (32-534).
ROBEY; (William), Hagerstown, Md.; X2 (9-30).
ROBINSON, EZEKIEL; (William5 and Parris5), Litchfield, N. H.; A1 (100-323).
ROBINSON, ISAAC; Barnstable, Tisbury, Mass.; B4 (18-45).
ROBINSON, JOHN (REV.); Leyden, Holland; B4 (17-207).
ROBINSON, THOMAS (REV.); Va.; V1 (14-106).
ROBINSON; notes; S4 (4-104).
ROBINSON; Baltimore, Md.; X2 (4-15).
ROBINSON; Coshocton Co., Ohio; Dt (8-37).
ROBINSON; (Benjamin), Stafford Co., Va.; W2 (21-409).
ROBINSON; (Charles), Middlesex and Caroline Cos., Va.; V3 (50-268).
ROBINSON; (Jeremiah), Trumansburg, N. Y.; Dt (4-64).
ROBINSON; (Michael), Spotsylvania Co., Va.; W2 (23-217).
ROBINSON; (Timothy); Dover, N. H.; Y1 (70-63).
ROBY; (Joseph), Lynn, Mass.; Brockport, N. Y.; E3 (6-442).
ROCKHILL; JM (2-2 and 3-14).
ROCKHOLD; Md.; X1 (32-371).
ROCKWELL, WILLIAM; (Family of Orin7); U (26-153).
ROCKWELL; Inscriptions, Cato, N. Y.;

SCHELLINGER, JACOB; New York, East
Hampton, N. Y.; A2 (68-132, 220);
S1 (32-108).
SCHENCK, MARTIN; N. Y.; A2 (68-33).
SCHENCK, ROELOF, JAN, and JOHANNES;
Dutch ancestry; A2 (68-114).
SCHEPMOES, JAN JANSZ; Dutch ances-
try; A2 (71-39).
SCHERMERHORN, JACOB JANSE; Schenec-
tady, N. Y.; S1 (26-268, 300).
SCHIFF, JACOB H.; New York; A2 (63-
151).
SCHMEIER, PHILIP; Bucks Co., Pa.; S1
(36-120).
SCHMIDT, JOHN-HENRY; Millington, N.
J.; S1 (27-520).
SCHNEIDER, HENRICH; Germantown, N.
Y.; S4 (1-317).
SCHNEIDER, JOHAN-DIETRICH; West Camp,
N. Y.; S4 (1-315).
SCHNELL; American colonists; M (33-
35).
SCHOOLEY, JOHN; Burlington Co., N.
J.; Z3 (2-9-247).
SCHOONMAKER, HENDRICK JOCHEMSEN; Al-
bany, N. Y.; OU (2-81, 121, 151,
183; 3-242).
SCHOONMAKER; (Cornelius-Benjamin),
Rochester, N. Y.; A2 (72-45).
SCHUREMAN, HARMEN; New York, N. Y.;
Dt (2-97, 117, 145, 163; 3-36, 57;
4-15, 37, 59, 81, 103, 117, 143,
191; 6-23, 53, 75, 131).
SCHUYLER, DAVID PIETERSON; Albany,
N. Y.; S1 (27-409); arms; A2 (65-
103).
SCHUYLER, PHILIP and DAVID; New
York; Dutch ancestry; A2 (69-3).
SCHWEYER, NICHOLAS; Kutztown, Pa.; M
(23-47).
SCLATER, JAMES (REV.); Charles Par-
ish, York Co., Va.; V3 (53-288).
SCOFIELD, DANIEL; Stamford, Conn.;
B4 (11-194).
SCOTT, JOHN; Roxbury, Mass.; S1 (21-
456); (Scottsville, N. Y., branch);
Dt (2-209).
SCOTT, JOHN; Brookfield, Mass.; Dt
(7-87, 129; 8-19, 31, 79).
SCOTT, JOHN; Bucks Co., Pa.; Z3 (4-
6-20).
SCOTT, JOHN (CAPT.); Orange Co.,
Va.; W2 (19-485).
SCOTT, RICHARD; Providence, R. I.;
arms, English data and descendants;
A1 (96-3, 192).
SCOTT; Petersburg, Va.; V1 (16-244).
SCOVILL, JOHN; Haddam, Conn.; S1 (32-

81).
SCRASE, ANN; Pa.; English origin; P
(13-274).
SCROPE, LE; baronial family; S1 (36-
771).
SCUDDER, THOMAS; Salem, Mass.; A1
(100-222).
SCUDDER; Almanac items (Benjamin),
Springfield, N. J.; cont.; Z3 (64-
20, 100, 168, 219).
SEAL, JOHN [JAN CELES]; New York, N.
Y.; A2 (66-234).
SEALBY; Maryport, Cumberland Co.,
Eng.; ancestral to Joseph, Vine-
land, N. J.; B5 (30-186).
SEAMAN, JOHN; Hempstead, N. Y.; B4
(11-197).
SEAMANS, THOMAS; (Thomas[3]), Rehoboth,
Mass.; B4 (15-54).
SEAMANS;(Isaac), Virgil, N. Y.; S1
(25-425).
SEARLE, JOHN and PHILIP; Boston and
Roxbury, Mass.; English ancestry;
B4 (16-88).
SEAVEY, WILLIAM; Isles of Shoals, Me.;
English origin; B4 (18-76).
SECOR, SECORD; see Sicard.
SEELEY, ROBERT (CAPT.); English data;
B4 (9-127; 16-43; 22-194); S1 (33-
65).
SEELEY; (Joseph), Sempronius, N. Y.;
E3 (3-32).
SEITZINGER, NICHOLAS; Reading, Pa.;
A2 (68-51).
SELDEN, SAMUEL; Va.; W2 (18-291).
SELIJNS, HENRICUS (REV.); New York;
Dutch ancestry; A2 (63-111, 309;
72-310); arms; A2 (64-146; 72-227).
SELKRIGG, WILLIAM; Waterbury, Conn.;
Dt (9-37, 83).
SELLMAN, JOHN (Sir); All Hallow's Par-
ish, Md.; X2 (11-49).
SEMPLE, JAMES (REV.); New Kent County,
Va.; V1 (15-130).
SEVERANS, JOHN; Salisbury, Mass.; S1
(25-299).
SEWELL, HENRY; Newbury, Mass.; Eng-
lish data; B4 (17-55).
SEXTON, GEORGE; Westfield, Mass.; B2
(10-3, 30,46, 59; 11-1, 17, 29, 43;
22-23).
SEYMOUR, RICHARD; Hartford, Conn.; S1
(27-336).
SHADDOCK; Essex Co., Va.; V3 (47-259).
SHAFFER; notes; X2 (9-23).
SHANDS, THOMAS and WILLIAM; Va.; V1
(15-196).
SHAPLEIGH, ALEXANDER; Kittery, Maine;

Al (95-180, 264, 324; 96-27, 196);
English origin; Al (100-176).
SHARMAN; (Robert, Rev. soldier, Ga.,
Va.); Vl (14-174).
SHARP, JOHN, HUGH and WILLIAM; Bur-
lington Co., N. J.; Bl (15-8).
SHARPE, PETER (DR.); Talbot Co.,
Md.; Xl (37-324).
SHARP, ROBERT; Brookline, Mass.;
English origin; Al (98-205).
SHARP, THOMAS; Newton, N. J.; Bl
(15-8).
SHARPE; (Gov. Horatio), Md.; Xl (31-
215).
SHATTUCK, WILLIAM; Watertown, Mass.;
S4 (3-148); S1 (23-216).
SHATTUCK, (Widow) DAMARIS; Salem,
Mass.; S1 (25-281).
SHAW, ABRAHAM; Dedham, Mass.; S1 (31-
672).
SHAW, JOHN; Plymouth, Mass.; S1 (36-
507).
SHAW, JOHN; Boston, Mass.; (Nathani-
el3, Fairfield, Conn.); B4 (22-
262).
SHAW; Cape May, N. J.; B7 (2-167 ff.).
SHEAFE; Family of Edmund, Cranbrook,
Kent; B4 (15-69); 22-85); S1 (32-
119).
SHEFFIELD, EDMUND; Roxbury, Brain-
tree; S1 (26-40).
SHELBY, EVAN; Pa.; (Col. Isaac of
Md.); Xl (27-128).
SHELDON, ISAAC; Northampton, Mass.;
S1 (20-54).
SHELDON, JOHN; Providence, R. I.;
WF (1-33).
SHELTON; Amherst County, Va.; W2 (16-
605).
SHEPARD, RALPH; Dedham, Malden,
Mass.; S1 (26-103); (Maj. John4);
Stoughton, Mass.; Al (98-285; 99-
81).
SHEPARD, THOMAS (REV.); English an-
cestry of wife (Margaret Stoute-
ville); Al (100-73).
SHEPARD; (Stephen), Acton, Mass.; S1
(23-313).
SHEPPARD, DAVID, THOMAS and JOHN;
Cohansey, N. J.; Irish connections;
B4 (15-15); B5 (27-362; 28-17; 30-
207).
SHEPPARD, ROBERT (MAJ.); James City
Co., Va.; V3 (47-367).
SHERMAN, JOHN (REV.); Watertown,
Mass.; B4 (20-129).
SHERMAN, JOHN (CAPT.); Watertown,
Mass.; S1 (26-166).

SHERMAN, MARY (LAUNCE); Watertown,
Mass.; English and royal lines; B4
(21-169).
SHERMAN, WILLIAM; (Ebenezer of Marsh-
field); D (30-165).
SHERMAN; (James), Charlestown, Mass.;
Al (91-268).
SHERWOOD, THOMAS; Fairfield, Conn.;
Al (92-203, 303).
SHERWOOD; (probate of Philip, 1685),
Old Rappahannock Co., Va.; Vl (23-
116, 278).
SHINNICK, MICHAEL; Oxford, Pa.; B4
(17-79); 19-45, 176).
SHIP; (will of Lemuel, 1788), Carol-
ine Co., Va.; V3 (47-177).
SHIPLEY, ADAM; Anne Arundel Co., Md.;
S1 (37-144).
SHIPP; (Richard), Woodford Co., Ky.;
N3 (43-310).
SHIPP; (Thomas), St. Anne's Parish,
Essex Co., Va.; Vl (28-226).
SHIPPEN, EDWARD; Philadelphia, Pa.;
(N. J. descendants); Z3 (4-1-30).
SHOEMAKER, CHRISTOPHER; Bible records,
Licking Co., Ohio; O (3-216).
SHOLES, JOHN; Groton, Conn.; S3 (13-
3-7).
SHORT; Ulster Co., N. Y.; A2 (70-
357).
SHORT; (William), Surry Co., Va.; Vl
(18-132).
SHORTRIDGE, RICHARD; Portsmouth, N.
H.; S1 (30-176).
SHUCK; (Frederick), Alexandria, Va.;
W2 (18-252).
SHUCK; Penn.; Ky.; N3 (44-101).
SIBLEY, JOHN; Salem, Mass.; S1 (22-
454, 516).
SICARD, AMBROISE; New Rochelle, N. Y.;
A2 (68-313).
SILVESTER, RICHARD; Weymouth; cont.;
Al (86-84, 120, 286).
SIMKINS; Greenwich, N. J.; B5 (25-9,
50).
SIMMONS, JOHN; (Remembrance2), Free-
town, Mass.; B4 (21-94).
SIMMONS; (will of Moses, 1691); D (31-
60).
SIMONDS; (Caleb); B4 (15-54).
SIMONS, BENJAMIN; Bible records,
Charleston, S. C.; J (37-142).
SIMPSON, WILLIAM; Portsmouth, N. H.;
S1 (32-365).
SIMPSON, WILLIAM (DR.); Madison Co.,
Ala.; S1 (36-675).
SIMPSON; Frederick Co., Md.; El (10-
35).

I.; B4 (11-22).
SMITH; (Nicholas and Francis); Essex County, Va.; V1 (14-17).
SMITH; (Samuel, Gread Nine Partners, N. Y.); S5 (10-1-11).
SMITH; (William), Barren Co., Ky.; N3 (37-172).
SMITH; (Ancestry of Mary-Cooke), Va.; V1 (22-259).
SMITH; (Gov., N. C.); H1 (1-22).
SMITH; Inscriptions, Hatfield and Hadley, Mass.; E3 (7-137); Anne Arundel Co., Md.; X2 (4-7); Alfred, Me.; A1 (95-394).
SMOOT, WILLIAM; York County, Va.; U (24-104, 152; 25-13, 63, 112, 152; 26-8; 27-93, 128, 169; 28-29, 83, 126, 181).
SNEAD; (will of Samuel), Va., 1687; V1 (21-55).
SNELL, THOMAS; Bridgewater, Mass.; A1 (100-336).
SNELL; American colonists; M (33-35).
SNOW, NICHOLAS; Eastham, Mass.; S1 (19-562; 36-514); English data; B4 (14-229).
SNOW; (James of Bridgewater); D (31-17).
SNOW; (Stephen of Eastham); D (31-37).
SNOWDEN; (Lt. Jonathan), Md.; X1 (31-259).
SNYDER, MARTIN; Saugerties, N. Y.; OU (1-21).
SNYDER; (Christian), Pa., Md.; X2 (5-4).
SOMERS, JOHN; Gloucester Co., N. J.; B7 (1-306; 2-68).
SOMES, MORRIS; Gloucester, Mass.; English origin; B4 (21-180).
SONMANS, PETER; Perth Amboy, N. J.; Dutch-Scots origin; Z3 (57-230).
SORRELL; Amherst County, Va.; E1 (10-35).
SOULE, GEORGE; Plymouth; D (30-120); (Ebenezer6), Spencertown, N. Y.; Ng (5-179).
SOUTHALL, EDWARD; Spotsylvania Co., Va.; V3 (45-277).
SOUTHALL; Va.; V1 (13-65); V3 (46-166).
SOUTHALL; Charles City Co., Va.; W2 (20-306, 397).
SOUTHERLAND; Halifax Co., N. C.; V3 (47-52).
SOUTHGATE, RICHARD; Bible record; Combs, Essex, Eng.; Leicester,

Mass.; A1 (90-374).
SOUTHMAYD, WILLIAM; Gloucester, Mass.; S1 (32-136).
SOUTHWICK, LAWRENCE; Salem, Mass.; Shelter Island; S1 (20-118).
SOUTHWORTH, CONSTANT and THOMAS; Plymouth; English origin; A1 (86-260); 97-359); arms; A1 (93-395); correction; A1 (99-77).
SPALDING, EDWARD; Chelmsford, Mass.; Z2 (16-43).
SPANGLER [SPENGLER]; (Matthias, Frederick, Md.); S1 (31-334).
SPARROW, RICHARD; Eastham, Mass.; S1 (19-245; 22-113; 26-532; 27-357); D (32-49).
SPAULDING; (probate of John), Plainfield, Conn., 1709; B4 (19-218).
SPEAKE; (Lt. Joseph), Md.; X1 (31-256).
SPEARS; (George), Rockingham Co., Va.; N3 (37-83).
SPEER, GORDON; Huntingdon Co., Pa.; ancestry; Col (5-68).
SPENCE, PATRICK; Westmoreland Co., Va.; V1 (15-268).
SPENCE; Va.; V1 (13-134).
SPENCER, GERARD; Haddam, Conn.; Dt (8-7); English ancestry; S1 (33-548); (Thomas5, Canandaigua, N. Y.; E3 (2-63); (probate of Thomas), Saybrook, Conn., 1700; B4 (19-218).
SPENCER, NICHOLAS; Va.; N3 (34-371).
SPENCER, WILLIAM (ENS.); Surry Co., Va.; V3 (47-370).
SPOFFORD, JOHN; Rowley, Mass.; English origin; A1 (99-174).
SPOTSWOOD; Va.; descent from Robert Bruce; V1 (21-173).
SPOTSWOOD; letters, Va.; V1 (19-227).
SPRAGUE, RALPH; Charlestown, Mass.; (Rev. Edward5), Monadnock, N. H.; S1 (37-28).
SPRAGUE, WILLIAM; Hingham, Mass.; S1 (26-131).
SPRAGUE; Duxbury, Mass.; B4 (15-109).
SPRINGER, CARL CHRISTOPHERS; Wilmington, Del.; Swedish origin; B4 (18-91); family tree and Bible records; O (2-179; 8-625).
SPRINGSTEEN; New York; A2 (66-92).
SPROAT, ROBERT; Middleboro, Mass.; S1 (22-520).
STAATS, PIETER JANSEN; Brooklyn, N. Y.; A2 (66-191).
STACIE; co. Essex, Eng.; U (24-14).
STAGG; co. Dorset, England; A1 (100-216).

STAIGE, THEODOSIUS (REV.); Charles
Parish, Va.; B4 (10-146).
STALLYON, EDWARD; New London, Conn.;
M (25-97); S1 (20-429). See
Stollyon.
STANDISH, MYLES (CAPT.); Plymouth,
Duxbury; A1 (87-149); note; B4
(22-190); will; S4 (1-154).
STANDISH, THOMAS; Wethersfield,
Conn.; WF (1-36).
STANGE, FREDERICK; Detroit, Mich.;
S1 (25-130).
STANLAKE; (will of Richard, 1691);
D (31-62).
STANLEY, TIMOTHY; Hartford, Conn.;
WF (1-209).
STANNARD; Saybrook, Conn.; estates;
B4 (19-218).
STANSBURY; Baltimore County, Md.;
X2 (3-1); Bible records, Ga., Ky.;
X2 (5-5).
STANTON, GEORGE; New York, N. Y.;
OU (3-275, 311, 333, 370; 4-17).
STANTON, THOMAS; Stonington, Conn.;
alleged English ancestry; B4 (14-
86); (estate of Anna), Stoning-
ton, Conn., 1688; B4 (19-219);
(estate of Theophilus), 1705; B4
(19-220).
STANTON, THOMAS; Stafford Co., Va.;
V1 (15-250).
STARBUCK, EDWARD; Nantucket, Mass.;
S1 (25-284; 36-815).
STARK, JOHN; Londonderry, N. H.; S1
(19-116).
STARK; (estate of John), New London,
1689; B4 (19-220).
STARKWEATHER; (estate of John),
Preston, Conn., 1703; B4 (19-221).
STARR, THOMAS (DR.); Cambridge,
Mass.; A1 (89-172, 279, 374; 90-
152, 269; 91-71, 286; 92-365; 93-
92, 355; 94-66, 168, 238, 346;
95-127, 252, 384; 96-271, 366;
97-344).
STATION; Albany Co., N. Y.; A2 (72-
142).
STEARNS, ISAAC; Watertown, Mass.;
S1 (23-338).
STEBBINS, ROWLAND; Northampton,
Mass.; S1 (20-140; 24-263).
STEBBINS; (will of John), New Lon-
don, Conn.; B4 (20-190).
STEELE, JOHN; Farmington, Conn.; S1
(26-559).
STEELE; (Augusta County, Va.); V1
(13-127).
STEELMAN, JAMES; Gloucester Co., N.

J.; B1 (13-26).
STEGER, FRANCIS-GEORGE; Goochland Co.,
Va.; S1 (36-683).
STEINHAUER, PHILIPP and FRIEDRICH;
Philadelphia, Pa.; German ancestry;
S1 (33-228).
STELLE; (Pontius-Delare); M (25-111);
C5 (2-141).
STELWAGON, FREDERICK and JOHN; Mont-
gomery Co., Pa.; P (14-292; 15-112).
STEPHENS; (Thomas), Simsbury, Conn.;
Dt (4-35, 57, 77, 99; 5-65).
STEPHENS; co. Gloucester, Eng.; S1
(21-296).
STEPHENS; Brixton, co. Devon, Eng.;
S1 (25-294).
STEPHENS; (Cornwall, Eng.; Mich.); S1
(29-451).
STERLING; JM (2-1-3).
STEVENS, FRANCIS; (John[3] of Rehoboth
& Attleboro); A1 (97-259).
STEVENS, WILLIAM; Talbot Co., Md.; X1
(39-342).
STEVENS; (Thomas), Malden, Mass.; A1
(98-368).
STEVENS; Wills, Killingworth, Conn.;
B4 (20-190).
STEVENSON; JM (4-1-1; 4-2-9; 4-3-17;
4-4-25; 5-1-33; 5-2-41; 5-3-49; 6-
1-1; 6-2-9; 6-3-17; 6-4-25; 9-2-15;
9-3-21).
STEVENSON; (Samuel), Pisgah, Ky.; N3
(37-306).
STEWART, EDWARD; Millington, Kent Co.,
Md.; X2 (13-41).
STEWART, JOHN; Bible record (John),
Ireland; Maine; Ill.; V1 (20-178).
STEWART ; Family records; des-
cendants of Henry-Wilbur[8]; Dt (10-
3?).
STEYMETS, CASPAR; New York, N. Y.;
Z3 (4-1-13, 77, 164).
STIBBS; Henstridge, co. Somerset,
Eng.; A1 (92-67).
STICKNEY, WILLIAM; Rowley, Mass.; S1
(31-172).
STIER, HENRI-JOSEPH; Annapolis, Md.;
Belgian ancestry; X1 (38-123).
STILLE, CORNELIS JACOBSEN; New York,
N. Y.; Dt (3-79).
STILLMAN, GEORGE; Wethersfield, Conn.;
(George[2], Westerly, R. I.); Ng (5-
206, 216, 242; 6-282, 298).
STILLMAN; (Benjamin[2] of Wethersfield,
Conn.); B4 (10-18).
STILLWELL; (Nicholas), Cape May Co.,
N. J.; B7 (2-51, 172).
STINCHCOMB, NATHANIEL; Anne Arundel

Co., Md.; Ohio branch; M (28-8).
STINCHCOMB; Md.; M (20-69).
STIRLING; Scotland; C5 (1-1-26).
STOCK, JOHN; Family record (Germany
to Mass.); B5 (24-161).
STOCKDELL; (John), Madison Co., Va.;
V3 (50-270).
STOCKER, ANTHONY; Philadelphia; S1
(27-75).
STOCKETT, THOMAS; Md.; X2 (4-31).
STOCKING, GEORGE; Hartford, Conn.;
S1 (31-188).
STOCKTON, RICHARD; Flushing, N. Y.;
S1 (26-74); M (31-29).
STOCKTON, RICHARD; Burlington Co.,
N. J.; Z3 (4-9-124).
STODDARD, RALPH; (Family of Calvin
W.3); U (26-151).
STODDER, RALPH; Groton, Conn.; M
(24-133).
STOKES, CHRISTOPHER; Gloucester Co.,
Va.; V1 (13-187).
STOKES, THOMAS; Burlington Co., N.
J.; B1 (12-73); English ancestry;
S1 (34-500); Z3 (59-96).
STOLLYON; New Haven, Conn.; England;
B4 (16-138). See Stallyon.
STONE, GREGORY; Cambridge, Mass.;
S1 (32-147).
STONE, THOMAS; New Kent Co., Va.; M
(24-126).
STONE; Calvert County, Md.; M (21-
86).
STONER; (Michael of Boonesborough,
Ky.); N3 (31-271).
STOOTHOFF, ELBERT ELBERTSE; (Wilhel-
mus3, Brooklyn, N. Y.); A2 (69-
321).
STORM, DIRCK; (Abraham5, Clarkstown,
N. Y.); Dt (9-111); note on ori-
gin; A2 (70-153, 235).
STORY, ROBERT; New York; P (14-199).
STORY, WILLIAM; Mass.; S1 (19-114).
STORY; N. C.; P (12-93).
STOUTENBURGH, PIETER; New York, N.
Y.; S1 (27-408).
STOW, JOHN; Roxbury, Mass.; S1 (30-
733); A1 (93-296).
STOWELL, SAMUEL; Hingham, Mass.; S1
(28-103); Z (78-498).
STRATTON, JOHN; East Hampton, N. Y.;
B4 (17-20).
STRATTON; American colonists; C5
(1-2-17).
STRATTON; (William), London and Ten-
terden, Eng.; B4 (16-140).
STRIBLING; St. Paul's Parish, K.
George County, Va.; W2 (13-31).

STRICKLAND, EDMUND; Newtown, N. Y.;
B4 (21-85).
STRICKLAND, JOHN; Jamaica, N. Y.; B4
(11-81, 145, 197; 14-117); John
and Edmund; B4 (19-44; 20-207,
210).
STRICKLAND, PETER; Flatbush, N. Y.;
B4 (21-88).
STRICKLAND, THWAITE; Dedham, Mass.;
Hartford, Conn.; B4 (21-89).
STRICKLAND; Sizergh, Westmorland,
Eng.; ancestral to Washington and
Carleton; A1 (96-99); list of
families ancestral to Walter
Strickland; A1 (96-197); d'Eyn-
court and Fleming; A1 (96-307).
STRINGFELLOW; (will of Henry, 1815),
Culpeper Co., Va.; Bible records
(Robert); V1 (27-39).
STRINGHAM, PETER; (Family of Wil-
liam5); U (26-146).
STRODE, GEORGE; (Richard), Chester
Co., Pa.; M (31-76).
STROH; (Nicholas-John), Dauphin Co.,
Pa.; S1 (24-424).
STRONG, JOHN; Northampton, Mass.; S1
(20-160; 22-372; 31-176); (wives
of John2 and John3); B4 (12-76);
correction to Genealogy; Dt (3-
217).
STRONG; (will of John), Lebanon,
Conn.; B4 (20-192).
STRONG; Inscription, Portland, Conn.;
B4 (11-182).
STROTHER, WILLIAM; Richmond Co., Va.;
English ancestry; S1 (36-712);
royal line; S1 (36-773).
STROTHER; Rockingham Co., Va.; V1
(21-201).
STROTHER; (Benjamin), Stafford Co.,
Va.; V1 (19-224).
STROZIER, PETER; Ga.; M (24-94).
STRYKER, JAN; New York; A2 (74-62).
STUART; King George Co., Ga.; M (29-
68, 69).
STUDSON; (estate of William, 1699);
D (34-54).
STURGEON, JEREMIAH; Harrisburg, Pa.;
S1 (22-385).
STURGIS, EDWARD; Yarmouth, Mass.; S1
(20-564; 23-491).
STURMAN, THOMAS; Westmoreland Co.,
Va.; W2 (16-635); 17-99).
STURTEVANT, SAMUEL; Plymouth; S1 (21-
451).
STUYVESANT, PETER; arms; A2 (64-
142).
STYMETS, CASPAR; Casparus3, New

York, N. Y.; A2 (72-133).
SULLIVAN; Inscription, Laurens Co.,
S. C.; M (25-67).
SUMMERS; Md., Va.; W2 (14-247).
SUMNER, WILLIAM; Dorchester, Mass.;
English origin and identity of
wife; B4 (19-156).
SUMNER; notes; S4 (5-13).
SUMNER; (Capt. Ebenezer); Dt (3-
151).
SUMPTER; Va.; W2 (16-672).
SUTLIFF, ABRAHAM; Scituate, Mass.;
S1 (32-167); notes; Dt (3-127).
SUTPHEN, DIRCK JANSEN; Flatbush, N.
Y.; Bible record (Abraham R.5);
Dt (5-141).
SUTTON, GEORGE; Scituate, Mass.;
Perquimans Co., N. C.; A1 (91-65).
SUTTON, JOHN; Hingham, Rehoboth,
Mass.; A1 (91-61).
SUTTON, JOSEPH; Port Chester, N. Y.;
S1 (20-91).
SUTTON; (will of John, 1692); D (31-
64).
SUYDAM [HENDRICK RIJCKEN]; Flatbush,
L. I.; A2 (67-58); arms; A2 (67-
63).
SWAIN, ISAAC; Youngstown, N. Y.; U
(28-37).
SWAN, WILLIAM; Swan's Point, Va.; W2
(18-254).
SWART, TEUNIS CORNELISZE; Schenecta-
dy, N. Y.; S1 (35-129, 139).
SWAZEY; Southold, N. Y.; Chester, N.
J.; B4 (11-51).
SWEETSER, SETH; Charlestown, Mass.;
(Seth of Annapolis, Md.); X1 (27-
139).
SWETT; Marblehead, Mass.; A2 (70-
276).
SWICKARD, DANIEL; Somerset, Pa.; O
(4-339).
SWIFT, THOMAS; identity of wife; B4
(19-162).
SWIFT, WILLIAM; Sandwich; D (30-110);
English ancestry; B4 (17-101).
SWING; Southern N. J.; B4 (17-101).
SWISHER; (John), N. J., Ohio; O (8-
652).
SYMMES, ZECHARIAH (REV.); Charles-
town, Mass.; English data; B4 (12-
67).
SYMONDS, JOHN; Salem, Mass.; English
origin; A1 (96-205).

TABB; Gloucester Co., Va.; V3 (42-
155).
TABER, PHILIP; Portsmouth, R. I.; S1

(31-374); B2 (22-29).
TAFF, PETER; Richmond Co., Va.; V1
(17-101).
TAFF; N. Y.; S1 (27-528).
TAFT; ancestry of William-Howard);
B4 (22-205).
TAINTOR, JOSEPH; Sudbury, Mass.; S1
(26-443).
TALCOTT, JOHN; Hartford, Conn.; Eng-
lish origin; S1 (36-448).
TALIAFERRO, ROBERT; Va.; W2 (12-306;
13-268); V3 (44-349; 50-270).
TALIAFERRO; Caroline County, Va.; V1
(26-105).
TALIAFERRO; Essex Co., Va.; V1 (18-
163).
TALIAFERRO; (notes, Charles, Sarah);
V1 (21-127, 183, 192).
TALIAFERRO; Stratton Major Parish;
W2 (23-218).
TALLMAN; (John M.), N. Y., Col.; Col
(2-67).
TANDY, HENRY; Old Rappahannock Co.,
Va.; V1 (14-114).
TANDY, WILLIAM; York County, Va.; V1
(14-113).
TANEY; origin of name; M (26-53).
TANNER; (William, Cornwall, Conn.,
Sennett, N. Y.); B4 (22-259).
TARNE, MILES; Boston; English clue;
A1 (86-258).
TATHAM; Letters of William (1752-
1819), Va.; W2 (16-162, 362).
TAYLOR, DANIEL; Saybrook, Conn.; B4
(23-211).
TAYLOR, DANIEL (REV.); King William
County, Va.; W2 (14-48, 248); Lu-
nenburg Co. branch; V3 (50-266).
TAYLOR, ISAAC; Rockbridge Co., Va.;
(Gen. Nathaniel3); N4 (12-28).
TAYLOR, JAMES; New York, N. Y.; S1
(24-412).
TAYLOR, JAMES; Caroline Co., Va.; N3
(36-95).
TAYLOR, JAMES; Kent Co., Va.; Ken-
tucky branch; N3 (36-330).
TAYLOR, JOHN; Hadley, Mass.; A2 (64-
408).
TAYLOR, JOHN; Md.; X2 (9-17).
TAYLOR, JOHN; Utah; cont.; U (23-
71, 112; 24-19, 166; 25-19).
TAYLOR, PHILLIP; Accomac, Va.; Md.;
X1 (33-280).
TAYLOR, RICHARD; Yarmouth, Mass.; S1
(28-439).
TAYLOR, THOMAS; Bible record; S. C.;
M (23-42).
TAYLOR; JM (8-1-4; 8-2-9; 8-3-18; 8-

4-34; 9-1-1; 9-2-9; 9-3-25; 9-4-
33; 10-1-1; 10-2-7; 10-3-15; 10-
4-20; 11-1-1; 11-2-10; 11-3-19).
TAYLOR; Md.; X2 (13-58).
TAYLOR; Bristol Parish, Va.; W2 (16-
1).
TAYLOR; Northumberland Co., Va.; V3
(47-81).
TAYLOR; Orange Co., Va., Ky.; N3
(33-70).
TAYLOR; (Col. James), Orange Co.,
Va.; V3 (46-231; 54-339).
TAYLOR; (John), Alexandria, N. J.;
S1 (25-110).
TAYLOR; (John of Caroline); V3 (46-
285).
TAYLOR; (Matthew), Cecil Cq., Md.;
X2 (9-1).
TAYLOR; (Rawleigh), Va., Ohio, Ky.,
Iowa, Ind.; W2 (16-485).
TAYLOR; (Rolley of Culpeper Co.,
Va.); W2 (15-313).
TAYLOR; (will of William), Overwhar-
ton, Stafford Co., Va.; V1 (25-
131).
TAYLOR; (Zachary), Carlisle, Ill.,
Col.; Col (3-5).
TEARSE, PETER-BAILEY; Ballston, N.
Y.; S1 (27-346).
TEASDALE; historic; early settlers;
M (27-71).
TEFFT, JOHN; Westerly, R. I.; B4
(17-235).
TEN BROECK; (will of Wessel, Ulster
Co., N. Y., 1705); OU (7-86).
TEN EYCK, COENRAET; New York; A2 (63-
152, 269, 321; 64-87; 65-190; 72-
267, 270 to 272, 277 to 280).
TENNISON; deeds (Henry), Amherst
Co., Va.; Z (80-584).
TERHUNE; notes; A2 (64-87).
TERHUNE; (Roelof), Gravesend, N.
Y.; A2 (69-83).
TERRY; (Daniel), Brookhaven, N. Y.;
S1 (26-428).
TERWILLIGER, EVERT DIRCKSEN; King-
ston, N. Y.; OU (7-116).
TETSELL, W. E. (REV.); Sterling,
Col.; English origin; Col (3-77).
TEUNISE, see Teunis Nyssen.
TEUNISSEN, TOBIAS; New York; A2 (64-
114).
THACHER, PETER; Boston, Mass.; roy-
al ancestry; S4 (2-251).
THATCHER; (will of Thomas, King
George Co., Va., 1750); V1 (18-234).
THAYER, RICHARD; Braintree, Mass.;
S1 (22-245).

THAYER, THOMAS; Braintree, Mass.; S1
(20-105; 34-679).
THEUS; (William-Randolph), S. C.; W2
(14-355).
THOMAS, JOHN; New Haven, Conn.; S1
(26-579).
THOMAS, WILLIAM; Marshfield, Mass.;
Dt (5-35).
THOMAS; London, Eng.; B4 (16-95).
THOMAS; Darby, Pa.; Z (67-643).
THOMAS; (Estate of Nathaniel), 1675;
D (34-35).
THOMAS; (probate of John, 1692); D
(31-64).
THOMAS; Marriage record (Nicholas),
Mt. Desert, Me.; A1 (91-196).
THOMAS, AP; (Will of William, Eliza-
beth City Co., Va., 1779); V1 (22-
229).
THOMES; (Cumberland Co., Maine); S1
(31-507).
THOMPSON, ANTHONY; New Haven, Conn.;
S1 (19-237; 22-104; 26-561); Ng
(4-152).
THOMPSON, GEORGE; Newburyport, Mass.;
Revolutionary Diary; Y1 (76-221).
THOMPSON, JOHN; Shropshire, Eng.;
Farmington, Conn.; U (24-18).
THOMPSON, JOHN; Brookhaven, N. Y.;
B4 (13-221).
THOMSON, JOHN (REV.); Va., N. C.; V3
(51-394).
THOMPSON, SAMUEL; Louisa Co., Va.;
Scots origin; N3 (36-42).
THOMSON, WILLIAM (REV.); New London,
Conn.; B4 (14-123).
THOMPSON, WILLIAM (REV.); Lawne's
Creek, Va.; V3 (51-200).
THOMPSON; Families of Brookhaven, N.
Y., and the Conn. coast; B4 (11-
184).
THOMPSON; Vt., N. Y.; M (24-42).
THOMSON; Petersburg, Va.; W2 (16-19).
THOMPSON; (will of Henry), Va.,
1691; V1 (21-57).
THOMSON; (Moses), Va., Ky.; W2 (21-
409).
THORNE, ANDREW; Me.; English origin;
A1 (96-91).
THORNE, WILLIAM; Flushing, N. Y.; Dt
(5-215).
THORNHILL; Goochland Co., Va.; V3
(48-66, 168).
THORNLEY, JOHN; King George Co.,
Va.; M (22-96).
THORNTON, JOSEPH; Newtown, Pa.; Eng-
lish ancestry; B4 (15-33, 146);
mother's ancestry; B4 (15-231).

THORNTON, WILLIAM; York Co., Va.; V3 (44-184).

THORNTON, WILLIAM; Stafford Co., Va.; S1 (36-752); (branch of King George Co., Va.); V1 (23-102).

THORNTON; St. Paul's Parish, K. George County, Va.; W2 (13-32); Orange Court House, Va.; W2 (14-248; 19-309).

THORNTON; Essex and Stafford Cos., Va.; W2 (15-96).

THORNTON; (Anthony), Va.; W2 (23-218).

THORNTON; (Will of Reuben, 1768); V3 (43-251); (notes, Reuben, Anthony); obituary notices; V1 (21-127, 178).

THORNTON; (Will of Rowland, King George Co., Va., 1741); V1 (22-231).

THORP, CHARLES; Stamford, Conn.; Bible record; B4 (12-259).

THORPE, JOSEPH; Surry Co., Va.; V3 (48-361).

THORPE, WILLIAM; New Haven, Conn.; S1 (26-78); B4 (20-237).

THORP; (Charles and Joel), Conn.; E3 (8-239).

THRELKELD; (John), Culpeper County, Va.; Scott County, Ky.; N3 (31-180).

THROCKMORTON, JOHN; Providence, R. I.; English ancestry; B4 (12-79); A1 (98-67, 111, 279); Blennerhasset ancestry; A1 (98-271).

THROCKMORTON, MORDECAI (CAPT.); King and Queen County, Va.; V3 (42-59).

THROGMORTON, THROCKMORTON; Halifax and Henrico Cos., Va.; V1 (16-124).

THROOP, WILLIAM; Bristol, R. I.; S1 (22-510).

THURSTON, EDWARD; Newport, R. I.; Pw (21-56); M (34-39).

TIBBETTS, HENRY; Dover, N. H.; A1 (98-57, 132, 215, 293; 99-52, 110, 244, 323; 100-34, 144); B4 (17-55).

TIBBS; (Col. Willoughby), Dumfries, Va.; W2 (17-304).

TIFFANY, HUMPHREY; Milton, Swansea, Mass.; B4.(10-138); English origin; A2 (63-3).

TILDEN, NATHANIEL; Scituate, Mass.; Pw (21-52).

TILDEN; Hebron, Conn.; Dt (3-173).

TILGHMAN; Letters, Md., 1697-1764; X1 (33-148).

TILLEY, JOHN; Plymouth; S1 (19-533).

TILLINGHAST, PARDON; Providence, R. I.; A1 (97-25); S1 (31-367).

TINKER; Lyme, New London; B4 (11-50).

TINKHAM; Plymouth; line from Peter Browne of Mayflower; Ng (5-210).

TIPPING, BARTHOLOMEW; Taunton, Mass.; B4 (23-174).

TIPTON, JONATHAN; Baltimore Co., Md.; Tenn.; N4 (1-67).

TIPTON; (Col. John), Shenandoah Co., Va.; Z (77-181).

TIPTON; Inscriptions, Dallas Co., Ala.; M (23-120).

TISDALE, JOHN; Taunton, Mass.; S1 (19-389).

TITUS, EDMUND; Westbury, N. Y.; A2 (77-97).

TITUS, ROBERT; Weymouth, Rehoboth, Mass.; S1 (31-380); (Joel7, Washington, Conn.); A1 (89-377).

TODD, CHRISTOPHER; New Haven, Conn.; S1 (32-128).

TODD, JOHN; Rowley, Mass.; B4 (21-94).

TODD, WILLIAM; Stafford Co., Va.; V1 (28-21).

TODD; notes; S4 (2-158).

TODD; King & Queen Co., Va.; N3 (38-112).

TOLER; Union County, Ill., marriages, wills; Z (79-156).

TOLLES, HENRY; (Amos), Bennington, N. Y.; Ng (3-155, 168, 194, 223, 240).

TOMES; Long Marston, co. Glouc., Eng.; S1 (35-89).

TOMLIN; (William), Cumberland Co., N. J.; L1 (5-29).

TOMPKINS, CHRISTOPHER; Gloucester County, Va.; W2 (13-225).

TOMPKINS, MICAH; Milford, Conn.; S1 (26-570).

TOMPKINS; (Nathaniel), R. I.; NE (1-224).

TOMPSON, ALICE (FREEMAN); English ancestry; B4 (13-1).

TOMSON, JOHN; (husband of Alice Freeman), Eng.; B4 (14-145).

TOMSON, JOHN; Plymouth; D (30-49).

TOMSON; Sulgrave, Northants, England; B4 (21-97).

TOPHAM, ABRAHAM; Newbury, Mass.; English origin; B4 (22-20).

TORREY, WILLIAM; Weymouth, Mass.; NE (2-177); English ancestry; S1 (24-260).

TORREY; (Nicholas), Rensselaer Co., N. Y.; Col (6-109).

TOURNEUR, DANIEL; Harlem, N. Y.; Dt

VAN WESTERHAUT, JAN; New York, N.
  Y.; Dt (2-97, 117).
VAN WICKLE, EVERT, JANSE; Flatbush,
  N. Y.; Somerset Co., N. J. branch;
  Z3 (54-118).
VAN WIJCK, CORNELIS, ABRAHAM and AN-
  THONI; coat-of-arms; A2 (64-366).
  See Van Wyck.
VAN WIJCKERSLOOT, SOPHIA; Albany;
  origin and arms; A2 (65-213).
VAN WYCK, CORNELIUS BARENTSE; (Fami-
  ly of Johannes3, New York); A2 (67-
  266). See Van Wijck.
VAN YSSELSTEYN, MARTEN CORNELISSE;
  Dutch origin; A2 (69-228).
VAN ZANDT; Harlingen; A2 (68-400).
VARLET, CASPAR; New York; Dutch an-
  cestry; A2 (71-117).
VAUGHAN, GEORGE; Middleboro, Mass.;
  B4 (23-24, 123).
VAUGHAN; Amherst Co., Va.; W2 (19-
  321).
VAUGHN; Edgar W. [Baker-Vaughn];
  London, Ontario; Dt (6-91).
VAULX; V3 (44-151).
VAUTRIN, ABRAHAM; Lehigh Co., Pa.;
  French origin; Dt (5-211).
VEATCH; Wills, Md.; Z (71-678).
VENABLE; (Nathaniel), Prince Edward
  Co., Va.; V3 (46-78).
VERDON, JACOB; New York; A2 (64-
  105); (Thomas4), Brooklyn, N. Y.;
  B4 (21-113).
VERDUGO, JOSE-MARIA; Calif.; B4 (22-
  40).
VERE, DE; Thrapston, co. Northamp-
  ton; S1 (36-701); Drayton, co.
  Northampton; S1 (36-710).
VERMULE, ADRIAN; Bergen Co., N. J.;
  Dutch ancestry; Z3 (4-12-354).
VER PLANCK, ABRAHAM ISAACSE; A2 (63-
  78).
VERPLANCK, JACOB ALBERTSZ; Rensse-
  laerwyck; Dutch origin and arms;
  A2 (69-226).
VER VEELEN, JOHANNES; Albany, N. Y.;
  B5 (24-153).
VESEY, GEORGE; Va.; V1 (13-61).
VICARS; (Anne), Bewdley, co. Worc.,
  Eng.; S1 (19-239; 22-106; 26-572).
VIELE, CORNELIS VOLKERTSZEN; New
  York, N. Y.; S1 (27-411).
VINSON; (John), Va., N. C., Tenn.;
  W2 (21-176).
VINTON, JOHN; Lynn, Mass.; S1 (21-
  316).
VIRDEN, HUGH; Sussex Co., Del.; Col
  (7-63).

VITTERY, GREGORY; Isles of Shoals,
  Me.; English origin; B4 (18-76).
VIVION, JOHN; Middlesex Co., Va.; V3
  (47-54, 56, 166).
VIVION, THOMAS; Isle of Wight Co.,
  Va.; V3 (46-352).
VON ALBADE, JOACHIM; New York; N4
  (2-81).
VON ROHR, GEORG K. H. F.; Freistadt,
  Wis.; Bergholtz, N. Y.; German an-
  cestry; S1 (35-739).
VOSCH; Holland; A2 (65-213).
VREELAND, MICHAEL JANSSEN; origin;
  arms; A2 (68-343).
VRIES, see de Vries.
VROOMAN, HENDRICK MEESE; Schenectady,
  N. Y.; S1 (35-145).
VROOMAN, PIETER, JACOB and HENDRICK;
  Albany, N. Y.; origin and arms; A2
  (67-142; 72-313).
VYALL; (estate of John, 1686), Swan-
  sea, Mass.; B4 (22-264).

WADDLE; Va.; W2 (17-123).
WADE; will of Isaac, Bedford Co.,
  Va., 1823; Col (5-95).
WADSWORTH, CHRISTOPHER; Duxbury,
  Mass.; S1 (28-570).
WADSWORTH; (will of Ignatius, 1806);
  M (21-71).
WAGENER, DAVID; Northampton Co., Pa.;
  P (13-261).
WAGGENER; notes; Ky.; V1 (21-129).
WAGGONER, JOHN; Essex Co., Va.; V1
  (20-244).
WAHULL; English barons; B4 (23-162).
WAKELEE, HENRY; Stratford, Conn.; S1
  (19-473).
WAKEMAN, SAMUEL; Hartford, Conn.; A2
  (70-112).
WALDRON, RESOLVED; New Harlem; B5
  (24-153); S1 (27-399).
WALDRON; New York, N. Y.; A2 (72-
  276, 289, 290).
WALKER, GEORGE; Philadelphia, Pa.;
  B4 (20-33; 23-239).
WALKER, GEORGE; Litchfield, N. Y.;
  Dt (10-15, 41, 73).
WALKER, JOHN; Pa.; Walker's Creek,
  Va.; N3 (34-286, 296).
WALKER, JOHN; Portsmouth, R. I.; S1
  (26-154); Dt (4-101).
WALKER, RICHARD (CAPT.); Lynn, Mass.;
  Z2 (14-99).
WALKER, ROBERT; Boston, Mass.; Eng-
  lish origin and wife; B4 (19-195;
  21-58).
WALKER; (David), Goochland Co., Va.;

WASHINGTON; Virginia; Newton Broms-
wold, Northants, Eng.; W2 (20-
404).
WASHINGTON; reinterments, George-
town, D. C.; M (28-43).
WASHINGTON; (Samuel), Jefferson Co.,
W. Va.; S1 (32-305).
WASHINGTON; St. Paul's Parish, K.
George County, Va.; W2 (13-32).
WASSON; Conn., N. Y.; B4 (23-85);
Maine; B4 (23-225).
WATERHOUSE, THOMAS; Dorchester,
Mass.; A1 (88-204).
WATERMAN, THOMAS; Roxbury, Mass.;
A2 (70-139, 345).
WATERS, BEVIL; Hartford, Conn.; S1
(31-187).
WATIES, WILLIAM; Berkeley Co., S. C.;
J (45-12).
WATKINS; (Francis), Prince Edward
Co., Va.; V3 (46-80).
WATKINS; (Diary of Joel, 1789, Va.,
Ky.); N3 (34-215).
WATROUS; (wife of Isaac), Lyme,
Conn.; Dt (5-21).
WATSON, ROBERT; Plymouth, Mass.; S1
(36-510).
WATTERS, WILLIAM (REV.); Md.; M (27-
95).
WATTS, JOHN; Boston, Mass.; B4 (16-
198).
WATTS; Col. and Rev. War services,
southern; V1 (15-32).
WEAVER; (Jan), Trenton, N. J.; S1
(24-268).
WEAVER; Inscriptions, Cambria, N.Y.;
Ng (4-128).
WEBB, EDMUND; Talbot Co., Md.; X1
(39-341).
WEBB, JOHN; Northampton, Mass.; B4
(23-129).
WEBB, JOHN; Saybrook, Conn.; B4 (22-
44, 200).
WEBB, RICHARD; Weymouth, Mass.;
(Rev. Joseph of Fairfield, Conn.);
B4 (19-208).
WEBB; marriages, Baltimore, Md.; X2
(17-51).
WEBBER, WOLPHERT; Holland; New York;
A2 (63-114, 116).
WEBBERS; (Jacob); A2 (65-89).
WEBER, JOHANN-WILHELM; Hempfield,
Pa.; S1 (23-319).
WEBER; Germany; S1 (35-394).
WEBSTER, JOHN (GOV.); Hartford,
Conn.; S1 (29-668); S1 (36-497); WF (1-
155).
WEBSTER, THOMAS; Hampton, N. H.; S1

(22-377).
WEBSTER; (Daniel), Fayette Co., Ky.;
V1 (26-76).
WEBSTER; (Rufus-Durkee), Sanbornton,
N. H., N. Y., Kan., Col., Va.;
Col (2-21).
WEEDON, GEORGE; Westmoreland Co.,
Va.; W2 (20-237).
WEEDON, JOHN; Westmoreland Co., Va.;
W2 (15-196).
WEEKES, FRANCIS; Oyster Bay, N. Y.;
B4 (9-77; 14-239; 15-118); Ng (2-
47).
WEEKES, GEORGE; Dorchester, Mass.;
English origin; B4 (23-82).
WEEKS; (Jonathan), Conn., Pa.; M (27-
104).
WEEKES; Christ Church, Middlesex Co.,
Va.; V3 (47-48).
WEISER, CONRAD; Berks County, Pa.;
Q1 (56-265).
WEISER, JOHANN-CONRAD; New York, Le-
banon, Pa.; Long Island branch; M
(25-38).
WELD, DANIEL; Sudbury, Eng.; Brain-
tree, Mass.; A1 (93-204).
WELD, JOSEPH (CAPT.); Roxbury, Mass.;
S1 (36-490).
WELLES, ALICE (TOMES); Royal and
titled ancestry; S1 (35-147).
WELLES, THOMAS (GOV.); Hartford,
Conn.; English data; S1 (35-85);
M (32-22); (will of John²); B4 (23-
90).
WELLES; English barons; B4 (18-149).
WELLS; (estate of Jonathan, 1688),
Hartford, Conn.; B4 (22-264).
WELLS; (Waterman), Newbury, Vt.; S1
(20-167).
WELTON, JOHN; Waterbury, Conn.; S1
(19-468; 32-227).
WENZEL, HENRY; Braintree, Mass.; A1
(95-234, 312).
WEST, JOHN L.; Euclid, N. Y.; S1 (23-
503).
WEST, JOSEPH (GOV.); S. C.; Boston;
N. Y.; A2 (65-202; 66-89); J (40-
79).
WEST; (Benjamin), Dutchess Co., N.
Y.; Dt (5-176).
WEST; Barons De La Warr; England; B4
(18-211); V1 (21-172).
WEST; Pedigree, Va. Governors; W2
(14-351).
WEST; (Charles of Middleboro, Mass.);
A1 (91-371).
WEST; (Nathaniel), Concord, N. H.;
S1 (31-153).

WEST; (will of John), Stafford Co.,
Va., 1716; V1 (20-102).
WESTLAKE, JOHN; St. Thomas, Canada;
S1 (23-315).
WESTOVER, JONAS; Windsor, Killing-
worth, Conn.; B4 (17-151).
WESTVAEL, JURYAN; (Capt. Abraham
Westfall), Carroll Co., Ohio; O (4-
321).
WETHERBY; R. I.; (Isaac-Augustus,
portrait pointer); T9 (25-55).
WETHEREL; (John of Scituate); D (31-
16).
WEYBRECHT, JOHN T.; Alliance, Ohio;
S1 (23-384).
WHARTON; England; A1 (97-200).
WHEELER, OBADIAH; Concord, Mass.;
(Obadiah2); A1 (87-115).
WHEELER, ROGER; Md.; X2 (7-51; 8-19).
WHEELER, THOMAS; Milford, Conn.; S1
(32-211); corrections; B4 (10-132).
WHEELER, THOMAS (CAPT.); Concord,
Mass.; English data; B4 (12-4,
135); Thomas and brothers; Concord;
English data; B4 (14-1); (estates
of George, Thomas, Timothy), Con-
cord; B4 (14-131).
WHEELER; notes; S4 (5-29).
WHEELER; Preston, Conn.; B4 (20-127).
WHEELER; (Journal of Lieut. Rufus of
Rowley); Y1 (68-371).
WHELDON; (Joseph), Fairhaven, Mass.;
S1 (25-555).
WHILLDIN, JOSEPH; Cape May County,
N. J.; B7 (1-10, 17); L1 (4-40);
(Seth), Cumberland Co., N. J.; L1
(6-37).
WHIPPLE; (Abraham), Providence, R.
I.; S1 (22-523).
WHIPPLE; (Noah, Ashford, Conn.); pa-
rentage of Commodore Abraham; A1
(100-68).
WHISTLER, JOHN; Ireland; Md.; Z (68-
526).
WHITAKER, JONATHAN; Somerset Co., N.
J.; S1 (25-113).
WHITAKER; family notes; S4 (1-251).
WHITAKER; Warwick Co., Va.; V1 (25-
63).
WHITAKER; (John-Mills); U (23-114).
WHITCOMB, JOHN; Lancaster, Mass.; WF
(1-151).
WHITE, ANTHONY; New Brunswick, N. J.;
English ancestry; Z3 (2-7-107).
WHITE, GAWEN; Scituate, Mass.; B4
(17-198).
WHITE, GEORGE; Ipswich, Rowley, Mass.;
A1 (97-199).

WHITE, JOHN (ELDER); Hadley, Mass.;
S1 (20-128).
WHITE, NICHOLAS; Taunton, Mass.; B4
(17-196).
WHITE, ROBERT; Lancaster, Mass.; S1
(28-435).
WHITE, THOMAS; Weymouth, Mass.; B4
(17-197).
WHITE, WILLIAM; Plymouth, Mass.; (Re-
solved2 of Scituate); B4 (17-200);
(daughters of Resolved2); A1 (87-
115); (Peregrine2 of Marshfield);
B4 (17-202); D (30-145; 31-145).
WHITE; notes; S4 (5-64).
WHITE; (George), Rochester, Mass.; N.
Y., Pa., Ind.; X2 (13-36).
WHITE; (Henry), Md., N. Y.; S1 (6-
630).
WHITE; (Rev. John), Dorchester, co.
Dorset, Eng.; C5 (1-4-15).
WHITE; (William of Dartmouth, Mass.);
B4 (17-193).
WHITEHEAD; Southern Va.; V3 (44-358).
WHITING, JAMES; Va.; (branch of Pe-
ter); W2 (17-124).
WHITING, SAMUEL (REV.); Lynn, Mass.;
S1 (24-275; 36-485); (Fryeburg,
Me., branch); B4 (17-230); royal
ancestry of wife; S1 (36-528).
WHITING, WILLIAM; Hartford, Conn.;
WF (1-155).
WHITLEY; (Col. William, Va. and Ky.);
N3 (36-189).
WHITLOCK; (will of David, 1798), Han-
over Co., Va.; V1 (18-173); (will
of James, 1736), Hanover Co., Va.;
V1 (18-231).
WHITMAN, JOHN; Weymouth, Mass.; Dt
(4-93); (line to Marcus7); A2 (69-
364).
WHITMAN; (family of John-Alderman);
Tinmouth, Vt.; Dt (9-11).
WHITMER; (Family of Peter); Pa.; U
(26-106).
WHITNEY, JOHN; Watertown, Mass.; Eng-
lish data; B4 (10-84); S1 (28-144);
Royal lines; S1 (27-193 to 251);
items, Ohio; Dt (4-85).
WHITNEY, THOMAS; (Samuel8, Vt.,
Ohio); U (28-64).
WHITTAKER, EDWARD; Kingston, N. Y.;
A2 (70-111).
WHITTEMORE, THOMAS; Charlestown,
Mass.; S1 (30-721).
WHITTIER; (John-Greenleaf); Y1 (68-
353).
WHITTON; (will of William), Va.,
1730; V1 (21-123).

76 NAME INDEX

WICKES, THOMAS; Huntington, N. Y.;
B4 (9-77).
WICKES; (Capt. Lambert); Md.; X1
(27-1).
WICKHAM, THOMAS; Wethersfield, Conn.;
B4 (9-155).
WICKISER, ANDREW and CONRAD; Wilkes-
Barre, Pa.; M (27-102).
WIDGER; (Diary of Wm., Marblehead,
Mass., 1781); Y1 (73-311; 74-142).
WIGGIN, THOMAS (GOV.); Dover, N. H.;
marriage; A1 (100-336).
WIGGINS; (William), Tompkins Co., N.
Y.; S1 (35-135).
WIJNKOOP, CORNELIS; origin; arms; A2
(65-351; 66-68). See Wynkoop.
WILBORE, SAMUEL; Boston, Mass.; Eng-
lish origin; A1 (99-175).
WILCOX, EDWARD; Portsmouth, R. I.;
B4 (19-23, 177); A1 (87-73); S1
(20-550; 23-479); M (25-118).
WILCOX, HENRY; Talbot Co., Md.; S1
(32-551).
WILCOX; Amherst County, Va.; V1 (13-
268).
WILCOXSON, WILLIAM; Stratford, Conn.;
S1 (35-120).
WILDERMUTH, WILHELM; Berks Co., Pa.;
Greenfield twp., Ohio; O (8-644).
WILKESON, JOHN; Delaware; Samuel2,
Buffalo, N. Y.; Ng (4-94).
WILKINS; Cumberland, Md.; S4 (1-71).
WILKINS; (Hezekiah), Deering, N. H.;
S1 (24-126).
WILKINSON, (ANN [BIDDLE]); Letters
from Ky., 1788-89; Q1 (56-33).
WILLARD, SIMON (MAJOR); Charlestown,
Mass.; S1 (35-117).
WILLETTS, RICHARD; N. Y.; Cape May
branch; L1 (4-46).
WILLEY; Thorley, Herts, Eng.; A2
(68-399).
WILLIAM; abstracts of wills, Edge-
combe Co., N. C.; M (33-11).
WILLIAMS, JOHN; (Frederick-Granger6,
Warrensville, Ohio); U (28-36).
WILLIAMS, REYNEAR; New York; Kent
Co., Del.; Col (7-69).
WILLIAMS, RICHARD; Taunton, Mass.;
English ancestry of himself and
wife; B4 (9-136, 212; 10-20, 118).
WILLIAMS, RICHARD-ALLEN; Vineland,
N. J.; English origin; B5 (24-271).
WILLIAMS, ROBERT; Roxbury, Mass.;
NE (1-65, 216).
WILLIAMS, ROGER; Providence, R. I. S1
(24-121; 29-430); C5 (1-1-18);
English data; A1 (97-173, 176);

parentage; NE (1-20).
WILLIAMS, THOMAS; (Thomas2, New Lon-
don, Conn.); B4 (13-190).
WILLIAMS, THOMAS; Blandford, Peters-
burg, Va.; V3 (43-61).
WILLIAMS; (will of Thomas, 1696); D
(31-106).
WILLIAMS; Inscriptions, mostly Otse-
go Co., N. Y.; Dt (5-150).
WILLIS, HENRY; Westbury, N. Y.; A2
(77-100).
WILLIS, WILLIAM; Bible records, Ma-
plewood, N. J.; Z3 (2-13-142).
WILLS, DANIEL (DR.); Newcastle, N.
J.; English origin; Z3 (56-198).
WILMARTH, THOMAS; Braintree, Reho-
both, Mass.; S1 (31-376).
WILMOT, BENJAMIN; New Haven, Conn.;
S1 (26-565).
WILSON, FELIX; Jamestown, Va.; W2
(20-433).
WILSON, GEORGE; Fayette Co.; M (30-
95).
WILSON, NATHANIEL; Newton, Mass.; B4
(17-227).
WILSON, PHINEAS; Hartford, Conn.; B4
(14-46; 23-236).
WILSON, WILLIAM; Hampton, Va.; W2
(15-252).
WILSON, WILLIAM; Bible records, Mag-
nolia, Del.; Col (2-7; 7-1-6; 7-2-
4).
WILSON; Inscriptions, Dallas Co.,
Ala.; M (23-121).
WINANS, JOHN; Elizabeth, N. J.; A2
(68-139, 357).
WINDECKER, JACOB; Lowville, N. Y.;
S1 (36-422).
WING; (Will of John, 1699), Harwich,
Mass.; D (33-173).
WINN; Will of Thomas (1797); M (21-
133).
WINNE, PIETER; Kingston, N. Y.; A2
(70-159).
WINNE; Cherry Valley, Otsego Co., N.
Y.; B2 (13-36).
WINSLOW, JOHN; Boston, Mass.; Eng-
lish origin; S1 (19-534).
WINSLOW; notes; S4 (2-351).
WINSLOW; (will of Josiah), 1675; D
(34-33).
WINSOR, JOSHUA; Providence, R. I.;
S1 (24-115).
WINSOR; (Jeremiah), Smithfield, R.
I.; S1 (21-269).
WINSTON; Laurel Grove, Hanover Co.,
Va.; V3 (42-34); (will of William),
1781; V1 (19-219).

WINSTON; New Kent Co., Va.; V1 (20-99).
WINTHROP, JOHN; Marriage; A1 (88-301).
WINTOUR; Md.; X2 (7-38).
WISE, JOSEPH; Roxbury, Mass.; S1 (27-379); (Rev. John2, Ipswich); Y1 (81-201).
WISEMAN; N. C.; H1 (1-5).
WITBECK, JAN THOMASE; Albany, N. Y.; S1 (26-284).
WITHERS; Stafford, Va.; W2 (18-360); Z (68-493).
WITHERSPOON, ROBERT; Williamsburg, S. C.; S4 (2-117).
WITHERSPOON; (John), Thomaston, Me.; A1 (99-29).
WITHERSPOON; (John), Wilkes Co., N. C.; Z (78-499).
WITHINGTON, HENRY; Dorchester, Mass.; S1 (21-317).
WITMAN, JOHN; Reading, Pa.; S1 (24-90).
WITTEN; Cecil Co., Md.; N3 (37-117).
WODHULL, see Woodhull, Odell.
WOLCOTT, HENRY; Windsor, Conn.; S1 (9-791).
WOLCOTT; Oldenbarneveld, Oneida Co., N. Y.; B4 (17-32).
WOLCOTT; (Hannah Hawley-Nichols-Porter); B4 (14-13, 189).
WOLFE; (Samuel), Coshocton Co., Ohio; Dt (10-59, 103).
WOLL, JÖRGEN; New York, N. Y.; A2 (72-295).
WOMACK; Va.; V3 (43-268, 365).
WOOD, EDWARD; Charlestown, Mass.; A1 (99-77); (Thomas2), Rowley, Mass.; B4 (21-123).
WOOD, HENRY; Middleboro, Mass.; S1 (22-526).
WOOD, HENRY; Henrico, Va.; English origin; V3 (53-64).
WOOD, JOHN; Kingston, N. Y.; A2 (70-111).
WOOD, JOHN; Elizabeth City County, Va.; W2 (13-265).
WOOD, JONAS; Southampton, Huntington, N. Y.; English ancestry; B4 (11-148, 199).
WOOD, RICHARD; (Richard-Davis, Millville, N. J.); B5 (24-167).
WOOD, WILLIAM; Va.; W2 (12-140, 141).
WOOD, WILLIAM; Royal Oak, Mich.; Dt (4-181).
WOOD; Saratoga Co., N. Y., 1850 Census; M (34-117).
WOOD; (William, M. D.), Loudoun Co.,

Va.; X2 (11-33).
WOODBRIDGE, JOHN (REV.); Newbury, Mass.; S1 (20-400; 24-270).
WOODBURY, JOHN; Salem, Mass.; Z2 (14-75; 20-33); S1 (23-239).
WOODBURY, WILLIAM; Beverly, Mass.; S1 (34-629).
WOODFORD, THOMAS; Hartford, Conn.; Northampton, Mass.; S1 (26-558).
WOODHULL, RICHARD; Brookhaven, N. Y.; B4 (13-77; 14-237; 21-69).
WOODHULL; Mollington, co. Oxford, England; B4 (22-6).
WOODMAN, EDWARD and ARCHELAUS; Newbury, Mass.; English ancestry; A1 (97-281, 394).
WOODRUFF, JOHN; Southampton, N. Y.; English ancestry; Z3 (4-15-224); corrections of "Woodruffs of New Jersey"; Z3 (3-8-156).
WOODRUFF, MATTHEW; Farmington, Conn.; B2 (15-1).
WOODRUFF; (Ancestry of Wilford); U (24-13).
WOODS, MICHAEL; Va.; V3 (52-45); Dt (7-40).
WOODS, SAMUEL; (Daniel5), Corinth, Vt.; A1 (94-20).
WOODS, WILLIAM; Ireland; Baltimore, Md.; WF (1-220).
WOODS; (Michael), Goochland Co., Va.; V3 (51-366).
WOODSON, JOHN (DR.); Prince George Co., Va.; V3 (44-167); S1 (31-645); N3 (36-26).
WOODWARD, EZEKIEL; Ipswich, Mass.; S4 (1-241).
WOODWARD, HENRY; Northampton, Mass.; S1 (31-180).
WOODWARD, NATHANIEL; Boston, Mass.; S1 (23-503).
WOODWARD, THOMAS; Isle of Wight Co., Va.; English origin; V1 (26-91).
WOODWARD; Early settlers; W2 (14-178).
WOODWARD; Va.; V3 (41-76).
WOODWORTH, WALTER; (Abel), Lebanon, Conn.; Canaan, N. Y.; A1 (86-350).
WOOL, see Woll.
WOOLCOTT, JOHN; Kent, Md.; X1 (31-264).
WOOLDRIDGE, MICHAEL; Cuyahoga Co., Ohio; S1 (24-99).
WOOLLENS, JOSEPH; Philadelphia Co., Pa.; M (30-91).
WOOLLEY, URSULA (WODELL); Concord, Mass.; B4 (21-69).
WOOLSTON, JOHN; Burlington Co., N.

ABBE; (Jeremiah), East Windsor, Conn.; Dt (4-195).
ABBOTT; (William); A1 (89-292).
ABERCROMBIE; (James), Ala., S. C.; M (23-124).
ABERNATHY; (Robert), W. Va., Ohio; M (21-88).
ACKLEY; (Uriah); B5 (26-261).
ACREE; (Nathaniel-Benjamin), Va., Tenn.; A1 (100-252).
ADAMS; (Edward); X2 (6-27); (Edward), Dorchester Co., Md.; X2 (7-1); (Charles); X2 (6-37); (John); A1 (89-201); (Joseph), Me.; M (20-89); (Eli), Md., Ohio; M (28-40); (Philip-Collins); M (28-41); (Dr. Abel), New Marlboro, N. Y.; LI (1-119); (Kimble), Iowa; Z (70-1020); (Benjamin); Col (2-54); (William), Fairfax, Va.; M (28-89).
ADDISON; (William); B5 (21-382).
ADKINS; (Erastus); B2 (14-34); Dt (10-90).
AIKENS; (Wm.-James); B2 (17-32).
ALBRO; (John), R. I.; A1 (87-82).
ALEXANDER; (Ebenezer), Mass.; B4 (14-140).
ALLEN; (Gen. Elisha), Sanford, Me.; A1 (88-380); (Moses); A1 (90-375); (Parley), Dutchess Co., N. Y.; A1 (89-93); (Hezekiah), Fairfield, Conn.; B1 (13-40); (William P.); A1 (98-207); (John), Mellenville, N. Y.; Dt (9-10); (Daniel), R. I.; Z (69-628); (Thomas); Z (71-843); (Joseph), N. J.; Z (78-397); (William); M (20-89).
ALLISON; (John), Franklin County, Pa.; M (21-113).
ALMY; (Peleg); A1 (90-297).
AMES; (Benajah), Lyme, Conn.; B4 (13-197).
ANDERSON; (Robert); V1 (16-110); (William), Hanover Co., Va.; V3 (44-55); (John); Z (72-11-60).
ANDREWS; (Nathan); WF (1-144).
ANTERROCHES-D'; Elizabeth, N. J.; B1 (7-59, 62).
ARMSTRONG; Dt (8-118); (James); Orange Co., N. C.; Col (5-70).
ARNOLD; (David); Burkittsville, Md.; X2 (14-8); (George); B2 (12-19).
ASHTON; (John), King George Co., Va.; M (22-33).

ATEN; (Jan), New Brunswick, N. J.; B1 (13-42).
ATWOOD, JOHN; Mass., N. H.; M (22-30); (David), Alexandria, N. H.; B4 (10-229).
AYDELOTT; (George H.); Nelson Co., Ky.; P (13-99).
AYERS; (Robert); A2 (77-181); (Ezekiel), Woodbridge, N. J.; A1 (93-203); (Robert); A2 (76-126).

BABCOCK; (Madison E.), Brookfield, N. Y.; WF (1-143).
BACON; (Abel), Philadelphia; B5 (17-200); (Wilmon), Greenwich, N. J.; B5 (17-201, also 30-185); (Eber F.); A1 (90-203).
BADEAU; (Peter), N. Y.; B4 (11-234).
BADGER; (William), Va.; Z (71-844).
BAGGERLY; Md.; M (31-102).
BAILEY; (Ebenezer), Haverhill, Mass.; A1 (96-303).
BAIRD; (James); X2 (15-6).
BAKER; (Moses); B4 (12-118); (James), Mass., N. Y., Ohio; Dt (6-8); (Ezra); Dt (7-47); (Henry); X2 (16-41).
BALDWIN; (Thomas), Rehoboth, Mass.; A1 (91-389); (David, Abijah); LI (4-23.); (Ezra), Conn., Mass., Mich.; Dt (7-31); (Thomas), Conn., N. Y., Pa.; Ng (5-213).
BALL; (David), Kilmarnock, Va.; V3 (45-49); (John), Del.; E2 (1-22); (Nathan); Dt (5-187, see 177); (Charles C. P.); Dt (2-40).
BALLARD; (Horace); Dt (8-15).
BANCKER; (Gerrit), Schenectady, N. Y.; E4 (4-121).
BANNERMAN; (George), Fla.; M (21-67).
BANTA; (John); Z3 (56-57).
BARBER; (Luke-Philip), Md.; M (22-89); Inscriptions, St. Mary's Co., Md.; M (22-93); (Gideon); B5 (30-202); (Aaron); Dt (3-53); (Benjamin), R. I., N. Y.; E3 (8-250); (Rev. Jonathan); Springfield, Mass.; A2 (75-122); (John), Groton, Conn.; A2 (75-123); (Gideon); B5 (26-151).
BARCALOW; (Garret); Churchville, Pa.; A2 (74-101).

BARKER; (Mark); Al (89-287).
BARNES;(Thomas); P (13-112); (Jonathan), Yarmouth, Mass.; P (13-121); (Enos), Litchfield, Conn.; M (29-22).
BARNEY; (Cyrenius), Mass.; Al (96-92).
BARNITZ; (Jacob); X2 (10-4); (Charles A.); P (13-255).
BARRETT; (Joseph); E3 (6-442); (George B.); Dt (10-72).
BARRY; Cameron, Mo.; Col (6-101).
BARTLETT;(Stephen B.); Cheshire Co., N. H.; Ng (2-42); family chart (Oliver-Barker); Rochester, N. Y.; Ng (2-43); (Ichabod); Dt (2-20).
BARTRAM; (Thomas); Pa.; P (13-101).
BATDORF; (Casper), Lancaster Co., Pa.; M (23-87).
BATEMAN; (Adrian), Cedarville, N. J.; M (21-108); (Reuben); B5 (23-50).
BATES; (Isaac), Warren, Conn.; Al (94-204); (Nathan); Dt (10-102); Thomas; Z (73-8-84); (Nehemiah), Hingham, Mass.; Dt (6-135).
BAXTER; (Samuel), Zanesville, Ohio; Col (2-72); (Samuel); X2 (12-37).
BAYSE; (William); N3 (31-341).
BEACH; (Daniel), Conn.; M (20-11); (Daniel); Bl (10-22).
BEALL; (Samuel); M (24-87).
BEAN; (Durrel), Gilmanton, N. H.; Al (86-460); (Phinehas), N. H.; B2 (13-10); (Thomas); O (5-399); (Ahab); Z (73-3-87).
BEARCE; (Geo. W.); Al (95-93).
BEARDSLEY; (Levi), Otsego Co., N. Y.; Dt (3-104).
BEARMOR; (Lewis), N. J.; M (31-88).
BEATTY; (Robert); Al (89-93).
BEAUCHAMP; (Milton), Ky.; Al (94-91).
BECK; (Lancelot); Z (79-556).
BECKER; (Frederick), Pa.; P (11-291).
BEE; (Ephraim), N. J.; Bl (9-40).
BEEBE; (Heman), Canaan, Conn.; E3 (3-105).
BEECHER; (Darius), Woodbridge, Conn.; Dt (9-35).
BEEMER; (William), Sussex Co., N. J.; Dt (6-92).
BEERS; (Nathan, New Haven, Conn.);B4 (17-233).
BEIDELMAN; (Moses-DePew), Chemung Co., N. Y.; Dt (9-70).
BELL; (Charles); Col (6-118).
BELLSON; (Vetter); Z (72-6-80).
BEMAN; (Anson), Auburn, Ohio; M (32-84).

BENEDICT; (Norman); A2 (77-30).
BENHAM; (Gamaliel); Al (89-287); (Lyman), Bristol, Conn.; B4 (22-165).
BENJAMIN; (Benonia), Fairfield Co., Ohio; O (3-274, 275).
BENNER; (David); Al (89-287).
BENNETT; (Maccabees); B4 (11-233); (Isaiah S.), N. J.; M (22-42); (Albert); Dt (7-32).
BENTLEY; (Stephen-Treat); E3 (3-9).
BERRY; (John); X2 (13-31); (John), Essex Co., N. J.; P (13-273).
BERRYHILL; (Samuel G.); O (1-9).
BETTS; (Aaron); Al (88-93).
BIDLEMAN; (Christian), N. Y., Mich.; Dt (4-189).
BIGGS; (James M.); Col (2-71); (Andrew); Col (6-61).
BILLINGS; (Chester); Al (89-391).
BINGHAM; (Truman), Lempster, N. H.; B4 (13-197).
BIRDSALL; (Lewis), N. Y.; A2 (64-253); (Samuel); A2 (65-120); (Jacob); B2 (14-6).
BIRDSONG; (John); Z (71-845).
BIRNEY; (James-Gillspie); Al (89-91).
BISHOP; (Luther); Dt (7-37).
BITTING; (Ludwig), Pa.; S3 (13-4-7).
BIXBY; (Taylor); Dt (6-119).
BLACKMER; Bennington, Vt.; E3 (1-69); (Samuel), Conn., Vt.; E3 (3-57); (Joseph), Westmoreland, N. Y.; E3 (3-122).
BLACKWOOD; (James-Monroe), Ohio; O (6-518).
BLAIR; (Samuel, Jr.); WF (1-48).
BLAISDELL; (Ebenezer), also (Elijah); Al (90-204, 205).
BLAKE; J (37-38, 65); (Edward); Ll (1-38); (Samuel-Parkman); Al (95-392).
BLAKELEY; (Jotham); Dt (10-102).
BLAND; (Charles), Ky.; Z (71-559).
BLASER; (Peter), Berks Co., Pa.; M (32-25).
BLEDSOE; (T. W. M.); S3 (11-4-14).
BLODGET; (Alden), Stafford, Conn.; B2 (11-36); (Joshua), Stafford, Conn.; B2 (11-37).
BLOUNT; (Henry); Dt (6-22).
BLUNT; (William), Isle of Wight Co., Va.; W2 (13-189).
BOATWRIGHT; (James), S. C.; Z (71-1028).
BOERUM; (Martin); A2 (76-74).
BOGERT; (John-Griffith); A2 (75-102).

BOHON; (Garrett); N3 (31-342).
BOLLES; (Obed), Lisbon, N. Y.; Z (70-710).
BOLTON; (Joseph L.), Dover, N. H.; Al (89-204).
BOONE; (Humphrey), W. Va.; M (20-78).
BORDWELL; (Enoch); Ng (4-31).
BOTTOM; N3 (31-343).
BOULDIN; Va.; Vl (14-110).
BOULT; (Peter); Al (90-92).
BOURN; (Henry); Dt (9-137).
BOUSQUETTE; (George H.); Detroit, Mich.; Dt (10-95).
BOUTON; (Esaias), Norwalk, (Nathan), Troy; Al (87-84).
BOWEN; (John), N. Y., Pa., Neb.; B2 (19-23); (Noah); Al (87-393); (Joseph), Salem Co., N. J.; X2 (5-17).
BOWIE; (William); X2 (11-40).
BOWLES; (Jonathan), Lisbon, N. H.; Z (70-711); (John), Washington Co., Md.; Z (70-1021).
BOWLING; (Robert); X2 (9-28).
BOWMAN; (Abraham), Ky.; W2 (20-147); (Peleg R.), Vt., N. Y.; Dt (3-105); (Julius); Ng (4-55); (James H.); Ng (4-121).
BOYNTON; (John G.); Al (87-394).
BOYS; (John); Z (69-561).
BRACKETT; (James), Braintree, Mass.; E3 (5-329).
BRADFORD; (Zephaniah); Al (95-93); (Elijah); Ll (1-46); (James G.), Ohio; B4 (11-231); (Charles); Col (4-27).
BRADY; (Hugh), Huntington County, Pa.; P (12-79).
BRAINERD; (Jehu), Johnson, Ohio; Dt (4-152).
BRANCH; (Peter R.); Dt (3-10).
BRASHEARS; (Robert-Samuel), Md., N. C.; Z (80-153).
BRAY; (David-Sutton); Z3 (64-45).
BRAZIER; (Daniel); Al (89-200).
BREADY; (Solomon); P (13-102).
BRIDGES; (George), James City County; X2 (9-25).
BRIGGS; (Thomas) Dartmouth, Mass.; Al (91-380); (George-Wilson), Cedar Falls, Iowa; Col (1 No. 6).
BRIGHAM; (William), Princeton, Mass.; P (13-264).
BRININSTOOL; (Jacob), Blenheim, N. Y.; E3 (3-107).
BRISCOE; (Leonard); Z (73-5-89).
BROCK; (Mathew D.), Howell, Mich.; Dt (4-189); (John), Orange Co., N.

Y.; Dearborn, Mich.; Dt (4-190); (Barnet), Duplin Co., N. C.; M (21-63).
BRODHEAD; (Rev. Jacob); A2 (71-137).
BROMWELL; (H. P. H.); Col (2-34).
BROOKS; (Henry), Cumberland County, N. J.; M (21-109); (Sheppard), N. J.; B5 (30-206); (Thomas); B5 (30-216); (Solomon), Grafton, Mass.; Al (93-293).
BROWER; (Jacob P.), Dodge Co., Wis.; WF (1-215).
BROWN; (Lemuel); Al (89-386); (Simeon S.); B5 (18-292); (Parshal); B5 (20-251); (Hezekiah), Conn.; E3 (3-169); (Othniel), Stafford, Conn.; Al (91-374); (George O.), Fairfield, Me.; Col (6-10; also 1 No. 9); (Lewis F.), Ohio, Ind.; Col (2-38); (David), Woodbridge, N. J.; Bl (13-43); (Moses), Pa.; B2 (19-24); (Daniel), LI (3-86).
BROWNING; (Joseph); B4 (13-194); (Jeremiah), R. I.; Al (87-81).
BRUCE; (James); M (20-67); (Eli M.); B5 (21-391).
BRUNER; (Daniel), W. Va.; Col (1 No. 5); (Abram); Z (79-187).
BRUSH; (Alexander); Huntington, N. Y.; LI (3-56); (Nehemiah), LI (2-23); (Samuel), New Brunswick, N. J.; Bl (13-43).
BRYANT; (Bayley D.), Ky.; M (30-16); (John); X2 (9-26).
BUCKINGHAM; (Isaac), Baltimore, Md.; M (22-45).
BUCKLAND; (Timothy); Dt (3-190).
BULLARD; (Daniel), Canada, Ill.; Col (4-29).
BULLIS; (Geo. W.), Kinderhook, N. Y.; Dt (4-33).
BUMP; (Albert H.); Dt (3-212); (Benjamin), Greenfield, N. Y.; Dt (4-132).
BUNKER; (William); Al (94-203).
BURGE; (David), N. H.; B5 (17-202).
BURKHART; (Henry); Monroe Co., N. Y.; Dt (10-94, 111).
BURLINGHAM; (Andrew J.), N. Y., Va., Ill.; Dt (7-114).
BURLINGHAM; (Hopkins), Cranston, R. I.; Dt (9-125).
BURR; (Ozias); Al (96-196).
BURRELL; (Dexter); Dt (9-46).
BURROUGHS; (Isaac), Bridgeton, N. J.; M (21-110); (Davidson); Dt (3-211); (Col. Geo. T.), Mich.; Dt (5-151).
BURT; (David); E3 (5-329).

BURTON; (Richard, Conn.); M (20-
11); (Simon); Ng (2-31); (John-
Williams and Robert); Z (73-3-
74).
BURWELL; (Daniel), Milford, Conn.;
B4 (14-21).
BUSH; (Jeremiah), Clark Co., Ky.; Z
(70-209).
BUSHMAN; (Jacob); Ng (4-119).
BUTLER; (David C.), Pawnee City,
Neb.; B2 (14-24); (Jesse), Pompey,
N. Y.; Dt (10-35); (Norman G.),
Md.; X2 (17-39); (Benjamin), Rocky
Hill, Conn.; B2 (17-9); (Henry),
Baltimore Co., Md.; X2 (15-22);
(Joseph), Md.; X2 (16-65).
BUTTRICK; (Joseph), Concord, Mass.;
S3 (11-3-11).
BUTTS; (Thomas); E3 (4-41).
BUZBY; (Daniel), Downe, N. J.; B1
(14-24).
BYNUM; (Benjamin), Pitt Co., N. C.;
M (32-45).
BYRD; Va.; V3 (40-285, 374).
BYRNSIDE; (John), W. Va.; Z (70-58).

CALEF; (Stephen), Dorset, Vt.; Col
(1 No. 9).
CALKINS; (Simon), N. Y., Mich.; Dt
(9-98).
CANER; (Adron); Dt (5-43).
CANN; (John); P (13-265).
CANNON; (Isaac), S. C.; also (Col.
Geo.-Speake); M (25-69); (Le
Grand), Troy, N. Y.; Al (87-85).
CARD; R. I.; M (32-31).
CARLE; (Jacob); A2 (71-137).
CARLISLE; (Lewis-Moore), Russell-
ville, Ky.; Ng (4-117); (John,
James); N3 (31-343).
CARLL; (Silas); LI (1-121); (Alonzo
S.); A2 (77-169).
CARLOUGH; (Henry J.); Dt (9-78).
CARMAN; (James); Dt (5-165).
CARPENTER; (George W.), Attleboro,
Mass.; Ohio; Wis.; WF (1-218);
(Edward); P (14-178); (Hope); Dt
(5-57).
CARSON; (Thomas), Butler Co., Ky.;
V1 (15-255); (John); P (14-199).
CARTER; (John), Va.; V3 (42-163);
(Edward), Woburn, Mass.; Al (93-
390); (Elisha), Fitchburg, Mass.;
M (22-5).
CARTTER; (Harlehigh); Dt (10-81).
CARVER; (Timothy), Carmel, N. Y.;
B2 (20-2).
CARY; (Abel); O (1-80); Ohio; M (23-

67).
CAUTHORN; (Amos); M (31-28).
CENTRY; (William), Pa.; M (25-124).
CHALMERS; (Thomas-Hardie); P (14-
60).
CHAMBERLAIN; (Sullivan); WF (1-43);
(Luther), Kent, Conn.; Dt (6-74);
(Oliver-Perry), Belfast, N. Y.;
Dt (9-22).
CHAMBERLIN; (Laurel S.); N. Y.; Dt
(3-106); (Moses), Lunenburg, Vt.;
Dt (7-13).
CHAMBERS; (David); P (13-263).
CHANCE; (William), Md.; X2 (8-27).
CHAPMAN; (Jedediah), Westbrook,
Conn.; B4 (13-111); (Elias), Ash-
ford, Conn.; Al (100-333); (Wil-
liam), Groton, Conn.; T8 (4-30; 5-
2, 10; 6-11).
CHASE; (Ebenezer); Al (90-95).
CHATFIELD; (David), N. Y., Ohio; B4
(11-237).
CHERINGTON; (James B.); P (14-181,
301).
CHILD; (Samuel); Al (89-386); (John),
Philadelphia, Pa.; LI (4-24);
(John), Conn., N. H.; Z (70-716).
CHILTON; (John R.), Vt.; B4 (11-
231).
CHURCH; (Reuben P.); Ky.; Col (5-
69); (Ezra), Vt., Mass.; Dt (2-
140); (Asa), Mansfield, Conn.; Dt
(3-119); (Benjamin); Dt (3-39);
(John K.); L1 (5-28).
CHURCHILL; (Jonas), Shelby, N. Y.;
Dt (8-50).
CLAGGETT; (Charles), Md.; M (32-43).
CLARK; (Abner), Pa.; Al (89-380);
(William), Brookhaven, N. Y.; B4
(9-90); (Samuel); Al (89-296);
(Ephraim), Southington Conn.); B4
(10-54; also 14-140); (Sidney-Zi-
na), Northmoreland, Pa.; M (22-94);
(Elisha), Pawlet, Vt.; Al (90-380);
(Ephraim); Al (90-376); (John); O
(1-9); (Jeremiah), Milford, N. J.;
Col (2-86); (William), Albany Co.,
N. Y.; Dt (3-94); (Henry), Greene
Co., N. Y.; WF (1-145); (Charles),
Kingston, Ontario; Dt (6-37); (Lou-
is), Hanover City, Va.; M (31-9);
(William), Albany Co., N. Y.; Ng
(5-212); (Jeremiah); M (32-111);
(James), Monroe Co., Va.; Z (70-
58); (William), Long Island; Z
(74-7-56); (Daniel); B5 (27-373).
CLARKSON; (James), Woodbridge, N. J.;
Al (90-299).

CLEMENT; (Obadiah), Alexandria, N.
H.; B4 (10-230).
COBB; (Binney), Vt.; A1 (100-67);
(Herman); A1 (93-393); (John M.);
Dt (2-161).
COBIA; (Daniel), S. C.; M (21-59).
COBURN; (James F.), Salem, Mass.;
A1 (89-201).
COCKE; (Samuel), Goochland County,
Va.; M (20-12).
COCKS; (Henry), North Brunswick, N.
J.; B1 (13-45).
CODINGTON; N. J.; A1 (90-299).
COE; (William); A2 (71-139).
COFFIN; (Tristram), N. H.; A1 (87-
89).
COGSWELL; New Preston, Conn.; E3 (3-
170).
COLE; (James) Va.; V3 (40-374); (Jo-
seph), New London, Conn.; Dt (7-
17); (Isaiah), N. J., N. Y.; Dt (7-
38).
COLES; (Nathaniel); A2 (65-121; 75-
126).
COLLINGS; (Andrew); P (13-106).
COLLINS; (Andrew), Del.; X2 (6-13,
25); (John); B1 (20-70); (Jesse),
Green Briar Ridge, Va.; W2 (14-
242).
COLLYER; (Joel); B2 (10-65).
COLMAN; (Phineous), Newington, N. H.;
A1 (96-90).
COMBS; (John L.), Fauquier Co., Va.;
M (22-34).
COMFORT; (Richard); A1 (90-376).
COMINGO; (John); N3 (31-344).
COMPTON; (John); Z (73-5-89); (Je-
rome); Dt (9-127).
COMSTOCK; (Aaron); Dt (3-53).
CONANT; (Levi), Cambridge, Mass.; B2
(10-52); (Charles); Dt (5-86).
CONGDON; (John), Pownal, Vt.; B2 (12-
31).
CONGER; (David); A2 (77-181).
CONKLIN; (Joseph), Penfield, N. Y.;
Dt (8-16).
CONSTANTINE; (Joel), Ashburnham,
Mass.; B5 (21-332).
COOKE, COOK; (William), Northumber-
land, Va.; P (11-286); (John), Ply-
mouth, Mass.; S3 (12-3-9); (Conover-
Rezo); Col (6-4); (Elisha), Mass.,
N. J.; D (33-1); (David); B5 (18-
256); (Joseph), Shrewsbury, N. J.;
B1 (9-38); (Green); B1 (9-39);
(William), Warren Co., N. J.; M
(22-93); (Elisha), Sussex Co., N.
J.; M (22-41); (John); E3 (5-281).

COOLEY; (Jacob), Springfield, Mass.;
Dt (8-83).
COOMBS; (Asa); Z (75-11-68).
COOPER; (Lawrence-Entwisle); A1 (89-
202); (Charles); W2 (12-133);
(William); A1 (90-377); (Thomas);
A1 (100-66).
COPLAND; Bible and cemetery records
(Charles-Robert); Dt (7-127).
CORBIN; (George W.); O (3-246).
CORBYN; (Joseph P.); Dt (4-41).
CORDES; (John); J (41-39).
CORIELL, CORIEL; (Isaac); M (25-91);
(David); Z3 (64-44); B1 (14-55).
CORSON; (Robert), Cape May, N. J.;
L1 (1-39); (Peter), Cape May; L1
(3-29).
CORWIN; (David), Cutchogue, N. Y.;
LI (1-17).
COSINE; (Peter), Adams Co., Pa.; B1
(13-46).
COTTON; (Elihu), Middletown, Conn.;
B4 (14-18).
COURTNEY; (Thomas); X2 (14-64).
COVENHOVEN; B1 (13-72).
COVERT; (John); Dt (6-101).
COWEN; (Edward), Blair Co., Pa.; M
(33-64).
COX; (George A.), Fla.; M (28-42);
(John); P (14-186); (Moses); Z
(70-208).
CRANE; (Joseph); Dt (8-107).
CRANSON; (Caleb), Ashfield, Mass.;
A1 (98-282, 360).
CRAWFORD; (Benjamin); L1 (5-23).
CRENSHAW; (Nicholas); M (32-111).
CRESSE; (Jacob); L1 (5-26).
CREWS; (David), Hanover County, Va.;
M (21-69); (James), N. C.; M (22-
37).
CRITTENDEN; (Chauncey); E3 (2-153).
CROCKETT; (John); M (30-150).
CRONKITE; (Stephen); LI (1-87).
CROOM; (Jesse), N. C.; M (21-118).
CROSS; (Jason), Ypsilanti, Mich.;
B4 (9-153).
CROSSETT; (Richard); Dt (5-207).
CROSSMAN; (John H.); Ng (4-121).
CROUCH; (John M.), Sharon, Pa.; Ng (6-278).
CROWELL; (Seth), N. J.; B4 (10-126,
231).
CRUSER; (Abraham), New Brunswick, N.
J.; B1 (13-92).
CULVER; (James); B2 (10-44, 65);
(James), Livingston Co., N. Y.;
Ng (4-70).
CUMMINGS; (William A.); E3 (7-122).
CUNNINGHAM; (James); Boston; A1 (95-

393); (David), Kingston, Vineland;
B5 (21-323).
CURRIER; (H. M.), Haverhill, Mass.;
Al (89-199).
CURTIS; (Allen), Conn.; B4 (15-90);
(John), Conn., Vt., Canada; B4
(15-91); (Amos), Conn., Vt.; B4
(15-87).
CUSHING; (Samuel), Hingham, Mass.,
Cicero, N. Y.; Dt (8-50).
CUSHMAN; (Seth); A2 (67-368);(Ethi-
el); E3 (6-507).
CUSHNEY; (Richard H.), Johnstown,
N. Y.; E3 (4-121).
CUTTING; (Chauncey), Lyme, N. H.,
and Stanstead, Canada; Al (89-
290, 292).

DAINGERFIELD; (Le Roy), Va.; W2 (12-
41).
DAKIN; (Samuel-Dana), Utica, N. Y.;
Al (88-95).
DANA; (Schuyler), Vt.; Z (71-842).
DANIEL; (James-Cunningham); Z (71-
466).
DANN; (Jesse C.); Ng (3-132); (Hen-
ry A.); Ng (3-133).
DANNER; (Samuel), Chester, Pa.; Z
(71-1028).
DARBY; (Benjamin); Z (66-671).
DATER; (Philip); M (32-112).
DAVID; (John), Pa.; M (24-43).
DAVIS; M (22-64); (William), Dinwid-
die Co., Va.; W2 (16-98); (James
E.); N3 (31-344); (William), N.
C.; M (21-70); (Meredith, Ignati-
us); X2 (8-17, 29, 41); (John-
Maynard), Charleston, S. C.; J
(39-102); (Philip), Conn.; B4 (11-
55); (James); V3 (49-375); (Jo-
seph), Pa., Ohio; O (4-367); (Samuel B.), Logan Co., Ky.; M (30-
39, 50); (Peter); N. J.; M (31-
89); (Nathan), Farmington, Conn.;
Ng (3-226); (Samuel); Plymouth,
Pa.; P (14-65); (Thomas), Ala.;
Z (72-6-79); (John), Washington
Co., Va.; M (22-36); (Joshua); B2
(12-11); (Eliezer), Holden, Mass.;
Dt (3-16-31, 49, 71, 103); (Abisha); B5 (27-370); (Richard); B1
(19-86); (David); Dt (8-118).
DAWLEY; (Christopher-Harrington); E3
(6-425).
DAWSON; (Thomas); O (4-367); (William); J (41-40).
DEAN; (Isaac), Adams, Mass.; Al (100-
67); (Israel); B2 (16-21).

DECROLYER; (Joseph); Al (90-377).
DEGARMO; (B2 (10-44).
DEHART; (William W.), N. J.; M (31-
91).
DEMAREST; (David), Hackensack, N. J.;
B1 (11-1).
DEMERITT; (Ebenezer), N. H.; Al (87-
89).
DEMING; (Elijah); E3 (8-201).
DENIKE; (Robert); Dt (6-21).
DENNIS; (George); Dt (9-121).
DENSMORE; (Horace), N. H.; Al (89-
198).
DEPUY; (Jacobus); E3 (6-522).
DETRICH; (Ludwig), Pa.; M (25-124).
DEUEL; (Timothy), Dartmouth, Mass.;
B2 (15-35).
DEWEES; (John W.); Dt (6-40).
DEWEY; (Truman C.), Ellisburgh, N.
Y.; Dt (5-160); (David); E3 (6-
442).
DEZENG; (Frederick-Augustus), New
York; Al (89-389).
DIBBLE; (Samuel); Danbury, Conn.; B4
(19-117).
DICKERMAN; (Benoni), Ohio; B4 (10-
235).
DICKERSON; (Charles), Ovid, N. Y.;
Dt (5-104, 100).
DIFFENDERFFER; (Michael); X2 (14-40,
53; 15-4, 18).
DILLARD; (Joseph), Amherst County,
Va.; W2 (13-46).
DILLWYN, WILLIAM; (P (14-185).
DIMICK; (David); Al (89-293).
DINGLEY; (Abner); Al (89-398).
DISNEY; (Josiah-Rutter), Md.; X1 (29-
329); (Thomas); M (20-115).
DIX; (Jonathan), Waltham, Mass.; B1
(7-63).
DIXON; (John); A2 (71-139); (James-
Payson), Lebanon, Me.; Al (97-301);
(Thomas); Ng (4-70).
DOANE; (Joseph); Dt (2-62).
DOBBINS; (William N.), Bedford Co.,
Va.; O (3-274).
DONHAM; R. I.; Al (87-82).
DOPP; (Peter); Al (90-378).
DOWDNEY; M (20-69).
DOWNEY; (William, James), Pa.; M (25-
121, 122).
DOWNING; (David); Dt (5-159).
DOWNS; (Thomas), Ky., Ind.; X2 (4-
19, 27).
DRAGOO; (William); Z (72-9-89).
DRAKE; (Aaron); Al (90-298); (James),
Orange Co., N. Y.; B4 (23-187);
(Isaac-John); Dt (3-78).

DRAPER; (John), Sussex County, Del.;
E2 (1-31).
DRAWBAUGH; (George), Pa.; M (32-26).
DUBOIS; (Solomon); New York; A2 (73-287).
DUDLEY; (Guilford), Caroline Co.,
Va.; M (32-112).
DUNBAR; (Hamilton), Va., Ky.; M (29-27; 30-15); (James); J (41-30).
DUNHAM; (David-Gage); B1 (13-95);
(Samuel); Piscataway, N. J.; B1
(13-96); (Lewis); A2 (77-74);
(John L.); Dt (8-118).
DUNN; (William), Hartford, Vt.; M
(33-64); (Peter R.); N3 (31-345);
(John); Z (73-1-65).
DUPRÉ; (Thomas J. J.); J (39-81).
DUPUY; (Saffarine), Auburn, N. Y.;
A1 (90-378).
DURBOROW; (John); Baltimore, Md.;
WF (1-221).
DURKEE; (Wilks); Dt (6-120).
DUVALL; (John), Md.; M (29-71).
DWELLE; (Alphonso), Greenwich, N. Y.;
Z (74-5-37).
DYE; (William, Thomas), Stonington,
Conn.; Brookfield, N. Y.; WF (1-215); (Ezekiel); Dt (4-170).

EARL; (Gilberthorpe), Burlington, N.
J.; B1 (9-39); (Marmaduke); E3 (3-41).
EARLE; (Frederic); Dt (9-7).
EAST; (Isham), Stokes Co., N. C.;
Col (1 No. 6).
EASTON; (Robert); E3 (7-122).
EATON; (Joseph H.); Dt (8-64).
EBERLY; (John); O (3-245).
EDDOWES; England, Philadelphia; A1
(90-83, 92).
EDGERTON; (John M.); Dt (10-54).
EDMONDS; (Benjamin); B1 (13-96);
(Jeremiah); Cape May, N. J.; P (13-118).
EDMONSTON; B5 (17-154).
EDMUNDS; (Downs); L1 (1-44); (will
of Downs), Cape May, 1804; L1 (5-18); (Enoch); L1 (5-25).
EDWARDS; (Nathaniel); B5 (20-280);
(Robert), Northumberland Co., Va.;
W2 (21-406).
EELLS; (Nathaniel), Conn.; B4 (11-232); A1 (97-197).
EGBERT; (Enos), Elizabeth, N. J.; B1
(7-110).
ELDREDGE; (Killey); A1 (94-299).
ELDRIDGE; (William); P (13-116).
ELIAS; (Francis S.), Brattleboro,

Vt.; Ng (2-164).
ELLIOTT; K2 (20-313); (John-Tindle),
Ind.; Z (74-5-37).
ELLIS; (John); A1 (90-379); (Zaccheus), Middleboro, Mass.; M (29-24);
(Myron-Hawley), Saline, Mich.; Dt
(5-151); (Isaac), Harwich, Mass.;
B5 (19-120); (James); A1 (92-94).
ELY; (John G.); Middlesex Co., N.
J.; B1 (14-20); (Francis A.); A2
(76-76).
EMMONS; (William), Pa.; M (24-43).
ENGLE; Washington Co., Md.; M (25-98).
ENGLISH; (James M.); B5 (18-231).
ENLOW; (Jeremiah), Baltimore County,
Md.; X2 (3-30).
ENOS; (Newman); A1 (90-379).
ERGOOD; (Jesse), D. C.; M (25-86).
ESKRIDGE; (William), Northumberland
Co., Va.; W2 (21-407).
ETHERIDGE; (Samuel), Williamstown,
Mass.; E3 (3-138); (Samuel), N. Y.;
Mich.; Dt (4-75).
EUSTIS; (Joseph); B4 (17-61).
EVANS; (George W.); O (5-398); (Elias), South Reading, Mass.; A1 (87-90); (James); Dt (9-126); (Samuel), Pa., Mich.; Dt (8-66).
EVEREST; (Joseph), Salisbury, Conn.;
A2 (77-35).
EVERETT; (Joseph), Cecil Co., Md.;
V1 (28-184).
EVERY; (John), Pa.; M (24-43).
EWING; (Thomas); B5 (27-373).

FAESCH; (John-Jacob), Morris Co., N.
J.; B1 (14-21).
FAIRBANK; (Pearley); Col (1 No. 5).
FAIRCHILD; (Thomas); Z (72-10-98).
FAIRFIELD; (Stephen); B2 (14-19);
(John), Pittsfield, Mass.; B2 (17-10).
FAIRMAN; (Harry); Dt (8-109).
FALLEN; (William-James), Philadelphia, Pa.; B5 (27-289).
FARNSWORTH; (Joel), Washington, N.
H.; Wis.; WF (1-217).
FARRINGTON; (Lewis); A1 (93-394).
FAUNCE; (Asa), Me.; A1 (87-90).
FAUVER; (George), Tompkins Co., N.
Y.; Dt (9-91).
FEDTER; (Peter), Pa.; M (26-23).
FEEKS; (Charles), N. Y.; A2 (64-39).
FELLOWS; (Philip), Buffalo, N. Y.;
E3 (2-90).
FENDALL; (Thomas D.); A1 (89-92).
FENTON; (Edwin), Stafford, Conn.; B5

(19-39).
FERGUSON; (John); A2 (77-130).
FERNALD; (Archelaus); A1 (90-82).
FERRIS; (John), Dutchess Co., N. Y.;
    WF (1-83).
FIDLER; (Daniel), Allentown, N. J.;
    B1 (14-23).
FIELD; (Richard-Harrison), Kansas
    City, Mo.; Col (1 No. 6); (John
    A.), D. C.; M (26-24); (John, Jere-
    miah); A2 (72-47).
FILLER; (Joseph), Dublin, Ohio; O
    (4-354).
FINCH; (Caswell), Franklin Co., N.
    C.; M (29-24).
FINK; (James M.); A1 (90-380).
FISH; (Thomas), Dartmouth, Mass., Ob-
    long, N. Y.; S3 (14-2-14; 14-3-7);
    (Benjamin), Trenton, N. J.; B5 (18-
    345).
FISHER; (Joshua); P (13-254); (John),
    Yates Co., N. Y.; A1 (97-294).
FISKE; (Nathan); S3 (12-3-9).
FITCH; (William); A1 (90-380); (Dr.
    Samuel), Acton, Mass.; A1 (90-
    395).
FITZHUGH; (Philip), Caroline County,
    Va.; V3 (40-175); V1 (13-273);
    Prince William County, Va.; V3
    (40-375); King George County, Va.;
    V1 (16-44).
FITZ-RANDOLPH; (James); B1 (8-69);
    (Gilbert); A1 (91-192).
FLEMING; (Daniel), Ohio; O (8-671).
FOARD, RICHARD; (Charles-Tilden);
    Cecil Co., Md.; M (32-72).
FOOTE; (Reuben-Clark); Ng (4-118);
    (Nathaniel); E3 (5-345).
FORD; (John); Cecil Co., Md.; M (33-
    40); (William); Z3 (50-294); (Nor-
    man); B2 (12-20); (John-Odell);
    B4 (10-230).
FOREMAN; Wilmington, Del.; A1 (89-
    87).
FORKER; (Samuel); P (13-268).
FORMAN; (Robert), S. Amboy, N. J.;
    B1 (14-23).
FORTSON; (William), Ala.; Z (80-
    583).
FOSHAY; (William); A2 (75-37).
FOSS; (Levi), Leeds, Me.; A1 (100-
    69).
FOSSELMAN; (Philip), Pa.; A2 (67-
    367).
FOSTER; (Nathan), Barnstable, Mass.;
    D (32-177); (William); P (13-108);
    (Stewart), Winthrop, Me.; WF (1-
    146); (Henry); A2 (76-92); (Lem-

uel), Pittsfield, Mich.; Dt (5-
    109); (Alforde); Z (80-379).
FOUST; (John); M (20-117).
FOWLER; (Adolphus); A1 (96-200).
FOX; (James-Lenoir), Burke Co., N.
    C.; Col (5-100).
FRANCIS; (Joseph), Clermont County;
    M (20-69); (David); P (14-303).
FRANKS; (Isaac C.); O (3-245).
FREDERICK; (Thomas), Lisbon, Ohio;
    Dt (4-63).
FREEMAN; (Elisha), Norwich, Vt.; B4
    (10-127); (Zophar), N. J.; B4 (10-
    231); David), S. C.; M (21-62);
    (Samuel), Kennebunkport, Me.; A1
    (95-393).
FRENCH; (Thomas, 1738); A1 (86-112);
    (David); A1 (89-203); (Stephen B.);
    A2 (77-140); (John-Owen), Wood-
    bridge, Conn.; Dt (9-35).
FRINK; (Joseph-Colton), Scipio, N.
    Y.; A1 (89-93; 90-297).
FRISBEE; (Marcus W.); Delhi, N. Y.;
    Dt (6-46).
FROST; (Joseph), Conn.; E3 (3-170).
FULLER; (Joseph), Wrentham, Mass.;
    Westmoreland, N. H.; B2 (20-21);
    (Luther K.); B2 (20-22); (Alonzo
    D.); Dt (2-40); (Samuel), N. Y.;
    B2 (10-66); (Abial), Attleboro,
    Mass.; B4 (13-196); (Elijah), N.
    Y.; B4 (13-196).
FUNK; (John, Henry), Pa.; M (25-
    123, 124).

GAGER; (John), Clinton N. Y.; A1
    (89-381); (William), Clinton, N.
    Y.; A1 (94-203).
GAIGE; (Henry W.), Oneida Co., N. Y.;
    Dt (7-63).
GAILLARD; (Theodore); J (41-39).
GAINES; (Heirom), Va., Ga., Miss.;
    M (29-107).
GANONG; (Jeremiah); B2 (20-1).
GARDINER; (James); A1 (97-391).
GARDNER; (Joseph); B2 (15-30).
GARRETT; (Robert), Miss.; M (29-
    108); (William); B5 (23-61).
GARRISON; (Benjamin); Z (70-136).
GARVIN; (John), Va., Ky.; Col (2-8;
    also 6-11).
GARWOOD; (Daniel); B1 (20-70).
GAYER; (Percy-Frederick); X2 (12-
    37).
GAYLORD; (Theodore); A1 (89-287).
GEORGE; (Benjamin), Pa., Ohio; M (24-
    43); (James B.); X2 (10-39);
    (John); X2 (11-1, 17); (Sampson),

Cecil Co., Md.; M (32-70); (Stephen), Cecil Co., Md.; M (33-41).
GERMOND; (Barnard); Z (69-562).
GERRISH; (William), Berwick, Me.; Al (94-203).
GESNER; (William H.); LI (4-26).
GIBSON; (Wm. B.); Philadelphia; Al (90-388).
GIDLEY; (Hezekiah); E3 (2-58).
GIFFORD; (Hubbard), N. Y.; Z (72-8-86).
GILBERT; (Thomas); Al (97-394).
GILL; Boston, Mass.; Al (89-198); (Matthew); P (14-63).
GILLASPAY; (James); P (14-198).
GILLESPIE; (William); Dt (10-53).
GILLETT; (John), Ogden, N. Y.; E3 (4-9).
GILLISON; (Derry-Pitman), Me.; M (22-28).
GILMAN; (William); Al (90-299).
GILPIN; (Thomas); P (13-252).
GIST; (Joseph), Md.; X2 (15-35); (David C. R.); X2 (16-4); (Dow), London, Ohio; Z (70-457, 458).
GITHENS; (Thomas); P (14-62).
GLANN; (Gabriel), Downe, N. J.; B1 (14-24).
GLAZIER; (Capt. John), S. C.; Z (80-81).
GLENN; (George D.); Pa., Va.; M (30-63).
GLOVER; (Joseph); J (40-105).
GODARD; (Aaron); Al (99-75).
GODFREY; (James); B4 (12-119).
GODMAN; (James-Nicholls), Va.; M (26-27).
GOING; (Henry J.), Mass., Mich.; Dt (8-99).
GOKEY; (Peter); Moline, Mich.; Dt (9-74).
GOLDSBOROUGH; (Robert), Dorchester Co., Md.; X2 (10-13).
GOOCH; (John), Wells, Maine; Al (95-298).
GOOD; (David); P (12-83).
GOODELL; (Nathan S.); Sheboygan Falls, Wis.; WF (1-44).
GOODMAN; (Peter), Berks Co., Pa.; P (14-183, 185); (Peter); Z (75-7-29).
GOODSPEED; (Daniel), Constantia, N. Y.; Dt (2-20).
GOODWIN; (James W.); Al (98-206).
GOODYEAR; (Stephen); B4 (10-235).
GOOLD; (James), Mass., N. H.; Z (70-715).
GORDON; (Nathaniel); Al (89-199);

(William); M (27-31); (George), Antrim, Pa.; P (13-269).
GORHAM; (Charles-Truesdell), Danbury, Conn.; E3 (3-138); Al (91-382); (George), Stamford, Conn.; B4 (12-59).
GOTTSCHALD; (Daniel), Pa., Ohio; M (25-121).
GOULD; (David), Ipswich, Mass.; Al (89-94); (Elisha); Hull, Mass.; Al (87-91); (James F.), Dorchester, Mass.; Baltimore, Md.; X2 (7-16); (Amos), Henneken, N. H.; Ng (5-212).
GRAHAM; (George), Va., Washington, D. C.; M (32-41); (William), Pa.; Z (80-272).
GRANDEY; (Elijah); Dt (9-21).
GRANT; (Ulysses S.), Ohio; WF (1-217).
GRAY; (George); P (13-109); (Gabriel); W2 (13-192).
GREBILL; P (13-111).
GREEN; (Daniel); A2 (76-103).
GREENE; (Nathaniel), Boston; D (32-145); (John), Conn., Kans.; M (29-25); (John-Lynde); O (5-398).
GREER; (George), Lancaster, Pa.; M (24-12); (James); Dt (3-125).
GREGG; (David); Ky.; K2 (20-308).
GREGORY; (John); Col (7-71).
GRIDLEY; (Selah); A2 (75-40).
GRIFFEN; (Edward); B5 (20-249).
GRIFFITH; (Joseph), Mich.; Dt (4-7).
GRIGG; (Thomas); A2 (74-134).
GRIGGS; (Daniel); Dt (2-122).
GRISWOLD; (Philip); E3 (2-153).
GROFF [GROVE]; (Daniel), Reading, Pa.; M (25-94).
GUION; (John), N. Y.; B4 (11-234).
GUNN; (Nathaniel); Al (88-303).
GUNNISON; (Orlando-Frank), Lordville, N. Y.; Col (2-37; also 7-70).

HADLEY; (Stephen O.); Al (93-202); (Stephen), N. J., N. Y., Mich.; Al (93-203).
HAGERMAN; (Barrent); Al (90-391).
HAGLER; (Samuel), Xenia, Ohio; O (1-8).
HAIGHT; (Benjamin); B2 (10-10); (James), Cazenovia, N. Y.; B2 (16-7); (William), N. Y.; B2 (10-71; 16-8).
HAINES; (Samuel); M (29-138).
HALE; (David); B5 (21-391); (Ebenezer), Glastonbury, Conn.; B4 (15-

60).

HALL; (Edmund T.), Croydon, N. H.;
Sutton, Mass.; Al (89-202); (Timo-
thy), Cheshire, Conn.; B4 (22-166);
(Joseph); B4 (13-195); (Adam); Sus-
sex Co., Del.; P (13-102); (Wm. S.);
Dt (3-77).

HAMILTON; (John, 1726); N3 (37-82);
(Nathaniel-Thomas); Col (1 No. 5);
(David); Al (95-94).

HAMLIN; (Harvey); Cleveland, Ohio; WF
(1-222); (Russel); Al (90-380).

HAMMOND; (Samuel); E3 (8-201);
(Charles), Elkridge, Md.; WF (1-
221); (Calvin-Luther), Whitesboro,
N. Y.; Al (100-71); (Samuel); A2
(77-37).

HANCOCK; (Benjamin); Dt (10-36);
(John); B5 (18-344).

HAND; (Elisha); L1 (3-33); (Philip);
L1 (3-38); (Recompence); L1 (4-44);
(Jeremiah); L1 (5-23, 26); (Rob-
ert-Forest); A2 (77-140).

HANKINSON; (Thomas), Amwell, N. J.;
B1 (14-48).

HANNUM; (Othniel-Elliot), Peru, Mass.;
Col (6-36); (Perez); O (1-10).

HANSON; (Moses); B4 (12-119); (John);
X2 (14-63).

HARDENBERGH; (Jacob R.); B1 (14-67).

HARDER; (John), Claverack, N. Y.; E3
(6-447).

HARDESTER; (David); X2 (13-34).

HARDING; Surry County, N. C.; H1 (1-
131).

HARDWICK; (William), Ga.; Dt (9-115).

HARLOW; (Jonas); O (1-8); (James); O
(3-244).

HARMER; (Ebenezer); B5 (22-48).

HARNED; (Jonathan); Dt (2-2).

HARRIMAN; (James); B4 (12-120, 122).

HARRIS; (Pierson), N. J.; M (21-109);
(Silas), Otego, N. Y.; B2 (12-23);
(Levi); Al (90-94); (Champlin, Dr.
James); Dt (10-14); (Leonard W.),
Lebanon, N. H.; Al (92-204); (Levi);
B2 (17-10); (Asa), Saybrook, Conn.;
Al (93-298); (Milo), Salisbury,
Conn.; Dt (7-24); (Jordan); Z (69-
681); (Peter); Z (71-467); (Wil-
liam), Hanover Co., Va.; Z (71-
467).

HARRISON; E3 (4-25); (Elias), Pa.; Al
(90-381); (Joseph), Haddonfield, N.
J.; Al (93-295).

HART; (Luther-Wells), New Britain,
Conn.; E3 (3-138); Al (91-382); Al
(92-206); (Jesse), Vt.; Ohio; Dt (3-

159).

HASBROUCK; (Jacob I.); A2 (73-287).

HASEY; (Abraham); Al (93-391).

HASKELL; (William O.); B5 (23-100).

HASTINGS; (Richard C.); Al (89-203).

HATCH; (Thomas); E3 (8-201).

HATLER; (Philip); Z (71-1112).

HAVEN; (Rev. Samuel), Portsmouth, N.
H.; Al (89-197).

HAVENS; (Peter); Al (90-382); (Thomas); Col (2-53).

HAWKINS; (William), Derby, Conn.; Ng
(3-163); (James-King); A2 (77-
92).

HAYS; (James), Miss.; V3 (49-281);
(Leonard); X2 (4-5).

HAZZARD; (Cord); P (14-64).

HEAD; (Richard); Z (69-560).

HEARD; (Jethro); Z (74-5-38).

HEDDEN; (Cyrus); B1 (12-45).

HEDGES; (Jeremiah), Norwich, Vt.; B4
(10-127).

HEFFNER; (Jonas D.), Chester Co.,
Pa.; O (3-211).

HEFFRON; (John); A2 (77-74).

HEMPSTED; (Daniel, Samuel B.); A2
(77-184).

HENDERSON; (James), S. C.; M (23-
125).

HENKLE; (Rev. Eli), Pendleton Co.,
Va.; X2 (6-2).

HENRY; (William); E3 (5-297); (Wil-
son), Siloam, Miss.; M (27-19);
(Wm. S. B.); Gloucester Co., Va.;
M (29-92).

HERBERT; (Thomas, Daniel, Jacob,
Jonathan); B1 (19-83).

HETZER; (George-Marcus); O (2-106);
(Philip); O (5-435).

HEWITT; (Prentiss-Samuel), Stonington, Conn.; Al (89-93), 92-206);
(Jonas); Dt (6-102); (Fayette);
Ng (4-120); (Phipps W.); Ng (4-
35).

HEXT; (Philip); J (40-97).

HIBBEN; (Thomas), Pa.; Ohio; O (4-
294).

HIGGINBOTHAM; (Aaron), Va.; Z (80-
583).

HILL; (Jonathan); Walworth, N. Y.;
Al (90-382); (Abner), Guilford,
Conn.; Sunderland, Vt.; Al (98-
91); (Harvey), Conn.; Dt (4-8).

HINDS; (Jesse), Greenwich, Mass.;
B2 (13-11).

HINE, THOMAS; (William), Derby,
Conn.; B4 (11-127); (Aaron), Conn.,
Ohio; M (20-8).

HINCKLEY; (Benjamin); Dt (5-205).
HINTON; (George W.), Ala.; M (24-38).
HINZEY; (John), Pa.; B2 (13-9).
HITCHCOCK; (Bethuel); E3 (3-107).
HOAG; (Joseph); Al (89-89).
HOAGLAND; (Christopher), Steuben Co.,
N. Y.; Dt (5-205); (Jacob); Dt (5-
206).
HODGE; (Isaac); Dt (2-214); (Samuel),
Kittery, Me.; B5 (19-59, 65).
HOFFMAN; (Millman); B5 (24-160).
HOFMAN; (Leo), Md.; X2 (5-10).
HOGELAND; (Dirck); A2 (74-101).
HOGGE; (William); Al (90-383).
HOLBROOK; (Joseph), Wiscassett, Me.;
Al (89-292); (Peter); Al (94-204).
HOLBURT; (Charles); A2 (71-143).
HOLDEN; (Moses), Barre, Mass.; Al (89-
295); (Nathaniel), Shirly, Mass.;
Bl (19-10).
HOLLISTER; (John), Conn., N. Y.; B4
(10-234).
HOLLY; (Don C.), Jefferson Co., N. Y.;
B2 (15-11).
HOLMES; (Jabez); E3 (2-91).
HOLSTEAD; (Timothy), Shrewsbury, N.
J.; M (25-76).
HOLTER; (Jacob), Md.; M (23-20).
HOPKINS; (Jason); Dt (9-128); (Wil-
liam O.), Otsego, N. Y.; B5 (23-
100).
HORDENBROOK; (Hendrick); Bl (14-70).
HORRY; (Daniel), S. C.; J (39-129).
HORTON; (Stephen), N. Y.; B4 (11-236);
(Thomas), Pittstown, N. Y.; A2 (77-
168).
HOSKINS; (Elkanah); Z (70-716).
HOUGH; (Benjamin-Kent), Gloucester,
Mass.; Al (87-298).
HOUGHTELING; (Abraham); Al (89-388).
HOUSE; (Eleazer), Glastonbury, Conn.;
Al (91-374); (James H.); Bl (14-
71); (William-Corlette); Dt (3-9).
HOUSELL; (Matthias); Bl (14-71).
HOUSEMAN; (John-Moore), Ky.; W2 (12-
305).
HOUSTON; (James); Z (72-10-97).
HOW; (Ebenezer), Greenwich, Conn.;
Dt (4-121).
HOWARD; (John-Scott), Kinderhook, N.
Y.; WF (1-43); (George-Robert),
Wilkes Co., N. C.; Z (70-208); (Ol-
vin), N. Y., Pa.; Dt (3-94).
HOWE; (Edward), Dover, Vt.; Col (5-
101).
HOWELL; (Matthew); LI (1-18); (Jo-
seph), Coram, N. Y.; Greenville,
Ill.; LI (3-4); (Richard W.), Cam-

den, N. J.; P (14-179); (Walter),
Lansdale, Pa.; Al (89-87, 88).
HOWLAND; (Malachi), Cayuga Co., N. Y.;
Al (90-387).
HOYT; (Ezra-Randall), Rumford, Me.;
Wis.; WF (1-222); (Daniel), Ports-
mouth, N. H.; Al (98-206).
HUBBARD; (Ephraim); Al (88-96).
HUFF; (Charles) Kennebunkport, Me.;
Al (96-200).
HUGGINS; (Zadok), Dorset, Vt.; B4
(22-170).
HUGHES; (Ellis); Ll (2-48); (Jesse),
Cape May, N. J.; Ll (5-20); (Da-
vid), Cape May; Ll (5-22, 23).
HUGHLETT; (Thomas); X2 (6-27).
HUGUENIN; Bible records and inscrip-
tions (Abraham), S. C.; M (22-29).
HULL; (Gideon-Wakeman); New Bruns-
wick, N. J.; Bl (14-88);(Josiah);
M (23-19).
HULSE; (Caleb M.); LI (2-55).
HUMESTON; (Isaac), Conn.; B4 (14-19).
HUMPHRIES; (John F.); King George
Co., Va.; M (22-35).
HUMPHREY; (Robert Y.); Col (1 No. 4;
also 5-71).
HUNGERFORD; (Stephen); Dt (9-129).
HUNT; (John), Northampton, Mass.; Al
(88-204); (William), Luzerne Co.,
Pa.; M (25-116); (Ephraim and Fran-
cis); M (29-26); (Francis), Fal-
mouth, Me.; M (30-149); (Ephraim),
Falmouth, Me.; M (30-149); (Esaias),
N. J.; Bl (9-40); (John S.), Tully,
N. Y.; Dt (9-122).
HUNTER; (William-Forrest); O (5-419).
HUNTINGTON; (Moses); Al (100-255).
HUSTED; (Moses), Fairton, N. J.; B5
(17-174).
HUSTED; (Moses); B5 (27-322).
HUTSON; (James); O (4-354); (Joshua);
X2 (17-68).
HUVER; (Andrew), Eastern, Pa.; M (21-
95).
HYLAND; (John); Dt (2-215).
HYNN; (A. C.), Vt.; Al (90-374).

INGERSOLL; (Gideon); M (20-119).
INGRAHAM; (Benjamin), Chatham, N. Y.;
M (24-92); (Benjamin); M (25-61).
INNIS; (Henry); O (1-64).
IRWIN; (Stephen M.); Dt (4-76).
ISARD; (Henry); Ll (3-25). See
Izard.
IVES; (Butler), Sheffield, Mass.; Dt
(9-47).
IZARD; (Nicholas H.), Cape May Co.,

LANGDON; (Cornelius), St. Lawrence
Co., N. Y.; WF (1-40); (Seth); P
(13-257, 258); (John), Hempstead,
N. Y.; Al (97-290).
LANGSDON; (John C.); Dt (6-39).
LANING; (John); B5 (21-387).
LANPHERE; (Fitch); A2 (71-272).
LANSING; (Gerardus); A2 (71-230);
items; A2 (71-240).
LARGE; (Jacob), Hunterdon Co., N. J.;
B1 (14-90).
LARNED; (Abijah), Northumberland, N.
H.; M (29-39).
LARZALERE; A2 (76-182).
LATIMER; (Stephen); O (3-244).
LATTA; (Finley); A2 (77-45); (James),
N. Y.; M (26-24).
LAWRENCE; (Caleb), New York; Al (89-
389); (Richard, Robert); Dt (10-
47); (John), Yates Co., N. Y.; B4
(23-188); (Levi), Athol, Mass.; Dt
(10-109); (Elisha), Middlesex Co.,
N. J.; B1 (8-11); (Samuel); B5 (19-
93).
LAWS; (John), Md.; X2 (6-14, 25).
LAWSON; (Courtland), Ill., Ind.; A2
(67-367).
LEACH; (Andrew); Al (89-289).
LEAGUE; (James), Va., S. C.; M (23-
125).
LEAMING; (Christopher), Cape May
County, N. J.; B7 (1-119).
LEARY, JAMES; Milford, Mich.; Dt
(8-128).
LEATHERMAN; (Johann), Pa.; M (32-
26).
LEDINGHAM; Canada?; Dt (6-130).
LEE; (John); Ky.; Col (5-69).
LEFEVER; (David); Hopewell, N. Y.;
Dt (6-45); (Minard); Dt (8-81).
LEFFERTS; (Leffert); LI (4-27).
LEIGH; (Reuben-Harrington), N. Y.,
Minn.; Al (100-253); (Zebulon),
Montgomery, N. J.; B1 (14-91).
LEIPER, THOMAS; P (13-109).
LETTON; (Michael); X2 (14-19).
LEWIS; (Fielding), Va.; M (20-111);
(John); Va.; M (22-44); (Calvin),
Mich.; Dt (10-20); (Joseph), Ded-
ham, Mass.; Al (95-393); (Elisha),
N. Y.; Ontario; M (31-51); (El-
lis); P (14-92); (Jonas), Reading,
Mass.; M (29-40);(George); B1 (14-92).
LIGHTFOOT; (John A.); V1 (13-64).
LIGHTHIPE; (Charles); Z3 (50-395).
LIMING; (John), Cassville, W. Va.;
Col (1 No. 9).
LINCOLN; (James-Boone); Ng (6-256).

LINDLEY; (William), Z (73-7-71).
LINNEKIN; (John), B5 (26-151).
LINSLEY; (Israel), Branford, Conn.;
B4 (9-223).
LIPPERT; (Henry), Gettysburg, Pa.;
Col (6-117).
LIPPINCOTT; (Freedom); B1 (7-86);
(Seth); B1 (14-94).
LITTLE; (James); Al (90-396); (John
C.); L1 (5-29).
LITTLEPAGE; (Hardin); Z (71-961).
LIVINGSTON; (James); A2 (71-226).
LOCKE; (Elisha), Bath, N. H.; M (29-
40); (Josiah), Danvers, Mass.; M
(29-40).
LOCKWOOD; (Thomas); E3 (6-426).
LOKERSON; (Abraham L.); Al (90-390).
LOMBARD; (Solomon); M (29-26; 30-
150).
LONG; (Benjamin), Newbury, Mass.; B4
(17-62); (Elias); B2 (17-22).
LONGMUIR; (Gabriel), Chili, N. Y.;
Dt (6-16).
LONGSTREET; (Archibald C.); Dt (4-
169).
LONGYOR; (Zachariah); E3 (3-105).
LOOMIS; (Eber); E3 (1-27).
LORD; (Falmouth, Me.; M (30-149);
(Oliver H.), Me.; Al (97-299).
LORING; (Matthew); Boston; Al (90-
384).
LORTON; (Lewis R.); Dt (4-169).
LOSEY; (Philip); Dt (2-123).
LOUGHREY; (Andrew), Ohio, Ill.; Col
(1 No. 2).
LOVE; (Thomas), Sutton, Mass.; Z (71-
677).
LOVEJOY; (Abial); Al (89-390); (Hen-
ry), Andover, Mass.; B2 (20-34).
LOVELAND; (Joseph); Ng (4-55).
LOYD; (Willis); O (3-245).
LUCE; (Simeon), Martha's Vineyard,
Norwich, Conn.; Al (98-366).
LUKENS; (Evan); P (13-112).
LUMLEY; (James); Dt (3-165).
LUTZ; (Alexander); P (13-114).
LYON; (Daniel); Al (91-191); (Wil-
liam); Al (91-377);(Robert), Jef-
ferson Co., N. Y.; B2 (15-11); (Ja-
cob); WF (1-84).

MCAFEE; (Samuel); N3 (31-341).
MCCANDLESS; (James), Pittsburgh, Pa.;
Al (89-95).
MCCARTY; (Daniel), Miss.; M (29-108);
(Benjamin); Z (73-8-85).
MCCAULEY; (Nicholas J.); X2 (9-39);
(William H.), Armada, Mich.; Dt

92 FAMILY RECORDS

(4-54).
MCCAUSLAND; (William), Pa.; Z (69-358).
MCCLELLEN; (John); Dt (4-220).
MCCOUN; (Daniel); Oyster Bay, N. Y.; LI (1-88).
MCCULLOUGH; (William); Dt (5-125).
MCDONALD; (Harlem), Glenville, N. Y.; E3 (6-537).
MACDOWELL; (James), Scotland; M (29-63).
MCDUFFEE; (William), Charlestown, N. Y.; M (24-110).
MCELHENY; (John), Dryden, N. Y.; Dt (5-159).
MCELROY; (James M.), Pittsburgh, Pa.; Col (2-71); (John); Dt (4-105).
MCFARLAN; (James); P (13-139).
MACFEE; (James); W2 (13-61).
MCGARITY; (Andrew-Jackson), Fairfax Co., Va.; M (34-72).
MCGEE; (James); X2 (16-21).
MCGOWN; (John), Columbus, Ohio; O (1-31).
MCINTIRE; (Andrew), N. C.; M (21-118); (George); Al (92-205).
MCINTOSH; (Paskal Paoli), Ohio; B4 (14-140).
MCKEAN; (James); Ll (3-37).
MCKINNEY; (Charles), Va.; Z (72-3-73).
MCLALLEN; (Robert), Washington, Pa.; M (24-41).
MCLATCHEY; (Thomas); Al (89-197).
MCMASTER; (Hugh), Columbus, Ohio; O (1-30).
MCNABB; (Archibald); M (24-46).
MCPHERSON; (James S.); McPherson-ville; J (40-110).
MCREE; (James), New Brunswick, N. J.; Bl (13-92).

MACK; (Jacob); M (26-120).
MACKEY; (Benjamin), New Windsor, N. Y.; M (29-38).
MAGOFFIN; (John), Bedminster, N. J.; Bl (15-48).
MAHER; (Jeremiah), Claremont, N. H.; WF (1-82).
MALOTT; (Peter); X2 (4-21).
MANN; (James); P (13-258).
MANNING; (Jeremiah); Z3 (50-294).
MAPS; (Michael); Al (90-392).
MARBLE; (Ephraim), N. Y.; B4 (9-42).
MARIM; (Charles); Kent Co., Del.; P (13-104).
MARKS; (Peter), Pa.; M (27-93).

MARSH; (Isaac W.), Hartland, Vt.; M (29-28); (Joseph), St. Albans, Vt.; A2 (77-130); (Isaac W.); Hartland, Vt.; M (30-150).
MARSHALL; (Rufus); E3 (5-281).
MARSTON; (Thomas); Al (95-91); (James), Vineland, N. J.; B5 (22-132).
MARTIN; (Josiah); P (13-106); (James), N. J.; M (34-49); (James), Sussex and Middlesex Cos., N. J.; Bl (15-48); (John A.), Dutchess and Ontario Cos., N. Y.; Dt (4-123); (Joseph and Milton); Ky.; Ind.; X2 (14-4); (Merrick and Samuel), N. J.; M (31-91); (Stephen), Lisbon, N. H.; Z (70-714); (William); Z (71-843); (Elias); Z (78-102).
MASKELL; (Daniel, b. 1728); B5 (18-286).
MASSIE; (William, Va.); V3 (41-349).
MATHER; (Silas); Dt (10-108).
MATTERN; (John-Jacob), Pa.; M (20-88).
MATTHEWS; (Joseph); B4 (14-142).
MAXON; (Stephen); Z (72-7-76).
MAXSON; (William-Bliss), Philadelphia, Pa.; Bl (15-50).
MAY; (Benjamin), Pitt Co., N. C.; M (32-45); (George), Brattleboro, Vt.; Col 1 (No. 5).
MAYO; (Edmund), Hardwick, Mass.; B4 (12-117).
MEANS; (John); Boston; S. C.; Z (69-496); (David-Harper); Z (69-626).
MEEKER; (Jonathan), N. J.; Bl (8-91); (Elias T.); E3 (4-73).
MEREDITH; (William), Newark, N. J., Philadelphia, Pa.; M (25-73).
MESSICK; (Isaac), Sussex Co., Del.; X2 (5-21, 33, 43).
METCALFE; (John), Bourbon Co., Ky.; M (31-9).
MICHELL; (Thomas), Va.; V3 (42-164).
MILLER; (Thomas); Col (2-35); (Daniel), Pa., Ohio; M (21-89); (Hezekiah); Dt (2-162); Dt (3-126); (Hugh); Ll (3-37); (Aaron); Ll (5-25); (Isaac R.), Madison, Ind.; Ng (4-30); (Peter), Hawkins Co., Tenn.; Z (70-457).
MILLINGTON; (Samuel D.), South Shaftsbury, Vt.; E3 (1-69).
MILLS; (David), N. C., Ark.; Vl (25-146); (John), Whippany, N. J.; Bl (14-93).
MINER; (Elihu), East Haddam, Conn.; B4 (13-197).

MINOR; (Jehu), Woodbury, Conn.; B4 (9-225).
MITCHELL; (Rev. Wm.); Easton, Md.; Chester, Ill.; Al (90-298); (Isaac-Lappin); Dt (4-34); (Dummer), Kennebunkport, Me.; Al (96-200); Preble Co., Ohio; M (30-46).
MONFORT; (Peter); LI (2-109).
MONROE; (Jonathan), Mass.; Vt.; E3 (2-58).
MOODY; (Aaron); Al (88-206).
MOOR; (Robert); Dt (3-160).
MOORE; (Samuel-Preston), Pa.; P (11-288); (George), Hilltop, Durham, Eng.; Col (1 No. 8); (Daniel); Al (91-378); (Daniel), Levant, Me.; Al (94-201); (Samuel); P (14-304).
MOREY; R. I.; Al (87-81).
MORGAN; (Christopher); Groton, Conn.; Aurora, N. Y.; A2 (75-124); (William); Dt (2-215).
MORONG; (Thomas), Ala., Mass.; M (25-91).
MORRILL; (Moses); O (1-64).
MORRIS; (Jonathan, Samuel), Pa., Ohio; Z (74-6-35); (John), Clinton Co., Mich.; Dt (4-153).
MORSE; (Joseph), Hopkinton, Mass.; Al (95-201); (Alvin K.), Canterbury, Conn.; Dt (7-82).
MORTON; (John), N. J., N. Y.; B1 (15-51).
MOSELEY; (Joseph), Glastonbury, Conn.; Al (91-374); (Edward), Charlotte Co., Va.; V3 (48-353).
MOSER; (John-Reid); Brooklyn, N. Y.; Col (1 No. 1).
MOSHER; (Joseph), Dartmouth, Mass.; B2 (12-1); Al (91-379); (Ephraim); B2 (15-23); (Daniel), N. Y., Ill.; B2 (19-24); (Cornelius), Nobletown, N. Y.; B2 (19-33); (Aaron), Vt.; B2 (12-30); Dt (6-94); (Abraham); B2 (11-28); (Philip), Dartmouth, Mass.; Al (87-395).
MOSS; (James); Al (89-203).
MOTT; (Jacob); LI (3-57).
MUDGETT; (Elisha); Al (94-391).
MULFORD; (Enoch); B5 (27-370).
MUMFORD; (Thomas), New London, Conn.; Al (88-94).
MUNN; (Joseph); Al (89-302).

NALLE; (Martin); V1 (14-164).
NASH; (William), Norwalk, Conn.; Al (89-94)
NASON; (William), Portsmouth, N. H.; Al (88-376).

NEAL; (Charles A.); Al (90-83).
NEELEY; (Samuel) Pa.; M (21-115).
NEGUS; (Jonas), Weston, Vt.; Al (89-380).
NELSON; (John) Depford, N. J.; M (22-8); (Leader); Al (89-295).
NEVIN; (David), Pa.; M (25-125).
NEVIUS; (David), New Brunswick, N. J.; B1 (15-79).
NEWELL; (Dexter), N. Y.; M (28-96).
NEWSON; (Hobart); Ng (3-181).
NEWTON; (Samuel), Duplin County, N. C.; M (21-63); (Barnett), N. C.; M (21-65).
NICHOLS; (John), Chesterfield, N. H.; M (24-91); (George), N. Y., Minn.; Col (5-57); (Alexander H.); E3 (6-426).
NIGHTINGALE; (Isaac); P (13-268).
NOGLE; (Henry); Z (71-845).
NOLAND; (Stephen), Nicholasville, Ky.; B2 (10-28).
NORBURY; (Joseph), N. J.; B7 (1-67); L1 (1-45).
NORCROSS; (Benajah); Dt (10-101).
NORWOOD; (Nathaniel); Al (93-295).
NOYES; (Benjamin-Bosworth), R. I., Mich.; Dt (5-149).
NUTTER; (Joseph S.); Al (87-93).
NYE; (John-Peter); M (30-151).

OAKLEY; (Richard), Albany, N. Y.; Al (89-95).
OAKS; (George), Pa.; M (25-95); see also Ochs.
OATHOUSE; (William), Ontario Co., N. Y.; E3 (6-431).
OBENSHANE; (Samuel), Va.; M (20-32).
OCHS [OAKS]; (Leonhard); M (25-95).
ODEN; (Vincent), St. Mary Co., Md.; M (31-9).
ODLE; (James); Dt (5-164).
OFFUT; (Nathaniel), Md.; X2 (9-8).
OGDEN; (Benjamin), N. J.; M (22-8); (Gertrude-Gouverneur), N. J., Pa.; M (25-73); (David); A2 (76-124).
OLDS; (Daniel); Al (90-384).
OLNEY; (Epenetus), Providence, R. I.; Al (89-94); (Ezekiel), Willington, Conn.; Al (100-333).
OMANS; (Jonathan); Oakland, Mich.; Dt (8-127).
ORR; (John), Tenn., Iowa; M (25-66); (Gabriel), L1 (1-40).
ORRICK; B2 (10-12).
OSBORN; (Peter), Pa.; M (23-123).
OSBORNE; (Jonah); M (31-28).

POOR; (Samuel); A1 (88-302).
PORTER; (James M.), Ill.; B2 (17-24).
POST; (Peter), Angelica, N. Y.; Dt (9-22); (Nathan); A2 (77-77).
POTTER; (Thomas); Dt (8-127).
POWELL; (Rev. John), Granville, Ohio; M (24-43); (Joseph); B2 (12-19); (John-Peyton), Powhatan Co., Va.; Ala.; Z (71-466, 468).
POWER; (Arthur); Dt (2-207, 215).
PRATT; (Joseph); A1 (97-201).
PREDMORE; (Daniel); Dt (2-122).
PRESSLY; (David), S. C.; M (21-132).
PRESTON; (Levi), Salem, Mass.; M (21-110).
PRICE; (Ireland, Pa.); A1 (92-200); (John-Larens), Pa.; M (25-124); (George); A2 (76-124).
PRIEST; (John); M (28-31).
PROCTER; (Thorndike), Salem, Mass.; Y1 (70-31).
PROUDFIT; (David); B2 (19-34).
PULIS; (Conrad), N. Y., Pa.; B4 (11-235).
PUMPHREY; (Sylvanus), W. Va.; M (20-78).
PURDY; Ohio; B2 (10-54).

RADLEY; (John), N. J.; B1 (11-71).
RALES; (Francis-Henry); A2 (76-187).
RALF; (John), S. C.; Z (80-81).
RAMSEY; (George); Dt (5-27).
RANDOLPH; (Samuel), N. J.; Walworth, N. Y.; A1 (91-376); (Richard), Va.; W2 (15-429).
RASCO; (Wellington), Sand Lake, Mich.; Dt (9-73).
RATCLIFFE; (William); E2 (1-31).
RATLIFF; (William); X2 (9-25).
RAY; (William); E3 (1-52).
READ; (Joseph); A1 (100-258).
REDWOOD; (Abraham), Salem; P (11-292; 13-249).
REECE; (John); Dt (3-125).
REED; (Stephen), Westford, Mass.; Wethersfield, Vt.; E3 (8-201); (Samuel), Wendell, Mass.; Dt (5-87); (Zebulon), North Yarmouth, Me.; A1 (98-207).
REESE; (Daniel-Meredith); Cecil Co., Md.; M (33-42).
REESKIE; Dt (8-38).
REEVES; (Daniel), Lewis Co., N. Y.; E3 (1-120).
REID, WILLIAM; (Scotland; Benton, N. Y.; LI (3-87).
REIFF; (Jacob), Lower Salford, Pa.;

P (12-77).
REIGLE; (John), Clarence Center, N. Y.; Dt (8-129).
REX; (Michael); P (13-260).
REYNOLDS; (Solomon), Queensbury, N. Y.; B4 (17-63); (John); E3 (6-411); (Samuel); Dt (9-46).
RHEAD; (Robert D.); Dt (4-164).
RHODES; (Joseph), S. C., Ala.; Z (80-153).
RICE; (James), Caswell Co., N. C.; M (26-26); (James); Z (77-386).
RICHARDS; (Daniel); A1 (91-92).
RICHARDSON; (Daniel); A1 (92-204); (Richard); X2 (11-5); (Samuel); B4 (17-62).
RICHISON; (Richard), Chester Co., Pa.; P (14-66).
RIDGWAY; (Thomas); LI (1-121).
RIFE; (Abraham); B2 (12-19).
RIGGS; (Aaron); A2 (76-182).
RILEY; (Asher), N. Y. City; A1 (87-95).
RIPPLE; (Lewis); M (25-125).
RISDON; (Samuel), Burlington Co., N. J.; P (13-268).
RISH; (Simeon); Z (71-844).
ROBB; N3 (31-347).
ROBERTS; (Benjamin), Md., Ohio; X2 (12-35); (Allen), Ga.; Dt (9-116); (Zaccheus), Pa., Tenn.; Z (80-153).
ROBERTSON; (Jesse M.); Z (71-468).
ROBINSON; Manchester, Vt.; Dt (3-40); (Isaac); Ng (3-181); (Joshua); Dt (7-17).
RODGERS; (James); A2 (76-127).
ROGERS; (James); LI (1-121); (Charles); X2 (14-42); (James), Dauphin Co., Pa.; Z (70-1021); (Hope), Conn.; B4 (11-229); (Warren), Killingworth, Conn.; B1 (7-60); (Joseph), N. J., Mich.; B1 (10-24).
ROHRER; (Friedrich), Frederick Co., Md.; M (23-89).
ROLPH; (Joseph); A2 (71-142).
ROOME; (Benjamin); Z3 (50-395).
ROOSA; (Jan); OU (7-28); (Andries L.); OU (7-239); (John); A2 (77-65).
ROOT; (Benjamin), Greenfield; E3 (2-91).
ROSE; (David); E3 (5-330).
ROTZ; (Philip); Dt (9-44).
ROWLETT; (Matthew), Va.; Z (72-3-74).
ROYS; (Lent); Dt (9-127).
RUCKER; (John); Z (72-9-89).

RUGGLES; (Edward), Roxbury, Mass.;
B4 (17-115); (Eliezur), Oakland
Co., Mich.; Dt (9-16); (Joseph),
Roxbury, Mass.; B4 (15-108).
RUNYON; (John), New Brunswick, N.
J.; B1 (15-104).
RUSSELL; (Samuel-Davenport); A2 (76-
74).
RUTHERFORD; (James); L1 (1-41).
RYKER; (John), N. J.; B2 (11-28).
RYMES; (Samuel), Portsmouth, N. H.;
A1 (89-295).

SABIN; (William); Boston, Mass.; Ng
(3-151).
SACKETT; Dt (4-5, 27, 49, 71); (Ni-
ram), Dutchess Co., N. Y.; E3 (2-
106); (John I.); E3 (2-121).
SALISBURY; (Richard), Swansea,
Mass.; Woodstock, Conn.; B4 (15-
57); (Calvin); B4 (15-59).
SALTSMAN; (William); Z (72-12-69).
SAMMIS; (Silas); LI (1-122).
SAMSON; (David), Pike Co., Ohio; O
(8-636).
SANBORN; (Moses), New Chester, N.
H.; M (22-5).
SANDERS; (Lawrence); J (32-243);
(Stephen), Va.; Col (1 No. 9).
SANDS; (Daniel H.), Catskill, N. Y.;
LI (1-18).
SANFORD; (Abel), Wallingford, Conn.;
B4 (22-167).
SARGENT; (Sampson), Ohio; B4 (14-
138).
SAVAGE; (Solomon), Middletown, Conn.;
Dt (9-66).
SAVERY; (John), Plymouth, Mass., N.
Y. City; Dt (7-55).
SAWYER; (Jonathan), N. Y.; E3 (7-
169).
SAXTON; (Henry and Frederick A.);
E3 (3-9).
SAXTON; see Sexton.
SAYRE; (John); Dt (3-159).
SCHELL; (Joseph), Pa., Ohio; O (6-
484).
SCHELLINGER; (Enos); P (13-116);
(John); L1 (1-45).
SCHERMERHOORN; (Lucas), Raritan, N.
J.; B1 (16-18).
SCHUYLER; (Abraham), Plymouth, N.Y.;
P (13-267).
SCOFIELD; (Richard), Green, Ohio; Dt
(4-106).
SCOTT; (John); B4 (17-61); (William);
K2 (20-313); (Sylvanus), Smith-
field, R. I.; NE (3-67); (David),

Philadelphia, Pa.; Z (77-181).
SCOVIL; (Andrew); A1 (89-392).
SCRUGGS; Ky.; N3 (30-100).
SCUDDER; (Benjamin), Springfield, N.
J., from almanacs, 1780-; Z3 (63-
150, 219).
SCUDER; (Jacob), Lancaster Co., Pa.;
Dt (7-47).
SEARCH; (Lot); E3 (3-106).
SEAWARD; Md., Me.; A1 (88-381).
SEELEY; (John); O (4-355); (Richard);
M (22-12).
SEILER; (Jacob), Summit, Pa.; M (21-
122).
SELBY; (Zadok O.); X2 (3-26); (Law-
son L.), Md.; X1 (29-329); (Jo-
seph), Va., Ind., Iowa, Mo.; Col
(5-99).
SENSEL; O (3-244).
SEWARD; (David), Meredith, N. Y.; Dt
(8-25).
SEXTON; (Jared), Belvidier, N. J.;
Dt (7-27).
SEYLE; (John-Henry), S. C.; M (21-
60).
SEYMOUR; (Thaddeus); A1 (91-92);
(Thomas, Nathaniel); P (14-185).
SHAPLEY; (John); Dt (2-20; 7-134).
SHARP; (Jacob); N3 (31-347).
SHARTS; (Andrew N.), Hillsdale, N.
Y.; B4 (9-91).
SHATTUCK; (Alfred), Deerfield, Mass.;
B2 (10-64).
SHAW; (Benoni E.), Newport, Vt.; A1
(90-385).
SHELBY; (David); M (22-39).
SHELDON; (Gardner), South Kingston,
R. I.; B4 (12-59).
SHELL; (John); E3 (8-265).
SHEPPARD; (Hudson), Ohio; M (22-63);
(Furman); B5 (18-285); (John), Pa.;
M (25-89).
SHERRON; (Roger); P (13-264).
SHERWOOD; (Marcus), Conn., N. Y.;
Dt (9-10); (Nehemiah), Conn.; E3
(3-170).
SHIPLEY; (Greenbury); X2 (17-55).
SHIPPEN; (Charles); A1 (90-93).
SHOEMAKER; (Samuel), Del.; B2 (17-
20).
SHURTLEFF; (William); Marshfield,
Mass.; P (13-120).
SICKELS; (Robert); A1 (90-391).
SILVER; (John); A1 (91-93).
SIMMERMAN; (Thomas Q.); Col (1 No.
9).
SIMPERS; (William); Cecil Co., Md.;
M (32-71); (Jesse-Holliday); Ce-

cil Co., Md.; M (33-40).
SIMPSON; (Alva); X2 (16-42); (Ebene-
zer-Townsend); Ng (5-227).
SIPPLE; (Walker), Del.; E2 (1-31).
SKILLIN; (Simeon D.); LI (2-56).
SKINNER; (Elisha), Hartford, Conn.;
E3 (3-153).
SLATER; (Wilson), Ohio, Neb.; B2
(17-22).
SLAUGHTER; (Ezekiel), Va., Ohio; O
(8-636).
SLOVER; (Abraham A.), N. Y.; A2 (74-
12).
SMALLEY; (Abraham); M (25-92); (Jon-
athan); Bl (14-56).
SMITH; (George-Flintiff); Al (89-
196); (John), Shooter's Hill, Va.;
M (22-102); (Nathan), Conn.; M (22-
87); (Elijah); B5 (21-322; 24-219);
(John, Christopher); B5 (21-389);
(Samuel-Conover); A2 (67-366);
(John), Middleboro, Mass.; Al (94-
200); (George), Green, Ohio; Dt (4-
106); (John, Jr.); E3 (7-121);
Montague, Mass.; E3 (7-153); (Archibald); Somerset Co., Md.; Al (96-
205); (Elias); Mich.; Dt (5-188);
(John); Dt (5-27); (Elijah); B5
(27-371); N. Y.; A2 (64-40); (Joseph); Ll (3-34); (Samuel-Fair-
banks); Ng (4-140); (Erastus D.);
Ng (4-140); (Solomon), Bath, N.
Y.; Z (70-710); (David), Alburg,
Vt.; Z (70-1020); (Robert), S. C.;
Z (72-3-73); (Thomas); Z (73-5-
89); (Cyrus), Andover, Vt.; Al
(94-92); (Andrew), N. J.; B4 (9-
222); (William); A2 (76-189); (Ed-
ward-James), Romeo, Mich.; Dt (10-
68).
SMOCK; (Jacob); B2 (10-54).
SNAY; (Isaac), Panton, Vt.; B4 (10-
55).
SNIPES; (Maj. Wm.-Clay), S. C.; J
(34-85).
SNOW; (Daniel); B5 (21-391); (Si-
las), Lunenburg, Mass.; Al (95-
94); (Daniel); B5 (28-29); (Abra-
ham); P (14-303).
SNYDER; (David), Md., Pa.; M (24-
15).
SOLTER, see Sortor.
SOMMER; (Jacob); Al (91-193).
SOPER; (James H.), Stoneridge, N.Y.;
Al (89-95).
SORTOR; (John); Somerset Co., N. J.;
Bl (16-44); (George); Bl (16-47).
SPADER; (John); Bl (16-96).

SPEAR; (Abraham), Braintree, Mass.;
Al (89-94); (Lemuel); Al (91-194).
SPEARMAN; (William, Francis); B5 (21-
386).
SPENCER; (Lewis), E. Randolph, Vt.;
B4 (13-197); (Ichabod); Z (71-845).
SPINNING; Va.; B4 (11-6).
SQUIER; (Waite), Lanesboro, Mass.; P
(13-256).
SQUIRE; (Ellis); B4 (14-137).
STABLER; (Gottlieb); J (32-296).
STAFFORD; (Maurice C.); B5 (21-390).
STAMATS; (Orrin W.); X2 (16-4).
STANWOOD; (William), Brunswick, Me.;
Al (87-392).
STARK; (James), N. Y.; B4 (15-121).
STAUFER; (John-Fretz), Pa.; Dt (4-
41).
STEARNS; (Moses); Al (97-290).
STEBBINS; (John); Ng (4-31); (Jared);
Dt (10-13).
STEELE; (Joel), Bethlehem, Conn.;
Ontario Co., N. Y.; E3 (3-105);
(Samuel), Vt.; B4 (11-237).
STEPHENS; (Samuel), N. J.; M (25-
74, 76).
STEPHENSON; Lincoln County, Ky.; N3
(30-201).
STERLING; (James); Al (89-395).
STEVENS; (James); Al (89-202); (Wil-
liam), Conn.; B4 (11-236); (John),
Boston; Al (90-390); (Whiting),
Sanford, Me.; Al (97-299).
STEVENSON; (John), Baltimore Co.,
Md.; O (5-436).
STEWARD; (William), N. J.; B4 (10-
226).
STEWART; (Lt. John), Colrain, Mass.;
Al (91-195); (James); X2 (4-29);
(Abraham), St. Albans, Me.; Al (92-
301); (William), St. Louis, Mo.; O
(4-294).
STITES; (Page); Ll (1-43); (John),
Ll (6-41); (John), Cape May Co.,
N. J.; P (12-82).
STODDARD; (Robert); A2 (69-170);
(Elijah); B5 (24-259).
STONE; (Amos), Addison, Mich.; Dt (6-
123); (George-Washington), Pier-
mont, N. H.; Dt (9-97); (Samuel M.);
Pittsylvania Co., Va.; Z (69-428).
STOOTHOFF; (Garret, Johannis, Wil-
helmus); LI (2-76).
STOVER; (Samuel), Muskingum Co.,
Ohio; M (26-61, 62); (David), Shen-
andoah Co., Ohio; M (26-61); (Ste-
phen); Al (90-205).
STRATTON; (Benjamin), N. Y., N. J.;

M (21-111, 112); (George); L1 (5-26); (Levi); Ng (4-90).
STRICKLAND; (Joseph), East Granby, Conn.; A1 (91-195).
STROTHER; B2 (10-12); (William), Madison Co., Va.; V1 (27-45).
STUKES; (Joseph); J (39-143).
STURGIS; (Jedediah); A1 (92-205).
STURTEVANT; (John), Albany, N. Y.; Dt (6-81).
SUDDARTH; (Abraham); M (22-13).
SULLIVAN; (Owen), S. C.; M (25-130).
SUMMERS; (John), Md.; M (32-43).
SURDAM; (Seneca); Dt (2-182).
SUTTON; (Jonathan); Dt (2-123).
SWAIN; (John); A1 (94-202); (Jeremiah); B5 (27-290).
SWART; (Peter-Cuyler); B5 (27-372).
SWEARINGTON; (Samuel); Z (80-582).
SWEENEY; Ky.; N3 (30-100).
SWIFT; (Judah); A2 (71-140); (Nathaniel), Warren, Ohio; Dt (8-18); (Jabez); A1 (91-379).
SWINSON; (Jesse), N. C.; M (21-121).
SWISHER; (Jacob), Knowlton, N. J.; O (3-240).
SWITZER; (Henry); Reading, N. J.; Dt (5-195).

TABER; (Gideon), Westport, Mass.; M (21-123).
TALLMAN; (Matthew-Van-Alstyn); P (14-59); (Jonathan), Ohio; B4 (11-231).
TANDY; (Roger); Z (70-57).
TANNEHILL; (Samuel); Z (71-844).
TANNER; (Robert); M (29-64).
TAYLOE; (John), Va.; V1 (14-245).
TAYLOR; (Joseph), Bainbridge, Ohio; O (5-419).
TEAL; (Eli), L1 (3-37).
TEEL; (Aaron); L1 (1-40).
TEMPLE; (Enos), Lisbon, N. H.; Z (70-714).
TEN EYCK; (Anthony), N. Y. City; A2 (72-54).
TERHUNE; (Jacob J.); Z3 (56-59).
TERRELL, TERRILL; (George), Newtown, Conn.; B4 (15-60); (George); Dt (5-190); (Thomas); Z (73-1-64).
TERRY; (Joseph); A1 (92-304).
THARP; (Andrew); Z (72-8-87).
THATCHER; (Samuel); Va.; M (33-64).
THOMAS; (Hiram-Munson), Volney, N. Y.; Dt (5-101); (David); P (13-101); (Daniel); P (14-64); (Zebulon), Middleboro, Mass.; A1 (100-67).

THOMPSON; (David), Douglas, Mass.; E3 (3-89); (William C.); A2 (71-139); (Benjamin), Arundel; A1 (99-81); (Stephen-Hurd); Z (70-1021); (Daniel), Newark, N. J.; B4 (10-55); (James), Newark, N. J.; M (30-114).
THORNE; (William A.), Vineland, N. J.; B5 (27-372).
THORP; (Henry), Conn.; B4 (11-232); (Stephen); B1 (18-71); (William); E3 (7-191).
TILDEN; (Asa); Ng (3-164).
TOMB; (Dr. Joseph); P (14-61).
TOMPKINS; (Daniel); E3 (2-75); (John); Dt (8-134).
TOOKER; (Daniel); B4 (12-56).
TORBERT; (William), Sussex County, Del.; E2 (1-31).
TOTTEN; (Peter), Westchester, N. Y.; E3 (5-250).
TOWNSEND; (John); P (12-82).
TRACY; (Isaac), Conn.; B4 (14-137).
TREFETHEN; (Henry); A1 (90-83); (Archelaus); A1 (91-91).
TREICHLER; (John); Ng (4-118).
TRIBBLE; (Rev. Andrew); V1 (18-60).
TRIGG; (Hiram), Tenn.; A1 (90-95).
TRIPP; (James); Z (72-7-76).
TRUESDELL; (Darius); E3 (6-426).
TRUMBULL; (Oliver); Dt (5-176).
TRYON; (William), Middletown, Conn.; A1 (89-94).
TUBBS; (Thomas J.); B2 (17-22).
TUCKER; (Robert), King & Queen Co., Va.; V1 (23-123); (Daniel L.), Windham, N. Y.; B2 (11-40).
TURCK; (Ahasuerus), N. Y.; A2 (66-49).
TURMAN; A2 (67-368).
TURNBULL; (Rev. George), Dinwiddie Co., Va.; W2 (16-99).
TURNER; (Miller), Newtown, Conn.; B4 (15-61).
TURPIN; (William); Z (66-672).
TUSSEY; (David), Petersburg, Pa.; M (23-46).
TWITCHELL; (Gilbert), Oxford, Conn.; B4 (17-115).

ULSH; (John), Pa.; Dt (3-168).
UNDERHILL; (Daniel); A2 (64-40).
UPTON; (Francis-Carr); Dt (5-125).

VAIL; (Micah); L1 (3-57).
VALENTINE; (Charles), Oyster Bay, N. Y.; B4 (17-63); (John-Jones); Spencer, N. Y.; Dt (7-4).

VAN AMRING; (William F.), N. Y., Pa.;
Al (89-392).
VAN ARSDALE, VANARSDELL; Bl (19-47);
(Jacob), N. J., N. Y.; Al (97-
295); (Symon Janson); N3 (31-348);
SSimon); N3 (31-349).
VANDERGRIFT; (Jacob), New Castle Co.,
Del.; E2 (1-22); see also A2 (64-
160, 410).
VAN DER LINDE; (Roelof), Schraalen-
burgh, N. J.; Bl (11-1).
VANDERPOEL; (Lourens); A2 (77-18).
VANDERVORT; (Richard); Dt (5-165).
VANDERVOORT; (Peter); A2 (71-139).
VANDEVANTER; (Cornelius M.), Va.,
Md.; M (25-90).
VAN DUZER; (John), New Cornwall, N.
Y.; Al (91-375).
VAN FOSSEN; (Nathan), Duncannon,
Pa.; M (20-71).
VAN GIESEN; (William), Plymouth,
Mich.; Dt (2-161); (Abraham); Dt
(8-107).
VAN GORDEN; (Enos S.); E3 (2-121).
VAN MATER; (Joseph), Monmouth Coun-
ty, N. J.; Bl (20-48).
VAN METRE; (Jacob), Frederick Co.,
Va.; Col (2-36).
VANNEVAR; (Ede); Al (98-279).
VAN NUYCE; (Cornelius), Somerset
County, N. J., Mercer County, Ky.;
N3 (31-347).
VAN STAY; (Hendrick Jansen), Flat-
bush, N. Y.; Bl (20-72).
VAN TUYL; (Abraham); A2 (71-141).
VAN VECHTEN; (Dirck Theunissen);
Bl (20-95).
VAN VLECK; (John); A2 (73-288).
VAN WAGENEN; (Garrit Artsen), N. Y.;
M (27-31, 94).
VAUGHN; (John); E3 (5-377); (Dan-
iel); E3 (6-411).
VERNOR; (Ezekiel E.); Z (71-845).
VICTROY; (Elihu); B2 (15-35).
VIELE; (Philip); OU (7-241).
VOORHEES; (Abraham), Lebanon, N. J.;
Bl (13-46).

WADDELL; (Alexander); O (2-106).
WADE; (Lewis), Providence, R. I.;
Al (87-393).
WAIT; (Samuel), N. Y., Wis.; Col
(4-28).
WALDO; (Harvey W.); Dt (7-63).
WALES; (Eli B.); Ll (1-42).
WALKER; (John, S. C.; M (25-25);
Va.; B4 (11-6); (Abraham), Pa.;
Dt (7-86); (Ashford), Orange Co.,
N. C.; Z (72-8-88); (Conrid),

Portage, N. Y.; Ng (4-38); (John),
Blount Co., Tenn.; M (31-76).
WALLACE; (Benjamin); Z (72-10-98);
(James); M (26-115).
WALLIS; (Samuel), Elkton, Md.; P (12-
79).
WALTERS; N. Y.; M (32-54).
WALTON; (Thomas), Newtown, N. Y.; Bl
(8-12); (Simon), Vt., Mich.; E3 (1-
132); (Jesse), Northampton Co.,
Pa.; Dt (6-7).
WARD; (Elias); O (5-398); (Oliver);
Ng (4-37).
WARE; (Samuel F.); Ll (1-40).
WARFORD; (Rev. John); P (14-61).
WARNER; (Amos); Dt (5-28); (Daniel),
Mass., Ohio; P (14-187); (William),
Pittsford, Vt.; Al (89-289).
WARREN; (Thaddeus), Westborough,
Mass.; D (34-138); (Oliver); Kil-
lingly, Conn.; LI (3-88); (Moses),
New London, Conn.; B4 (14-141).
WARRICK; (John), Ohio; O (7-595).
WASHINGTON; (Wm.-Augustine), Va.; Vl
(14-245).
WATKINS; B5 (17-154).
WATROUS; (Timothy); Z (78-294).
WATSON; (Dudley); Al (88-91); (Ste-
phen B.); B4 (13-194, 195); (How-
el P.); B5 (22-107); (Jewel); Al
(93-296); (Jesse L.), Bedford Co.,
Va.; Dt (6-39); (Joseph); Al (89-
86).
WATT; (Robert); Ll (3-34).
WATTERS; (William), Baltimore, Md.;
M (28-89).
WATTS; (Wm. D.), S. C.; also (John),
Va., S. C.; M (25-68); (Joseph);
Dt (2-207); (William-Thomas, also
William-Hix); Z (71-465).
WEAVER; (Christopher), N. Y.; B4 (11-
6); (David); P (13-259); (Abraham),
Esopus, N. Y.; B5 (22-111).
WEBB; (Ebenezer), N. Y.; Al (96-203).
WEBSTER; (John C.); E3 (5-297).
WEEKS; (John C.); Al (91-377); (Jo-
seph); Ng (2-58); (Beriah), Mar-
tha's Vineyard; B4 (10-259); (Wil-
liam-Jones), Oyster Bay, N. Y.;
Dt (8-91).
WEEMS; (David), Marshes Seat, Md.;
Xl (28-265).
WELCH; (Isaac), W. Va.; Col (1 No.
9).
WELLS; (Isaac-Newton); O (1-30);
(Asa); X2 (15-47); (Artemas), Lis-
bon, N. H.; Z (70-711); (Ichabod);
Z (72-1-67); (Jonathan), Conn.; Al
(86-454).

WELTON; (George-Smith); Ng (4-33).
WENDELL; (Ephraim), Albany, N. Y.; A2
(71-230).
WENGER; (Michael); M (30-80).
WESNER; (Henry-Philip), S. C.; M (21-
60).
WEST; (Elisha), Mt. Clemens, Mich.;
Dt (8-23).
WESTBROOK; (Richard), Mo.; Z (80-272).
WESTCOAT; (William), Pa.; P (11-289).
WESTCOATT; (David), N. J.; B5 (21-
389).
WESTCOTT; (David), Fairfield, N. J.;
M (22-12); (John); E3 (5-329).
WESTERVELT; (Dower I.); Z3 (56-57).
WETHERBEE; (Jeremiah), Rindge, N. H.;
A1 (89-391).
WHEATON; (Isaac), Cohansey, N. J.; B1
(9-132).
WHIPPLE; (Francis), Mass.; P (14-188).
WHITAKER; (John); Kingston, N. Y.; A2
(75-25).
WHITE; (John), Prince Fredericks Par-
ish, S. C.; J (36-18, 42, 89); S.
C.; J (32-301); (James), N. J.; B4
(10-226); (Simon); X2 (7-16); (Eb-
enezer); B2 (16-8); (Thomas), Wey-
mouth, Mass.; A1 (93-389); (John);
Cumberland Co., Pa.; P (14-58);
(Coleman-Read), N. C.; Z (69-682);
(William), Rochester, Mass.; D (31-
98).
WHITING; (Samuel-Danforth), Jefferson
Co., N. Y.; Dt (3-40).
WHITMAN; (Eliphalet); LI (2-23).
WHITNEY; (Rev. Peter); A1 (90-393);
(David), Concord, Mass.; Dt (9-70);
(Thomas), Md.; X2 (17-37); (Wm. A.),
Shelby, N. Y.; Dt (4-79); (Samuel);
Z (78-301).
WHITTIER, THOMAS; (Francis4, Stephen5);
A1 (89-88).
WIATT; (Solomon), Philadelphia, Pa.;
X2 (13-23); 14-1, 23).
WIDDIFIELD; (John); P (13-101).
WIEDERIGHT; (John); Ng (4-36).
WILBER; (Stephen); B2 (16-24).
WILBORE; (David); Dt (3-39).
WILCOX; (James); WF (1-41); (Martin);
Dt (6-71).
WILD; (Isaac); B5 (20-250).
WILES; R. I.; A1 (87-82).
WILEY; (Elisha); A1 (95-94).
WILKERSON; (Wm. S.), King George Co.,
Va.; M (22-35).
WILLETT; (Samuel), N. J.; M (31-92).
WILLIAMS; (Daniel), Preston, Groton,
Conn.; Dt (2-155).

WILLIAMSON; (Garret), Somerset Co.,
N. J.; B1 (15-103).
WILLIS; (Lewis), Orange County, Va.;
B2 (12-7); (Alvin); A2 (77-30);
Tilghman); Col (1 No. 9); (John);
P (14-198).
WILLITS; (Jonathan); A1 (91-378).
WILLMARTH; (Leonard); A1 (88-96).
WILLOUGHBY; (Amherst), Conn.; Vt.;
A2 (77-167).
WILLSON; (Samuel), Bethlemem, N. J.;
E3 (2-74).
WILSON; (Daniel), Billerica, Mass.;
A1 (89-195); (William), Williams-
burg, S. C.; J (34-173); (John-
Diamond), Mass.; M (25-92).
WILT; (Peter), Garrett Co., Md.; X2
(8-31).
WINEBERGER; (Jacob), D. C.; M (25-
88).
WINEGAR; (Gerret); Dt (3-211).
WINGATE; (John), Madbury, N. H.; A1
(89-83).
WINN; (Daniel), Wells, Maine; A1
(95-299).
WINTERS; (Christopher), Dutchess Co.,
N. Y.; E3 (3-185).
WIRE; (Peter), Ohio, Ind.; Dt (7-
111).
WISNER; (Thomas C.); Ng (4-34; in-
scriptions; Geneva, N. Y.; Ng (4-
69); Inscriptions, Niagara Co., N.
Y.; Ng (4-127).
WOLCOTT; (William); Z (72-1-66).
WOLF; (Jacob), Md.; M (25-93).
WOOD; (William), Baltimore, Md.; X2
(11-23); (Philip); Col (3-11);
(Enoch); Z (74-1-37).
WOODARD; (Elisha), Edgecombe Co.,
N. C.; M (31-29).
WOODRUFF; (David), Conn.; B4 (10-
128); (Noah), Hopewell, N. J.; M
(22-13); (Lewis), Cumberland Co.,
N. J.; B5 (22-41); (Nathaniel),
Litchfield, Conn.; M (29-23);
(Nathaniel), Suffolk Co., N. Y.;
Z (74-7-55).
WOODWARD; (Thomas); B1 (9-38).
WOOLLEY; (Joseph); Great Neck, N. Y.;
LI (2-111).
WOOSTER; (Henry, William), Fulton
Co., N. Y.; E3 (4-121).
WRIGHT; A2 (65-121); (Data L.), Say-
brook, Conn.; B4 (14-19); (Asa);
E3 (4-73); (Joseph); Dt (2-41);
(Richard), Decatur, N. Y.; Dt (8-
78).
WYCKOFF; (William); E3 (2-121).

WYCOFF; (Cornelius); B1 (15-92).
WYMAN; (Abraham); A1 (88-93).

YARRINGTON; (William); A2 (76-75).
YATES; (James-Gaines), Va., Tenn.;
   Z (69-562).
YEWELL; (James), Va., Ky.; W2 (19-
   235).
YORK; (John); L1 (6-40).
YOUNG; (George), E3 (2-75); (William),
   Va.; W2 (12-41); (William C.), New-
   ark, Ohio; O (5-399); (Peter P.);
   Ng (2-59); (Capt. John), Baltimore
   Co., Md.; X2 (16-15, 24, 52, 61).
YULE, JAMES; Md.; A1 (88-92).

ZIMMERMAN; (Adam), Burford, Ont.; Dt
   (10-108).
ZORNS; (Israel S.), Pa.; M (25-90).
ZUG; (Jacob), Pa., Md.; M (25-93).

ABBOT; (Samuel), Mass., N. H.; M (30-128).
ABELL; (Simon), Conn.; M (30-128).
ABERNATHY; (David), N. C., Tenn.; M (24-48); (Robert), Va., N. C.; M (30-129).
ABRAHAM; (James), N. J.; M (23-90); (Enoch), Pa.; M (31-11).
ACKLER; (Leonard), N. Y.; M (30-129).
ACKLEY; (Champion), Conn., Ohio; M (30-129).
ADAMS; (James), Mass., Vt.; M (30-28); (James), Mass.; M (30-29); (James), Mass.; Me.; M (30-29); (Micajah), N. C., Tenn.; M (27-96); (David), N. J., Ohio; M (30-129); (Heman), Mass., Ohio; M (30-130).
ADDIS; (Simon), N. J.; M (30-130).
ALDERSON; (Thomas), Va.; M (30-131).
ALDRICH; (Amasa), Mass., N. H.; M (30-131).
ALEXANDER; (Dr. James R.), Md., S. C., Ky.; M (30-52); (James), Conn.; M (30-131); (James), Va.; M (30-132).
ALLEN; (Caleb); Mass.; M (30-132); (Daniel), Conn.; M (30-132); (Ebenezer), Mass., N. H.; M (30-133); (Jacob), Mass.; M (30-133); (Joseph), Mass., N. Y.; M (30-133); (John), Mass.; M (30-133); (Nathan), Medfield, Mass.; M (30-134); (Nehemiah), Mass., Me.; M (30-135); (Samuel), N. J.; M (30-135); (Samuel), Va., N. C., Ky.; M (30-136); (Samuel), N. J.; M (30-136); (William), Pa., N. C., Ill.; M (30-136); (Zoheth), R. I.; N. Y.; M (30-136).
ALLGOOD; (John), Va., Ga.; M (30-137).
ALLISON; (John), N. C., Tenn.; M (22-112); (John), Pa.; M (22-112).
ALLYN; (George), Conn.; M (30-137).
ALVERSON; (John), Va., S. C.; M (30-138).
AMES; (Daniel), Conn.; M (30-138); (John), Conn., N. Y.; M (30-138).
AMLERSON; (William), Mercer, Pa.; M (30-30).
ANDERSON; (Thomas), Conn.; M (23-91); (Jacob), Va.; M (30-138); (James), Pa.; M (30-139); (Joseph), Va.; M (30-139); (William), Va.; M (30-139); (Joseph), Mass., N. Y.; Z (72-9-91).
ANDREAS; (Jeremiah), Conn.; M (30-140).
ANDREWS; (Amos), Mass.; M (30-140); (Robert), Mass., Me.; M (30-141); (William), Va.; M (30-141); (Timothy), N. Y.; Z (70-1024).
ANDROS; (Thomas), Conn., Mass.; M (30-141).
ANTILL; (Jacob), Va.; M (30-141).
ARMSTRONG; (James), Conn.; M (30-142); (William), Va.; M (30-143).
ARNOLD; (Fenner), Conn., Mass.; M (30-143); (Jonathan), N. Y., Pa.; M (30-143); (Moses), R. I., Conn.; M (30-144); (Benjamin), S. C.; Tenn.; Z (78-101); (Thomas); Z (77-661).
ARNOT; (Henry), N. J., Va.; M (30-144).
ASHBY; (John), Mass.; M (30-144).
ASTON; (Alexander), Pa., Va., Tenn.; M (22-114).
ATCHLEY; (Thomas), Va., N. J.; M (22-74; 30-145).
ATHEY; (Thomas), Va.; M (30-145).
ATKINS; (Edward), Va.; M (30-145).
ATWOOD; (John), Conn.; M (22-75).
AUMOCK; (William), N. J.; M (30-145).
AUSTIN; (Moses), N. H.; M (30-146).
AVERY; (Rufus), Conn.; M (30-146).
AYRES; (Robert), N. J.; M (30-146).

BACHELDER; (Samuel), Me., N. Y.; M (31-43).
BACON; (Simeon), Ware, Mass.; M (30-30).
BAILEY; (Ward), Mass., Vt.; M (22-114).
BAIRD; (John), N. J.; M (24-48).
BAKER; (Isaac), Md., Ill.; M (31-11); (Capt. Thomas); M (31-43); (Peter), N. Y.; M (33-21); (Thomas); Mass., N. H.; M (33-21).
BANNERMAN; (George), N. C.; M (21-69).
BARBEE; (Joseph), N. C., Ill.; Z (80-427).
BARKER; (Williams), Me.; M (22-115); (Jacob), S. C., Ill.; M (24-49).

BARNES; (John), Va., Ky.; M (31-44).
BARRETT; (Lewis and Samuel), Va.; M (24-49).
BATES; (Nehemiah), Mass.; M (24-49).
BATTERSHELL; (Freeman), Va., Ky.; Z (72-2-68).
BAUM; (Frederick), Pa.; Z (71-846).
BAYLEY; (Jeremiah), R. I.; M (31-11).
BEACH; (Nathaniel), Conn.; M (23-91); (Nathan), N. Y., Pa.; M (24-50); (Philo), Norfolk, Conn., Dover, Ohio; Dt (9-91); (Joseph), Conn., N. Y.; M (31-12).
BEAGLE; (John), N. Y.; Z (78-692).
BEAL; (Samuel), Mass.; M (22-115).
BEAM; (Michael), Va., Ohio; M (30-53).
BEASLEY; (Isham), N. C., Tenn.; M (30-31).
BEAZELY; (James), Greene Co., Va.; M (30-30).
BEEMAN; (Friend), Conn., Vt.; M (21-127, 128).
BELLOUS; (Charles), Mass., Vt.; M (29-28; 30-31).
BEMIS; (Isaac), Mass., N. Y.; M (23-48).
BENTON; (Jonathan), Conn., Mass.; M (31-12).
BICKLEY; (Charles), Va.; M (33-50).
BIDLACK; (Philemon), Conn., Pa.; M (33-50).
BIDWELL; (Ozias), Conn.; M (33-51).
BIGELAR; (Nicholas), N. J.; M (33-51).
BILL; (Jabez), Mass.; M (33-51); (Jonathan), Conn., N. Y.; M (33-51); (Roswell), Conn.; M (33-81).
BILLINGS; (Lemuel), Mass.; M (33-52).
BINGLEY; (Lewis), Va., Ill.; M (33-52).
BIRD; (Edmund), Mass.; M (33-52).
BIRDSEYE; (Thaddeus), Conn.; M (23-92); Z (79-364).
BISHOP; (Gabriel), N. Y.; M (23-93); (Henry), Va.; M (23-93); (Sylvanus), Mass., N. Y.; M (30-53); (James), Conn.; M (33-53); (Jared), Conn.; M (33-53).
BISSELL; (Benjamin), Conn.; M (33-53); (Ozias), Conn.; M (33-54).
BLACKBURN; (Clement), Va., Ala.; M (33-54).
BLACKFORD; (Nathan), N. J.; M (31-13).
BLACKMAN; (Zachariah), Conn., N. Y.; M (24-50; 33-54).

BLACKMAR; (Jacob), R. I., Conn.; M (31-13).
BLAIR; (Abraham), N. J.; M (33-54); (Samuel), N. C., Tenn.; M (33-55); (Thomas), Pa.; M (35-55).
BLAKE; (Joseph), Mass.; M (33-55).
BLAKELY; (James), Conn., N. Y.; M (34-31).
BLANCHARD; (Elias), N. Y.; M (33-123).
BLANTON; (Thomas), Va., Tenn.; M (34-31).
BLAUVELT; (Harman), N. J.; Z (72-1-70).
BLODGET; (Joshua), Mass., Vt.; M (31-14).
BLODGETT; (Abisha), Conn., N. Y., Pa., Va.; M (31-14).
BLUE; (Peter), Va.; M (34-31).
BOAZ; (James), Va.; M (34-31).
BOGLE; (Andrew), Pa., Tenn.; M (24-50).
BONTA; (Hendrick), N. Y.; Z (79-278).
BOONE; (Squire), S. C., Ky; Z (80-38).
BOSTON; (Winthrop), Me.; M (33-123).
BOULDIN; (Wood), Va.; Vl (16-133).
BOWEN; (Samuel), Mass., Me.; M (32-101); (William), Va.; M (32-101).
BOWLING; (Wm.-Ignatius), Md.; M (24-51).
BOYER; (Frederick), Pa.; Z (73-12-62; 77-386).
BRADEEN; (Robert), Maine; M (31-14).
BRADFORD; (Thomas), Conn.; M (31-15); (John-Angel), Va., S. C.; M (31-92).
BRADLEY; (James), N. Y.; M (24-51); (James), Pa., and (James), N. C., Tenn.; M (24-52); (Eber), Conn., Vt.; M (27-96).
BRADSHAW; (John), Va.; M (31-93).
BRAINARD; (Reuben), N. Y.; M (27-97).
BRANDON; (Benjamin), N. C., Ohio; M (34-32).
BRANK; (Robert), N. C., Ky.; M (30-32).
BRANT; (Christian), N. Y.; M (27-97).
BRASWELL; (Richard), N. C.; M (30-32).
BRATTON; (Bartholomew), Pa.; Z (72-5-68).
BREEZE; (John), Md., Ky.; M (31-15).

BREWER; (Henry), N. Y.; M (29-29);
(Henry); Va., Ohio; M (33-55).
BREWSTER; (James), N. Y., Pa.; M (31-
93).
BROCK; (Reuben), N. C.; M (33-123).
BROOKS; (Wm.), Va.; M (24-53); (Ele-
azer), Conn., Vt.; M (31-122);
(Nelson), Va.; M (31-93); (John
C.), N. Y.; M (33-22).
BROWER; (Henry), N. Y.; M (31-16).
BROWN; (Basil), Va.; M (32-101);
(John), Worcester, Mass.; M (32-
101); (Robert), Va., Ga.; M (32-
102); (Samuel), Va., Ill.; M (32-
102); (Stephen), Conn., N. Y.; M
(32-102); (Daniel), Va.; M (33-22);
(John), Pa.; M (33-23); (John),
Mass., Ohio; M (33-23); (Oliver),
Conn.; M (31-16); (George), Mass.,
Pa., N. Y.; M (31-94).
BROWNELL; (Gideon), R. I.; M (31-94).
BRUCE; (Benjamin), Va.; M (32-102).
BRUNSON; (Amos), Mass., N. Y.; M (31-
44).
BRUSH; (Josiah), Vt.; M (31-123).
BRYAN; (John); M (32-103).
BRYANT; (Alexander), Mass., N. Y.; M
(32-103); (Amasa), Mass., Vt.; M
(32-103); (William), N. C.; M (32-
103); (Jesse), Va., N. C.; M (31-
43, 124).
BRYDIA; (David), Conn., Vt.; M (32-
103).
BUCHANAN; (Alexander), N. Y.; M (27-
98).
BUMGARDNER; (David), Va.; M (28-63).
BURFORD; (John), N. C.; M (28-63).
BURKES; (Samuel), N. C., Tenn.; M
(32-104).
BURNHAM; (James), Hampton, Conn.; M
(22-16); (Josiah), Hampton, Conn.;
M (22-17).
BURRISS; (Solomon), N. C.; M (22-
54).
BURROUGHS; (Matthew), Vt.; M (30-146).
BURTON; (Thomas), Va.; M (27-98);
(James), Va.; M (31-124).
BURWELL; (Jere), Conn.; M (26-53a).
BUSH; (William), N. C.; M (22-55);
(James), Va., Ky.; M (39-29).
BUTLER; (Moses), Me.; M (24-53);
(Reuben), Va.; M (27-98).
BUTLERS; (William), Mass.; M (32-
104).
BUTT; (Archibald, Md.); M (20-56).
BUTTS; (Williams), Mass., N. Y.; M
(25-99).
BYINGTON; (Justus), Conn., Vt.; M

(24-54); (Samuel), Conn., Mass.;
M (31-124).
BYNUM; (Tapley), N. C.; M (22-55).

CADMAN; (George), R. I., N. Y.; M
(22-75).
CALLAHAN; (John), N. C.; M (32-
104).
CAMERON; (James), Va.; M (32-105).
CAMPBELL; (George), N. C.; M (22-
55); (McDonald), N. J., Ohio; M
(25-99); (William), S. C., Ky.,
Ind.; M (30-54); (Lawrence), Va.,
Ky.; M (32-29); (Enos), N. J.,
Ohio; M (32-105); (John), Conn.;
M (32-105); (John), Va., Tenn.; M
(32-105).
CAMPER; (Tilman), Va., Ky.; Z (70-
102b).
CANNON; (Nathaniel), Ga.; M (32-29).
CARBACH; (Peter), Pa., Ind.; M (32-
106).
CARDER; (Sanford), Va., Ohio; M
(25-99).
CARLISLE; (James); M (33-23).
CARLL; (John), Mass.; M (33-24); Z
(71-764).
CARLTON; (Lewis), Va., N. C.; M
(32-30).
CARNALL; (Patrick), Va.; M (25-100).
CARPENTER; (Hope), N. Y.; M (33-
25).
CARR [KERR]; (Robert), Pa., N. C.;
M (23-49); (Caleb), R. I.; M (32-
62).
CARSON; (James), Del., Me.; M (32-
106); (Walter), Pa., S. C., Ind.;
M (32-30; 33-25).
CASEY; (Archibald), Del., Ky.; M
(33-81); (James), Va.; M (33-81).
CASON; (William), S. C., Ga.; M
(32-31).
CASSELL; (Thomas), N. C.; M (33-
26).
CASWELL, (Samuel), Conn., N. Y.; M
(32-30).
CHADWICK; (Elihu), N. J., Pa.; Z
(71-846).
CHALFANT; (Solomon), Va.; M (25-
100).
CHAMBERLAIN; (Freegift), Pa., Ohio;
M (33-26); (Moses), Mass.; M (33-
26).
CHAMBERS; (Nathaniel), N. C., Ind.;
M (33-26).
CHAMPLIN; (Charles), Conn.; M (24-
55); (Joseph), Mass., R. I.; M
(24-56).

CHANDLER; (Samuel); M (27-22); (Shadrack), S. C., Va.; M (33-27).
CHANEY; (Abraham), Va.; M (33-27).
CHAPIN; (John), Conn., N. Y.; M (33-27); (Joseph), Mass.; M (33-28).
CHAPMAN; (Elijah), Conn.; Z (70-717).
CHAPPELL; (William), Va.; M (33-81); (Benjamin), Va.; M (33-81).
CHENOWETH; (Thomas), Md.; M (32-63).
CHERRY; (Henry), N. J.; M (33-28).
CHIDESTER; (Phineas), N. J.; M (33-28).
CHILD; (Timothy), Conn., N. Y.; M (30-33).
CHILDERS; (Pleasant), N. C., Ky.; M (33-29); (Goolsberry), Va., Ky.; Z (72-8-89).
CHILDRESS; (Benjamin), Va.; M (26-67).
CHILES; (Henry), Va.; M (26-67).
CHILTON; (John), Va.; M (24-56).
CHINA; (John), S. C.; M (33-29).
CHINN; (Perry), Va., N. C.; Z (70-717).
CHIVVIS; (William), N. Y.; M (33-29).
CHOICE; (Tully), Va., Ga.; M (33-55); see also Vl (14-176); (William), S. C.; Z (70-718).
CHRIST; (Adam), Pa.; M (25-100); (Henry), Pa.; M (26-67).
CHRISTIAN; (John), N. C., Tenn.; M (33-56).
CHRISTIE; (James), Pa., Va.; Z (70-1025).
CHURCHILL; (Caleb), Mass., Vt.; M (33-56).
CISNA; (Stephen), Pa.; M (33-82).
CLARK; (Theophilus), Mass., Vt.; M (23-50); (Elijah), Mass.; M (26-4); (Elijah), Va.; M (26-4); (Jonathan), Conn.; M (26-4); (Lawrence), R. I.; M (26-5); (Paul), Mass.; M (26-6); (Roswell), Conn.; M (26-67, 68); (William), Conn.; M (26-69); (Asa), Conn., N. Y.; M (32-63); (Elijah), Md., Ky.; M (33-29, 57); (William), Md.; M (33-57); (William), N. C., S. C.; M (33-57); (Gershom), Conn., Vt.; Z (79-279); (Hezekiah), Conn., N. Y.; Z (72-1-71); (Oliver), Conn., N. Y.; Z (71-764).
CLEAVER; (William), Va., Ky.; M (33-58).
CLEMENTS; (Clement), S. C.; M (26-69).
CLINTON; (James), S. C., Ky.; M (33-

58); E3 (7-169).
CLOUGH; (William), Mass.; M (33-58).
CLUTCH; (John), Nottingham, N. J.; M (34-61).
COBB; (Edward), Mass., Me.; M (33-59).
COBBS; (Robert), Va.; M (33-59).
COBLER; (Frederick), N. C., Tenn.; M (33-59).
COCKE; (William), Va.; M (20-56).
COE; (Jedediah), Guilford, Conn.; M (34-62).
COFFEY; (Ozbourn), Va., Ky.; (Reuben), S. C., Ky.; M (34-62).
COFFIN; (Nathaniel), Shapleigh, Me.; M (34-62).
COGHILL; (Thomas), Va.; M (33-60).
COIT; (Isaac), Preston, Conn.; M (34-63).
COLBURN; (Daniel), Mass.; M (26-69).
COLE; (Amos), Voluntown, Conn.; (Amos), Dighton, Mass.; (Azor), Ballston, N. Y.; (Jonathan), Weston, Conn.; (John), Conn.; (Thomas), Wilton, Conn.; M (34-63, 64); (Daniel), Va.; M (27-99); (James), Conn.; M (27-99); (Samuel), Mass., Canada; M (27-100).
COLEMAN; (Jacob), Va.; M (26-70); (John), N. Y.; M (27-100); (Leonard), N. J.; M (27-100); (John), Va.; M (24-56).
COLEY; (William), N. Y.; M (34-97).
COLFAX; (William), Conn.; M (33-82).
COLLIER; (Aaron), Va.; M (33-82); (John), Pa., Va.; M (34-97).
COLLINS; (Benjamin); R. I., Ohio; M (34-65); (Asahel), R. I.; M (32-31); (Elisha), Va., Ala.; M (34-98); (Thadeus), Mass., N. Y.; M (34-98); (William), Conn.; M (34-98).
COLVIN; (Levi), Clarendon, Vt.; M (34-65).
COMBES; (William), Va., Ky.; M (32-107); (Mahlon), Va., Ohio; M (34-100).
COMPTON; (Archibald), Va.; M (32-31); (Edmund H.), Md., Ky.; M (32-32).
COMSTOCK; (Theophilus), Conn., N. Y.; M (34-65).
CONANT; (Peter), Mass.; M (34-98, 99).
CONAWAY; (John), Va., Pa.; M (34-99).
CONDRY; (William); M (32-32).
CONE; (Reuben), Conn.; M (32-62).
CONGDON; (James), R. I.; M (32-61).
CONNELLY; (John), Me., Mo.; M (33-

60); Z (79-364).
CONNOR; (Philip), Va., Ind.; M (34-99).
CONRAD; (Adam), N. J.; M (32-32).
CONWAY; (John), Va., Ky.; M (34-100).
COOK; (Benjamin), Ga., Ala.; M (32-32); (David), N. J., N. Y.; M (32-63); (Elijah), Conn., N. Y.; M (32-63); (John), Va.; M (32-64); (Jonathan), N. Y.; M (32-64); (Moses), Conn.; M (32-64); (Uriah), N. H.; M (32-93); (William), Va., Ky.; M (32-93); (Zachariah), Va., Ohio; M (32-93); (Oliver), Conn.; M (22-55); (Abraham), Conn., Pa.; M (32-61).
COOLEY; (William), N. Y., Ohio; M (32-94).
COOPER; (James B.), N. J.; M (23-50); (John), N. J.; M (34-100); (Joseph), Mass., N. Y.; M (34-100); (Leonard), Va.; M (34-101); Z (71-1031).
COPELAND; (Isaac), Mass.; M (22-116).
COPES; (Parker), Va.; M (34-101).
COPLEY; (Daniel), Conn.; M (34-101).
COPPAGE; (John), Va.; M (34-101).
COPPEGE; (Thomas), Va.; M (34-102).
CORBIN; (Lewis), Va., Ky.; M (32-95).
CORN; (Jesse), Va., Tenn.; M (32-95); (William), Pa.; M (32-94); (George), Pa., Ky.; M (33-60).
CORNWALL; (Isaac), Conn.; M (33-60).
CORNWELL; (William), N. J., Pa.; M (34-102).
CORSE; (John), Del.; M (33-60).
COTTON; (James), Va.; M (25-100).
COVEL; (Henry), Conn., N. Y.; M (33-61).
COWDERY; (Asa), Conn.; M (32-95).
COWHERD; (Francis), Va.; M (23-51).
COX; (Isaac), Md.; M (26-54a); (George), Va.; M (32-96).
COY; (William, Md.); M (20-57).
CRANDALL; (John), R. I.; M (34-102).
CRANE; (John), N. J.; M (32-107); (John), Mass., Vt.; M (32-107); (Col. John), Mass.; M (32-107); (John), Mass., N. Y.; M (32-96).
CRANSTON; (Samuel), R. I.; M (26-70).
CRARY; (Joseph), R. I., Conn., Me.; M (22-17).
CRAWFORD; (John), N. Y.; M (22-19); (Patrick), Pa.; M (22-116); (Joseph), N. Y.; M (22-19); (James), Mass.; M (33-82).
CREEKBAUM; (Philip), Md.; M (33-61).

CREEL; (John), Va.; M (33-83).
CREEMER; (William), N. J.; M (30-33).
CRESWELL; (Andrew), Va.; M (33-83).
CREVELING; (Andrew), N. J.; M (26-130).
CRITCHFIELD; (John), Va.; M (33-83); (William), Pa., Ohio; M (33-61).
CRUM; (John), Md., Pa.; M (33-62).
CUMMINGS; (John), Md., Va.; M (23-51); (James), Mass.; M (34-135); (Thomas), R. I., Conn.; M (34-135, see 102).
CUMMINS; (Harmon), S. C.; M (21-46).
CUNNINGHAM; (William), Va.; M (34-102); (Ansel), Va., Ga.; M (34-135).
CURD; (John), Va., Ky.; M (34-135).
CURRANCE; (William), Pa., Va.; M (25-100).
CURRIER; (Samuel), Pa.; M (34-135).
CURTIS; (Benjamin), Conn.; M (34-137); (Frederick), Conn., N. Y.; M (34-137); (Giles), Conn., Mass.; M (34-137).
CUSHMAN; (Isaac), Pa.; M (34-138).
CUTTING; (Jonas), Mass.; M (26-71).

DALTON; (Isaac), Mass., N. H.; Z (78-245).
DARBY; (Benjamin), S. C., Ala.; M (34-138).
DARROW; (Jedidiah), N. Y.; M (33-62).
DAVIS; (Benjamin), N. C., Ga.; M (21-128); (William), Md., Pa.; M (23-51); (Thomas), Md., Ohio; M (26-35a); (Zachariah), Pa.; M (34-138).
DAWSON; (Joseph), Md.; M (32-107).
DAY; (Joel), Mass.; Z (71-165); (William), S. C.; M (21-46); (Lewis), Mass., Conn., Ohio; S3 (13-3-8).
DAYTON; (Jonathan), N. J.; M (34-138).
DEAVER; (John), Md.; M (23-52).
DEGRAAF; (Isaac), N. Y.; M (23-94).
DEMOSS; (Peter), Va., Ky.; M (32-108).
DENNISTON; (John); N. J.; M (28-31).
DEVENY; (Aaron), N. C.; Z (70-718).
DICKENSON; (Griffith), Va., Ga.; M (26-35a).
DICKEY; (Ebenezer), N. C., Ky.; M (30-34).
DICKSON; (Thomas), N. C.; M (21-129).
DILLINGHAM; (Paul), Mass.; Vt.; M

(30-54).
DOLLINGER; (John), Pa.; S3 (9-6-9).
DORLAND; (Peter), N. J.; M (33-62).
DORR; (William), Mass., Me.; M (33-83).
DOYLE; (John), Md., Tenn.; M (24-56).
DUNCAN; (Charles), Va.; M (22-76).
DUNNING; (John), Mass., Me.; M (30-54); (Michael), N. Y.; M (30-55).
DURANT; (Thomas), Mass.; M (33-84).
DURHAM; (Matthew), Ga.; Z (78-293).
DUVAL; (William), Va.; M (26-54a).

EASTER; (John), Md., Va.; M (32-108).
EATON; (Thomas), Mass., N. Y.; M (25-116).
EDDY; (Asa), Conn., N. Y.; M (26-36a).
EDWARDS; (John), Mass.; M (33-84).
EIOTT; (John), N. C., Ala.; M (30-56).
ELBERT; (John L.), Md.; M (30-55).
ELGIN; (Walter); Va.; M (30-56).
ELLIOTT, ELLIOT; (John), Va., N. C.; M (20-120); (Ezekiel); M (26-113); (Jacob), N. Y.; M (30-56).
ELLIS; (Jesse), Md., Pa., Ohio; M (23-53).
ELLSWORTH; (John), M (27-23).
ELTON; (Bradley), Conn.; M (30-34).
EMERSON; (Jonathan); M (26-113).
EMERY; (Eliphalet); M (26-113).
ENOS; (Joseph), R. I., N. Y.; M (26-36a).
ERSKINE; (John); M (26-113).
ERWIN; (David); M (26-114).
EVAN; (Thomas), Va.; M (26-37a).
EVANS; (Eldad), N. H., N. Y.; M (30-56); (Zachariah), Md., Ky.; M (30-57); (Philip), S. C.; M (21-47).
EVERSEY; (Adam), N. Y.; M (32-108).

FALLIS; (Isaac), Pa., Ky.; M (26-55a).
FARLEY; (who?); M (26-114).
FARNUM; (Samuel); M (26-114).
FARRELL; (James), Va.; M (22-77).
FAST; (Christian), Md., Pa., Ohio; M (26-55a).
FERGUSON; (John), Md.; M (20-57); (Robert), Va.; M (20-57).
FIELD; (Dennis), Middlesex Co., N. J.; M (30-113).
FIELDS; (John), N. C.; M (22-77).
FILLEBROWN; (Samuel S.), Mass.; Z (71-1032).

FLANAGAN; (David), N. C.; M (30-58).
FLEENOR; (Michael), Va.; M (30-58).
FOLKNER; (Ezekiel); Z (79-156).
FORD; (Alexander), Md.; M (20-58); (Elisha), S. C.; M (20-58); (John), Md.; M (20-59); (Thomas), N. J.; M (20-59); (Joseph), M (26-115); (William), Va.; M (30-58).
FOSTER; (Asa), Conn., N. Y.; M (22-78); (John), Pa.; M (23-53); (Daniel); M (26-115).
FOWLER; (Amos), Conn.; M (24-57).
FRANCE; (Peter), Md.; M (27-101).
FRANK; (George), Pa.; M (33-123); (John), M (28-31).
FRANTZ; (Adam); Pa.; M (28-32).
FREEMAN; (Israel), N. J., N. Y.; Z (70-719).
FRENCH; (Samuel), Conn.; M (20-60, 61); (John); M (26-116).
FULLER; (William), Mass.; M (22-79); (John), M (26-116); (Samuel); M (26-116); (Elisha), Mass.; Z (70-1025).
FURBER; (Caleb), Del.; M (28-63).

GALLUP; (Amos), Conn.; Z (70-1026).
GARDNER; (William), Conn., N. Y.; Z (70-719).
GIBBONEY; (Alexander), Lancaster Co., Pa.; M (27-64).
GIBSON; (John), Md., Tenn.; M (23-54).
GILLAM; (Robert), S. C.; Z (73-7-72).
GILMAN; (Joseph); M (26-116).
GLIDDEN; (David); M (26-117).
GODMAN; (Williams), Va.; M (26-37a).
GOSS; (John); M (26-117).
GRACE; (William), Md., Ind.; Z (71-242).
GRANT; (William), S. C.; M (21-47).
GRAVES; (Whitney), Conn.; M (22-80).
GREACEY; (John), N. C., Tenn.; Z (71-765).
GREENTREE; (Benjamin), Md.; M (22-80).
GREENWAY; (William), Va., Tenn.; M (33-84).
GREER; (Henry), Pa.; M (30-34).
GRIDER; (John), N. C.; M (22-81).
GRIFFITH; (Samuel), Md.; M (23-54).
GRISWOLD; (Andrew), Conn.; M (26-37a); (Jabez), N. Y.; M (26-39a).
GROSH; (Michael), Md., Va.; M (26-39a).
GROVE; (Samuel), N. J.; M (23-55).
GUNN; (Eli), Mass.; M (34-103).
GURLEY; (Jeremiah), N. C.; M (22-81).

GUSTIN; (Josiah); M (26-117).

HADLEY; (Jonathan), M (27-23).
HAGEY; (John), Tenn.; M (26-57a).
HALE; (Amon), Md., Tenn.; M (23-55).
HALL; (James), Conn.; M (24-57).
HALLOCK; (Daniel), Southold, N. Y.; M (20-94).
HAMILL;(Robert), Pa.; M (22-117).
HAMILTON; (Abner), Va., Ky.; M (23-94).
HAMNER; (John), Va., Ky., Ind.; M (30-58).
HARDING; (Ede), N. J., Pa.; M (22-118); (Henry), Va., Ind.; M (22-118).
HARPER; (Wm.), Pa.; M (24-57); (Wm.), Pa.; M (24-58); (Daniel); M (27-23).
HARRELL; (Joel), N. C., Ky., Ill.; M (24-58).
HARRIS; (Robert), N. C.; M (22-82); (John), N. C., S. C.; M (30-59); (Joshua), Va., Ky.; M (34-103).
HARRISON; (Benjamin), Ga.; M (22-83); (Matthew), N. J., N Y.; M (30-113); (John), Pa.; Z (79-557).
HART; (Adams), N. C.; M (24-58).
HASKELL; (Caleb), Mass.; M (22-119).
HATCH; (Mason); M (27-24).
HAWKINS; (Philemon), N. C. M (24-59).
HAWLEY; (James), Conn.; M (2 3-95).
HAWTHORN; (Joseph), S. C., Ill.; M (24-59).
HENDERSON; (William), Va.; M (22-119; 34-103).
HERBERT; (Thomas), N. J., Ohio; M (34-103).
HERING; (Ludwig), Pa.; S3·(9-6-9).
HERMANY; (Jacob), Pa.; M (28-63).
HERNDON; (William), Va.; (two); M (23-56); (John), Va., Ky.; M (33-124); (James), N. C.; Z (80-428).
HERRIMAN; (Jacob); M (28-64).
HIBBARD; (Thomas); M (27-24).
HILL; (Isaac), N. C., Ga.; M (24-59); (Daniel), N. C., Tenn.; M (34-32); (Robert), N. C.; M (24-60).
HILLAN; (James), N. C.; M (22-83).
HINMAN; (Timothy), Conn., Vt.; Z (71-89).
HIPPLE; (John), Pa.; M (34-103).
HITE; (George), Va.; M (22-56).
HITES; (John), France; Ohio; M (24-**60).**

HODGES; (John), Va., S. C.; M (21-132); Will of John (1835); M (21-133); (Joseph), N. C.; Z (73-11-63).
HODGKINS; (Samuel), Pa., Md., Ky., Ohio; M (22-119).
HOLBROOK; (Amos); M (27-25).
HOLCOMBE; (Philemon), Va., Tenn.; M (22-84); (John), Va.; M (26-39a).
HOLLAND; (Wm.), N. C.; M (24-61); (Edward), Md.; M (34-65).
HOLLINGSWORTH; (Henry), N. C.; M (24-61); (Zebedee), N. C.; M (24-62).
HOLLOWAY; (James), Va., Ky.; M (22-120).
HOOD; (James), Md.; M (20-120).
HOOVER; (Jacob), Va.; (Jacob), Pa., Va.; (Michael), Va.; (Thomas), Va.; M (34-65, 66).
HOPKINS; (Dennis), N. C.; M (22-85); (Levi), Mass., Va.; Z (73-4-85).
HOUSER; (Andrew), S. C.; M (24-62).
HOUSTON; (James), N. C.; (two); M (23-57); (Archibald), N. C., Tenn.; Z (71-90).
HOWE; (David), S. C., Ky.; M (24-63).
HOWELL; (Arthur), N. J.; Z (71-847).
HOYT; (Seth), Mass., Vt.; M (24-63).
HUBBARD; (William), S. C.; M (21-50).
HUBER; (George), Pa.; M (34-103).
HUDSON; (James), N. C.; M (24-64).
HUGHES; (William), S. C.; M (21-50).
HUGHLETT; (Wm.), N. C.; M (24-64).
HULL; (David), Conn., N. Y.; Z (79-364).
HUNT; (Thomas), Md., Tenn.; M (24-66); (William), N. Y.; Z (71-766).
HURLBUT; (Stephen), Conn.; Z (73-4-84).
HUTCHINSON; (Wm.), N. C.; M (24-66).
HUYCK; (William), N. Y.; M (20-121).

ISBELL; (Garner), Pa., Conn.; M (32-108).

JACK; (John), Pa.; M (20-121).
JACKSON; (Samuel), N. C.; M (24-66); (John), Mass., Me.; Z (71-243).
JACOBY; (Philip), Pa.; M (22-20).
JENKINS; (James), S. C.; M (24-67).
JENNINGS; (Benjamin), Pa.; M (30-59).
JETER; (Littleton), Va., Ky.; Z

(72-4-87).
JOHNSON; (Jesse), N. C., Tenn.; M
(24-67); (Wm.), Va., N. C.; M (24-
68); (Wm.), N. C., Fla., Ala.,
with inscriptions; M (21-124, 125).
JOHNSTON; (Thomas), Pa., Ind.; Z (71-
469); (William), Ga.; Z (72-8-89).
JONES; (William), Vt.; M (30-60); N.
J., N. Y., Pa., Canada; M (30-60);
Conn., N. Y.; M (30-60); N. Y.; M
(30-60); (Jacob), Orange Co., N.
Y.; M (34-66); (Solomon), Mass.;
M (32-109); (Ambrose), Va., Ky.;
M (34-104).
JORDAN; (James), Mass., Me.; Z (71-
470).
JOY; (Samuel), Mass., Me.; M (23-1).

KARR; (Peter), N. J.; M (33-85).
KEATLEY; (Christopher), Pa.; M (23-
2).
KEELER; (Nathaniel), N. Y.; M (22-
85).
KEEN; (Jesse); Mass.; M (30-60).
KELLEY; (Moses), Md.; M (20-94);
(William), Md.; M (20-95).
KERR; (John), N. J., Ohio; M (23-
96).
KIBBE; (Lemuel), Conn.; Z (71-90).
KILBOURN; (Benjamin), Pa., Tenn.; M
(23-2); (Elisha), Mass.; M (23-2).
KINCHELOE; (Thomas), Va., Ky.; Z
(72-6-77).
KING; (Nathan), N. C.; M (23-3);
(Robert), N. C.; M (23-3); (Thom-
as), Pa.; Tenn.; M (23-4); (Wil-
liam), Pa.; Tenn.; M (23-4);
(Jesse), Va.; M (30-61); (Jonah),
Conn.; Z (71-243); (Baxter), N.
C.; Z (80-428).
KINNISTON; (David), Mass., N. Y.; Z
(71-91).
KROM; (John G.), N. Y.; Z (73-10-
74).

LAMPHIER; (James), Conn.; M (28-94).
LAMSON; (Thomas), Mass., Vt.; Z (71-
767).
LANDON; (Laban), N. J., Pa.; Z (73-
7-71).
LANDRUM; (Thomas), Va., Ga.; M (22-
86).
LANHAM; (Thomas), Md., Ky.; M (23-
96).
LAWRENCE; (Benjamin), S. C.; Z (73-
10-74).
LEE; (Tho.), N. J.; M (24-68); (Joseph), N. J., Ind.; Z (80-39);

(Richard-Evers), Norfolk, Va.; W2
(17-525).
LEHMAN; (Christian), York, Pa.; S3
(11-1-14).
LEWIS; (William), Conn.; M (22-58);
(William), Me.; M (22-57); (Ephra-
im), Conn.; M (22-57); (Thomas),
Va., Ky.; M (23-58).
LIBBY; (William), Mass.; Z (70-1027).
LITZINGER; (Henry), Md.; M (23-5).
LOOMIS; (Jerome); Phelps, N. Y.; M
(29-73).
LORD; (Joseph), Conn., N. Y.; M (23-
58).
LOUGEE; (John), Gilmanton, N. H.; M
(29-73).
LOVEJOY; (Samuel), Methuen, Mass.; M
(29-73).
LOVELACE; (Gersham), N. J.; M (33-
85).
LOW; (Samuel), N. Y.; M (23-5); (Hen-
ry); Md., Va.; Z (71-848).
LOWELL; (Wm.), Amesbury, Mass.; M
(29-73).
LOWER; (John), N. Y.; Z (80-503).
LUND; (Jesse), Londonderry, N. H.; M
(29-73).
LYON; (Jacob), Mass.; M (34-104);
(Noah), Conn., N. Y.; Z (71-244).

MCALLISTER; (Joseph), Va.; M (22-86).
MCBRIDE; (James), Salem, Pa.; M (34-
67).
MCCLEAN; (Neal), N. Y.; Z (72-4-88).
MCCLURE; (William), Va.; M (23-6);
(William), Pa.; M (23-6).
MCCLURG; (Robert and Samuel), Ohio;
M (29-73).
MCCOY; (John), Vt., N. Y.; M (29-74).
MCGEE; (John), N. J., Ky.; M (29-29).
MCKEAN; (Hugh), N. H., N. Y.; M (29-
74).
MCKIE; (Daniel), Va., Tenn.; M (34-
104).
MCMAHON; (Archibald), S. C.; M (21-
51); (Peter), S. C.; M (21-52).
MCMURTRY; (John), Pa., Tenn.; Z (71-
1032).
MCNEILL; (Daniel), N. H., Pa.; M (29-
74).
MACPHERSON; (John), Pa.; M (28-95).
MAGOON; (Joseph), N. H., Canada; M
(29-75).
MALLETT; (Lewis), Conn.; M (23-6,
59).
MANN; (John), Vt., Ind.; M (29-75);
(Joshua), Mass.; M (33-85).
MARCUM; (Thomas), N. C.; Z (71-1032;

80-428).
MARSH; (Jonathan); Douglas, Mass.; M (29-75).
MARSHALL, Benjamin (alias of Benjamin Greentree).
MARTIN; (Jireh), N. H.; M (29-75); (Joseph), Va.; Z (72-2-69).
MATTOON; (Ebenezer), Amherst, Mass.; M (34-66).
MEEKER; (Jonas), N. J.; Z (73-12-62).
MELTON; (William), N. C.; M (22-20).
MERRITT; (Daniel), N. C.; Z (71-245).
MESLER; (Simon), N. J.; M (23-97).
MIDDLETON; (John), Va.; Z (72-11-62).
MILLER; (Daniel), Va.; M (20-122); war record (Joash), Pa., Ohio; O (6-500).
MITCHELL; (Amasa), Va.; M (23-7); (Solomon), S. C., Tenn.; M (28-95).
MIXTER; (Timothy), Mass.; M (24-69).
MOORE; (William), N. J.; M (33-86).
MORGAN; (James), N. J.; Z (72-12-70); (James), N. C., Tenn.; Z (80-82).
MORTON; (David), S. C.; M (21-52).
MOSELEY; (Samuel), N. C.; M (20-17); (Joseph), Va., S. C.; M (21-130).
MOSHER; (Christian), Pa.; M (21-130).
MOSS; (David), N. Y.; M (23-97); (Daniel), Conn.; M (20-18).
MULFORD; (Benjamin), N. J.; M (20-18).
MUNN; (Francis), R. I., Ohio; M (21-131).
MURPHY; (William), Va.; M (20-18).
MUSGROVE; (Samuel), Lancaster Co., Pa.; M (34-67).

NANNY; (David), N. Y.; M (20-19).
NARAMORE; (Asa), Mass.; M (20-20).
NEARING; (John), Conn.; M (20-20).
NEEDHAM; (John), Mass.; M (20-21).
NELSON; (John), Va.; Tenn.; M (22-21); (John), Va., S. C.; M (30-61); (Henry), Mass.; M (33-86).
NEVILL; (James), Va., Ky.; Z (73-12-61).
NEWBURY; (Jeremiah), Conn., N. Y.; M (22-21).
NEWELL; (Thomas), N. Y.; M (28-96).
NEWMAN; (Edmund), Va.; M (20-21).
NICHOLS; (Isaac), Mass.; M (20-22); (Isaac), N. Y.; M (20-22; 30-62).
NOBLE; (William), Pa.; M (20-23).
NORCROSS; (John), Pa.; M (20-24).

NORMAN; (Thomas), Va.; M (33-86).
NORRIS; (John), Va.; M (20-24).
NORTON; (Freeman), Mass., N. Y.; M (26-39a); Z (73-11-62).
NORVELL; (Lipscomb), Va., Tenn.; M (23-98).
NOURSE; (James), Mass.; Z (70-166).

O'BANNON; (Thomas), Va.; M (28-96).
O'BRIEN; (Daniel), Md.; S3 (13-2-4).
ODALL; (John), N. H.; M (28-96).
ODELL; (William), N. Y.; M (28-96).
OKESON; (Nicholas), N. J.; M (20-122).
OLCOTT; (Jared), Conn.; M (20-123).
OLDFIELD; (William), N. Y.; M (28-97).
OLDS; (Reuben), Mass.; M (23-8).
OLIVER; (Alexander), Mass.; M (20-124); (Richard N.), N. J.; M (28-97).
O'NEAL; (Constantine), Pa., Ill.; Z (70-720).
O'NEIL; (Henry), N. J., Pa.; M (23-8).
ORVIS; (Roger), Conn.; M (20-24).
ORWIG; (George), Pa.; M (28-97).
OSBORN; (Joshua), Conn., Ohio; M (22-23); (Thomas), Conn.; M (22-24); (Joseph), N. J., Ohio; Z (73-11-63).
OSBORNE; (Abraham), N. J.; M (22-22); (Jonathan H.), N. J.; M (22-22).
OSTRANDER; (John), N. Y.; M (20-25).
OTIS; (Isaac), Mass.; M (20-25).
OWENS; (Uriah), N. Y.; M (20-26); (Uriah), N. Y., Ohio; Z (73-2-66).

PAIGE; (Foster), Mass.; M (33-86).
PAINTER; (Henry), Md.; M (20-124); (John), Pa.; M (20-125).
PALMER; (Elias), N. Y.; M (26-40a).
PARK; (Amaziah), Conn.; M (20-125); (Rufus), Conn.; M (20-127).
PARKER; (Jesse), Va.; M (20-127); (Joseph), N. H.; M (20-128); (Jotham), Cheshire, Norfolk, Conn.; Dt (8-26); (Abel), Conn., Vt.; Z (73-7-73).
PARKS; (Nathan), Conn.; M (20-126).
PARROTT; (Christopher); M (32-102).
PASCHAL; (George), S. C., Ga.; M (23-8).
PASLEY; (Thomas), Va., Ky.; Z (71-1118).
PATTEN; (Benoni), Vt., N. H., N. Y.; M (29-132); (John), Arundel, Me.;

Al (96-89).
PATTERSON; (Robert), N. J.; M (20-129); (Robert), Va.; M (20-130).
PATTIE; (William), Va.; M (20-128).
PATTON; (John), Pa.; M (20-130).
PAXTON; (Samuel), Va.; M (20-131).
PEARCE; (Rouse), R. I.; M (20-131).
PECK; (Samuel), R. I.; M (23-9); (Elisha); M (30-34).
PEDDY; (Andrew), N. C.; Z (74-1-47).
PEIRCE; (Joseph), Mass.; M (20-132); (Samuel), Conn., Vt.; Z (71-849).
PENDLETON; (Micajah), Va.; M (20-133).
PERKINS; (Abraham), Conn.; M (26-40a); (Daniel), Conn., Vt.; M (26-41a); (Reuben), Conn., N. Y.; M (26-41a).
PERRIGO; (David), N. Y., Vt.; M (23-10).
PERRY; (John), N. J.; M (26-41a); (Thomas), N. J., Pa., Ohio; M (26-42a).
PERSINGER; (Jacob), Va.; M (20-134).
PETREE; (Peter), N. C., Ky.; M (26-42a).
PETTY; (William), N. C.; Ala.; M (26-42a).
PFEIFFER; (John-George), Pa.; M (20-134).
PFIFER; (Martin), N. C.; M (26-42a).
PHILE; (Philip); P (11-300).
PHILLIPS; (Mark), N. C.; M (26-43a); (Levi), S. C.; M (21-53).
PHIPPS; (Benjamin), N. C., Va.; M (20-134).
PIATT; (Jacob), N. J.; M (20-135); (William), N. J.; M (20-135).
PITCHER; (Gottlieb), N. Y.; M (23-98).
PLUM; (John), N. Y.; M (20-136).
POINDEXTER; (David), Va., N. C.; M (33-87).
POLAND; (Joseph), Mass.; M (23-10); (Seward), Mass.; M (21-35); (John), N. J.; M (29-133).
POMEROY; (Luther), Mass.; M (21-36).
PONDER; (Amos), S. C.; M (23-11).
POOL; (James), Va., S. C.; M (26-43a).
PORTER; (John), Mass.; M (21-37; 23-12).
POST; (George), Conn.; M (21-37); (Isaac), N. Y.; M (21-38); (Henry), N. J.; M (26-43a).
POTTER; (Lemuel), Conn.; M (26-43a).
POWELL; (Levin), Va.; M (26-44a).

POWER; (James), Md., Pa.; M (26-44a).
PRATHER; (Thomas), N. C.; M (26-45a).
PRATT; (Asa), Mass., N. H.; M (26-45a); (Jonathan), Conn., N. Y.; M (26-45a); (Laban), Mass.; M (26-46a); (Paul), Mass.; M (26-46a); (William), Conn.; M (26-46a).
PRESTON; (Daniel), N. Y.; M (26-46a); (Noah), Conn., N. Y.; M (26-47a); (Othniel), N. Y.; M (26-47a); (Moses), Va., Ky.; M (21-38).
PULLEN; (William), Va., Ky.; Z (74-1-48; 78-649).
PUTNAM; (Howard), Mass.; M (26-48a).
PYRON; (William), N. C.; M (26-48a).

QUARTERMAN; (John), Pa.; M (20-65).
QUINN; (Benjamin), Va., Ky.; Z (72-4-88).

RADER; (Michael), Jackson Co., Va.; Z (77-182).
RAINBOULT; (Adam), N. C., Ind.; M (24-114).
RAINS; (John), N. C., Tenn.; M (24-114).
RANDALL; (Jacob), Mass., N. Y.; M (26-128).
RANDOLPH; (Zedekiah F.), N. J.; M (21-38).
RANKIN; (Robert), N. C., Tenn.; (William), N. C.; M (24-115).
RANKINS; (Robert), Va., Ala.; M (24-116).
RAYMOND; (David), Conn.; M (26-128); (Nathaniel), Conn.; M (26-128); (Joshua), Conn.; M (26-129); (Enoch), N. Y.; M (21-40).
READ; (David), N. J.; M (20-66).
READING; (John), N. J., Pa., Ky.; M (29-133).
REAMER; (David), Pa., Ind.; M (26-48a).
RECKIE; (Andrew), N. Y.; M (26-49a).
REDINGER; (John), Pa.; P (11-291).
REDMAN; (Benjamin); X2 (4-28, 29).
REED; (Abraham), Mass.; M (21-76); (Philip), Pa.; M (20-66); (Ebenezer), N. Y.; M (21-76); (Isaiah), N. J.; M (21-77); (James), Pa.; M (21-78); (Jonathan), Mass.; M (21-78, 79); (Samuel), Mass.; M (21-79); (William), Pa.; M (21-79); (Zadock), Mass.; M (21-80); (Joseph), S. C.; M (23-99).
REWALT; (John), Pa.; M (26-49a).

REYNOLDS; (Gamaliel), Conn., N. Y.;
    M (22-87); (Allen), N. H., N. Y.;
    M (21-80); (James), Conn.; M (21-
    81); (Robert), Mass., Vt.; M (21-
    81); (James), R. I.; Z (71-470).
RHODES; (John), R. I.; M (21-82);
    (Joseph), N. Y.; M (21-83).
RICE; (Eben), Mass., Vt., N. Y.; M
    (21-83); (Jacob), Conn., N. Y.; M
    (21-83); (Samuel), Va., Ky.; M (21-
    84); (William B.), Va., Ky.; M (21-
    84); (Benjamin), Mass.; M (24-116);
    (Josiah), Mass.; M (24-117).
RICHARDS; (Samuel), Farmington,
    Conn.; M (24-117); (John), Va.; M
    (21-85).
RICHEY; (James), N. H.; M (24-118).
RICHIE; (James), Va., Tenn.; M (24-
    118).
RICHMOND; (Amaziah), Mass., Vt.;
    (two of name); M (24-119); (Ezra),
    Mass.; M (24-121); (Nathaniel),
    Mass., Ind.; Z (72-5-67).
RIDLEY; (George), Mass.; M (22-120).
RIGGAN; (Francis), N. C.; M (24-121).
RIGSBY; (Jesse), N. C.; M (24-122).
RINGO; (Cornelius), S. C., Ky.; Z
    (71-472).
ROBERTS; (Edward), Va., Ky.; M (24-
    122); (James), Md.; M (24-122);
    (Luke), Conn., Vt.; M (24-123);
    (Thomas), Va., Ky.; M (24-123);
    (Gideon), Conn., N. Y.; M (23-59).
ROBINS; (William), N. J., Ohio; M
    (26-50a).
ROBINSON; (John), Va., Ga.; Z (70-
    721).
ROOT; (Abel), Windsor, Vt.; Erie Co.,
    Pa.; M (24-96).
ROSAMOND; (Samuel), S. C.; M (21-
    131); (James), S. C.; M (21-56);
    will of James (1806); M (21-133).
ROSE; (Jacob), Schoharie, N. Y.; M
    (24-96); (John), Surry Co., N. C.;
    M (24-98).
ROWELL; (Daniel), N. H., Ohio; M (26-
    130); (William), N. H.; M (26-130).
ROWLEY; (Timothy), N. Y.; M (33-87).
RUSK; (James), Pa., Ohio; M (29-134).
RUSSELL; (Philip), Va., Ill.; M (23-
    68); (James), Pa., Ohio; M (24-69);
    (Enoch), Va.; M (23-68).
RYERSON; (George G.); N. J.; M (29-
    135).

SADLER; (David), S. C.; M (21-53).
SAGE; (Enos), Conn.; M (23-99);
    (James), Va.; M (23-100).

SALMON; (Nathaniel), N. J.; Z (72-
    2-69).
SANFORD; (William), N. J.; M (33-
    124); (Elihu), Conn.; Z (71-92).
SAXON; (Lewis), S. C.; M (21-58; 23-
    13).
SAXTON; (James), Mass.; M (33-87).
SCOFIELD; (William), Conn., N. Y.;
    M (28-97); (Gideon), Conn.; M (28-
    98).
SCOTT; (William), Ridgefield, Conn.;
    Z (77-717).
SEAMAN; (Hezekiah), N. Y., R. I.; Z
    (79-280).
SEARING; (Daniel), N. Y.; M (23-16).
SHATTUCK; (Nathaniel), Mass., Vt.; M
    (24-70).
SHAW; (Abraham), Mass.; M (24-70);
    (Nathaniel), Mass.; M (24-71);
    (Nathan), N. J.; M (24-71).
SHAWN; (Frederick), Md., Ohio; M (23-
    16).
SHAY; (Timothy), Westchester Co., N.
    Y.; M (24-98).
SHED; (David), Mass., Vt., N. Y.; M
    (24-99).
SHELTON; (William), Va.; M (33-87).
SHERMAN; (John), R. I.; S3 (12-4-9).
SHIMER; (Isaac), Pa.; Z (71-1119).
SHORT; (Siloam), Conn.; M (24-124).
SIBLEY; (Daniel), Sutton, Mass.; M
    (24-100).
SIDDALL; (Stephen), Va., Ga.; M (24-
    100).
SIFERT; (Peter), Pa., Ohio; M (24-
    124).
SISLER; (Michael), Pa.; M (24-101).
SKINNER; (Israel), Hebron, Conn., N.
    Y.; M (24-101); (Samuel), Bedford
    Co., Ohio; M (24-103); (William),
    Dorchester Co., Md.; M (24-103).
SLOANE; (Robert), N. C.; M (21-66).
SMICK; (Christian-Carl), Pa.; M (28-
    98).
SMITH; (William), N. J.; M (28-99);
    (William), S. C., Ga.; M (28-99);
    (James), Chester Co., Pa.; S3 (11-
    1-14); (Griffith), Pa.; Z (72-5-
    67).
SOUTHARD; (Henry), Pa., N. Y.; M (23-
    69).
SPALDING; (Joseph), Conn., Vt.; M
    (23-70); (Josiah), Conn.; M (23-
    70; 26-50a).
SPARKS; (Matthew), N. C., Tenn.; Z
    (80-554).
SPEAKE; (Richard), S. C., Ga.; M (26-
    51a).

STACY; (John), N. Y.; Z (71-166).
STALEY; (Henry), N. Y.; M (23-100).
STANLEY; (Dennis), N. H.; M (24-124).
STARKWEATHER; (Ephraim), Conn., N. Y.; M (26-51a).
STEELMAN; (Zephaniah), N. J.; M (23-17).
STEPHENSON; (David), S. C.; M (34-68); (James), N. C., Ind.; M (34-105).
STEWART; (John), Pa., Ohio; M (23-101).
STIFF; (James), Va.; M (29-135).
STINSON; (James), Ohio; M (23-71).
STINSON [STEVENSON]; (John), Pa., Md., Ky.; M (24-125).
STOCKNEY; (Patrick), Baltimore Co., Md.; M (24-99).
STOCKTON; (James), N. J.; M (23-71).
STONE; (Thomas), Va.; M (24-72); (William), R. I.; M (29-136); (Henry), Va.; M (34-105); (Nathaniel), R. I.; M (34-105); (Samuel), N. Y.; M (34-106).
STONER; (Philip), Md., Pa.; S3 (13-2-5).
STOUGHTON; (Shem), Conn.; M (28-100).
STOUT; (John), N. J., Pa.; M (34-106).
STRAHAN; (Gregory), Pa.; M (28-100).
STRIBLING; (Clayton), S. C.; M (34-106).
STROZIER; (Peter), Ga.; Z (79-557).
STURTEVANT; (Lemuel), Mass.; M (28-101).
SWEET; (Rufus), North Kingston, R. I.; M (24-104).
SWIFT; (Thomas), Va.; M (34-106).
SWISHER; War record (Capt. Abraham), N. J., Ohio; O (6-500).
SYDNOR; (Fortunatus), Va.; M (26-130).

TAFF; (Peter), Va.; M (23-101).
TAGGART; (Patrick), Pa.; M (31-16).
TALIAFERRO; (Richard), Va., Ala.; M (24-72).
TALLMAN; War record (Benjamin), Pa., Ohio; O (6-501).
TATE; (John), Ireland, Pa., N. C., Ga.; M (24-72).
TAYLOR; (Archibald), Va., Ind.; M (24-126); (Daniel), N. J., Pa., Va.; M (24-127); (Jonathan),

Conn.; M (24-127); (James), Va.; M (25-7).
THAYER; (David), Conn.; M (23-72).
THOMPSON; (Lawrence), Va., N. C.; M (25-8).
THORN; (Samuel), N. Y.; M (31-17).
TICE; (Elias), N. J.; M (26-131); (Jacob), N. J.; N. Y.; M (31-17).
TIFFANY; (Thomas), Mass., Pa.; M (26-129).
TILTON; (John), N. J., Ohio; M (34-68).
TIPPE; (Uriah), Pa., Ohio; M (33-88).
TODD; (Samuel), Mass., Vt.; M (23-101).
TOWERS; (John), Fairfax Co., Va.; M (34-68).
TOWNSEND; (John), Va., Ky.; Z (72-5-66).
TOZER; (Richard), Conn.; M (28-101).
TRABUE; (Daniel), Va., Ky.; M (28-102).
TRACY; (Daniel), Conn., Mass.; M (33-88).
TRASK; (Thomas), R. I., Me.; M (28-103); (Retire), Mass.; M (28-102).
TRAZVANT; (Dr. John), Va.; M (33-62).
TUCKER; (John), Va., Ky.; M (34-106); (Reuben), Va.; Z (71-92).
TURNER; (James), N. C.; abstract from will; Z (80-429).
TYLER; (George), Va.; M (34-69, 107); (Daniel), Va., Ohio; Z (71-246).
TYREE; (William), Va.; M (33-88).

UFFORD; (Samuel M.), Conn.; M (28-103).
ULLMAN; (Frederick), Pa.; M (28-103).
UNDERWOOD; (John), Del., N. C.; M (33-88).
UPSON; (Ezekiel), Conn.; M (33-89).
UTTER; (Solomon), N. Y.; M (29-29; 30-35).

VAIL; (Jonathan), N. Y.; M (29-30; 30-36).
VANCLEAF; (Peter), N. J., Ohio; M (33-89).
VAN DOREN; (Abraham), N. J., N. Y.; M (29-136).
VAN HOUTEN; (Tunis), N. Y.; M (34-107).
VAN SCOY; (Abraham), N. Y.; Z (71-1033).

VAN TASSEL; (Cornelius), N. Y.; M
(34-32).
VAN TASSELL; (John), N. Y.; M (26-
58a).
VAN VRANKEN; (Derick), N. Y.; M (26-
51a).
VAUGHAN; (William), Va.; M (34-33).
VEGHTE; (Henry), Franklin, N. J.; M
(34-69).
VERMILIA; (Jacob M.), N. Y.; Z (71-
1033).
VERNER; (John), S. C.; M (21-54).
VIALL; (Nathaniel), R. I.; M (32-
109); (Samuel), Mass., Vt.; M (32-
109).
VORHEES; (Peter), N. J.; M (30-36);
(Peter L.), N. J.; M (30-36).

WADSWORTH; (John), Conn.; M (23-101).
WAGSTAFF; (William), Va., Pa.; M (26-
52a).
WAKELY; (Abel), Conn.; M (23-102).
WALKER; (Edward), N. C., Tenn.; M
(23-102).
WALLACE; (Cornelius), N. Y.; M (26-
52a).
WALLIS; (Benjamin), N. C.; M (23-
102).
WALTMAN [WALCKMAN]; (Michael), Md.;
M (23-103).
WALTON; (Capt. John), N. J.; Bl (8-
11).
WAPLES; (Samuel), Va.; M (23-103).
WARD; (Edward), Md., Ohio; M (23-104).
WARDWELL; (Jacob), Stamford, Conn.; M
(23-127).
WARFIELD; (Joseph), Md.; M (34-69).
WARNER; (Moses), Mass.; M (23-127);
(Seth), Mass., N. Y.; Z (71-472).
WARNOCK; (John), S. C.; M (21-54).
WASH; (John), Ga., Mo.; M (34-33);
(Thomas), Va.; M (34-34).
WATERMAN; (Asa), Conn., R. I.; M (23-
18); (John), Conn., N. Y.; M (23-
18); (Luther), Conn., Ohio; M (23-
18).
WATERS; (John), N. H.; M (23-127);
(Richard), Md.; Z (71-167).
WATKINS; (Stephen), Mass.; M (23-128);
(Stephen), Md., Pa.; M (34-70).
WATSON; (Evan T.), Va., Ky.; M (30-
114).
WAY; (Selah), Conn., N. Y.; Z (71-
473).
WEATHEN; (Willis), N. C.; M (23-128).
WEAVER; (William), N. C.; M (23-128).
WEBB; (Ebenezer), Conn., N. Y.; M (25-
8); (John), Me.; M (25-11); (Jesse),

N. C.; M (25-10); (Moses), Conn.;
Z (71-768).
WEISE; (Adam), Pa.; M (25-12).
WEISS; (Jacob), Pa.; M (25-12).
WELLS; (Benjamin), Conn.; M (23-
129).
WENTWORTH; (Paul), Me.; M (34-34).
WERDEN; (Jesse), Conn., N. Y.; M
(23-129).
WERTZ; (George), Md., Pa.; M (23-
130).
WHEATLEY; (Andrew), Conn.; M (23-
130).
WHEELER; (John), Va., N. C.; M (23-
131); (James); Va.; Ind.; M (30-
114).
WHEELOCK; (Adam), Mass.; M (23-132).
WHITE; (Samuel), N. J.; M (23-132);
(William), Pa.; M (26-59a);
(John), Va.; Z (72-7-72); (John),
Conn., Ohio; Z (80-555).
WHITEHEAD; (Aaron), N. J.; M (30-
115).
WICKLIFFE; (Charles), Va., Ky.; M
(33-89).
WILCOX; (Stephen), Conn., Pa.; Z
(78-691).
WILCOXEN; (Daniel), N. C., Ky.; M
(23-133).
WILEY; (William), N. C.; M (23-133).
WILKINSON; (William), Va.; M (34-
34).
WILLBORN; (Isaac), Orange Co., N.
C.; Z (78-692).
WILLIAMS; (John), Va., N. C.; M (23-
134); (John), N. Y.; M (23-135);
Moses), S. C.; M (23-135); (James),
Va., Ky.; M (23-134); (Abel), Pa.,
Ohio; M (34-34); (Benjamin), Md.,
Ky.; (Charles), Md.; (Edward),
Md., N. C.; (Elisha), Md.; M (34-
70); (Thomas), Pa.; M (25-13);
(John); Lancaster, Pa.; M (30-
115); (Charles), Md.; Z (72-7-73);
(John), Va., Ky.; Z (71-167).
WILSON; (Robert), N. C.; M (24-23);
(John), S. C.; M (21-55).
WINFREY; (Philip), Buckingham Co.,
Va.; S3 (11-3-7).
WINSTEAD; (Mandley), N. C.; M (24-
25).
WINSTON; (Anthony), Va.; M (24-25).
WISE; (Henry), Md.; M (24-26).
WISEMAN; (Joseph), Pa., Va.; M (24-
26).
WITHERS; (James), Va.; M (24-27).
WITHERSPOON; (John), Pa., N. C.; M
(24-27).

WOOD; (Aaron), Va., Md., N. C.; M
(24-28); (John), Va., S. C.; Z (71-
168).
WOODWORTH; (Joseph), Conn., N. Y.; Z
(72-5-68).
WRIGHT; (Samuel), New York; M (24-
29).
WYMAN; (Henry), Mass., Me.; M (34-
71).
WYNN; (William), Va.; M (26-53a).

YEAGER; (John), Va.; M (25-13).
YEATON; (John), Mass.; M (23-136).
YEOMAN; (Solomon), N. C., Fla.; M
(23-136).
YOUNG; (David), N. J.; M (23-136);
(Christian), Orange Co., N. Y.; M
(34-71); (Guy), Albany) N. Y.;
Stafford, Vt.; M (30-115); (John),
R. I., Mass.; Z (72-8-88); (John),
Mass., Me.; Z (77-7-73); (Robert),
Va., Ky.; Z (71-768).

ZECHMAN; (George), Bern, Pa.; M (34-
71).

Quaker Soldiers, Delaware; Z (75-7-
7, 23, 50).
Consult also the individual states
in the Place Index; and Revolutionary War and Soldiers in the Topic
Index.

ALABAMA
Claiborne, Monroe Co.; Inscriptions; Z (77-722).
Dallas County; Inscriptions; M (21-124; 23-119).
Jefferson County; Rev. War soldiers; M (24-35).
Lawrence County; Marriage records, 1822-26; M (27-21); marriage bonds, 1818-23; Z (79-609).
Madison County; Deed Book; Z (77-723, 760).
Mobile; Inscriptions of northerners; Al (100-75).
Morgan County; Marriage records, 1822-47; M (23-45).
Wilcox County; Inscriptions; Z (77-721).

BERMUDA
Genealogical notes; V1 (23-176, 259;24-50, 113, 220, 282; 25-44, 136, 206, 278; 26-33, 107, 189, 295; 27-47, 144, 231, 319; 28-33, 112, 170, 254).
Historical; W2 (17-176, 317; 18-13).
American privateering; Y1 (82-174).

CALIFORNIA
Immigration from R. I.; S1 (26-232).
Maine natives, 1850 Census; Al (91-276, 319).
Passengers on the Capitol, 1849; Al (91-198).
Records of "Forty-Niners"; Al (90-32).
Voyage, San Francisco from New York, 1853; Al (91-312).
Pasadena; Inscriptions; S3 (9-1-15; 6-5-4).

CANADA
Province of Quebec; Inscriptions; Al (87-395).

CENTRAL AMERICA
Colonists from United States; M (28-29).

COLORADO
Sources; Col (1 No. 2).
Members of Col. Soc., S. A. R.; Col (2 Nos. 9, 10).
Census of 1860; Col (3-27).
Arapahoe County; probate, 1864-1870; Col (2-6, 24, 55, 65, 81; 3-8, 71, 78; 4-4, 113; 5-24,

COLORADO (continued)
59, 90; 6-2, 89, 108; 7-1-29; 7-2-29; 7-88, 103).
Marriages, 1869; Col (7-99).
Arvada, Jefferson Co.; Inscriptions; Col (1 Nos. 1, 2, 3).
Boulder County; Marriages, 1874-1875; Col (1 Nos. 7, 8, 9).
Inscriptions; Col (5-102; 6-12, 42, 90, 119; 7-78).
Marriages, 1863-1884; Col (7-72, 111).
Boulder; Inscriptions, Catholic Cemetery; Col (5-47).
Buffalo Park, Jefferson Co.; Inscriptions; Col (1 No. 3).
Central City; First Cong. Church records; Col (5-64).
Colorado Springs; First Cong. Church records, 1874-; Col (3-22).
Conifer, Jefferson Co.; Inscriptions; Col (1 No. 5).
Denver; Marriages, 1859-1867; Col (2-17, 41, 51, 73; 4-114; 5-34, 72, 104; 6-5, 38, 68, 102; 7-1-14; 7-2-13).
Deaths, 1862-; Col (2-74).
Douglas County; Marriages, 1864-1916; Col (3-116; 4-11, 39, 63, 119; 5-19, 49, 86, 108; 6-26, 57, 94, 121).
El Paso County; Marriage certificates; Col (6-8).
Franktown, Douglas Co.; Historical; Col (3-72).
Inscriptions; Col (3-81).
Georgetown; Police Judge's Deeds, 1874-; Col (3-23, 74, 98; 4-5, 106, 113a; 6-3).
Logan County; Marriages, 1887-89; Col (2-59).
Morgan County; Marriages, 1889-1896; Col (2-9, 25).
Morrison, Jefferson Co.; Inscriptions; Col (1 No. 4).
Niwot, Boulder Co.; Inscriptions; Col (5-13).
Ovid, Sedgwick Co.; Inscriptions; Col (2-11, 27).
Park County; Marriages, 1881-82; Col (2-77).
Pine Grove, Jefferson Co.; Inscriptions; Col (1 No. 5).

COLORADO (continued)
  Rocky Ford; soldiers' graves; Col
    (7-19).
  Sedgwick County; Marriages, 1889-
    1900; Col (1 Nos. 5, 6).
  Sedgwick, Sedgwick Co.; Inscrip-
    tions; Col (1 No. 7).
  West Creek, Douglas Co.; Inscrip-
    tions; Col (3-9, 18).
CONNECTICUT
  Sources; C5 (1-4-1).
  Towns and counties; S1 (24-401).
  Early Items from Winthrop Journal;
    B4 (9-54; 23-62, 124, 231).
  French and Indian War; A1 (94-225).
  Items showing migrations; B4 (19-
    47).
  List of Orderly Books etc., French
    & Indian War; A1 (95-18).
  Revolutionary soldiers; B4 (17-
    175).
  Stephen Matthews' Co., 1776; B4
    (11-191).
  Barkhamsted; Church records, 1781-;
    T8 (8-13, 18, 27; 9-20, 24; 10-
    3,13, 20, 29).
  Berlin; Deaths (Peck record), Ken-
    sington, 1823-52; T8 (3-4-2).
    Inscriptions; E3 (2-185).
  Branford; Church records, 1688-
    1706; B4 (9-31).
    Vital records, Vols. I and II;
    B4 (12-100).
    Early town records; B4 (12-112).
  Brooklyn; Inscriptions; A1 (100-
    330).
  Danbury; items from deeds; B4 (22-
    191).
  East Granby; Names in Owen Ac-
    count Books; Dt (3-11).
  East Haddam; Militia Company,
    1771-2; B4 (15-167).
  East Hartford; Church records,
    1802-14; T8 (6-18).
  Fairfield; Families; B4 (Supple-
    ment
    Tryon attack, 1779; T8 (2-4-2).
  Farmington; Vital records, before
    1700; B4 (9-174).
    Land records; B4 (11-111).
  Franklin; Inscriptions; A1 (86-
    372).
  Glastonbury, Inscriptions; A1
    (86-46, 157, 314).
    Names in Goodrich account book,
    1803-; Dt (8-119).
  Griswold; Second Cong. Church
    records, 1826-61; T8 (3-2-2;

CONNECTICUT (continued)
    4-2, 18, 25; 6-11).
  Groton; Chapman record; T8 (4-30;
    5-2, 10).
  Guilford; Vital records; B4 (13-
    88, 181, 242; 15-184; 16-180;
    17-127, 191, 255; 18-128; 19-
    33).
    Christ Church (Ep.) records,
    1807-34; T8 (5-20, 27; 6-3).
    St. John's Church, records; T8
    (6-4, 13, 26; 7-5).
  Hartford County; court records,
    1700-2; B4 (23-114).
  Hartford; Burials (Goodwin record),
    1689-98; T8 (3-1-3).
    Inscriptions, South Ground; T8
    (7-15, 20, 25).
    First Baptist Church, marriages,
    1813-25; T8 (7-30; 8-2).
  Kent; Tax list, 1744; B4 (11-57).
  Killingly; Inscriptions; A1 (100-
    328).
  Killingworth; Vital records, Vol.
    I; B4 (12-35).
    Church records, 1807-53; T8 (7-
    5, 12).
    Early deeds; B4 (23-113).
  Lebanon; Church records, 1711-13;
    T8 (1-3-3).
    Marriages by J. P., 1789-1814;
    A1 (91-196).
    Inscriptions; A1 (98-300).
  Ledyard; Marriages and deaths (pri-
    vate record), 1801-18; T8 (3-3-
    3).
  Lisbon; Inscriptions; A1 (86-388).
  Lyme; Vital records;B4(10-217; 12-64).
    Land records; B4 (22-260).
  Middletown; Vital Records, Vol. I;
    B4 (12-155, 210; 13-31).
    Proprietors, 1673; B4 (10-109).
  Milford; Vital records, 1653-1718;
    B4 (9-100, 159).
    Early town and land records; B4
    (10-34; 12-170, 173; 16-238).
    Church admissions, 1639-87; B4
    (16-28).
  Monroe; Inscriptions; B4 (11-53;
    12-51).
  Montville; Inscriptions; A1 (98-
    286).
  Naugatuck; Gunntown burials; B4
    (13-21, 166).
  New Haven; Early miscellaneous i-
    tems; B4 (20-122; 21-120).
    Baptist Church, marriages, 1831-
    34; T8 (8-12).

CONNECTICUT (continued)
Newington; Inscriptions; E3 (2-169).
New London; Episcopalian petition,
1727; B4 (9-233).
Probate records, files before
1710; B4 (9-230; 10-35, 101, 166-
215; 11-30, 103, 153; 12-33, 115,
151; 13-106, 164, 246; 14-16,
103, 184, 246; 15-104; 17-118;
18-121; 19-218; 20-190).
North Parish, 2nd Church baptisms
and marriages, 1722-40, 1784-98;
NE (1-42, 186, 213).
New Milford; Note; B4 (10-257).
Norwich, New London Co.; Marriages,
1781-1801; M (22-53).
Newent church records; T8 (6-30;
7-4).
Diary of Jabez Fitch; D (30-161;
31-44; 32-167; 33-73, 128, 176).
Prospect; Inhabitants, 1805; B4
(14-183).
Ridgebury; Marriages, 1769-85; B4
(19-211).
Ridgefield; Patriots, 1776; B4 (10-
49).
Salem, New London Co.; Inscriptions;
A1 (89-243).
The "Discontinuers"; S1 (26-12).
Saybrook; Indian deeds; T8 (1-2-2).
Land records; B4 (16-240).
Sharon; Probate records, 1757-59;
B4 (10-170); items; B4 (22-192).
Southbury; Militia company, 1774;
B4 (19-21).
Stafford; Marriages; B4 (13-248).
Some residents, 1800, 1810; Dt
(9-54).
Stamford; Vital and Town Records;
B4 (10-40, 110, 174; 11-32, 87,
157, 220).
Stratford; Early proprietors; B4
(11-56).
Cong. Church records; B4 (13-
270; 14-126).
Voluntown; Marriage and Court rec-
ords, 1751-76; A2 (65-301).
Wallingford; Vital records; B4 (14-
22, 109).
Items from church records; B4
(16-188).
Militia company, 1777-78; E3 (8-
336).
Washington; Marriages, 1779-80; M
(23-60).
Waterbury; Historical; S1 (32-7).
Waterford; Inscriptions; A1 (94-
394; 98-287).

CONNECTICUT (continued)
Wethersfield; Notes on early fam-
ilies; B4 (10-51, 52).
Vital records, 1635-80; B4 (9-
27; 10-104).
Wilton; Census, 1733; A2 (70-151).
Windham; Probate Items; B4 (23-
228).
Windsor; Matthew Grant record,
1666; T8 (2-2-3).
Wolcott; Inscriptions; B4 (12-50).
Woodbridge; Petition 1780; B4 (11-
192).
Woodbury; Church records, 1670-
1718; B4 (9-17; 21-222, 265; 22-
56).
Items; B4 (17-173).
DELAWARE
Sources; Z (75-4-47).
Assessment of settlers, Delaware
River, 1677; B1 (13-3).
Depositions; E2 (1-6, 12, 22).
Guardianships, orphans; E2 (1-7).
Migration records; E2 (1-6, 12).
Penn and Calvert claims; X1 (29-
83).
Signers of the Oath of Allegiance;
Z (75-9-53; 75-10-69; 75-11-71;
75-12-65; 76-67).
Wills; E2 (1-5).
Kent County; Marriage evidences;
E2 (1-3, 10, 19, 26).
Probate records; Z (79-324).
Orphans' Court; E2 (1-14, 29).
Newcastle County; Marriage evi-
dences; E2 (1-1, 9, 17, 25).
Tax-lists, 1776; E1 (10-25, 44,
50).
Orphans' Court; E2 (1-13, 21,
30).
Sussex County; Inscriptions, Mil-
ton; F (13-108).
Marriage evidences; E2 (1-4, 11,
20, 28).
Wills; E2 (1-16, 23).
Orphans' Court; E2 (1-15, 32).
Depositions and Births; E2 (1-
29).
DENMARK
Research; U (24-156; 30-59).
Early kings; M (31-53).
DISTRICT OF COLUMBIA
Vital Items, National Intelligen-
cer, Washington, 1805-23; M (26-
33, 63a, 110; 27-6, 37, 75, 106;
28-17, 24, 43, 66, 109; 29-1,
45, 96, 123; 30-9, 63, 96, 121;
31-3, 33, 73, 104; 32-14, 46,

DISTRICT OF COLUMBIA (continued)
97; 33-15, 72; 34-13, 89, 130).
Vital items, newspapers, Washington; M (28-13, 55).
Georgetown; Inscriptions; M (23-85, 104).
Washington; Christ Church records;
M (28-26).

ENGLAND
Corporation Records; B4 (10-69).
Court-Rolls; B4 (9-80).
Deeds enrolled; B4 (9-199).
Feudal genealogy; B4 (19-2).
Gleanings; A1 (88-386).
Probate Records; Z3 (3-5-1; 3-6-148; 3-7-85).
Quaker records; U (24-61); M (34-73).
Records in London; U (27-16).
Research; U (24-61).
Churston Ferrars, co. Devon, Parish Register, 1589-1653; A2 (63-259, 351; 64-46, 298, 396; 65-82, 182).
Ockley, Surrey; extracts from parish registers, with special reference to Guilford, Conn., surnames; T8 (4-10).
Yorkshire; Rawmarsh residents, 1379; A2 (68-311).

FRANCE
Peasant families; U (29-167).
Terms of Nobility; B4 (9-152).

GEORGIA
Items; E1 (10-7).
Sample of death statistics, 1850, from census schedules; M (31-47).
Vital items from newspapers, 1769-95; Z (69-370).
Dawson, Terrell County; Inscriptions; Z (80-151).
Greene County; wills and marriage licenses; Z (66-310).
Midway; Inscriptions; A1 (95-13).
Richmond County; Marriage licenses, 1791-97; E1 (10-1).
Warren County; Rev. soldiers buried; Z (74-12-47).

GERMANY
Sources; U (27-10, 12; 30-5); S1 (33-222).
Palatines; Emigrants from Nassau-Dillenburg; M (29-41); Origin of Palatines; M (31-25).

HAWAII
Genealogy; U (24-4).

HOLLAND
Background of emigration to America; M (29-81).
Dutch settlers; M (29-81).
Dutch Colonial Names; Ng (3-258).
Dutch-English names; Z3 (4-9-375).
Dutch Christian names; OU (1-231).
New England names at Amsterdam; B4 (20-125).
Prefixes to Dutch surnames; OU (9-342).
Location of Archives; U (23-110).

HUNGARY
Kings of House of Arpad; A1 (96-138, 304); M (30-115).

ILLINOIS
Lawrence County; Marriages and inscriptions; Z (68-500).
Lincoln, Logan Co.; Marriages; B1 (19-12).
Marshall, Clarke Co.; Church records; Z (80-40).
Tazewell County; School children, 1865; M (30-24).

INDIANA
Genealogical background; M (29-142).
Gibson County; Marriages performed by Rev. Alexander Devin; Z (77-333).
Jefferson County; Wills and Administrations,1811-1852; Z (79-108).
Mount Carmel, Franklin Co.; Inscriptions; M (20-14).
Orange County; Quaker records; M (31-115).
Parke County; Account book names; Z (77-536).
Richmond; Inscriptions, Beulah Pres. Church; Z (80-327).
Smith township, Whitley Co.; Inscriptions and genealogical notes of families; M (33-117; 34-20).
Vincennes District; Heads of families to 1783; M (29-144).

IRELAND
Records at Belfast; M (34-41).
Anglo-Norman and Scots families in; S1 (20-349).
Gaelic names; S1 (21-415).
Irish in New England before 1700; A1 (90-165).
Ulster King of Arms; A2 (75-78).

KENTUCKY
Genealogical background; M (29-142).
Acts and Legislative Journals,

KENTUCKY (continued)
216, 303; 32-1, 139, 244, 320;
33-39, 151, 212).
Inscriptions, Bethel Pres. Church-
yard; N3 (31-168).
Macedonia Christian Church; N3
(36-291).
Frankfort; Bibliography; Dt (5-1);
N3 (40-1, 155).
Early landowners; N3 (43-107).
Garrard County; Early settlers; N3
(30-335).
Great Crossings, Scott Co.; Bapt-
ist Church records, 1795-1801;
N3 (34-3, 173).
Hardin County; Marriages, 1792-
1825; N3 (42-54, 144).
Jefferson County; Abstracts of rec-
ords; Vl (13-196).
Inscriptions, Penn. Run Pres.
Churchyard; N3 (30-393; 31-71).
Knox County; Early Marriages; Z
(69-122, 248).
Lawrence County; Marriages, 1822-
59; N3 (35-60, 179).
Leitch Station, Campbell Co.; His-
torical; N3 (36-359).
Lexington; Bibliography; N3 (44-
151, 259).
Historical notes; N3 (40-107,
253, 353; 41-44, 107, 250, 310;
42-26).
Light Infantry Co., War of 1812;
N3 (42-263).
Lincoln County; N3 (32-351).
Items, County Court Order Books,
1781-92; N3 (42-215).
Probate records, 1780-1805; N3
(39-315).
Bibliography; N3 (35-339).
Madison County; Wills, 1784-1813
(miscellaneous); B2 (10-35; 12-
28).
Marriages, 1779-1817; B2 (10-55,
69; 11-6, 51; 12-4, 21).
Early history; N3 (31-119).
The Blue Lick; Vl (13-50).
Marriage records; N3 (37-184; 38-
25, 131, 221, 295; 39-10, 157,
278).
Madisonville, Hopkins Co.; Inscrip-
tions; S3 (9-5-10).
Mason County; Marriage bonds, 1797-
98; Z (78-552; 80-333, 381, 429,
555, 586).
Maysville, Mason Co.; Marriage
Bonds; Z (79-32, 189, 326, 365,
465, 557, 611, 655; 80-42, 83,

KENTUCKY (continued)
273).
Mercer County; Inscriptions, Old
Mud Meeting House; N3 (33-266).
Probate records; N3 (37-94, 214).
Muhlenberg County; Marriage rec-
ords, 1799-1836; N3 (30-260, 373).
Nelson County; Inscriptions, Cox's
Creek Baptist churchyard; N3 (30-
187).
Newport; Baptisms, Meth. Church,
1869- ; Dt (6-30, 77).
Pendleton County; Inscriptions,
Peter Demoss Plantation; N3 (39-
408).
Pike County; Marriage records,
1822-65; N3 (35-220).
Scott County; Land Patents, George-
town Area; N3 (41-172).
Smithland, Livingston Co.; Inscrip-
tions; N3 (41-231).
Woodford County; Inscriptions, Pis-
gah churchyard; N3 (32-178).
Items; K2 (20-10).
MAINE
Counties and towns; Sl (25-380).
Huguenot settlers, Kennebec Valley;
NE (3-17).
Journal of Jeremiah Hacker, from
1837; B5 (17-204).
Marriages by Nathaniel Thwing,
1777-1816; M (29-108).
Marriages by Rev. Enoch M. Fowler,
1843-77; Al (91-383).
Natives in California (1850 Census);
Al (91-276, 319).
Acton; Inscriptions; Al (92-94).
Alewive; Inscriptions; M (24-20).
Alfred; Inscriptions; M (24-18); Al
(91-222).
Bangor; Items; NE (1-1).
Benton; Inscriptions; Al (91-391).
Berwick; Marriage records; Z (69-
367).
Bucksport; Inscriptions; Al (91-
198).
Cushing; Inscriptions; Al (91-90).
Marriages, 1789-1847; Al (90-89).
Dedham; Inscriptions; Al (89-297,
300).
Edgecomb; Inscriptions; Al (87-82).
Eliot, York Co.; Inscriptions; M
(26-40).
Goodwin death record, 1820-1840;
Al (97-141, 265).
Town officers, 1810; Al (97-300).
Fort Pownal; Entries, 1772-77; Al
(90-85).

MARYLAND (continued)
  Militia during Revolutionary War
    (name list); X2 (13-53, 59; 14-
    9, 24, 58; 15-26, 40, 57; 16-8,
    28, 43, 71; 17-3, 24); M (32-68).
  Mills, Taverns, Forges, Furnaces,
    list 1795; X1 (31-155).
  Next of Kin; El (10-49).
  Private Manors; X1 (33-307).
  Quakers; X1 (29-101).
  Refugees from St. Domingo, 1793;
    X1 (38-103).
  Revolutionary pensions; M (32-53).
  St. John's College, Annapolis, stu-
    dents 1789-95; X1 (29-305).
  Ships and shipping; X1 (33-334; 34-
    46, 270, 349).
  Stamp Act Controversy; X1 (27-79).
  Surnames, Hall of Records, Annapo-
    lis; M (33-67; 34-11, 80).
  Witchcraft; X1 (31-271).
  Allegany County; Marriages, 1791-
    96; M (20-52).
  Annapolis; List of records to 1800;
    X1 (35-74).
    Diary of William Faris, 1792-
    1804; X1 (28-197).
  Anne Arundel County; Deaths, Meth.
    Church; X2 (5-29).
    Militia, 1779; X2 (4-9).
  Baltimore County; Abstracts of
    wills; Z (65-505).
    Assessment list, 1798; X2 (5-
    35).
    Early records; X2 (5-44).
    Founders; X2 (6-9, 20; 7-53; 8-
    14).
    Inscriptions, Garrisonville; M
    (25-59).
    Inscriptions, Harrisonville; M
    (25-61).
    Land records, 1671-86; X1 (27-
    123; 28-44, 345; 29-116, 299;
    30-271; 31-36, 242; 32-30, 286;
    33-176; 34-284; 36-315).
    Land records; X2 (6-40; 7-9, 18,
    35; 9-20, 33, 43; 10-8; 11-10,
    25, 31; 13-12).
    List of articles in "Baltimore,
    Note Book of History"; X2 (10-
    23).
    White servants, 1772-74; X1 (33-
    126).
  Baltimore; City churches, 1819;
    X2 (14-33).
    City government, 1800; X2 (13-50).
    First Unitarian and Universalist
    church; X2 (17-13).

MARYLAND (continued)
    Colombia Avenue Meth. Ep. Church,
    marriages, 1842; X2 (14-62).
    Inscriptions; began in "Notes on
    History" (vol. 1, p. 32, and
    cont. through vol. 2, 1939-40),
    pub. R. F. Hayes, 3526 Roland
    Ave., Baltimore; cont. in X2
    (12-13, 21, 43, 58; 13-7, 24, 43,
    68; 14-6, 45; 15-10, 42, 60; 16-
    5, 35, 48, 67; 17-9, 18, 43,
    58).
    Churchyards; C5 (1-4-8; 2-105).
    Items from newspapers, 1796,
    1800; X2 (15-24).
    Items, St. James' Roman Cath.
    Church records; X2 (13-5).
    Fire company, 1846; X2 (13-49).
    In 1830; the Peale Museum; X1
    (27-115).
    Journal of Robert Mills, 1816;
    X1 (30-257).
    New Jerusalem Church marriages
    1793-4; X2 (5-30).
    Town Battalion and Militia, 1779;
    X2 (6-4).
    Privateers, 1812-15; X1 (34-165).
    Revolutionary Militia; X2 (15-
    12).
    Swedenborgian church; X2 (17-12).
    Vital items, from newspapers,
    1834-35; X2 (3-2); 1828; X2 (3-
    4); 1837-38; X2 (3-27); 1841; X2
    (10-7; 13-19).
    Vital items, Federal Gazette; X2
    (16-12); Sun; X2 (16-66).
    War of 1812; X1 (39-177, 199,
    293; 40-7, 137); M (33-108).
    Wards; X2 (16-34).
  Calvert County; Court houses and
    records; X1 (27-36).
    List, early land-holders; X2 (3-
    5, 12, 23, 28; 4-3, 11, 18).
  Caroline County; Marriage licens-
    es, 1774-81; M (23-33).
    St. John's Parish, list of sur-
    names; X2 (4-4).
  Cecil County; Soldiers, 1740; M
    (34-128).
  Charles County; Early Court (Vi-
    tal) records; X2 (3-5, 15, 23,
    27; 4-4, 6, 12, 18, 26; 5-2, 12,
    28, 42; 6-6, 24, 35).
    Court Records, names 1658-1662;
    X2 (3-29).
    Militia, 1777; X2 (3-25; 4-25;
    5-27).
  Dorchester County; Justices,

MASSACHUSETTS (continued)
Dedham; Revolutionary notes; Z3
  (1-9-86).
Duxbury; Vital records; D (29-
  172; 30-37, 79, 172; 31-66).
Eastham and Orleans; Vital records; D (31-172; 32-39, 61, 111,
  171; 33-11, 80, 132, 181; 34-58,
  134, 183).
Essex County; Town origins; Y1
  (81-1, 138, 257).
  Prison, 1764; Y1 (68-299).
Gloucester; Historical; S1 (31-
  461).
  Ship registers, 1789-1875; Y1
  (77-363; 78-41, 177, 387; 79-
  65, 176, 293, 387; 80-71, 180).
Granville; Deaths, 1813-21, Cooley Diary; M (26-125).
Green's Harbor; Sketch; S1 (26-
  376).
Hadley; Early settlers; C5 (2-1);
  Inscriptions; C5 (2-38, 73).
Hampshire County; Abstracts (selected) of early probate rec-
  ords; M (32-35).
Harwich; Vital records; D (33-60,
  146; 34-24, 67, 102).
Haverhill; Families, 1783; Y1 (82-
  137).
  First Baptist Church; Y1 (82-
  193).
  Journal of Elizabeth Cranch,
  1785-6; Y1 (80-1).
Ipswich; Orderly Book of Capt. Ab-
  raham Dodge, 1776; Y1 (80-37,
  111, 208, 368; 81-87, 152).
Lancaster; Mary Rowlandson's narra-
  tive, 1675; S1 (27-45).
Malden; Warnings out, 1678-1794; A1
  (92-46).
Marblehead; Commerce, 1665-1775;
  Y1 (68-117).
  Documents; Y1 (68-280; 70-365).
  Commoners' Records, 1652-1745;
  Y1 (78-65, 284; 79-81).
  Town Records, 1648-83; Y1 (69-
  207).
  Historic; Y1 (82-229).
  Commoners' Records, 1652-1710;
  Y1 (77-68, 161, 267, 339).
  Great Neck; historical; Y1 (73-
  203).
Marshfield; Vital records; D (29-
  103, 154; 30-129, 146; 31-19,
  70; 32-103).
  Church records, 1705-19; D (31-
  117, 161; 32-12).

MASSACHUSETTS (continued)
  Deaths from church records; B4
  (17-236).
Middleboro; Vital records; D (29-
  183; 30-6; 31-133, 188; 32-3, 85,
  135, 162; 33-39, 75, 155; 34-123,
  155).
Middlesex County; Data from early
  Court Files; A1 (86-348).
Monson; First Cong. Church records,
  1762-74; B4 (12-26).
Nantucket; Death records; A1 (100-
  47, 152, 184, 277).
Newbury; Historical; Y1 (81-261).
  Warnings, 1734-76; Y1 (69-36).
  Historical; S1 (31-389).
  Revolutionary War items; Y1 (76-
  279).
  Men in Shays' Rebellion, 1786; Y1
  (77-183).
Newburyport; Ship registers, 1789-
  1870; Y1 (70-69, 185, 283, 387;
  71-81, 167, 267, 351; 72-159,
  261; 73-89).
  Privateers, 1781; Y1 (72-236; 76-
  285).
Norfolk County; Land records; Y1
  (68-88, 186, 359; 70-147).
Norwell; Inscriptions; D (32-107).
Oxford; Huguenots; S1 (27-63).
Plymouth Colony; Land records; D
  (32-45; 34-22, 80, 161).
  Mayflower descents, false, D (34-
  14).
  U. S. Presidents of Mayflower
  descent; D (31-53).
  Probate Records; D (33-35, 160;
  34-33, 73, 112).
Plymouth County; Abstracts of Probate; D (30-68, 138, 184; 31-15,
  60, 100, 159; 33-79; 34-36, 181).
  Abstract of Deeds; D (31-41, 179;
  32-33; 33-18; 34-29, 85, 176).
Plymouth; Vital records; D (29-125;
  30-73, 115, 188; 31-2, 109, 182;
  32-21, 129; 33-33, 140, 179; 34-
  7).
  Vital entries from Prince's Annals; D (30-1).
  Mayflower; S1 (26-23).
Reading; Early marriages; B4 (16-
  135).
Rehoboth; Early counterfeiting; A1
  (97-22, 103, 251, 310).
  Early data; A1 (98-317).
  King Philip's War; A1 (99-93).
  List of inhabitants, 1689; A1 (97-
  313, see 319).

MASSACHUSETTS (continued)
  Epidemic and deaths, 1694; Al
    (96-249, 345).
  Lists, King Philip's War; Al (99-
    93).
  Roxbury; Capt. Andrew Gardner's
    Co., Canada expedition, 1690; Al
    (99-307).
  Salem; Heller's Reformed Church-
    yard; Z (79-650).
  Ministers of First Church; NE (1-
    28).
  Town records; Yl (68-33, 153, 209,
    305; 69-65, 137).
  Vessels out, 1812; Yl (68-30).
  Hides imported, 1775; Yl (68-32).
  Shipping records, 1750-69; Yl
    (68-49, 241, 337; 69-49, 155).
  Privateers, Rev. War; Yl (68-147).
  Private armed ships, 1799; Yl
    (71-120).
  Privateers, War of 1812; Yl (78-
    241, 348; 79-371; 80-79, 158).
  St. Peter's Church (with Inscrip-
    tions); Yl (80-229, 334; 81-66).
  Merchants of 1800 and their ves-
    sels; Yl (80-261).
  Salisbury; West Parish, Historical;
    Yl (82-97).
  Sandwich; Vital records; D (30-58,
    99).
  Sheffield, Berkshire Co.; Marriages
    and deaths, 1731-80; M (27-42).
  Springfield; Vital records, 1640-
    81, corrections; Al (87-301); B4
    (9-44).
  Ms. genealogies, see Z (74-9-46).
  Suffolk County; Probate Index,
    1686-92; B4 (12-175, 222; 13-98;
    14-34).
  Swansea; List of inhabitants, 1689;
    Al (97-320, see 325).
  Taunton; List of inhabitants, 1689;
    Al (97-327).
  Topsfield; Historical; Yl (81-270).
  Truro; Church records; D (29-130,
    163; 30-28, 53, 105, 156; 31-29,
    54).
  Uxbridge; Marriages, 1868-75; Al
    (89-241).
  Wareham; Vital records; D (31-125,
    153; 32-179).
  Warwick; Grantees of Gardner's Can-
    ada; Al (99-307).
  Watertown; "colonial beehive"; Sl
    (26-18).
MICHIGAN
  Location of family records; Dt (2-

MICHIGAN (continued)
    13, 47, 69).
  Newspaper vital records, 1817-30;
    Dt (3-14, 29, 55, 69, 91, 111,
    135, 157, 179, 201; 4-3, 29, 47,
    69, 91, 113, 135, 157, 179, 201;
    5-3, 25, 47, 69, 91, 113, 135,
    157, 179, 201).
  Deaths in Chautauqua Co., N. Y.
    newspapers; Dt (7-44).
  Bedford; Assessment Roll, 1845; Dt
    (7-33, 63).
  Calumet; Interments, 1894-99; Dt
    (8-125; 9-23, 49, 79, 105, 132).
  Cass County; Marriages; Dt (5-5,
    161).
  Concord, Jackson Co.; Inscriptions;
    Dt (7-43).
  Dearborn; Inscriptions, Wallace-
    ville; Dt (2-55, 75).
  Detroit; Quit-rent Book, 1771-2;
    Ng (2-62).
  Eaton County; School records; Dt
    (4-147, 159).
  Fairgrove, Tuscola Co.; Inscrip-
    tions, Watrousville; Dt (3-101,
    121, 143, 151).
  Hartford, Van Buren Co.; Inscrip-
    tions; Dt (5-77, 99).
  Hillsdale County; Rev. and War of
    1812 families; Z (78-598).
  Isabella County; Deaths, 1867-8;
    Dt (7-11).
  Keeler, Van Buren Co.; Inscrip-
    tions; Dt (6-17, 35).
  Kent County; Marriage items; Dt
    (3-93).
  Macomb County; Marriages; Dt (5-
    33, 51, 85, 97, 119).
  Inscriptions; Dt (7-109).
  Midland County; Deaths; Dt (10-38).
  Oakland County; Inscriptions, Big-
    ler Cemetery; Dt (10-64).
  Deaths and marriage items, Gaz-
    ette, 1846-7; Dt (8-43, 67).
  Plymouth; Inscriptions; Dt (2-101).
  Redford, Wayne Co.; Poll list,
    1839; Dt (7-121).
  Assessment roll, 1845; Dt (7-91).
  Royal Oak, Oakland Co.; Lamphere
    School records (1844); Dt (9-8).
  Utica, Macomb Co.; Cemetery lot
    owners; Dt (6-9, 47, 63, 103,
    125).
  Vermontville, Eaton Co.; Inscrip-
    tions; Dt (8-65).
  Volinia, Cass Co.; Civil War rec-
    ords; Dt (4-13).

MICHIGAN (continued)
Warren; Inscriptions; Dt (4-97,
115, 141, 161, 185, 207; 5-13,
29).
Washtenaw County; Inscriptions
near Crooked Lake; Dt (6-16).
MISSISSIPPI
Amite County, Census of 1816; M
(33-104; 34-9, 55).
Baldwyn, Lee Co.; Inscriptions;
M (22-48).
Lowndes County; Marriage records,
1830-52; M (22-61).
Natchez; Wills; Z (67-649).
Noxubee County; Inscriptions, mar-
riage records; M (26-28).
Starkville; Inscriptions; M (33-71).
Tupelo, Lee Co.; Inscriptions; M
(22-46).
Warren County; Marriages, 1836; Z
(78-296).
MISSOURI
Ralls County; Settlers from Ken-
tucky; N3 (43-342).
Randolph County; Marriages, 1829-
39; Z (76-711; 77-334, 477; 78-
103, 455).
Wills; Z (78-452).
NEBRASKA
Census, 1854; First District; B2
(13-1); Second District; B2 (13-
13); Third District; B2 (13-18);
Fourth District; B2 (13-25);
Fifth District; B2 (13-32);
Sixth District; B2 (13-34).
Census 1855; see counties.
Vital entries, newspaper files,
1857-62; B2 (11-8, 41; 12-3;
16-22).
Butler County; Census, 1869; B2
(22-30).
Cass County; 1855 Census; B2 (15-
6); 1856 Census; B2 (17-1).
Deaths, 1859-60; B2 (22-24).
Marriages, 1855-7; B2 (18-24,
35).
Deaths, 1869-70; B2 (20-23, 32).
Clay County; Census, 1856; B2
(17-14).
Cuming County; 1865 Census; B2
(22-6).
Dakota County; Census 1856; B2
(19-4).
Dodge County; Census 1855; B2 (15-
26); Census 1856; B2 (17-15).
Marriages, 1856-1859; B2 (10-
29).
Douglas County; Census 1855; B2

NEBRASKA (continued)
(15-17); Census 1856; B2 (17-25;
18-1, 17).
Marriage licenses, 1856-70; B2
(11-14, 38; 12-8, 34; 13-23, 38;
14-20; 15-28).
Falls City; Inscriptions, Pearson's
Point; B2 (10-74).
Lancaster County; Census, 1856; B2
(17-13).
Marriages, 1869-71; B2 (10-14,
37, 72; 11-24; 13-10; 16-9, 23,
36; 17-34; 18-11).
Probate abstracts, 1872-3; B2
(15-33).
School census, 1875; B2 (12-16).
Nemaha County; Census, 1856; B2
(16-13).
Otoe County; Census, 1856; B2 (16-
25); Census, 1865; B2 (19-13, 25;
20-3, 15, 25; 21-1, 19, 25).
Deaths, 1859-60, 1869-70; B2 (19-
21, 35).
Pawnee County; Census 1855; B2 (14-
4); Census 1856; B2 (16-6).
Platte County; Census, 1856; B2
(17-19).
Richardson County; Census 1855; B2
(14-1); Census 1856; B2 (16-1).
Marriages, 1857-67; B2 (10-8,
49).
Stanton County; Census, 1869; B2
(22-20).
Washington County; Census, 1855;
B2 (15-25); Census, 1856; B2 (18-
28).
NETHERLANDS, see Holland.
NEW HAMPSHIRE
Index of family names in N. H.
town histories; NH (Dec. 1946).
Counties and towns; Sl (25-83).
Newspaper vital items; M (24-106;
25-84).
Rev. War Pensions; M (24-107; 26-6,
33a, 113; 27-22; 29-37).
Alton; Inscriptions; Al (90-397).
Barnstead; Inscriptions; Al (86-
111).
Concord; Deaths, 1792-1836; Al (92-
268, 309).
First Bapt. Church; Historical;
NE (3-1).
Dover; Orderly book, Capt. Samuel
Hodge, 1760; B5 (18-299).
Gilsum; Latter-day Saints; U (25-
105; 26-63, 111, 157).
Grafton County; Probate items; Z
(70-137).

NEW HAMPSHIRE (continued).
Hudson; Church records, 1738-95;
 Al (91-252).
Madbury, Strafford Co.; Inscrip-
 tions; Al (87-342).
 Deaths, 1785-90; Al (89-83).
Plaistow; Marriage licenses, 1767-
 73; Yl (73-195).
Salem; Marriages, 1740-; B4 (16-
 116, 228).
Strafford; Inscriptions; Al (86-
 111).
NEW JERSEY
Sources; Bl (8-1, 25, 49, 73); Z3
 (2-12-139; 2-13-149).
Genealogical Dictionary; Bl (Vols.
 10 to 20, passim).
Reference list; history; Z3 (55-
 21).
Historical Records Survey; Bl (11-
 25).
List of genealogies, N. J. Hist.
 Soc.; Z3 (3-3-19).
Manuscript collections; Z3 (2-13,
 321).
Assessment of settlers, Delaware
 River, 1677; Bl (13-3).
Census, "New Sweden," 1693; Bl (13-
 63).
Capt. Jedediah Swan's Co.; Z3 (4-
 2-36).
Diary of Joseph Lewis; Z3 (62-35,
 106, 167, 217).
Divorce records; Bl (9-2).
Early emigrants to the West; Z3
 (4-10-387).
Early patentees; Z3 (2-3-110).
History of counties; Z3 (52-69).
Indentured servants, west N. J.,
 1676-7; Z3 (3-1-149).
Indentures of Apprentices, 1676-
 77; Bl (16-89).
Inscriptions; Z3 (3-2-118).
List of officers, Rev. War; Z3 (1-
 7-110; 1-8-65).
Loyalists; Z3 (4-11-77, 213, 289,
 433; 4-12-1, 147).
Licenses, 1683-4; Bl (18-93).
Marriage licenses 1727-40; Bl (14-
 73; 15-19, 52, 74; 16-19, 42,
 70, 93; 17-21, 45, 70, 96; 18-
 23, 45, 69, 94; 19-22, 45, 70,
 95; 20-22, 44, 67, 94).
Moravian records, 1742-62; Bl (13-
 20, 29).
Muster Roll, Capt. Conway's Co.,
 1776; Bl (12-13).
Obituary notices, Rev. soldiers;

NEW JERSEY (continued)
 Z3 (4-13-325).
Original stockholders, west N. J.,
 1691; Z3 (3-6-129).
Patentees, 1683-96; Z3 (4-15-231,
 372).
Rev. Pension applications; Z3 (4-
 5-236; 4-6-89, 166; 4-7-25, 134,
 227; 4-8-30, 306; 4-9-49; 4-10-
 182, 312).
Pensioners; Z3 (4-16-28); Bl (8-
 74).
Petition, 1780; M (34-75).
Quartermaster-General's receipt
 book, Rev. War; Z3 (4-11-364).
Rev. soldiers buried in Ohio; Z3
 (4-2-97).
3d Regt., N. J., 1776; Z3 (1-2-
 102; 1-9-183).
St. Domingan refugees; Z3 (62-197;
 63-73).
Silversmiths, 1623-1800; Z3 (61-
 145, 249; 62-100).
Alexandria; German Reformed Church,
 marriages 1796-1802, baptisms
 1763-1802; JM (3-4-1).
Arcola; Inscriptions; Z3 (4-2-168).
Atlantic County; Inscriptions; Bl
 (7-15, 52, 81; 9-82; 10-61; 11-
 21).
Auburn, Salem Co.; Inscriptions;
 Bl (13-70).
Basking Ridge, Somerset Co.; Pres-
 byterian Church, baptisms, 1795-
 1817; Bl (7-33, 75).
Bayonne; Inscriptions, Constable's
 Hook; Z3 (3-10-29).
Bedminster, Somerset Co.; Inhabi-
 tants, 1773-5; Z3 (54-116).
Bergen County; Record sources; Z3
 (2-3-175).
 Inscriptions, Old Tappan; Z3 (4-
 2-61).
 Huguenot inscriptions; Z3 (3-6-
 141).
 Inscriptions; Z3 (3-7-19, 106; 3-
 8-26, 147; 3-9-59; 3-10-73).
 Loyalists; Z3 (62-30).
 Ramapo Lutheran Church records;
 Z3 (3-8-1, 69).
Bridgeton; Inscriptions; B5 (17-4,
 145, 188).
 School, 1832; B5 (18-287).
Bridgewater, Somerset Co.; Inscrip-
 tions; Bl (12-86).
Burlington County; Vital records,
 1682-1701; B4 (15-179).
 Birth records, 1770; Z3 (4-3-55,

NEW JERSEY (continued)
108, 173, 205).
Cape May County; Assessors' lists,
1774, 1778, 1784; B7 (1-91).
Abstracts of Deeds; B7 (1-229;
2-25).
Cold Spring Church; B7 (2-203);
records of church; L1 (2-21).
Partial Census, 1704; B7 (2-
164).
Diary of Jacob Spicer, 1755-56;
Z3 (63-37, 82, 175).
Early settlers, 1750-1777; B7
(1-69).
List Pilgrim descendants; B7 (1-
23).
Rev. War and soldiers; B7 (1-
46).
Oaths of Allegiance, 1778; B7
(1-53).
Early county records; B7 (1-269,
316).
Early physicians; B7 (1-131,
190).
Ear marks; L1 (6-33).
First land purchasers; B7 (2-
229).
Inquest, 1740; B7 (2-41).
Landowners, 1778, 1784; B7 (1-
146).
Marriages; B1 (11-81).
Members of Legislature, 1697-
1942; B7 (2-160).
Memorandum Book (Jacob Spicer),
1757-64; B7 (1-109, 162, 182).
Methodists; B7 (1-199).
Miscellaneous records; B7 (1-
245).
Petitions and orders; B7 (1-239).
Soldiers, War of 1812; B7 (1-
179; 2-201).
Tax lists, 1751, 1768; B1 (14-
32, 59); B7 (2-74).
Tax list, 1768; B1 (14-59).
Vessels built; B7 (1-289).
Voters, 1848; B7 (2-3).
Chester, Morris Co.; Inscriptions;
B1 (11-4, 39, 65).
Cumberland County; Inscriptions,
M. E. churchyard, Tuckahoe River;
M (21-104).
Letters to Elizabeth Beatty Fith-
ian, 1772-1802; B5 (17-13, 155,
181, 212; 18-245, 278, 317, 346;
19-31, 49).
Militia list, 1806; B1 (15-14,
41, 70, 93).
Oaths of Allegiance; Z (80-272,

NEW JERSEY (continued)
328).
Place names; B5 (23-52).
Prominent men; B5 (24-216).
Reeves book of births, 1801-31;
B5 (24-247, 264; 25-27, 57, 90).
School records, Stow Creek; B5
(24-263).
Tax list, 1751; B1 (14-36).
Wills; M (29-17).
Baptist Church records, Divid-
ing Creek; B5 (30-203).
Demarest; Inscriptions; Z3 (4-1-
108).
Dividing Creek; Inscriptions; B5
(21-246; 22-5, 58).
Downs; Township records, 1773-
1817; B5 (26-152, 210, 225, 262;
27-338; 28-32).
Dumont, Bergen Co.; Inscriptions,
North Schraalenburgh yard; B1
(12-31, 60).
East Brunswick, Middlesex Co.; In-
scriptions, Cheesman Ground; B1
(15-90).
Egg Harbor; School census, 1832-
4; Z3 (3-8-134).
Elizabeth; Residents, 1771-89; Z3
(4-15-84).
St. John's Church, baptisms,
1820-26; B1 (7-56).
Englewood; Inscriptions; Z3 (4-1-
88).
English Creek, Atlantic Co.; Inscriptions; B1 (8-17).
Essex County; Marriages, 1794-
1814; B1 (9-4, 74; 11-13, 32,
68, 92; 12-19, 41, 64, 87).
Death records, 1772-7; Z3 (4-9-
159).
Evesham; Diary of Rev. John Hunt,
1770-1800; Z3 (52-177, 223; 53-
26, 111, 194, 251).
Fairfield, Cumberland Co.; Christ
Church founders, 1708; Z3 (3-6-
177).
Fairton; Inscriptions; B5 (18-261,
293, 356; 19-3, 67, 75, 137; 20-
178, 190, 227, 257; 21-309, 342,
365).
Franklin, Somerset Co.; Inscriptions, Voorhees-Nevius Ground;
B1 (15-65).
Freehold, Monmouth Co.; freeholders, 1748 and 1755; B1 (16-83).
Gloucester County; Rev. War soldiers; B1 (10-4).
Tax list 1687; B1 (13-10).

NEW JERSEY (continued)
    Residents, 1757; Z3 (3-3-171;
    3-4-41).
    Subscribers to Academy, 1817;
    Z3 (3-6-71).
New Stockholm; Early settlers; Z3
    (4-15, 487).
Northampton, Burlington Co.; Cen-
    sus, 1709; Z3 (1-4-33).
North Brunswick; Inscriptions; B1
    (16-24).
Nottingham; Town records, 1692-
    1710; Z3 (58-22,124, 179).
Ocean County; Inscriptions; B1 (7-
    1, 45).
Orange; Canal petitioners, 1837;
    Z3 (4-13-351).
Orangeburg; Inscriptions; Z3 (3-
    10-68).
Paramus, Bergen Co.; Inscriptions;
    B1 (8-39, 64, 87).
    Baptismal Records, Ref. Dutch
    Church; Z3 (50-206, 298, 396;
    51-51, 191, 162 sic page number
    repeated; 52-19, 108).
Pilesgrove, Salem Co.; Inscrip-
    tions; B1 (13-85).
Piscataway, Middlesex Co.; In-
    scriptions, Runyon ground; B1
    (16-41).
    Birth records; Z3 (3-2-73, 169;
    3-3-10).
    Marriage and death records,
    1688-1805; Z3 (4-4-33).
    St. James' Church; A2 (68-82).
Pompton; Early settlers; Z3 (4-4-
    44).
    Inscriptions, Dutch Church,
    1830-85; Z3 (3-2-23).
Port Elizabeth; Inscriptions,
    Friends' Graveyard; B5 (22-136).
Princeton; Sketch; S1 (26-23).
    Burials, Stony Brook Graveyard;
    Z3 (51-134).
    Graduates of Princeton College,
    1749; Dt (4-127).
Ramapo Tract; Early settlers; Z3
    (50-375).
Ramsey; Inscriptions, Union Ceme-
    tery; Z3 (4-1-112).
Raritan Landing; Early settlers;
    Z3 (54-85, 197).
Roadstown, Cumberland Co.; Cohan-
    sie Baptist Church records,
    1757-1835; B5 (23-56, 104, 140;
    24-162, 194, 235, 274; 25-3,
    38).
Saddle River; Inscriptions; Z3

NEW JERSEY (continued)
    (4-2-164).
Salem County; Early settlers; Z3
    (3-9-38, 85).
    List, court officers 1692-1849;
    Z3 (1-4-37).
    Penn's Neck Church records; Z3
    (1-3-112).
    Inscriptions; B1 (7-9).
    Marriages Canton Bapt. Church,
    1818-20; P (12-10).
Sayreville, Middlesex Co.; Inscrip-
    tions; B1 (15-23).
Scotch Plains; Baptist Church, mem-
    bers 1747-1814; B1 (7-65).
Second River; Dutch Church records;
    Z3 (3-1-178; 3-2-65, 131, 177).
Somerset County; Freeholders,
    1753; B1 (17-87; 18-13, 47).
    Inscriptions; B1 (9-17, 59).
    Beekman Cemetery Inscriptions,
    Montgomery; B1 (14-17).
    Inscriptions near Liberty Cor-
    ner, Bernards township; B1 (16-
    65).
    1st Regt., 1807; Z3 (4-13-324).
Sussex County; Inscriptions; B1 (7-
    26, 47, 84, 106; 12-21).
Swedesboro, Gloucester Co.; In-
    scriptions, Trinity Churchyard;
    B1 (13-33, 66, 81).
    Funerals 1793-99; B1 (14-81).
Tewkesbury, Hunterdon Co.; Fair-
    mount Churchyard Inscriptions;
    B1 (12-15, 35, 66).
Tuckahoe, Atlantic Co.; Inscrip-
    tions, Baptist Yard; B1 (11-24).
Union County; Inscriptions; Z3 (4-
    9-167, 275, 381; 4-10-59, 201);
    B1 (9-3).
Vineland; Bibliography of Maps, B5
    (23-134).
    Early houses; B5 (20-195, 237,
    261; 21-295, 344, 368, 229; 22-
    33, 42, 131; 23-170, 45, 85).
    First Pres. Church; Historical;
    B5 (30-198).
    Hotel registers, 1864-67; B5 (19-
    100, 131; 20-170, 209, 285; 21-
    307, 334, 383, 219; 22-30, 49,
    75, 143; 23-174, 70, 101, 111;
    24-148, 184, 245, 255; 25-35, 45,
    103, 126; 26-161, 204, 242, 269;
    27-310, 343; 28-13).
    Inscriptions, Baptist Graveyard;
    B5 (18-238).
    Journal of Charles K. Landis; B5
    (17-1, 143, 169, 197; 18-225,

NEW YORK (continued)

Franklin, Delaware Co.; Cong.
Church records; E3 (5-199, 215,
232, 248, 263, 279, 295, 311,
327, 343, 359).
Bapt. Church records; E3 (4-119,
136, 151, 167, 183; 5-359).

Franklin, Dutchess Co.; Census of
1800; A2 (69-248). See Patterson.

Frederick, Dutchess Co.; 1800 Census; A2 (66-389).

Fredericktown, Putnam Co.; baptisms, 1757; E3 (8-296).

Friendship; Baptist Church records; E3 (7-53, 69, 85).

Genesee County; Early settlers; E3
(1-4, 16, 28, 42).
Inscriptions, East Bethany; E3
(8-201).

Gilead, Putnam Co.; Pres. Church
records; E3 (8-229, 245, 261,
277, 295, 321).

Good Will, Orange Co.; Presbyterian Church records; E3 (3-7, 21,
37, 53, 69, 85, 101).

Goshen, Orange Co.; Census, 1800;
A2 (63-405).
Marriages; Z (68-248).

Granville, Washington Co.; Records; E3 (1-138; 2-6, 27, 43);
Inscriptions; E3 (4-155).

Greene County; Inscriptions, Kiskatom, Catskill; A2 (71-359,
360).

Greenwich; Church records; E3 (2-
35, 55, 71, 87, 103, 119, 135,
151, 166).

Herkimer County; Early settlers,
1797 deed; Dt (7-14).

Hillsdale, Columbia Co.; Inscriptions; A2 (70-209).

Hopewell, Ontario Co.; Inscriptions; E3 (1-139).

Howell's; Baptist Church records;
E3 (2-167, 181; 3-5).

Hudson, Columbia Co.; Methodist
Church records; E3 (3-120).
Inscriptions; E3 (3-155, 171,
186; 4-10, 26, 42).

Hume, Allegany Co.; Inscriptions;
Ng (6-292).

Huntington; Note; B4 (10-258).
Inscriptions, Crabmeadow; LI (1-
116).

Ischua, Cattaraugus Co.; Inscriptions; Ng (3-243).

Jefferson County; Inscriptions,
Rodman; E3 (5-203).

NEW YORK (continued)

Katsbaan, Ulster Co.; Reformed
Church records; OU (7-111, 151,
184, 215, 245, 272, 310, 342,
372; 8-23, 56, 81, 118, 148, 180,
211, 245, 280, 305, 342, 372; 9-
20, 51, 83, 112, 153, 182, 218).
Marriage records; Z (68-692).
Records, 1802-06; A2 (76-146).

Kinderhook; Names in account book,
1819-31; Ng (4-104).
Dutch Church marriages; Z (69-
436).

Kingston, Ulster Co.; Reformed
Dutch Church baptisms, 1809-14;
OU (1-122, 219, 279; 2-61, 86,
188, 311).
Civil Marriages, 1667-72; OU (1-
350).

Kirkland, Oneida Co.; Inscriptions,
Chickery Corners; M (27-47).

Lee, Washington Co.; Inscriptions;
E3 (3-90).

Lexington, Green Co.; Inscriptions;
A1 (92-162).

Lima; Inscriptions; E3 (3-107).

Lodi, Seneca Co.; Inscriptions; Dt
(4-9, 29, 51, 64).

Long Island; Early towns; S1 (26-
388).

Loonenburg [Athens]; Zion Lutheran Church records, 1705-40; A2
(73-64, 109).

Lowville, Lewis Co.; Inscriptions;
E3 (8-268, 283, 307, 339).

Mexico, Oswego Co.; Inscriptions;
E3 (7-124, 140, 155, 171, 187; 8-
203, 219).

Middle Granville, Washington Co.;
Church records; E3 (6-502, 517,
533, 549, 565; 7-5, 21, 37).

Middle Island; Marriages, 1818-87;
B4 (19-110).

Minisink, Orange Co.; Census, 1800;
A2 (63-79).

Monroe County; Settlements of estates; E3 (6-553, 569; 7-9, 25,
41, 57, 74, 89, 105).

Newburgh; Palatine settlers; OU (3-
97; 9-103).

New Cornwall, Orange Co.; Census
1800; A2 (64-293).

New Paltz, Ulster Co.; Inscriptions, Huguenot Ground; OU (1-
88, 119, 188, 246, 281).

Newstead; Members of Temperance
Society, 1831; E3 (1-141).

Newtown; Town records, 1659-88; A2

OHIO (continued)
23; 3-256).
Taverns, 1806-47; O (1-69).
Tax list, 1810; M (26-13); O (6-483).
Gallia County; Tax list, 1810; O (6-508).
Gallipolis; Historical; O (4-313).
Geauga County; Tax list, 1810; O (6-510).
Greene County; Marriages, 1803-5; O (4-292).
Tax list, 1810; O (7-591).
Guernsey County; Tax list, 1810; O (7-613).
Hamilton County; Tax list, 1810; O (8-655).
Harrison County; Inscriptions, near Cadiz; M (21-32).
Haven's Corners, Franklin Co.; Inscriptions; O (3-223, 247).
Highland County; Tax list, 1810; O (8-639).
Holmes County; Census 1830; Z (68-250, 504).
Hooker, Fairfield County; Inscriptions; O (4-317).
Jackson County; Early settlers; O (4-381).
Inscriptions, Buckley Cemetery; O (1-89).
Jefferson County; Letters in post-office, Knoxville; O (2-190).
Newspaper notices; O (2-164, 176; 3-202).
Knox, Columbiana Co.; Inscriptions; O (3-226).
Licking County; Inscriptions, Beard-Green Cemetery; O (1-75).
Inscriptions, Swisher Cemetery; O (2-123).
Madison County; Jury and tax lists, 1810; M (28-36).
Marietta; First settlers; O (1-74).
Miami County; Quaker records; Z (68-560, 628, 691).
Miflin, Franklin Co.; Historical; O (3-241).
Monroe; Inscriptions; Dt (7-63).
Montgomery County; German inhabitants, 1806; M (25-64).
Muskingum County; Vital items, newspaper, 1817-18; O (3-254).
New Salem; Letters in Post Office, 1817; O (2-165).
Pickaway County; Owners of Va. Military Lands, 1822; O (4-295).
Index of Wills, 1810-37; O (4-

OHIO (continued)
334).
Private death entries; Col (1 No. 3).
Inscriptions, small yards near Williamsport; O (8-646).
Plain, Franklin Co.; Historical; O (3-242).
Inscriptions, Maplewood Cemetery; O (7-602).
Preble County; Early settlers; Z (69-568).
Reynoldsburg, Franklin Co.; Historical; O (2-169).
Inscriptions; O (7-582).
Steubenville; Letters in Post Office, 1817; O (2-141).
Tarlton, Pickaway Co.; Early settlers (1830); O (2-97).
Trumbull County; Early Probate abstracts; M (34-77, 126).
Warren County; Inscriptions; M (26-58).
Marriage, death and other items, Western Star; O (5-403, 429).
Washington County; Census, 1810; Z (80-424, 509, 551, 585, 654).
Waynesville, Warren Co.; Friends' records; Z (76-714).
Worthington; St. John's Church; historical; O (4-289).
OKLAHOMA
Inscriptions, various; Z (79-280).
Bartlesville, Washington Co.; Inscriptions; Z (78-391).
Craig County; Landrum Cemetery; Z (80-378).
ONTARIO
London; Inscriptions; Dt (7-71).
PENNSYLVANIA
Sources for German genealogy; M (34-113).
Sources for Scotch-Irish genealogy; M (33-114).
List of Collections, Genealogical Society of Pa.; P (13-320).
Source material; Z (80-580).
Anglican clergy in Revolution; Q1 (63-401).
Briefs of title; P (14-223).
Burial places of Penn. War of 1812 soldiers; M (32-4).
Divorce, colonial; Q1 (57-175).
Eastern; list of Reformed Church records; P (13-90).
Emigration from; Q1 (55-134).
Iron plantations, early; Q1 (57-117).

PENNSYLVANIA (continued)
Land records; P (12-111).
Licenses to settle on Susquehanna
River; P (11-268).
Marriage licenses, 1784-91; Q1 (55-
259).
The Northwestern lands, 1790-1812;
Q1 (60-131).
Provincial Conference, 1776; Q1'
(58-312).
Quakers in Rev. War; Z (76-145).
Reformed Church records; Z (77-
244).
Susquehannah River, land licenses;
P (12-62).
Vital records, note; A2 (68-270).
Western; Index of Estates; A2 (68-
147, 261, 365; 69-48, 137, 257,
386).
Allegheny County; Inscriptions
(near Wilkinsburg); M (23-113).
Marriages by Rev. Abraham Boyd;
M (21-89).
Amityville, Berks Co.; Inscriptions;
M (21-18).
Ayr, Fulton County; Inscriptions;
M (22-106).
Bedford County; Abstract of Pro-
bate; P (11-260; 12-56, 145).
Rev. War soldiers; M (24-112).
Rev. monument near Saxton; M
(24-112).
Tavern keepers, 1791-96; Col (2-
45).
Oaths of Allegiance, 1778; Col
(2-83).
Bedford, Bedford Co.; Inscriptions;
M (24-83).
Berks County; Marriages (by Matthi-
as Kaler), 1791-1824; P (11-295);
Marriages, 1811-49; P (14-285);
Marriages, 1771-1811; M (24-38).
Richard Penn's manor, and early
purchasers; Q1 (58-193).
Bradford County; Early families; Z
(80-148).
Brooks County; Marriages by Isaac
Hicks, J. P., 1823-36; P (12-
160).
Bucks County; Probate abstracts;
Ng (4-132).
Butler County; Marriages by Rev.
Abraham Boyd; M (21-89).
Carlisle; Inscriptions; P (12-88).
Chambersburg; Newspaper items,
1802-1805; P (11-276; 12-71).
Chester County; Marriages, 1811-
38; P (13-134); Marriages, Faggs

PENNSYLVANIA (continued)
Manor, 1781-87; P (14-72).
Churchtown; Rev. soldiers buried;
Z (76-139).
Delaware County; Rev. Quaker Patri-
ots; P (13-130).
Derry, Westmoreland Co.; Tax Lists,
1786, 1798; M (24-73, 78).
Dunbar, Fayette Co.; Marriages,
1805-48; Z (76-398, 583; 77-53).
Ephrata Community; Inscriptions; M
(29-55, 60).
Erie County; Inscriptions; M (24-
41); Z (69-366).
Fayette County; Original pension
claims; Z (75-11-69).
Franklin County; Salem Ref. Church
records; Z (69-502).
Germantown; Letters, 1738; Q1 (56-
9).
Naturalization, 1692; M (28-7).
Greene County; Index of wills,
1796-1825; Col (3-104).
Greenwich, Columbia Co.; Marriages,
1822-35; P (13-228).
Huntington, Blair Co.; Marriages,
1787-1823; P (12-48).
Indiana County; Inscriptions, near
Cramer; M (22-111; 23-23).
Jefferson, Greene Co.; Inscriptions;
Col (3-92).
Lancaster County; Inscriptions, Sa-
lem Lutheran Churchyard, Kissel
Hill; M (34-42); Inscriptions,
Willowstreet Mennonite Cemetery;
M (34-118); Inscriptions, Millers-
ville; M (34-78).
Inscriptions, West Lampeter; M
(20-81, 84, 85).
Inscriptions, St. Paul's Church-
yard, Manheim; M (30-109).
Inscriptions, Bangor Parish,
Churchtown, Caernarvon township;
M (30-103).
Inscriptions, Bromberger Cemetery;
M (33-70).
Rev. soldiers buried, New Holland;
Z (78-500).
Rev. soldiers buried, Leacock; Z
(75-4-51; 75-5-38).
Rev. soldiers buried, Old Welsh
Graveyard; Z (78-695).
Rev. soldiers buried, Old Fierre
Graveyard; Z (77-476).
Donegal Pres. Churchyard; Z (77-
763).
Forrey Graveyard; Z (79-188).
Strickler Graveyard; Z (79-188).

PENNSYLVANIA (continued)
Tax lists, 1751-57; M (21-1).
Wills; Z (73-8-81; 73-9-69;
73-10-72; 73-11-61; 73-12-60;
74-1-46; 74-2-36; 74-3-39; 74-
9-43; 74-11-54).
Burial records, 1748-49; M (20-
15).
Inscriptions, First Pres. Grave-
yard; M (20-54).
Church records (excerpts); M
(24-17).
Lawrenceville, Tioga Co.; Benefac-
tors to Pres. Church, 1847; M
(31-87).
Lebanon County; Inscriptions,
Walmer's Cemetery; M (26-49,
119).
Litchfield, Bradford Co.; Inscrip-
tions; Dt (6-93).
Lost Creek; Marriages, 1845-71; P
(11-251).
Luzerne County; Historical; S1
(24-159).
Petitioners for erection, 1794;
Pw (21-28).
Lycoming County; Inscriptions,
Taylor Cemetery; Dt (7-79).
Marlborough, Chester Co.; Mar-
riages, 1715-36; P (12-93).
Mercersburg, Franklin Co.; Church
records, 1769-1811; P (14-237;
15-35).
Mifflin County; Pioneers; Z (80-
271).
Mifflin, Cumberland Co.; Marriag-
es, 1824-26; M (25-93).
Mifflintown; Marriages, 1845-71;
P (11-251).
Mill Creek, Huntingdon Co.; In-
scriptions; M (26-47).
Monroe County; Inscriptions, Ha-
milton Union Churchyard; M (28-
58).
Montgomery County; Inscriptions,
Barren Hill; P (13-72, 231; 14-
53, 172, 276; 15-103).
Inscriptions, Upper Merion; P
(14-257; 15-70).
Northern Liberties; Marriages,
Baptist Church, 1820-29; P (12-
10).
Northumberland County; Probate
records; P (13-48, 193; 14-22,
150, 247; 15-46).
Parkesburg; Inscriptions; M (32-
86).
Philadelphia County; Marriages,

PENNSYLVANIA (continued)
1845-54; P (14-170).
Tavern licenses, 1832; M (30-102).
Philadelphia; Colonial clockmakers;
Q1 (56-225).
Colonial shipbuilding; Q1 (56-
156).
Vital items, newspapers; M (28-
75).
Deaths from Ladies Literary Port
Folio, 1828-9; P (13-225).
Diary (Grace Growden Galloway),
1778-79; Q1 (55-32).
Early fire defences; Q1 (56-355).
General Hospital, historical; Q1
(52-32).
Index to Families in North Ameri-
can; B4 (15-92).
Inscriptions; P (12-170; 13-35;
14-3, 144).
Marriages, 1828-32; P (12-127;
13-93).
Minute Book of Trustees, St. Ma-
ry's Church, 1814-18; G1 (43-
246).
Old St. Augustine's (R. C.); G1
(44-289).
Quaker records; P (11-230; 12-30,
151; 13-24, 210; 14-34, 160, 267;
15-99).
Quaker marriages, 1682-1714; Z3
(1-9-19).
Providence, Bedford Co.; Inscrip-
tions; M (27-95).
Redstone; Bapt. Church marriages; Z
(75-7-30).
Shawnee, Monroe Co.; Inscriptions;
A2 (77-20).
Sullivan County; Inscriptions, Ed-
kin Cemetery (Shrewsbury); Dt (7-
80).
Susquehanna County; Marriages and
Deaths, 1816-49; Pw (22-125).
Sussex County; Abstracts of wills;
P (11-215; 12-21, 191; 13-81,
238).
Tioga and Columbia Counties; Mar-
riages, 1854-83; P (14-50).
Todd, Huntingdon Co.; Inscriptions;
M (20-86).
Venango County; Genealogical items;
M (20-90).
Washington County; Early settlers;
Z (80-367).
Westmoreland County; Inscriptions
near Ligonier; M (22-25; 23-23).
Inscriptions near Pleasant Unity;
M (22-27).

SOUTH CAROLINA (continued)
  Refugees, 1781; J (34-78).
  Spanish documents concerning
    settlement; J (37-49, 91, 131).
  Stoney Creek Church records,
    1743-60; J (38-21).
  Colleton County; Inscriptions; J
    (38-107; 40-36).
  Dorchester; Inscriptions; J (40-
    112).
  Edisto; Inscriptions; J (40-108).
  Georgetown; Vital items; J (32-
    193).
    Inscriptions, Prince George Win-
    yah; J (31-184, 292).
  Grahamville; Inscriptions; J (41-
    84, 94).
  Grenadier Co., 2nd Regt.; Z (79-30).
  James Island County; Inscriptions,
    Stiles Point; J (38-74).
  Laurens County; Inscriptions; M
    (21-56; 25-67).
  Lewisfield Plantation; Inscrip-
    tions; J (42-81).
  McCormick County; Guillebean Ceme-
    tery Inscriptions; J (32-314);
    Inscriptions, Willington; J (34-
    113).
  Marion County; Inscriptions; J (39-
    100).
  Pawley's Island; Inscriptions; J
    (40-64).
  St. Helena Island, Beaufort Co.;
    Inscriptions; J (35-34).
    Diary of Ebenezer Coffin, 1816;
    V3 (54-117).
  St. Matthew's Parish; Records of
    Rev. Paul Turquand, 1770-71; J
    (33-180).
  St. Stephen's Parish; Minutes of
    vestry from 1754; J (45 – 65, 156,
    217; 46-40, 93).
  Sampit; Inscriptions, Northampton
    Plantation; J (39-173).
  Welsh Neck; Baptist Church; mem-
    bers; Z (79-155).
  Yeamans Hall; Inscriptions; J (38-
    99).
SOUTHERN COLONIES
  Notes; B4 (11-42; 15-95).
  Harvard College; Early students
    from the South; W2 (13-1).
SWEDEN
  Genealogical sources; J (29-97).
  Noble families in U. S.; M (29-
    139).
  Emigrants to Delaware, New Jersey;
    B1 (13-1, 13).

SWEDEN (continued)
  Emigrants to N. Y.; M (30-79).
TENNESSEE
  First inhabitants; S1 (27-14).
  Settlers on Cherokee lands, 1819;
    M (33-65).
  Indian attacks and massacres; Z
    (65-551).
  Capt. Jacob Tipton's Co., St.
    Clair's Campaign, 1791; N4 (3-
    150).
  Pensioners of the Revolution and
    War of 1812; Z (77-715).
  "State of Franklin"; S1 (29-321).
  Blount County; Marriage bonds; Z
    (68-555).
    Early land owners; M (33-1, 38).
  Greene County; Index to early
    wills; Z (80-650).
    Marriage bonds, 1783-1807; Dt (2-
    109, 133, 167, 177, 199; 3-3,
    27, 47); Z (69-769; 72-12-71; 73-
    1-67; 73-2-67; 73-3-88; 73-4-85;
    73-5-90; 73-6-59).
  Knox County; New Prospect Pres.
    Church; N4 (7-50).
    Newspaper marriage notices, 1791-
    1813; N4 (11-116).
  Roane County; Rev. soldiers buried;
    Z (68-688).
  Warren County; Inscriptions; M (32-
    73).
TEXAS
  Brownsville; Inscriptions; Dt (7-
    15).
  Washington County; Residents, 1837;
    M (32-87).
UTAH
  Davis County; Census, 1851; U (28-
    51, 104, 169; 29-45).
  Great Salt Lake County; U. S. Cen-
    sus, 1851; U (29-133, 179).
  Iron County; U. S. Census, 1851; U
    (29-65, 130).
VERMONT
  Counties and towns; S1 (25-534).
  Death records from Vermont Journal;
    Z (67-394).
  Barton; Vital records; Z (66-529;
    67-244).
  Bennington; First Cong. Church rec-
    ords; E3 (2-147, 163, 179; 3-3,
    19, 35, 51, 67).
    Inscriptions; E3 (4-57, 74, 90,
    106, 123, 138).
  Chittenden County; School list,
    1829-32, Jericho, Underhill,
    Richmond, Essex; Dt (7-21).

VERMOUNT (continued)
  Fairfield; Cong. Church records;
    B4 (12-86).
  Ferrisburgh; Inscriptions; A1
    (95-202).
  Orwell; Vital items, 1809-10,
    from an almanac; Dt (3-145).
  Poultney; Baptist church records;
    E3 (7-101, 117, 133, 149, 165;,
    8-197, 213).
  Underhill Flats, Chittenden Co.;
    Inscriptions; Dt (5-212).
  Wallingford; Inscriptions; E3 (1-
    71).
  Weathersfield Bow; Inscriptions;
    S3 (14-3-8).
VIRGINIA
  List of family papers, Library of
    College of William and Mary; W2
    (20-388).
  List of families in Baltimore Sun;
    Z (73-2-62).
  Counties and parishes 1774; Z (72-
    6-75).
  County records in State Library;
    Z (77-600, 659, 719).
  List of Parish Registers in State
    Library; Z (75-12-61).
  Acadians in; V3 (40-241).
  Baptist vital records; M (28-121).
  William Byrd Title Book; V3 (48-
    31, 107, 222, 328; 49-37, 174,
    269, 354; 50-169, 238).
  Clergy list, 1758; W2 (17-39).
  Clergy of the Established Church,
    Revolutionary period; V3 (41-11,
    123, 231, 297); 1785-1814; W2
    (19-397).
  County Court records; V3 (54-3).
  Churches, Northumberland and Lan-
    caster Cos.; V3 (54-137, 233).
  Colonial parish acts; W2 (18-106).
  Council and General Court records,
    1642-45; W2 (20-62).
  Council of War, 1756; M (25-45).
  County court records; N3 (38-360).
  Early colonists; E1 (10-37, 68).
  Early records pertaining to Indi-
    ans; W2 (16-589).
  Early settlers; V3 (51-71).
  Immigrants from Isle of Wight,
    1621; V3 (40-80).
  Immigrants, 18th Century; W2 (23-
    344).
  Items from Colonial Decisions; W2
    (20-545).
  Items 1677-89 from Order Book,
    Stafford, King George, Prince

VIRGINIA (continued)
  William, Westmoreland Cos.; W2
    (23-525).
  List of County Surveyors; V3 (50-
    368).
  Marriages; E1 (10-13, 27).
  Militia Officers, 1698; V3 (49-
    304).
  Miscellaneous documents; M (24-34).
  Wills; Z (75-2-52).
  Notes from county records (before
    1700); V3 (50-366).
  Notes from Albemarle, Amherst and
    Buckingham Cos.; E1 (10-26).
  Organization of colony and coun-
    ties, 1726; V3 (48-141).
  Original counties; V1 (16-76).
  Parishes and ministers, 1680; W2
    (17-466).
  Pay roll, Capt. Tho. Watkins'
    Troop, Gen. Sawyer's Brigade; V1
    (19-168).
  Orderly Book, Militia, War of 1812;
    V3 (46-146, 329).
  Parishes and Rectors, 1785-1814;
    W2 (19-424).
  Rev. War soldiers; E1 (10-29, 47).
  Revolutionary Pensioners, 1786;
    W2 (15-395; 16-534).
  Richard Taliaferro's Co., 1779; M
    (24-104).
  Roll of Co. I, York Rangers, 32d
    Regt., Hunter's Brigade, Confed-
    erate Army, 1861-3; W2 (14-235).
  Settlements on Eastern Shore; V3
    (50-193).
  Shipping; E1 (10-1).
  Soldiers from Prince Edward Coun-
    ty, Rev. War; W2 (15-138, 403).
  Southwestern, early history; W2
    (17-501).
  Supreme Court records, 1806-09; W2
    (12-167; 13-49; 14-24).
  Students at Litchfield Law School;
    W2 (21-35).
  Tithables 1755 between Bush River
    and County Line; V1 (45-50).
  Workmen at Great Falls for the Po-
    tomack Co., 1786, pay roll; M (20-
    5).
  Accomack County; Early items; V3
    (44-52).
  Albermarle County; Notes from di-
    ary of Rev. Robert Rose, 1750-1;
    V1 (23-63).
  Alexandria; Economic history; W2
    (12-104).
  Amelia County; Marriage bonds; Z

VIRGINIA (continued)
(66-513, 582, 665; 67-53, 123,
154, 247, 389, 578).
Order Book, 1735-40; V1 (22-
185).
Revolutionary soldiers; W2 (15-
397).
Amherst County; Probate records,
1773-77; E1 (10-52).
Marriage certificates; E1 (10-
57).
Augusta County; Militia, 1758; Z
(78-497, 550, 595, 645, 693).
Settlers from England; 1739-
40; M (25-46).
Early settlers; M (25-50, 53).
Court records; M (29-30).
Companies organized 1756; M
(25-70).
Revolutionary soldiers, buried
Bethel Church; W2 (15-405).
Aylett; Ledger accounts, 1781-2;
W2 (17-49).
Bedford County; Vital records; W2
(14-36).
Items from Order Book, 1774-82;
Z (75-7-31; 75-8-40; 75-12-60;
76-59, 141, 216).
Berkeley County; Dissenters' Peti-
tion; Dt (4-73).
Botetourt County; Rev. claims; Z
(69-471).
Boydton, Mecklenburg Co.; Histo-
rical; V3 (50-108).
Brunswick County; Militia, 1757;
V3 (50-360).
Petition, 1778; M (34-85).
Rev. patriots; Z (68-244).
Wills, 1732-97; Z (69-438).
Buckingham County; Accounts of
planters; W2 (13-180).
Courts Martial, 1832-41; W2 (12-
193).
Buffaloe Settlement, Prince Ed-
ward Co.; settlers; V3 (49-234).
Campbell County; Marriages, 1800-
1810; V3 (40-44, 155).
Revolutionary Ensigns, 1782; M
(27-19).
Caroline County; Revolutionary
soldiers; W2 (12-221).
Marriages, 1819, and a few 1797-
1828; V1 (14-166).
Cedar Creek, Hanover County; Qua-
ker Meeting House, historical;
W2 (19-293).
Charles City Co.; Excerpts from
records, 1655-66; V3 (43-144,

VIRGINIA (continued)
347).
Charlotte County; List of Justices;
W2 (21-178).
Militia; V1 (22-189; 23-191).
Revolutionary records, 1782; V1
(20-119, 184).
Cumberland County; Election list
and voters, 1804; Marriages,
1806-9; W2 (22-61).
French War soldiers, 1757; W2
(19-230).
Marriage Bonds; Z (65-40, 110,
301, 432, 626, 737).
Court records, 1794; W2 (14-181,
315).
Cumberland; Miscellaneous records,
1780-86; W2 (12-39).
Dinwiddie County; Colonial churches;
W2 (23-249).
Methodist marriages, 1818-19; V3
(50-67).
Probate records, 1784-1826; M (30-
43).
Dunmore County; Military Co. (Rev.
War); Rev. records; V3 (44-102,
246).
Purchasers of salt, 1776; V3 (49-
342).
Elizabeth City County; Churches;
W2 (21-371).
Index to Wills, 1730-1800; W2
(13-34).
Marriages; W2 (14-95).
Elk Creek District; Men in service,
1782; M (34-76).
Essex County; Ages of children,
1698; W2 (18-120).
Churches (historical); V3 (53-1).
Court records; W2 (18-297).
Election Poll, 1741; W2 (22-54).
Marriage licenses, 1692-95; V1
(13-99).
Notes from diary of Rev. Robert
Rose, 1747-9; V1 (23-62).
Rent roll, 1704 (annotated); W2
(21-397).
Rent roll, 1715; W2 (18-203).
Fairfax Co.; Militia in French and
Indian War; Z (79-32).
Notes from Order Book, 1756-63;
E1 (10-8).
Frederick County; Militia lists,
1755-58; M (27-56).
Fredericksburg; Thornton-Storke
inscriptions; W2 (19-187).
Germania; 1714 colonists; V3 (40-
317; 41-41).

VIRGINIA (continued)
Taverns; W2 (16-339).
Pittsylvania County; Vital rec-
ords; W2 (14-36).
Marriage bonds, 1767-87; Z (70-
722).
Prince Edward County; Abstracts
of wills; Z (75-1-50).
Soldiers, Revolutionary and Co-
lonial; W2 (15-138, 403).
Prince George County; Baptist
records; V3 (41-97).
Colonial churches; W2 (23-249).
Items 1715-20; El (10-53).
Court items, 1811-13; V1 (15-
273).
Prince William County; records
recently discovered; W2 (21-
183).
Richmond County; Ages of children,
1698; W2 (18-207).
Churches; historical; V3 (53-1).
Roanoke County; Marriage bonds,
1838-40; M (27-34).
Rockbridge County; Inscriptions,
Old Providence Church; W2 (16-
88).
Marriages, 1783-89; V1 (13-261).
Rockingham County; Court Orders,
1778-81; B4 (11-4).
Russell County; Abstracts of
wills, 1803-60; V3 (40-177,
287).
Salem, Roanoke Co.; Marriage
bonds, 1838-9; M (29-34).
Spotsylvania County; Marriage
licenses; Z (80-188).
The mouth of Massaponax; V1 (13-
175).
Stafford County; Abstracts, Deed
Book, 1722-28; V1 (19-45).
Index of Probate, 1664-1760; V1
(20-182; 22-37).
Probate records, 1692; V3 (47-
22, 126, 248, 335).
Deaths, 1715-30, St. Paul's; V1
(20-121, 181).
Inscriptions, "Edge Hill"; M
(25-59).
Inscriptions, "Rock Raymond"; M
(25-60).
Inscriptions; V1 (27-278).
Miscellanea; B2 (10-67).
Order Books, 1690-92; V3 (44-
191, 296; 45-11, 171, 243, 367;
46-26, 126, 222, 316).
Survey of records; V3 (53-215).
Staunton; Marriage bonds, 1802-;

VIRGINIA (continued)
V1 (25-217, 289).
Surry County; Index to Will and ·
Deed Book, 1730-39; W2 (12-281).
Early records; W2 (19-531).
Colonial churches; W2 (20-285).
Sussex County; Colonial churches;
W2 (20-285).
Warwick County; Churches; W2 (21-
371).
Early records; V1 (25-52).
Westmoreland County; Marriages,
1691-2; W2 (23-85).
Miscellanea; B2 (10-34).
Letters of Lawrence Butler, 1788-
93; V3 (41-24, 111).
West Point; Baptist churchyard;
W2 (12-43).
Weyanoke, Charles City Co.; V1
(16-85).
Williamsburg; William and Mary Col-
lege accounts, 1784-91; W2 (14-
9).
Winchester; (Account book of Anna
Smith, 1815-24); M (23-44).
York County; Colonial churches;
W2 (19-159).
Losses in Revolution; W2 (15-
173).
Petitions, 1776-1861; W2 (18-
119).
Yorktown; Colonial innkeepers; W2
(23-8).
WEST INDIES
New Providence; (Gov. Elias Has-
ket, 1702); Y1 (71-216).
WEST VIRGINIA
Northern; Index of Estates; A2
(68-147, 261, 365; 69-48, 137,
257, 386).
Bath, Morgan Co.; Purchasers,
1777-98; W2 (16-347).
Berkeley County; Abstracts of
wills, 1775-77; Z (65-296).
Rental list, 1780; M (20-33).
Hardy County; Abstracts of Wills;
Z (74-9-47).
Marriages (Baker, Simmons, Whet-
zel, 1806-36); M (24-136).
Marion County; Graves of Rev. sol-
diers; Z (77-55).
Monongalia County; Marriage bonds;
cont.; Z (66-50, 150, 314, 679;
67-49, 518; 68-559).
Miscellaneous wills; Z (80-548).
Rev. list of claims; Z (68-559).
Randolph County; Inscriptions; M
(32-28, 74; 33-13, 43).

WISCONSIN

Revolutionary War and Soldiers
(continued)
Bamford's Diary; X1 (27-240).
British Campaign, 1777, Mary-
land; X1 (33-3).
British orderly book, 1780-81; H2
(9-57, 163, 273, 366).
Buried in Arlington Cemetery; M
(29-145).
Contemporary painters; S1 (32-
639).
Deaths of Rev. soldiers from Am-
erican Advocate, 1810-27; Z
(68-695).
Diary of George Norton, 1777-78;
Y1 (74-337).
Diary of William Widger (Mill
Prison, Eng., 1781); Y1 (74-
22).
Diplomas of the Soc. of the Cin-
cinnati; S1 (29-7).
Discharges; W2 (21-344).
Expedition to Portsmouth, Va.;
1779; W2 (12-181).
Follett Diary, Wyoming Massacre;
S3 (9-3-2; 9-4-3).
French soldiers killed at York-
town; W2 (12-70).
Gen. Duportail at Valley Forge;
Q1 (56-341).
Journal of Dr. Lewis Beebe, Can-
ada Expedition, 1776; Q1 (59-
321).
Lee's Legion; V1 (13-285; 15-
256).
Letters of Major Baurmeister,
Philadelphia Campaign, 1777-8;
Q1 (59-392).
Letters of Josiah Adams of New-
bury, Mass.; Y1 (77-143).
Letter from Marion to Greene,
1782; J (36-111).
Letters (Sage collection); J (38-
1, 75).
List, British prisoners; Z3 (3-3-
85).
Members of the Cincinnati, Va.
and Ky.; N3 (32-199).
Navy officers; M (32-1).
Order Book of Col. Peter Horry;
J (35-49, 112).
Pension records, abstracts; in-
dexed individually herein un-
der names.
Pension records; Z (65-325).
Pensioners, 1787; V3 (50-163).
Invalid pensioners, 1792; LI (3-
14).

Revolutionary War and Soldiers
(continued)
Pensioners, 1891; X2 (16-51).
Phillips' Expedition to Va.; 1781;
W2 (12-191).
Prisoners taken to St. Augustine,
Fla.; Z (73-3-85).
Putnam's Command, Bunker Hill; Y1
(68-330).
Sailors on the Bon Homme Richard; M
(32-65).
Service items, mostly Va.; E1 (10-
10).
Siege of Yorktown; W2 (12-229).
Subscribers to a Loan to Congress,
1780; M (22-110; 23-22).
The Continental Army; W2 (12-79;
13-85).
Wheeler Journal, Ticonderoga; Y1
(68-371).
Royalty and Peerage
Royal ancestry; B4 (9-93).
Albreda of Lorraine; A1 (99-256).
Ancestry of wives of King Edward I;
B4 (9-362).
Capet; medieval ancestry; A1 (99-
130).
Carolingians; origin; A1 (98-303).
The Conradins; A1 (99-facing 242).
Countess Lucy; B4 (10-125).
Descents from the Cid; B4 (9-99).
Descent of Deighton family from
King Edward I; B4 (9-212).
House of Rurik (Russia); B4 (9-13).
Hungarian ancestry of Queen Philip-
pa; A1 (96-138, 304); M (30-115).
Identity of Agatha; M (28-105).
Kings of Ireland; B4 (9-98).
Pelham royal lines; B4 (19-197).
Plantagenet; mediaeval ancestry; A1
(99-34).
Rich, barons; B4 (21-234; 22-27).
Ruffin royal descent; V1 (22-242;
23-130; 25-64).
Toeni, de; English barons; A2 (74-
25).
See also in Name Index; Amundeville,
Aton, Aucher, Baliol, Barne, Bar-
rington, Bruce, Camville, Darcy,
d'Eyncourt, Drummond, Dunbar,
Eure and Vesci, Fettiplace, Fien-
nes, FitzHugh, Giffard, Gorsuch,
Greystoke, Gubion, Gunne, Hast-
ings, Harlakenden, Ingoldsby,
James, Lancaster (barons), Lin-
coln (earls), Ludlow, Makernes,
Marbury, Marmion, Marshall, Myt-
ton, Newburgh, Pelham, Percy,

Royalty and Peerage (continued)
Rich, Scrope, Sheafe, Tomes,
Twigden, Vere, Wahull, Warren,
West.
Ships and Shipping
American vessels at Archangel,
1810; Y1 (68-378).
Building of the Massachusetts,
1787; Y1 (74-239).
17th Century, Maryland; X1 (33-334).
Naval Battle, Delaware Bay; B7 (2-
58).
See Newburyport, Salem, Jamestown;
also E1 (10-61) for "Ships in
Port." See also Passenger Lists.
Source material; U (28-25).
Status of Professional Genealogists;
B4 (20-1).
Terms, "servant"; S3 (17-2-12).
"Mr." in Virginia; W2 (19-142).
Tradition and Family History; B4 (9-
1).
Trusts and Estates; P (15-1).
Use of an alias in England; B4 (17-
68).
Use of "y" for "th"; E1 (10-67).
Use of law reports; B4 (18-100).
Vital Records
Centralization of Vital Records in
the Various States; A1 (90-9).
Deaths, American Weekly Mercury,
1724-1746; Q1 (58-37).
Obituaries from Presbyterian maga-
zine, 1831-58; M (20-98, 114).
War of 1812
Burial places, soldiers (mostly
Penn.); M (33-78; 34-84).
Captains at North Point and Fort
McHenry, 1814; X2 (6-5).
Richmond Washington Vols. (Capt.
Booker), muster roll; V3 (49-
228).
Capt. Jacob Hartsell's Co., East
Tenn.; N4 (11-93; 12-118).
Pension record (Jacob Lehman, Pa.);
S3 (9-6-10).
Pension Applications: Blackmar; M
(22-31). Caruthers, Dorr; M (22-
58). Neely; M (22-59). Miller;
M (22-73). Barr, Campbell; M
(26-62). Failing, Flesher, Laird,
Peet, Scofield; M (26-63). Mose-
ley, Stewart, Vankirk; M (26-64).
Austin; M (31-18). Banister,
Blair, Bowers; M (31-19). Brooks,
Campbell, Clark, Clemons; M (31-
20). Cline, Criswell, Cooley,
Cooper, Cushwa, Drennan, Fox, Har-

War of 1812 (continued)
per, Heter, Irvin; M (32-78ff.).
Jackson, Meacham, Rogers, Sut-
ton, Van Valkenburgh, Yount); M
(33-19 ff.). Beaver, Cooper,
Deem, De Hass, Demoss, Downing,
Foster, Fox, Frailey, Frost,
Fruit, Glascock, Harrington,
Harrod, Johnston, O'Riley, Port-
er, Schell, Ullery, Adkins, At-
kins;. M (33-106ff.; 34-51ff.).
William the Conqueror; companions
at Hastings; B4 (21-111).
World War I
American Overseas Cemeteries; S1
(26-381).
German sailors died in N. C.; H1
(1-138).

INDEX

TO

GENEALOGICAL PERIODICALS

Volume III

together with

"MY OWN INDEX"

By

DONALD LINES JACOBUS, M.A.

PREFACE

Index to Genealogical Periodicals, Volume III

The present small volume has been prepared largely
in response to the inquiries and requests of librarians,
who have found the two earlier volumes useful in locating
genealogical material which has appeared in the serial
publications.

The first volume, published in 1932, covered the
chief genealogical periodicals through 1931, except those
which provided their own complete general indexes such as
the first fifty volumes of the New England Historical and
Genealogical Register, and the earlier volumes of Collections of the Essex Institute. The second volume, published in 1948, covered the fifteen years, 1932 to 1946
inclusive, and included a few titles (completely) which
were overlooked in the first volume.

The third volume, presented herewith, covers most of
the periodicals devoted to genealogy or with genealogical
sections for the six years, 1947 to 1952 inclusive. The
indexer now lays down the task, feeling that his efforts
have been of great aid to many seekers and that he now
deserves a rest from his labors, but with the hope that
some altruist may assume the thankless task and continue
an index of this type.

Few have any idea of the amount of work involved in
preparing and publishing such an index. The actual indexing, on index slips, consumes an incredible amount of
time. Much of this has to be done in libraries. Some
magazines are behind schedule, and when at last the final
issue of a volume is received by the library, the entire
volume may be whisked off promptly to the binders before
the indexer can get a chance to consult the final issue.
The 1951 volume of one magazine was called for three
times at a New Haven library in the winter of 1952-3, but
was still at the binder's, and finally had to be indexed
in a Hartford library.

Because of extremely high rates for letterpress
printing, this volume, like the last one, is lithoprinted. The preparation of "master copy" for this process is
tedious, fussy work, and the standard rates are high.
For this operation I have been fortunate in securing the
services of Miss Helen M. Pfeifer, at somewhat more mod-
erate rates.

Demand for a book of this type is limited, and an
edition of only 300 copies is printed. It is hoped that
enough copies will sell in the first six months to cover
out of pocket costs: for preparation of the master copy
and the actual printing and binding; for mailing cartons
(or cost of wrapping); for postage; and for such adver-

tising as may be required. If the entire edition is
eventually sold, the "profit" will be extremely poor pay
by prevalent wage scales for the personal time of the indexer.

"My Own Index"

Over the years, I have indexed some of the numerous
pedigree books which contain data on a number of families
ancestral to the compilers. This was done for my own
use, and despite the incompleteness and selective nature
of this Index, I have found it extremely useful.

It covers a number of books, some old, some recent,
which deal chiefly with families of New England and New
York, but all families in the selected books are included
in the Index, hence a few families of other sections will
be found. Considering the selective, even personal, as-
pects of the Index, I have hesitated to publish it. Several genealogical friends, both amateur and professional,
who have known me to locate "buried" data in record time
by use of "My Own Index," have urged me to make it available to themselves and others. I have therefore decided
to include it in the present volume.

Without further apology, I will merely add that I
know some first-class books are omitted, while perhaps
half a dozen which are not quite first-class are included.

KEY TO PERIODICALS

A1   The New England Historical and Genealogical Register. Vols. 101-106. 1947-1952.

A2   The New York Genealogical and Biographical Record. Vols. 78-83. 1947-1952.

B1   The Genealogical Magazine of New Jersey. Vols. 21-24, and Vol. 25, Nos. 1, 2, 3. 1946-1949 and through July 1950 (published March 1953 but so dated).

B4   The American Genealogist. Vols. 24-28. 1948-1952.

B5   Vineland Historical Magazine. Vols. 31-36. 1946-1951. (The Oct. 1951 issue was published Dec. 1952.)

Col   The Colorado Genealogist. Vols. 8-13. 1947-1952.

Dt   The Detroit Society for Genealogical Research Magazine. Vols. 10 (No. 5)-16 (No. 2). 1947-1952 (Dec.).

J   South Carolina Historical and Genealogical Magazine. Vols. 48-53. 1947-1952.

K2   The Filson Club History Quarterly. Vols. 21-26. 1947-1952.

M   National Genealogical Society Quarterly. Vols. 35-40. 1947-1952.

N3   Register of Kentucky State Historical Society. Vols. 45-50. 1947-1952.

NAH   Publications of the Norwegian-American Historical Association. Studies and Records. Vols. 1-17. 1926-1952.

Ng   The Niagara Frontier Genealogical Magazine. Vol. 7, Nos. 1, 2. 1948. (These two issues published after a suspension of two years; again suspended.)

O1   Bulletin of the Historical and Philosophical Society of Ohio. Vols. 1-10. 1943-1952.

P   Publications of the Genealogical Society of Pennsylvania: name changed 1948 to The Pennsylvania Genealogical Magazine. Vol. 15 (nos. 2, 3) to Vol. 19 (no. 1). Spring 1947 through Sept. 1952.

T9   New York Historical Society Quarterly Bulletins. Vols. 31-36. 1947-1952.

V1   Tyler's Quarterly Historical and Genealogical Magazine. Vols. 29-32. 1947-1951. (Succeeded by Tyler's Quarterly, Vol. 1, 1952, not included herein, address 126 Third Ave., No., Nashville, Tenn.).

V3   The Virginia Magazine of History and Biography. Vols. 55-60. 1947-1952.

X1   Maryland Historical Magazine. Vols. 42-47. 1947-1952.

X2   Maryland Genealogical Bulletin. Vols. 18-21. 1947-

1950. (Discontinued.)
Yl   The Essex Institute Historical Collections. Vols.
      83-88. 1947-1952.
YA   Your Ancestors. Vols. 1 to 6 (No. 9). Nov. 1947
      to Sept. 1952. (Box 57, Station C, Buffalo, N.
      Y.)
Z3   Proceedings of the New Jersey Historical Society.
      Vols. 65-70. 1947-1952.
Z4   The Atlantic County Historical Society. Yearbooks,
      Vol. 1 (Nos. 1, 2, 3, 4); Vol. 2 (No. 1). 1948-
      1952.

                        RECENT INDEXES

      N. B. Note that some of the old indexes, such as
Munsell's (1900, Supplement 1908), and the catalogue of
genealogies in the Library of Congress (now far out of
date) still have their usefulness. Also, indexes of a
regional nature, such as Swem's Virginia Index. Attention is here called to three recent indexes:

AGI   The American Genealogical Index. 47 vols. 1942-
      1952. A full-name index covering many family
      histories and other genealogical source material.
      Very important when seeking a specific name (both
      given name and surname).
Yl   Essex Institute Historical Collections. Index,
      Vols. 68-85. 1931-1949.
Z   Daughters of the American Revolution Magazine.
      Genealogical Guide: Master Index of Genealogy in
      the D. A. R. Magazine, Vols. 1-84. 1892-1950.
      (This index is so comprehensive that we have not
      included this Magazine in our present index.)
      Address 1776 D Street, N. W., Washington 6, D. C.

ABBOTT, GEORGE; Andover; English
data; A1 (106-233).
ACHINGBACK, ACHENBACH; Pa.;
M (35-43).
ACYE, WILLIAM; Rowley, Mass.;
English ancestry; B4 (24-15).
ADAMS, HENRY; (John3), Worcester;
Dt (14-63); (Erastus6), Lever-
ett, Mass.; Dt (15-102).
ADAMS, JEREMY; Great Egg Harbor
branch; A2 (80-245); Z4 (1-91,
136; 2-176).
ADAMS, RICHARD; cont.; B4 (24-
193).
ADAMS; ancestry of William H.
and Alva, governors of Colora-
do; Col (8-9; 13-43).
ADAMS; (Elkanah), Pittsylvania
Co., Va.; N3 (47-262).
ADGATE; Norwich, Conn.; Philadel-
phia; B4 (25-171).
ALBADA [ANDRIES JOCHEMSEN1; New
York; B1 (21-1).
ALDEN, JOHN; Duxbury; A1 (102-
82).
ALEXANDER, JOHN; Chester Co.,
Pa.; YA (3-367, 441, 465, 487).
ALEXANDER; Cecil Co., Md.; N. C.;
P (16-85).
ALEXANDER; (Robert), Fishkill,
Lansing, N. Y.; YA (2-17, 37,
69, 117, 147).
ALLEN, HOPE; Boston, Mass.; A1
(102-177, 263).
ALLEN; Bible record (Henry W.),
Scipio, N. Y.; A2 (83-91).
ALLEN; Bible record (Jonathan);
Dt (15-111).
ALLING, ROGER; New Haven; Eng-
lish ancestry; B4 (27-7).
ALLISON; Bible records (William);
A2 (79-20).
ALSTON, JOHN; Woodbridge, N. J.;
B1 (23-49).
AMELUNG, JOHANN FRIEDRICH; Bal-
timore; X1 (43-155).
AMES [EMES], THOMAS; (Ezra5),
Framingham; T9 (35-231; 36-66).
AMMONS; ancestry of Elias-Milton
and Teller, governors of Colo-
rado; Col (13-75).
AMUNDEVILLE; English baronial

family; A1 (103-282).
ANDERSON, JOHN (COL.); Freehold, N.
J.; B1 (23-5); Scotch ancestry; B1
(24-3); see Andris.
ANDERSON; (will of George, 1791),
Somerset Co., N. J.; B1 (25-72).
ANDREWS, SAMUEL; Biddeford, Me.;
(James), Marblehead; (William),
Marblehead, Salem; A1 (104-176;
105-153).
ANDREWS, SAMUEL; Mansfield, N. J.;
B1 (24-51, 73; 25-10, 35, 55).
ANDREWS, WILLIAM; New Haven, Conn.;
B4 (24-53).
ANDRIS [ANDERSON, ANDRUS], JOACHIM;
Elizabethtown, N. J.; other fami-
lies; B1 (21-1, 40, 72; 22-7, 37,
51, 79; 23-5, 29, 54, 81; 24-9,
31).
ANDRUS, JOHN; (Joshua), Newington;
B4 (28-214).
APPLETON, SAMUEL; wife's maternal
ancestry; B4 (27-208); see Wheat-
hill.
APPLETON; Bible records (Isaac), New
Ipswich; A1 (106-153).
ARGALL, SAMUEL (SIR); Va.; V3 (59-
162).
ARNER, JOHANN ULRICH; Whitehall, Pa.;
Swiss ancestry; M (38-101).
ARNOLD; Family record (Ebenezer);
Dt (13-17).
ASHBY, WILLIAM; Newburyport, Mass.;
Y1 (84-15).
ASPINWALL, PETER; Muddy River; Eng-
lish data; A1 (105-94).
ATCHISON, JOHN; Lancaster Co., Pa.;
M (36-35).
ATKINS; (Dudley); Newburyport, Mass.;
Y1 (85-151).
ATKINSON, CORNELIUS; Northumberland
Co., Pa.; Dt (13-123).
AUDLEY [ODLIN], JOHN; Boston; B4
(26-228).
AUDLIN, EDWARD-BRIGHTMAN; Mich.;
Bible record; Dt (12-128).
AYLSWORTH, see Elsworth.
AYRES; (Simeon); A2 (82-117).

BACON, MICHAEL; Woburn; B4 (27-97).
BACON; Bible record (Abner), Putney,
Vt.; A1 (101-257, 327; 102-73).

BLANCHARD; Bible records (David),
N. Y.; A2 (82-173).
BLOOMFIELD, THOMAS; Woodbridge,
N. J.; Dt (13-82).
BLOWERS; Rev. Pension (Robert),
Pequannock, N. J.; B1 (25-16).
BODGE, HENRY; Kittery, Me.; A1
(101-97); wife of Henry[2],
Charlestown; A1 (102-74); cor-
rection; A1 (106-234).
BODINE; (will of John, 1702, Sta-
ten Island); A2 (80-216).
BOEKENOOGEN [BOEKENHOVE], JAN
WILLFMSZ; Germantown, Pa.;
Dutch ancestry; P (17-45).
BOGARDUS, ANNEKE JANS; New York;
B4 (24-65).
BOLLING; (Stith), Surry Co., Va.;
V3 (56-210).
BONNELL; Bible record (Abner), N.
J.; Z3 (66-44).
BOOKER; Bible record (James), N.
C.; A1 (104-167).
BOSWORTH, ZACHEUS; Boston, Mass.;
B4 (24-80).
BOTTS, THOMAS; Stafford Co., Va.;
(family of Benjamin-Gaines);
V1 (31-44).
BOUDINOT; (Elias), Philadelphia;
Z3 (67-253).
BOURNE; London; ancestral to Ap-
pleton; B4 (27-208).
BOWER, JONAS; Southampton, L. I.;
B4 (26-211).
BOWERMAN; Bible record (Samuel),
Saratoga Co., N. Y.; Dt (15-
130).
BOWERS; (George), Mass., Del.; A1
(106-41).
BOWES, GEORGE; Bible record; Wis.;
Col (10-57).
BOWLES, JAMES; St. Mary's Co.,
Md.; X1 (46-173).
BOWLING; (Robert), Fairfax Co.,
Va.; X2 (19-11).
BOYD, NATHANIEL; New Windsor, N.
Y.; YA (2-185).
BRACKETT; Sampler record (Will-
iam); B5 (34-70).
BRADFORD, WILLIAM; (Gershom[4]); A1
(101-296).
BRADFORD; Fauquier Co., Va.; Ky.;
N3 (48-291).
BRADT [BRATT], ALBERT ANDRIES;
Albany, N. Y.; B4 (24-231; 25-
168).
BRAINERD, DANIEL; (David[3] and

John[3]), N. J.; Z4 (1-65).
BRANDON; (Sir William), Norfolk, Eng-
land; A1 (103-102).
BRATT, NOAH; Baltimore; X2 (20-31).
BRAYTON, FRANCIS; Portsmouth, R. I.;
B4 (27-97).
BRENT; Bible records (William-Leigh),
Charles Co., Md.; X2 (21-52).
BREVARD, JOHN; Cecil Co., Md.; N. C.;
P (16-91).
BREVITT, JOSEPH (DR.); Md.; X1 (43-
81).
BREWTON, ROBERT; S. C.; addenda; J
(48-164).
BRIDGEMAN; (Isaac), Coventry; B4
(28-65).
BROKAW; Bible record (George R.),
Monroe Co., N. Y.; B1 (24-82).
BRONSON, RICHARD; Farmington, Conn.;
YA (2-213, 269).
BROUGH, EDWARD; Marshfield; B4 (27-
1).
BROUGHTON; (John), Wells, Vt.; Ng
(7-368).
BROUWER, ADAM; Brooklyn, N. Y.;
cont.; B4 (24-23, 96, 161; 26-56).
BROWNE, CHAD; correction to genealo-
gy; A1 (105-234); B4 (28-210).
BROWN, HENRY; R. I.; B4 (25-249).
BROWN, JOHN (REV.); Va., Ky.; with
Irish origin; K2 (26-3).
BROWNE, NICHOLAS; Reading, Mass.;
English data; A1 (103-234).
BROWN, RICHARD; (Tristram[3]), Norwich;
B4 (28-245).
BROWN; (Ephraim), Coventry; B4 (28-
245).
BROWN; (Stephen); Col (9-103).
BROWN; Bible records (Anson), Mass.;
M (40-31).
BROWN; Bible record (David-Ogden),
Kalamazoo, Mich.; Dt (11-11).
BROWN; Bible records (William), Va.,
Ill.; Col (11-99).
BROWN; Rev. Pension (Ezra), Morris,
N. J.; B1 (24-16).
BROWNSON; Manchester, Vt.; A1 (105-
73).
BRUEN, OBADIAH and MARY; English and
royal ancestry; B4 (26-12).
BRUYN, DE, FRANÇOIS; New Utrecht, N.
Y.; B4 (25-209).
BRYAN, JOHN and BERNARD; Fairfax Co.,
Va.; X2 (19-11; 21-5).
BRYAN; marriages, Va.; M (38-46).
BRYAN; Family record (Thomas), Md.;
X2 (19-53, 72; 20-59).

BRYANT; Bible records (Allen);
  M (35-32).
BUCHANAN, SAMUEL; Washington Co.,
  Va.; V3 (55-291).
BUCHTEL; ancestry of Henry-Augus-
  tus, governor of Colorado; Col
  (13-97).
BUCK, ENOCH; Wethersfield;(John2),
  Cape May, N. J.; B5 (34-60).
BUCK, HENRY; Wethersfield;
  (Henry2), Cohansey, N. J.; B5
  (34-55).
BUCK, ISAAC (LT.); Scituate,
  Mass.; B4 (24-104).
BULKELEY, PETER; Bible record
  (Sturgis); A2 (79-121).
BULLARD; (Jonathan3, Watertown);
  B4 (25-161).
BULLITT; (Cuthbert and Thomas),
  Va., Ky.; K2 (24-137).
BUNCE; Bible record (Sylvanus),
  Hunter, N. Y.; A2 (82-173).
BUNDY, JOHN; Taunton; B4 (27-1).
BURCHAM; (David), Hardin Co.,
  Ky.; N3 (47-163).
BURCHAN, ROBERT; Philadelphia;
  P (19-28).
BURKHART; Bible record (Henry);
  A2 (79-20).
BURRELL; Bible record (Dexter);
  Dt (14-75).
BURT; (Matthew), Edgefield, S. C.;
  M (38-104).
BURTON, ROBERT and WILLIAM; Ac-
  comack Co., Va.; Sussex Co.,
  Del.; P (18-143).
BURWELL, LEWIS; York Co., Va.;
  V3 (55-171).
BUSHNELL; (Joseph), Norwich; B4
  (27-99).
BUTLER, JAMES; Boston, Mass.;
  cont.; B4 (24-258).

CALDWELL, JAMES; Londonderry; A1
  (104-198).
CALEY; Bible record (Matthias);
  Dt (13-128).
CALKINS; (Israel), Conn., N. H.;
  B4 (26-55).
CALVERT; (George), Md.; X1 (45-
  271).
CAMERON; Rev. Pension (Alexander),
  Hanover, N. J.; B1 (24-13).
CAMPBELL, ROBERT; Voluntown,
  Conn.; Lebanon, N. Y., branch;
  YA (2-145, 181, 211, 241, 267),
CANFIELD; Rev. Pension (Dennis),

N. Y., Vt.; M (35-29).
CARLETON, EDWARD; Rowley; English
  note; A1 (106-89); (Samuel4),
  Salem; Y1 (96-144).
CARMAN, JOHN; (Richard4), Woodbridge,
  N. J.; A2 (81-101).
CARPENTER; Spotsylvania Co., Va.;
  Shelby Co., Ky.; N3 (49-256, 258).
CARR, ROBERT and CALEB; Newport, R.
  I.; A1 (102-203).
CARRICO, ABEL and Peter; Charles
  Co., Md.; K2 (25-217).
CARRINGTON; Bible record (Thomas),
  Md., Ky.; X2 (18-69).
CARRUTH, ADAM, ALEXANDER, WALTER;
  Hanover, Pa.; Irish origin; A1
  (106-111).
CARY; Cooperstown, N. Y.; YA (3-421).
CASE; (John, Glastonbury); B4 (25-
  205).
CASSEL; Bible records (Arnold); B5
  (34-25).
CASSON; Bible records (Robert); YA
  (3-346).
CATON, RICHARD; Baltimore Co., Md.;
  X1 (43-280).
CHANDLER, ROGER; Duxbury; B4 (27-1).
CHAPMAN, ROBERT; Stephen-Brewster8,
  Kans.; Col (10-63).
CHAPMAN; (Jonathan), New London,
  Conn.; Newfield, N. Y.; Dt (11-21).
CHAPMAN; Bible record (James Y.); Dt
  (11-171).
CHATTERTON; Bible records (Abraham);
  A2 (83-5).
CHENEY, RICHARD; Anne Arundel Co.,
  Md.; V1 (30-43).
CHENNELL, see Quennell.
CHRISTAL; (Richard), Wayne Co., Ky.;
  Dt (15-123).
CHRISTIAN, GILBERT; Va., Ky.; N3
  (47-304).
CHURCH, RICHARD; Plymouth; (Joseph4);
  Dt (12-7).
CHURCH; (Seth-Green), Norwich, Conn.;
  Dt (11-22).
CHURCHILL, EDWARD; Fishkill; B4 (27-
  102).
CHURCHILL, WILLIAM; New York; B4
  (27-102).
CHURCHILL; Bible record (William H.);
  A2 (82-49).
CLAIBORNE, WILLIAM; Va.; English
  origin; V3 (56-328, 431).
CLAIBORNE; (Thomas), King William
  Co., Va.; V3 (58-237).
CLAPP, JOHN (CAPT.); Flushing; B4

COURTNEY; (Michael), Va.; X2 (19-4).
COVENHOVEN, WOLFERT GERRITS; (Peter3), Atlantic Co., N. J.; Z4 (1-50); Rev. Pension (Albert); M (35-93); addenda; A2 (80-53, 245; 81-123, 172, 225; 82-34, 89, 175, 211; 83-86, 147, 237). Bible record (James); A2 (81-92).
COWGILL; Rev. Pension (Daniel), Va., Ohio; M (35-93).
COWHERD; Rev. Pension (James), Va., Ky.; M (35-93); (Jonathan), Va.; M (35-93).
COX, ISRAEL, GABRIEL and FRIEND; Md., Va., Ky.; K2 (22-75).
CRABTREE; Rev. Pension (William), N. C.; M (35-94).
CRAIK, JAMES, (DR.); Alexandria, Va.; V3 (55-318).
CRAMPTON, DENNIS; Guilford, Conn.; YA (2-61, 89, 113, 139).
CRANDALL; Rev. Pension (George), N. Y.; M (35-94); (Simeon), R. I., Conn.; M (35-94).
CRANE; Rev. Pension (Jonathan), Morris, N. J.; B1 (24-87).
CRANSTON, JOHN; R. I.; B4 (25-249).
CRAVEN, THOMAS; Ringoes, N. J.; B1 (21-57).
CRAVEN;(Tunis), Washington, D. C.; P (16-57).
CRAW, ROBERT; Newport; B4 (27-216).
CREED, RALPH; Surry Co., Va.; English origin; V3 (56-73).
CRITTENDEN, ABRAHAM; (Timothy5, Vt., Mich.); Dt (12-87, 115).
CROFOOT, CROFUT; Rev. Pension (Ephraim), M (35-95); (Seth), Conn.; M (35-95).
CROM, GYSBERT; Marbletown; A2 (81-197);(Floris); Haverstraw; A2 (82-118).
CROSSTHWAYTE, CHARLES; Boston; B4 (26-215).
CROWDER; Rev. Pension (Sterling), Va., Ky.; M (35-96); (William), Va.; M (35-96).
CROWELL; Bible record (Zadock), Chatham, Mass.; A2 (82-80).
CROWNINSHIELD, (DR.), JOHN CASPAR; letters, Salem, Mass.; Y1 (83-112); family; A1 (102-189; 103-152; 104-285; 105-234); German

origin; B4 (25-220).
CROY, MATTHIAS; Belmont Co., Ohio; Col (9-15).
CUERTON, RICHARD; Merion, Pa.; B4 (27-223).
CURRAN; Family record (Edward), Utica, N. Y.; Dt (10-125).
CURTIS, JOHN; Del.; A1 (106-42).
CURTIS, RICHARD; (Edmund6); Macomb Co., Mich.; Dt (12-95; 14-58).
CURTIS, SAMUEL; Salem Co., N. J.; with English origin; P (19-54).
CUSHMAN, ROBERT; (Isaac3), wife; B4 (26-144); (Allerton), Plympton; B4 (24-104).
CUSTIS; (Daniel-Parke), Md.; V3 (57-164).
CUVILJE, ARIAENTJE; New York; M (35-65).

DAINS; Corrections, children of Ebenezer2; Dt (14-88).
DALE; John and James, Somerset Co., Md.; P (16-96).
DAMEN, JAN JANSZEN; New York; M (35-65).
DANIELL, ROBERT; Watertown, Cambridge; Dt (15-127).
DART; Conn.; addenda; A2 (82-115).
DAVANT; Bible records (James); M (37-59).
DAVIE, HUMPHREY; addenda; B4 (25-63).
DAVIES, SAMUEL; Boston; Dt (14-45).
DAVIS; (Robert), DeKalb Co., Ga.; J (53-52).
DAVIS; (Thomas), Coventry; B4 (28-246).
DAVIS; Bible record (Elias), N. Y.; Dt (15-56).
DAVIS; Rev. Pension (Thomas), Chester, N. J.; B1 (24-71).
DAWSON; Rev. Pension (William), Pa., Ky.; M (35-29).
DAY; Rev. Pension (Moses), Chatham, N. J.; B1 (23-28).
DAYTON, RALPH; South Jersey, addendum; B4 (26-128).
DAYTON; Bible record (Isaac N.); Dt (15-24).
DEADMAN, HENRY; Lancaster Co., Va.; V3 (56-208).
DEAN; (Dr. Ezra), Biddeford, Me.; B4 (24-193).
DEAN; Bible record (Henry H.); A2 (78-81).
DEAN; Rev. Pension (John), Va.; M

(35-29).
DEANE; Rev. Pension (John), Va.,
Ala.; M (35-30).
DEARBORN, GODFREY; Hampton, N. H.;
Dt (11-6, 45).
DE GROOT; Rev. Pension (William),
N. J.; M (35-30).
DE L'STAGE, PIERRE; Laprairie; Dt
(14-93).
DENN, JOHN; Salem Co., N. J.; Col
(9-20).
DENNIS; (Schooley), Sussex Co., N.
J.; Dt (12-39).
DENSLOW, HENRY; Windsor, Conn.;
A2 (78-2, 74, 117, 173; 79-22,
84, 156, 209; 80-33, 105, 142,
230; 81-31, 106, 156, 207).
DESHLER; Bible record (George-
Wagener), New Brunswick, N. J.;
B1 (24-86).
DEVOS, WALRAVEN JANSEN; Delaware;
A2 (82-70).
DEWALL; Rev. Pension (Thomas),
Morris, N. J.; B1 (25-16).
DEWEY; (Rollin C.), Mass., Ind.;
Col (12-87).
DIBBLE, THOMAS, JOHN, ABRAHAM;
Conn.; YA (2-143, 179, 209, 239,
265; 3-291, 312, 361, 369, 391,
413, 439, 463, 485; 4-509, 533,
555, 575, 597, 623, 630; 5-649,
673, 701, 729, 755, 783; 6-809,
835, 863).
DICKERMAN, THOMAS; Dorchester;
B4 (26-165).
DICKERSON, PHILEMON; (Mahlon),
Morris Co., N. J.; Z3 (68-
297).
DICKINSON; Bible records (Oris-
Buckner), Ky., Ind.; M (35-32).
DICKINSON; Bible record (Thomas-
Passmore), Jonesville, Va.;
Mich.; Dt (15-145).
DICKINSON; Rev. Pension (John),
Del., Ind.; M (35-30).
DIGGES; (Joseph), North End, Ma-
thews, Va.; Vl (32-306).
DIMOCK; (Henry), Limington, Me.;
B4 (24-194).
DITLOF, CLAES; New York; B4 (25-
162).
DIXON, JOHN; Hanover Co., Va.;
English origin; V3 (56-76).
DOANE; Bible record (David), Vt.;
Dt (14-17).
DOBELL; Bible record (Joseph);
Col (9-35).

DODGE, TRISTRAM; New Shoreham; B4
(26-228).
DODSON; 1790 Census; Md.; X2 (18-
45).
DOLBEARE, EDMUND; Boston; English
data; A1 (104-318).
DOLLES, WILLIAM; Cohansey, N. J.;
B5 (33-174, 182).
DONALSON; Rev. Pension (James),
Chatham, N. J.; B1 (23-28).
DONALDSON; Rev. Pension (William);
M (35-53).
DOOLITTLE; Bible records (Benjamin);
Col (13-39).
DORRANCE, JOHN; Chamberburgh, Pa.;
X2 (20-3, 19; 21-63).
DOTY; Rev. Pension (Samuel), Pa.; M
(35-30).
DOUD; Rev. Pension (Samuel-Miles),
Vt., Ohio; M (35-53).
DOUGLAS, WILLIAM; (John[4]), Saybrook;
B4 (27-212).
DOUGLASS; (William), Fauquier Co.,
Va.; V3 (57-328).
DOUGLASS; Bible record (Caleb), New
London, Conn.; Dt (13-25).
DOUVRES, DE [or Chilham]; baronial
house; A1 (105-36).
DOW; (John-Blasdel), Bethany, N. Y.;
Dt (15-87).
DOYLE; Rev. Pension (Henry), Pequan-
nock, N. J.; B1(25-19).
DRAKE, JOHN; Windsor; English clue;
B4 (26-156).
DRAKE; Rev. Pension (Nicholas), Jef-
ferson, N. J.; B1 (24-72).
DU BOIS, GUALTHERUS (REV.); New York;
Dutch ancestry; A2 (82-134).
DUCKWALL; Clermont Co., Ohio; O1 (10-
254).
DULEY; Bible record (James), Algoma,
Mich.; Dt (13-106).
DUNCAN, GEORGE; Londonderry; Y1 (86-
247; 87-242; 88-1).
DUNHAM; Bible records (Jacob), New
Brunswick, N. J.; B1 (25-71).
DUNN; Bible record (John); Ng (7-
373).
DUNNING, ANDREW; Brunswick, Me.; Col
(10-75, 103; 11-51, 55, 115).
DUNNING, JOHN; Chenango Co., N. Y.;
Col (11-91).
DUNNING, THEOPHILUS; genealogy;
cont.; Col (8-17, 53, 77, 111; 9-
22, 23, 45, 73, 115; 10-37, 111;
13-6).
DUNSHEE, JOHN; Bible record; A2 (80-

EVANS; Rev. Pension (Andrew), N.
C., Tenn., Ky., Ind.; M (36-
32); (David), Smithfield, R.
I.; Plymouth, N. Y.; M (36-32).
EVERETT, Philip; Eastern Shore,
Md.; Dt (13-33; 15-33).
EVERETT; Rev. Pension (William),
Va., Tenn.; M (36-33).
EVERITT; Rev. Pension (John), N.
C., Ga.; M (36-33).
EWELL, HENRY; Scituate, Mass.;
Dt (12-65; 14-58).
FAGAN, NICHOLAS; Philadelphia;
P (18-73).
FAIRBAIRN; Bible and other rec-
ords (John), Baltimore; X2
(21-19, 41, 47).
FAIRCHILD; Bible records (James
H.), Shaudaken, N. Y.; Col (11-
41).
FAIRCHILD; Rev. Pension (Nathan-
iel), N. J., N. Y.; M (35-57).
FARNHAM, RALPH; Andover, Mass.;
YA (3-477; 4-501, 525, 547,
567, 589, 615; 5-641, 665, 693,
721, 747, 775; 6-801, 827, 855).
FARNSWORTH; Bible record (Thomas),
Alden, N. Y.; Ng (7-339).
FAUT [FAUN]; Rev. Pension
(George), Va., Tenn.; M (35-
57).
FAUVER; Rev. Pension (George), N.
J., Ohio; M (35-57).
FEAKE, JUDITH and TOBIAS; Yar-
mouth; English data; B4 (27-
69).
FEGINS; Rev. Pension (James),
Va., Ohio; M (35-58).
FELLOWS; Rev. Pension (John),
Mass., N. Y.; M (35-58).
FENN, BENJAMIN; Milford, Conn.;
B4 (24-129).
FENNER, ARTHUR and WILLIAM; R.
I.; B4 (25-250; 26-229).
FERRIS, JEFFREY; (John3), Green-
wich; B4 (26-126); (James2,
James3); B4 (26-230); (Benja-
min3), Stamford; B4 (28-96).
FIELD, ABRAHAM; Westmoreland Co.,
Va.; M (35-31).
FIFIELD, WILLIAM; (John, King-
ston, N. H.); B4 (25-27).
FILSON, JOHN; Chester Co., Pa.;
K2 (26-251).
FINDLAY, SAMUEL; Philadelphia;
P (16-3).
FINDLEY; Rev. Pension (Joseph-

Lewis), Pa., Ohio; M (35-58).
FINLEY, ROBERT and JAMES; Chester
Co., Pa.; YA (1-7, 19; 2-9, 27,
47, 79, 101, 129, 169, 199, 233,
259, 335).
FINLEY; Rev. Pension (William),
Mendham, N. J.; B1 (25-16).
FLEMING; Bible record (Thomas R.);
Dt (11-127).
FLENNER; Bible records (Abraham);
M (36-114).
FLINT; (Asher), Conn., N. Y.; A2
(83-247).
FLOOD; Rev. Pension (William), Va.,
Ohio; M (35-58).
FLOURNOY; Rev. Pension (James), Va.;
M (35-58).
FOBES, JOHN; Duxbury, Mass.; B4
(24-7).
FOLTS; Family record (John), Pa.,
Md.; X2 (20-12).
FOOS [FUSS], NICHOLAS; Berks Co.,
Pa.; P (18-87).
FORCE; Rev. Pension (Joseph), Han-
over, N. J.; B1 (24-89).
FORD; (Joseph), Ipswich, Windham;
Dt (15-116).
FORD; Bible record (Isaac); Dt (14-
126).
FOSTER; Rev. Pension (James), Md.,
Va.; M (35-59).
FOWLER, HENRY; (David4), N. Y.,
Pa.; A2 (83-101); (Reuben4),
Cortlandt, N. Y.; A2 (83-106).
FOWLER; (Jonathan), Coventry; B4
(28-66).
FOWLER; Rev. Pension (Caleb), Conn.,
Ohio; M (35-59).
FOX; (Boaz), Clark Co., Ky.; N3
(45-159).
FRANKLIN; early settlers, Md.; X2
(18-46).
FRAZEE, JOSEPH; Elizabeth, N. J.;
B4 (24-37, 128).
FREEMAN; (Robert), Culpeper Co.,
Va.; V3 (56-211).
FRENCH, GEORGE; Prince George Co.,
Md.; B4 (17-23).
FRENCH, STEPHEN; Dorchester; (Sam-
uel3, Weymouth); B4 (25-23).
FRENCH; Bible record (James), S.
C., Tenn., Ala.; M (36-36).
FRENCH; Rev. War (William), Mass.,
Ohio; M (35-59).
FRENEAU, ANDREW; Bergen Co., N. J.;
Z3 (65-117).
FRIEND; (Christian), Philadelphia,

GIBBS; Family record (William);
Dt (13-102).
GIBBS; Rev. Pension (Spencer), N.
Y.; M (39-30).
GIBSON; Rev. Pension (John), N.
C., Tenn.; M (37-28).
GIDDINGS; Rev. Pension (John),
Mass., Vt.; M (38-95); (Joseph),
Conn.; M (38-95).
GIFFARD; baronial family; Al
(105-292; 106-76).
GIFFORD; Rev. Pension (Gideon),
R. I., N. Y.; M (38-96).
GILBERT, JOHN; Taunton; English
ancestry; B4 (27-9).
GILBERT, THOMAS; Wethersfield; Dt
(14-79).
GILBERT; Rev. Pension (Allen),
Conn., N. Y.; M (38-96); (John),
Conn., N. H.; M (38-96); (John),
Conn.; M (38-96); (Theodore),
Mass., N. Y.; M (38-96); (Asa),
Conn.; M (39-30).
GILDERSLEEVE, RICHARD; (George-
Whitfield), Ohio, Col.; Col
(12-63).
GILES; Rev. Pension (Aquila), Md.,
N. Y.; M (37-28); (Samuel),
Mass., N. Y.; M (37-28).
GILLESPIE; Summerhill, Pa.; Dt
(13-28).
GILLETT, JEREMIAH (SERGT.); Sims-
bury; (Milford, Wethersfield,
Newtown, Southington); B4 (25-
174, 200; 26-52, 169; 27-99).
GILLETT, JONATHAN and NATHAN;
Windsor, Conn.; cont.; Al (101-
43, 153, 237, 283; 102-236).
GILLET; Rev. Pension (Benoni); M
(39-30).
GILLIAM; (John), Hanover Co.,
Va.; V3 (58-123).
GILLUM; Rev. Pension (Jonathan),
Pa., Va.; M (35-60).
GILMAN; Bible record (Charles),
N. J.; B1 (21-12, 25).
GILMORE; Bible records (William),
Pelham, Mass.; Al (106-315).
GILPATRICK; Rev. Pension (Nathan-
iel), Me.; M (39-67).
GIST; Rev. Pension (Thomas), N.
C., Tenn.; M (38-97).
GIST; correction of X2 (16-4);
X2 (21-66).
GIVENS; Rev. Pension (James), N.
C., Tenn.; M (39-99); (Samuel),
N. C.; M (39-67).

GLADSON; Rev. Pension (William),
Hanover, N. J.; B1 (24-89).
GLANN; (Lazarus, Gabriel); Cumber-
land Co., N. J.; B5 (32-116).
GLANVILLE; English mediaeval fami-
ly; Al (102-292; 103-155).
GLASSCOCK; Rev. Pension (Robert),
Va.; M (39-99).
GOODSPEED; English data, addendum;
Al (105-153).
GOODWIN; Rev. Pension (Benjamin),
Mass., Me.; M (37-61); (Thomas),
Va.; M (37-61, 81).
GORDON; Rev. War (Archibald), Md.,
Pa.; M (36-34).
GORHAM, JOHN; wife of Joseph[3],
Stratford; B4 (26-83, 184); (Na-
than[4]), Canterbury; B4 (28-153).
GORIN; Rev. Pension (John), Va.,
Ky.; M (37-62).
GOSNELL; Rev. Pension (Benjamin),
Va., Ind.; M (37-62).
GOSNOLD, ANTHONY and BARTHOLOMEW;
Jamestown; V3 (57-307); English
data; Al (104-27; 105-5).
GOSS, PHILIP; Roxbury, Lancaster;
Dt (13-93).
GOSSETT, PETER; Cumberland Co.,
Pa.; N3 (49-139).
GOTT, CHARLES; (Daniel[2]), Wenham,
Mass.; B4 (24-57).
GOUGH; (Harry-Dorsey), Anne Arun-
del Co., Md.; X1 (45-33).
GOULD, JOHN; Elizabethtown, N. J.;
Dt (13-133).
GOULD; (Nehemiah), Groton, Mass.;
B5 (36-153).
GRAFF; (John), Philadelphia; P (19-
24).
GRAHAM; Rev. Pension (George), N.
J., Pa.; M (37-62).
GRAMPS; Rev. Pension (John P.), N.
Y.; M (40-32).
GRANSDEN; Tunbridge, Kent; B4 (26-
61).
GRANT, DAVID; Somerset Co., N. J.;
Z3 (65-35).
GRANT, MATTHEW; Windsor; wife; Al
(102-153).
GRAY, JOHN; (Jonathan[3]), Pelham,
Ashfield, Mass.; Al (101-173).
GRAY, JOHN; Worcester, Mass.; Dt
(16-1, 37).
GRAY; Rev. Pension (John), Va.,
Ohio; M (35-60).
GRAY; Rev. Pension (John), N. H.;
M (35-61).

GREEN, BARTHOLOMEW; Cambridge; (Samuel2, family of printers); A1 (104-81).

GREENE, JOHN; Warwick, R. I.; English ancestry; A1 (103-185).

GREEN, THOMAS; (Rev. Jacob), Hanover, N. J.; Z3 (69-115).

GREEN; (William), Groton; Dt (15-18).

GREEN, GREENE; Rev. Pension (Fortunatus), Va.; M (37-62); (Joseph), Va.; M (37-63); (James), R. I., Pa.; M (37-63); (Lewis), Va., Ky.; M (37-63); (James), R. I., N. Y.; M (37-87); (Robert), Md., Mo.; M (35-61).

GREER, ROBERT; York Co., Pa.; Wilkes Co., Ga.; P (15-170).

GREGG; origin and early colonists; P (16-31).

GREGORY; Rev. Pension (Stephen), Conn., Pa.; M (37-63); (Thomas), N. C.; M (37-87).

GRIFFIN; Bible record (Robert-Burns), Md., Mass.; X2 (18-39, 54; 19-9).

GRIFFIN; Rev. Pension (Joseph), S. C.; M (37-87).

GRIFFIS; Rev. Pension (Southard), R. I.; M (37-87).

GRIFFITH; eastern Penn.; P (18-114).

GRIFFITH; Rev. Pension (Nathan), Mass., Vt.; M (37-88).

GRINER; Rev. Pension (John M.), Ga.; M (40-111).

GRISCOM, ANDREW; Philadelphia; Co1 (9-20).

GRUBER, JOHN ADAM; German ancestry; (John2), Md.; X1 (47-89).

GRUMMAN, JOHN; Fairfield; maternal ancestry; B4 (27-37).

GUARD; Rev. soldier (Daniel), Roxbury, N. J.; Dt (10-130).

GUILFORD, JOHN; Hingham, Mass.; Dt (11-69, 123).

GUTHRIE, EDWARD; King & Queen Co., Va.; V3 (57-88).

GUYER; Rev. Pension (John), Pa.; M (37-61).

GWATHMEY; (Owen), Va., Ky; K2 (25-125, 317).

HACKETT, JABEZ; (Samuel3), Raynham, Wareham, Mass.; B4 (24-191).

HAGAMAN; Bible records (Henry), New Hackensack, N. Y.; A2 (83-5).

HAGER; Rev. Pension (Joseph), N. Y.; M (37-88); (Henry), N. Y.; M (39-99).

HAGERMAN; Rev. Pension (Barnet), Pa., Ohio; M (38-97).

HAIR; Rev. Pension (John), Mass.; M (38-97).

HALES, JOHN; Georges Creek, Del.; B4 (27-229).

HALL, DAVID; Philadelphia; P (19-21).

HALL, JACOB; Tacony, Pa.; (Levi4); B5 (36-161).

HALL, WILLIAM; Salem Co., N. J.; P (19-56).

HALL; Rev. Pension (John), Va.; M (37-88); (William), Pa., Md.; M (37-89); (Benajah), N. Y.; M (38-97); (Nathaniel), Conn.; M (39-99); (William), N. C., Mo.; M (39-100).

HALLAM, ROBERT; Henrico Co., Va.; English data; V3 (56-325).

HALLENBECK; Bible record (William); A2 (80-239).

HALLET; (Andrew2); B4 (26-193).

HALSEY, THOMAS; Southampton; English data; B4 (26-216).

HAMBLIN; Rev. Pension (Levi), Conn., Ohio; M (35-61).

HAMILTON; Rev. Pension (James), N. C.; M (37-89); (John), Md.; M (37-89); (John-Agnew), Md.; M (37-90); (William), Hanover, N. J.; B1 (24-90).

HAMLIN; Rev. Pension (John), Huntington, N. J.; Ohio; M (36-34); (Levi), Conn., Me.; M (37-90).

HAMMER; Rev. Pension (George), Md., Ind.; M (39-130).

HAMMON, AMBROSE; Rappahannock Co., Va.; (John5, Va., Ky.); K2 (23-202); Goochland Co., Va.; N3 (50-35).

HAMMOND, WILLIAM; Watertown; English data; A1 (106-83, 315).

HAND, JOHN; East Hampton, L. I.; wife's English origin; B4 (26-61, 151).

HANDS, BENJAMIN; Middletown; B4 (25-204).

HANDY; Rev. Pension (Levin), Md.; M (39-130).

HANNAH; (Hugh), Bethlehem, Conn.; B4 (27-253).

HANNEY; Rev. Pension (John), Pa.;
M (36-34).
HANSFORD; Rev. Pension (William),
Va., Ky.; M (38-98).
HARDY; Bible records (William-
White); Dt (11-8).
HARLESS; Rev. Pension (Phillip),
Va.; M (38-128).
HARLOW, WILLIAM; B4 (26-144);
(Nathaniel2), Plympton, Mass.;
B4 (24-105; 25-152).
HARLOW; Rev. Pension (Ansel),
Mass.; M (38-128).
HARRIS, THOMAS; East Hampton, N.
Y.; (Cumberland Co., N. J.); A1
(105-56, 155).
HARRIS, THOMAS; East Hampton, N.
Y.; (Thomas2), Fairfield, N. J.;
P (17-79); (Nathaniel2), Hope-
well, N. J.; P (17-91); addenda;
P (18-81); noble ancestry; B5
(35-88); Cumberland Co., N. J.;
A1 (105-56, 155); Bible records
(Ephraim, Abijah, Samuel); B5
(35-88).
HARRIS, THOMAS; Middletown, Conn.,
and Washington Co., N. Y.,
branch; Dt (11-16, 39).
HARRIS; Boston families; A1 (105-
190, 242; 106-15).
HARRIS; (Rev. Samuel), Hanover
Co., Va.; V3 (57-328).
HARRIS; Bible record (Henry); Dt
(15-111); (Robert); N3 (46-
454).
HARRIS; Rev. Pension (Edward),
Va.; M (37-90); (Richmond), N.
C., Ky.; M (37-90); (Samuel),
Va., Ky.; M (36-67).
HARRISON, ANDREW; St. Mary's, Es-
sex Co., Va.; V3 (55-85).
HARRISON, RICHARD; Branford,
Conn.; English ancestry; B4
(25-263).
HARRISON; (will of Richard,
1716), Calvert Co., Md.; X3
(46-644).
HARRISON; Rev. Pension (Abijah),
N. J.; M (38-128); (Joseph),
Md., Tenn.; M (38-128); (Rich-
ard), Va.; M (37-90).
HART, THOMAS; Hanover Co., Va.;
Ky. branch; K2 (21-228, 327).
HART; (Thomas), Md., Ky.; K2 (24-
28).
HARTLEY; (George-Harland); Loyal-
ist, S. C.; J (51-45).

HARTMAN; Rev. Pension (Christopher),
N. J., Ohio; M (35-61).
HARTSHORNE, RICHARD; Middletown, N.
J.; Z3 (67-126).
HARTWELL; Rev. Pension (Oliver),
Conn., N. Y.; M (38-128).
HARWOOD; Rev. Pension (James), N. C.;
M (38-129).
HASKELL, ROGER; (John4), Dudley; B4
(28-68); John2, Middleboro; Wood-
stock; B4 (28-71); (Rev. Abel7);
Dt (13-51).
HASKELL; Rev. Pension (Prince),
Mass., Ohio; M (39-67).
HASKINS, WILLIAM; (Samuel2), Taun-
ton; B4 (28-252).
HATCH, PHILIP; York, Me.; YA (3-393,
415, 489; 4-511, 535, 557, 577,
599, 625; 5-651, 675, 703, 731,
757, 785; 6-811, 841).
HATCH, THOMAS; (Ebenezer4, Plymouth);
B4 (25-154).
HATHAWAY, NICHOLAS; (Rodman-Barney),
Col.; Col (13-62).
HATHAWAY; Rev. Pension (Theophilus),
Hanover, N. J.; B1 (24-13).
HAUCK; Rev. Pension (George-Michael),
Va.; M (35-62).
HAUGHT; Rev. Pension (Peter), Va.;
M (37-111).
HAVENS, WILLIAM; (William5), Sag
Harbor, N. Y.; A2 (78-32).
HAWKINS, WILLIAM; Boston; B4 (27-
21).
HAWKINS; Bible records (Ebenezer),
Conn., Vt.; Dt (12-106).
HAWLEY; Bible record (James), Strat-
ford; A2 (82-210).
HAWKINS; Rev. Pension (John), Va.;
M (38-98).
HAWTHORN; Rev. Pension (John), S. C.,
Ky.; M (37-111).
HAWTHORN; Rev. Pension (Robert), S.
C., Ill.; M (35-98).
HAY; Rev. Pension (David), N. J.; M
(35-62).
HAYDON; Rev. Pension (John), N. J.,
Pa.; M (37-111).
HAYES; Rev. Pension (Henry), Va.,
Ky.; M (37-111).
HAYFORD; (John), Farmington; A2 (83-
101).
HAYNES, WILLIAM; Salem; (Jonathan2);
Newbury; B4 (27-129, 187).
HAYNES; Bedford Co., Va.; N3 (49-
388).
HAYNES; Rev. Pension (Joseph), N.

C., Tenn.; M (37-112).
HAYNESWORTH; (Richard), Sumpter,
S. C.; V1 (30-206).
HAYS; (William), Hardin Co., Ky.;
N3 (47-163, 261).
HAYWARD; Rev. Pension (James),
Mass., N. Y.; M (39-130);(Seth),
Mass.; M (39-131); (Solomon),
Mass.; M (39-131).
HAZARD; Philadelphia; X1 (46-44).
HEADLEY; Rev. Pension (Carey), N.
J., Ohio; M (37-112).
HEAL; Rev. Pension (John), Me.; M
(38-129).
HECK; Rev. Pension (Youst), Pa.,
Va.; M (35-98).
HEERMANS; Bible record (Gerrit),
Kingston; A2 (83-40).
HEGEMAN, ADRIAEN; Denys2, Flat-
bush, N. Y.; B1 (25-49).
HEIFNER; Rev. Pension (Jacob);
Md., Ohio; M (36-67).
HENCHMAN, DANIEL; Boston, Mass.;
·A1 (102-266, 277).
HENDERSON; Family record (Joseph),
Va., Ohio, Ind.; Dt (13-46).
HENRY; (will of Rev. Patrick,
1777), Hanover Co., Va.; V3
(58-120).
HENRY; Rev. Pension (Robert),
Pa., Tenn.; M (38-98).
HERRINGTON; Rev. Pension (Daniel);
Pa., Md., Ill.; M (36-67).
HERRMAN, AUGUSTINE; New York; A2
(78-130).
HESTON; Bible and other records
(Zebulon); Mass., Pa.; Dt (13-
148).
HEULINGS; Bible record (Michael),
Philadelphia; Dt (14-116).
HEVERIN; Bible records (William),
Del.; P (17-110).
HEWITT; Rev. Pension (Daniel),
Conn., N. Y.; M (38-98).
HEYER; additions and corrections;
A2 (80-243).
HIBBS; (Mahlon-Nicholas), Ottum-
wa, Iowa; Col (9-91).
HICKOX; Rev. Pension (Giles),
Conn., N. Y.; M (38-99).
HICKS; Rev. Pension (Daniel), R.
I.; M (38-99).
HILL, ANTHONY; Scarsdale, N. Y.;
Dt (13-37).
HILL, CHARLES; New London, Conn.;
Dt (14-28).
HILL, HUMPHREY and THOMAS; Va.;

V3 (56-323).
HILL; (Calvin), Barry Co., Mich.; Dt
(13-88).
HILL; (Ebenezer), Windham; Goshen;
Dt (15-147).
HILL; Manchester, Vt.; A1 (105-73).
HILL; St. Joseph Co., Mich.; Dt (14-
113).
HILL; Bible record (George C.), Vt.;
A1 (101-331).
HILL; Rev. Pension (John); R. I.;
M (36-68); (William), N. Y.; M (36-
68); (Frederick), Pa., Md.; M (37-
112).
HILLS; Rev. Pension (Zimri), Conn.,
Ohio; M (38-99).
HILYARD; Bible records (Henry); B5
(31-71).
HINE, THOMAS; Milford; B4 (26-111;
27-40).
HINMAN, EDWARD; (Zechariah3), Dur-
ham; B4 (26-256).
HINMAN; Rev. Pension (Benjamin),
Conn., N. Y.; M (38-129).
HITER; (James), Jessamine Co., Ky.;
N3 (47-244).
HITT, ELIPHALET; Boston; B4 (27-95).
HOADLEY; Rev. Pension (Thomas),
Mass., Vt.; M (35-98).
HOAGLAND; Inscriptions, Somerset Co.,
N. J.; B1 (21-8).
HOAGLAND; Rev. Pension (Richard), N.
J.; M (38-130).
HOBART, EDMUND; Hingham; B4 (27-94).
HODGES; Rev. Pension (Isaac), Mass.;
M (38-100).
HOFFMAN; Rev. Pension (Cornelius);
Pa.; M (36-68).
HOGG, JAMES; N. C.; Ky.; K2 (21-5).
HOLCOMBE, THOMAS; Windsor; alleged
English ancestry; B4 (26-109);
corrections to genealogy; B4 (28-
32).
HOLLAND; Rev. Pension (Drury), Va.;
M (37-112); (Jacob), Md., Va.; M
(38-130).
HOLLISTER; Rev. Pension (David),
Conn., N. Y.; M (37-91); (Joseph),
Conn.; M (38-100).
HOLLYDAY; (Col. James), Queen Anne's
Co., Md.; X1 (45-95).
HOLMES; (John), Prince William Co.,
Va.; V1 (29-195).
HOLST, LAURENS LAURENSZ; New York; P
(17-54).
HOMAN; Rev. Pension (Eber), Pa., N.
J.; M (38-130).

HOOFMAN; Rev. Pension (Christian),
Pa., Va.; M (38-131).
HOOKE; Rev. Pension (George), Va.,
Ind.; M (38-33).
HOOMERY, JOHN; R. I.; B4 (25-
168).
HOOPES; Bucks Co., Pa.; addenda;
B4 (27-88).
HOPKINS, STEPHEN; Plymouth; A1
(102-46, 98, 197, 257; 103-24,
85, 166, 304; 104-52, 123, 213,
296; 105-32, 100, 306).
HOPKINS; Rev. Pension (Ebenezer),
Vt., Ohio; M (38-131); (George),
Conn., N. Y.; M (39-100); (Tim-
othy), R. I.; M (39-100).
HORN; Bible record (Daniel); Col
(9-79).
HORNER; John and Isaac; Burling-
ton Co., N. J.; English ances-
try; B1 (22-25, 55, 89).
HOSMER; Rev. Pension (John),
Mass.; M (39-101).
HOTTEL; Bible record (Jacob); Dt
(13-132).
HOUGH; Rev. Pension (William),
Va., Ohio; M (35-62); (John),
Va., Pa.; M (39-31).
HOUSE; Rev. Pension (Andrew),
Pa., Ohio; M (39-31).
HOW, HOWE; Rev. Pension (John),
Va., Ky.; M (39-31); (Daniel),
Mass., Vt.; M (39-130); (Dav-
id), Md.; M (35-63).
HOWARD; (Enos), Hillsdale, N.
Y.; cont.; Ng (7-345).
HOWELL, EDWARD; (Maj. Silas6), N.
J., Ohio; O1 (10-322).
HOWELL; Bible records (Charles),
Ky., Ill.; Col (11-99).
HOWELL; Bible record (George);
A2 (81-142); (Parshall), N. J.,
Mich.; Dt (15-26).
HOWLAND, ARTHUR; Marshfield; A1
(104-221).
HOWLAND, JOHN; Plymouth; B4 (24-
118).
HOXTON, WALTER; Anne Arundel
Co., Md.; English data; V3
(60-115).
HOYT; Family record (David); Dt
(12-71).
HUBBARD, GEORGE; (John3), Glas-
tonbury; B4 (27-48).
HUBBARD, JOHN; additions to B4
(23-221); B4 (24-36).
HUBBARD; Windsor; B4 (27-59).

HUBBELL, RICHARD; (Ithamar, Great
Barrington); B4 (25-254, 261).
HUDGES; Rev. Pension (Anthony), Va.;
M (39-102).
HUDSON; Rev. Pension (Elisha),
Mass.; M (39-101).
HUFF; Rev. Pension (John), Va.; M
(39-102).
HUFFAKER; (Andrew), Tenn., Mo.; Col
(9-99).
HUGHES; Rev. Pension (James), Md.,
Pa.; M (35-63); (Joseph), Md.,
Mo.; M (39-68).
HULL, JOSEPH; R. I.; B4 (28-211).
HUMPHREY, MICHAEL; Windsor; French
relatives; B4 (28-12).
HUMPHREY; co Essex, Eng.; B4 (26-
153, 217).
HUMPHREY; Bible record (William),
Hempstead; A2 (82-78).
HUNN, NATHANIEL; Boston; A1 (106-
41).
HUNT, ENOCH; (Benjamin4), Braintree,
Mass.; A1 (101-332); (John), Wa-
tertown, Mass.; Dt (13-3, 39, 65,
97, 129).
HUNT, RALPH; Newtown, L. I.; B4
(26-1).
HUNT, THOMAS; (Solomon4), Woodbridge,
N. J.; B4 (27-89).
HUNT; Rev. Pension (George), R. I.,
N. Y.; M (35-63); (Josiah), Chat-
ham, N. J., B1 (23-86).
HUNTER, JAMES; Fredericksburg, Va.;
V3 (56-3).
HUNTER; Rev. Pension (Nathaniel),
Conn.; M (39-102).
HUNTLEY, JOHN; Lyme, Conn.; cont.;
A1 (101-56, 141, 199; 102-235);
YA (2-13, 31, 51, 81, 103, 131,
171, 201, 235, 261; 3-287, 308,
329, 357, 385, 407, 433, 457, 481;
4-505, 529, 551, 571, 593, 619; 5-
645, 669, 697, 725, 751, 779; 6-
805, 831, 859).
HURD; (Daniel), Denver, Col.; Col
(9-78).
HURDLE; (John N., Noble); Md., X2
(20-47).
HURLBUT; Rev. Pension (Daniel),
Conn.; M (39-102).
HURST, HENRY; Northumberland Co.,
Va.; V1 (31-113, 200, 277; 32-59,
246).
HURST; (Lt. John), Putnam Co., Ind.;
Col (9-100).
HURST; Bible records (John), Md.,

KEATINGE, GEORGE and HENRY S.;
Baltimore; X2 (18-50).
KEECH; Bible record (George); Dt
(15-72).
KEECH; Rev. Pension (Jeremiah),
R. I.; M (36-70).
KEEN, see Kyn.
KELLY, JOHN; Southwark, Pa.; P
(16-53).
KELLY; Rev. Pension (Jared), Han-
over, N. J.; Bl (24-88).
KENDRICK, WALTER; Louisville,
Ky.; K2 (22-268).
KENDRICK; Bible records (John),
N. H., N. Y.; Col (8-14).
KENDRICK; Rev. Pension (John),
Ga.; M (39-103).
KENNEDY; (John), Rowan Co., N.
C.; Tenn.; N3 (45-129).
KENNERLY; Rev. Pension (Samuel);
Va.; M (36-101).
KENNEY; Rev. Pension (Thomas),
Me.; M (37-64).
KENNON, RICHARD; Henrico Co.,
Va.; English data; V3 (56-324).
KENRICK; Hillsdale, Mich.; Eng-
lish ancestry; B4 (24-220).
KENT; Rev. Pension (John); Conn.,
Mass.; M (36-70).
KENTON; Rev. Pension (Simon),
Va., Ohio; M (35-99).
KENYON, ROGER; R. I.; B4 (27-221).
KEPLER; (Peter), Crawford Co.,
Pa.; Dt (16-7, 41).
KERBY; Rev. Pension (Jesse); Va.,
Ky.; M (36-101).
KERNINE; Rev. Pension (Eder),
Jefferson, N. J.; Bl (24-72).
KESTER; Rev. Pension (Peter), Pa.;
M (38-36).
KETCHAM; Bible record (William);
Ng (7-367).
KEY; Rev. Pension (Tandy); Va.; M
(36-101).
KIBBE; Rev. Pension (Frederick);
Conn.; M (36-101).
KIBBES; Rev. Pension (Israel),
Conn., Vt.; M (36-102).
KIDD; Rev. Pension (James), Va.,
Ga.; M (36-102).
KILBY, JOHN; Boston; B4 (27-193;
28-34).
KILGORE; Rev. Pension (Charles),
Va.; M (35-122; 36-71).
KIMBERLY, THOMAS; New Haven,
Stratford; English origin and
descendants; Al (102-102, 315);

B4 (28-85).
KINCAID; Bible records (Paul-Reed);
Dt (12-107).
KING; (Robert, Rev. War); N3 (47-
260).
KING; New Kent Co., Va.; V3 (57-88).
KINGMAN, HENRY; Weymouth; Al (105-
22).
KINGSMAN; (Nathaniel), Salem, Mass.;
Yl (85-9, 101).
KINNEY; Family record (Lewis), N.
Y.; YA (3-373).
KINNEY; Rev. Pension (John), N. J.;
Bl (24-17).
KINSEY; (James), Burlington, N. J.;
P (19-37).
KIP; Bible record (Jacob), New York;
A2 (83-164).
KIRKENDALL; Rev. Pension (Samuel),
N. J.; M (36-121).
KIRKPATRICK; Somerset Co.,
N. J.; YA (2-55, 85, 107, 135,
173, 203).
KIRKPATRICK; Rev. Pension (James);
N. J.; M (36-71); (Robert), S. C.,
Tenn.; M (36-71).
KIRTLAND, NATHANIEL; Lynn, Mass.;
B4 (25-1).
KITCHEN, JOHN; Salem; Al (106-38).
KLEIN; Bible record (Philip); M (37-
60).
KNIGHT; (George-Franklin), Miss.,
Col.; Col (8-91).
KNIGHT; (John), Newington, N. H.; Al
(102-74).
KNIGHT; Rev. Pension (Robert), R.
I.; M (36-102); (Dr. John), Va.,
Ky.; M (36-102).
KNOWLES; Rev. Pension (Seth), Conn.,
N. Y.; M (37-29).
KOLLOCK, JACOB; Lewes, Del.; Bl (22-
49).
KROM; Rev. Pension (Simon), N. Y.;
M (37-29).
KUNTZ; Rev. Pension (Daniel), Pa.;
M (37-64).
KYN [KEEN], JORAN; New Sweden; addi-
tions to genealogy; Al (105-48).

LACEY; Rev. Pension (Samuel), Chat-
ham, N. J.; Bl (23-86).
LADD; Bible record (Carlos E.), Am-
sterdam, N. Y.; Dt (15-24).
LA DU; inscriptions, Warners, N. Y.;
Dt (12-42).
LA DUE; inscriptions, Weedsport,
Mich.; Dt (11-128).

LAFRANCE; Bible record (Willis-
Breese), Elmira, N. Y.; Ng (7-
360).
LAKE, JOHN; John (Freehold, N.
J.); A2 (80-97).
LAKE; Tiverton; B4 (27-220).
LAKE; Rev. Pension (Daniel), R.
I., N. Y.; M (40-143).
LAMB; Bible record (John), N. J.;
Z3 (66-42).
LAMBERT; (Jonathan), Salem; Y1
(88-150).
LAMMAS; Rev. Pension (Dye), Conn.,
Me.; M (39-104).
LANE; (Aaron), Somerset Co., N.
J.; (Ohio; O1 (9-164).
LANG, JOHN; Boston; A1 (105-74).
LANGDON; Bible record (Ira),
Windsor, Vt.; Dt (11-32).
LANGFORD; Family record (George),
Westmoreland, Oneida Co., N.
Y.; Dt (10-125).
LAPHAM, JOHN; Dartmouth, Mass.;
B4 (24-1, 122, 180, 242).
LARABEE, GREENFIELD; (John3),
Windham; B4 (28-247).
LARD; Rev. Pension (John), N. J.;
M (39-104).
LATHROP; Manchester, Vt.; A1 (105-
73).
LATTIMORE, HUGH and CLEMENT;
Northumberland Co., Va.; V1 (32-
134).
LAUNE; Bible record (Stephen P.);
A2 (80-165).
LAWMAN; Bible record (Barnard);
Col (9-113).
LAWRENCE, THOMAS; N. Y.; (Jona-
than5, Stephen, Samuel), S. C.;
J (53-77).
LAWRENCE, THOMAS; Philadelphia;
B4 (27-91).
LAWRENCE; St. James, Southelmham,
co Suffolk; cont.; B4 (24-56).
LAWRENCE; Bible records (John),
Warren, Ohio; Dt (12-99).
LAZELL, JOHN; Hingham; additions;
A1 (105-153).
LEACH; (Ebenezer), Coventry; B4
(28-246).
LEE, THOMAS; Lyme, Conn.; B4 (25-
249).
LEE, WALTER; Westfield, Mass.;
(Nathaniel, Broome Co., N. Y.);
B4 (25-252).
LEE, WILLIAM; Burlington, N. J.,
Philadelphia; B4 (27-114).

LEE, WILLIAM; Hempstead; B4 (27-114).
LEE; (Woodbridge, N. J.); B1 (23-50).
LEE; Rev. Pension (William), Pa.,
Ohio; M (38-65); (William), Lyme,
Conn., Canaan, N. Y.; Dt (13-145).
LEEDS; Rev. Pension (Jeremiah), N.
J.; Z4 (2-198).
LEEK, PHILIP; (Ebenezer2), East
Hampton, L. I.; B4 (26-213).
LEGARE, FRANCIS; Braintree, Mass.;
B4 (25-1; 26-29).
LEGG; Rev. Pension (David), Mass.;
M (39-131).
LEMAY; (will, William, 1784), Han-
over Co., Va.; V1 (32-30).
LEMON; Rev. Pension (Matthias S.),
Pa.; M (40-33).
LEONARD [LEONARDSON], SOLOMON;
Bridgewater; B4 (27-1).
LEONARD; Rev. Pension (Samuel), Mor-
ris, N. J.; B1 (24-43).
LEVERETT; (Hudson3), Boston; B4 (25-
160).
LEWIS, JOHN; Gloucester Co., Va.; V3
(56-195).
LEWIS, THOMAS; Saco, Me.; English
ancestry; A1 (101-3); Herring an-
cestry; A1 (101-81); ancestry of
wife Elizabeth Marshall; A1 (101-
86).
LEWIS; (Samuel), Coventry; B4 (28-
246).
LEWIS; Bible records (Judson-Whit-
ing); Dt (16-24).
LEWIS; Rev. Pension (John), Morris,
N. J.; B1 (24-44).
LINDSLEY; Rev. Pension (Joseph), Mor-
ris, N. J.; B1 (24-41).
LINKLETTER, GEORGE; Warwick, N. Y.;
arms; A2 (80-16).
LIPPERT, HENRY; Adams Co., Pa.; Col
(11-63).
LIPPINCOTT; (Freedom), Burlington
Co., N. J.; B1 (25-1).
LITTLEFIELD; correction to genealogy;
A1 (105-234).
LITTLEPAGE, THOMAS; Va.; England; V3
(56-72).
LIVINGSTON; Family record (Peter Van
Burgh), New York; A2 (79-190).
LOCK; Rev. Pension (John), Pequan-
nock, N. J.; B1 (25-19).
LOCKETT; Mecklenburg Co., Va.; Hen-
derson Co., Ky.; N3 (49-403).
LOGAN; (John), Henderson, Ky.; N3
(46-451).
LONG, JOSEPH; (William3), Coventry;

B4 (28-247).
LONG; settlers in New England;
A1 (104-36).
LONG; Sampler record (Joel); Dt
(13-26).
LCNG; (Samuel), Va., Ky.; N3
(49-374; 50-187).
LORE, RICHARD; (Seth, Hezekiah),
Cumberland Co., N. J.; B5 (31-
54; 32-85).
LOVING, ADAM; Halifax Co., Va.;
V3 (56-213).
LOW; (Samuel), Warren; B4 (28-
212).
LOW; (Seth), Salem, Mass.; Y1
(85-215).
LUDDEN; (Joseph), Braintree; Dt
(15-55).
LUM, JOHN; English data; B4 (28-
55).
LUTHER; (Hezekiah[2]); Swansea; B4
(27-139).
LYNDE; Boston; note; B4 (24-258).
LYON; Rev. Pension (Jonas), Pe-
quannock, N. J.; B1 (25-18).
LYTLE; family record (Nathaniel);
N3 (48-74).

MCCLIMANS; Bible record (John),
Pa., Ohio; Dt (15-11).
MCCORD; Rev. Pension (John), S.
C.; M (40-33); (William), Va.,
Ind.; M (39-131).
MCCRACKEN, THOMAS; Mt. Bethel,
Pa.; M (40-64).
MCDONALD; Family record (Rich-
ard); Dt (10-129).
MCKAY; Family record (Alexander),
Hadley, Mass.; Dutchess Co., N.
Y.; Dt (11-26).
MCKEAN; Rev. Pension (William),
Pequannock, N. J.; B1 (25-17).
MCKNITT, JOHN; Somerset Co., Md.;
P (16-75).
MCLEAN; Bible records (William);
Col (13-4).
MACWITHEY, MCQUIVEY; (Nathan),
West Springfield, Mass.; B4
(26-195; 27-187).
MALLORY, PETER; Vermont and Cana-
dian branches; B4 (26-206; 28-
191).
MANCHESTER, THOMAS; Portsmouth,
R. I.; A1 (101-175, 308, 329;
102-10, 314; 104-167; 105-75);
Dt (11-93).
MANN, RICHARD; Scituate; (Thom-

as[2]); B4 (27-220).
MANSFIELD, JOHN; Hingham; B4 (25-
157).
MANSFIELD, ROBERT; (John[2]), Lynn,
Mass.; B4 (24-57).
MANSSON, HANS; Pa.; N. J.; A2 (79-
113).
MAPLE; Rev. Pension (Stephen), N.
J., Pa.; M (40-34); (William),
Pa.; M (39-132).
MARBLE; Bible record (Samuel), Md.,
Ohio; Col (10-57).
MARCY; Woodstock, Conn.; correction;
Dt (15-102).
MARKHAM; (will of John, 1804), Staf-
ford Co., Va.; V1 (31-180).
MARRS; (William), Sussex Co., N. J.;
Dt (12-39).
MARSHALL, JOHN; Va.; V1 (30-137).
MARTIN; Bradford, Vt.; A1 (105-154).
MARTINDELL; (James), Rev. soldier,
S. C.; cont.; Dt (11-12, 35, 73,
97, 119; 12-13).
MASON; (CAPT.) JOHN; Windsor; B4
(26-84, 185).
MASON; inscriptions, Gunston Hall,
Va.; V1 (32-32).
MASSEY; Bible records (Thomas); P
(16-121).
MATHEWS, ALEXANDER; Augusta Co., Va.;
V1 (32-46).
MATHIS; (will of John, 1824), Gallo-
way, N. J.; Z4 (1-154).
MATLACK; Bible record (William); B5
(35-130).
MAUZY, JOHN; Stafford Co., Va.; V1
(31-182); V3 (58-112).
MAVERICK, JOHN; (Samuel-Augustus),
Texas; A1 (102-163).
MAY, GEORGE; Mays Landing, N. J.; Z4
(1-70).
MAYO; (Rev. John); Cape Cod, Boston;
A1 (103-32).
MEEK; Bible record (William), Pales-
tine, Ohio; Dt (14-50).
MELCHER; Bible record (Nathaniel);
A2 (78-171).
MELVILLE; (ancestry of Herman); A2
(80-194).
MERAUGH, DENNIS; Falmouth; Coventry
branches B4 (28-67).
MERWIN; Family record (Ebenezer); B4
(26-192).
MICKLES; Bible record (Peter); A1
(82-146).
MIDDLETON, ROBERT; Prince Georges
Co., Md.; P (19-91).

NOLL, JUSTUS PETER; N. Y.; Bible
record; Dt (15-36).
NORMAN; Bible record (Thomas); Dt
(11-63).
NORTON, GEORGE; Salem; (Isaac),
L. I.; B4 (26-226).
NORTON; Saybrook; B4 (26-161).
NOYES, NICHOLAS; (Josiah4), Fal-
mouth, Me.; B4 (24-32).

OBITTS; Bible record (Jacob), Ant-
werp, N. Y.; Dt (14-115).
ODELL, WILLIAM and URSULA; Con-
cord, Mass.; English data; B4
(26-8).
OLIVER, WILLIAM; Elizabeth, N. J.;
B4 (24-37).
O'NEIL; Rev. Pension (Con), Mend-
ham, N. J.; B1 (25-18).
O'RORKE, CONSTANTINE; Herkimer
Co., N. Y.; A2 (78-167).
ORR; Bible records (John); A2 (82-
173).
OVIATT; Tring, Herts, Eng.; B4
(24-128).
OYSTERBANKS; Bible record, Fair-
field; B4 (26-192).

PACKER, JOHN; Groton; B4 (28-175).
PAGE, JOHN; Watertown, Mass.; Eng-
lish ancestry; A1 (101-242; 105-
25).
PAINE, JOHN; Newport, R. I.; B4
(24-70).
PALGRAVE, RICHARD (DR.); Charles-
town; English ancestry; A1 (102-
87, 312); Plantagenet descent;
B4 (25-24); Wingfield ancestry;
A1 (103-287).
PALMER, JOHN; Bucks Co., Pa.; ad-
denda; B4 (27-89).
PALMER, MICAH; Branford; (Rev.
Solomon); YA (4-608; 5-633).
PALMER, WALTER; Stonington, Conn.;
YA (1-59, 87, 111, 137, 177,
207, 237, 263; 3-289, 310, 331,
359, 387, 409, 435, 459).
PALMER, WILLIAM; Wethersfield,
Branford, Westchester; B4 (26-
95, 170).
PALMER; (Deborah), Stephentown,
N. Y.; B4 (24-59).
PALMER; (John), Detroit, Mich.;
Dt (10-121).
PALMER; co Essex, Eng.; B4 (26-
155).
PALMETER; Rev. Pension (Jonathan),

Conn., N. Y.; M (40-143).
PANTIER; Bible records; X2 (21-3).
PARKER; Bible record (Joel); A1
(106-316).
PARKER; Bible record (Stephen A.),
Orford, N. H.; Dt (12-41).
PARMELEE; Bible record; Dt (14-78).
PARMINTER; Rev. Pension (Nathaniel),
Mass., N. H.; M (39-132).
PARSELL; Rev. Pension (Swain), Jef-
ferson, N. J.; B1 (24-88).
PARSONS, JOSEPH; (Jonathan3), North-
ampton, Mass.; B4 (26-71, 210; 27-
60, 188; 28-98).
PARSONS; Wisconsin; A1 (101-328).
PATTEE, WILLIAM; Topsham, Vt.; (Rev.
Elias); Dt (11-59).
PATTERSON, WILLIAM; Baltimore; Dt
(11-33).
PAUL; (Nathan), Greenwich, N. J.; B1
(23-73).
PAYNE, WILLIAM; Boston, Ipswich; Eng-
lish data; A1 (103-183; 106-83).
PEARSE, JOHN; Daniel2, wife; B4 (26-
57).
PEARSON, JOHN; Rowley, Mass.; Y1
(83-289).
PEARSON; Bible records (George), Al-
bany; A2 (81-49).
PEASE; Rev. Pension (John), Conn.; M
(40-34).
PECK; Family record (Willard), Hud-
son, N. Y.; Dt (10-125).
PEIRCE, JOHN; Watertown; B4 (27-98);
(Ruth4), marriages; B4 (26-162).
PENFIELD, SAMUEL; Lynn, Bristol; A1
(101-75).
PENNOCK, JAMES and SAMUEL; Lyme, He-
bron; B4 (27-211).
PENNOYER; Bible record (Gould S.),
Stamford; A1 (103-153).
PEPPERELL; (Sir William); A1 (104-
252; 106-156).
PERCY, GEORGE; Jamestown; V3 (57-
227).
PERKINS, NICHOLAS; Goochland Co.,
Va.; V1 (30-216, 282).
PETER, ROBERT; Georgetown; V3 (57-
173).
PETTUS, THOMAS; V1 (29-140).
PHILLIPS; Rev. Pension (David), N.
J.; M (40-34).
PIKE; (Samuel), Muscle Cove; B4 (26-
157).
PILE, THOMAS; Pilesgrove, N. J.; P
(19-59).
PILLSBURY; correction; A1 (103-317).

PINHORNE, WILLIAM; N. Y., N. J.;
Z3 (66-156).
PITMAN, NICHOLAS; Va.; V1 (32-234).
PITNEY; Morris Co., N. J.; Z4 (2-191).
PLUMLEY, JOHN; Bucks Co., Pa.;
English origin; B4 (28-78).
POELLNITZ, FREDERICK CARL, BARON
VON; Saxony; S. C.; A2 (80-130).
POND, SAMUEL; (Nathaniel3), Stamford; B4 (28-96).
PORTER, EDWARD; Boston; B4 (27-19).
PORTER; Bible record (James); A1
(106-316).
PORTER; Bible record (Nathaniel),
Conn., N. Y.; A2 (82-31).
POWELL, NATHANIEL; Jamestown, Va.;
V3 (60-515).
POWELL, THOMAS; Va.; (Richard3),
Amherst Co.; V1 (30-49).
POWELL; early Virginia settlers;
V1 (31-53).
PRATT, JOHN; Hartford; English
clue; B4 (26-157).
PRENTICE, VALENTINE; (Joseph4),
Preston; B4 (28-86).
PRETEMAN, THOMAS; Del.; B1 (22-49).
PREWITT; Va.; notes; V3 (58-137;
60-330).
PRICE; Rev. Pension (Rice), Morris, N. J.; 31 (24-44).
PRINGLE, ROBERT; Charleston, S.
C.; J (50-91).
PRITCHARD; Bible records (Amos);
Dt (16-22).
PROCTOR; Rev. Pension (Little-Page), Va., Ill.; M (40-35).
PROVOOST; Bible record (David),
Rye, N. Y.; YA (3-317, 346).
PRUDDEN, PETER (REV.); addendum;
B4 (26-232).
PRUETT; Va.; V3 (57-329).
PUTNAM, JOHN; Salem, Mass.; English ancestry; A1 (102-39,
192, 312); B4 (24-257).

QUARRELL; England; B4 (24-215).
QUATTLEBAUM, PETER; Pa.; S. C.;
J (48-1, 84, 167, 219; 49-41,
104, 170, 231).
QUENNELL; co. Surrey, Eng.; B4
(26-156).
QUIGLEY; (Isaac), N. J., Pa.,
Mich.; Dt (14-105).

QUIGLEY; Bible records (Elijah); A2
(78-134).
QUINCY; Bible record (Horatio G.),
Chesterfield, Me.; A1 (105-235).

RADCLIFFE, JOHN; Albany; A2 (80-67,
146, 209; 81-24).
RADLEY; Rev. Pension (William), Chatham, N. J.; B1 (23-26).
RANDOLPH; Family record (William),
Elkton, Ohio; Dt (15-26).
RATHBECK; Horncastle, co. Linc.; A1
(103-185).
RAWLINGS; (Asahel), Greene Co.,
Tenn.; X2 (19-35).
RAWLINGS; Rev. Pension (John), N. H.;
M (36-113).
RAY, SIMON; Braintree; English data;
A1 (104-107); additions; B4 (27-221).
RAY; Rev. Pension (James), Mendham,
N. J.; B1 (25-16).
RAYBURN, HENRY; Montgomery Co., Va.;
Col (8-33).
RAYMOND [RAYMENT], RICHARD, JOHN,
WILLIAM; Beverly, Mass.; B4 (24-157); (Daniel, Baltimore.); X1 (44-111).
REABURN; (Edward), Augusta Co., Va.;
Col (11-119; 12-17, 43, 75, 103;
13-23, 46, 78, 107).
READE, ESDRAS; Boston, Woburn; English data; B4 (28-149).
REED; (Nathan, Norwalk, Conn.); B4
(25-63).
REED; Rev. Pension (Benjamin), Mass.;
M (40-112); (Benjamin), Conn.; M
(40-144).
REEDER; Bible record (John); A2 (79-109).
REEVES, WALTER; (Biddle4), Woodbury,
N. J.; Dt (14-87).
REEVES; Inscriptions, N. J., Mich.;
Dt (14-47, 49).
REINECKER; (will of Conrad, 1810),
Md.; X2 (19-55).
REMINGTON; Bible record (Thomas),
East Greenwich, R. I.; A2 (78-73);
Dt (13-25).
REMSEN; Bible record (John); A2 (78-81).
REYNOLDS, FLECTIOUS; Salem, Middleboro; Dt (15-93).
REYNOLDS; Bible records (Samuel), N.
Y.; Dt (14-75).
RHOADES, JOHN; Scarsdale, N. Y.; Dt
(13-38).

213).
SAUNDERS, TOBIAS; Saugus; B4 (28-212).
SAWYER, JOHN; Lyme, Conn.; Dt (13-63).
SAWYER; Bible records (Dr. Jacob), Carlisle, Pa.; M (36-115).
SAXTON, see Sexton.
SCARBOROUGH; (wife of Col. Edmund); Va.; V3 (57-90).
SCHENCK; (Martin), N. Y., N. J.; A2 (83-238).
SCHIPPER, GERRIT; artist; origin and family; A2 (83-70).
SCHUTT; Rev. Pension (James), N. Y.; M (35-100).
SCHUYLER, DAVID; (Peter-David4), Albany, Canajoharie; B4 (27-125); (Arent), Albany; Z3 (65-126); Bible record (Anthony), Geneva, N. Y.; A2 (83-91).
SCOBEY; Rev. Pension (James), Chester, N. J.; B1 (24-71).
SCOTT, JAMES; Caroline Co., Va.; V1 (30-272).
SCOTT, JOHN (CAPT.); Southampton, L. I.; B4 (27-216).
SCOTT; Bible records (Gavin), York Co., Pa.; M (36-116).
SCOTT; Bible record (John); Ng (7-372).
SCRIVENER, MATTHEW; Jamestown; V3 (57-311).
SCRUGGS, THOMAS; Beverly, N. Y.; B4 (24-156).
SCUDDER; almanac jottings; Springfield, N. J.; cont.; Z3 (65-47, 104, 152, 198).
SCUDDER; Bible records (Benjamin), Huntington, N. Y.; N. J.; Z3 (66-38).
SCUDDER; Rev. Pension (Philip), Chatham, N. J.; B1 (23-87).
SEALBY; (Joseph); cont.; B5 (31-21).
SEARLE, JOHN; Springfield, Mass.; Dt (14-7, 33, 65, 101, 139; 15-13, 41, 73, 103, 135).
SEAVER; (Joshua), Roxbury; Dt (15-55).
SEAY; Rev. Pension (James), Va., S. C.; M (40-36).
SEVERANCE; Revolutionary pensions; Dt (13-107).
SEVERSMITH; see Smith, Nicholas.
SEXTON, GEORGE; Westfield, Mass.;

Dt (11-47, 67); Ng (7-340).
SHANKS; (Christian), Bourbon Co., Ky.; N3 (49-83).
SHARP; Bible record (James-Taylor), Coatesville, Pa.; Col (9-37).
SHARPE; (Gov. Horatio), Md.; X1 (46-8).
SHATTUCK; (Alfred), Deerfield, Mass.; Mich.; Dt (11-117).
SHAW, ABRAHAM; Dedham; English data; A1 (106-50).
SHAW; (John), Annapolis, Md.; X1 (42-35).
SHEFFIELD, ICHABOD; Newport, R. I.; A1 (104-3, 243; 105-75).
SHELDON, JOHN; Kingstown; (Isaac2); B4 (27-222).
SHELDON, JOHN; Providence; B4 (27-222).
SHELLY; Raynham, Taunton, Mass.; B4 (24-190).
SHELTON, DANIEL; Bible record (Elisha); A2 (79-121).
SHEPARD; Bible record (Simeon), Newtown, Conn.; A1 (106-72).
SHEPPARD, DAVID; (David2); B5 (31-61; 32-78, 122).
SHEPPARD; Bible record (Ephraim); B5 (31-28).
SHERRADEN; Bible records (Henry); Dt (12-99).
SHERWOOD, THOMAS; Fairfield, Conn.; YA (3-337, 365, 417, 443, 455, 479; 4-503, 527, 549, 569, 591, 617; 5-643, 667, 695, 723, 749, 777; 6-803, 829, 857); B4 (27-156).
SHERWOOD; Bible records (Edward); X2 (21-3).
SHIER; Palatinate, Ireland, U. S.; Dt (12-61, 91, 117; 13-7, 43, 69, 99).
SHIPMAN, EDWARD; Saybrook, Conn.; B4 (24-53).
SHIPP, JOSIAH; Essex Co., Va.; V1 (29-50).
SHIRTS; Bible record (Michael); Col (12-66).
SHORT; Stafford Co., Va.; V1 (32-208).
SHORTT; (Philo), Va., Md.; X2 (18-67).
SHYROCK; (Mathias), Md., Ky.; N3 (50-111).
SIBOUTSZEN, HERCK; New York; B4 (27-107).
SIKES; (Nathaniel), Monson, Mass.;

Dt (10-138).
SILLIMAN; Bible records (Isaac);
Philadelphia; P (18-142).
SIMPKINS, NICHOLAS; Boston; B4
(28-87).
SIMPSON, JOHN and THOMAS; Pax-
tang, Pa.; P (17-59).
SINNICKSON, ANDREW; Penns Neck,
N. J.; P (19-64).
SKILLMAN; Bible record (Henry S.);
B1 (21-94).
SKINNER; Bible records (Edmund
B.); M (36-114).
SLAUGHTER; Bible record (Samuel),
Ga.; M (36-36).
SMITH, ABRAHAM; Charlestown;
(John2, Killingworth); B4 (25-
124).
SMITH, ANDREW; Hopewell, N. J.;
B4 (24-102); Z3 (65-141).
SMITH, BARTHOLOMEW; Huntington,
L. I.; B4 (25-68).
SMITH, JOHN; Mespat, L. I.; B4
(25-66).
SMITH, JOHN (SERGT.); Milford
Conn.; B4 (25-102).
SMITH, JOHN (YE SMITH); Milford,
Conn.; B4 (25-91).
SMITH, NICHOLAS; Milford, Conn.;
B4 (25-94).
SMITH, PETER; Hempstead; (Heze-
kiah4), Newton, N. J.; B1 (22-
73).
SMITH, RICHARD; Wethersfield; B4
(25-126; 26-55).
SMITH, RICHARD; Lyme; B4 (25-
140).
SMITH, RICHARD; R. I.; B4 (27-
222).
SMITH, ROGER; East Hampton, L.
I.; B4 (25-93).
SMITH, THOMAS; Guilford, Killing-
worth; B4 (25-123).
SMITH, WALTER; Milford, Conn.;
B4 (25-117).
SMITH, WILLIAM; Jamaica, L. I.;
B4 (25-70; 26-58).
SMITH; (Adam C.), Ky.; Mo.; Dt
(16-11, 33).
SMITH; (Benjamin), Taunton;
Westminster, Vt.; Dt (15-7).
SMITH; (James), Canterbury, Suf-
field; B4 (28-251).
SMITH; (John, Ashford, Conn.);
B4 (25-200).
SMITH; (Nathaniel), Stafford Co.,
Va.; N3 (47-49, also 43).

SMITH; (Silas-Sanford), Utah; Col
(8-62).
SMITH; (Guilford, Conn.); B4 (25-
92).
SMITH; (Lyme, Conn.); B4 (25-143).
SMITH; (Stratford, Conn.); B4 (25-
122).
SMITH; Bible record (Henry), Madison
Co., N. Y.; A2 (81-141).
SMITH; Bible records (Jeremiah);
Jonesboro, Tenn.; Mo.; Col (8-13).
SMITH; Bible records (Samuel A.); X2
(21-31).
SMITH; Pension record (John P.),
Claverack, N. Y.; Dt (13-141).
SMITHSEN, RICHARD; Glastonbury; B4
(25-139).
SNAPP, LAWRENCE and JOHN; Shenandoah
and Frederick Cos., Va.; V1 (32-
234).
SNELLING; Boston; A1 (105-54).
SOMERS, JOHN; Great Egg Harbor, N.
J.; Z4 (1-18).
SOUTHARD; Bible records (Timothy);
M (40-31).
SPAULDING, EDWARD; (John2, Conn.
descendants); B4 (24-222; 26-168).
SPEAR, GEORGE; (Joseph3), Dorchester,
Mass.; A1 (101-174).
SPENCER, WILLIAM, THOMAS, MICHAEL,
GERARD; English ancestry; B4 (27-
80); genealogy; B4 (27-161; 28-56,
108, 256); wife of Thomas; A1
(105-197).
SPENCER; (John and Thomas), Dutchess
Co., N. Y.; Dt (12-139).
SPOOR, JAN WYBESSE; Schenectady, N.
Y.; YA (5-677, 705, 733, 759, 787;
6-813, 839, 867).
STAATS [JAN PIETERSZEN]; Brooklyn,
N. Y.; B1 (25-25).
STACY; Bible record (William); Dt
(15-98).
STANBOROUGH, JOSIAH; East Hampton,
L. I.; wife's English ancestry;
B4 (26-61).
STANTON; (Thomas), Canterbury, Conn.;
B4 (26-41).
STAUFFER; families, Penn.; P (15-
216).
STEELMAN; Burlington Co., N. J.; A2
(79-113).
STEENBURGH; Rev. Pension (Elias), N.
Y.; M (37-29).
STERN; (will of Peyton, 1800, and
David, 1797); Caroline Co., Va.;
V1 (30-256).

STEVENSON; Rev. Pension (John), N.
C.; M (35-122).
STIER; (Baron Henry), Md.; X1
(45-271).
STILES; Bible record (Isaac); B5
(35-135).
STILES; Rev. Pension (Hezekiah),
N. J., Ohio; M (37-29).
STOCKWELL, QUINTIN; Suffield,
Conn.; YA (3-491; 4-513, 537,
559, 579, 601, 627; 5-653, 679).
STONE; Rev. Pension (William),
Mass.; M (37-30).
STORY; (Elisha), Boston, Mass.;
Y1 (83-59).
STOUFFER; families, Penn.; P (15-
216).
STOUT; (George), Mich.; M (36-
114).
STOUT; Family record (Hervey-
Bliss), Ind.; M (38-123).
STOUT; Rev. Pension (John), N.
J.; M (35-122; 37-31).
STOVER; family, Penn.; P (15-216).
STOVER; Bible record (William);
A2 (78-171).
STRACHEY, WILLIAM; Jamestown, Va.;
V3 (57-115); Sutton Court, co.
Somerset, Eng.; V3 (59-275).
STREET, NICHOLAS (REV.); New Ha-
ven; maternal ancestry; B4 (27-
9).
STRETCHLEY; (John), Lancaster
Co., Va.; V3 (57-79).
STRICKLAND, JOHN; Philadelphia; P
(18-137; 19-39, 66).
STROTHER; Ky.; N3 (49-386).
STRYKER, JAN; (Peter2), Flatbush;
(Peter4), Somerset Co., N. J.;
(Peter4), New Brunswick; A2 (82-
196); (Hendrick), Flatbush; A2
(83-101).
STUART; royal Stuarts in America;
A1 (104-173; 105-72, 183; 106-
75, 235).
SUMMERS; Rev. Pension (John);
Va., Ky.; M (36-103); (Shubill),
Conn., N. Y.; M (37-31).
SUNDERLAND; England and Maryland;
A1 (101-26).
SUYDAM [HENDRICK RYCKE]; A2 (78-
37).
SWADDLE [SWATHEL], JOHN; Middle-
town, Conn.; Dt (11-66).
SWAIN, HENRY and JEREMIAH; Charles-
town, Mass.; B4 (24-254).
SWARTWOUT; Bible record (John-

Bernardus); New Hackensack, N. Y.;
A2 (83-5).
SWEERS, CORNELIUS; Philadelphia; P
(16-45).
SWETLAND; Rev. Pension (Luke), Pa.;
M (36-103).
SYDEBOTTOM; Rev. Pension (John); Va.,
Ky.; M (36-103).

TALIAFERRO, ROBERT; Va.; identity
of wife; V3 (56-208); King George
Co., Va.; V1 (30-46).
TANNER; Rev. Pension (Josiah), S. C.;
M (35-122).
TAYLOR, JAMES; St. Stephen's Parish,
New Kent Co., Va.; V1 (29-127).
TAYLOR, JOHN; (Rev. John), Va., Ky.;
N3 (46-541; 47-21).
TAYLOR; (David), Concord, Mass.; B4
(24-58).
TAYLOR; Bible records (Thaddeus);
Col (8-15); (Solomon); B5 (36-149).
TAYLOR; Rev. Pension (Richard); Va.;
M (36-104).
TEDFORD; (Alexander and Robert),
Tenn.; Col (13-104).
TEMPLETON, THOMAS; Schenectady; A2
(80-52).
TERRELL; (Fleming), Va., Mo.; V3 (58-
194).
TERRILL, ROGER; Milford, Conn.; B4
(25-37; 26-55); (Lewis4), Windham;
B4 (28-247).
THAYER, RICHARD; (Joshua5), Williams-
burg, Mass.; A1 (101-332; 102-76).
THOMAS, JOHN; Marshfield, Mass.; A1
(101-72).
THOMAS, THOMAS; Cecil Co., Md.; M
(40-140).
THOMAS; Bible record (Alanson); Dt
(15-145).
THOMAS; Rev. Pension (Henry), Pa.,
Ind.; M (37-31).
THOMPSON; (Roger), Hanover Co., Va.;
V3 (58-237).
THOMPSON; Bible records (Alexander),
Maine, Calif.; A1 (103-154).
THOMPSON; Rev. Pension (Alexander),
Pa., Ind.; M (37-91, 114); (Alex-
ander), Pa.; M (37-113).
THONG, WALTER; New York; English an-
cestry; A2 (83-196).
THROCKMORTON; English ancestry; A1
(101-290).
THRUSTON; (Charles-Mynn); Va.; La.;
K2 (21-168, 228, 327).
THURLOW; (Edward, Baron); natural is-

sue; B4 (28-168); T9 (36-411).
THWING, JOHN3; Boston; B4 (24-
259).
TIBBALS, THOMAS; (Ebenezer), Dur-
ham, Conn.; Dt (11-65).
TILGHMAN; (Tench); Md.; X1 (42-
71).
TILGHMAN; Bible records (Samuel
Ogle), Md.; X2 (21-19).
TILLEY, JOHN; Plymouth; B4 (24-
118).
TILTON; Rev. Pension (John); Egg
Harbor, N. J.; Z4 (1-105).
TINDALL; Rev. Pension (James), N.
C., Ga.; M (39-132).
TINGEY, THOMAS (COMMODORE); Santa
Cruz; Philadelphia; P (16-46).
TOBEY, THOMAS; Joshua5 (Hudson,
N. Y.); B4 (26-30).
TOBIAS; Bible record (Jacob),
Vt.; B4 (24-258).
TODD; (Patrick), Laurens, S. C.;
M (38-104).
TOMM; Rev. Pension (Henry); Md.;
M (39-32).
TONG; Rev. Pension (William),
Md., Mo.; M (37-91).
TOOKER; Bible record (Elias), N.
J.; Z3 (66-46).
TORKSEY, PHILIP; Albemarle Co.,
N. C.; Ng (7-365).
TOSH; (William), South Kingston;
B4 (28-212).
TOTTEN; Bible records (Joseph),
New York; A2 (81-48).
TREIBLE; Bible records (Peter
M.); A2 (78-134).
TRENCHARD, GEORGE; Salem, N. J.;
P (19-3); (John); B5 (34-41).
TRIPLETT; (Daniel), Culpeper Co.,
Va.; V1 (31-50).
TRIPLETT; (John), Culpeper Co.,
Va.; V3 (55-289).
TROLINGER; Rev. Pension (Henry),
Va., N. C.; M (37-113).
TROUTMAN; (John-Michael and
George-Peter), Md., Ky.; K2
(24-199).
TRUMAN; Va. ancestry of Pres.
Harry S.; cont.; V1 (29-51,
195; 30-35).
TRUMBULL [TRUMBLE], JOHN; Rowley;
Conn. branches; Dt (15-3, 37,
69, 99, 131); (wife of John, the
painter); T9 (36-411).
TRUMBULL; Bible record (Stephen);
Dt (13-26).

TRUXTON, THOMAS; Jamaica, N. Y.; P
(17-3).
TSCHUDY; genealogy; cont.; V1 (29-
74, 130, 212, 274; 30-68, 212; 1-
27).
TUCKER; Rev. Pension (John), Va.; M
(37-92, 114).
TURNER; (Edward), Madison Co., Ky.;
N3 (45-166).
TURNER; (Hiram-Beede), Me., Col.;
Col (12-88).
TURNER; (Thomas), N. C., Ky.; K2 (25-
33).
TURNER; Rev. Pension (Lewis), S. C.,
Ala.; M (35-122); (Andrew), N. C.,
Ill.; M (37-92).
TYLER, ROBERT; Calvert Co., Md.; V1
(30-35).

UPSHUR; Northampton Co., Va.; V3
(57-173).

VALENTINE, ROBERT; Chester Co., Pa.;
Bible record; P (16-121).
VALENTINE; Bible records (Abraham);
A2 (82-31).
VALLANCE, JOHN; Philadelphia; P (19-
32).
VAN ALEN, LAURENS and PETER; Albany;
A2 (81-4, 113, 179, 243; 82-51,
104, 148, 244).
VAN ANTWERP, DANIEL JANSE; New York;
cont.; A2 (79-49, 161, 219; 80-19,
99, 167, 198; 82-117).
VAN ARSDALE; (Cornelius), Flatlands;
A2 (79-82; 82-115).
VAN BENSCHOTEN; Rev. Pension
(Jacques), N. Y.; M (38-65).
VAN DER LINDE; Holland; ancestral to
Van Elslant; B4 (28-29).
VAN DER VEER, CORNELIS JANSZ; Flat-
bush; Dutch ancestry; A2 (79-76).
VANDERVEER; Rev. Pension (Joseph),
N. J., Ohio; M (38-66).
VAN DERWARKER; Rev. Pension (Martin),
N. Y.; M (35-123).
VAN DEUSEN; Bible record (Bernard);
A2 (80-240).
VAN DOORN [CLAES DITLOF]; N. Y., N.
J.; B4 (25-162).
VAN DYKE; Rev. Pensions (all of
name); M (40-77, 111).
VAN ELSLAND, CLAES JANSEN; New York;
B4 (28-29).
VAN EPS; Rev. Pension (Abraham I.),
N. Y.; M (38-66).
VAN GELDER; addendum; A2 (80-53).

VAN HORNE; Rev. Pension (Abraham),
N. J., N. Y.; M (38-67).
VAN KLEECK, BALTUS; Bible record
(James); Dt (11-4).
VAN KOUVENHOVEN, see Covenhoven.
VAN METEREN, JAN JOOSTEN; Kings-
ton, N. Y., Burlington, N. J.;
A2 (81-197).
VAN OOSTEN, CORNELIS JANSZ; Flat-
bush; B4 (25-192).
VAN RENSSELAER, KILIAEN; Dutch an-
cestry; B4 (28-178).
VAN SICKLEN; Bible record (Abra-
ham); A2 (78-129).
VAN VARICK, RUDOLPH (REV.) and
JAN; New York; Dutch ancestry;
B4 (27-70).
VAN VOORHEES; Bible records (Al-
bert), Somerset Co., N. J.; Bl
(21-90).
VAUCHERE, JEAN CLAUDE; Natchez;
Dt (14-93, 135).
VAUGHAN, SAMUEL; Philadelphia; V3
(57-168).
VERHAGEN, JOSYNTJE; Kingston,
Flatbush; B4 (25-192).
VIALL, JOHN; Boston, Wickford;
(Samuel², Salem, Bristol); B4
(25-159; 27-222).
VICKERS, VICKERY; N. J.; B5 (34-
17).
VIGNE, GUILLAUME; New York; M
(35-65).
VILLEPONTOUX, PIERRE; New Rochelle,
N. Y.; St. James Parish, S. C.;
J (50-29).
VISBOOM; Holland; ancestral to Van
Varick; B4 (27-160).
VOARE, RICHARD; Windsor; with Eng-
lish clue; B4 (26-65).
VOORHEES; Hopewell, N. J.; Z3 (65-
83).
VOORHEES; Bible record (Abraham);
Somerset Co., N. J.; Bl (21-70).

WADSWORTH; Family record (John),
Conn.; Dt (11-26).
WAGER, ANDREW; Boston, Mass.; Al
(102-263); Sir Charles; R. I.;
Al (102-276).
WAKEFIELD; Rev. Pension (Henry);
N. C., Tenn.; M (36-72).
WALKER; (Jesse), Buckingham Co.,
Va.; Vl (32-54).
WALKER; Family record (Abraham-
Boice); Ng (7-372, 383).
WALKER; Bible record (John), Dart-

mouth; Dt (15-53).
WALKER; Rev. Pension (John); Pa.,
N. Y.; M (36-104); (William), N.
C., Ga.; M (37-31).
WALLER, JOHN; King William Co., Va.;
English origin; V3 (59-337, 458).
WALLER; wills, Stafford Co., Va.;
Vl (31-263).
WALLER; Rev. Pension (Nelson), Del.;
M (35-123).
WALLIN; Bible records (John); B5
(31-71).
WALTER; Rev. Pension (Nicholas),
Pa.; M (38-28).
WALTON; Rev. Pension (Silas), N. Y.;
M (38-36).
WARD, JOHN; Newport; B4 (26-229).
WARD, WILLIAM; (Nehemiah), Attle-
boro; Al (102-153).
WARD; (Josiah), Westfield, N. Y.;
Col (9-104).
WARD; (Seth), Abbington, co. Cam-
bridge; V3 (56-70).
WARD; co. Essex, Eng.; B4 (26-155).
WARD; Bible records (Caleb); Col (8-
15).
WARE; L. I.; N. J.; B5 (32-135; 33-
207).
WARNER, ANDREW; Hartford; English
records, self and wife; B4 (26-
152, 217); (John²); B4 (27-153).
WARNER, JOHN; Farmington; B4 (27-
153); (John³), Suffield; Dt (14-
37, 73).
WARNER; Inscriptions, Chautauqua
Co., N. Y.; Dt (11-64).
WASGATT; (Davis), Monson, Mass.; B4
(24-47).
WASHINGTON; English data; Al (103-
198); B4 (26-50).
WASHINGTON; connection with Amunde-
ville; Al (103-282).
WASHINGTON; (Mildred, Mrs. Willis);
V3 (56-42).
WATERBURY, JOHN; Stamford; B4 (27-
241; 28-96).
WATERHOUSE [WATROUS], JACOB; New
London; Al (104-186).
WATKINS; Rev. Pension (Leonard), Md.;
M (36-121).
WATLINGTON; Halifax Co., Va.; N3
(47-309).
WATSON; Rev. Pension (Larner), Va.;
M (36-122).
WEARE; Rev. Pension (Jeremiah), Me.;
M (38-131); (William), Conn.; M
(38-132).

WEATLEY; R. I.; item; Al (103-
234).
WEBB, JOHN; Northampton, Mass.;
cont.; B4 (24-178).
WEBB, JOHN; Saybrook, Conn.; B4
(24-171).
WEBB, RICHARD; Stamford; B4 (25-
194; 26-55).
WEBB; Inscriptions, Germantown,
Tenn.; M (39-91).
WEBSTER, JOHN (GOV.); Hartford,
Conn.; English ancestry; B4
(24-197).
WEED, JONAS; Stamford; (Sarah3);
B4 (28-96).
WEEDEN; co. Cheshire, Eng.; Al
(106-87).
WELCH; Rev. Pension (Thomas), Pa.,
Tenn.; M (36-34); (William),
Me.; M (36-72).
WELLER, RICHARD; Windsor; English
notes; B4 (26-248; 27-26, 192).
WELLES, THOMAS (GOV.); ancestry
of wife, Alice Tomes; B4 (28-
164).
WELLS, FRANCES; Wethersfield; B4
(28-227).
WELLS, HUGH; Wethersfield; B4
(28-227).
WELLS; Bible record (John); A2
(81-143).
WELLS; Rev. Pension (John), Md.,
Va.; M (38-132).
WELSH; Bible record (Peter); Col
(9-8).
WENDELL; Rev. Pension (Ahasuer-
us), N. Y.; M (38-132).
WENTWORTH; Rev. Pension (Ben-
ning), Mass., Ohio; M (36-72);
(William), N. H.; M (38-132).
WEST, ANTHONY; Northampton Co.,
Va.; V3 (58-396).
WEST; (Edward), Va., Ky.; K2
(21-301).
WEST; Bible records (John-Hunter),
Shrewsbury, N. J.; B1 (21-90).
WEST; Rev. Pension (Thomas), Va.,
Pa.; M (37-32); (Thomas), Va.,
Ky.; M (37-32); (Willis), N.
C.; M (37-32); (Timothy), Mass.,
N. H.; M (39-32).
WESTCOTT, STUKELEY; (Samuel4),
Norwich, Conn.; B4 (24-54).
WETHERILL, CHRISTOPHER; Burling-
ton, N. J.; B4 (24-75); royal
ancestry; Al (24-269; 25-155).
WHEELER, GEORGE; (William4), Can-

ton, Mass.; Al (104-244).
WHEELER, WILLIAM; Baltimore Co.,
Md.; M (37-59).
WHEELER; co. Bedford, England; B4
(27-35, 119; 28-139, 257).
WHEELER; (Lewis), Athens, N. Y.; Dt
(10-137).
WHETEHILL; Calais; ancestral to Ap-
pleton; Al (102-5, 241; 103-5).
WHIPPLE; Bible records (James),
Providence; Al (102-313).
WHITCOMB, JOHN; (Hezekiah3), Lancas-
ter; Dt (15-18).
WHITE, JOHN; (Oliver6), Windsor; B4
(27-16).
WHITE, JOHN; Watertown, Mass.; (I-
saac3); Y1 (83-14).
WHITE, THOMAS; Weymouth; (Danbury,
Conn.); B4 (25-24); (Benjamin3),
Middleboro; B4 (27-204); (Micah5),
Abington; B4 (28-83).
WHITE, WILLIAM; Plymouth; B4 (27-
204).
WHITE; (Hugh), Clay Co., Ky.; N3
(50-242).
WHITEHEAD; Bible records (John),
Scotland; Mich.; Dt (12-126).
WHITENACK; Bible records (Cornelius);
Montgomery, N. J.; B1 (21-91).
WHITING; (Nathan), Williamstown,
Mass., Schoharie Co., N. Y.; Al
(104-63).
WHITLEY, SOLOMON; Augusta Co., Va.;
(William), Ky.; K2 (25-101, 210,
300).
WHITTEMORE, THOMAS; Malden; Al (106-
31, 89, 191, 262).
WHITTINGTON, WILLIAM (CAPT.); Northampton Co., Va.; N3 (47-314).
WILCOX, EDWARD; R. I.; YA (1-1, 11;
2-1, 19, 39, 71, 93, 121, 155,
187, 221, 249; 3-277, 298, 319,
347, 375, 397, 423, 447, 471; 4-
495, 519, 541, 561, 583, 609; 5-
635, 659, 687, 715, 739, 767; 6-
793, 819, 847); B4 (24-260; 26-
230).
WILCOX, JOHN; Hartford; YA (1-15; 2-
5, 23, 43, 75, 97, 125, 159, 191,
225, 253; 3-281, 302, 323, 351,
379, 401, 427, 451, 475; 4-499,
523, 545, 565, 587).
WILCOX; (David), Canaan, N. Y.; YA
(2-92).
WILCOX; Bible record (Abel E.), Guilford, Conn.; Dt (11-3).
WILCOXSON, WILLIAM; Stratford, Conn.;

YA (1-3, 13; 2-3, 21, 41, 73,
95, 123, 157, 189, 223, 251; 3-
279, 321, 349, 377, 399, 425,
449, 473; 4-497, 521, 543, 563,
586, 611; 5-637, 661, 689, 713,
741, 769; 6-795, 821, 849).
WILDER, THOMAS; (William4), Bol-
ton; Dt (15-18).
WILDIN; Bible record (Jeremiah);
B5 (32-128).
WILKINSON, LAWRENCE; Providence;
alleged royal ancestry; B4
(26-28).
WILKINSON, WILLIAM (REV.); Va.,
Md.; V3 (57-316).
WILKINSON; Bible records (Henry-
Lee), Green Co., Ga.; M (36-
115).
WILL, MICHAEL; York Co., Pa.; V1
(32-139).
WILLARD; Bible record (Azel),
Vt.; Dt (14-15).
WILLETS, RICHARD; Hempstead; A2
(80-112).
WILLETT, THOMAS; Flushing; A2
(80-1, 83, 150, 220).
WILLETT, THOMAS (CAPT.); New Eng-
land, New York; A1 (80-41).
WILLIAMS, JOHN; Newport, R. I.;
B4 (24-72).
WILLIAMS, NATHANIEL; Boston; B4
(28-215).
WILLIAMS, ROGER; Providence; B4
(28-197); YA (1-5, 17; 2-7,
25, 45, 77, 99, 127, 161, 193,
227).
WILLIAMS, WILLIAM; (William-
George), Buffalo, N. Y.; V3
(57-165, 171).
WILLIAMS; (Elisha), Frederick
Co., Md.; V1 (32-313).
WILLIAMS; (Samuel), Northampton
Co., Va.; V1 (31-92, 187).
WILLIAMS; Bible records (Dr.
Chauncey), LaFayette, N. Y.;
A1 (106-313).
WILLIAMS; Bible record (Ebene-
zer), Groton, East Windsor; A2
(82-31).
WILLIAMS; Bible record (Elijah);
A2 (81-93).
WILLIAMS; Bible record (Isaac);
YA (5-711, 737).
WILLIAMS; Rev. Pension (Lewis),
Pa., Ohio; M (36-122).
WILLIAMSON; Bible record (Nicho-
las, Kort, Jeremiah); Graves-

end, N. Y.; B1 (21-93).
WILLIS, HENRY; Va.; V3 (56-42).
WILLS; Rev. Pension (William), Va.,
Ky.; M (39-32).
WILSON, JOHN; Woburn; (Francis),
Rehoboth; B4 (27-60).
WILSON; (James), Bedford Co., Va.;
Dt (14-133).
WILSON; (James), Cambridge, S. C.;
M (40-121).
WILLSON; (John), Coventry; B4 (28-
250).
WILSON; (Rev. Obed), Bingham, Me.;
A1 (103-296).
WILSON; Bible record (James), Scot-
land; Mich.; Dt (12-126).
WILTBANK, HERMANUS FREDERICK; Lewes,
Del.; P (18-3, 131).
WINDS; (will of Barnabas, 1708,
Southold); A2 (80-216).
WINGATE; (Joseph-Ferdinand), Mass.,
Me.; P (16-56).
WINGFIELD, THOMAS; York River, Va.;
V3 (60-305).
WINGFIELD; co. Suffolk, Eng.; ances-
tral to Palgrave; A1 (103-287).
WINKETT; Bible record (Samuel), Md.,
Pa.; M (37-86).
WINNE; Bible records (Martin); Dt
(15-114).
WINTHROP, JOHN; Boston; A1 (103-
246).
WITCHELL; Rev. Pension (Jacob), Mor-
ris, N. J.; B1 (24-15).
WITHAM, HENRY; Gloucester, Mass.;
YA (6-837, 865).
WOLFE; (Samuel); Coshocton Co., Ohio;
cont.; Dt (10-131).
WOLFE; Bible records (Jacob), Bran-
don, Mich.; Dt (12-108).
WOOD, HENRY; (Barnabas3); Middleboro,
Mass.; B4 (24-187).
WOOD, JOHN; (William2), Newport; B4
(26-230).
WOOD, JOSEPH; Frederick Co., Md.;
(Woodlawn, Ky., branch); N3 (47-
171).
WOOD, RICHARD; Philadelphia; P (19-
60).
WOOD; (David), Albemarle Co., Va.;
N3 (46-455).
WOOD; (Joseph), Ellington, Conn.; B4
(27-16).
WOOD; Pension and Bible record (Le-
vi), Bridgewater, Mass.; Dt (13-
142); (James), Swansea, Mass.; Dt
(13-143); (James), Alstead, Mass.,

Dt (13-144); (Thomas), Hebron,
Mass.; Dt (13-144).
WOODRUFF; Bible records (Theo-
dore); Dt (16-23).
WOODS; (Richard), Roxbury; Dt
(15-55).
WOODWARD, NATHANIEL; (Israel[3]),
Swansea, Newport; Al (104-73).
WOODWARD, RICHARD; (Amos[5]), Can-
terbury; Dt (15-57).
WOODWORTH, WALTER; (wife of Jo-
seph[4]), Little Compton, R. I.;
Al (101-175, 329).
WOOLFOLK; (Robert), Caroline
Co., Va.; Paducah, Ky.; K2 (25-
126).
WOOLSEY, GEORGE; heirs of Noah[5],
Marlborough, N. Y.; B4 (26-
200).
WORDEN; Bible record (George),
Manlius, N. Y.; Dt (11-96).
WRAY, GEORGE; Fort Ann, N. Y.;
A2 (78-49).
WRIGHT; Rev. Pension (Jarrett),
Va., Ky.; M (38-133).
WYATT, EDWARD; Nathaniel of Stam-
ford; Al (103-150).
WYETH; Rev. Pension (Joshua);
Mass., Ohio; M (36-122).

YARDLEY, GEORGE (SIR); Jamestown,
Va.; V3 (55-259); Vl (31-82).
YELVERTON, JOHN and ANTHONY;
Chester, New Paltz; B4 (28-176).
YOUMANS; Bible record (Frederick),
N. J., N. Y.; A2 (81-95).

ZEHNDER; Bible record (George F.);
B5 (32-115; 33-186).
ZERN; (William), Pa., Col.; Col
(13-87).
ZUTPHEN, Count of; Al (104-206).

(40-116).
Tattnall County; 1810 Jury List;
  M (39-89).
HOLLAND
  Arms of families of Dutch des-
  cent; A1 (106-4).
ILLINOIS
  Edgar County; settlers from Vir-
  ginia; M (36-73; 38-1, 41,
  76).
  Montgomery County; settlers be-
  fore 1840; M (39-37, 72; 40-
  53, 92, 118).
INDIANA
  Jefferson; residents, 1825; M
  (35-3).
IRELAND
  Sources; B4 (28-129, 236).
KANSAS
  Pioneer memories; Col (10-63).
KENTUCKY
  Sources; M (38-74).
  Genealogical research; M (37-
  65).
  Newspaper death and marriage
  items; N3 (45-188).
  Confederate soldiers buried at
  Camp Douglas, Ill.; N3 (46-
  404).
  Marriages and deaths in The
  Commentator, 1826-   ; N3
  (50-134).
  Migrations across Ohio River;
  K2 (25-24).
  Early cabinet makers; N3 (49-
  337; 50-130).
  Bullitt County; Inscriptions,
  Catholic Cem., Deatsville; K2
  (24-365).
  Caldwell County; deaths, 1852-
  59; N3 (45-171).
  Calloway County; deaths, 1852-
  59; N3 (45-235).
  Campbell County, 1852-59; N3
  (45-249).
  Campbell County; Inscriptions;
  N3 (45-199, 267, 341).
  Carroll County; Deaths, 1852-
  59; N3 (45-352).
  Carter County; Deaths, 1852-
  59; N3 (45-358).
  Casey County; Deaths; N3 (46-
  410).
  Christian County; death rec-
  ords; N3 (46-496).
  Clark County; death records; N3
  (47-229).

Crittenden County; death records;
  N3 (46-588).
Cumberland County; death records;
  N3 (46-656).
Daviess County; death records; N3
  (47-72).
Edmonson County; death records; N3
  (47-144).
Estill County; death records; N7
  (47-325).
Fayette County; list of records;
  N3 (47-250); death records; N3
  (48-65).
Fleming County; death records; N3
  (48-173).
Floyd County; death records; N3
  (48-267).
Franklin County; death records; N3
  (48-361).
Fulton County; death records; N3
  (49-60).
Gallatin County; death records; N3
  (49-153).
Garrard County; death records; N3
  (49-245).
Grant County; death records; N3
  (49-389).
Graves County; death records; N3
  (50-57).
Grayson County; death records N3
  (50-165).
Green County; death records; N3
  (50-261).
Greenup County; death records; N3
  (50-347).
Jefferson County; Jeffersontown,
  Cumberland Pres. Church records;
  Dt (12-133).
Lexington; bibliography; cont.;
  N3 (45-39).
Mercer County; wills; cont.; N3
  (47-202; 50-152).
Mt. Sterling; Inscriptions, French
  Cemetery; N3 (47-243).
Nelson County; Rolling Fork Bap-
  tist Church; historical; In-
  scriptions; N3 (46-459).
Transylvania Company personnel; K2
  (21-3).
MAINE
  Vital records, diaries of Rev. Ja-
  cob Richardson Scott; M (39-40);
  marriages by Rev. Obed Wilson of
  Bingham, 1814-39; A1 (103-235);
  baptisms and funerals; A1 (103-
  296).
  Charlotte; Vital Records; A1 (101-

(13-137; 14-21); Inscriptions,
Bruce; Dt (14-23); Early mar-
riages; Dt (12-26); Inscrip-
tions, Washington; Dt (11-49;
14-82); Inscriptions, Ray;
Dt (11-81).
Michilimackinac County [Macki-
nac, Cheboygan, etc.]; 1820
Census; Dt (15-19, 47, 77).
Monroe County; 1820 Census; Dt
(14-51, 83, 109).
Oakland County; Inscriptions,
Bald Eagle Lake Cem., Brandon;
Dt (14-81).
Osceola County; Inscriptions,
Sacred Heart Cem., Evart; Dt
(14-81).
St. Clair County; Marriages,
1838-48; Dt (11-77, 101, 138;
12-21, 47); Inscriptions,
Caswell; Dt (15-81).
Shelby, Macomb Co.; Inscrip-
tions; Dt (11-105).
Wayne County; 1820 Census; Dt
(13-19, 47, 83, 113).
MISSISSIPPI
Revolutionary Pension records;
M (40-4).
Adams County; Census, 1816; M
(37-95; 38-13, 49, 80).
MISSOURI
Cape Girardeau County; early
settlers; Inscriptions; M (39-
10, 60, 75, 119; 40-15, 56,
98, 129).
NEW HAMPSHIRE
Marriages, 1838-42; 1858-83; A1
(103-43, 47, 48).
Chichester; inscriptions; A1
(105-295).
New Castle; tax list, 1763; A1
(105-112).
Piermont, Orford, Lyme; births,
1768-1820; A1 (104-21).
NEW JERSEY
Genealogical Dictionary; cont.;
B1 (21-1, 40, 72; 22-7, 37,
51, 79; 23-5, 29, 54, 81; 24-
9, 31, 51, 73; 25-10, 35,
55); Abbreviations used; B1
(24-57).
List of Bible records, Gen. Soc.
of N. J.; B1 (22-47; 23-47;
24-23, 95).
Family historians; B1 (25-48).
Marriage Licenses; cont.; B1
(21-9, 48, 64, 95; 22-23, 69;

23-21).
Emigration to California 1849; Z3
(70-17).
Atlantic County; early deeds; Z4
(1-11, 103); Census, Atlantic
City, 1855; Z4 (2-207); Inscriptions; Z4 (2-210); Revolutionary items; Z4 (1-108); Galloway
bounds; Z4 (1-156).
Bergen County; petition, 1796; Z3
(65-195); Inscriptions, Van Bus-
kirk Ground, Washington Twp.; B1
(24-65).
Cape May; Baptist marriages, 1808-
22; B1 (23-1); see Egg Harbor,
Friends Vital Records.
Cumberland County; Baptist Church
records, Dividing Creek; B5 (31-
29); Baptist Cem. Inscriptions,
Bridgeton; B5 (34-32, 61; 35-
90, 127; 36-158, 193).
Egg Harbor; Friends Vital Records;
Z4 (1-28, 33, 75, 121, 161);
Ear marks; Z4 (1-117).
Essex County; Coffins, 1761-1831;
B1 (24-80); Rev. War soldiers;
Z3 (66-183).
Fairfield; Dutch Church, name list,
1804-33; B1 (25-5).
Gloucester County; Sealing Docket,
1746-48; M (35-101; 36-16);
Deptford, tax on dogs, 1773; B1
(22-17); Griggstown; historical;
Z3 (66-105).
Hopewell, Maidenhead, Six Mile
Run; baptisms, 1710-15; B4 (26-
26).
Hunterdon County; Inscriptions; B1
(23-71).
Mendham; churches and records; Z3
(67-141).
Mercer County; Lawrence Twp.; In-
scriptions; B1 (21-81); East
Windsor Twp.; Inscriptions; B1
(21-83).
Middlesex County; North Brunswick
Twp.; Inscriptions; B1 (23-75);
Baptist marriages, South River,
1805-26; B1 (24-39).
Monmouth County; petition, 1781; M
(35-38); Church records (Dutch),
Freehold and Middletown; B1 (22-
1, 31, 59, 85; 23-11, 43, 67,
91; 24-19, 45, 49, 91; 25-20, 42,
61); Adelphia, Howell Twp.; Inscriptions; B1 (21-84; 22-19, 43,
63, 93; 23-15, 36, 61, 88); Cof-

fin accounts, 1756-1808; B1
(24-68).

Morris County; poll list, 1776;
Z3 (66-114); Revolutionary
Pension files; B1 (23-25, 85;
24-12, 41, 71, 87, 95; 25-16,
31, 67).

New Brunswick in 1825; Z3 (68-
93, 194, 322).

Ocean County; Inscriptions,
Whitesville; B1 (24-25).

Piscataway; Ear marks; B1 (21-
75; 22-12, 41, 71, 92; 23-19,
41, 65, 95; 25-14).

Secaucus, Hudson Co.; Inscriptions, Abel Smith Farm; A2
(78-132).

Somerset County; Inscriptions,
Hoagland Ground, Montgomery;
B1 (21-8); Inscriptions,
Nevius Ground, Montgomery; B1
(23-51).

Sussex County; Marriages, 1773-
1804; B1 (24-1).

Woodbury; Inscriptions, Reeves
Cemetery; Dt (14-47).

NEW YORK
Marriages, 1839-65, Middlesex,
Geneva, Victory, Gates, Penfield; Dt (13-51); Funerals,
1839-65; Dt (13-77); baptisms, 1839-65; Dt (13-115).

Albany; list of church records;
A1 (100-311).

Bainbridge, Chenango Co.; early
settlers; Dt (11-23).

Broome County; Windsor; church
founders; Dt (14-77).

Burlington Flats, Otsego Co.;
Inscriptions; A1 (101-230).

Cattaraugus County; Inscriptions, Abbott Cemetery; Ng (7-
335).

Cayuga County; Inscriptions,
Cato; A2 (80-10, 75).

Chateaugay; marriages records,
1846-55; Dt (14-14).

Claverack; Dutch Church records;
cont.; A2 (81-39, 81, 166,
233; 82-43, 108, 140, 202;
83-8, 73, 169, 204).

Edmeston, Otsego Co.; Inscriptions; A1 (101-92).

Erie County; Inscriptions,
Evans Center; YA (2-183, 219,
245; 3-275).

Fishkill, Dutchess Co.; church

marriages, 1731-   ; A2 (83-
93, 156, 231).

Fredonia; residents, 1825; Ng (7-
366).

Fulton County; Kingsboro, church
members, 1804; B4 (27-215).

Greene County; account book names,
Catskill area, 1753-82; Dt (16-
49).

Hempstead; Willett and Hicks correction; A2 (80-18).

Hopewell, Dutchess Co.; Marriages,
Church records; A2 (78-161; 79-
17).

Jefferson County; Inscriptions,
Champion; Dt (16-25).

Loonenburg [Athens], Greene Co.;
Church records; A2 (82-15, 81,
161, 227; 83-24, 109, 132, 240).

Long Island; source material; M
(36-61).

Newfield, Tompkins Co.; Inscriptions; Dt (11-20).

Newtown; Census, 1698; B4 (24-
133).

New York; sources; A1 (106-244).

New York; Trinity Church records;
cont.; A2 (78-28, 112; 79-148;
81-18, 96, 218; 82-98, 156; 83-
42).

New York; reburials in Woodlawn
Cemetery; A2 (80-15).

New York; Deaths, 1795-   ; A2
(81-146, 203).

New York; probate recor s; A2 (81-
44).

Otsego County; inscriptions, West
Burlington; A1 (104-43); Laurens; YA (5-765; 6-791, 817,
846); near Morris; YA (3-445,
469; 4-493, 517, 539, 559, 581,
607).

Palmyra; inscriptions; Dt (13-75).

St. Lawrence County; inscriptions,
DePeyster; A1 (104-93).

Saugerties; Katsbaan Church records; cont.; A2 (78-58; 79-29,
93, 204; 83-19).

Warren County; Inscriptions, Glen
Falls; Dt (16-21).

Warren; Inscriptions; A1 (100-316;
103-315).

Whitehall; inscriptions; A1 (106-
106).

Yonkers; St. John's Epis. Church
records, 1820-46; A2 (79-179).

NORTH CAROLINA

Sources; M (39-46).
Craven County; Inscriptions,
Tuscarora; M (39-91).
NOVA SCOTIA
Cumberland; records, 1765-71;
B4 (24-50).
OHIO
Butler County; marriages, 1803-
7; O1 (6-57, 110; 7-134).
Cincinnati; Inscriptions, Col-
umbia Bapt. Cemetery; O1 (5-
4-41).
Clermont County; Inscriptions,
Miami Twp; O1 (6-107, 108,
109; 7-60); near Mulberry;
O1 (6-56, 110); Union Twp;
O1 (7-58); Bethel, Tate Twp;
O1 (7-132, 195, 261); Goshen
Twp; O1 (7-199); small
grounds; O1 (7-198, 199); Ba-
tavia region; O1 (6-54, 55);
Batavia Twp; O1 (7-264; 8-68);
Franklin; O1 (10-253).
Granville; births, 1814-22; B4
(24-115).
Greene County; Inscriptions,
Spring Valley; O1 (8-327).
Hamilton County; Inscriptions;
Anderson Twp; O1 (6-53, 104;
7-193; 8-69, 149); North Bend;
O1 (7-53); Mariemont; O1 (8-
151); Symmes Twp; O1 (6-168;
7-55); Columbia Twp; O1 (7-
59); Duck Creek Bapt. Cemete-
ry; O1 (8-146); Springdale;
O1 (8-230, 328; 9-77, 167,
328; 10-78, 170); Camp Denni-
son; O1 (10-250).
Trumbull County; probate ab-
stracts; cont.; M (35-72; 36-
5, 76; 37-45; 38-24; 39-83).
Warren County; Inscriptions,
Maineville; O1 (9-75); Mur-
doch; O1 (9-247, 326).
ONTARIO
Vital Statistics, Chatham
Journal 1841-44; Dt (13-13);
Essex County families; Dt (14-
127).
PENNSYLVANIA
Sources; M (28-1).
Schwenckfelders; sources; M (39-
33).
German Reformed Church records;
M (37-33).
Mennonites; M (35-88).
Roster of Scouts and Spies

(1792); M (36-105).
Berks County; Baptisms, Lutheran
Church, Albany; M (39-105; 40-
10, 60, 101, 125).
Chester County; rate list for New-
lin, 1795; M (39-82); Rev. War
Pensioners, 1840; M (37-86).
Clairon County; Inscriptions; M
(36-83).
Fulton County; Inscriptions, Knobs-
ville; M (39-112).
Lancaster County; Millersville
Cem. inscriptions; M (35-73; 36-
7); Carpenter's Church Cem.; M
(36-42); Maytown Churchyard; M
(37-71); Salem Churchyard; M
(38-9, 53); Conestoga Cem.; M
(39-71).
Mercersburg, Franklin Co.; church
marriages, 1769-1812; P (15-
187).
Middle Smithfield, Monroe Co.; Inscriptions; A2 (79-123).
Montgomery County; Inscriptions,
St. Peter's, Barren Hill; P (15-
198; 16-108).
Philadelphia [Holmesburg]; Crispin
Cemetery; P (16-23).
Washington County; marriages,
1825-6; M (36-78); Rangers,
1793; M (37-43).
York County; families; M (38-57).
RHODE ISLAND
Additions and Corrections to Aus-
tin's Gen. Dict.; cont.; B4 (24-
69; 25-249; 26-54, 228; 27-216).
Block Island; notes on early fami-
lies; A1 (105-183, 249; 106-
103).
Portsmouth; items, Friends' Rec-
ords; A1 (103-231).
Tiverton; mortuary list, 1772-
1824; A1 (105-213).
SOUTH CAROLINA
Sources; M (40-81).
Manuscripts in S. C. Hist. Society;
cont.; J (48-48, 177).
Marriages, Abbeville and Anderson
Cos.; M (40-120).
Marriages and death notice, The
City Gazette; J (48-12, 76, 134,
198; 49-15, 76, 153, 208; 50-14,
71, 127, 204; 51-24, 97, 164,
243; 52-48, 107, 180, 233; 53-
48, 113, 172, 241); Greenville
Mountaineer; J (49-57, 119; 50-
46, 101, 156, 216; Pendleton

Messenger; J (48-35, 112).
German Protestants, 1794; J (51-75).
Beaufort County; Inscriptions; J (51-171).
Charleston; records of St. Philip's Parish; J (48-26); organists, St. Michael's; J (53-146, 212).
John's Island; Inscriptions; J (50-163).
Laurens County; Inscriptions, Duncan's Creek; J (49-225).
Marlboro County; marriage licenses, 1788-1826; M (40-51).
St. Bartholomew's Parish; J (50-173); Vestry minutes, 1822-40; J (51-10, 78, 145, 229; 52-34).
Springville, Darlington Co.; J (53-190).
TENNESSEE
Signers of Constitution, 1834; M (37-11).
TEXAS
First Census, 1829-36; M (40-49, 95, 122).
VERMONT
Probate Districts; B4 (27-65).
Marriages, 1843-57; 1873-5; A1 (103-44, 48).
Fairlee, West Fairlee, Bradford; births, 1768-1820; A1 (104-21, 114; 262; 105-155).
Wells; poll list, 1782; Dt (13-132).
VIRGINIA
Parochial and County Court records; V3 (56-125).
Rent rolls (Lord Fairfax), 1746-76; M (39-113).
Emigrants to Edgar Co., Ill.; M (36-73).
Governors, 1606-1940; V1 (32-1, 153, 262).
Vital records, diaries of Rev. Jacob Richardson Scott; M (39-40).
Lincoln Militia, 1782; N3 (49-396).
Albemarle Parish; V1 (31-147).
Buckingham County; militia, 1775; V3 (56-206); marriage bonds, 1785-94; V3 (57-82).
Caroline County; churches; V3 (58-457).
Charles City County; court rec-
ords, 1762-4; V3 (59-103).
Cobham, Surry Co.; Historical; V3 (57-252).
Culpeper County; wills; N3 (50-369).
Denbigh, Warwick Co.; church; V3 (57-286).
Elmington, Gloucester Co.; V3 (55-247).
Gloucester County; land holdings, Ware Neck; V3 (60-64).
Greenbrier County; Petition, 1777; M (38-119).
Henrico and Chesterfield Counties; colonial churches; V3 (55-45, 147).
Isle of Wight County; marriages, 1773-4; V1 (32-29).
Middlesex County; Militia, 1730; V3 (57-80).
Northampton County; sources and records; M (35-33).
Spotsylvania County; churches; V3 (58-442).
Stafford County; missing Will Book K; V3 (57-67).
Westmoreland and King George Counties; churches; V3 (56-154, 280).
WEST VIRGINIA
Intermont; Hebron Lutheran Church; M (38-6, 53).
Berkeley County; selective records; N3 (50-276).
WISCONSIN
Marriages, Hudson, 1855-63; M (40-89).

French and Indian War
  Diary of Benjamin Glasier of
    Ipswich, 1758-60; Y1 (86-65).
  Journal of Ashley Bowen, 1759-
    61; cont. (70-266); Y1 (88-
    336).
  Deaths, French Prison Camps,
    1757-58; B4 (25-157).
Genealogy
  American Society of Genealogists;
    P (15-161).
  General; P (17-33).
  Emigration Routes; Col (11-33).
  High School activities; M (35-
    71).
  Hints for amateurs; M (37-100).
  Age of girls at marriage; B4
    (27-116).
  Directories in the Library of
    Congress; cont.; B4 (27-142).
  National Archives; M (36-37);
    A1 (105-42).
  Realty rights of husbands and
    wives; A1 (102-254; 103-153).
  Genealogy for amateurs; A1
    (103-95).
  Frequency of given names; Dt
    (8-59).
  Right of Privacy; B4 (25-145).
  Memorial spoons; A2 (80-194).
  County atlases listed; M (37-
    4).
  Perpetual Calendars; B4 (28-
    188).
  Quaker sources; M (38-37).
Heraldry
  College of Arms; P (15-153).
  Roll of Arms; A1 (106-163, 258).
  Information; Ng (7-354); M (40-
    1).
  See Holland under Place Index.
Norway, Surnames; NAH (12-1);
  Quakers of 1825; NAH (1-60).
Revolutionary War and Soldiers
  Some items are in Place Index
    under states and counties.
  Index of Pensioners; M; separ-
    ately paged; cont.; Vols.
    35-40.
  Order book of Lt.-Col. Francis
    Barber, 1779; Z3 (65-61, 143,

209; 66-48, 122, 197).
  Connecticut Rolls; B4 (26-79).
  Conn. soldiers proved by pension
    records of other soldiers; M
    (35-108).
  Kentucky soldiers in Battle of
    Blue Licks; N3 (47-247).
  Items in Family Pioneer (Bruns-
    wick, Me.), 1833-4; A1 (104-
    205).
  Mass. soldiers, proof in pension
    records of other soldiers; M
    (35-20).
  Chester Co., Pa.; Pensioners,
    1840; M (37-86).
  Mississippi pensioners; M (40-4).
  Papers of Capt. John Currier,
    Amesbury, Mass.; Y1 (84-254,
    349).
  Capt. Samuel Griffith's Pay Roll,
    1777, Md.; M (36-87).
  Maryland Troops, Battle of Harlem
    Heights; X1 (43-1).
  Basil Waring's Militia Co., 1777,
    Maryland; M (36-4).
  Regimental Book of Capt. James
    Bentham, 1778-80; J (53-13, 101,
    161, 230).
Royal or ruling families
  Brabant; B4 (25-224; 26-188; 28-
    23).
  Counts of West Friesland and Hol-
    land; M (36-80).
  Agatha wife of Eadward Atheling;
    A1 (106-52).
  Counts of Gelres and Zutphen; A1
    (104-206).
  Carolingians, early; A1 (101-109).
  Theophano; B4 (26-186, 233).
  Bernadotte; A1 (103-251).
  Baliol; A1 (106-273).
  Plantagenet; descent from German
    Emperors; A1 (101-37); descent
    from Kings of Hungary and Em-
    perors of the East; A1 (101-77).
  Capet; early ancestry; M (39-69).
  Early Tsars of Bulgaria; B4 (27-
    31).
  Grand Princes of Kiev; B4 (28-91,
    177).
Ships and Shipping Lists

MY OWN INDEX

As already explained in the Preface, this is a selective index of families treated in certain pedigree or ancestral books which deal chiefly with New England and Long Island families. Sometimes the best account in print is found in one of these books. In other cases the account may merely be based on earlier and more comprehensive publications, such as a family history. Often the account gives references to other printed sources where data will be found on the family under discussion.

We have followed the precedent of Savage in stating only the names of <u>towns</u>, following the names of the founders of each family. Since most of those in the index were New England settlers, it is believed that this will be ample to identify the family for the searcher.

KEY

ANDERSON, MARY AUDENTIA SMITH
1. Ancestry and Posterity of Joseph Smith and Emma Hale. Independence, Mo., 1929.
AVERY, SAMUEL PUTNAM
1. The Warren, Little, Lothrop, Park, Dix, Whitman, Fairchild, Platt, Wheeler, Lane and Avery Pedigree of Samuel Putnam Avery. New York, 1925.
BOARDMAN, WILLIAM F. J.
1. The Ancestry of William Francis Joseph Boardman. Hartford, 1906.
BOOTH, CHARLES EDWIN
1. One Branch of the Booth Family. New York, 1910.
CONSTANT
1. The Journal of the Reverend Silas Constant....of ...Yorktown, N. Y. By Emily Warren Roebling, ed. Josiah Granville Leach. Philadelphia, 1903.
CORY, CHARLES HENRY, JR.
1. Lineal Ancestors of Captain James Cory and of his Descendants. 1937.
2. Lineal Ancestors of Rhoda (Axtell) Cory, mother of Captain James Cory. 1937.
3. Lineal Ancestors of Susan (Mulford) Cory, wife of Captain James Cory. 1937.
4. Lineal Ancestors of Susan (Kitchell) Mulford, mother of Mrs. Susan (Mulford) Cory. 1937.
5. Lineal Ancestors of Rufus Rennington Young and Jane Vosburgh. 1937.
CRAWFORD, HANNAH-LOUISE-MACNAIR
1. Maternal Ancestry of Charles Whiting MacNair. Boston, privately printed, 1912.

DAVIS, WALTER GOODWIN
    1. The Ancestry of Lydia Harmon. Boston, Mass., 1924.
    2. The Ancestry of Lieut. Amos Towne. Portland, Me.,
            1927.
    3. The Ancestry of Sarah Stone. Portland, Me., 1930.
    4. The Ancestry of Bethia Harris. Portland, Me.
            1934.
    5. The Ancestry of Sarah Miller, Portland, Me. 1939.
    6. The Ancestry of James Patten. Portland, Me., 1941.
    7. The Ancestry of Joseph Neal. Portland, Me., 1945.
    8. The Ancestry of Annis Spear. Portland, Me., 1945.
    9. The Ancestry of Phoebe Tilton. Portland, Me.,
            1947.
    10. The Ancestry of Joseph Waterhouse. Portland, Me.,
            1949.
DE FOREST, L. EFFINGHAM [and ANNE LAWRENCE]
    1. Moore and Allied Families. The Ancestry of William
            Henry Moore. New York, 1938.
    2. Our Colonial and Continental Ancestors. The Ances-
            try of Mr. and Mrs. Louis William Dommerich.
            New York, 1930.
FERRIS, MARY WALTON
    1. Dawes-Gates Ancestral Lines. Chicago, 1931, 1943
            (2 vols.)
FLAGG, ERNEST
    1. The Founding of New England. Hartford, 1926.
GOLDTHWAITE, CHARLOTTE
    1. Boardman Genealogy 1525-1895. Hartford, 1895.
GOODWIN, NATHANIEL
    1. Genealogical Notes. Hartford, 1856.
HOLMAN, ALFRED L.
    1. Blackman and Allied Families. Chicago, 1928.
HOLMAN, MARY LOVERING
    2. Ancestry of Charles Stinson Pillsbury and John
            Sargent Pillsbury. Concord, N. H., 1938.
    3. The Scott Genealogy. Boston, 1919.
    4. Ancestry of Colonel John Harrington Stevens and
            his wife Frances Helen Miller. Concord, N. H.,
            1948. [Completed by Winifred Lovering Holman.]
HOLMAN, WINIFRED LOVERING
    5. Ancestry of Colonel John Harrington Stevens and
            his wife Frances Helen Miller. Vol. II. Con-
            cord, N. H., 1952.
HORTON, BYRON BARNES
    1. The Ancestors and Descendants of Zachariah Eddy
            of Warren, Pa. Rutland, Vt., 1930.
JACOBUS, DONALD LINES
    1. An American Family: Botsford-Marble Ancestral
            Lines. New Haven, 1933.
    2. The Waterman Family. Volume I. Descendants of
            Robert Waterman of Marshfield, Mass. New Haven,
            1939.

3. The Granberry Family and Allied Families. New
   Haven, 1945.
4. ed. Ancestry of Thomas Chalmers Brainerd. Montreal, 1948.
5. Hale, House and Related Families. Donald Lines
   Jacobus and Edgar Francis Waterman. Hartford,
   1952.

LINZEE, JOHN WILLIAM .
1. The History of Peter Parker and Sarah Ruggles of
   Roxbury, Mass. and their ancestors and descendants. Boston, 1913.

MORRIS, MYRTLE M.
1. Joseph and Philena (Elton) Fellows Their Ancestry
   and Descendants. n. d. (1941).

MORSE, REV. ABNER [A. M.]
1 to 3. The Genealogy of the Descendants of Several
   Ancient Puritans. Boston, 1857, 1859, 1861.

SELLECK, LILLIAN LOUNSBERRY (MINER)
1. One Branch of the Miner Family with extensive notes
   on the Wood, Lounsberry, Rogers and fifty other
   allied families of Connecticut and Long Island.
   New Haven, Conn., 1928.

SEVERSMITH, HERBERT FURMAN
1. Colonial Families of Long Island, New York and
   Connecticut. Mimeographed, 25 copies. Vol. 1,
   1939. Vol. 2, n. d. Vol. 3, 1948. [Further
   volumes are planned.]

SHEPPARD, WALTER LEE, JR.
1. The Ancestry and Descendants of Thomas Stickney
   Evans and Sarah Ann Fifield his wife. Privately printed, 1940.

STARR, FRANK FARNSWORTH
1. Goodwin-Morgan Ancestral Lines. 1915.
2. The Newberry Family. Hartford, 1898.
3. The Olcott Family. Hartford, 1899.
4. The Roberts Family. Hartford, 1896.
5. The Edward Jackson Family. Hartford, 1895.
6. The Thomas Spencer Family. Hartford, 1896.
7. The Williamson and Cobb Families. Hartford, 1896.

TINGLEY, RAYMON MEYERS
1. Some Ancestral Lines. Rutland, Vt., 1935. [To
   be used with caution]

UNDERHILL, LORA ALTINE WOODBURY
1. Descendants of Edward Small and the Allied Families. Cambridge, 1910. [After this was added
   to the Index, a second edition was published
   (1934) in which the same family names appear,
   but the page numbers given apply to the first
   edition.]

VINTON, JOHN ADAMS
1. The Giles Memorial. Boston, 1864.
2. The Vinton Memorial. Boston, 1858.

WATERMAN, EDGAR FRANCIS; see Jacobus.
WHITE, JOHN BARBER
   1. Ancestry of John Barber White. Haverhill, 1913.

ABBE, JOHN; Wenham; Jacobus 3.
ABBOT, GEORGE; Rowley; Booth 1.
ABELL, ROBERT; Rehoboth; Jacobus 3; Booth 1.
ACKERLY, ROBERT; Southold; Seversmith 1.
ACKLEY, NICHOLAS; Hartford Haddam; Ferris 1 (2-33).
ADAMS, HENRY; Braintree; Jacobus 3; Jacobus 4; Vinton 2; Booth 1; Morse 1 (p. 1).
ADAMS, JAMES; Londonderry; Holman 2.
ADAMS, JAMES; Westerly; Holman 1.
ADAMS, JEREMY; Hartford; Seversmith 1.
ADAMS, WILLIAM; Ipswich; Tingley 1; Seversmith 1.
ADGATE, THOMAS; Norwich; Jacobus 3; Jacobus 4.
AKERLEY, see Ackerly.
ALDEN, JOHN; Plymouth; Horton 1; Crawford 1 (p. 45); Jacobus 4; Vinton 2.
ALDRICH, GEORGE; Braintree, Mendon; Tingley 1.
ALEXANDER, GEORGE; Windsor, Northampton; de Forest 2.
ALLANSON, RALPH; Scarborough; see Dixon; Davis 5 (pp. 63-69).
ALLEN, ANDREW; Lynn, Andover; Holman 2.
ALLEN, EDWARD; Ipswich, Suffield; Starr 1 (2-113).
ALLEN, GEORGE; Sandwich; de Forest 1.
ALLEN, JOHN (CAPTAIN); Charlestown; Flagg 1 (p. 263).
ALLEN, JOSHUA; Windham; Jacobus 3.
ALLEN, MALCOLM; Botetourt Co., Va.; White 1.
ALLEN, SAMUEL; Braintree; Vinton 2.
ALLEN, SAMUEL; Windsor; de Forest 2; Jacobus 5.
ALLEN, WILLIAM; Salem, Manchester; Tingley 1; Jacobus 3.
ALLEN, WILLIAM; Salisbury; de Forest 1; Jacobus 3.

ALLERTON, ISAAC; Plymouth, New York, New Haven; Underhill 1 (2 - 596); Holman 3 (p. 190); Seversmith 1.
ALLYN, MARGARET (WYATT); English ancestry; Crawford 1 (p. 75); Flagg 1 (p. 358).
ALLYN, MATTHEW; Cambridge, Hartford, Windsor; Crawford 1 (p. 66); Flagg 1 (pp. 267, 221, 307); Jacobus 4.
ALLYN, ROBERT; Manchester, New London; Holman 1; Jacobus 2 (pp. 603-606); Jacobus 3.
ALVORD, ALEXANDER; Windsor, Northampton; de Forest 1; see Booth 1.
ALVORD, BENEDICT; Windsor; White 1.
ANDERSON, SAMUEL; Blandford; Jacobus 4.
ANDREWS, JOHN; Farmington; Flagg 1 (pp. 224, 184, 160, 147).
ANDREWS, NICHOLAS; Marblehead; Ferris 1 (2-57).
ANDREWS, ROBERT; Ipswich; de Forest 2; Davis 8.
ANDREWS, THOMAS; Hingham; Underhill 1 (2-686).
ANDREWS, WILLIAM; New Haven; White 1.
ANGELL, THOMAS; Providence; Tingley 1.
ANNIS, CORMAC [CHARLES]; Newbury; Wells; Davis 8.
APPLETON, SAMUEL and JUDITH (EVERARD); Ipswich, Rowley; Boardman 1 (pp. 314, 292); Flagg 1 (pp. 282, 242, 307, 315, 391); Jacobus 3; Davis 9.
ARCHER, SAMUEL; Salem; Tingley 1.
ARMITAGE, JOSEPH and GODFREY; Lynn; Seversmith 1 (p. 155).
ARMITAGE, THOMAS; Sandwich, Hempstead, Oyster Bay; also Yorkshire, Eng., families; Seversmith 1.
ARNOLD, JOHN; Hartford; Jacobus 4.
ASHTON, JAMES; Providence; Tingley 1.
ASLETT [ASSELBEE], JOHN; Rowley, Andover; Jacobus 3; Sheppard 1.
ATKINSON, THEODORE and JOHN; Boston

and Newbury; Holman 2.
ATWATER, DAVID and JOSHUA; New
    Haven; Holman 4.
AVERY, CHRISTOPHER; New London;
    Jacobus 3.
AVERY, WILLIAM (DR.); Dedham,
    Boston; Avery 1 (p. 195); Jaco-
    bus 3.
AXTELL, THOMAS; Sudbury; Cory 2
    (p. 1).
AYER, JOHN; Salisbury, Haverhill;
    Holman 2; de Forest 1; Jacobus
    3; Sheppard 1.

BABCOCK, see Badcock.
BACKUS, WILLIAM; Saybrook, Nor-
    wich; de Forest 1; Jacobus 3;
    Jacobus 4; Jacobus 5.
BACON, NATHANIEL; Middletown; de
    Forest 1.
BACON, MICHAEL; Dedham; Holman 4.
BADCOCK [BABCOCK], ROBERT (CAPT.);
    Dorchester, Milton; Jacobus 3;
    Holman 5.
BAGLEY, ORLANDO; Salisbury; Holman
    2; Anderson 1.
BAILEY, JAMES and RICHARD; Rowley;
    Holman 2.
BAILEY, JOHN; Salisbury; Davis 9.
BAKER, EDWARD; Lynn; Ferris 1 (1-
    67).
BAKER, JOHN; Ipswich; Tingley 1;
    Anderson 1.
BAKER, RICHARD; Dorchester; Cory
    2 (p. 56).
BALCH, JOHN; Salem; Ferris 1 (1-
    70); Tingley 1.
BALDOCK; Sussex, Eng.; Jacobus 4.
BALDWIN, JOHN "SR."; Milford; de
    Forest 1; White 1.
BALDWIN, JOSEPH; Milford, Hadley;
    Booth 1.
BALDWIN; Buckinghamshire, Eng.;
    ancestral to Conn. Baldwins;
    Seversmith 1.
BALDWIN, GEORGE; Hempstead; Sever-
    smith 1.
BALDWIN, SARAH [w. Searle and Ed-
    wards]; Springfield; Holman 3
    (p. 247).
BALDWIN, SYLVESTER; Milford;
    Flagg 1 (p. 249).
BALDWIN, TIMOTHY; Milford; Jaco-
    bus 1 (p. 29).
BALL, FRANCIS; Springfield; Hol-
    man 4.
BALL, JOHN; Concord; White 1.

BALLARD, WILLIAM; Lynn; de Forest 2.
BANCROFT, JOHN; Lynn; Booth 1.
BANGS, EDWARD; Plymouth, Eastham;
    Ferris 1 (2-61).
BARBER, JOHN; Boston; White 1.
BARBER, THOMAS; Windsor; Morris 1;
    White 1.
BARDEN, JOHN; Marshfield, Barnstable,
    Middleboro; Tingley 1.
BARKER, ROBERT and JOHN; Duxbury,
    Marshfield; Tingley 1; Seversmith 1.
BARLOW, JOHN; Fairfield; Booth 1.
BARLOW, THOMAS; Fairfield; Selleck
    1.
BARNARD, BARTHOLOMEW; Hartford;
    Starr 1 (1-47).
BARNARD, THOMAS; Salisbury; Holman
    2.
BARNES, JOSHUA; Yarmouth; Southamp-
    ton; Seversmith 1.
BARNES, THOMAS; New Haven, Middle-
    town; Morris 1; Jacobus 4; Ander-
    son 1.
BARNES, WILLIAM; Salisbury, Ames-
    bury; Holman 2.
BARNEY, JACOB; Salem; Holman 4.
BARRETT; Suffolk and Norwich, Eng.;
    Jacobus 5 (p. 648).
BARTLETT, JOHN; Marblehead; Ferris
    1 (2-71).
BARTLETT, RICHARD; Newbury; Holman
    2.
BARTLETT, ROBERT; Plymouth; de For-
    est 1.
BASSETT, DAVID; Boston; Jacobus 2
    (pp. 609-610).
BASSETT, WILLIAM; Lynn; Flagg 1 (pp.
    250, 212, 178, 157).
BATCHELDER, JOHN, HENRY and JOSEPH;
    Salem; Ferris 1 (2-97); Holman 3
    (p. 207).
BATCHELDER, WILLIAM; Charlestown;
    Seversmith 1.
BATES, CLEMENT; Hingham; Cory 4.
BATES, JAMES; Dorchester; Booth 1.
BAYLEY, JOSEPH; Huntington; Sever-
    smith 1.
BEACH, THOMAS; Milford; Anderson 1.
BEAMON, SIMON; Springfield; Starr 1
    (1-141); Ferris 1 (2-105).
BEAMON, WILLIAM; Salem, Saybrook;
    Ferris 1 (2-117).
BEAMSLEY, WILLIAM; Boston; Ferris 1
    (1-84); Sheppard 1.
BEARD, (WIDOW) MARTHA; Milford; Mor-
    ris 1.
BEARDING, NATHANIEL; Hartford; Mor-

BOSWORTH, EDWARD; Hingham; Tingley 1; Anderson 1.
BOSWORTH, HANNIEL; Ipswich, Haverhill; Ferris 1 (1-105).
BOTSFORD, HENRY; Milford; Jacobus 1; de Forest 1.
BOURNE, THOMAS; Marshfield; Jacobus 2 (pp. 615-624); de Forest 1; Jacobus 3.
BOWEN, GRIFFITH; Boston; Linzee 1 (p. 511).
BOWEN, RICHARD; Salem, Rehoboth; White 1.
BOWLES, JOSEPH; Wells; Sheppard 1.
BOYKIN, JARVIS; Charlestown, New Haven; Boardman 1 (p. 239).
BOYLSTON, THOMAS; Watertown; Vinton 2.
BOYNTON, WILLIAM and JOHN; Rowley; Holman 2; White 1.
BRACY, THOMAS; New Haven, York; Davis 3.
BRADFORD, ROBERT; Beverly; Davis 4.
BRADFORD, WILLIAM; Plymouth; Crawford 1 (p. 31); Jacobus 2 (pp. 625-630); Jacobus 3; Jacobus 4.
BRADISH, ROBERT; Boston; Jacobus 4.
BRADLEY, (WIDOW) ELIZABETH; New Haven, Guilford; Morris 1.
BRADLEY, (MARY m. THOMAS LEAVER); Rowley; Sheppard 1.
BRADLEY, WILLIAM; New Haven; de Forest 1; White 1; Anderson 1.
BRADSTREET, HUMPHREY; Ipswich; White 1.
BRAGG, EDWARD; Ipswich; Holman 2.
BRAINERD, DANIEL; Hartford, Haddam; Ferris 1 (2-129); Jacobus 4.
BRANCH, PETER; Marshfield; Holman 3 (p. 270).
BRANDON, WILLIAM; Weymouth; Jacobus 3.
BRASS, [HENDRICK PIETERSZEN]; New York, Flatlands; Seversmith 1.
BREAD [BREED], Allen; Lynn; de Forest 2.
BRETT, WILLIAM; Bridgewater; (William3, Norwich, Conn.); Jacobus 2 (p. 631).
BREWER, DANIEL; Roxbury; Ferris 1 (1-108); Booth 1.
BREWER, THOMAS; Roxbury, Hampton; Sheppard 1.
BREWSTER, FRANCIS; New Haven; (Rev. Nathaniel, Brookhaven); Seversmith 1.
BREWSTER, WILLIAM (ELDER); Plymouth; Ferris 1 (2-143); Selleck 1; de Forest 1.
BRIDGE, EDWARD; Roxbury; Ferris 1 (1-113).
BRIGHAM, ANNE and CONSTANCE (w. Simon and Robert Crosby); Holman 2.
BRIGHAM, THOMAS; Cambridge; Morse 2 (p. 1).
BRILL, ANNA MARGARETHA [wid. Johannes]; Fishkill; Seversmith 1.
BROCKLEBANK, (WIDOW) JANE; Rowley; Anderson 1.
BRONSON, JOHN; Hartford, Farmington; Boardman 1 (pp. 252, 177); de Forest 2.
BROOKS, THOMAS; Haddam; Jacobus 4.
BROOKS, WILLIAM and GILBERT; Scituate, Rehoboth; Tingley 1.
BROWN, ANDREW; Scarborough; Boston; Davis 5 (pp. 47-61); Davis 10.
BROWN, EDWARD; Ipswich; Jacobus 3; Tingley 1.
BROWN, [GEORGE] and CHRISTIAN (HIBBERT); Salisbury; Davis 1.
BROWNE, JOHN; Duxbury, Taunton; Jacobus 3 (p. 340).
BROWN, JOHN; Ipswich; Davis 9.
BROWNE, JOHN; Milford; Cory 2 (p. 277).
BROWN, JOHN; Pemaquid; Jacobus 4.
BROWNE, NATHANIEL; Middletown; de Forest 1.
BROWNE, NICHOLAS; Lynn, Reading; de Forest 2.
BROWNE, RICHARD; Watertown; White 1.
BROWNE, THOMAS; Newbury; Holman 2.
BROWNE, WILLIAM; Gloucester; Ferris 1 (1-120).
BROWNING, THOMAS; Salem, Topsfield; Davis 2; Jacobus 3.
BRUCE, GEORGE; Woburn; Sheppard 2.
BRUEN, OBADIAH; Marshfield, Gloucester, New London, Newark; Cory 4; White 1.
BRUSH, RICHARD and THOMAS; Huntington, Southold; Seversmith 1.
BRYAN, ALEXANDER; Milford; Starr 1 (2-283); Selleck 1; Seversmith 1.
BRYANT, JOHN (LIEUT.); Plymouth; Jacobus 2 (pp. 632-635).
BUCK, EMANUEL; Wethersfield; Boardman 1 (p. 190).

BUCKLAND, WILLIAM; Hingham, Rehoboth; Anderson 1.
BUELL, WILLIAM; Windsor; Starr 1 (1-124); Booth 1.
BULL, ROBERT; Saybrook; Ferris 1 (2-159).
BULL, THOMAS (CAPT.); Hartford; Booth 1.
BULLARD, BENJAMIN and GEORGE; Watertown; Morse 1 (pp. 10, 38, 46 3/4).
BUMSTEAD, THOMAS; Boston; Ferris 1 (1-123).
BUNNELL, WILLIAM; New Haven; Anderson 1.
BURBANK, JOHN; Newbury; Booth 1.
BURGE, JOHN; Weymouth, Chelmsford, Dorchester; Holman 2.
BURNAP, ROBERT; Roxbury, Reading; de Forest 2.
BURNHAM, ROBERT, JOHN and THOMAS; Ipswich, Boston, Dover; Holman 2; Ferris 1 (1-129).
BURNHAM, THOMAS; Hartford, Windsor; Flagg 1 (pp. 239, 193, 165); Seversmith 1.
BURROWES, WILLIAM; Providence; Seversmith 1.
BURSLEY, JOHN; Weymouth, Barnstable; Holman 3 (p. 235); Jacobus 3.
BURT, HENRY and ULALIA (MARCH); Springfield; Holman 4; Booth 1; Jacobus 5.
BURWELL, JOHN; Milford; Boardman 1 (pp. 282, 223, 145); Cory 2 (p. 291).
BUSHNELL, FRANCIS; Guilford; Ferris 1 (2-163); Jacobus 3; Seversmith 1.
BUSWELL, ISAAC; Salisbury; Holman 2.
BUTLER, JAMES; Lancaster, Woburn, Billerica; White 1.
BUTLER, JOHN; Hartford, Branford; White 1.
BUTLER, RICHARD (DEA.); Hartford; Booth 1.
BUTTERWORTH, HENRY; Weymouth; Holman 4.
BUXTON, ANTHONY; Salem; Jacobus 3.

CADY, NICHOLAS; (Ebenezer[4], Canaan, N. Y.); Jacobus 2 (p. 612).
CAESAR, PAUL WILHELM; New York;

de Forest 2.
CAKEBREAD, THOMAS; Watertown, Sudbury; Ferris 1 (1-663).
CALDWELL, ALEXANDER; Litchfield, N. H.; Holman 2.
CALKINS, HUGH; Gloucester, New London, Norwich; Cory 1 (p. 278); Jacobus 3.
CALL, THOMAS; Charlestown; Ferris 1 (1-132); Tingley 1.
CAMP, NICHOLAS, EDWARD, WILLIAM; Milford; Boardman 1 (pp. 148, 213, 228, 141); de Forest 1; Morris 1.
CANFIELD, THOMAS; Milford; Boardman 1 (pp. 226, 147, 94, 74, 59); Morris 1.
CAPEN, RADIGONE (CLAPP) [w. John]; Dorchester; Holman 3 (p. 229).
CARLETON, EDWARD; Rowley; Holman 2; Sheppard 1 (also ancestry of Edward's mother, Jane Gibbon).
CARPENTER, JULIANA [w. Morton] and Alice [w. Southworth, Bradford]; Wrington, Somerset, Eng.; Holman 3 (p. 284); Jacobus 4.
CARPENTER, WILLIAM; Rehoboth; Seversmith 1; Holman 4.
CARTER, NICHOLAS; Stamford, Newtown, L. I.; Cory 1 (p. 332).
CARTER, THOMAS; Charlestown; Ferris 1 (1-142); Holman 4.
CASE, JOHN; Simsbury; Goodwin 1; de Forest 1.
CASS, JOHN; Hampton; Tingley 1.
CATLIN, THOMAS; Hartford; Booth 1.
CHALKER, ALEXANDER; Guilford, Saybrook; Ferris 1 (2-175).
CHALLIS, PHILIP (LIEUT.); Ipswich, Amesbury; Holman 2.
CHAMBERLAIN, EDMUND, THOMAS and WILLIAM; Roxbury, Chelmsford, Malden, Woodstock, Billerica; Linzee 1 (pp. 540, 370, 227).
CHAMPION, HENRY; Lyme; Anderson 1.
CHAMPION, THOMAS; Hempstead; Seversmith 1.
CHANDLER, EDMUND; Scituate, Duxbury; Underhill 1 (2-854).
CHANDLER, WILLIAM; Roxbury; Booth 1.
CHAPIN, SAMUEL; Roxbury, Springfield; Starr 1 (2-123).
CHAPLIN, HUGH; Rowley; Holman 2.
CHAPMAN, EDWARD; Windsor; Starr 1 (1-155); Ferris 1 (2-181).
CHAPMAN, RALPH; Marshfield; Holman 4.
CHAPMAN, ROBERT; Saybrook; Ferris 1

(2-185); Booth 1.
CHARLES, JOHN; Branford; Jacobus 3.
CHASE, AQUILA; Hampton, Newbury; Holman 2; Davis 8.
CHATER, JOHN; Newbury; Davis 5.
CHATTERTON, WILLIAM; New Haven; Boardman 1 (p. 174).
CHEEVER, EZEKIEL; New Haven, Boston; de Forest 2.
CHENEY, JOHN; Newbury; Holman 2; Davis 9.
CHESTER, LEONARD; Wethersfield; Goodwin 1.
CHIDSEY, JOHN; East Haven; Anderson 1.
CHILD, BENJAMIN, EPHRAIM and WILLIAM; Watertown, Roxbury; Linzee 1 (pp. 545, 381).
CHIPMAN, JOHN; Plymouth, Barnstable; Anderson 1.
CHITTENDEN, WILLIAM (MAJOR) and JOANNA (SHEAFFE); Guilford; Flagg 1 (p. 295, 311, 341); Morris 1.
CHURCH, RICHARD; Hartford, Hadley; Jacobus 4; Jacobus 5.
CHURCH; Runwell, co Essex, Eng.; Davis 4.
CHURCHILL, JOHN; Plymouth; de Forest 1.
CHURCHILL, JOSIAH; Wethersfield; Jacobus 4; Booth 1.
CLAPP, ROGER (CAPT.); Dorchester; Ferris 1 (1-155); White 1.
CLAPP, THOMAS, NICHOLAS, JOHN, EDWARD; Dorchester, Weymouth, Scituate; Holman 3 (p. 224); Davis 7; Holman 4.
CLARK, DANIEL; Windsor; Goodwin 1.
CLARK, EDWARD; Haverhill; Ferris 1 (1-177).
CLARK, GEORGE "JR."; Milford; Selleck 1.
CLARK, JAMES; New Haven; Boardman 1 (p. 244).
CLARK, JOHN (ELDER); Hartford, Saybrook, Milford; Boardman 1 (pp. 303, 290); Ferris 1 (2-201); de Forest 1; Jacobus 3; Jacobus 4; Jacobus 5.
CLARK, ROWLAND; Dedham; Tingley 1.
CLARK, THADDEUS; Falmouth; Tingley 1.
CLARK, WILLIAM; Dorchester, Northampton; Jacobus 2 (pp. 637-640).

CLARK, WILLIAM; Hartford, Haddam; Ferris 1 (2-207).
CLARK, WILLIAM; Watertown, Woburn; Sheppard 1.
CLAUSEN, DIRCK; New York; Tingley 1.
CLEEVE, GEORGE; Falmouth; Tingley 1.
CLEMENTS, ROBERT; Haverhill; Holman 2; Sheppard 1.
CLESSON, Northampton, Deerfield, Holman 3 (p. 250).
CLOICE, JOHN; Watertown; Holman 4.
CLOUGH, JOHN; Salisbury; Holman 2.
COBB, HENRY; Plymouth, Barnstable; Starr 7 (p. 37); Anderson 1.
COBB, JOHN and AUGUSTINE; Taunton; Jacobus 3.
COCHRAN, JAMES; Topsham; Holman 2.
COE, ROBERT; Watertown, Wethersfield, Stamford, Newtown, Jamaica, Hempstead; Ferris 1 (2-211).
COFFIN, TRISTRAM (GOV.); Haverhill, Nantucket; Holman 2.
COGAN, MARY [w. Roger Ludlow] and ELIZABETH [w. John Endecott]; Chard, co. Somerset, Eng.; Seversmith 1.
COGSWELL, JOHN; Ipswich; Ferris 1 (1-188); Jacobus 3.
COIT, JOHN; Marblehead, New London; Starr 1 (2-433); Selleck 1; Ferris 1 (1-191).
COLBURN, NATHANIEL; Dedham; Tingley 1.
COLBY, ANTHONY; Boston, Salisbury; Holman 2; Jacobus 2 (p. 8); Anderson 1.
COLCORD, EDWARD; Hampton, Exeter; Sheppard 1.
COLEY, SAMUEL; Milford; Starr 1 (2-163).
COLFS [COLVER], JACOBUS; New York; Seversmith 1.
COLLIER, WILLIAM; Plymouth, Duxbury; de Forest 1; Booth 1.
COLLINS, EDWARD; Cambridge, Charlestown; Starr 1 (2-383); Boardman 1 (pp. 294, 242); Jacobus 4; Seversmith 1.
COLLINS, JOHN; Boston; Holman 4.
COLLYER, JOSEPH; Hartford; Starr 1 (1-64).
COLYER [CALJER], JOCHEM; New York; Seversmith 1.
COMSTOCK, WILLIAM; Wethersfield, New London; Selleck 1; Holman 4.
CONANT, ROGER; Plymouth, Nantasket, Cape Ann, Salem, Beverly; Ferris 1

(2-221).
CONDIT, JOHN; Newark; Cory 2 (p. 143).
CONE, DANIEL; Hartford, Haddam; Ferris 1 (2-231).
CONEY, JOHN; Boston; Holman 3 (p. 165); also Coney Genealogy.
CONKLING, ANANIAS; Salem, South-old, East Hampton; Cory 3 (p. 156).
CONNER, CORNELIUS; Salisbury; Holman 2.
CONVERSE, ALLEN; Salem, Woburn; Holman 4.
COOK, HENRY; Salem; White 1.
COOKE, AARON; Dorchester, Windsor, Northampton; de Forest 2.
COOKE, FRANCIS; Plymouth; Under-hill 1 (1-443); Ferris 1 (2-239).
COOKE, JOSEPH and GEORGE; Peb-marsh, co. Essex, Eng.; Cam-bridge; Davis 4.
COOKE, JOSIAH; Plymouth, Eastham; Ferris 1 (2-503).
COOKE, THOMAS; Guilford; Starr 1 (2-437).
COOPER, JOHN; Boston, Lynn, South-ampton, L. I.; Selleck 1; Sever-smith 1.
COOPER, JOHN; East Haven; White 1.
COOPER, THOMAS; Hingham, Rehoboth; White 1.
COOPER, THOMAS; Springfield; Jaco-bus 5.
COPP, WILLIAM; Boston; Holman 2.
COREY; (N. J. and Penn. branch); Ferris 1 (2-259). See Cory.
CORNISH, JAMES; Saybrook, Windsor, Northampton, Westfield, Sims-bury; de Forest 1.
CORNISH, THOMAS; Gloucester, Exe-ter, Newtown; Cory 1 (p. 231); Seversmith 1.
CORNWELL, WILLIAM; Middletown; Booth 1.
CORY [COREY], JOHN; Southold; Cory 1; Seversmith 1.
COTTON; Landwade, co. Cambridge, Eng.; Seversmith 1 (p. 612).
COULTMAN, JOHN; Wethersfield; Flagg 1 (p. 231).
COUSIN, THOMAS; Hingham; White 1.
COUSINS, ISAAC; Rowley, Haver-hill, Portsmouth; Davis 1.
COWES, GILES; Stoke-in-Teignhead, co. Devon, Eng.; Ipswich; Davis

4.
COWLES, JOHN; Hartford, Farmington, Hatfield; Flagg 1 (pp. 296, 269, 222, 183); Morris 1; Booth 1.
COX, MOSES; Hampton; Sheppard 1.
COX, WILLIAM; Newcastle Co., Del.; Holman 3 (p. 294).
COXE, MOSES; Hampton; Holman 2.
CRAFTS, GRIFFIN; Roxbury; Jacobus 3; Linzee 1 (p. 455).
CRAM, JOHN; Exeter, Hampton; Davis 9.
CRANE, BENJAMIN; Wethersfield; Ja-cobus 3.
CROCKER, WILLIAM and JOHN; Barnsta-ble; Anderson 1.
CROMWELL; England and New England; Seversmith 1.
CROMWELL, JOHN; Charlestown; Sever-smith 1.
CROSBY, CONSTANCE (BRIGHAM); Row-ley; Holman 2; Sheppard 1.
CROSS, JOHN; Wells; Sheppard 1.
CROSS, ROBERT; Ipswich; Davis 9.
CROSS, WILLIAM; Windsor, Wethers-field, Fairfield; Selleck 1.
CROSWELL, THOMAS; Charlestown; Flagg 1 (p. 255).
CUDWORTH, JAMES (GEN., DEPT.-GOV.); Scituate; Holman 3 (p. 259).
CULVERWELL, THOMAS; Norwich; Jaco-bus 2 (p. 645).
CUMMINGS, ISAAC; Ipswich, Topsfield; Linzee 1 (pp. 279, 204, 166).
CURRIER, RICHARD; Salisbury; Holman 2.
CURTIS, THOMAS, RICHARD, WILLIAM, JOHN; Scituate; Holman 3 (p. 267); White 1.
CURTIS, WILLIAM; Roxbury; Linzee 1 (pp. 469, 463).
CURTIS, ZACHEUS; Salem, Boxford, Arundel; Davis 2, 3; Anderson 1.
CURTIS; (Elnathan), New Milford, Stockbridge; de Forest 1.
CURWEN, GEORGE (CAPT.); Salem; Vin-ton 1.
CUSHMAN, ROBERT; Plymouth; Under-hill 1 (2-511); Jacobus 2 (pp. 646-647).
CUTLER, JAMES; Watertown, Lexington; Ferris 1 (1-198).
CUTLER, JOHN; Hingham; Jacobus 4; Morse 2 (p. 229).
CUTLER, ROBERT (DEACON); Charles-town; Flagg 1 (p. 285).
CUTT, RICHARD; Portsmouth; Sheppard

1.
CUVELLIER [CUVILJE], ADRIENNE [w.
Vigne and Damen]; New York;
Seversmith 1.

DANE, JOHN; Roxbury, Ipswich;
Ferris 1 (1-239); Tingley 1;
Sheppard 1.
DANFORTH, NICHOLAS; Cambridge;
Ferris 1 (2-279), (1-250).
DAVENPORT, THOMAS; Dorchester;
Ferris 1 (1-271).
DAVIS, JAMES; Newbury, Haverhill;
Holman 2.
DAVIS, JENKIN; Lynn; de Forest 2.
DAVIS, JOHN; Ipswich, Gloucester;
Ferris 1 (1-280).
DAVIS, JOHN; Huntington, L. I.;
Seversmith 1 (p. 870).
DAVIS, SAMUEL; Boston, Braintree;
Jacobus 3.
DAVIS, WILLIAM; Roxbury; Holman 3
(p. 242).
DAVIS; (David of Westbury, N. Y.);
Seversmith 1.
DAWES, WILLIAM; Boston; Ferris 1
(1-11).
DAY, ANTHONY; Gloucester; Ting-
ley 1.
DAY, ROBERT; Cambridge, Hartford;
de Forest 2; Booth 1; Jacobus
5.
DAY, ROBERT; Ipswich; Holman 2.
DAYTON, RALPH; New Haven, East
Hampton; Seversmith 1.
DEANE, STEPHEN; Plymouth; Jaco-
bus 4.
DEERING, SAMUEL; Braintree; Davis
8.
DEMING, JOHN; Wethersfield; Starr
1 (2-229); Booth 1.
DENISON, JOHN; Ipswich; de Forest
1; Jacobus 3.
DENISON, ROBERT; Milford, Newark;
Boardman 1 (pp. 238, 168).
DENISON, WILLIAM; Roxbury; Jaco-
bus 3.
DENSLOW, NICHOLAS; Windsor; An-
derson 1.
DENYSE [NYSSEN], THEUNIS; Flat-
bush, Brooklyn; Seversmith 1.
DEVEREUX, JOHN; Salem, Marble-
head; Ferris 1 (2-285).
DEVOTION, EDWARD; Roxbury; Lin-
zee 1 (p. 334).
DEWITT, PIETER JANSZEN; Bushwick;
Seversmith 1.

DEWOLF, BALTHASAR; Lyme; Morris 1;
Anderson 1.
DEXTER, RICHARD; Charlestown, Mal-
den; Flagg 1 (p. 289).
DICKERMAN, THOMAS; Dorchester; White
1.
DICKINSON, NATHANIEL; Watertown,
Wethersfield, Hadley; Boardman 1
(pp. 246, 176, 106); de Forest 2;
Booth 1.
DIMMOCK, THOMAS; Barnstable; Jacobus
3.
DIMOND, THOMAS; Fairfield; Cory 3
(p. 162).
DINGMAN, ADAM; Albany; Jacobus 2 (pp.
715-718).
DISBOROUGH, NICHOLAS; Hartford;
Starr 1 (2-201).
DIX, EDWARD; Watertown; Avery 1 (p.
113).
DIXEY, WILLIAM; Beverly; Davis 3.
DIXON, ANNE; (w. Allanson); Davis 5
(pp. 71-80).
DIXON, WILLIAM; Cambridge; Holman 4.
DOANE, JOHN; Plymouth, Eastham; Fer-
ris 1 (2-299); de Forest 1; Jaco-
bus 4.
DOD(D), DANIEL; Branford; Cory 2 (p.
192); Seversmith 1.
DODD, EDWARD; Hartford; Booth 1.
DODGE, RICHARD and WILLIAM; Salem,
Beverly; Ferris 1 (2-315); Jacobus
3; Booth 1.
DODSON, ANTHONY; Scituate; Tingley
1.
DOMMERICH, LOUIS FERDINAND; New
York; de Forest 2.
DORCHESTER, ANTHONY; Windsor, Spring-
field; Starr 1 (2-59); Booth 1.
DOUGLAS, WILLIAM; Ipswich, Boston,
New London; Selleck 1.
DOW, THOMAS; Newbury, Haverhill; Hol-
man 2.
DOWNING, EMANUEL; Salem; Ferris 1
(1-315); Tingley 1; Jacobus 5.
DRAKE, JOHN; Windsor; White 1.
DRAPER, JAMES; Roxbury; Jacobus 3.
DRIVER, ROBERT; Lynn; de Forest 2.
DRUMMOND; Philadelphia, Pa.; Holman
3 (p. 313).
DRURY, HUGH (LIEUT.); Sudbury, Bos-
ton; Holman 5.
DUDLEY, WILLIAM; Guilford; Jacobus
4.
DUMBLETON, JOHN; Springfield; Jaco-
bus 5.
DUNCAN, SAMUEL; Boston, Roxbury;

Holman 3 (p. 157).
DUNSTER, HENRY (REV.); Scituate;
   Holman 4.
DUNTON, ROBERT and SAMUEL; Read-
   ing; Sheppard 1.
DUTCH, OSMUND; Gloucester, Ips-
   wich; Davis 9.
DUTTON, JOHN; Anderson 1; [see B4
   (19:207)].
DUTY, WILLIAM; Rowley; Anderson
   1.
DWIGHT, JOHN; Dedham; Goodwin 1.
DYER, WILLIAM; Boston, Newport;
   White 1.
DYER, WILLIAM; Dorchester; Under-
   hill 1 (3-1151).

EARLE, RALPH (CAPT.); Portsmouth;
   Holman 3 (p. 238).
EASTMAN, ROGER; Salisbury; Holman
   2.
EATON, JOHN; Salisbury, Haverhill;
   Holman 2.
EATON, WILLIAM and JONAS; Reading;
   Jacobus 3.
EDDY, SAMUEL (and JOHN); Plymouth,
   Swansea; Horton 1.
EDENDEN, see Iddenden.
EDGE, ROBERT; York; Davis 8.
EDMANDS, WILLIAM; Lynn; Holman 3
   (p. 159).
EDWARDS, ALEXANDER; Springfield,
   Northampton; Holman 3 (p. 246).
EDWARDS, WILLIAM; Hartford; Good-
   win 1; Jacobus 5.
EDWARDS; Northants, Eng.; Holman
   4.
EGGLESTON, JANE (———); Woburn;
   Ferris 1 (1-285).
ELIOT, ANDREW; Beverly; Ferris 1
   (2-331).
ELLERY, WILLIAM; Gloucester; Fer-
   ris 1 (1-288).
ELLIS, JOHN; Dedham; Holman 3 (p.
   192).
ELLISON, LAWRENCE; Braintree;
   Hempstead; Seversmith 1.
ELMES, RADOLPHUS; Scituate; Ting-
   ley 1.
ELTON, JOHN; Middletown; Morris
   1.
ELY, NATHANIEL; Springfield; Ja-
   cobus 5.
EMERSON, ROBERT; Haverhill; Hol-
   man 2.
EMERY, JOHN; Newbury; Davis 5
   (pp. 19-26); Holman 2; Davis 9;

Sheppard 1.
ESTOW, WILLIAM; Newbury, Hampton;
   Davis 3.
EVANS, DAVID; Charlestown, Concord;
   Sheppard 1.

FAIRBANK, JONATHAN; Dedham; White 1.
FAIRCHILD, THOMAS; Stratford; Avery
   1 (p. 137); Morris 1.
FARNUM, RALPH; Ipswich, Andover;
   Sheppard 1; Booth 1.
FARRAND, NATHANIEL; Milford; Cory 4.
FARRAR, THOMAS; Lynn; Flagg (pp.
   253, 315); de Forest 2.
FAUNCE, JOHN; Plymouth; de Forest 1.
FAWNE, JOHN; Haverhill; Holman 2.
FAXON, THOMAS; Braintree; Linzee 1
   (p. 520); Vinton 2.
FELCH, HENRY; Gloucester, Boston;
   Sheppard 1.
FELLOWS, WILLIAM, RICHARD and SAMU-
   EL; Ipswich, Hadley, Salisbury;
   Morris 1.
FELTON, ELEANOR (THROWER) [wid.
   John]; Salem; Tingley 1.
FENN, BENJAMIN; Dorchester, Milford;
   Flagg 1 (p. 207).
FENNER, ARTHUR, JOHN and WILLIAM;
   Providence, Saybrook; Flagg 1 (p.
   316); Morris 1.
FENNO, JOHN; Dorchester, Milton;
   Jacobus 3.
FERNALD, (DR.) RENALD; Portsmouth;
   Davis 10.
FIELDER, STEPHEN; Roxbury; Linzee 1
   (p. 218).
FIFIELD, WILLIAM; Hampton; Sheppard
   1.
FISHER, ANTHONY and JOSHUA; Dedham,
   Dorchester, Medfield; Tingley 1;
   Jacobus 3.
FISHER, THOMAS; Dedham; Holman 3
   (p. 198).
FISKE, PHINEHAS (CAPT.); Wenham;
   Booth 1.
FITCH, JAMES (REV.); Saybrook, Nor-
   wich, Lebanon; Jacobus 2 (pp. 648-
   657).
FITCH, JOSEPH; Windsor; Selleck 1.
FITCH, SAMUEL; Hartford; Selleck 1.
FITCH, THOMAS; Norwalk; Selleck 1.
FITTS, ROBERT and RICHARD; Ipswich,
   Newbury; Tingley 1.
FLAGG [FLEGG], THOMAS; Watertown;
   Flagg 1 (pp. 195, 166, 150, 142,
   138, 136, 316, 401, 363).
FLEET, THOMAS; Huntington; Sever-

Booth 1.
GILDERSLEEVE, RICHARD; Hempstead;
Jacobus 5.
GILES, EDWARD; Salem; Vinton 1.
GILL, JOHN; Salisbury; Holman 2.
GLEASON, THOMAS; Watertown, Cambridge, Charlestown; White 1.
GLENN, THOMAS; Boston, Chester;
Tingley 1.
GOADE, [JOHN]; [London]-Abigail;
Salem; Ferris 1 (1-315); Tingley 1.
GODFREY, GEORGE; Eastham; Ferris
1 (2-367); Jacobus 4.
GODFREY, PETER; Newbury; Holman
2.
GODFREY, WILLIAM; Watertown, Hampton; Sheppard 1.
GOFF, PHILIP; Wethersfield; Flagg
1 (pp. 226, 185); Selleck 1.
GOLDHATCH; Ashford, Kent; Seversmith 1.
GOOCH, JOHN; York, Wells; Holman
5.
GOODALE, RICHARD; Newbury, Salisbury; de Forest 1; Jacobus 3.
GOODALE, ROBERT; Salem; Davis 1;
Holman 3 (p. 210).
GOODENOW, THOMAS; Sudbury; White
1.
GOODHUE, WILLIAM; Ipswich; White
1.
GOODMAN, RICHARD; Cambridge,
Hartford, Hadley; de Forest 2.
GOODRICH, WILLIAM and JOHN; Wethersfield; Goodwin 1; Boardman
1 (pp. 182, 108, 113, 82, 65);
Goldthwaite 1; Flagg 1 (pp.
262, 218, 219, 181, 317, 375);
Jacobus 3; Holman 4; Jacobus 5.
GOODWIN, OZIAS and WILLIAM; Hartford; de Forest 1; Goodwin 1;
Booth 1.
GOODWIN, RICHARD; Gloucester;
Tingley 1.
GORE, JOHN; Roxbury; Ferris 1 (1-320).
GORHAM, RALPH; Duxbury; Jacobus
3.
GOULD, FRANCIS; Braintree; Jacobus 4.
GOULD, JOHN; Charlestown; Vinton
1.
GOULD, ZACCHEUS; Weymouth, Lynn,
Topsfield; Anderson 1.
GOULDING, PETER; Boston; Morse 1
(p. 201).

GRANGER, LAUNCELOT; Newbury, Suffield; Jacobus 1 (p. 129).
GRANT, MATTHEW; Dorchester, Windsor;
Starr 1 (1-100); Ferris 1 (2-371).
GRANT, THOMAS; Rowley; Holman 2; Jacobus 3; Booth 1.
GRAVES, GEORGE; Hartford; Ferris 1
(2-381); Booth 1.
GRAVES, THOMAS. (CAPT.); Charlestown;
Jacobus 3; Booth 1.
GRAVES, THOMAS; Hartford, Hatfield;
Boardman 1 (pp. 275, 193); Holman;
4; Jacobus 5.
GRAY, THOMAS; Marblehead; Tingley 1.
GREELEY, ANDREW; Salisbury; Holman
2.
GREEN, THOMAS; Malden; Vinton 2.
GREENAWAY, JOHN; Dorchester; Holman
3 (p. 204).
GREENE, WILLIAM; Woburn; Ferris 1
(1-331); Holman 4; Holman 5.
GREENHILL, SAMUEL; Hartford; Seversmith 1.
GREENLEAF, EDMUND (CAPT.); Newbury;
Holman 2.
GREGSON, THOMAS; New Haven; Flagg 1
(pp. 202, 317).
GRIFFIN, HUGH; Sudbury; Ferris 1 (1-639).
GRIFFIN, HUMPHREY; Ipswich; Davis 8.
GRIFFIN, MATTHEW; Charlestown; Flagg
1 (pp. 254, 214, 179).
GRIGGS, THOMAS; Roxbury; Tingley 1;
Jacobus 1; Linzee 1 (pp. 474, 350).
GRISWOLD, EDWARD; Windsor, Killingworth; Ferris 1 (2-399); Jacobus
2 (pp. 664-669); Jacobus 3; Booth
1.
GRISWOLD, MICHAEL; Wethersfield;
Morris 1.
GROMBRIDGE; co Sussex, Eng.; Seversmith 1.
GROUT, JOHN; Watertown, Sudbury;
Ferris 1 (1-663); Morse 1 (p. 135).
GROVER, THOMAS; Malden; Ferris 1 (1-337).
GRUMMAN, JOHN; Fairfield; Holman 4.
GUILD, JOHN and SAMUEL; Dedham, Haverhill; Tingley 1.
GUNN, JASPER (DR.); Milford; Jacobus 1 (p. 42); de Forest 2.
GUNN, THOMAS; Dorchester, Windsor,
Westfield; Ferris 1 (2-407).
GUNNE; co. Gloucester, Eng.; Holman
4.
GURLEY, WILLIAM; Northampton; Goodwin 1.

GUTTERSON, WILLIAM; Ipswich; Ferris 1 (1-344).
GYLES, JOHN, JAMES and THOMAS; Boston; N. J.; Salem; Vinton 1.

HACKLEY, PETER; New London; Jacobus 2 (pp. 672-674).
HADLOCK, NATHANIEL; Watertown; Jacobus 3.
HAFF, LOURENS; New York; Seversmith 1.
HALE [HEALD], JOHN; Concord; Anderson 1; Booth 1 [Enfield Hales erroneously derived from this source]; Jacobus 5.
HALE, RICHARD; Swansea; Jacobus 5.
HALE, ROBERT; Charlestown; Jacobus 5.
HALE, SAMUEL; Wethersfield; Jacobus 5.
HALE, THOMAS; Charlestown and Norwalk; Jacobus 5.
HALE, THOMAS; Newbury; Holman 2; Davis 9.
HALE, TIMOTHY; Suffield; Jacobus 5.
HALL, JOHN; Roxbury, Hartford, Middletown; de Forest 1; Morris 1; Jacobus 4.
HALL, JOHN; Boston, Hartford, New Haven, Wallingford; Boardman 1 (pp. 233, 165); White 1.
HALL, JOHN; Scituate, Marshfield; Davis 7.
HALL, JOHN; Yarmouth; Jacobus 3; Jacobus 4.
HALL; Stratford-on-Avon, co. Warwick, Eng.; Seversmith 1.
HALSEY, THOMAS; Lynn, Southampton; Starr 1 (2-319); Seversmith 1.
HALSTEAD, JONAS; Hempstead; Seversmith 1.
HALSTEAD, NATHANIEL; Dedham; Holman 2.
HAMBLIN, WILLIAM; Boston; Jacobus 4.
HAMILTON, HUGH and JOHN; Rutland, Hopkinton, Blandford; Jacobus 4.
HAMLET, WILLIAM; Cambridge, Billerica; Holman 2.
HAMMOND, WILLIAM; Watertown; White 1.
HANCHETT, THOMAS (DEA.); Wethersfield, Northampton, Suffield;

Booth 1.
HANFORD, [JEFFREY] and EGLIN (HATHERLY); Scituate; Holman 4.
HANSON; Austerfield, York, Eng.; Jacobus 4.
HAPGOOD, SHADRACH; Sudbury; Morse 2 (p. 111).
HARCOURT, RICHARD; Oyster Bay; Seversmith 1.
HARMON, JAMES; Salem, Saco; Davis 1 (p. 6).
HARMON, JOHN; Springfield; Booth 1.
HARMON, JOHN; Saco, York; Davis 1 (p. 9).
HARMON, JOHN; Wells; Davis 1 (p. 12).
HARRADEN, EDWARD; Ipswich, Gloucester; Ferris 1 (1-347).
HARRIMAN, LEONARD; Rowley; Holman 2.
HARRINGTON, ROBERT; Watertown; Holman 4.
HARRIS, JOHN; Isles of Shoals, Ipswich; Davis 4.
HARRIS, MARTHA (LAKE); Ipswich; Davis 4.
HARRIS, THOMAS; Charlestown; Davis 4; Morris 1; Jacobus 4; Booth 1.
HARRIS, THOMAS and WILLIAM; Salem, Providence; Tingley 1.
HARRIS, WALTER; Weymouth, New London; Selleck 1.
HARRISON, RICHARD; New Haven, Branford; Boardman 1 (pp. 166, 100, 76); de Forest 1; Cory 2 (p. 157).
HART, JOHN; Salem, Marblehead; Davis 3.
HART, STEPHEN (DEA.); Hartford, Farmington; Flagg 1 (pp. 258, 216, 180, 158, 146, 140, 137).
HARVEY, WILLIAM; Boston; Holman 2.
HASENBROECK; Holland; Seversmith 1.
HASKELL, ROGER, WILLIAM and MARK; Beverly, Gloucester, Norwich; Davis 3 (pp. 3-4); Jacobus 2 (pp. 675-676); Ferris 1 (1-351).
HASKINS, see Hoskins.
HASKINS, JOHN; Dorchester, Windsor; White 1.
HASSELSE, PIETER; see Pieterse.
HASTY, DANIEL; Portsmouth, Scarborough; Davis 1.
HATCH, JOHN; Portsmouth; Underhill 1 (1-317).
HATCH, PHILIP; York; Davis 8.
HATCH, WILLIAM; Scituate; Holman 3 (p. 215); Davis 7.
HATHERLY, TIMOTHY; Scituate; Holman

4.
HAVILAND, WILLIAM; Newport, Flushing; Seversmith 1.
HAWKES, ADAM; Lynn; Jacobus 3.
HAWLEY, JOSEPH; Stratford; Ferris 1 (2-411); Holman 4.
HAYDEN, JOHN; Braintree; Vinton 2.
HAYWARD, ROBERT; Dorchester, Windsor, Hartford; Ferris 1 (2-417).
HAYWARD, SAMUEL; Charlestown, Malden; Ferris 1 (1-355).
HAYWARD, WILLIAM; Weymouth, Braintree; Holman 4.
HAZELTINE [HAZELTON], ROBERT and JOHN; Salem, Rowley; Holman 2; Sheppard 1.
HAZEN, EDWARD; Rowley; Jacobus 3; Booth 1.
HEALD, see Hale.
HEARD, JOHN; Kittery; Underhill 1 (1-303).
HEATH, BARTHOLOMEW; Haverhill; Holman 2.
HEATH, WILLIAM and ISAAC; Roxbury; Davis 8.
HELME, THOMAS; Brookhaven; Selleck 1.
HENRY; (Sergt. William); Berlin; Booth 1.
HERRICK, HENRY; Salem, Wenham Beverly; Ferris 1 (2-421).
HEWINS, JACOB; Dorchester; Morse 2 (p. 164).
HEWITT, see Huit.
HIBBERT, ROBERT; Salem, Beverly; Tingley 1; de Forest 2.
HICKS, JOHN; Newport, Newtown, Hempstead; Seversmith 1.
HICKS, ROBERT; Plymouth; de Forest 1.
HIDDEN, ANDREW; Rowley; Anderson 1.
HILL, JOHN; Guilford; de Forest 1.
HILL, PETER; Saco; Sheppard 2.
HILLS, WILLIAM; Roxbury, Hartford; Cory 4; Jacobus 5; Seversmith 1.
HILTON, EDWARD; Exeter; Holman 2.
HINE, THOMAS; Milford; Morris 1.
HINSDALE, ROBERT; Dedham, Medfield, Hadley, Deerfield; Jacobus 4.
HITCHCOCK, LUKE; Wethersfield; Jacobus 5.
HOBART, EDMUND; Hingham; Jacobus

3.
HODGE, JOHN and CHARLES; Killingworth, Windsor, Lyme; Anderson 1.
HODGES, GEORGE; Cambridge, Salem; Tingley 1.
HOLBROOK, RICHARD; Dorchester, Huntington, Milford; Cory 4.
[Daniel and John; Roxbury; Morse 1 (pp. 92, 90); sons of Richard.]
HOLBROOK, SAMUEL; Weymouth; Morse 1 (p. 93).
HOLBROOK, THOMAS; Weymouth; Holman 3 (p. 222); Davis 7; Vinton 2; Morse 1 (p. 48).
HOLDEN, RICHARD and JUSTINIAN; Watertown, Cambridge; Ferris 1 (1-360).
HOLGRAVE, JOHN; Salem; Jacobus 3.
HOLLISTER, JOHN; Wethersfield, Conn.; Goodwin 1; Jacobus 5.
HOLMAN, WILLIAM; Cambridge; Holman 2; Linzee 1 (p. 236).
HOLMES, GEORGE; Roxbury; White 1.
HOLMES, JOHN; Plymouth; de Forest 1.
HOLMES, WILLIAM; Marshfield; Vinton 1.
HOLTOM, JOHN; Springfield, Lyme; Goldthwaite 1.
HOLTON, WILLIAM; Northampton; Holman 4.
HOLYOKE, EDWARD; Boston (Chelsea); Holman 2; Jacobus 5.
HOOD, RICHARD; Lynn; Flagg 1 (p. 251).
HOOKER, THOMAS (REV.); Hartford; Flagg 1 (pp. 248, 317, 318, 377).
HOPKINS, JOHN; Hartford; Goodwin 1.
HOPKINS, STEPHEN; Plymouth; Ferris 1 (2-443); Jacobus 4.
HOPKINS, WILLIAM; Stratford; Booth 1; Seversmith 1.
HORSFORD, WILLIAM; Dorchester, Windsor; Seversmith 1.
HORTON, JOHN; Boston, Eastham; Jacobus 4.
HOSKINS, WILLIAM; Plymouth, Taunton; Jacobus 3.
HOTCHKISS, SAMUEL; New Haven; Anderson 1.
HOUGHTON, RALPH; Lancaster, Milton; White 1.
HOUSE, NATHANIEL; Lebanon; Jacobus 5.
HOUSE, SAMUEL and HANNAH (m. Lothrop); Eastwell, Kent, Eng.; Barnstable; Jacobus 4; White 1.
HOUSE, WILLIAM; Glastonbury; Jacobus 5.
HOVEY, DANIEL; Ipswich; de Forest 2.

HOWARD, THOMAS; Ipswich; Tingley
1.
HOWE, JAMES and ABRAHAM; Roxbury,
Ipswich; Tingley 1.
HOWELL, EDWARD; Lynn, Southampton;
Starr 1 (2-333); Seversmith 1.
HOWKINS, ANTHONY; Windsor, Farm-
ington; Flagg 1 (p. 259).
HOWLAND, JOHN, ARTHUR and HENRY;
Plymouth; Marshfield; Duxbury;
Jacobus 3; Davis 8; Anderson 1.
HOWLETT, THOMAS; Ipswich; Jacobus
3; Linzee 1 (p. 286).
HOYT, JOHN; Salisbury, Amesbury;
Davis 1; Holman 2.
HOYT, SIMON; Dorchester, Scitu-
ate, Windsor, Stamford; Constant 1.
HUBBARD, GEORGE; Watertown; Cory 2.
HUBBARD, GEORGE; Hartford, Middle-
town; Holman 4.
HUCKINS, THOMAS; Boston, Barnsta-
ble; Anderson 1.
HUDSON, RALPH; Cambridge; Tingley
1.
HUGHES, RICHARD; Guilford; de
Forest 1.
HUIT, EPHRAIM; Windsor; de Forest
2; Booth 1 ["Hewitt"].
HULL, GEORGE; Dorchester, Wind-
sor, Fairfield; Ferris 1 (2-
453).
HULL, ISAAC; Beverly; Ferris 1 (2-
467).
HULL, JOSEPH (REV.); Weymouth,
Barnstable, Dover, Isles of
Shoals; Holman 3 (p. 236); Ja-
cobus 3.
HUMISTON, HENRY; New Haven;
White 1.
HUMPHREY, MICHAEL; Windsor, Sims-
bury; Starr 1 (1-78); Ferris 1
(2-471).
HUNGERFORD, THOMAS; Hartford,
New London; Ferris 1 (2-477).
HUNLOCK, JOHN; Boston; Tingley 1.
HUNT, JOHN; Northampton; Flagg 1
(p. 205).
HUNT, WILLIAM; Concord, Marlboro;
Anderson 1.
HUNTINGTON, SIMON; Windsor, Say-
brook, Norwich; Jacobus 2 (pp.
669-670); Jacobus 4; Jacobus 5.
HUNTLEY, JOHN; Lyme; Anderson 1.
HURLBUT, THOMAS; Wethersfield;
Morris 1.
HURST, JAMES; Plymouth; Anderson
1.

HUTCHINS, JOHN; Newbury, Haverhill;
de Forest 1.
HUTCHINS, JOHN; Haverhill; Jacobus
3.
HUTCHINSON, [EDWARD] and SUSANNA;
Exeter, Wells; White 1.
HUTCHINSON, RICHARD; Salem; Holman
2.
HUXLEY, THOMAS; Hartford, Suffield;
Morris 1.
HYDE, SAMUEL; Cambridge, Newton;
White 1.
HYDE, WILLIAM; Saybrook, Norwich;
Booth 1.

IBROOK, RICHARD; Hingham; Jacobus 3;
Davis 8.
IDDENDEN, EDMUND; Scituate, Boston;
Sheppard 1.
INGALLS, EDMUND; Lynn; Holman 2;
Sheppard 1.
INGERSOLL, JOHN; Hartford, Northamp-
ton, Westfield; Goodwin 1; Flagg 1
(pp. 174, 227, 155, 377).
INGRAHAM, RICHARD [Wm., John & Jar-
ret]; Rehoboth; Tingley 1.
IVORY, WILLIAM; Lynn; de Forest 2.

JACKSON, EDWARD; Newton; Starr 5;
Linzee 1 (p. 401).
JACKSON, HENRY; Fairfield; Morris 1.
JACKSON, JOHN; Newton; Linzee 1 (pp.
401, 269).
JACKSON, WILLIAM and NICHOLAS; Rowley;
Tingley 1.
JACOB, RICHARD; Ipswich; Jacobus 3;
Davis 9.
JAGGER, JEREMY; Wethersfield, Stam-
ford; Selleck 1.
JAMES, (WIDOW) ANNA; Marshfield;
Tingley 1.
JAMES, PHILIP; Hingham; Tingley 1.
JAQUES, HENRY; Newbury; Davis 9.
JEGGLES, WILLIAM; Salem; Tingley 1.
JENNEY, JOHN; Plymouth; Underhill 1
(1-488); Holman 3 (p. 286).
JENNISON, WILLIAM (CAPT.) and ROBERT;
Watertown; Ferris 1 (1-369); Vin-
ton 1.
JEWETT, JOSEPH and MAXIMILIAN; Row-
ley; Holman 2; Sheppard 1.
JOHNSON, DAVY; Weymouth; Tingley 1.
JOHNSON, JAMES; Plymouth, Middle-
town, East Hampton; Ferris 1 (2-
485).
JOHNSON, JOHN; Roxbury; Jacobus 4,
Holman 4.

JOHNSON, JOHN and EDMUND; Andover, Hampton; Sheppard 1.
JOHNSON, WILLIAM; Charlestown; Holman 4.
JOHNSON, WILLIAM [WINGLE]; New Haven; White 1.
JOHNSTON, JAMES AND JOHN; Scarborough, Stroudwater, Me.; Davis 6 (pp. 89-104).
JONES, HUGH; Salem; Tingley 1.
JONES, LEWIS; Watertown; Goodwin 1.
JONES, NATHANIEL; Ipswich; Davis 4.
JONES, RICHARD and DOROTHY (m. Sears); Dorchester; Jacobus 4.
JONES, THOMAS; Hingham, Hull, Manchester; Tingley 1.
JORDAN, FRANCIS; Ipswich; Holman 2.
JORDAN, STEPHEN; Ipswich; Davis 9.
JOSLIN, THOMAS; Hingham, Lancaster; Holman 1; White 1; Holman 4.
JUDD, THOMAS; Farmington, Northampton; Flagg 1 (pp. 238, 191, 164, 149, 378); Jacobus 4; Booth 1.
JUDSON, WILLIAM; Stratford, Conn.; Goodwin 1.
JUNG, JOHAN MATTHAUS; West Camp; Cory 5.

KEEN, JOHN; Hingham; Tingley 1.
KEENEY, WILLIAM; Gloucester, New London; Selleck 1.
KEIGWIN, JOHN; Stonington; Holman 1.
KELLEY, JOHN; Newbury; Holman 2.
KEMBER; Brixton, co. Devon, Eng.; Holman 2.
KENDALL, FRANCIS; Charlestown; Woburn; Ferris 1 (1-375); Holman 4.
KENDRICK, JOHN; Ipswich; Holman 2.
KENNEDY, WILLIAM; Preston; Holman 1.
KENT, JOHN; Suffield; Goodwin 1.
KETCHAM, EDWARD; Southold, Stratford; Holman 4.
KETTLE, JOHN; Salem, Gloucester; Tingley 1.
KEYSER, GEORGE; Lynn, Salem; Holman 2.
KILBORNE, GEORGE; Roxbury, Rowley; Davis 3.
KILBOURNE, THOMAS; Wethersfield; Ferris 1 (2-509); (1-369, footnote); Jacobus 5.
KIMBALL, RICHARD and HENRY; Watertown, Ipswich; Holman 2; Davis 9; White 1.
KIMBERLY, THOMAS; New Haven; Jacobus 5.
KING, CLEMENT; Marshfield, Providence; Tingley 1.
KING, THOMAS; Sudbury, Marlboro; White 1; Holman 4.
KINGSBURY, HENRY; Ipswich, Rowley, Haverhill; de Forest 1; Jacobus 3.
KINGSBURY, JOHN and JOSEPH; Dedham; de Forest 1.
KINNE [KENNEY], HENRY; Salem; Tingley 1.
KINNEAR, HENRY; Center and Warren Cos., Pa.; White 1.
KIRBY, JOHN; Lynn, Sandwich, Middletown; Boardman 1 (p. 266); Flagg 1 (pp. 275, 326); Morris 1; Booth 1.
KIRBY; Little Munden, co. Herts, Eng.; Holman 2; Davis 9.
KIRTLAND, PHILIP; Lynn; Ferris 1 (2-517).
KITCHELL, ROBERT; Guilford, Newark; Cory 4.
KITCHEREL, SAMUEL; Hartford; de Forest 2; Jacobus 4.
KNAPP, WILLIAM; Watertown; White 1.
KNIGHT, ALEXANDER; Ipswich; Ferris 1 (1-397).
KNIGHT, JOHN; Watertown, Sudbury, Charlestown; Holman 4.
KNIGHT, JOHN and RICHARD; Newbury; Holman 2; Davis 9.
KNIGHT, WALTER; Nantucket, Cape Ann, Boston; Tingley 1.
KNOWLTON, JOHN WILLIAM and THOMAS; Ipswich; Tingley 1; Jacobus 3.

LAFLIN, CHARLES; Westfield; Jacobus 4.
LAKE; North Benfleet, co. Essex, Eng.; Davis 4.
LANE, JOB; Malden; Avery 1 (p. 171).
LANGTON, GEORGE; Wethersfield, Northampton; Booth 1.
LANGTON, ROGER; Ipswich, Haverhill; Tingley 1.
LARCOM, MORDECAI; Ipswich, Beverly; Tingley 1.
LARKIN, EDWARD; Charlestown; Holman

MCCOLLUM, DUNCAN; Southampton,
Middletown; Holman 4.
MCCURDY, ROBERT and JAMES; Lon-
donderry, N. H.; Holman 2.
MACFARLAND,FURTHE; Hingham;
Tingley 1.
MCKENNEY, JOHN; Scarborough; Un-
derhill 1 (1-339).
MCLAFLIN, ROBERT; Wenham; Jacobus 4.
MCNAIR, JOHN; Allen, Northampton
Co.; Crawford 1 (p. 25).
MACK, JOHN; Salisbury, Concord,
Lyme; Anderson 1.
MALLORY, PETER; New Haven; Ander-
son 1.
MALTBY, WILLIAM; New Haven, Bran-
ford; Anderson 1.
MANSFIELD, ROBERT; Lynn; de For-
est 2.
MANWARING, OLIVER; Salem, New
London; Selleck 1.
MARBLE, JOHN; Charlestown; Jaco-
bus 1.
MARBURY, ANNE [w. William Hutch-
inson]; Boston; R. I.; White 1.
MARCH; Devonshire, Eng.; Holman
4.
MARCY, JOHN; Roxbury, Woodstock;
Jacobus 3.
MARINER, ANDREW; Dover, Boston,
New London, New York; Underhill
1 (3-1103).
MARKHAM, WILLIAM; Hartford, Had-
ley; Booth 1.
MARRETT, THOMAS; Cambridge; Ja-
cobus 3.
MARSH, JOHN; Salem; Jacobus 3.
MARSH, JOHN; Hartford; de Forest
1; de Forest 2.
MARSHALL, JOHN; Boston; Vinton 1.
MARSHALL, THOMAS; Lynn; de Forest
2.
MARSHALL; Tidd St. Mary, co Lin-
coln, Eng.; Seversmith 1 (p.
607).
MARSHFIELD, THOMAS; Windsor; Ja-
cobus 5.
MARSTON, WILLIAM (CAPT.); Salem,
Hampton; Davis 3; Holman 2;
Tingley 1.
MARTIN, SAMUEL; see Phebe Bisby.
MARVIN, MATTHEW and REINOLD;
Hartford, Norwalk; Flagg 1 (pp.
293, 333); Ferris 1 (2-575);
Jacobus 3; Jacobus 4; Jacobus 5.
MASON; Cheltenham, co Gloucester,
Eng.; Davis 4.

MASON, HUGH; Watertown; White 1.
MASON, NICHOLAS; Farmington, Say-
brook, Wethersfield; Starr 1 (2-
455).
MASURY [MAJORY, LE MESSURIER], LAU-
RENCE, BENJAMIN, MARTIN, JOSEPH,
WILLIAM; Salem; Tingley 1.
MATHER, RICHARD; Dorchester; Good-
win 1; Jacobus 3.
MAVERICK, JOHN (REV.); Dorchester;
Holman 3 (p. 184); Tingley 1.
MAY, JOHN; Roxbury; Ferris 1 (1-413).
MEACHAM, JEREMIAH; Southold, East
Hampton, Salem; Jacobus 3.
MEAKIN, THOMAS; Boston; Boardman 1
(pp. 208, 137).
MEARS, ROBERT; Boston; Ferris 1 (1-
426).
MEIGS, VINCENT; New Haven, Guilford;
Anderson 1.
MELLENS, RICHARD; Weymouth, Charles-
town; Flagg 1 (pp. 288, 257).
MELYN, CORNELIUS; New York, Staten
Island; Cory 3 (p. 337).
MERRIAM, GEORGE and JOSEPH; Concord;
Cory 2 (p. 29); Anderson 1.
MERRICK, WILLIAM; Plymouth, Duxbury,
Eastham; Ferris 1 (2-581).
MERRILL, JOHN and NATHANIEL; New-
bury; Holman 2; Sheppard 1.
MESSENGER, ANDREW; New Haven, Green-
wich, Jamaica; Selleck 1.
METCALF, MICHAEL; Dedham; Goodwin 1.
MEYER, JOHAN LUDWIG; Hamilton; Ting-
ley 1.
MILES, RICHARD; New Haven; Holman 4.
MILLER, JAMES; Charlestown; White 1.
MILLER, JOHN; Salem; Cape Porpoise;
Davis 5 (pp. 1-12).
MILLER, THOMAS; Rowley, Middletown;
de Forest 1; Holman 4.
MILLER, THOMAS; Springfield; Jacobus 5.
MILLETT, THOMAS; Dorchester,
Gloucester, Brookfield; Holman 3
(p. 201).
MILLS, JOHN; Boston, Braintree; Fer-
ris 1 (1-441); Vinton 2.
MILLS, SIMON; Windsor, Simsbury;
Starr 1 (1-114).
MINER, THOMAS; Charlestown, Hingham,
New London, Stonington; Selleck 1;
Jacobus 3.
MITCHELL, CHRISTOPHER; Kittery; Un-
derhill 1 (1-1295).
MITCHELL, EXPERIENCE; Duxbury,
Bridgewater; Underhill 1 (1-353).
MITCHELL, MATTHEW; Charlestown, Con-

cord, Saybrook, Wethersfield,
Stamford; Ferris 1 (2-589);
Cory 4.
MITCHELL, THOMAS; New Haven; Fer-
ris 1 (2-589).
MITTON, MICHAEL; Falmouth; Ting-
ley 1.
MOODY, JOHN and FRANCES (m. Kil-
bourn); Hartford; Jacobus 5 (p.
653).
MOORE, ALEXANDER; New York, New
Brunswick; de Forest 1.
MOORE, ISAAC; Farmington; Booth 1.
MOORE, JOHN; Sudbury; Ferris 1
(1-446); Holman 5.
MOORE, JOHN; St. Thomas Parish,
Charleston, S. C.; Flagg 1 (pp.
152, 143, 334).
MOORE, THOMAS; Dorchester, Wind-
sor; Flagg 1 (pp. 302, 279,
379); White 1.
MOORES, EDMUND; Newbury; White 1.
MORGAN, JAMES; New London; Jaco-
bus 3.
MORGAN, ROBERT; Salem; Tingley 1;
but see Davis 3.
MORLEY, THOMAS; Westfield, Glas-
tonbury; Jacobus 4.
MORRIS, LEWIS; Shrewsbury; Morris
1.
MORRISON, DANIEL; Newbury; Rowley;
Davis 8.
MORSE, ANTHONY and WILLIAM; New-
bury; Holman 2.
MORSE, SAMUEL; Dedham, Medfield;
see also Jasper (ancestry of
wife, Elizabeth (Jasper) Morse;
Tingley 1; Holman 5.
MORTON, GEORGE; Plymouth; de For-
est 1; Holman 3 (p. 282).
MOSES, JOHN; Portsmouth; Davis 10.
MOSS, JOHN; New Haven, Walling-
ford; Boardman 1 (pp. 228, 164,
98).
MOULD, HUGH; Barnstable, New Lon-
don; Starr 1 (2-427); Selleck 1.
MOULTON, JOHN; Hampton; Holman 2.
MOULTON, ROBERT; Charlestown,
Salem; Ferris 1 (1-452); Ting-
ley 1.
MOUSALL, RALPH (DEA.); Charles-
town; Flagg 1 (p. 303).
MOYCE, JOSEPH; Salisbury; Holman
2.
MULFORD, JOHN; Salem, Southampton,
East Hampton; Cory 3 (p. 1).
MULLINS, WILLIAM; Plymouth; Craw-

ford 1 (p. 50); Jacobus 4.
MYGATT, JOSEPH; Hartford; Goodwin 1.
MYRICK, JAMES and JOHN; Charlestown,
Newbury; Holman 2.

NASH, ROBERT; Charlestown; Holman 3
(p. 180).
NASH, SAMUEL; Plymouth; Tingley 1.
NASH, THOMAS and MARGERY (BAKER);
New Haven; Flagg 1 (pp. 245, 204,
309); Anderson 1.
NEAL, JOHN; Scituate, Brunswick;
Davis 7.
NEALE, FRANCIS; Maine, Salem; Davis
3 (p. 58).
NEALE, JOHN; Salem; Davis 3.
NEEDHAM, EDMUND; Lynn; de Forest 2.
NELSON, JOHN; Flatbush, Mamaroneck;
Constant (p. 410).
NETTLETON, SAMUEL; Branford; Holman
4.
NEWBERRY, THOMAS and JOANE (DABI-
NOTT); Dorchester; Starr 2; Flagg
1 (pp. 281, 311, 336).
NEWCOMB, ANDREW; Boston; de Forest
2.
NEWCOMB, FRANCIS; Boston, Braintree;
Ferris 1 (1-459); Davis 8.
NEWELL, THOMAS; Farmington; Starr 1
(1-181); Flagg 1 (p. 233); Morris
1.
NEWHALL, ANTHONY and THOMAS; Lynn;
Flagg 1 (p. 284); de Forest 2.
NEWTON, RICHARD; Sudbury, Marl-
borough; de Forest 1; Holman 4.
NEWTON, ROGER (REV.); Hartford, Farm-
ington, Milford; Flagg 1 (pp. 206,
175).
NICHOLS, CYPRIAN; Hartford; de For-
est 1.
NICHOLS, THOMAS; Salisbury, Amesbury;
Holman 2; White 1.
NICHOLSON, EDMUND; Marblehead; Ferris
1 (2-595).
NILES, JOHN; Braintree; Vinton 2.
NOBLE, THOMAS; Westfield; Booth 1.
NORCROSS, JEREMIAH and JOHN; Water-
town, Cambridge; Jacobus 3.
NORMAN, RICHARD; Salem, Marblehead;
Davis 3; Tingley 1.
NORTH, JOHN; Farmington; Flagg 1 (pp.
232, 188, 162, 148, 141); Booth 1.
NORTHAM, JAMES; Wethersfield; Booth
1.
NORTHEND, EZEKIEL; Rowley; Holman 2.
NORTON, GEORGE; Salem, Gloucester,
Wenham; [Brookhaven, L. I.]; Sel-

leck 1; Morris 1.

NORTON, JOHN; Branford, Farmington; Booth 1.

NOTT, JOHN; Wethersfield; Goodwin 1.

NURSE, FRANCIS; Salem; de Forest 2.

NYE, BENJAMIN; Sandwich; Holman 3 (p. 273).

OBER, RICHARD; Beverly; Ferris 1 (2-605).

OLCOTT, THOMAS; Hartford; Starr 3.

OLMSTEAD, JAMES; Braintree, Cambridge, Hartford; Starr 1 (1-181); Ferris 1 (2-611); Anderson 1.

OLMSTEAD, RICHARD; Cambridge, Hartford, Norwalk; Selleck 1; Flagg 1 (p. 337); Morris 1.

ORDWAY, JAMES; Newbury; Holman 2.

OSBORN, THOMAS; New Haven, East Hampton; Cory 1 (p. 238); Cory 3 (p. 201).

OSBORNE, JOHN; Weymouth, Braintree; Tingley 1.

OSGOOD, JOHN; Andover; Holman 2; Tingley 1; Sheppard 1.

OSGOOD, WILLIAM; Salisbury; Holman 2.

PABODY, JOHN; Plymouth, Bridgewater; Tingley 1; Jacobus 4.

PADDOCK, ROBERT; Plymouth; Jacobus 4.

PAINE, WILLIAM; Watertown, Ipswich, Boston; Flagg 1 (p. 283); see also White 1.

PAINE, WILLIAM; New Haven; Anderson 1.

PALGRAVE, [RICHARD]; Southold; Ferris 1 (2-621).

PALMER, HENRY; Haverhill; Holman 2.

PALMER, JOHN; Rowley; Holman 2; Anderson 1.

PALMER, WALTER; Charlestown, Rehoboth, Stonington; Selleck 1; Jacobus 3.

PALMER, WILLIAM; Plymouth, Duxbury; Anderson 1.

PALMER, WILLIAM; Yarmouth, Newtown, L. I.; Selleck 1.

PANTRY, WILLIAM; Cambridge, Hartford; Starr 1 (2-311); Selleck 1.

PARK, RICHARD; Cambridge, Newtown;

Avery 1 (p. 89).

PARKE, ROBERT; Roxbury, New London, Stonington; Holman 1; Jacobus 3.

PARKER, JACOB, (JAMES, ABRAHAM, JOHN and JOSEPH); Woburn, Chelmsford; Ferris 1 (1-464, see also 499).

PARKER, SAMUEL; Dedham; Linzee 1 (pp. 184, 160, 152, 148).

PARKER, WILLIAM; Scituate; Holman 3 (p. 263).

PARKER, WILLIAM; Saybrook; Jacobus 3.

PARLOW, THOMAS; Beverly, Middleboro; Tingley 1.

PARRATT, FRANCIS; Rowley; Holman 2.

PARSONS, JOSEPH; Springfield, Northampton; Ferris 1 (2-625); Holman 4.

PARTRIDGE, JOHN and WILLIAM; Medfield; Tingley 1.

PATTEN, HECTOR; Saco; Davis 6 (pp. 11-41).

PATTEN, MATTHEW; Biddeford; Davis 6 (pp. 1-9).

PATTEN, ROBERT; Arundel; Davis 6 (pp. 49-77).

PATTEN, WILLIAM; Boston; Davis 6 (pp. 43-47); Linzee 1 (p. 480).

PATTEN, WILLIAM; Wells; Davis 6 (pp. 79-104).

PEABODY, see Pabody.

PEABODY, FRANCIS (LIEUT.); Hampton, Topsfield; Jacobus 3.

PEARCE, JOHN; York; Davis 3.

PEASLEY, JOSEPH; Newbury, Haverhill, Amesbury; Holman 2.

PECK, JOSEPH; Hingham, Rehoboth; White 1.

PECK, JOSEPH; Milford; Morris 1.

PECK, PAUL (DEACON); Hartford; Flagg 1 (p. 225).

PEIRCE, JOHN; Watertown; Holman 4.

PEIRCE, THOMAS; Charlestown; Sheppard 1.

PEMBER, THOMAS; New London; Jacobus 2 (pp. 677-678).

PENGRY, MOSES (DEACON); Ipswich; Holman 2.

PENNIMAN, JAMES; Braintree; Vinton 2.

PENOYER, ROBERT; Stamford, Mamaroneck; Selleck 1.

PERIGO, ROBERT; Lyme; Jacobus 3.

PERKINS, ABRAHAM and ISAAC; Hampton; Holman 2.

PERKINS, JOHN; Boston, Ipswich; Holman 2; Ferris 1 (1-484).

PERKINS, JOHN; Ipswich; Jacobus 3.

PETERS, ANDREW; Ipswich, Andover; Sheppard 1.
PETTEE, WILLIAM; Weymouth; Morse 2 (p. 147).
PETTYJOHN, JAMES; Hungar's Parish, Va.; Ferris 1 (2-643).
PHELPS, WILLIAM; Dorchester; Windsor; Holman 3 (p. 252).
PHILBRICK, THOMAS; Watertown, Hampton; Tingley 1.
PHILLIPS, WILLIAM; Taunton; Cory 2 (p. 92).
PHIPPEN, DAVID; Hingham, Boston; Tingley 1.
PHIPS, SOLOMON; Charlestown; Morse 1 (p. 95).
PIERCE, RICHARD; Muscongus; Jacobus 4.
PIERSON, ABRAHAM (REV.); Lynn, Southampton, Branford, Newark; Cory 4.
PIETERSE [PIETER HASSELSE]; Bergen; Tingley 1.
PILLSBURY, WILLIAM; Dorchester, Newbury; Holman 2.
PINDER, HENRY; Ipswich; Holman 2.
PINNEY, HUMPHREY; Dorchester, Windsor; Ferris 1 (2-659).
PINSON, THOMAS; Scituate; White 1.
PIPER, NATHANIEL; Ipswich; Holman 2.
PITKIN, WILLIAM; Hartford; de Forest 1.
PLATT, RICHARD; New Haven, Milford; Selleck 1; Avery 1 (p. 151); Anderson 1; Holman 4.
PLATTS, SAMUEL and JONATHAN; Rowley; Holman 2.
PLUMB, JOHN; Wethersfield, Branford; Flagg 1 (pp. 209, 337).
PLYMPTON, THOMAS and ELIZABETH; Sudbury; Ferris 1 (1-493).
POMEROY, ELTWEED; Dorchester, Windsor, Northampton; Flagg 1 (pp. 211, 177, 339); Holman 4.
PONTUS, WILLIAM; Plymouth; de Forest 1.
POORE, JOHN; Newbury; Holman 2.
PORTER, JOHN; Windsor; Goodwin 1; Boardman 1 (p. 306); Booth 1.
PORTER, RICHARD; Weymouth; Jacobus 3.
PORTER, THOMAS (DEACON); Farmington; Flagg 1 (p. 270).
POST, STEPHEN; Cambridge, Hartford, Saybrook; Ferris 1 (2-667); Booth 1.

POTTER, NICHOLAS, Lynn, Salem; de Forest 2.
POTTER, WILLIAM; New Haven; Ferris 1 (2-671); White 1.
POULTER, MARY [wid. John]; Billerica; Ferris 1 (1-499).
POWELL, THOMAS; New Haven; de Forest 1; Anderson 1.
POWER, WALTER; Concord, Littleton; Jacobus 4.
PRATT, JOHN; Cambridge, Hartford; Starr 1 (1-1).
PRATT, MATTHEW; Weymouth; Underhill 1 (2-727); Cory 2 (p. 37).
PRATT, WILLIAM; Cambridge, Hartford, Saybrook; Ferris 1 (2-675); de Forest 1; Jacobus 3; Jacobus 4; Jacobus 5.
PRENCE, THOMAS (GOV.); Plymouth, Duxbury, Eastham; Ferris 1 (2-683).
PRENTICE, HENRY; Sudbury, Cambridge; Ferris 1 (1-502); Sheppard 1.
PRESCOTT, JOHN; Watertown, Lancaster; White 1; Holman 4.
PRESTON, WILLIAM; New Haven; Anderson 1.
PRICHARD, ROGER; Springfield, New Haven; White 1; Anderson 1.
PRINCE, ROBERT, REBECCA (and BETHIA); Salem; Ferris 1 (1-519).
PRINCE, THOMAS; Gloucester; Ferris 1 (1-510).
PRIOR, JAMES; Boston; Holman 3 (p. 158).
PRITCHARD, ROGER; Wethersfield, Springfield, Milford, New Haven; de Forest 1.
PROCTOR, JOHN; Ipswich; Tingley 1.
PRUDDEN, JAMES; Milford; Starr 1 (2-163).
PRUDDEN, PETER (REV.); Milford; Starr 1 (2-163).
PUFFER, GEORGE; Braintree; Tingley 1.
PUTNAM, JOHN; Salem; Ferris 1 (1-521).
PYNCHON, WILLIAM; Roxbury, Springfield; Crawford 1 (p. 54); Jacobus 4; Jacobus 5.

QUINBY, ROBERT; Amesbury; Holman 2.

RAND, ROBERT; Charlestown; Sheppard 1.
RANDALL, JOHN; Westerly; Holman 1.
RAPALJE, JORIS JANSEN; New York,

Brooklyn; Tingley 1.
RAYMOND [RAYMENT], JOHN and
  WILLIAM; Glastonbury, co. Som-
  erset, Eng.; Beverly; Davis 4;
  Ferris 1 (2-697).
RAYMOND, RICHARD; Salem, Say-
  brook; Selleck 1.
READ, THOMAS; Sudbury; Holman 4.
READ, WILLIAM; Weymouth, Boston;
  Jacobus 3.
READE; Wickford, co. Essex, Eng.;
  Davis 4.
REDDING, JOSEPH; Ipswich; Ander-
  son 1.
REED, WILLIAM; Weymouth; Jacobus
  3.
REES, ANDRIES; New York, Albany;
  de Forest 1.
REMINGTON, JOHN (LIEUT.); Rowley;
  Holman 4.
REYNOLDS, JOHN; Wethersfield;
  Selleck 1 (p. 108).
RICE, EDMUND; Sudbury, Marlboro;
  White 1; Holman 5.
RICHARDS, THOMAS; Dorchester,
  Weymouth; Jacobus 3; Jacobus 4;
  Morse 3.
RICHARDSON, EZEKIEL, SAMUEL,
  THOMAS; Woburn; Vinton 2.
RIGGS, EDWARD; Roxbury; Cory 2
  (p. 251).
RILEY, JOHN; Springfield; Jacobus
  5.
RIPLEY, WILLIAM; Hingham; Jacobus
  3.
RISING, JAMES; Suffield; Jacobus
  4.
ROBBINS, RICHARD; Charlestown,
  Cambridge; Jacobus 3.
ROBERTS, HUGH; Gloucester, New
  London, Newark; Cory 1 (p.
  260).
ROBERTS, JOHN; Simsbury; Starr 4;
  Ferris 1 (2-711).
ROBERTS, SIMON and HUGH; Boston
  and Gloucester; Underhill 1 (2-
  923).
ROBERTS, WILLIAM; Oyster River;
  Davis 1.
ROBINSON, GEORGE; Rehoboth; Ting-
  ley 1.
ROBINSON, JOHN (REV.); Leyden,
  Holland; Isaac, Plymouth and
  Barnstable; Vinton 1.
ROBINSON, JOSEPH; Andover; Shep-
  pard 1.
ROBINSON, WILLIAM; Dorchester;

Ferris 1 (1-528).
ROCKWOOD, RICHARD; Braintree; Morse
  1 (p. 103).
ROE, HUGH; Weymouth, Suffield; Ja-
  cobus 4.
ROGERS, JOHN; Scituate, Marshfield;
  Tingley 1; Davis 7.
ROGERS, THOMAS; Plymouth; Jacobus 4.
ROGERS, WILLIAM; Wethersfield, Hemp-
  stead, Huntington; Selleck 1.
ROGERS; Boxted, Eng.; Tingley 1.
ROLFE, HENRY and JOHN; Ipswich;
  Holman 2.
ROOT, THOMAS; Hartford; Jacobus 2
  (pp. 643-644).
ROOTS, JOSIAH; Salem, Beverly; Ja-
  cobus 3.
ROPER, WALTER; Hampton, Ipswich;
  Davis 9.
ROSE, ROBERT; Wethersfield, Bran-
  ford; White 1.
ROSE, THOMAS; Stonington, Preston;
  Holman 1.
ROSS, JAMES; Sudbury; White 1.
ROSS, THOMAS; Cambridge; Holman 2.
ROSSITER, EDWARD; Dorchester; Cory
  2 (p. 116).
ROUND, JOHN; Yarmouth, Rehoboth,
  Swansea; Tingley 1.
ROUSE, JOHN; Duxbury, Marshfield;
  Tingley 1.
ROWAN, ANDREW; Haverhill; Holman 2.
ROWE, JOHN; Gloucester; Tingley 1.
ROWELL, THOMAS; Salisbury, Ipswich,
  Andover; Holman 2.
ROWLEY, HENRY; Barnstable; Anderson
  1.
ROYCE, ROBERT; Stratford, New Lon-
  don; Starr 1 (1-295); Flagg 1 (pp.
  234, 189); Jacobus 3; Anderson 1.
RUDD, JONATHAN; Hartford, Saybrook;
  Jacobus 3.
RUGGLES, THOMAS; Roxbury; Linzee 1
  (pp. 454, 453, 452, 448, 329, 215,
  173, 155).
RUSCOE, ROGER; Hartford, Norwalk;
  Flagg 1 (p. 340).
RUSSELL, GEORGE; Hingham; Tingley 1.
RUSSELL, JOHN; Cambridge, Wethers-
  field, Hadley; Boardman 1 (pp.
  272, 192, 118).
RUTTER, JOHN; Sudbury; Ferris 1 (1-
  534).

SAFFORD, THOMAS; Ipswich; Davis 9.
SAGE, DAVID; Middletown; Flagg 1
  (pp. 230, 187); Booth 1.

ST. JOHN, MATTHIAS; Dorchester, Windsor, Norwalk; Selleck 1.

SALMON, WILLIAM; Southold; Cory 3 (p. 176).

SAMPSON, ABRAHAM; Duxbury; Horton 1.

SAMPSON, HENRY; Duxbury; Vinton 1.

SANDELL; Basildon, co. Essex, Eng.; Davis 4.

SANFORD, ANDREW; Hartford, Milford; de Forest 1.

SANFORD, ROBERT; Hartford; Starr 1 (1-72).

SANGER, RICHARD; Watertown; Morse 1 (p. 123).

SARGENT, WILLIAM; Newbury, Hampton, Amesbury; Holman 2.

SAWYER, THOMAS; Lancaster; Holman 1; Holman 4.

SAWYER, WILLIAM; Amesbury, Newbury; Underhill 1 (1-327); Holman 2.

SAWYER, WILLIAM; Reading; de Forest 2.

SAXTON, RICHARD; Windsor; Starr 1 (1-133); Ferris 1 (2-717).

SAYLES, JOHN; Providence; Flagg 1 (p. 200).

SAYRE, THOMAS; Lynn, Southampton; Cory 1 (p. 305); Holman 4.

SCHELLINGER, JACOB; New York, New Haven, New London, East Hampton; Cory 3 (p. 270).

SCOTT, BENJAMIN; Braintree; Holman 3 (p. 323).

SCOTT, BENJAMIN; Cambridge, Rowley; Holman 3 (p. 325); Booth 1.

SCOTT, JOHN; Roxbury; Holman 3 (p. 3).

SCOTT, JOHN; Springfield; Jacobus 5.

SCOTT, JOHN; North Carolina; White 1.

SCOTT, JOSEPH; Rowley; Holman 3 (p. 343).

SCOTT, THOMAS; Ipswich; Holman 2; Davis 9.

SCROGGS, THOMAS; Great Yarmouth, co. Norfolk, Eng.; Salem; Davis 4; Ferris 1 (2-721).

SCUDDER, THOMAS, JOHN, ELIZABETH; Salem, Barnstable; Jacobus 4.

SEABROOK, ROBERT; Stratford; de Forest 1.

SEALIS, RICHARD; Scituate; White 1.

SEARLE, JOHN and JOANNA; Springfield; Booth 1.

SEARLE, WILLIAM; Ipswich; Davis 4; Holman 2.

SEARS, RICHARD; Yarmouth; Jacobus 4.

SEDGWICK, ROBERT; Charlestown; Goodwin 1.

SEDLEY, JAMES; Weymouth; Tingley 1.

SEEBER, WILLIAM; Canajoharie; Jacobus 1 (p. 126).

SELDEN, THOMAS; Hartford; Jacobus 4.

SENDALL, SAMUEL; Newbury, Boston; Tingley 1.

SEVERSMITH, NICHOLAS; Milford; Huntington; Seversmith 1.

SEXTON, GEORGE; Windsor; Booth 1.

SEYMOUR, RICHARD; Hartford, Norwalk; Flagg 1 (pp. 236, 190, 163, 340); Ferris 1 (2-727).

SHAFER, JOHANNES MATTHIAS; Hamilton; Tingley 1.

SHATSWELL, WILLIAM, JOHN and THEOPHILUS; Ipswich; Holman 2; Davis 8.

SHATTUCK, WILLIAM; Watertown; White 1.

SHEAFFE; Cranbrook, Kent; Cory 4 (pp. 1-30); Morris 1.

SHELDON, GODFREY; Saco, Scarboro; Sheppard 1.

SHELDON, ISAAC; Windsor, Northampton; Starr 1 (2-171); Holman 4.

SHEPARD, RALPH; Malden; Jacobus 4.

SHEPARD, SOLOMON; Salisbury; Holman 2.

SHEPARD, WILLIAM; Taunton; Ferris 1 (1-541).

SHEPARDSON, DANIEL; Charlestown; Ferris 1 (1-545).

SHERBURNE, HENRY and JOHN; Portsmouth; Davis 10.

SHERMAN, EDMUND; Watertown, Wethersfield, New Haven; Boardman 1 (pp. 218, 144, 92); Anderson 1.

SHERMAN, WILLIAM; Plymouth; Holman 3 (p. 211).

SHERMAN; (Capt. John, Nantucket); Jacobus 2 (p. 679).

SHERWOOD, THOMAS; Wethersfield, Fairfield; Selleck 1.

SHERWOOD, THOMAS; Stratford; de Forest 1.

SHIPMAN, EDWARD; Saybrook; Ferris 1 (2-733).

SHIRLEY, JAMES; Chester; Tingley 1.

SIBBORN, JOHN; Boston; Sheppard 1.

SIGGINS, JOHN; P e n n . ; White 1.

SILSBEE, HENRY; Salem, Ipswich, Lynn; Jacobus 3.

SILVER, THOMAS; Newbury; Davis 9.

SIMPSON, ALEXANDER; Flatlands,
Staten Island; Cory 1 (p. 295).
SKELTON, SAMUEL (REV.); Salem;
Jacobus 3.
SKINNER, JOHN; Hartford; Brain-
tree, Essex; Jacobus 5 (p. 748).
SKINNER, THOMAS; Boston; Holman 3
(p. 182).
SLEGHT, HENDRICK CORNELISE; Flat-
bush, Brooklyn; Tingley 1 (p.
337).
SLUMAN, THOMAS; Norwich; Jacobus
3; Booth 1.
SMALL, EDWARD; Kittery; Underhill
1 (1-3).
SMALL, JOHN; Salem; Jacobus 3.
SMITH, ARTHUR; Hartford; Booth 1.
SMITH, CHRISTOPHER; Providence;
Tingley 1.
SMITH, EDWARD; New London; Jaco-
bus 3.
SMITH, FRANCIS; Roxbury; White 1.
SMITH, HENRY (REV.); Wethersfield;
Goodwin 1; Jacobus 5.
SMITH, HENRY; Hingham, Rehoboth;
White 1.
SMITH, HENRY; Springfield; Jaco-
bus 4.
SMITH, HUGH; Rowley; Starr 1 (2-
99).
SMITH, JAMES; Weymouth; Jacobus 3.
SMITH, JOHN; Watertown; White 1.
SMITH, JOHN (Quartermaster); Dor-
chester; Holman 1.
SMITH, JOHN; Lancaster; Selleck 1.
SMITH, JOSEPH; Hartford; de Forest
2; Booth 1.
SMITH, LAWRENCE; Dorchester; Hol-
man 4.
SMITH, NEHEMIAH; New London; Jaco-
bus 2 (pp. 621-623); Jacobus 3.
SMITH, NICHOLAS; see Seversmith.
SMITH, ROBERT; Ipswich, Rowley,
Topsfield; Davis 2; Anderson 1.
SMITH, SAMUEL (LIEUT.); Wethers-
field, Hadley; Holman 4.
SMITH, SIMON; Haddam; Jacobus 4.
SMITH, THOMAS (CAPT.); Boston ?;
Ferris 1 (1-548).
SMITH, WILLIAM; Hartford, Wethers-
field, Middletown, Farmington;
Starr 1 (1-191).
SNOW, ANTHONY; Plymouth, Marsh-
field; de Forest 1.
SNOW, NICHOLAS; Plymouth, Eastham;
Jacobus 4.
SNOW, RICHARD; Woburn; Ferris 1

(1-552).
SNOW, THOMAS; Boston; Holman 3 (p.
200).
SOUTHWORTH, ALICE (CARPENTER); Ply-
mouth; Jacobus 4.
SPARROW, RICHARD; Plymouth, Eastham;
Ferris 1 (2-763).
SPEAR, GEORGE; Braintree; Davis 8.
SPENCER, GARRARD; Cambridge, Lynn,
Hartford, Haddam; Goodwin 1; Fer-
ris 1 (2-769); Holman 1; Jacobus
4; Booth 1.
SPENCER, THOMAS; Hartford; Goodwin
1; Starr 6; Morris 1.
SPENCER, WILLIAM; Cambridge, Hart-
ford; Goodwin 1; de Forest 1.
SPINNING, HUMPHREY; New Haven; An-
derson 1.
SPOOR, JAN WYBESE; Albany, Niskayu-
na, Livingston Manor, Linlithgo;
de Forest 1.
SPRAGUE, FRANCIS; Plymouth, Duxbury;
Holman 3 (p. 241).
SPRAKE, NICHOLAS; Billerica; Holman
2.
SQUIRE, EDITH (m. Adams), ANNE (m.
Purchase); Somerset, Eng.; Jacobus
4).
STACY, SIMON; Ipswich; Ferris 1 (1-
558).
STANDISH, MYLES (CAPT.); Plymouth,
Duxbury; Holman 1; Horton 1.
STANDISH, THOMAS; Wethersfield;
Boardman 1 (p. 207).
STANDLAKE, DANIEL; Scituate; White
1.
STANLEY, JOHN, THOMAS, TIMOTHY; Cam-
bridge, Hartford; Flagg 1 (pp.
297, 300, 299, 272, 341); Morris
1; Booth 1.
STARR, COMFORT (DR.); Boston; Booth
1.
STEBBINS, EDWARD and EDITHA; Spring-
field; Booth 1.
STEBBINS, ROWLAND; Springfield,
Northampton; Starr 1 (2-21).
STEDMAN, THOMAS; New London; Flagg 1
(pp. 274, 228, 186, 161, 347).
STEELE, JOHN and RACHEL (TALCOTT);
Cambridge, Hartford, Farmington;
Starr 1 (1-239); Boardman 1 (pp.
199, 133); Flagg 1 (pp. 291, 261,
347).
STEPHENS, see Stevens.
STERLING, WILLIAM; Bradford, Haver-
hill, Lyme; Holman 2.
STEVENS, DIONIS; (w. Tristram Cof-

THOMPSON, JOHN; New Haven; de Forest 1.
THOMPSON, JOHN; East Haven; Anderson 1.
THOMPSON, WILLIAM; Sudbury; Ferris 1 (1-591).
THOMSON, JOHN; Plymouth, Barnstable, Middleboro; Jacobus 2 (pp. 684-687).
THOMSON, THOMAS; Hartford, Farmington; Starr 1 (1-205); Flagg 1 (pp. 260, 217, 312, 348); Holman 4; Booth 1.
THRALL, WILLIAM; Windsor; Ferris 1 (2-793).
THROOPE, WILLIAM; Barnstable, Bristol; Holman 4.
TIBBALS, THOMAS; Milford; de Forest 1.
TIDD, JOHN; Charlestown, Woburn; Ferris 1 (1-596); Holman 4.
TIFFANY, HUMPHREY; Rehoboth, Milton, Swansea; Jacobus 3.
TILDEN, NATHANIEL; Scituate; Davis 7.
TILLEY, JOHN; Plymouth; Jacobus 3; Anderson 1.
TILLINGHAST, PARDON; Providence; Flagg 1 (pp. 199, 168).
TILTON, WILLIAM; Lynn, Ipswich; Davis 9.
TINGLEY, SAMUEL; Malden; Tingley 1.
TISDALE, JOHN; Duxbury, Taunton; Jacobus 3.
TITUS, ROBERT; Weymouth, Rehoboth, Huntington; Selleck 1.
TOMES; co. Gloucester, Eng.; Holman 4; Jacobus 5 (p. 779).
TOMPKINS, RALPH; Dorchester, Salem; Tingley 1.
TOMPSON, ALICE (FREEMAN); Roxbury; Jacobus 3; Holman 4.
TOOTHAKER, ROGER; Plymouth Co.; Holman 2.
TOPPING, THOMAS; Wethersfield, Milford, Southampton, Branford; Selleck 1; Morris 1.
TOWER, JOHN; Hingham; Davis 8.
TOWNE, WILLIAM; Salem, Topsfield; Davis 2; de Forest 2; Holman 4.
TOWNER, RICHARD; Branford; Anderson 1.
TOWNSEND, THOMAS; Lynn; de Forest 2.
TRACY, STEPHEN; Plymouth, Duxbury; Ferris 1 (2-799); Jacobus

2 (pp. 688-690).
TRACY, THOMAS (LIEUT.); Salem, Wetherfield, Saybrook, Norwich; Jacobus 2 (pp. 691-700); de Forest 1; Jacobus 3.
TRAPP, PHILIP; Springfield; Tingley 1.
TRAVERS, HENRY; Newbury; Tingley 1.
TREAT, MATTHIAS; Wethersfield; Goodwin 1.
TREAT, RICHARD; Wethersfield, Milford; Goodwin 1; Starr 1 (2-247); de Forest 1; Booth 1; Jacobus 5.
TROWBRIDGE, THOMAS; New Haven; Flagg 1 (pp. 203, 173, 331, 350).
TRULL, JOHN; Billerica; Holman 2.
TRUMBULL, JOHN; Roxbury, Rowley; Holman 2; Morris 1.
TRY, MICHAEL; Fairfield; Holman 4.
TRYON, WILLIAM; Wethersfield; Jacobus 4.
TUCKER, MORRIS; Salisbury, Tiverton; Holman 2.
TUCKER, ROBERT; Weymouth, Gloucester, Milton; Jacobus 3.
TUELL, RICHARD; Boston; Tingley 1.
TULLER, JOHN; Simsbury; de Forest 1.
TUPPER, THOMAS; Lynn, Sandwich; Holman 3 (p. 278).
TURNER, HUMPHREY; Scituate; Selleck 1; Holman 3 (p. 264).
TURNER, JOHN; Sussex Co.; Morris 1.
TUTTLE, JOHN; Boston, Ipswich; Ferris 1 (1-600); Jacobus 5.
TUTTLE, RICHARD; Boston; Jacobus 5.
TUTTLE, WILLIAM; New Haven; de Forest 1; White 1; Anderson 1; Jacobus 5.
TWISDEN, JOHN; Scituate, York; Davis 7.
TWITCHELL, JOSEPH; Dorchester; Morse 1 (p. 247).
TYBBOT, WALTER; Gloucester; Ferris 1 (1-607).

UPHAM, JOHN (DEACON); Weymouth, Malden; Flagg 1 (pp. 286, 256, 215, 351); Ferris 1 (1-611).
UPSON, ELIZABETH (————); Sudbury; Ferris 1 (1-639).
UPTON, JOHN; Lynn, Salem; de Forest 2.

VAN ALSTYNE, JAN MARTENSE; New York, Kingston, Kinderhook; Cory 5.
VAN BUREN, CORNELIS MAESSEN; Rensselaerswyck; Cory 5.

VAN CORTLANDT, OLAF STEVENSE;
New York; Constant (p. 424).
VANDERHORST, JOHN; Charleston, S.
C.; Flagg 1 (pp. 170, 153,
382).
VAN GLAHN, GERD CHRISTOPH; West
Haven; de Forest 2.
VAN HORN, CHRISTIAN BARENTSEN;
New York; Tingley 1.
VAN VLIET, ADRIAN GERRITSE; King-
ston; Jacobus 2 (pp. 701-708).
VAN VOORHEES, STEVEN COERTE,
Flatlands, L. I.; Cory 1 (p.
298).
VAN WAGENEN, [AERT JACOBSEN];
Kingston; Jacobus 2 (pp. 709-
711).
VARNEY, WILLIAM; Ipswich; Ting-
ley 1.
VAUGHAN, GEORGE; Scituate, Mid-
dleboro; Jacobus 2 (pp. 733-
734).
VAUGHN, WILLIAM; Portsmouth;
Sheppard 1.
VAUGHAN; Bristol, Lebanon; Jaco-
bus 2 (pp. 612-614).
VENTRES, WILLIAM; Farmington,
Haddam; Ferris 1 (2-805).
VERY, (Widow Bridget); Salem; de
Forest 2.
VINTON, JOHN; Lynn; New Haven;
Vinton 2; Anderson 1.
VORCE (see Force); Sudbury; Fer-
ris 1 (1-643).
VORE, RICHARD; Windsor; de For-
est 1.
VOSBURGH, ABRAHAM PIETERSEN;
Rensselaerswyck, Albany, King-
ston; Cory 5.
VROOM, CORNELIS PIETERSEN; New
York; Tingley 1.

WADLEIGH, JOHN; Saco, Wells; Hol-
man 2.
WADSWORTH, WILLIAM; Hartford;
Flagg 1 (pp. 298, 271, 223,
351).
WAKEFIELD, JOHN; Boston; Holman
4.
WAKEMAN, FRANCIS; Worcester, Eng.;
[John, Samuel & others, New
Haven]; Jacobus 4.
WALDO, CORNELIUS; Ipswich, Chelms-
ford; Jacobus 3.
WALDORF, ANTHONY; Nauright; N. J.;
Morris 1.
WALDRON, RICHARD; Dover; Sheppard

1.
WALKER, JOHN; Penn.; White 1.
WALKER, RICHARD; Lynn; Sheppard 1.
WALKER, THOMAS; Boston; Holman 4.
WALKER, "Widow"; Rehoboth; Jacobus
3.
WALTON, GEORGE; Dover, Portsmouth,
Great Island; Davis 1.
WARD, ANDREW; Wethersfield, Fair-
field; Goodwin 1; Anderson 1.
WARD, GEORGE; New Haven, Branford;
Cory 4.
WARD, JOHN; Newport; Flagg 1 (pp.
197, 167, 151).
WARD, JOYCE (Widow); Wethersfield;
Flagg 1 (p. 304); Cory 2 (p. 211).
WARD, WILLIAM; Middletown; Morris 1.
WARDWELL, WILLIAM; Boston; Davis 8.
WARHAM, JOHN (REV.); Dorchester,
Windsor; Flagg 1 (p. 368); Jaco-
bus 3; Jacobus 5.
WARNER, ANDREW; Hartford, Hadley;
Starr 1 (1-17).
WARNER, WILLIAM; Ipswich; Linzee 1
(pp. 430, 303, 209); Jacobus 4;
Ferris 1 (1-649).
WARREN, RICHARD; Plymouth; Avery 1
(p. 15); Holman 1; de Forest 1.
WARREN, SAMUEL; Westchester; Con-
stant (p. 434).
WARRINER, WILLIAM; Springfield;
Booth 1.
WATERBURY, JOHN; Watertown, Stam-
ford; Selleck 1.
WATERHOUSE, JACOB; Wethersfield, New
London; Boardman 1 (pp. 288, 240,
169, 101).
WATERHOUSE, RICHARD; Portsmouth;
Davis 10.
WATERMAN, ROBERT; Marshfield; Jaco-
bus 2; de Forest 1; Jacobus 3.
WATERS, LAWRENCE; Watertown, Lan-
caster, Charlestown; White 1; Hol-
man 4.
WATSON, ROBERT; Plymouth; Tingley 1.
WATSON, ROBERT; Leicester; (Mat-
thew², Barrington); Jacobus 3.
WATSON-CHALLIS, see Challis.
WATTS, HENRY; Saco; also Anne (w.
Dixon); Davis 5 (pp. 81-90).
WATTS, RICHARD; Hartford; de Forest
1; Holman 4.
WATTS alias Mercer, Samuel (Lieut.);
Andover; Holman 2.
WEARE, PETER; York; Holman 5.
WEBB, CHRISTOPHER; Braintree; Vin-
ton 1; Booth 1.

WEBB, RICHARD; Stamford; Selleck
1.
WEBBER, WOLFERT [ANNEKE JANS];
New York; Tingley 1.
WEBSTER, JOHN (GOV.); Hartford,
Hadley; Goodwin 1; Flagg 1 (p.
247); de Forest 1; de Forest 2.
WEBSTER, JOHN; Boston, Ipswich;
Holman 2; Sheppard 1.
WEBSTER, NICHOLAS; Stamford; Sel-
leck 1.
WEBSTER, THOMAS; Hampton; Shep-
pard 1.
WEEKS, GEORGE; Dorchester; Holman
4.
WELD, BARBARA (CLAPP) [w. Joseph];
Dorchester; Holman 3 (p. 229).
WELD, JOSEPH (CAPT.); Roxbury;
Linzee 1 (pp. 502, 488, 355,
220, 180); Morris 1; Jacobus 4;
Booth 1.
WELLER, RICHARD; Windsor, North-
ampton, Deerfield; de Forest 1.
WELLES, HUGH; Wethersfield; Flagg
1 (p. 266).
WELLES, THOMAS (GOV.); Cambridge,
Hartford, Wethersfield; Goodwin
1; Starr 1 (1-219); Flagg 1 (p.
290); Jacobus 1 (p. 30); Holman
4; Booth 1; Jacobus 5.
WELLINGTON, NICHOLAS; Newbury;
Tingley 1.
WELLS, ISAAC; Scituate, Barnsta-
ble; Holman 4.
WEST, TWIFORD; Marshfield, Rowley,
Ipswich; Holman 2.
WESTCOTT, STUKELEY; Salem, Prov-
idence, Warwick; Selleck 1.
WESTWOOD, WILLIAM; Cambridge,
Hartford, Hadley; de Forest 2.
WETMORE, THOMAS; Wethersfield,
Middletown; de Forest 1.
WHALE, PHILEMON; Sudbury; Ferris
1 (1-660).
WHEELER, JOHN; Hampton, Salisbury,
Newbury; Holman 2; Davis 8.
WHEELER, MARGERY; (w. Thomas
Thayer); Holman 2.
WHEELER, MOSES; New Haven, Strat-
ford; Starr 1 (2-91); Avery 1
(p. 163).
WHEELER, THOMAS; Milford; Cory 4.
WHIPPLE, MATTHEW and JOHN; Ips-
wich; Holman 2; Jacobus 3; White
1.
WHITCOMB, JOHN; Dorchester, Scit-
uate, Lancaster; Holman 3 (p.

254); Tingley 1; White 1; Holman 4.
WHITE, GAWEN; Scituate; Davis 7;
White 1.
WHITE, JOHN; Salem, Lancaster; White
1; Booth 1.
WHITE, JOHN; Lynn, Southampton; Sel-
leck 1.
WHITE, JOHN (Elder); Hartford; Booth
1.
WHITE, ROBERT; Elizabeth; Ferris 1
(2-809).
WHITE, [ROBERT]; Essex, Eng.; [John
of Hartford and others]; Starr 1
(2-395); Jacobus 4; White 1.
WHITE, THOMAS; Weymouth; Vinton 2.
WHITE, WILLIAM; Ipswich; Tingley 1.
WHITEHEAD, DANIEL; Hempstead, Smith-
town, Huntington, Newtown; Selleck
1.
WHITING, WILLIAM; Hartford; Goodwin
1; Starr 1 (2-351); Flagg 1 (pp.
201, 172, 154, 144, 139); Selleck
1; Crawford 1 (p. 10); Jacobus 4.
WHITMAN, JOSEPH; Stratford?, Huntington; Selleck 1.
WHITMAN, ZACHARIAH and JOHN; Milford
and Weymouth; Avery 1 (p. 121).
WHITMORE [WETMORE], JOHN; Wethersfield, Stamford; Booth 1.
WHITRIDGE, WILLIAM; Ipswich; Tingley
1.
WHITTIER, THOMAS; Salisbury, Haver-
hill; Holman 2.
WICKHAM, THOMAS; Wethersfield; Jaco-
bus 4.
WIGHT, THOMAS (DEACON); Dedham, Med-
field; Tingley 1.
WIGNALL, ALEXANDER; Watertown; Ting-
ley 1.
WILCOX, JOHN; Hartford; Boardman 1
(p. 279); Jacobus 5.
WILDER, THOMAS; Charlestown; White
1; Holman 4.
WILFORD, GILBERT; Haverhill; Holman
2.
WILKINSON, EDWARD; Milford; de For-
est 1.
WILLARD, SIMON (MAJOR); Concord,
Charlestown; Holman 4.
WILLEY, ISAAC; New London; Booth 1.
WILLIAMS, JOHN; Scituate; Tingley 1.
WILLIAMS, JOHN; Windsor; Seversmith
1 (p. 1391).
WILLIAMS, ROBERT; Boston; Tingley 1.
WILLIAMS, ROGER (REV.); Providence;
Flagg 1 (pp. 244, 357).
WILLIAMSON, TIMOTHY; Marshfield;

Starr 7 (p. 5).

WILLIS, GEORGE; Hartford; Morse 2 (p. 181).

WILMOT, BENJAMIN; New Haven; Anderson 1.

WILSON, JAMES; Chester; Tingley 1.

WINCHESTER, JOHN; Hingham, Brookline; White 1.

WINSLOW, JOSIAS; Plymouth, Marshfield; de Forest 1.

WINTHROP, ELIZABETH (READE); England; Davis 4.

WISWALL, THOMAS; Linzee 1 (pp. 262, 189).

WITHINGTON, HENRY (ELDER); Dorchester; Cory 2 (p. 68); Booth 1.

WITT, JOHN; Lynn; Holman 4.

WOLCOTT, HENRY; Windsor; Boardman 1 (p. 308); Flagg 1 (pp. 280, 241, 194); de Forest 1.

WOOD, EDMUND; Wethersfield, Hempstead, Huntington; Selleck 1.

WOOD, EDWARD; Charlestown; Flagg 1 (p. 287).

WOOD, JONAS "HALIFAX"; Wethersfield, Hempstead, Southampton, Huntington; Selleck 1.

WOOD, NICHOLAS; Dorchester, Braintree, Medfield; Tingley 1; Morse 1 (p. 131).

WOOD, THOMAS; Rowley; Booth 1.

WOODBURY, JOHN and WILLIAM; Salem, Beverly; Ferris 1 (2-823); Tingley 1.

WOODFORD, JOSEPH; Farmington; Starr 1 (1-168); Flagg 1 (p. 192); Morris 1.

WOODFORD, THOMAS; Roxbury, Hartford, Northampton; Starr 1 (2-183); de Forest 2; Holman 4; Jacobus 5.

WOODHULL, RICHARD; Jamaica, Setauket; Selleck 1.

WOODRUFF, MATTHEW; Farmington; Flagg 1 (p. 237).

WOODWARD, EZEKIEL; Boston, Ipswich; Ferris 1 (1-667).

WOODWARD, HENRY; Dorchester, Northampton; Ferris 1 (2-841); Flagg 1 (p. 210); Holman 4.

WOODWARD, PETER; Dedham; Jacobus 2 (pp. 734-735).

WOODWARD, RICHARD; Watertown; Jacobus 3.

WORMWOOD, WILLIAM; York; Davis 8.

WORTH, LIONEL; Salisbury, Newbury; Holman 2.

WORTHINGTON, NICHOLAS; Hatfield; Goodwin 1.

WRIGHT, ABEL; Springfield; de Forest 2; Jacobus 4.

WRIGHT, DOROTHY and (son) Edward; Sudbury; Ferris 1 (1-678).

WRIGHT, RICHARD; Saugus, Braintree; Davis 7.

WRIGHT, SAMUEL (DEA.); Springfield, Northampton; Booth 1.

WRIGHT, THOMAS; Wethersfield; Boardman 1 (pp. 253, 211, 179, 107, 81); Flagg 1 (pp. 294, 264, 358).

WYATT, JOHN; Ipswich; Holman 2.

WYATT, JOHN; Windsor, Farmington, Haddam; de Forest 2.

WYATT, MARGARET [w. Matthew Allyn]; Devon, Eng.; Jacobus 4.

YOUNG, see Jung.